THE NAZI PARTY

THE NAZI PARTY

A SOCIAL PROFILE
OF MEMBERS AND LEADERS
1919-1945

Michael H. Kater

Harvard University Press
Cambridge, Massachusetts
1983

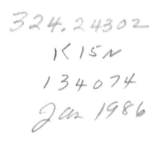

Library of Congress Cataloging in Publication Data

Kater, Michael H., 1937–
The Nazi Party.

Includes indexes.
1. Nationalsozialistische Deutsche Arbeiter-Partei.
2. National socialism.
3. Germany – Social conditions.
I. Title.
JN3946.N36K37   1983   324.24302   82–15814
ISBN 0-674-60655-8

For Jane Fair and Frank Falco,
composers, teachers, and
jazz musicians par excellence,
whose artistry and friendship are
a constant source of inspiration

ACKNOWLEDGMENTS

In 1973–74 I was in Munich on sabbatical leave. An old friend from Heidelberg days, Professor Wolfgang Schieder, now at the University of Trier, asked me to participate in a panel he was organizing for the West German Historical Association meeting in Brunswick in October 1974. I was to speak on changes in the social composition of the Nazi movement during Hitler's coming to power. Out of my paper for the Brunswick conference — a preliminary examination of occupations and classes chiefly in the Nazi party membership — grew further articles over the next eight years: articles on the SS, on the Brown Shirts, on the Hitler Youth, and on the party itself, always with a view to comparing the social structure of each group with that of the general population and finding out what had motivated these particular Germans to become followers of Hitler when they did.

My resolve to collect material for this book and finally write it was, in part, the consequence of the encouragement of friends and colleagues in Canada, the United States, West Germany, and Austria. Richard Bauer, then acting director of the Berlin Document Center, opened the vaults of that massive archive to me until his untimely death in February 1976. The present director, Major Daniel P. Simon, could not have been more helpful in later years. His two assistants, Werner Pix and Egon Burchartz, ably guided me through the impressive records. In assembling my statistical data there, I was loyally aided for two summers by Hans Oppermann of the Toronto Goethe Institute. Archivists in more than thirty West German and Austrian archives advised and assisted me as my research proceeded, among them, first and foremost, Dr. Heinz Boberach of the Federal Archive in Koblenz. I was fortunate to have the opportunity to peruse many books and articles in the well-stocked Munich Institute of Contemporary History, where Professor Martin Broszat and Hellmuth Auerbach looked after me. In addition, I made use of the large bibliographical collection in the Bavarian State Library. Most of the printed material came to me through the good offices of York University's interlibrary loan service, whose three marvelous and never-tiring experts, Mary Hudecki, Susan Partridge, and Gary MacDonald, deserve my gratitude.

The research for this book involved the gathering of machine-readable mass data, computer processing, and multiple statistical analyses, an extremely time-consuming and expensive process. I could not have attempted it without funding and institutional support. The Killam Program of the Canada Council (Ottawa) freed me from all academic responsibilities for two years and provided more than generous research funds. Also very supportive in a variety of ways were the Guggenheim Foundation (New York), the Alexander von Humboldt-Stiftung (Bonn), the Grants and Leave Fellowship programs of the Canada Council (Ottawa), and the Social Science and Humanities Research Council of Canada (Ottawa). York University has consistently been magnanimous, notably in supporting computer programming and technology.

Special thanks must go to Rolf and Helga Steffensmeier of Wiedenbrück, West Germany, who year after year faithfully provided me with a dependable automobile that enabled me to accomplish the complex, geographically widespread research within relatively short time spans.

Many scholars have helped me research this book. Their advice has been not only thematic, technical, and bibliographical, but also supportive, inspiring, and morale-boosting. For the sake of brevity I can only mention those who have aided me most significantly. They are Geoffrey Barraclough, Gunnar C. Boehnert, Gerhard Botz, Werner Conze, Hans-Werner Gensichen, John R. Gittins, Richard F. Hamilton, Ernst Hanisch, Eike Hennig, Georg G. Iggers, Konrad H. Jarausch, Hartmut Kaelble, Bruce Kidd, Peter R. Knights, Jürgen Kocka, George L. Mosse, Albert D. Mott, Nobuo Noda, Gerhard A. Ritter, Ronald Rogowski, Wolfgang Schieder, Lawrence D. Stokes, Henry A. Turner, Jr., and Hans-Ulrich Wehler.

A few scholars have gone beyond the call of duty to facilitate the publication of this book. Gerhard Arminger and Michael Cowles shared their expert knowledge of statistics and computer technology. I hope that the statistical tables in this book will do justice to their efforts; any mistakes are, however, my own. Three distinguished experts in the field of Nazi studies have read all or parts of the completed manuscript and have made valuable suggestions for improvement: Hans Mommsen, Gerhard L. Weinberg, and especially William S. Allen, who also commented intelligently on parts of the ongoing research during an American Historical Association annual meeting in Dallas years ago.

Words of thanks are due to the people who helped me write and produce this book. Katarina Rice of Harvard University Press proved to be a very perceptive and sympathetic editor; she was a joy to work with. Dorothy and Leonard C. Whitney's editorial guidance at an earlier stage was invaluable; they themselves know best what they have done to improve the manuscript. Finally, Aida D. Donald, editor for the social sciences at Harvard Press, must be thanked, not only for her awesome professionalism but also for her patience, constant admonition, and personal encouragement over the years.

Any scholar with a wife and two pre-teenage daughters knows what it means to write a book and try to keep the family together at the same time. My younger daughter, Anja, was born in Toronto on the very same day I returned from that historic conference in Brunswick in the fall of 1974. Since then, the patience of Barbara, Eva, and Anja Kater has defied any attempts at description.

The assistance of many individuals has enabled me to publish this book. I am grateful to all of them. Although I have benefited from their understanding, criticism, and advice, they cannot be held responsible for any mistakes the book may still contain. That responsibility is mine alone.

CONTENTS

ABBREVIATIONS

ADGB	Allgemeiner Deutscher Gewerkschaftsbund; General German Trade Union
AfA	Allgemeiner freier Angestelltenbund; General free White-Collar Workers' Union
BDM	Bund Deutscher Mädel; League of German Girls
BNSDJ	Bund Nationalsozialistischer Deutscher Juristen; League of National Socialist German Jurists
BVP	Bayerische Volkspartei; Bavarian People's Party
DAF	Deutsche Arbeitsfront; German Labor Front
DAP	Deutsche Arbeiterpartei; German Workers' Party
DDP	Deutsche Demokratische Partei; German Democratic Party
DHV	Deutscher Handlungsgehilfen-Verband; German Shop Clerks' Association
DNVP	Deutschnationale Volkspartei; German National People's Party
DVP	Deutsche Volkspartei; German People's Party
HJ	Hitlerjugend; Hitler Youth
KdF	Kraft durch Freude; Strength through Joy
KPD	Kommunistische Partei Deutschlands; Communist Party of Germany
KVD	Kassenärztliche Vereinigung Deutschlands; Association of German Health Insurance Physicians
NPEA	Nationalpolitische Erziehungsanstalten; National Political Training Schools
NS-Hago	Nationalsozialistische Handels-, Handwerks- und Gewerbeorganisation; National Socialist Tradesmen's and Craftsmen's Association

NSBO	Nationalsozialistische Betriebszellenorganisation; National Socialist Shop Organization
NSDAP	Nationalsozialistische Deutsche Arbeiterpartei; National Socialist German Workers' Party
NSDStB	Nationalsozialistischer Deutscher Studentenbund; National Socialist German Student Union
NSLB	Nationalsozialistischer Lehrerbund; National Socialist Teachers' League
NSS	Nationalsozialistischer Schülerbund; National Socialist Upper-School Students' League
NSV	Nationalsozialistische Volkswohlfahrt; National Socialist People's Aid
OKH	Oberkommando des Heeres; Army High Command
RÄK	Reichsärztekammer; Reich Physicians' Chamber
RDB	Reichsbund der Deutschen Beamten; Reich League of German Civil Servants
RF	Reichsführung; Reich Leadership
RNS	Reichsnährstand; Reich Nutrition Estate
SA	Sturmabteilungen; Stormtroopers
SPD	Sozialdemokratische Partei Deutschlands; Social Democratic Party of Germany
USPD	Unabhängige Sozialdemokratische Partei Deutschlands; Independent Socialist Party of Germany
WHW	Winterhilfswerk; Winter Aid

THE NAZI PARTY

INTRODUCTION

Exactly half a century ago Adolf Hitler's National Socialist German Workers' Party (NSDAP) assumed political power in Germany. Earlier histories of the Nazi party have dealt with its political, economic, or institutional aspects, but most of them have not attempted to determine its social structure.[1] The purpose of this book is to describe the party's structure and to provide a social profile of both its general following and its leadership cadres for the period 1919–1945. Such an analysis should empirically test the widespread conception that the Nazi party was preeminently a lower-middle-class phenomenon, an assumption that, if simply taken for granted, would impede the progress of scholarly investigation into the class-related origins and subsequent history of National Socialism.[2]

The comparative method was employed in constructing the social profile of the Nazi party. The structure of the peer group or groups of the Nazi party was compared, as directly as possible, with the structure of German society as a whole, by using the social system of the Reich as a backdrop against which to view the party profile. Information on the German nation was obtained from the Reich censuses of 1925, 1933, and 1939; data on the NSDAP were drawn mainly from the party's membership lists and official publications pertaining to both members and leaders.[3]

The comparison is based on the principle of inequality, which has been used by sociologists since the time of Marx, Sombart, and Weber as the most reliable means for determining what is called social ranking or stratification.[4] This principle assumes the existence of differences in the quality of life experienced by the various groups or segments that make up the social hierarchy. Obviously, the identification of these groups (both the major groups, or social "classes," and the subgroupings of which they are composed) is a major task. Valid criteria for judging status must be used, criteria (such as occupation or inherited wealth) on which a scholarly consensus exists. The same set of criteria has of course been applied both to the population as a whole and to the Nazi party.

For the purposes of this study, German society during the first half of the twentieth century is perceived, in accordance with Max Weber's models, as a three-layered, hierarchical construct comprising, in a vertical array, as in a pyramid, a very large lower layer (called the "lower class"), a somewhat smaller middle layer (the "lower middle class"), and a very small upper layer (the "upper middle class" or "elite").[5] These layers consist of groupings of people that are based primarily on occupation; in other words, occupation is the chief criterion of hierarchical status. This primary criterion or variable—occupation—may itself be weighted according to the type of training or education required for it, as well as the expertise connected with it. It may, furthermore, be evaluated in terms of prestige, which depends not only on training but also on the nature of the work performed (for example, whether it is done indoors or outdoors) and on the remuneration it commands. All of these factors relating to occupation—training or education, expertise, nature of the work, and remuneration—are important in determining the vertical ranking of the occupations. They determine the arrangement of these occupations, and hence of the individuals who perform them, in the three-layered construct of society.

The upper layer of this trichotomy is further affected by three criteria that are not related to occupation: inherited wealth, titled birth, and political power. Inherited wealth was and still is a time-honored mark of high standing. Titled birth was for centuries synonymous with power in European society, but after World War I it became little more than a symbol of historic prestige; yet, though merely suggesting power, it continued to carry weight. A hypothetical (but typical) case of a young man born into the lower nobility of imperial society will illustrate this point. He joined the army at the height of World War I and by virtue of his high social station instantly received an officer's commission. After demobilization, however, since he had neither a trade nor a higher education and his family had lost its fortune, he was obliged to accept the precarious existence of a traveling salesman. But eventually, solely because of his name, he was elevated to the well-paid position of manager.[6] The third and last mark of high status is access to political power. This type of distinction was bestowed upon a number of German workers and craftsmen who had become trade union officials or Social Democrats and who suddenly found themselves holding the reins of government after the revolution of 1918.[7]

Two important questions arise in connection with the vertical division of society into a lower class, a lower middle class, and an upper middle class or elite (including the aristocracy). First, is it accurate to use the word "class" in this way? And second, how were these classes related to the historical lower, middle, and upper classes of eighteenth- and nineteenth-century German society?

In answer to the first question, "class" is used only for lack of a better term: unfortunately, since Marx's day, the word has been so inflated ideologically that it has lost its original nonpolemical connotation of "estate," as in the "Third Estate" of eighteenth-century France. But Marx viewed society dichotomously; he drew the line between the classes of the powerful and of the powerless, between the exploiters and the exploited. In his analysis, the second class would eventually overthrow the first. Hence his concept of class always contained an antagonistic quality. For these reasons it would be better to use the word "layer," or *Schicht,* but this would not be practical. It should be understood, however, that the meaning of *Schicht* is implied whenever the term "class" is employed in this book.

To answer the second question, the three classes treated in this study must be seen in sociohistorical perspective. It is not too difficult to relate the lower class to its historical antecedents, but the historical predecessors of the middle and upper layers of the pyramid are more complex.

The lower class is vaguely coterminous with the lower classes of nineteenth-century Germany, which Marx within his dialectical frame of reference called the proletariat, or propertyless workers. Since Marx, however, the term "lower class" has predominantly denoted blue-collar wage earners in the broad sense. Refinements of meaning abound beyond the general category.[8]

The general term "middle class" or *Mittelstand* can be traced back to the late eighteenth century, when it was used to refer to the healthy center core of society. This included the preindustrial workers, or craftsmen, and, by geometric logic, excluded both the social outcasts below (criminals, vagrants, and "dishonorable" professionals such as prostitutes and gravediggers) and the elite above (the socially and politically powerful).[9] Later, after the 1848–49 revolution, *Mittelstand* was applied to all those above the workers; it included primarily the independent tradespeople, merchants, artisans, and peasants, as well as, to a lesser degree, the liberal (academic, learned) professionals and entrepreneurs. Later still, the growing number of white-collar employees and civil servants (of any but the highest ranks) were also identified as middle class. At the beginning of the twentieth century German social scientists singled out those white-collar clerks and bureaucrats as the *Neue Mittelstand* (new middle class) in contradistinction to the *Alte Mittelstand* (old middle class) of the self-employed. This division between new and old amounted to the creation of a classifying device indicating horizontal separation. The order it meant to establish did not imply a ranking on a scale of values but rather a formal, nominal ranking based on two fundaments, operation and function, and the device was applied solely to the middle class. Yet it posed a problem because at that time the middle class was generally understood to be a stratum located between an upper and a lower layer, and the principle of horizontal subdivision seemed out of place in the vertical or pyramidal model. Moreover, the difficulties of conceptualizing the divisions in German society were compounded when the middle-class members of the twentieth-century elite continued to be counted among the *Mittelstand*.

Another complication was the division of the middle class into the *Oberer* (upper) and the *Unterer* (lower) *Mittelstand*. This theoretical device, first used by Gustav Schmoller at the end of the nineteenth century, definitely separated the liberal professionals, the wealthy entrepreneurs, and the members of the higher bureaucracy (insofar as they had not already been included among the ruling elite) from the rest of the middle class. It moved them closer to the historic upper class with which they had become increasingly identified during the second half of the nineteenth century. At the same time, of course, this new view changed the horizontal pattern of categorization back to a vertical pattern, resulting in a lower middle class that was composed, on the one hand, of small and intermediate merchants, independent craftsmen, and peasants (the self-employed — the *Alte Mittelstand*), and, on the other, of small and medium employees and civil servants (the salary-dependent — the *Neue Mittelstand*).

As for the upper layer of German society, in the pre-Marxian epoch the original German upper class had been the ruling elite — that is, the aristocracy. In the course of time, however, the professionals, who were initially counted among the classical nineteenth-century *Mittelstand,* became more prominent and more visible in German society. They excelled because they combined the two characteristics of *Bildung* and *Besitz. Bildung,* meaning higher (though not necessarily formal) education, can also be translated as "refined knowledge" or "cultivation," and it qualified its holder for the higher occupations; *Besitz* simply means property. Toward the end of the nineteenth century, the social and political importance of the aristocracy diminished in direct proportion to the social elevation of the professionals (*Besitz- und Bildungsbürgertum*), who had emerged during the revolution of 1848–49 but showed an even sharper profile during the Wilhelmine phase, in post-1871 German history. By 1914, this new professional, entrepreneurial, and administrative elite with varying degrees of in- herited or acquired wealth was clearly discernible as an "upper bourgeoisie," and it ranged almost alongside the traditional ruling elite of aristocratic lineage. During the Weimar Republic (according to many sociologists) this group detached itself from its lower-middle- class neighbors and became the self-contained upper middle class.[10] At the same time the former aristocracy, having lost both its political power and its traditional privileges through the neutralization of titles (1918), began to merge with the upper middle class to form the new cream of society—the social, cultural, and economic elite.[11]

This broad, historically grounded view of the German class system in the early twentieth century will serve as the basis of the structural analysis in this study. In summary, it supports the tripartite, vertical division of Weimar and Third Reich society into a lower class, approx- imating the German term *Unterschicht*; a lower middle class, the *Unterer Mittelstand,* including both the *Neue* and the *Alte Mittel- stand*; and the elite, comprising the *Oberer Mittelstand* and the former aristocracy.

Each of the three classes can be divided into occupational subgroups (see table 1). The lower class contains three subgroups: (1) unskilled workers; (2) skilled workers whose skills were generically related to the traditional or newer artisanal crafts (craft workers or craftsmen); and (3) other skilled workers. In the lower middle class there are six subgroups: (4) master craftsmen, that is, independent, self-employed artisans; (5) independent professionals who were not academically trained; (6) lower and intermediate employees; (7) lower and intermediate civil servants; (8) self-employed merchants; and (9) self-employed farmers, vintners, and fishermen. Finally, the elite in- cludes five subgroups: (10) managers; (11) higher civil servants, who usually had a university education; (12) academically trained profes- sionals; (13) senior upper-school and university students; and (14) en- trepreneurs. The number ascribed to each of the subgroups in a class is not intended to give it any particular rank within that class.

These diversified subgroups have already been defined within their historical settings by an earlier generation of historians, sociologists, and statisticians. The greatest definitional problems have arisen in connection with the overlappings between groups and consequently between classes. In selecting the occupational subgroups for this study, definitions have been sought that, especially in the borderline cases, will meet with the greatest possible scholarly consensus. Nevertheless, as Theodor Geiger warned in 1932, mistakes in this procedure cannot be ruled out, and not everyone will be satisfied.[12]

The occupational labels and the numbers of gainfully employed (in the case of students, eventually employable) persons in the following subgroups were obtained from the 1933 German census and census-related statistical records (showing a total of just over 27 million such persons of both sexes) and from the Nazi party membership lists.

Everybody appearing as a laborer on the census and party lists fell naturally into subgroup 1 (unskilled workers), because the occupation of laborer or worker hardly ever implied either training or acquired skills. Also included under this rubric were semiskilled workers, household servants, and agricultural laborers, as well as miners and persons such as hardeners (*Härter*) whose occupational label connoted a type of operation that did not require training or expertise.

Whenever it was provable, or even conceivable, that a worker might have undergone formal training in order to acquire a journeyman's certificate or a master craftsman's diploma, he was transferred to subgroup 2, that of skilled (craft) workers, as were apprentices in the same trades. Also assigned to subgroup 2 were the more traditional types of skilled artisans who need not have acquired either one of these diplomas, such as bakers and smiths, whose crafts had become firmly established in precapitalist times. Finally, this subgroup includes jobs connected with industrialization (which gained ground rapidly after the unification of Germany in 1871) that developed an artisanal character either because they incorporated diversified types of formal training on the traditional pattern or because they made it possible for individuals to be employed in a workshop. Two examples of such workers were the machine-fitter (*Maschinenschlosser*) and the electrician (*Elektromechaniker*).

The third subgroup (other skilled workers) is made up of blue-collar occupations that could not be linked to the trades but nevertheless entailed a certain degree of specialization based on training and experience, such as the foremen among miners.

It is assumed that the members of the three subgroups of the lower class possessed a certain amount of the class consciousness or pride that is implied by Marx's notion of the proletariat. But their class consciousness was much more closely allied to their desire for economic betterment than to any scheme for overthrowing the higher classes. Generally, a worker's class consciousness prevented him from being upwardly mobile. Workers were usually more interested than were the members of the other two classes in the mundane side of life, typically spending more money on food and beer and enjoying popular forms of recreation such as soccer.[13]

In the early 1900s Georges Sorel in France and Robert Michels in Germany touched off a controversy as to the feasibility of classifying the most highly trained and specialized workers—the "labor aristocracy"—as members of the lower middle class rather than the lower class. The existence of a labor aristocracy cannot be denied, but it is difficult to identify such a subgroup. For, although the criteria of high skills and concomitantly high wages might suggest that these people belonged to the lower bourgeoisie, their subjective class mentality, if it were measurable, would clearly militate against such ranking. Contemporary, as well as the more recent, scholarly wisdom holds that such people should be classified among the workers—that is, as members of the lower class.[14]

The first subgroup of the lower middle class (4) consists of the independent master craftsmen. These master craftsmen, who were close to the labor aristocracy of the working class, could descend into that class if they lost their status of self-employment as the result of industrialization. On the other hand, if they received an unusually large income or owned a sufficiently large production shop, they could rise into the elite, with wealth serving as the decisive criterion of status. Master craftsmen, in fact—as well as the entire lower middle class—were distinguished by this potential for extremely negative or extremely positive social mobility.[15]

These self-employed artisans, traditional members of the old middle class, had economic independence in their own shops (by virtue of their ownership of the means of production), as well as employer status and the independent ability to market their own products. Thus many of their socioeconomic interests were identical to those of the self-employed merchants (subgroup 8); and for the sake of sociohistorical analysis the two subgroups have often been treated together as *Kleine und Mittlere Gewerbetreibende* (small and intermediate businessmen), or *Gewerblicher Mittelstand*.[16] Further, it is difficult for the researcher who comes upon artisanal designations on the Reich statistical rosters or in the Party membership lists to know how to differentiate between the wage-earning craftsmen (subgroup 2) and the independent or master craftsmen (4).[17] For the purposes of this study, all craftsmen—such as bakers and machine-fitters—were initially counted as one integral, horizontally defined social unit.[18] They were later divided vertically into two groups according to a formula, proposed during the mid-1920s, by which 36.6 percent of all craftsmen in the Reich, approximately 1.32 million, were self-employed. As an example, 36.6 percent of all bakers on the lists were assumed to have been master craftsmen (subgroup 4), and the rest were treated as skilled (craft) workers (subgroup 2). Since this formula had to be applied to both the highly aggregated data in the population records and the more diversified data in the Nazi membership samples, a certain degree of bias was incorporated in the construction of both subgroups. Though this was regrettable, it was preferable to the bulk treatment of all artisans, self-employed or wage earners, as a self-contained, homogeneous body.[19]

Nonacademic professionals constitute subgroup 5. Generally, they defy classification by the standards of either the new or the old middle class; but if anything they belong more in the latter. Midwives, masseurs, master builders, and dentists not educated at a university were typical of this subgroup, as were certain kinds of engineers, artists, and writers. Engineers' names on the Nazi lists that lacked the affix *Diplom.-Ing.* or *Dr.-Ing.,* which connoted academic schooling, were automatically included in this group. In the case of the census records, however, the total mass of engineers was trisected according to a formula based on type of education or training. University-trained engineers were ranked with the academic professionals in subgroup 12 of the elite class (they could also have been treated as managers); polytechnic-trained (professional) engineers were classified with subgroup 5; and technicians with subgroup 6 (lower and intermediate employees).[20] The figures for artists, actors, musicians, and singers on the statistical records were prorated, one-third being allocated to subgroup 12 (elite), and two-thirds to subgroup 5. All dancers were assigned to subgroup 5. In the Nazi membership lists, however, the division of these occupations was linked, somewhat arbitrarily, to the region of residence. If an artist or musician came from a large city (having at least 100,000 inhabitants), he was ranked with subgroup 12 (elite); and all others were ranked with subgroup 5.[21]

The sixth subgroup is made up of the lower and intermediate (petty) employees who formed the bastion of the new middle class. By definition they were salaried and thus dependent for their livelihood on merchants, entrepreneurs, large corporations, or municipal or state administrations.[22] On the archival lists and records they were typically designated as salesmen or saleswomen, shop clerks, office clerks, and, within the category of technical employees, technicians (*Techniker*) or foremen (*Werkmeister*). Marxist scholars have always insisted that such white-collar workers belong to the working class, since they are economically dependent on an employer.[23] Yet not only did the white-collar workers branch off historically from the mass of blue-collar workers (laborers) in the nineteenth century and hence develop different socioeconomic interests, but in the early twentieth century the majority of them emphatically resented being confused with the working class.[24] Largely engaged in quasi-intellectual rather than physical tasks, they felt much more akin to their slightly more elevated new-middle-class cousins, the lower civil servants (subgroup 7), whose job tenure, gradated promotion and pay schedule, and governmental authority they envied.[25] These petty employees took pride in the way they dressed, which usually was not merely white-collar but actually fastidious (consider the dapper salesmen in today's department stores), and in what they considered to be a sophisticated life-style. In this area they strove to emulate their employers and to foster close relationships with them during the working hours. Upwardly mobile in principle, they aspired to become employers themselves, or (if they were women) employers' wives through hypergamy, or civil servants. But sometimes their potentially negative mobility carried them downward to the working class from which many of them had come. It was because they were often so familiar with the workers' milieu that they so heartily eschewed it.[26]

Just as the lower and intermediate employees worked against the intrusion of ordinary laborers into their ranks, so did the lower and intermediate civil servants (subgroup 7) work against intrusion by petty employees. In addition to job tenure, a logical, scaled system of salaries, and symbols of authority such as uniforms, these administrators (coincident with the second stratum of the new middle class) were blessed with pension and social insurance benefits as well as universally recognized titles and ranks. Moreover, the attainment of a certain rank brought the secure feeling that the next rung on the professional ladder would be reached within a calculable period of time. This element of rationality inherent especially in modern (post-1871) German bureaucracy infused the consciousness of even the lowliest state servant with professional pride. Because of their fixed scale of ranks, the occupations of the civil servants are among the easiest to categorize.[27]

Subgroup 8 is composed of the merchants, pillars of the old middle class, who could be easily distinguished from both the workers and the large-scale entrepreneurs (subgroup 14, in the elite). The description *Kaufmann* (merchant) on membership lists and in census records clearly refers in most cases to independent shopkeepers (including innkeepers) who marketed natural or manufactured products or rendered services in accordance with the rudiments of rationality on which modern capitalism relies. It was more difficult to spot the cases in which commercial employees, such as the proverbial *Handlungsgehilfen* (shop clerks), had upgraded themselves on the Nazi party rosters by changing their status description to *Kfm.,* short for merchant.[28] How often this was done is not known, as no mechanism was available to screen such entries; consequently, the group of Nazi merchants may have been smaller than the files suggest, and that of petty employees correspondingly larger. All that can be done is to indicate the margin of error that the statistical method permits. The opposite error was also possible, resulting in insufficient upgrading, but here an adjustment was attempted through the use of income or wealth as a status criterion. For instance, a very high volume of trade, a costly inventory (in wholesale businesses), or the independent control of considerable investment input (garage and service facilities in the case of an automobile dealership) might single out certain merchants as entrepreneurs rather than *Kleine* or *Mittlere Gewerbetreibende,* and thus align them with the elite. For reasons of professional self-esteem, such people invariably identified themselves accordingly by using indications like wholesaler or car dealer. But in the Reich statistical records, where no such differentiating method was used, the entrepreneurs were unavoidably lumped together with ordinary merchants and dealers. Because of this defect, yet another formula was employed by which 2.6 percent was deducted from the total number of merchants in the census and added to the number of entrepreneurs (subgroup 14).[29]

Self-employed farmers, fishermen, and vintners, all of the old middle class, composed the last subgroup (9) of the lower middle class. In this case, when the Nazi party files were being used for research, only the head of the family was counted. Entries such as farmer's son were treated as "no job indication," as was family help.[30] As in the case of the wealthier merchants in the previous subgroup, 2.6 percent of all the farmers in the census records were assumed to have been large landowners and were counted as entrepreneurs. No adjustment was necessary for the large Nazi landowners, who cited their occupation accurately on the party lists.[31]

As for the third main group, the elite, the managers (subgroup 10) must be linked generically to the white-collar workers of the new middle class, for they were simply those salaried employees who had reached the top—the most responsible positions in businesses of appreciable size. Typically, they were men of the twentieth century and, in Germany, their numbers increased after World War I with the founding of large cartels and trusts. So far, this occupational sub-group, the German manager (*Prokurist, Direktor,* or *Geschäfts-führer*), has hardly been subjected to sociological analysis, and in the West German Federal Republic, *Leitende Angestellte* (business ex-ecutives) are only now being recognized as a separate social group with justifiable claims to special privileges, such as generous social in-surance.[32] Because managers have been found to resemble en-trepreneurs (owners) in life-style, political and economic philosophy, and frequently in income—in fact, the lines between them in terms of functionality have often been excessively blurred—sociologists have often treated them collectively as "business leaders."[33]

The higher civil servants in the next subgroup (11), while sharing many of the basic characteristics of their humbler colleagues (subgroup 7), usually stood apart from them because of a university degree (or, alternately, an aristocratic family background and atten-dant wealth), or because of executive duties and concomitantly higher pay. A part of this group consisted of upper-school (*Gymnasium*) teachers, many with doctorates, and of university lecturers and pro-fessors. The tenured full professors were the cream of the elite during the Weimar Republic and until well after World War II; but whether they held this status during the Third Reich is open to question.[34]

Similar in structure and social character to these higher-ranking bureaucrats were the self-employed, academically trained profes-sionals (subgroup 12). The German intelligentsia has often been por-trayed as outside the class system. But such an interpretation would be valid only under two conditions: if the professionals for lack of an in-digenous money supply had fallen to subsocietal depths and hence become part of the *Lumpenproletariat;* or if the intellectuals, forming a creative intelligentsia, were, by virtue of their critical distance from society, freewheeling, suspended above class lines.[35] In any case, in this study they will be treated formally, no matter what their income, ideology, or life-style, as members of the upper middle class, or the elite. This subgrouping of professionals includes physicians, lawyers, architects, and the various doctors of letters or science who had their own consulting firms, like the proprietors of an engineer's consulting firm or a chemical laboratory.[36] The profession of engineer, however, presented definitional problems. Academically educated engineers were easy to find in the party listings because they always identified themselves as such by using the appropriate suffixes. (Title-conscious Germans were apt to use whatever high-sounding label was defensible, as is still the case particularly in Austria.)[37] But an *Ing.-Grad.*—that is, a professional engineer graduated from a technical college ranking below a university—would simply have called himself *Ingenieur*. Technicians (*Techniker*), on the contrary, were not difficult to identify. In dealing with the census records, a fairly reliable formula of 1930 was used to determine the number of engineers at each professional level. Out of the total number of about 200,000 engineers, 60,000 were estimated to have been *Diplom-Ingenieure*, 90,000 *Ingenieure (grad.)*, and 50,000 technicians.[38]

In German society, upper-school and university students customarily belong to the social elite, because of the prestigious and well-paying professions they may look forward to after graduation.[39] University students were naturally not included in the census records of gainfully employed persons, but since they represented a social segment that lent itself easily to class assignment, statistical figures on students were culled from tables for 1933 published by the Statistisches Reichsamt and were added to the census figures to form subgroup 13.[40] University students, as well as a handful of senior upper-school students, were also found in the party files.

The last subgroup (14) of the elite is the entrepreneurs. For German society as a whole, 2.6 percent of all the merchants, farmers, owners, and leaseholders on the census rolls were presumed to have been in the highest income bracket. And in the party lists, they were readily identified by the titles they gave themselves: factory owners (*Fabrikanten*), entrepreneurs (*Unternehmer*), wholesale dealers (*Grosshändler*), and estate owners (*Gutsbesitzer*). This subgroup can be equated with Theodor Geiger's "capitalists," although his category is somewhat larger numerically than the one arrived at here.[41]

This detailed analysis of 27,047,899 socially classifiable persons of both sexes in Germany in 1933 results in the following class breakdown:[42]

Class	Number	Percent
Lower	14,758,322	54.56
Lower middle	11,537,226	42.65
Elite	752,351	2.78

The percentage of 54.56 for the lower class may seem relatively high, but it is not so large as Karl Martin Bolte's figure would have been for 1933—59.9 percent—if his study (like this one) had omitted family help from the arithmetic.[43] Conversely, the percentage of 2.78 for the elite appears somewhat low in comparison with other counts or estimates; still, it is not totally out of line. For the West German society of 1958-59, Harriett Moore and Gerhard Kleinig found that 6 percent of the population ranked themselves with the "upper crust" (*Ober-*

schicht) and the "upper middle crust" (*Obere Mittelschicht*). Ralf Dahrendorf recently fixed on an elitist figure of 5 percent for the postwar European societies, "according to the criteria of prestige, of income and of influence." Morris Janowitz calculated an upper-class portion of 4.6 percent for West German society in 1955. For Weimar society, Carl Dreyfuss mentioned 3.3 percent. Geiger's ("capitalist") designation of the elite, which was based on the testing of theoretical concepts by empirical research, produced a percentage of only 0.84.[44]

Thus far, in laying the groundwork for this book on the social profile of the Nazi party, attention has been paid to the class groupings and occupational subgroups of the whole German society, as based, in the main, on the census of 1933. This has been done because sociographic data about the general population are needed to provide the backdrop, or norms, against which to view and analyze the sociography of the Nazi party.[45] Comparable data on the party were drawn from several types of sources. One was a fragmented Nazi membership list for the fall of 1923, comprising 4,726 cases, which was augmented by primary data printed in secondary sources.[46] The second was a representative sample of 18,255 cases, all of them Nazi members during the period from 1925 to 1945, selected systematically from the Nazi Party Master File in the Berlin Document Center. (This file, about 80 percent complete, contains the membership cards for several million National Socialists; altogether there are approximately 8.5 million cards in two separate but overlapping sets.) Of these 18,255 cases, only 15,343 could be used to compare Nazi class structure with the structure of German society as revealed by the Reich statistical (census) data. The rest had to be discarded for lack of classifiable characteristics; this category included party functionaries, members with no job indication, the unemployed (only two such entries were found for the entire time span), pensioners, and housewives (2,912 *N*).[47] But these remaining cases could still be used whenever any of four specific variables were in question: sex, age, year of NSDAP entrance, and size of region.

The third type of party source was the lists of self-contained local or regional groups of party members and functionaries. Their names either had been published by entrenched Nazis in semiofficial commemorative chronicles after January 1933 or were discovered in the West German archives. Such lists usually showed the Nazis' names and party numbers and sometimes their places of residence. Hence it was necessary to search further for information regarding each candidate's occupation and date of birth, as well as to verify the time of party entrance and place of abode during that period. This was done, through very time-consuming and costly processes, in the Berlin Document Center. Data were collected in this fashion for "party comrades" from Bochum, Thuringia, and other venues, for *Gauleiter* (regional party leaders), for *Kreisleiter* (district party chiefs), and for various other groups in the party hierarchy.

On the basis of these data gathered from Nazi party sources, five variables were established for use in statistical analysis. The first variable, sex, was easily created on the fundament of candidates' Christian names. The second, occupation, was more problematical because of the difficulties inherent in self-evaluation. As the candidates entered their names on the membership lists, they naturally indicated their professions to the Nazi record keepers according to their subjective status image, which usually, but not always, coincided with the objective fact. Some highly specialized workers, for instance, wishing perhaps to impress the functionaries of a party that craved recognition as a labor movement, represented themselves as only *Arbeiter* (subgroup 1) rather than as *Handwerker* (2 or 4). Conversely, some candidates styled themselves merchants when in reality they were only sales clerks.[48] The third variable was residence, which included three subdivisions arranged according to size. The first, large city, comprised all towns with a population of over 100,000; the second, small town, was composed of those having between 10,000 and 100,000 inhabitants; and the third, country, was applied to communities of less than 10,000 people. This division resulted in a relatively facile coding procedure, which permitted quick perception of the size of towns from compactly published census records that excluded all places with a population below 10,000.[49] The system proved to be useful because it showed up the gradations between the least and the most populous areas, and hence made clear the differences resulting from regional peculiarities. As one critic has recently argued, a somewhat finer grid might have been even more useful.[50] The fourth and fifth variables were the year of entrance into the Nazi party and the age at the time of entrance. The latter was computed on the basis of information about members' dates of birth, readily available in the Berlin Document Center files.

Besides setting up variables to be used in statistical analysis, it was necessary to use a prosopographical approach in order to answer many questions relating to the development of the National Socialist party as a social phenomenon. Naturally, a simple listing of the occupations found in the party at any given period would not have sufficed; it was also desirable to know something about the motives of the men and women who signed up as members in varying strengths over time to make for a very irregular growth of the party from 1919 to 1945 (figure 1). Because this information was not contained in the raw data presented in tables or figures, it was essential to turn to selected primary documents, such as private letters and official memoranda. Several of these were found in the post–World War II anthologies, some even in translation; but the great majority had to be sought from archives, mostly in West Germany. Memoirs published after 1933 by "Old Fighter" (*Alte Kämpfer*) Nazis with distinguished records as pioneers of the movement in the "Time of Struggle" (*Kampfzeit*), 1919–1933, contributed important details to the composite picture of social makeup and psychological motivation. Questions regarding the role of women in the party, which have never before been asked with any degree of thematic consistency, were posed, and some of them were at least partially answered. An explanation of the age factor, as it affected the party's development from the earliest beginnings to the end, also had to be part of the exercise. And finally, something previously untried and hence of special significance was an analysis of the leadership strata along sociological lines. To what extent, it was asked, did the sociography of the Nazi functionaries differ from that of the Nazi rank and file?

In view of the incomplete nature of the existing social histories of the Nazi party, two particular problem areas have been given special consideration.

First, every facet of the sociology of the Nazi movement prior to 1933 (prior to Hitler's coming to power) has always been treated either in close correlation with, or through heavy concentration on, voting behavior before that year. One reason for this has been the relative accessibility of data pertaining to the Weimar Republic's regional and national elections. Although it has been valid to attempt such analyses, it has often been wrongly assumed that sociographic trends based on voting behavior may be readily used to make inferences about the characteristics of the party's membership structure. The likelihood of such a congruence does exist, but it has never been empirically proved.[51]

The second problem is related to the first. It has been the fashion to characterize the pre-1933 Nazi party, on the basis of electoral statistics, as a "typical" lower-middle-class phenomenon, and even to imply that the other classes represented in it were negligible.[52] From this conclusion the axiom was derived that the lower middle class exhibited propensities for fascism, and, as a corollary, that fascism could be identified by the sum total of lower-middle-class characteristics, as shown, for instance, by a specific code of behavior or cultural pattern. Although it cannot be denied that classes in Germany were distinguishable by traits of collective mentality — an assumption that will be put to use in this study — one must beware of the a priori equation of sociocultural attitudes and political preferences.[53] More care is needed in examining both the lower class and the elite in their relation to the National Socialist movement. "Historical evidence shows," wrote the pioneering scholar Wolfgang Sauer in 1967, "that support of fascism may not be confined to the classical elements of the lower middle class (*Mittelstand* — peasants, artisans, small businessmen, and so forth), but may extend to a wide variety of groups in the large field between the workers on the one hand and big business, the aristocracy, and the top levels of bureaucracy on the other."[54] Testing the validity of that statement and furnishing still more of what Sauer calls the "historical evidence" are two of the most important concerns of this book.

I

SOCIAL COMPOSITION OF THE NAZI PARTY'S RANK AND FILE
1919-1945

1

THE BEGINNING

1919 TO THE BEER HALL PUTSCH
NOVEMBER 1923

Part I of this book investigates the social composition of the rank and file of the Nazi party from its beginning in 1919 to Hitler's downfall in 1945. This aspect of Nazi party history can best be examined by dividing the party's history into five periods: 1919–1923, 1923–1930, 1930–1933, 1933–1939, and 1939–1945. In the first period the Nazi party got its start, developed promisingly in Bavaria, and fell victim to Hitler's abortive Putsch against the German government in November 1923. In the second period Hitler managed not only to resurrect the Nazi party but also to enlarge and develop it beyond the narrow confines of the state of Bavaria. In the third period the party's growth appeared to be greatly aided by the economic depression that affected all of Germany at the beginning of the 1930s. The end of this period also marked the end of the National Socialist "Time of Struggle," which coincided with the life span of the Weimar Republic. In January 1933, at the beginning of the fourth period, Hitler was not only the leader of a mass party but also the head of the national government. Because his party was the official, monopolistic state party of the Third Reich, its social composition underwent certain changes. Further changes occurred in the fifth and last period, from 1939 to 1945, when the party had to endure the pressures of a world war and finally to struggle for survival—a struggle that was lost even before the Nazi act of capitulation to the Allied victors on May 8, 1945.

The analysis in this chapter assigns each of several thousand known Nazis to one of the fourteen occupational subgroups that made up the three social classes in Germany between the world wars. The outcome is a series of percentages that indicate, when set against the occupational and class structure of German society as a whole (presented in table 1), whether the subgroups and classes were overrepresented or underrepresented in the party in relation to their representation in the entire population. To enhance this statistical analysis, discussion centers on the reasons why certain of the occupational and class groupings in Germany were attracted to the Nazi party while others were not. Data on party members have been drawn from fifteen membership lists; eight of these pertain to the Munich chapter, two to the Reich as a whole, and the rest to the Nazi chapters in five South German towns: Rosenheim, Passau, Landshut, Mannheim, and Ingolstadt.[1]

THE WORKERS

When the German Workers' Party (DAP) was founded by toolmaker Anton Drexler and his fellow workers in the Munich railway workshops on January 5, 1919, its name clearly indicated that it would appeal especially to the German working class.[2] There is convincing evidence that the DAP's leadership—which after September 1919 included a twenty-nine-year-old Austrian, Adolf Hitler—was at great pains to attract workers not only in Munich and its environs (the center of party activity) but also in the industrial areas to the North and West.[3] That large numbers of workers attended Nazi party rallies and membership meetings in Munich and its hinterland from 1919 on is amply documented by both contemporary government records and private eyewitness accounts.[4] In North and Northwest Germany the appeal began in 1920, when, incidentally, the DAP's name was changed to National Socialist German Worker's Party (NSDAP). In that year workers in Dortmund in the industrialized Ruhr Valley were attracted to the party; in 1921 members came from Hattingen, not far from Dortmund, and the rubber works of Hanover in Lower Saxony. In 1922 workers in Hagen, again in the Ruhr district, joined up. In the same year working-class members of Nazi chapters were reported in Göttingen, and in the North Sea port of Bremen a local paper informed its readers in November that workers were flocking to the new Nazi movement "in droves."[5]

If, in the first few years of the party's existence, the Nazi leaders in Munich were not entirely satisfied with the modest progress they were making among the workers, this was due mainly to the party chiefs' peculiar concept of the working class in German society and of what its socioeconomic objectives should be.[6] Their views stood in marked contrast to the philosophy of traditional Marxism, embodied in the political catechisms of the leftist parties of the early Weimar Republic, the Social Democrats (SPD) and the more militant Independent

Socialists (USPD) and Communists (KPD). Although the SPD had long forsaken Marx's and Engels's more orthodox ideal of the political class struggle, all the leftists subscribed to the idea of achieving social betterment by such economic means as labor strikes.[7] The Nazis, by contrast, resisted the idea of an economic division of society into exploiters and exploited. In place of such an economically based class struggle, whose reality and necessity they denied, they visualized a contest that would be determined by biological criteria: the pure-blooded "Aryan" Germans abused by racially "alien" Jews.[8] Racist anti-Semitism was thus at the basis of the Nazi definition of the worker, a definition that was officially echoed in the party's program of February 24, 1920. (This, the so-called Feder Program, had been drawn up by Drexler, Hitler, and the crank economist Gottfried Feder.) In principle, the worker was anybody who was of unadulterated German blood and who toiled, with his brain or his hand, to make an honest living. The natural enemy of the worker was not the historic captain of industry or the heavy-industrialist tycoon of more recent times but rather the Jewish banker or petty dealer who was thought to live unproductively by collecting interest on the money he had craftily garnered from honest German folk. The Feder Program as well as Hitler's speeches earmarked the exponents of "finance capital" as the purveyors of "interest slavery." Every good German, including by implication the "worker of the hand," was viewed as having been "enslaved."[9]

These planks in the Nazi platform, which neither recognized the German workers' historical heritage nor did anything to further their rightful claims against capitalists and the bourgeois class, were ill received by many. The Feder Program did not satisfy the workers with political grievances, including those who were clamoring for the recapture of the colonies. No more did it satisfy those with economic grievances: "profit-sharing in the great industries" (paragraph 14 of the Program), a goal that was well out of reach, seemed decidedly unrealistic to most German workers. Nor would these workers have benefited from the leasing of chain stores to small businessmen (paragraph 16); on the contrary, working people welcomed the price advantages that rationalization and large-volume buying in the five-and-ten stores had afforded them in the past. And "interest slavery" was a term that meant nothing to people who were not accustomed to borrowing and thus had no recollection of having been forced into making exorbitant interest payments.[10]

In actuality, the average worker was in no danger from the Jews, the purported instigators of interest bondage. The worker simply did not understand the Nazis' association of Semitism with high-volume capitalism and undue profit gains. He did not find himself in danger of seduction by international Jewry, whose representatives he did not even recognize, except, perhaps, for those at the helm of the unions, and the union leaders were generally trusted. The worker rarely read Jewish-controlled newspapers, and if he did, it was beyond his capabilities to determine in what sense they were "Jewish" and why, by virtue of that fact, they were "bad." He could not visualize "Judas, the World's Enemy" (Drexler's phrase), who had supposedly been preying on the workers of Europe since the outbreak of the Great War. The more firmly the German worker was entrenched in one of the traditional leftist parties, the less time he had for racism and anti-Semitism, which, as Franz Neumann has said, were substitutes for the class struggle.[11]

As for the issues dearest to the workers' hearts, the Nazi party's position did it more harm than good. The NSDAP remained ambivalent on the question of unions, approving of them only as corporate institutions without economic or political bargaining power. On the question of industrial strikes, the Nazi leaders tended toward noninvolvement, avoiding any hard-line policy. At a time when the German labor scene was highly volatile, when the workers were constantly ready to strike, such an insecure stance almost amounted to political self-defeat among the proletariat.[12] On this issue, as on others, it was far better for the workers to stay with the traditional parties, in particular the SPD and the small but growing KPD. As Theodor Geiger astutely observed in 1932, socialism of the Nazi type could not catch on with the bulk of the workers: they had long been accustomed to varieties of "concrete socialism" that offered them far more than Nazi theory.[13] And repeated Nazi attacks against Marxist parties and "Bolshevism" could do nothing to change their allegiance.[14]

What, then, about the workers who actually did join the Nazi party between 1919 and 1923? Where did they come from, why did they join, and how many of them were there? As table 2 shows, workers began to join the Munich party in 1919, before Hitler was a member. The lower class as a whole was always underrepresented in the NSDAP (compared with its representation in the total population in 1933: 54.56 percent), but the two subgroups of skilled workers—who in terms of mentality and living conditions were close to the lower middle class—tended to be overrepresented, and the subgroup of unskilled laborers tended to be underrepresented (compare tables 2 and 1).

The fluctuations that occurred in the strength of the workers' contingents between 1919 and 1923 could not be called statistically meaningful, and there does not appear to have been a preponderance of country laborers over city workers, or vice versa. It is certain, however, that these Nazi workers viewed the NSDAP as a right-of-center alternative to the SPD or the KPD and that they fitted the model of Drexler and Hitler. They were men of nationalist leanings with peculiar, ingrown prejudices against Jews; they were disenchanted (like the well-known "social imperialist" August Winnig) with Marxist ideology and practice as seen in the leftist parties; and they were proud of the title "worker" as opposed to "proletarian."[15] Above all, a goodly number of them must have harbored hopes of upward social mobility that were not typical of their class. They may have partially fallen prey to the gradual process of "embourgeoisement," which was so poignantly described by the sociologist Robert Michels in the early twenties. Having adopted parts of the value system of the lower middle class, these workers could not help suffering from certain maladies characteristic of that group, such as a marked propensity toward ultranationalism, which the Nazis happened to cater to. In all probability, these were the "better workers" to whom a Munich police report of September 1920 referred — people with proved skills, well established in their occupations, but possibly afraid of falling back into a more impoverished and much more class-conscious proletariat.[16] On the whole, then, although the NSDAP from 1919 to 1923 contained a considerable number of members from the working class, it was not by any means a workers' party, as Drexler and perhaps even Hitler might have fancied it to be.

THE LOWER MIDDLE CLASS

National Socialism has been presented as a prototypical lower-middle-class phenomenon in the scholarly literature of the West. Since World War II the most authoritative exponent of this thesis has been the U.S. political scientist Seymour Martin Lipset.[17] To date, there is not much empirical evidence to substantiate this view for the period preceding the Putsch of November 1923. The data do reveal that a number of typical lower-middle-class occupations, notably those of master craftsman and merchant, tended to be overrepresented in the NSDAP, and that the lower-middle-class character of the party was strengthened when farmers started to join the Nazi movement in 1922–23. Further, the figures for Munich in 1920–21, Ingolstadt in 1922–23, and the Reich (mainly South Germany) in the autumn of

1923, which show that more than half the members of the party in those areas came from the lower middle class, strongly suggest that this class was overrepresented in the party as a whole (compare tables 2 and 1).

Table 2 shows that the urban, and later also the small-town and rural, merchants and artisans (craftsmen) of the old middle class were a substantial source of strength for the early party. These occupational subgroups (4 and 8) had begun to suffer economically during World War I, when their shop assistants had been drafted and their profits had dwindled in the wake of price controls, shortages in raw materials, and credit restrictions. These difficulties lingered after the war's end and were compounded by new problems, even though the demand for craftsmen increased as a result of the general need for repairs. But as the postwar inflation progressed, small businesses became more difficult to operate. A further threat was the growth of modern factories, department stores, and cooperatives, which could manufacture and sell goods more cheaply than the family-directed businesses. Credit and raw materials remained scarce. Although the degree of harm done to small shopkeepers and craftsmen by the pre-1924 inflation was often overestimated prior to the publication of Heinrich August Winkler's illuminating study, the fact remains that these people *thought* they were being made to suffer unduly, and hence, in searching for redress, they turned away from the democratic ideals of the newborn Weimar Republic.[18] Moreover, in the countryside, retailers and tradesmen had even more reason to fear competition from rationalized business procedures in the cities than did their urban counterparts, who were better able to adapt to the changing times.[19]

Why the farmers, the third large group of the old middle class, did not find their way into the Nazi party until comparatively late in the 1919–1923 period has never been convincingly explained (table 2). One possible reason is that before 1920 the DAP or NSDAP had little influence outside Munich and so could not have reached peasants or farmers.[20] Another reason, suggested by Werner T. Angress in 1959, may be that the peasants, who constituted 65 percent of the population of Bavaria by 1918–19, did not begin to suffer economically until 1923 because they were still able to get relatively high prices for their foodstuffs; the tide turned in that year, however, when currency stabilization reduced the barter value of produce from the land, and farmers started to flock to the NSDAP.[21] But this line of reasoning contains several flaws. Studies more recent than Angress's have shown that farmers had been suffering economically at least since the end of

World War I: their cattle had been decimated and their soil exhausted, and the state regulatory measures that hurt them were not lifted until 1922. There was harmful competition from agricultural imports from abroad, and the tight credit squeeze irked the peasants as well as the small merchants and tradesmen.[22] As for the currency stabilization ordinances that might have hurt the farmers, they did not really take effect until after 1923. Yet all the peasants who came to the party in this early period joined before November 9, 1923. Probably they started joining after Hitler began to refer to them in public in July 1923. The most plausible reason for the peasants' hesitancy until then appears to have been their political mores. Tradition-minded South German farmers needed time in which to develop trust in a movement that had originated in a big city and was said to appeal to workers. They may have mistaken the NSDAP for a Marxist party of sorts, born in the aftermath of the Bavarian Soviet Republic, while they themselves were used to a pattern of order and stability tempered with ultramontanism, which was available to them through the political ideology of the Bavarian People's Party (BVP) closely linked with the Catholic Church.[23]

As for the representatives of the so-called new middle class (the lower civil servants and the lower employees, or office clerks), their absolute numbers in the Reich population significantly increased after the occupational census of 1907 because of the inflated wartime administration and the implementation of republican democracy after 1918, and because of further advances in the industrialization of the economy.[24] The lower employees or white-collar workers (subgroup 6) appear to have been represented in the NSDAP in almost equal proportion to their numbers in the Reich, although in Ingolstadt in 1922–23 they were overrepresented. The lower civil servants (subgroup 7), however, were always overrepresented. (Compare tables 2 and 1.) Even though the statisticians of both the Weimar Republic and the Third Reich usually combined the two occupations and entered them in the same slot, the sociopolitical interests of the subgroups were by no means identical. Since long before the founding of the Wilhelmine Empire (1871), lower civil servants had been distinguished by a sense of duty to the state that not only was the hallmark of their officialdom but also provided the rationale for their sinecurial privileges — old-age pensions, job tenure, and a fair measure of health and other welfare protection. These privileges tied the lower civil servants to the government they were serving at any given time; yet in the case of the Weimar Republic many were unable to identify the new, pluralistic party government with the old, stable, monarchic order. Inasmuch as they had doubts about this, and insofar as they looked upon the ill-fated revolution of November 1918 as merely a first (albeit unsuccessful) step in the direction of a Marxist dictatorship of the sort already witnessed during the Eisner regime in Munich, they feared for their future. To them the Nazi emphasis on nationalist virtues as expressed in the Feder Program (paragraphs 1–6) was sufficient to present the NSDAP as a patriotic bulwark. And the bad effects of the staggering inflation added an economic reason for discontent: while lower civil servants were on fixed salaries, the real value of their monthly pay dwindled each time they received it. Just as they were dreading the impending cutbacks in their pensions, Hitler promised them relief.[25] And in 1923 Jakob Sprenger, an intermediate state official and a future Nazi Gauleiter, was delegated to look after the affairs of public servants within the Nazi leadership.[26]

The clerks (lower employees or white-collar workers) were one rung below the civil servants on the German social scale. In addition to the economic problems they faced, which were tied to inflation and in this sense were not dissimilar to those of the officials, they existed in a situation of potential social flux. Always in danger of lapsing into the proletariat that they despised, they emulated the lower civil servants, aped their mannerisms and life-style, and hoped eventually to be raised to their status in society. They were especially jealous of the officials' economic benefits such as tenure and pension rights.[27] But they also envied the independent merchants in their role as employers of shop assistants.[28]

If the workers of the lower class who were attracted by the Nazi party platform had difficulty in comprehending its anti-Semitic utterances, the members of the lower middle class did not. Indeed, the anti-Jewish propaganda seemed to be tailor-made for them. Even before the Feder Program was made public early in 1920, the National Socialists had identified the Jews as the perpetrators of all the economic and political ills befalling the country.[29] To the small craftsman and shopkeeper the Jew was the instigator (and owner) of a system of factories and chain stores that threatened their livelihood. Feder's paragraphs 13, 14, and 16 addressed themselves to this problem. The farmers, too, who could look back on a firm tradition of rural anti-Semitism in the 1880s and 1890s, especially in Hesse where the Jew-baiter Dr. Otto Böckel had been politically active on their behalf and consequently had become a local legend, were taken in by the stereotype of the Jewish cattle dealer as well as that of the Jewish-Marxist revolutionary in the city.[30] They stood to gain by points 17 and 18 of the party program, which called for land reform, abrogation of "soil interest charges" and real estate speculation, and capital punishment of (Jewish) "usurers" and "confidence men." Insofar as the Feder Program succeeded in associating everything dishonest and corrupt in the national polity explicitly or implicitly with a perverse Jewish ethic, it also appealed to the white-collar workers, whose most significant professional organization, the German Shop Clerks' Association (DHV), had been decidedly anti-Semitic since its beginnings in the early 1890s.[31] Finally, the civil servants received satisfaction from paragraph 6 of the program, which relegated tenure privileges for state offices expressly to "citizens" (non-Jewish Germans) and castigated the "corrupt" parliamentary system of the new republic. It was a common belief in illiberal rightist circles that this republic was the product of a Jewish conspiracy to trap the guileless German people after the shameful capitulation of November 1918.[32]

THE ELITE

The sparse data presented in table 2 indicate that the German elite — the upper middle class and former aristocracy — were consistently overrepresented in the NSDAP since its very beginnings. Evidently, a large percentage of these upper-class members consisted of high-school and university students (subgroup 13): over 50 percent in the Munich chapter 1920–21, and more than 33 percent in the entire Reich in the fall of 1923. Even in Ingolstadt and its surroundings, which had a comparatively small local student population, almost half of the upper-class members within the local NSDAP chapter in 1922–23 came from the student body (table 2). It is tempting to disregard many of the university students as social drifters who, temporarily displaced after returning from the war in 1918–19 and from Freikorps action thereafter, sought refuge in the institutions of higher learning, only to drop out later and fall back into the lower middle class, if not the proletariat. Indeed, between 1918 and 1923 the student population at German universities and technical colleges rose dramatically from 20,000 to 125,000.[33] But even if half of all the students are discounted, the upper layers of society would still have been overrepresented in the NSDAP up to the time of the Beer Hall Putsch.

The reasons for the students' attraction to Drexler's and Hitler's party are obvious. Still emotionally attached to the monarchic order that had allegedly been "stabbed in the back" by Marxist-revolutionary forces, these former "front-line soldiers" embraced Hitler's nationalist slogans with a fervor of which only disillusioned youth is capable. The NSDAP's anti-Semitism blended smoothly with the tradition of Jew-baiting that had prevailed in university seminars and student fraternities long before World War I. The sense of frustration and futility that engulfed many would-be academics because of economic uncertainties could be sublimated by joining the more militant ranks of the growing NSDAP, especially its activist sports and fighting organizations, such as the budding Stormtroops (Sturmabteilungen — SA). As early as November 1922 the official Nazi newspaper, *Völkischer Beobachter,* called for a meeting of radical *völkisch* students in a Munich pub. Toward the end of that year, veteran army lieutenant Rudolf Hess, at the time a senior university student himself, formed an SA student battalion as part of the SA regiment in Munich. As recent scholarship has shown, it is virtually impossible to divest the early Nazi student movement of its military element; these students, more often than not, thought of themselves as officers first, and may even have entered the Nazi party after indicating their military rank rather than their student status and academic discipline on the membership rosters.[34]

As academic hopefuls striving for privileged socioeconomic status in German society, the students were readily identifiable with the broader segments of the upper middle class and former aristocracy, even if they had originally come from a lower-middle-class or proletarian background, as was increasingly the case.[35] Other representatives of the upper strata of German society joined the Nazi party not so much for its activist appeal, which was a decisive factor for the students, as for its antiliberal attitudes that were distinctly opposed to the new republic. Art impresario Ernst Hanfstaengl, piano manufacturer Carl Bechstein, publishers Julius Lehmann and Hugo Bruckmann, university professor Karl Alexander von Müller, aristocrat Count Ernst zu Reventlow, and even representatives of heavy industry, such as Dr. Karl Burhenne of the Siemens works, came to regard Hitler and his Nazis very favorably. Although the relationship was often tenuous — rich patrons would make intermittent financial contributions without ever publicizing their support for the Nazis — it was significant if for only one reason. The NSDAP was being seriously tested as an alternative to the ultraconservative Deutschnationale Volkspartei (DNVP), in the search for ways to turn back the clock and reestablish the old imperial order with its proved system of economic stability and social privilege. Thus the Nazi party appeared to a large number in Germany's higher circles as a useful tool for achieving reactionary goals.[36] By 1922, when Hitler was introduced to the members of a conservative and influential club in Berlin, his party had already achieved an impressive record of membership connections with entrepreneurial and manager circles in Munich.[37] Avraham Barkai has advanced a cogent argument in favor of the view that the economic planks in the Feder Program made it easy for the Nazis to assume an anticapitalist air without really offending the protagonists of large industry, large-scale farming, and commerce.[38]

Although the party leadership did little to encourage academics and well-educated professionals to join the NSDAP, this subgroup (12) was heavily overrepresented (compare tables 2 and 1).[39] As with the students, more of the Nazi intellectuals tended to come from large cities, particularly Munich, than from small towns or the countryside. Donald M. Douglas's published data, for instance, point to a high percentage of artists from Schwabing, a bohemian suburb of Munich, who should be included in this group.[40] The motives that led intellectuals and academically trained professionals to join the NSDAP are less obvious than those governing the university and upper-school students. However, as Juan J. Linz has pointed out, National Socialism as a form of fascism did have a certain esthetic appeal for the intellectual, an appeal that was as much grounded in his hatred of what were considered the vulgarities of Bolshevism as in his contempt for late nineteenth-century bourgeois liberalism, which he looked upon as degenerate. Many, including Ernst ("Putzi") Hanfstaengl, scion of a famous Munich art publishing house, delighted in the unsophisticated behavior of Adolf Hitler and his cronies and thought it fashionable to identify themselves with such earthy ways. Among the more prominent personages who came into contact with the Nazi party rather early in its history were Emil Nolde the artist, who joined in 1920, and the Benedictine abbot Alban Schachleitner, who was to consecrate the banners of the SA. But the alliance between the Nazis and the intellectuals was, at best, a tenuous one. Before long Nolde was to become the victim of Alfred Rosenberg's diatribes, and the nationalist writer Arthur Moeller van den Bruck, whose June Club Hitler visited in 1922, could not be wooed by the Führer. Characteristically, Moeller is said to have accused Hitler of not being able to "give his National Socialism any intellectual basis."[41]

The upper-middle-class (elite) subgroup that was most reluctant to join the Nazi party was the higher civil servants (11). In Munich in 1920–21 they were overrepresented, but by the end of 1923 their enthusiasm had fallen off (tables 2 and 1). These upper-level administrators, who shared the reservations of many academically trained professionals concerning Hitler's fundamental anti-intellectualism, also felt duty-bound to the new order that they represented, even though it was distastefully republican. The proverbially apolitical attitude of the German higher civil servant essentially prevented him from taking violent action against the state, whether it was authoritarian or democratic.[42] Without question the upper-echelon bureaucrats who did become party members had first to overcome such scruples, but they were not driven by merely ideological motives. Since the end of World War I upper civil servants had harbored severe economic grievances. In times of inflation their salaries were cut back much more, proportionately, than those of intermediate or even lower civil servants. They were often virulently anti-Semitic, especially if they found themselves in competition with Jews at the government level, or, as was increasingly the case with the professors (who, like most teachers, enjoyed civil-servant status), in the universities. One of the German scholars who pledged allegiance to Adolf Hitler in those early years was the natural scientist Johannes Stark, a Nobel laureate. And among those who were killed in the skirmish of November 9, 1923, was a Bavarian Supreme Court justice, Theodor von der Pfordten.[43]

The events of November 8 and 9, 1923, brought the history of the Nazi party to a sudden halt. Hitler, whose Munich Putsch against the central government in Berlin had resulted in dismal failure, was tried in a Bavarian court of law and sentenced in April 1924 to five years' imprisonment. Had any of the close observers of that trial been in a position to speculate about the future of the Nazi movement, they might well have concentrated on three significant circumstances. First, at the time of its proscription by national and state authorities in November 1923, the party had had 55,287 members (figure 1). For a political formation with a life of less than five years, such a high membership was remarkable, even though most of it was centered in South German Bavaria. It remained to be seen what these members would do while their leader was in jail. Second, the fact that General Erich Ludendorff, one of the most venerated heroes of World War I, participated in the Putsch on Hitler's side was symptomatic of the extent of the support the Nazi party had been receiving from the upper echelons of society. Could this kind of support be sustained or, indeed, expanded in the years to come, if the NSDAP should experience a resurrection? Such a resurrection, of course, was bound up with the personal fate of Adolf Hitler. The third factor of interest, then, was how the party's leader would fare, in the immediate and distant future, at the hands of the Bavarian justice officials. It was known that the Bavarian minister of justice in 1924 was entirely sympathetic to the Austrian's cause. (A decade later, he would pursue a career as Nazi justice minister for the German Reich.) Hence it was not unreasonable to expect that Hitler would be freed from prison long before his five-year term was up. In fact, the judgment condemning him included a clause that left open the possibility of an early parole.

2

THE MIDDLE YEARS
1924 TO THE FALL ELECTIONS
OF 1930

On December 20, 1924, after only nine months of detainment in his Landsberg cell, Hitler was released, just in time to spend Christmas at the spacious residence of the Hanfstaengls pondering the revival of his political party. During his imprisonment the party—illegal as its status was—had been under the caretakership of its chief ideologist, the expatriate Baltic architect Alfred Rosenberg, who was also the editor of the party's newspaper, *Völkischer Beobachter.* Rosenberg had not been generally trusted by the other leaders, and he lacked the Führer's charisma. In the South, Rosenberg had been opposed by such men as Dr. Wilhelm Frick, Captain Ernst Röhm, and General Ludendorff; in the North and Northwest, rival groups had sprung up under various labels, one led by the Landshut pharmacist Gregor Strasser, another by the young Rhenish journalist Dr. Paul Joseph Goebbels, and another by the Prussian aristocrat Albrecht von Graefe. Hitler's first important task was to assure himself once again of the allegiance of these men and to neutralize their motley organizations while he set out to rebuild the NSDAP from his Munich base. Late in February 1925 Hitler called for a new beginning by rescinding all pre-1924 party memberships and issuing new membership numbers to old and new adherents; for himself (the original party's fifty-fifth member) he reserved number 1.

The NSDAP had established its South German (Bavarian) reputation as a political protest movement that thrived on the disappointments of people of all classes. Although for the vast majority of Germans the second half of the 1920s turned out to be a comparatively tranquil period, not everyone in the Reich was satisfied. This was fortunate for Hitler, whose undeniable political genius included the ability to manipulate circumstances in order to augment the membership of his party.

For two reasons he began his work in the northern part of Germany. First, the Nazi cover organizations north of Bavaria, chiefly under the leadership of the highly intelligent and sober-minded Gregor Strasser, had reached a significantly greater number of industrial workers during the interregnum than had the Bavarian group. Unquestionably, Strasser's own proworker sympathies had had a good deal to do with this. Over the months following February 1925 Hitler was able to utilize Strasser's excellent organizational network and to extend Strasser's campaign among the workers in the North. Second, the disillusioned social subgroups that were most open to Nazi propaganda (such as the farmers in Schleswig-Holstein) happened to exist in much higher density in the North than in the South. This meant that Hitler hardly ever lacked a target group suitable for his political purposes, chief among which was his intention to topple the national government in Berlin not by coup d'etat but by legal, parliamentary means. He needed, therefore, to enlist as many Germans as possible from all walks of life.

The following analysis of the social composition of the Nazi members between 1923 and 1930 is largely based on Nazi party membership lists from various parts of the Reich. On these lists, two categories of members have been identified.

The first category (as was the case in table 2) consists of members of established standing. The frequencies indicated for these member groups connote almost total membership at the time in question, because in each case only a few members' data could not be statistically processed. It is justifiable, therefore, to treat the frequencies for the North German cities of Hamburg and Brunswick, the four Ruhr towns of Barmen, Langerfeld, Mülheim, and Mettmann, the southern Bavarian small town of Starnberg, and the East Prussian provincial capital of Königsberg as total memberships of local party chapters, counted cumulatively from the time of their establishment in the post-1924 period (table 4).

The second category is that of NSDAP joiners or newcomers. Figures for newcomers often pertain only to the year in which the candidates joined the Nazi party. They represent either the total number of joiners in that particular year (as do the Studentkowski frequencies for the Reich, 1925–1930, in table 3) or a sample of such joiners (the Madden frequencies for the Reich, 1925–1929, also in table 3). Because Studentkowski's and Madden's criteria of social definition may have differed, the figures for the two types of joiners are not statistically compatible, and comparisons from year to year must be made separately for each type.

By the same token, direct comparisons between the two categories of members and joiners are not possible for any given year, because the total membership accumulated by the end of that year obviously differed from the new membership between the first and the last day of that year. Still, it is defensible to treat joiners' values in cumulative terms for a certain year if the values for all previous years are known. Taking Madden's sample, it is fair to say that by his standard of selection all unskilled workers made up no more than 26.6 percent and no less than 20.8 percent of all Nazi party members extant in 1927 (table 3).

As well, frequencies are given for two separate samples — Greater Bochum in the West (Ruhr Valley), and the state of Thuringia in the East — for the 1925–1928 period (table 5). These frequencies, which have been broken down by region, may be viewed as those of established members within the perimeters of the time period, but it would be improper to use them as the basis for generalization either for any one year or for the Reich membership as a whole.

A final word of caution is needed with regard to the high turnover rate in the NSDAP's membership between 1923 and 1930. Many would-be Nazi party members joined the NSDAP for trial purposes only; they stayed for a few months or a few years and then dropped out. Many joined and rejoined several times, and of those who left before 1933 many returned for good after Hitler's appointment as Chancellor. During certain phases of the Weimar Republic, the overall dropout rate amounted to as much as 50 percent of the total membership. This tells the student of Nazism a good deal about the provisional character of the Nazi party in these years. But it also raises a methodological question because many of the members shown in the statistics for established Nazi party comrades and new joiners may only have been representative of the social composition of the party at certain points in time, rather than over the entire time span indicated in a table. No statistical technique has so far been devised to adjust for possible distortions in this case. One is therefore forced to accept the figures at face value. Keeping this reservation in mind, it is to be hoped that future scholarship can remove the potential for error and present the picture more accurately.

THE WORKERS

After the disastrous November 1923 Putsch, the National Socialists intensified their efforts to attract new members from the working class. In 1924 the leaders of the Nazi surrogate formations in North and Northwest Germany, who had strong leftist leanings, appealed to the thousands of industrial workers who were concentrated in the Ruhr as well as in such northern cities as Bremen, Hamburg, and Hanover. And when Hitler reestablished the NSDAP early in 1925, he recognized the opportunity to attract a large following in the Ruhr and expressly pledged himself to win over the laborers.[1]

Because of the party's initial difficulties in administering the resurrected NSDAP, the campaign to enlist workers north of Bavaria did not get under way until 1926. Then concerted efforts were made in the Ruhr, especially in such industrial centers as Essen, Bochum, Dortmund, and Wuppertal-Elberfeld. These efforts were directed by five leftists exponents of the Feder Program: Josef Terboven, Joseph Goebbels, Karl Kaufmann, and the brothers Gregor and Dr. Otto Strasser. Late in the same year, the campaign spread to North Germany when Goebbels, who had become Gauleiter of Berlin, started to canvass the pro-Communist proletarian districts of the capital. In 1927 Gustav Seifert, the founder of the first party chapter in Hanover, redoubled his efforts to win over the workers in the giant Continental rubber plant there. Up to 1930 special appeals were also made to blue-collar workers in the seaport of Bremen, in the Saxon metropolis of Dresden, throughout the countryside of East Prussia, and southward in the industrial centers surrounding Frankfurt. By 1927 the NSDAP had once again begun to spread its proworker propaganda in the South, first in Franconia and finally in Munich itself. There, in March, Hitler addressed a crowd in the arena of the Krone Circus and all but blamed the suffering of the working class on the German bourgeoisie.[2] Unlike such men as Kaufmann and the Strasser brothers, who were genuinely interested in the fate of the working class, Hitler held to his original view of the German proletariat, stressing the necessity for a homogeneous *Volksgemeinschaft* (people's community) in which the elements of class interest and class struggle would be replaced by a sense of unity fostered by the collective consciousness of mutual blood ties. In this program, Jews still figured prominently as the archenemy of true German socialism.[3]

In spite of its leaders' efforts, the Nazi party achieved little overall success among the blue-collar population of the Reich until the Reichstag elections of September 1930. Except for the pockets of concentrated working-class support in the Ruhr (at Bochum, Barmen, Mettmann, Langerfeld, and Mülheim-Ruhr), the lower class was generally underrepresented in the party. And although the percentage of new workers joining the NSDAP peaked in 1926 and 1927 (table 3), these figures were still not very high. Finally in 1928 the party leaders realized the futility of their approach to the working class and began to direct their propaganda toward other segments of society, even though this meant a concomitant drop in cumulative working-class membership.[4]

The data in table 4 for 1925-1929 tend to support a thesis that has already been convincingly advanced with regard to state (Landtag) and national (Reichstag) elections: there existed a negative correlation between workers living in heavily industrialized urban centers (such as Hamburg) and membership in the NSDAP. (This would imply, of course, a positive correlation between such workers and membership in the KPD or possibly the SPD.) Further, the data in table 5 suggest that those workers who did become attached to the NSDAP tended to live in small communities and villages, even though they may have commuted to the big cities for employment. This was particularly evident in the Ruhr district. For the Bochum region as a whole, among NSDAP members who lived in the country or in a small town there was a larger percentage of workers (48.5 and 41.6) than among members who lived in the mining city itself (32.2). The magnitude of the percentage, in fact, appeared to correspond with the distance of the place of residence from the city.

Localities other than those in the Ruhr Valley were no different.[5] In Berlin the proletariat favored the KPD rather than the NSDAP. In Saxony, where Nazi workers tended on the whole to live in rural rather than industrial settings, Plauen seems to have been the only large center whose working class gave the Nazi party substantial support. Other Nazi worker strongholds were Hesse-Nassau, Mecklenburg-Lübeck, East Hanover, the Palatinate, and Pomerania, all of them regions in which the agrarian way of life predominated and there were few large industrial cities. The Munich historian Günter Plum has stated with good reason that for the Nazi-inclined worker, whether he commuted to the city or worked on a farm, it was residence in a rural environment that was decisive, enabling him to tie himself to the soil either by owning some property, such as a small house and garden, or by aspiring to do so. Commuters, whose mixed culture of farming (at home) and industrial labor (at work) made them a sort of hybrid group, rejected the value system of the fully industrialized, houseless and rootless big-city worker and identified instead with the lower-middle-class mentality that was marked by the petit bourgeois pride of small land ownership in the country.[6]

A further isue is the effect of unemployment. As has been repeatedly asserted by scholars, the NSDAP won over a respectable number of unemployed workers during the post-1924 period.[7] Hard documentary evidence shows not only that the Nazis made an effort to attract the unemployed but also that the unemployed came to them for help. It is not always clear, however, whether these jobless men and women were members of the industrialized urban proletariat.[8] In the Ruhr, for example, within the period 1924–1930 (a time of generally rising industrial unemployment throughout Germany), the shorter period between 1924 and 1927 was relatively secure for workers.[9] Yet it was precisely during these years—especially in 1926 and 1927—that in the Reich as a whole the Nazis attracted a higher percentage of workers than at any other time before the Great Depression. After 1927, when unemployment increased, the rate at which workers joined the Nazi party declined (table 3). In view of the Communists' efforts on behalf of the industrial unemployed as well as the Nazis' failure to make inroads among the miners' shop stewards, who were obsessed with the fear of dismissal, it is fair to assume the existence of a positive correlation between KPD membership and industrial unemployment in urban areas, as well as the likelihood of a similar correlation between NSDAP membership and unemployment among workers in small towns and the countryside.[10] These assumptions are corroborated indirectly by membership statistics for the KPD in 1927 (whose job categories diverge somewhat from those used here), which show that at a time of relative economic stability more than 80 percent of the Communist party members belonged to the working class.[11]

Further evidence that before 1930 the NSDAP fared comparatively poorly among the industrial proletariat is revealed by its actions with regard to labor unions and strikes. In 1925 the attempts of Nazi party leaders in the North to establish a trade union were foiled by Hitler's personal indifference, but in 1929 the National Socialist Shop Organization (NSBO) was finally established in the Knorr Pneumatic Brakes plant in Berlin.[12] The NSBO gained ground only gradually, however, especially in the urban centers of the Ruhr, and it seems to have attracted a much higher percentage of white-collar workers than would be expected of a union with genuine proletarian interests. In some smaller industrial towns, in fact, the growth of the NSBO was stymied, if not altogether prevented, by the dearth of Nazi worker members. As the highest administrative officer of the party in the district of Stade, which had a low density of industrialization, wrote to his superiors in Hanover in the spring of 1930, "Because of the small number of NSDAP members in the individual factories, the formation of special [Nazi] workers' associations has not yet been possible."[13]

The Nazis' failure in their labor union policy was closely related to their attitude toward strikes, which continued to be ambiguous. On the one hand, the party condemned participation by its members in the strike-breaking operations of Technische Nothilfe (Technical Emergency Aid), an institution established by the republican government in 1919, and emphasized this in propaganda appeals to the workers. On the other hand, with the exception of the modest moral support given in newspaper articles to strikers in Thuringia and the Ruhr and Saar valleys in 1927, the party did not encourage its members to strike.[14] In November 1928, when about 250,000 steel workers in the Ruhr were locked out, the Nazis at first took no action at all and subsequently paid only lip service to the cause of the suffering workers. At the same time, of course, the KPD was reaping the full political harvest of the event by organizing a vigorous protest. Again, the Nazi leaders totally abstained from involvement in a strike in Saxony early in 1930, but in October they were compelled to allow their proletarian membership to participate in the big metal workers' strike in Berlin.[15] Obviously, a so-called workers' party that failed to formulate exact principles governing unions, strikes, and lockouts could hardly expect to attract the bulk of the industrial proletariat, especially when its fiercest political rival at the opposite end of the ideological spectrum had staked its whole political future on such issues.

THE LOWER MIDDLE CLASS

Notwithstanding their appeals to the workers after February 1925, the Nazis vigorously resumed their overtures to the traditional representatives of the old middle class, the small artisanal shopkeepers and independent merchants. As in earlier years they attacked Jews and chain stores, but they also geared their propaganda to such specific grievances of the mid-twenties as the credit policy adopted by banks and savings institutions after the financial stabilization of 1924, the new real estate tax of the same year, the salary increases for civil servants in 1927, and such state welfare measures as the introduction of unemployment insurance in 1927. Moreover, the Nazi leaders clamored for a protectionist policy and continued to bewail the ill effects of the postwar inflation. Not surprisingly, the extant documents indicate that the Nazi propaganda effort was concentrated on the old middle class between 1928 and 1930, just after the appeal to the workers had proved futile. Unrest was growing among shopkeepers and independent tradespeople as the Great Depression was approaching.[16]

As H. A. Winkler has remarked, these shopkeepers and artisans did not fare after 1924 as badly as they pretended; they appear to have been compensated for losses due to inflation by specific gains and benefits, such as those resulting from real estate ownership. In fact, Winkler's data support the hypothesis that small businesses did quite well in the wave of economic prosperity that swept over much of the German economy between 1923 and 1929.[17] Yet it is equally correct to stress, as Jeremy Noakes has done, that small business people suffered from a feeling of neglect and sociopolitical isolation, driving them away from the moderate conservative right toward the Nazi radical right.[18] In spite, too, of the undeniable prosperity experienced by the majority of small businessmen between 1924 and 1929, a sizable minority encountered serious difficulties. There were simply too many retailers in business after 1924, and so the less competitive were faced with reduced incomes. Additionally, female help was becoming increasingly difficult to get because of the lure of better-paying jobs in the more efficient chain stores and cooperatives. These two factors increased the fear that many master cobblers and small-town greengrocers already had of such big-city enterprises and hastened their own failure. The number of such bankruptcies increased as the thirties approached and heralded the advent of total economic collapse.[19] As early as 1925 small business people (master craftsmen and merchants), easily convinced of the villainy of the Jews, began to join the Nazi party in at least representative numbers. After 1928 they joined with renewed vigor, primarily for socioeconomic reasons, even if as a consequence their shops were boycotted by their anti-Nazi customers and their businesses stood a fair chance of failure in the short term (tables 3 and 1).[20]

As table 3 shows, another lower-middle-class subgroup, the small farmers, appears to have been underrepresented in the Nazi party from 1925 through 1927, as it had been in the earliest years of the DAP and NSDAP. But in 1928 the small farmers started flocking to Hitler's movement in much greater numbers than their representation in the Reich population would justify (tables 3 and 1).[21] More than in the case of the other occupational subgroups, this development was due to the interaction of two factors: the small farmers' socioeconomic plight and the parallel propaganda efforts of Nazi manipulators. The general German agricultural crisis did not begin until 1927, but it had regional forerunners. An unhealthy trend away from the soil was evident as early as 1924–25, especially among the farmers' younger sons and daughters and female help, who were being drawn to the cities or overseas. By 1925, this difficulty was accompanied by an increase in indebtedness due to enforced mechanization. At the same time, cheap credit was becoming less readily available. And by 1927, farm income was declining, foreclosures were becoming common, and peasants were finding themselves unable to compete against cheaper foreign foodstuffs, such as the Belgian dairy products imported to the left bank of the Rhine, or the Danish beef and butter and the Polish pork coming to North and East Germany. In the same year, the farmers of Schleswig-Holstein were seriously affected by a very sudden fall in the price of pork that eventually triggered other price collapses — beef in 1930–31 and cabbage in 1931–32. Just at the beginning of the 1930s the agricultural depression had reached its climax in North and Northwest Germany, was making inroads among the small farmers in the East (for instance, in East Prussia), and was affecting the Bavarian peasants who earlier had been comparatively well off.[22]

When the conventional parties and the farmers' lobbies failed to respond quickly and effectively to the peasants' cries for help, small agricultural estate owners, especially those in the North, resorted to mass demonstrations and other methods of self-help frequently marked by violence.[23] It was this mood of despair that the Nazis exploited when they began their propaganda campaign in the countryside in 1925. Late in that year, Seifert and Major Karl Dincklage started touring the villages and talking to farmers near Hanover in Lower Saxony in an attempt to win party members as well as subscribers to the *Völkischer Beobachter.*[24] A few months later, in 1926, the first Nazi agitators appeared among the small farmers and vintners of western Hesse.[25] Later still, in 1927, Hinrich Lohse, the Gauleiter of Schleswig-Holstein, published an article in the Nazi yearbook that purported to analyze the deteriorating situation in agriculture for the benefit of the North German farmers who were already noticeably agitated.[26] At the end of that year Hitler made a speech in Hamburg to representatives of the Northwest German agricultural interests. The Führer, it was clear, was beginning to focus on an important potential membership group.

The following year, 1928, marked the watershed in the party's efforts to enlist farmers. Early in that year Nazi campaigns got under way in Thuringia, Mecklenburg, and Baden. When the officers of the local peasants' association in Oldenburg, North Germany, drew up a fourteen-point program for agrarian reform, it was quickly seized upon by Nazi infiltrators. The National Socialists were then getting ready for their first important Reichstag election, to be held in May, and they increased their efforts to attract new members in all the rural areas of the Reich. In this connection, Hitler made a wise tactical move when on April 13, 1928, he corrected point 17 of the Feder Program to make it agree with the larger farmers' interests. After the election, which brought fewer proletarian votes than expected, the change in the party line became obvious: a memorandum drawn up by the Bielefeld Nazi leaders, for example, instructed local members "to concentrate on the open country from now on" and to place less emphasis on the big cities.[27] A collection of flyers pertaining to East Prussia has survived from that time; they are laced with anti-Semitism and were obviously designed to indoctrinate the farmers with the latest Nazi wisdom on the agricultural demise, including its remedies.[28] Some of the suggestions anticipated the Nazi agricultural program of March 6, 1930.

This new program, much less radical than might have been expected and therefore attractive even to the moderates among the farmers, promised solutions to a whole host of problems that had been fiercely discussed in previous months. Besides a reform of the credit system, price decreases for fertilizers and hydroelectric power, and long-awaited protectionist concessions and tax benefits, it included a sociopolitical reevaluation of the peasant community that flattered the farmers' self-image.[29] In May 1930 Richard Walther Darré, an expert on colonial farming and a recent addition to the Nazi leadership core, established the party's Agrarian Political Apparatus, whose main purpose was to implement the clauses of the March program.[30] The NSDAP had meanwhile been making further progress among the farmers on a wide front — in East Prussia, in the southwestern Rhenish states that had always been dominated by the Catholic Center Party, and gradually even in Bavaria, where the power of the ultramontane Bavarian People's Party was hard to dislodge.[31] When the NSDAP won its first overwhelming success at the polls in September 1930, it was clear even to the most skeptical observer that the German farmers bore a major responsibility for Hitler's victory.[32]

Table 3 (which deals with party joiners) shows that the first important segment of the new middle class, the lower civil servants (subgroup 7), was overrepresented at the Reich level as newcomers to the NSDAP in three of the six years under consideration: 1925, 1926, and 1929. Table 4 reveals that in six out of eight self-contained communities this subgroup was overrepresented in local party chapters between 1925 and 1929. And table 5 indicates that between 1925 and 1928 every third Nazi party member in the cities of the state of Thuringia was a lower civil servant. Again on the local level, in the summer of 1927 four out of eighteen Nazis in the little Franconian town of Dinkelsbühl were petty state officials, as were three out of twenty-seven Nazis in the upper Bavarian *Kreisstadt* (district center) of Starnberg.[33] These ratios signaled the beginning of a membership trend that continued from the mid-twenties up to Hitler's assumption of power

in 1933 — a chronic overrepresentation of lower civil servants, especially lower-grade school teachers, in the Nazi party.[34]

Some of the causes of this trend date from the early years of the
Weimar Republic, when the lower civil servants began to be disenchanted with what they considered to be a Marxist-prone parliamentary democracy in which the state's authority could not be properly
manifested.[35] Although Hitler already had emphatically rejected a
civil servant's career for himself, he again made his views clear in 1926
in the first volume of *Mein Kampf*. There he hurled invectives against
"drivel in the parliaments or diets" and against collusion between Jews
and the administrative officers of the state.[36] The civil servants'
customary attitude of political neutrality was thus threatened by a
sense of sociopolitical anomie. The situation was not helped when on
December 1, 1929, in addressing the civil servants, the Prussian Social
Democratic Minister of the Interior, Albert Grzesinski, praised the
achievements of the November Revolution of 1918, which had
ushered in the hated Weimar Republic.[37]

The public envied the lower and medium officials because they,
along with the upper civil servants, had received a salary increase on
December 16, 1927. In fact, this measure had done no more than correct the notorious underpayment that had existed since stabilization in
1924, and it was long overdue. But the lower civil servants were irked
because their higher-placed colleagues had received disproportionately
greater increases. They were also disgruntled in 1930 by a special levy
made on their salaries, with further reductions in the offing.[38] Matters
came to a head in June 1930 when the government of Prussia, led by
the SPD, decided to outlaw membership by state officials in both the
radical parties, the NSDAP and the KPD, and subsequently used this
decree to effect the dismissal of particularly vocal Nazi members from
state office. Neither the timid Reich authorities under the temperate
Chancellor Dr. Heinrich Brüning nor most of the *Länder* (state) governments followed suit, and the Nazis still enjoyed comparative freedom in the non-Prussian states; but the traditionally constitutional
government of Baden emulated the Prussian decree.[39] It is true that at
the end of January 1930 a National Socialist government had been installed in Thuringia under State Minister Dr. Wilhelm Frick, and that
in this small enclave Nazi officials of all ranks were faring well.[40] Yet
at the same time, in German states such as Prussia and Baden,
schoolteachers who openly professed Nazi ideals in the classrooms, as
well as police lieutenants and government inspectors whose Nazi
membership was on record, were subject to stern disciplinary action
and dismissal from office.[41] Such suffering as this among the lower

civil servants bolstered their subjective awareness of martyrdom for a lofty cause, making them adhere to the Nazi movement even more tenaciously, if somewhat clandestinely, and leading to a corresponding growth in Nazi membership. Moreover, the knowledge that by 1929 many pro-Hitler civil servants had infiltrated the governments of certain cities in North Germany, such as Göttingen, gave many loyal followers of the Führer the confidence that upon the coming of the Third Reich they would all be amply rewarded with state sinecures.[42]

The strong representation of the second important segment of the new middle class, the white-collar employees (occupational subgroup 6), in the Nazi party from 1925 to 1930 (see tables 3–5) may be interpreted as a direct outcome of the economic uncertainty of that period, especially the layoffs and dismissals that resulted in widespread unemployment.[43] As in the years immediately following World War I, after 1923 the rate of growth of the white-collar work force had been higher than that of the industrial and agricultural laborers.[44] Thus, in 1923 when layoffs and dismissals started to affect the white-collar group (the lower and intermediate clerks), disproportionately more of them lost their jobs than did the blue-collar laborers working in factories and industrial plants. These reductions in the work force had three major causes: (1) between the economic stabilization of 1924 and the summer of 1925 thousands of white-collar workers were dismissed; (2) a temporary economic recession in the next year (1925–26) led to bankruptcies and further releases of sales and technical clerks from the work force; (3) as factories and trading companies turned to specialization, rationalization, and mechanization, more and more clerks, particularly sales and office personnel, became redundant and were laid off.[45] From the middle to the late twenties, more blue-collar workers than clerks, in absolute numbers, were fired from their jobs, but as a group the clerks suffered more consistently in that time period, lacking the seasonal fluctuations that often afflicted but sometimes benefited the workers. Even more important, after the implementation of unemployment insurance in 1927 jobless laborers stood to receive disproportionately more dole and social welfare benefits than white-collar employees, if only because of the massive influence of their unions. By contrast, the most significant organization of white-collar employees, the German Shop Clerks' Association (DHV), was based predominantly in small towns and thus represented the lower-middle-class values usually associated with a small-town milieu.[46] These circumstances were sufficiently important to tilt a large segment of the white-collar work force toward National Socialism, especially when after 1929–30 their conservative lobby, the DHV, became more openly defiant of the right-of-center bourgeois parties and slowly strengthened its connections with the NSDAP through such middlemen as Dr. Albert Krebs, the erstwhile Nazi leader of Hamburg.[47] Thus, although the class-conscious industrial worker tended to rally to the KPD during intermittent stretches of unemployment, the unemployed white-collar worker had a tendency to move in the opposite direction toward National Socialism.[48]

THE ELITE

According to the figures in tables 3–5, German upper-school and university students (subgroup 13) continued to be overrepresented in the Nazi party after 1924. In terms of absolute numbers, there were far fewer university students in Germany from 1925 to 1929 than before the time of stabilization.[49] Nevertheless, in a period of relative socioeconomic stability for most sections of society, including those workers who held down steady jobs, the students suffered acute hardship: the part-time job market was depressed, the patronage usually offered by the fraternity system was harder to come by, and state offices and welfare agencies neglected students. As a result, in February 1926 a small band of disillusioned students, under the leadership of the would-be revolutionary Wilhelm Tempel of Leipzig, founded the National Socialist German Student Union (NSDStB). This organization gradually gained momentum, especially after the more urbane Baldur von Schirach replaced Tempel in the summer of 1928.[50] Toward the end of the twenties, as many German students began to regard themselves as a "potential proletariat," more and more of them supplemented allegiance to the fraternities with membership in the NSDStB and the NSDAP, even though their elitism kept them from rubbing shoulders too openly with their comrades from the lower middle and lower classes.[51] Half of the entire German student body may have joined the Nazis by 1930, although precise figures on this subject have never been found. Still, it is certain that between 1925 and 1930 the rate of growth among Nazi students in the Reich was much greater than for German students as a whole.[52]

For Nazi university students 1926 was an important year. For large-scale business executives and entrepreneurs (subgroups 10 and 14), however, it was an even more important year because it marked, during the second historical phase of the Nazi movement, the beginning of an amicable relationship between Hitler and German industry and commerce. Significantly, the data in table 3 for Nazi joiners in the Reich show that support for the party among the entrepreneurs was on the upswing after 1926. The figures in tables 4 and 5 qualify this trend. They indicate that managers and entrepreneurs tended to join the Nazi party not in large commercial centers such as Hamburg, nor in heavily industrialized areas like the Ruhr (Barmen, Langerfeld, Mülheim), but rather in less obvious places such as Brunswick, the small town of Starnberg south of Munich, the city of Königsberg in East Prussia, and the state of Thuringia. Therefore, it would be misleading to interpret the continuous overrepresentation of businessmen in the NSDAP as the result of an intimate relationship between Hitler and the magnates of banking and heavy industry, as most East German and a few West German historians have been fond of doing.[53] Even though such contacts did exist, their importance was negligible when compared with the support for Hitler that came from light industry and intermediate-size entrepreneurial and commercial establishments.

It cannot be denied that as early as 1925 Hitler was once more on the lookout for pecuniary backing for his party from financially powerful sources. He may well have thought of using Gregor Strasser's and Karl Kaufmann's influential positions in the Ruhr in 1924–25, when he was writing *Mein Kampf* and reestablishing the party. The point has been made that although Hitler lashed out against the upper bourgeoisie in his book, he was careful not to intimidate potential donors by passing precipitate judgments on the German economy. At this time, in fact, Gregor Strasser was already receiving subsidies from industrial circles in the Ruhr.[54] Even though National Socialist propaganda was aimed at the workers in these years, directors and owners of factories were in touch with the Nazi leaders in the Ruhr as early as the fall of 1925, attempting to sound out their political intentions. In Langerfeld near Wuppertal one factory owner was reported as having approached the party in September with the aim of becoming a member, but not without "previously examining our [Nazi] goals a little more closely."[55] The following spring (1926), Hitler, having been largely barred from public appearances by the Länder governments, began a series of private speaking engagements before some of the Ruhr magnates with the obvious purpose of inducing them to donate money. A month or two earlier, in February, he had also addressed a select forum of conservative-minded representatives of industry and politics at the exclusive Nationalclub in Hamburg, where he was enthusiastically applauded.[56]

It was probably in April 1927, during another speech to industrial and commercial leaders, that the Führer met Emil Kirdorf, the most prominent Ruhr magnate he had met up to that time. Yet although the aging Kirdorf was still a towering figure on the industrial scene, he had recently lost some of his influence and was by no means the ty-coon—the top representative of corporate industrial power in western Germany—that he has been reputed to have been. And though Kir-dorf, who was personally sympathetic toward Hitler, became a party member in 1927 and made a single donation of 100,000 marks, he eventually reverted to the German National People's Party (DNVP) that was his home base, mainly because of the Nazis' continued appeal to the workers.[57] Through Kirdorf, Hitler was able to meet other influential leaders of the Ruhr group in the summer and fall of 1927; in particular, he had the chance to express cautiously conservative views on the economy, including the desirability of increasing national exports and opposing Bolshevism.[58]

Hitler's contacts with the Ruhr leaders of heavy industry continued from the end of 1927 into the early 1930s, but he spoke to represen-tatives of other German entrepreneurial interests as well. A good ex-ample is his speech to over two hundred notables in Nuremberg on December 8, 1928, in which he wooed his audience by making critical remarks about Jews and republican democracy.[59] Yet even though in the preceding April Hitler had modified point 17 of the Feder Program (calling for the forceful expropriation of real estate owners) in order to please both entrepreneurs and farmers, especially large-scale farmers, there is no evidence that as a consequence a significant number of industrial leaders either became party members or con-tributed large amounts of money to the NSDAP.[60] Hence it would be grossly incorrect to say that in the formative years of the late twenties the party was becoming the political handmaiden of capitalist interests in the Reich.[61] Attempts by cadres of the regional NSDAP leadership to make contact with corporate industry remained ill-conceived and clumsy.[62] The money from industry that did reach the NSDAP came instead from the smaller manufacturers, who in some cases also joined the party. Albert Pietzsch was one of these. The engineer and owner of an electrochemical factory in Munich, he sought and acquired a party badge in 1927 because he felt ostracized by Munich high society. Small-scale manufacturers often approached the Nazis because they resented the big tycoons who supplied them with raw materials on un-favorable terms. Finally, many an intermediate entrepreneur or manager threw in his lot with the movement in anticipation of future material rewards. Thus all the available evidence points to the assump-tion that it was the heads of family businesses, the representatives of light and manufacturing industry, and the wealthy wholesale mer-chants who made up the bulk of the entrepreneurs referred to in tables 3–5.[63] Within this group must also be included a growing number of large-scale farmers, particularly those from east of the Elbe, who were beginning to suffer from the agrarian crisis and were starting to blame the DNVP, as well as their lobby, the Reichslandbund (Reich Farmers' League), for failing to deal effectively with the economic difficulties. After 1929 such sentiments were aggravated by resentment over the government's acceptance of the Young Plan committing Germany to several decades of reparation payment, which was considered harmful to all landed interests.[64]

After 1924 the academically trained professionals, including "intellectuals" of all sorts (subgroup 12), were not attracted to Hitler's movement in such large numbers as before the Putsch (tables 2–5). When the NSDAP moved into North and Northwest Germany, it did not appeal to the academic elite there as much as it had earlier to those in Munich, where the Schwabing artists and bohemian intellectuals had found it easy to sympathize with Hitler, the frustrated artist who had turned politician. The more sober-minded German professionals and literati living outside Bavaria tended to be repelled by Hitler's diatribes against the upper bourgeoisie, contained in the second volume of *Mein Kampf* (1927), and by the general vapidity of National Socialist doctrine.[65] "It would help the national *völkisch* cause considerably," wrote the former Heidelberg lecturer in philosophy, Dr. Arnold Ruge, in 1927, "if its ideas could be metaphysically grounded."[66] In the second half of the 1920s, intellectuals, especially those living north of Munich, found it difficult to associate with a party that so openly despised them and insulted their sensibilities.[67] Finally, because of the cultural and esthetic differences that customarily separated the layers of German society, a party like the NSDAP that was dominated (in absolute terms) by the lower-middle-class elements remained distasteful to intellectuals, who despised the materialistic value system of the common people as manifested by gutter language and primitive jokes.[68]

Nevertheless, the German intelligentsia still remained overrepresented in the NSDAP until 1930. The first reason for this was that scores of intellectuals looked upon themselves as having been socially and politically displaced after 1918 and again after stabilization in 1924–25; thus they put themselves squarely within the German tradition of cultural pessimism that criticized the entrenched order. They strove for basic simplicity, for a life in the country as opposed to the city, for the social and cultural attributes of an elitist minority rather than of the mass. Often they faced psychological problems of adjustment within their immediate environment; they were the "odd men out." Such persons regarded Nazism as an antidote to the evils of modernity brought on by war and revolution. They joined the Nazi party out of a perverted Social Darwinian feeling of admiration for Hitler, the dictatorial strongman who would cleanse the nation of its ills and build something new. Among those who thought in these terms, not all of whom became Nazi party comrades, were the writers Ernst Jünger (who never joined) and Arnolt Bronnen (who did).[69]

Second, as the party leadership realized the futility of its efforts among the working class and began to pay more attention to the bourgeoisie, the upper layers of society quite naturally came within its purview. This was no doubt facilitated by Hitler's own somewhat cynical attitude toward the industrial leaders, from whom he wanted not only money but moral and political support. It is from this perspective that the party's conscious efforts to win over the academically oriented professional groups should be viewed. The Nazis catered to these groups' specific interests either vocally or, as in the case of the physicians and lawyers, through action, forming National Socialist ancillary organizations under the cloak of professional lobbies.[70] In this context, the appointment in July 1928 of Baldur von Schirach, scion of a noble family from Weimar, as head of the Nazi Student Union assumes a deeper meaning. So also does Alfred Rosenberg's attempt to found a Society of German Culture at the Reich Party Rally in Nuremburg in the summer of 1927, and Adrian von Renteln's founding of a Nazi Upper-School Students' League (NSS) in 1929.[71]

After 1924 the higher civil servants (subgroup 11), unlike the university-educated professionals, not only kept their level of representation in the Nazi party well above that of the Reich as a whole but also increased their proportion in the NSDAP (tables 1–5). It is true, however, that in the main their political allegiance remained with the monarchical DNVP and the German People's Party (DVP), or the more liberal German Democratic Party (DDP), which took a sharp swing to the right in 1930 after fusing with the conservative wing of Artur Mahraun's Young German Order in July of that year.[72] It is also true that between 1924 and 1930 the economic situation of the higher civil servants was much better than it had been in 1923–24 (especially after the salaries were increased in 1927), even though many of them continued to suffer severely from aftereffects of the inflation. And the prolonged Nazi calls for a cut in higher administrative salaries and a concomitant reduction in the number of higher civil servants were ill designed to attract tenured judges, university professors, and upper-school teachers to the NSDAP.[73]

But there were other issues working in favor of the National Socialists that more than neutralized these factors. The higher civil servants were affected by the same syndrome of sociocultural alienation after the apparent failure of democracy as were the intellectuals, to whom they were linked by academic background and a strong sense of superior social status. Hence, in those circles, the Nazis' harangues against the evils of Weimar did not fall on deaf ears. The National Socialists also argued successfully against the party patronage extended by the SPD to senior civil servants after 1918 on purely political grounds, particularly in Prussia. Bent on exploiting the mandarins' feelings of frustration to the full, representatives of local NSDAP chapters made advances to regional administrators known to be of a reactionary disposition – for example, in Essen in March 1930. And an increasing number of upper-school teachers, notably in North Germany, were inclined to actively support the recently established National Socialist Upper-School Students' League at their institutions of learning.[74]

In the fall of 1930 the second phase of the Nazi party's Time of Struggle came to an end. Hitler had successfully rebuilt his movement after the disaster of 1923. In so doing, neither had he lost the traditional allegiance of the lower middle class and the elite, both of which continued to be overrepresented, nor had he missed the chance to win over more blue-collar workers. In 1926–27, in fact, it had looked as if the worker newcomers to the NSDAP would increase their share at the expense of the lower middle class, whose loyalty to the Nazi cause was becoming proverbial. Whether this phenomenon – the temporary swelling of the workers' percentage – was linked to economic factors is still in doubt because the years from 1926 to 1928 were not years of extraordinary hardship for laborers in the Reich as a whole.

During the second half of the 1920s Hitler had used external circumstances to develop his party internally, to enlarge it, and to groom it as a "democratic" base for participation in political elections. Locally, regionally, and even nationally this post-Putsch formula worked. Out of a total of thirty Landtag and Reichstag elections from the spring of 1925 until the summer of 1930, the NSDAP was successful in sixteen, with at least one mandate. In 1929 a significant breakthrough occurred when the party won an absolute majority in the municipal elections of Coburg in northern Franconia. And after a fortunate Landtag election return in Thuringia, Hitler's old Bavarian associate, Wilhelm Frick, was appointed Thuringian Minister for the Interior early in 1930.

Finally, at the national elections of September 14, 1930, Hitler's

National Socialists captured 107 of 577 seats, up from 12 in the 1928 election, to become the second largest party in the Reichstag. By that time Dr. Heinrich Brüning, a Centrist, was Chancellor; his appointment without parliamentary backing by Reich President Paul von Hindenburg in March 1930 and his subsequent emphasis on emergency decrees for governance hastened the downfall of parliamentary democracy in the Weimar Republic.[75] By that time also the economic depression in Germany was well under way. In retrospect, it appears sadly ironic that Brüning, a politician with at least a basic understanding of the democratic process, was installed as Chancellor by presidential fiat, whereas Hitler, who despised parliamentary democracy altogether, managed in the fall of 1930 to get his party duly elected by the best of the Republic's remaining constitutional devices.

3

THE RISE TO POWER
SEPTEMBER 1930 TO 1933

After his phenomenal victory in the Reichstag elections of September 1930, Hitler of course hoped that the President would appoint him Chancellor of the Weimar Republic. Although Hindenburg disliked him, Hitler knew that Hindenburg respected him as the leader of the second largest Reichstag party. There were three unresolved issues, however. First, Hitler's party was smaller than the SPD. Second, although the conservative Hindenburg was opposed on principle to offering the chancellorship to a Social Democrat, he might in this case feel bound by the spirit of democracy that he had neglected by appointing Brüning to the chancellorship. Third, Hitler was not qualified for public office because he was not a German citizen. He was actually stateless, having lost his Austrian citizenship in 1925; he could not take a seat in the Reichstag and was even liable to be deported until the newly established Nazi government in Brunswick made him a naturalized German by handing him a nominal state office in February 1932.

These delicate political circumstances hardly provided a firm base for an aspiring dictator who, at a time of national socioeconomic trouble, wanted to assume control of the central government. In this political quest more "democratic" backing for the NSDAP was essential. As it happened, the economic chaos appeared to be just what Hitler needed to carry him to the top. In 1922–23 he had ridden the wave of social and economic turmoil in Bavaria, using it to manipulate Germans to help him topple the government by force. A similar use of force after the September 1930 elections was out of the question, but there were signs that the economic crisis would increase the mass of Hitler's followers—over 100,000 in the fall of 1930 (figure 1)—until the NSDAP became, in electoral terms, the largest party in the land.

Such an increase might be accompanied by certain changes in the social composition of the party that could have important consequences for Hitler's political career: a greater share of workers to bolster the "mass appeal," and a larger number of the influential personages who were wont to curry favor with politicians. In any event, a larger party in terms of both electoral potential and membership would certainly enhance Hitler's chances for success.

The analysis of the growth and social makeup of the NSDAP from 1930 to 1933 rests on data from a (combined) membership list for NSDAP party chapters in the East Prussian small towns of Deutsch-Krone and Klausdorf and on similar data for the Holstein small town of Eutin. In addition, data from lists for the two Franconian villages of Pahres and Eltersdorf, near Nuremberg, were used (table 6). The membership frequencies from the lists in table 6 should be read, like the values for Königsberg in table 4, as total memberships calculated cumulatively. Values for the Reich (1930–1932) were also used and were treated as yet another sample of joiners that could easily be broken down by region (table 6). These figures, incidentally, should be viewed like Madden's figures in table 3, but without the potential for cumulative inferences because of the lack of corresponding, statistically compatible information for the period 1925–1930.

THE WORKERS

The increase in the percentage of workers among the newcomers (joiners) in the Nazi party that was evident between 1929 and 1933 must be viewed against the background of the Great Depression.[1] This disaster left hardly any social group in Germany untouched except the beneficiaries of large capital and investment holdings. For wage and salary earners it meant a steady decrease in real income, a reduction in welfare benefits despite increases in the state insurance premiums, and, above all, a steep escalation of both unemployment and sporadic part-time work.[2] In order to posit a causal relationship between the depression and the increasing percentage of worker newcomers in the NSDAP, one would have to establish two facts: that the workers suffered more than other social groups, and that it was this greater degree of suffering that induced them to join the Nazi party. At a superficial level a case can be made for both presumptions. Previous scholarship has proved that the industrialized Ruhr, particularly its mining area, was affected more acutely by the depression than the other regions of Germany. It is also known that the proportion of industrial workers was largest in the metropolitan areas of the Ruhr. Further, it can be shown that the workers were much more drastically afflicted with joblessness and short-term employment than were the other societal segments. Finally, it is clear that the growth of the sector of unemployed workers in the Reich population corresponded with the increase in Nazi party membership after September 1930.[3] And conversely, toward the end of the period, at the time of the Reichstag elections of November 6, 1932, when there was a slight easing of the economic plight of workers, particularly in the Ruhr, the NSDAP received fewer working-class votes than expected. Simultaneously, the rate at which laborers joined the NSDAP dropped somewhat and the rate at which members left the NSDAP to join the KPD increased.[4]

But the situation of the workers in the NSDAP during this period of extreme economic hardship and heightened political polarization cannot be properly examined without using a wider frame of reference that includes the two leading Marxist parties, the SPD and the KPD. In regard to this wider framework, the documents and critical sociohistorical literature suggest, first of all, that between 1929 and 1933, although the basic pattern of interrelationship between the industrial urban proletariat and Marxism (as well as the converse of that relationship in the countryside) did not change in principle, more workers, in relative and absolute figures, left the Marxist parties for the radical right than ever before.[5] This tendency was less pronounced in the large cities, where workers were more likely to be unemployed; but the net gain for the Nazis in absolute numbers was such as to correspondingly decrease the percentages of other newcomer groups in the party.[6] Second, the shift of socialist-oriented workers to the NSDAP appears to have affected the SPD less than the KPD, in terms of membership as well as voting habits. In switching to one of the two radical parties, SPD members seem to have favored the KPD over the NSDAP.[7] In this connection, further consideration should be given to three important phenomena: the exchangeability of the NSDAP and the KPD as adequate vehicles of radical political expression; the ineptitude of the slowly ossifying Social Democratic structure; and the proselytizing effect of National Socialist palliatives, expressed in word as well as deed.

The political similarity of the KPD to the NSDAP in this period of crisis made switches from the one to the other much more common than had previously been the case. Often, for example, the patrons of a local tavern acted as a unit and changed their political persuasion overnight. This switching process resulted, on the one hand, from the KPD's long-standing failure to bring about, by parliamentary means, any lasting improvement in the socioeconomic situation of the working class.[8] On the other hand, it can be traced to a gradual fusing in the early thirties of the public images of the two radical camps: the Nazis, like the Communists, had perfected the dubious art of street-fighting, especially in the large industrial areas; they subscribed to a similar honor code (which was respected by the other party); and they professed a specific myth of martyrdom for the "cause."[9] In addition, the Communists and Nazis borrowed propaganda from each other, occasionally supported each other on social and political issues in the lower government councils, and collaborated in strike action, most notably during the Berlin transport strike of November 1932.[10]

Much of the Nazi propaganda was directed squarely against the SPD, and the Nazi leadership scored remarkable success in drawing working-class members away from that party to its own ranks. This was particularly true in the small towns, such as Northeim near Hanover, where laborers normally favored the SPD over the Communists, and in the countryside, where the agricultural laborers were naturally attracted to the NSDAP. In fact, in the early thirties, when the Communist party's growth rate was lower than that of the Nazi party but still positive, the SPD experienced a negative rate of growth. This development was intimately connected with depression-related factors, such as the refusal by the left wing of the SPD in March 1930 to support a proposal by the DDP and the Center Party for a future decrease of unemployment insurance benefits. The result was the fall of the Great Coalition cabinet under Hermann Müller.[11] Moreover, the SPD-controlled trade union Allgemeiner Deutscher Gewerkschaftsbund (ADGB) was losing favor with the workers, as indicated by the steady drop in membership from 1921 to 1932. The ADGB lost momentum not only because it associated itself with the Brüning administration in accepting a decrease of wages on December 14, 1931, but also because of the SPD's weak showing in elections throughout the entire period.[12] In this connection it is significant that the NSDAP picked up support among workers in the countryside and in moderately industrialized regions such as Saxony and Thuringia, where the SPD-controlled unions were least efficiently organized and where street demonstrations called by the SPD were in utter disarray, in comparison with those of the two more radical parties.[13]

The Nazi party's relatively large measure of success with the workers from 1930 to 1933 was undoubtedly linked to both the sharpening of its propaganda tools and its welfare activities among the destitute, which convinced many workers in all regions of Germany of the Nazis' "sincerity." The recurring necessity for election preparation at intermediate as well as major levels compelled the Nazi leadership to refine its propaganda techniques and, especially, to replace sheer rhetoric with constructive plans for change.[14] Hence, although the hate slogans against the Republic and the bourgeois and workers' parties by no means disappeared from Nazi posters and leaflets, there was remarkably little mention of the Feder Program, a scheme that had never impressed the proletariat.[15] Instead, concrete proposals appeared for quick solutions to the pressing issues of the moment, and in this vein Brüning's emergency decrees were branded as destructive to the workers. In a typical Prussian newspaper article of March 1932, Hitler addressed himself to the agricultural working population by stressing its priorities: the need to increase wages in money and in kind; the desirability of halting mechanization and rationalization on large estates; and the desirability of offering small-scale homesteads to laborers.[16] Workers of all levels could see that the Nazis were attempting to diversify their approach, that they were speaking to agricultural laborers as well as to Ruhr miners, and that they were being very careful not to offend the sensibilities of any specific group.[17]

By this time the Nazis had no choice but to come out boldly and unequivocally in favor of strikes, holding out the possibility of strike action as bait in their attempt to enlarge the membership of their own union (NSBO). There is no question about the effectiveness of this policy: although the Nazis remained opposed to the conventional trade unions, NSBO membership increased from 39,000 late in 1931 to approximately 400,000 at the end of the Republic.[18] The Nazis also played their part in setting up soup kitchens for the unemployed, and, like East Prussia's Gauleiter Erich Koch, they pushed for special unemployment relief measures in municipal councils.[19]

Despite the Nazis' efforts at the start of the thirties to attract the workers—efforts that at a time of unusual hardship brought them a proportionately greater influx of working-class members than in the previous period, even in the face of competition from the KPD and the SPD—they still could not claim to be a workers' party. The NSDAP profited only incidentally from unemployment among the workers, and the lower class as a whole was still underrepresented in the party although it increased in absolute numbers (tables 6 and 1). Because the Nazis still would not shed their middle-class image, the SPD and especially the KPD, using propaganda tactics and benefit relief programs of their own, continued to reap the political harvest on the left until Hitler forced them out of existence during the Third Reich.[20]

THE LOWER MIDDLE CLASS

Altogether, from 1930 to 1933, the rate at which newcomers from the lower middle class joined the NSDAP was not quite so high as in the preceding period, although the lower middle class as a whole was still overrepresented among both party joiners and old members. Even though tabular comparisons are difficult to make, percentage figures for key occupational subgroups such as merchants and farmers can be shown to have declined.[21]

For the old-middle-class subgroups of artisans and small or intermediate merchants (4 and 8), the socioeconomic situation had not changed basically, although it is certain that after September 1930 their difficulties were exacerbated by the developing crisis.[22] These two groups were just as prone to exaggerate their economic suffering as they had been during the inflationary period. The small businessmen who were badly hurt by the crisis, as well as those who were badly frightened by it, were likely to turn to the NSDAP, especially since they found the political alternatives, such as the Economic Party (Wirtschaftspartei) disappointing.[23] For, although only 1 percent of all retail businesses were forced into bankruptcy in 1932, the record year of business failures, the actual number of failures was large. As William S. Allen has argued, it was large enough to frighten those businessmen who were still solvent into registering a protest by voting for or joining the radical right.[24] Usually the bankruptcies resulted directly from staggering interest rates, accompanied by conditions of deflation and a very tight credit market. Inevitably, net profits fell rapidly. In 1932 German independent craftsmen realized only 33.5 percent of their 1928 profit level.[25] East Prussian tobacco retailers are a case in point. Early in 1931 they found themselves unable to increase their profit margins because of competition from wholesale dealers who were believed to be resorting to unsavory business practices in the purported tradition of their Polish-Jewish ancestors.[26] The tobacco merchants were not the only ones to suffer; many other small businessmen seem to have been equally hard hit.

If the economic crisis did supply the main motive for these groups' allegiance to National Socialism, then the retail merchants in the countryside, who would have been better off than those in the large cities, should not have joined the party with such frequency. For the period 1930–1932 table 6 does reveal a remarkably lower percentage of Nazi merchant newcomers in the country than in the cities or small towns; but this pattern was not duplicated by the craftsmen newcomers. Perhaps craftsmen based in the country were less able than rural merchants to rely on the comparatively secure economic infrastructure of the countryside because they were more closely connected with industry in the city and so were more susceptible to crisis.[27] Another very different possibility could be that the causal relationship indicated here between the effects of the depression and the fluctuations in the NSDAP membership percentages was far more tenuous than has previously been believed.[28]

In any case, the NSDAP again did its best to prove that it had the answers to all the ills of the depression. As before, it capitalized on the rampant anti-Semitism and also played up fears of Communism to the best of its ability. It continued its campaign against chain stores and consumer cooperatives and urged Nazi housewives to buy only from Nazi merchants. In contrast to the vague promises contained in its Feder Program, the party now called for plentiful credit, for various insurance and welfare plans, and especially for the establishment of selective training and examination mechanisms to restrict the competitive market. Insofar as it was designed to benefit the craftsmen, this program at the high point of its development was very similar to the corporative ideology propounded by the Austrian scholar Othmar Spann and, farther afield, to that of Italian fascism.[29] Slowly, as the NSDAP managed to infiltrate such small-business associations as the Main Organization of the German Retail Trade, at both the regional and national level, and even created an apparatus within the party to deal with problems through propaganda, National Socialism began to emerge as the only viable political alternative to the previous lobbies and formations, notably the Economic Party. This situation, however, lasted only until the fall of 1932, when Hitler, for strategic reasons, replaced Dr. Otto Wilhelm Wagener, the party exponent of corporative ideas, with Dr. Walther Funk, who was much more attuned to the interests of industry and commerce. This change signaled the end of the liaison between small business and Nazism that had begun in the early twenties.[30]

By comparison with the previous period, the decline in the percentage of farmer newcomers to the Nazi party between 1930 and 1933 was slight, but there was a decline.[31] Indeed, it can be shown that in the last few years of the Weimar Republic the small farmers or peasants were no better off than they had been in the late twenties, with the possible exception of the last quarter of 1932; and, in fact, 1931 stands out as the peak year of the agrarian crisis. Interestingly, Nazi party newcomers from among the peasantry appear to have dropped off in numbers in 1932 as compared with 1931, according to a preliminary count I made in 1976.[32]

The negative developments in the economic sector after September 1930 brought distress to many farmers. The vicious circle of crop failures, credit shortages, low prices for agricultural products, low tariffs, rising taxes, bankruptcies, and falling net profits could not be stopped. The most serious crop failure was the low grain harvest of 1931, especially in the East, including Silesia. Wholesale cattle prices dropped alarmingly, plunging from the 1930 rate of 12 percent above the base level of 1913 to 17 percent below that level in 1931, and then to 36 percent below it in 1932. By 1931, cries for higher tariffs were rising from every corner of the country, including the hitherto less susceptible German South. Foreclosures became inevitable, and by June 1931 the collective debt of German farmers had reached the staggering figure of three billion dollars.[33]

The Nazi leadership, using the efficient party institutions built up by Richard Walther Darré, consistently directed its propaganda against so-called foreign influences (epitomized by the Young Plan), the governments in Berlin and the Länder capitals, and the traditional farmers' organizations, and continued to focus on the most contentious current issues. By the fall of 1931, at the nadir of rural prosperity, the Nazis succeeded in dislodging the Reichslandbund in the state elections in Hesse. This marked not only the beginning of the downfall of Germany's most powerful peasants' lobby but also the Nazis' final breakthrough among the peasantry of Bavaria, who, tied to Catholic interests in both the Reichslandbund and the Bavarian particularist parties, had been slow in coming over to the Nazi movement.[34] On December 18, 1931, Darré's lieutenant, Werner Willikens, joined the presidium of the Reichslandbund, making use of the National Socialist art of gradual infiltration of existing bourgeois institutions for manipulatory purposes. Here, as in the small-business associations, corporative ideas became firmly established.[35]

It is not clear whether the final months of 1932 brought the farmers sufficient economic alleviation to induce them to once again turn their backs on the Nazi party. Regional reports for the autumn of 1932 indicate that although the harvest of some crops had increased, further declines in wholesale prices had compounded the already existing problems of marketing. On the other hand, the Weimar Republic had begun to take some sluggish action with regard to tariff protection and the suspension of foreclosures.[36] In areas such as East Prussia the Nazis were campaigning among the local farmers in a last desperate effort, pulling out all the stops before the Reichstag election of November. And in Hesse, Franconia, Swabia, and Bavaria the NSDAP scored record highs in both of the Reichstag elections of that year. But if the rate of Nazi recruitment among the farmers was really declining in North and West Germany at that time (which might account for the slight drop in the peasants' percentage at the end of 1932), it is certain that the potential for membership in South Germany had not yet been exhausted.[37] For whereas Upper Bavarian Catholics still tended to shy away from party membership but found nothing wrong with voting for the NSDAP in elections, their Franconian comrades, around Nuremberg for instance, had long been embracing the NSDAP with enthusiasm. If the party had had a little more time in Bavaria to drive home the effects of the rural depression before Hitler came to power, it might have been able to remove the last traditionally motivated qualms among Bavarian ultramontane farmers and induce them finally to sign up as members at party headquarters.[38]

The lower and intermediate civil servants (subgroup 7) tended to be somewhat underrepresented in the NSDAP after September 1930 (tables 6 and 1). Their percentage among the newcomers actually declined until mid-1932, at which time it shot up again. Shortly before Hitler's assumption of power, 10 percent of all German civil servants were said to have joined the Nazi movement.[39] The reasons for this are complex. Whereas it was comparatively easy for the Nazi leadership to gear its propaganda machine to the specific needs of most middle-class groups, especially after the onset of the depression, it was difficult to do this in regard to the lower (as well as upper) civil servants because some of the most extreme measures initiated against civil servants by the Brüning cabinet happened to be in accord with the Nazis' own philosophy. The first cost- and staff-cutting ordinances of the Berlin government directed against state officials came in late 1930, but more severe measures followed in 1931, such as the emergency decree of August 24 that further reduced the salaries of municipal and government bureaucrats. As a result, disappointment and bitterness spread among Germany's administrators at every level and soon found expression in many public rallies.[40]

In the uniquely unhappy case of these civil servants, particularly the lower ones, the Nazi leaders committed a strategic blunder. They failed to reconcile the bureaucrats' desires with those of the other occupational strata whom the party was also endeavoring to win over but whose vested interests were somewhat opposed to those of the state officials. As it turned out, in this particular instance the Nazis' policy of trying to meet everybody's needs led to polarization, with the result that one group could only be satisfied at the expense of another. For example, Nazi support of the much publicized issue of special financial cutbacks for civil servants during the depression alienated those officials but found favor with the peasants, independent crafts-men, and merchants, to whom the Nazis were also appealing. The Nazis' stance, voiced by their Reichstag spokesman, Jakob Sprenger, in the parliamentary session of December 19, 1930, was hypocritical: earlier, before the September elections, they had openly condemned such cuts.[41] At a propaganda meeting in Insterburg (East Prussia) on October 12, 1930, the NSDAP speaker, Karl Maria von Wedel, had rebuffed many potential civil-service sympathizers when he unabashedly condoned further salary reductions. One Nazi critic wrote, "News of this attitude by the NSDAP toward the civil servants had spread like wildfire among the officials of the town, so that their former enthusiasm for the NSDAP has been severely dampened, if they are not altogether opposed to the party by now."[42] In other cases, lower civil servants such as teachers and policemen were subjected to pressure by local party chapters to induce them to join the party under the threat that their careers might otherwise be in jeopardy after the Nazis had taken over. Similar threats were already being implemented in regions where the Nazis held power locally—in Brunswick, Thurin-gia, and the Franconian town of Coburg. It stands to reason that in such trying times, when the Nazi leadership was under pressure to meet the sociopolitical demands of almost every sector of society, the social groups that had been the early targets of Hitler's inbred prej-udices would eventually fare worse than the others.[43] This was especially evident on those occasions when simple-minded party leaders like Hermann Esser expressed their opinions officiously in public and paid no heed to the need for a balanced propaganda effort as advocated by more sober-minded functionaries like Gregor Strasser.[44]

Men like Strasser attempted to counteract the disastrous effects of such a self-defeating policy by continuing the attitude of benevolence toward civil servants that had been pursued in earlier years. Late in 1931 a conscious effort was made by the NSDAP leadership to im-prove the party's image among the state administrators. Averring that the Nazis' policy toward civil servants was being discredited by the professional lobbies and bourgeois parties, NSDAP leaders reem-phasized the pro-civil-servant planks of the Feder Program and gradually came around to recognizing the remuneration demands of the lower officials—the point of greatest contention.[45] This effort was intensified in the spring of 1932, when a Prussian state election, a Reichstag election, and two presidential elections finally provided am-ple opportunity for the Nazi leaders to make their stand unmistakably clear to Germany's state officials. At a time when these officials had been thoroughly demoralized by the failure of governments and parties alike to meet their individual needs and allay their fears of the future, the NSDAP came out unequivocally in favor of tenure (even for female officials), higher salaries, and decent living quarters. The party added weight to its statement by strongly criticizing Brüning's emergency legislation, the SPD party patronage system said to be practiced by members of the higher civil service echelons, and the negative ramifications of such "foreign influences" as the Young Plan, which had supposedly condemned the German state railway employees to slavery through its system of reparation guarantees.[46]

The new regime of Chancellor Franz von Papen, which began in June 1932, altered the situation for the Nazis, for the various restrictions imposed on the openly activist Nazi public servants by the states of Prussia and Baden, and sporadically by other state governments, were either revoked or could be openly ignored. (This was even more the case after Papen's forceful takeover of the Prussian government in July.) As a consequence of the new situation, as well as of the Nazis' more vigorous efforts on behalf of the civil servants, the absolute number of Nazi newcomers from that group began to rise again and continued to do so until the very day of Hitler's assumption of power. This process was also aided by a modest expansion of the National Socialist officials' lobby that had been formally instituted by Sprenger in 1931. By the fall of 1932, Nazi activities in the interest of the civil servants had increased noticeably, ranging from special party meetings for civil servants of Nazi persuasion to outright attempts at conversion among those who were still unconvinced. Particular attention was paid to the public school teachers, who had special grievances of their own in addition to the problems suffered by other civil officials. On April 2 and 3, 1932, when 20,000 teachers (the great majority of whom came from the lower schools) attended a Nazi Teachers' League rally in Berlin, they gave impressive testimony of the strength of the Nazi movement within Germany's lower officialdom. The crowd assembled in the capital represented approximately 7 percent of all the teachers then working in the Reich, even though only a little more than half of them were bona fide members of the NSDAP, doubtless because of the disciplinary sanctions that had been imposed upon teachers up to that time.[47]

The percentage of white-collar workers (lower employees or clerks — subgroup 6) who joined the party between September 1930 and 1933 was also somewhat lower than it had been in the preceding period.[48] This can be attributed to their new relationship to the blue-collar

workers in day-to-day situations. Clerks who were out of work, often
for a much longer time than the laborers, were now forced to work
alongside laborers doing odd jobs or to mingle with them in the
welfare lineups of the large cities. This association was bitterly
resented by the clerks. So, after 1929, as they became aware of the
larger influx of blue-collar workers into the NSDAP, the clerks tended
to stay away from the Nazi party more than before, although their
socioeconomic prospects had not essentially changed since the late
twenties. For these clerks, there was to be no social mixing with the
workers, not even in the NSDAP, lest they might become easy prey to
the process of proletarianization that they had so dreaded in the past.

In the cities and towns, however, the lower clerks in the Reich
came to the party more readily than in the countryside (table 6), a
situation that was exactly the reverse of the workers'. This seems to indicate that although unemployment brought less distress in absolute
terms to white-collar workers than to laborers (despite the clerks'
lower chances of advancement), unemployment nevertheless served as
the prime cause of the clerks' drift to the NSDAP, for it occurred with
much greater frequency in the metropolitan areas than in the country.
As in the case of the retail merchants, clerks in the countryside were
better able than those in the city to withstand the crisis, including the
effects of unemployment. The support of the agrarian infrastructure,
which might include a small plot of privately owned land, was more
solid than anything the city could provide and thus made survival in
the village easier than in the big city.[49]

THE ELITE

Between 1929 and Hitler's assumption of power in January 1933
the attraction of the NSDAP as a political alternative to other
bourgeois parties increased considerably for the upper middle class
and former aristocracy. If this fact is not demonstrable by statistical
data, that is because many members of the upper levels of German
society still preferred to express their sympathy for National Socialism
through methods other than outright party membership, such as electoral support.[50] The reasons for such seemingly contradictory
behavior varied. Whereas the upper civil servants in such states as
Prussia and Baden were prohibited from joining the Nazis by decree,
many intellectuals and academics had a natural dislike for the National Socialists' continued use of a parliamentary strategy on their
quasi-legal road to power. And entrepreneurs often preferred to make
clandestine financial contributions to the party instead of joining it, in

order to avoid harming their businesses. Hence the silent minority support that the NSDAP enjoyed within the upper echelons from 1930 to 1933 is less apparent from membership statistics than from private letters or confidential protocols of business proceedings that have survived in the archives. Collectively, the elite remained clearly over-represented in the party (tables 6 and 1).[51]

There is little doubt that the September elections of 1930, in which the right-of-center bourgeois parties lost significantly to the Nazis, solidified business executive and entrepreneurial interest in the NSDAP (subgroups 10 and 14). In the historical literature a great deal has been made of the fact that Hitler owed his success in early 1933 to the backing he received at decisive moments from distinct business groups with vast political influence. Again, although it can be argued that the great industrialists were not without responsibility for Hitler's coming to power, the strength of their association with the Nazi party is still as questionable as the consistency of their long-range support. Moreover, if one takes into account the effects of the depression, which were of relatively small concern to the big industrialists in the Ruhr or Upper Silesia, it is more likely that support for Hitler came, as before, from small and intermediate businessmen, who stood to suffer heavy personal losses and consequently could have looked upon the NSDAP as a savior from total economic ruin.[52]

After September 1930, influential lobbies representing heavy industry (such as the Ruhrlade) intensified their connections with the party and contributed funds to various chapters. The reports vary; but it is likely that Walther Funk, the party's intelligent intermediary between heavy industry and the NSDAP, not only established new and important links with industry but also handled certain financial transactions. Other personalities from the world of big business who surfaced in 1930–31 without necessarily becoming party members were Fritz Thyssen, Hugo Stinnes, Paul Reusch, Albert Vögler, Fritz Springorum, and, in the role of a more direct spokesman for this group, August Heinrichsbauer. But as was true for the preceding periods, there is no evidence that the Nazis received sufficiently large sums of money from these circles to sustain the party financially.[53]

Again, all the available evidence suggests that while Hitler was bent on winning over big business with the aid of suitable lieutenants, the magnates themselves moved cautiously, considering any support for the Nazi party, especially financial contributions, as merely a possible alternative to their donations to the bourgeois parties, which had by no means ceased.[54] After all, it was sound policy to have more than one iron in the fire. During Papen's brief chancellorship (June–

November 1932) big business quite naturally rallied around the so-called Cabinet of Barons and saw in its members the ideal political representatives. Papen was relentless in his opposition to organized labor. It was only after his fall, and subsequently because of General Kurt von Schleicher's muddled pseudo-socialist measures, that Hitler, with the forceful backing of Papen, emerged as a genuine political candidate for the industrialists. Hence, in December 1932 and January 1933 there was a further strengthening of the rather weak relationship between National Socialism and industry, which in late January would lead to Hindenburg's appointment of Hitler as Chancellor.[55]

The gradually mounting encouragement rendered to the Nazis after September 1930 by the small and intermediate businessmen was more significant for the development of the NSDAP as a social phenomenon than the periodic financial or political support of large industry. Not only were small businessmen (such as owners and managers of family enterprises) much more likely to sign up as party comrades, but their local and regional influence on behalf of the NSDAP reached more deeply and carried farther than that of the elusive magnates.[56] Characteristically, the party adjusted its administrative machinery to these conditions when the need was realized. At the beginning of 1931 Dr. Wagener took over the economic-political department of the NSDAP, reporting directly to Konstantin Hierl. Wagener, like his fellow functionaries who were dealing with questions concerning the old middle class, emphasized a corporative approach to economic problems, holding that only a horizontal organization of business interests within the NSDAP that favored a harmonious, organic relationship between employers and employees would cure the country of its socioeconomic ills. Although this approach did not appeal to big businessmen because their economic philosophy continued to be based on a recognition of the traditional vertical organization with its cleavage between capitalists and proletariat, an organization that militated against any form of worker participation in business decision-making, it did appeal to small-scale entrepreneurs, who tended to look upon corporative forms of organization as a potential guarantee against harmful disputes and subsequent work stoppages.[57]

Wagener (who, interestingly enough, remained at his post only until September 1932, shortly before the rapprochement between Hitler and big business) appealed particularly to representatives of light industry, manufacture, and whole-sale distributing and services. They operated in the shadow of the big cartels and could least afford costly lockouts—the favorite economic weapon applied by heavy industry such as mining against the mass of workers, particularly in 1928.[58]

Typical of these groups were the intermediate textile manufacturers of Saxony, such as the self-made Martin Mutschmann (the Gauleiter), the thermometer makers in Thuringia, and the Rhenish iron wholesalers represented by Otto Wolff. Wherever these circles, threatened as they were by rising debts and falling profits, severed their political ties with the DVP or the DNVP, they not only voted for the NSDAP but often contributed money to it, even though on an irregular basis.[59] If such local donors chose to remain anonymous and stay outside the party, it was mainly because they were afraid of business repercussions from protagonists of the bourgeois right, who were still suspicious of the "socialist" ingredients in the Nazi movement. In some areas, small-scale entrepreneurs even had to beware of boycotts instigated by Communists, like that imposed on the owner of a construction company in East Prussia. Consequently, expenditures for the Nazi party were hardly ever reflected in a firm's business records.[60] Similarly, the large-scale entrepreneurial farmers, especially in East Germany, formed an ever-growing group of loyal supporters of the Nazi party. Like the struggling urban businessmen, and despite governmental support schemes, they were much more seriously affected by the depression than the great industrialists and hence would have had reason to exchange their political allegiance to the DNVP or the Catholic Center Party for a working alliance with the NSDAP.[61] This often, but not necessarily, resulted in formal party membership.[62] Thus it comes as no surprise that in the winter of 1932–33 the large landowners who were prominent in the Reichslandbund, already controlled by the Nazis, played an instrumental role in Hitler's assumption of power.[63]

Executives and entrepreneurs, whether small or great, as well as other representatives of the upper strata of German society, were encouraged in their positive attitude toward National Socialism by the party's gradual rapprochement with the two established churches, particularly the Protestant church. This occurred after 1929, even before the important election of September 1930 in which the spectacular losses of the traditional right-wing parties convinced many church-minded upper-bourgeois and aristocratic Germans that the NSDAP warranted a closer look.[64] Officially, the party still upheld paragraph 24 of the Feder Program of February 1920, stating that although it professed to support a "positive Christianity," there was to be general tolerance of religious beliefs and no confusion of religion with politics. This aim was, in fact, reiterated in early 1925 when Hitler reestablished the party.[65]

But after 1929 the NSDAP became frankly interested in the churches for strategic reasons. The effect of the 1930 election on the bourgeois camp was not lost on its seasoned propagandists, as subsequent efforts, notably during the various elections of 1932, were to show.[66] From the party's point of view, two approaches were feasible, and both were tried more or less simultaneously in the last two years of the Weimar Republic. One entailed taking an active interest in church (predominantly Protestant) institutions and attempting to influence regional church developments. For example, in Prussia in 1932 the NSDAP participated in Protestant church elder elections with a separate list of "Protestant National Socialists," who were directed by Brandenburg's Gauleiter Wilhelm Kube. The other approach meant active support in the establishment of specifically National Socialist church groups, such as the one that sprang up among *völkisch* Lutherans in Berlin in 1931.[67] Another possibility, to organize Protestant pastors in Nazi formations analogous to the corporate associations and interest lobbies in small business and professional circles, was discarded for reasons of "political neutrality," although many Protestant clergymen did join the Nazi party on an individual basis between 1929 and 1933 and even put their services at the disposal of regional Nazi party administrators.[68]

The results of this remarkable liaison between established Protestantism and the Nazi party were in the long run beneficial to Hitler and his lieutenants, although he himself never seems to have displayed a great personal interest in it.[69] The situation was somewhat peculiar in that Hitler was formally a Roman Catholic and was surrounded largely by Catholic advisers. Although this fact disturbed some conservative Lutherans who were concerned about German Protestants' survival in a Catholic-dominated Third Reich, it was mainly the spokesmen of the Catholic hierarchy who, in conjunction with the Center Party in the West as well as the Bavarian People's Party in the South, heartily opposed Hitler and the National Socialist ideology.[70] They felt especially provoked by party philosopher Alfred Rosenberg's anti-Catholic diatribes, published in 1930 in his book *The Myth of the Twentieth Century*.[71] If the book created less stir among Protestant leaders, it was because their specific sensibilities were not so strongly violated. For although Martin Luther, for instance, was condemned for certain medieval twists in his thinking, he was not assailed in the manner of the "Jewish" St. Paul but appeared instead as a Germanic hero.[72] Moreover, since Hitler himself did not seem to have thrown his full official weight behind Rosenberg's antireligious arguments, Protestants, insofar as they chose to do so, found it easy to discard them as just the private opinion of one radical Nazi functionary.[73]

The gradually improving relationship between the Nazi leadership and the Protestant church was undoubtedly instrumental in drawing academically trained professionals and intellectuals (subgroup 12) to the party in greater numbers after 1929.[74] Although it is difficult to ascertain statistically whether the contingent of student Nazi newcomers (subgroup 13) actually increased, it can be proved that students continued to be overrepresented in the party (table 6). The physical and mental suffering engendered by the depression was beginning to drive more German academics and academic hopefuls into Hitler's camp. Among them were unemployed university graduates or students just before graduation with no jobs in sight who may previously have supported the DVP or the DNVP. Despair was rampant by 1931. In the summer of that year, Nazi university students captured the majority in Reich student self-government (Deutsche Studentenschaft) elections at the annual convention in Graz. In October, a German youth leader, then indubitably anti-Nazi and considering emigration to escape from economic misery, expressed his thoughts in a private letter to a friend: "As the plight of approximately one thousand young academics whose number will climb from year to year is being ignored, my doubts are mounting whether this is the same fatherland which I once served as a seventeen-year-old volunteer and for which tens of thousands of the worthiest of my generation have shed their blood in Flanders and God knows where else. As desperation takes hold of me, I can almost feel how the soil will be fertilized with Hitler's lethal ideas, and for many, the harvest has already begun."[75]

Although local and regional Nazi leaders still harbored doubts about the usefulness of new party comrades drawn from the conventional elite, whose thinking they often found difficult to understand, they made the most of the situation by accommodating the newcomers in their party chapters and occasionally by providing jobs for them.[76] Thus by 1932 a symphony orchestra staffed entirely by unemployed musicians was being supported by the party.[77] At the same time, great care was taken to enlarge and refine the Nazi professional associations, such as the League of National Socialist German Jurists (BNSDJ), founded in 1928, and also to develop new ones, like the Fighting Association of German Architects and Engineers, created in the summer of 1931.[78] Professionals in the health services, such as physicians and pharmacists, had a solid economic motive for joining the Nazis: their earnings were falling because of the decrease in returns from the expanded public insurance system. And many physicians who were prospering feared attempts at totally socialized medicine, which some colleagues of Marxist persuasion were favoring.[79] Lawyers, especially younger ones, suffered from the overcrowding of their profession. Luckily for some, as violent confrontations—particularly with the Communists—escalated all over the Reich, the Nazi party had an urgent need for lawyers to defend Stormtrooper terrorists in the republican courts. At the same time, however, the NSDAP realized that lawyers formed a professional group whose members had to avoid giving the impression of being too closely linked to the Nazis for fear of being rejected by their more conservative peers as well as by the government agencies.[80] This once again raised a problem that the Nazis had faced earlier: how to appeal to members of the upper echelons of society who could not or would not join the party outright but who nevertheless made no secret of their sympathy with Nazism and tried to express that feeling in other ways.[81] This, it should be stressed, is the main reason why the strength of Nazi influence within the upper circles was even greater than is indicated by the membership statistics displayed in the tables in this book.

Accompanying the socioeconomic disillusionment of these upper societal segments, but now heightened by visions of imminent doom, were the same sentiments of cultural alienation that had been evident in earlier years. With the apocalypse in sight, many German intellectuals, whose critical faculties were dulled by their penchant for the irrational, reveled in their cynical rejection of the highly touted accomplishments of the democratic Republic, most of all the parliament. In 1932, when Ernst Jünger composed his fascist treatise "The Worker," praising the manly ideals of elitism and brutal war, and when Oswald Spengler declared that one might as well vote for Hitler for President, more and more academics turned to the NSDAP as the dictatorial alternative to what they had come to loathe as democratically administered chaos. These tendencies were quite naturally increased by the fears of Bolshevism that had chronically beset the upper classes since the defeat of 1918.[82] However, by late 1932 (as evidenced by the election of November 6), the Nazi party had lost some of its favor with intellectuals and other representatives of the elite because academics had come to feel that Hitler—for whatever reason—not only was wasting too much effort on the workers but was himself clinging too rigidly to parliamentary devices on his way to power.[83]

Up to the end of 1932 the NSDAP was also slowly making headway among the higher civil servants (subgroup 11). The case of the Prussian pastors has already been mentioned. Upper-school teachers, alarmed by such economic strictures as salary cuts, were also turning to the Nazis, covertly at first, but more openly under the reign of

Chancellors Papen and Schleicher in 1932. By the beginning of 1933 there were disproportionately more upper-school teachers in the NSDAP than lower-school teachers, for many of the latter found it difficult to sever their ties with liberal and leftist parties.[84]

Among the faculties in the universities the drift to the Nazis was not so obvious. Professors were reluctant to identify themselves publicly with a group that was more and more taking on the outward appearance of a mass party; their sense of elitism tended to direct them back to the ivory tower, which more often than not meant political neutrality. Besides, the traditional political haven for higher academics had been and still was the monarchical DNVP. It was more common for the younger than the older faculty members to sport Nazi party membership pins in their lapels; most of them were untenured, and they were often products of the Nazi Student Union. Thus, at the Technical University of Brunswick only one full professor had joined the party before January 1933, while two senior lecturers and seven graduate assistants had become members. Nevertheless, the number of converts to Nazism among the professors, often motivated by anti-Semitism, was growing, especially in 1932, and even if most of them chose to remain outside the party, the evidence suggests that in their heart of hearts they had switched their allegiance to Hitler.[85]

Finally, by 1932 more and more higher bureaucrats (also in subgroup 11) were changing over to National Socialism.[86] Their reasons were as diverse as those of the academic professionals, and not dissimilar. Like the academics, the judges and district administrators were concerned about the threat of Bolshevism posed by the growing number of Communists in Germany's big cities. They worried about the government's notorious inability to control economic and political turmoil, and while many may have appreciated that Brüning's cabinet already had gone a long way toward investing the higher bureaucracy with greater powers to ensure implementation of decree legislation, a goodly number felt that this was not enough. Their understanding of "law and order" called, above all, for a greater commitment to the concept of the German nation as symbolized by the Hohenzollern dynasty, and a much sharper rejection of the concept of the Weimar Republic. The more cynical state officials even went so far as to advocate the abrogation of judicial independence for court judges. Professor Carl Schmitt's acid criticism of the workings of the democratic constitution in daily parliamentary practice was finding a ready audience.[87]

These officials, too, were suffering acutely from the salary cuts necessitated by Brüning's and even Papen's emergency decrees.[88] Increasingly suspicious of colleagues whose only credentials seemed to be their good standing as members of the SPD, the bureaucrats listened eagerly to the Nazis' harangues. Although the National Socialists had condemned high salaries for upper civil servants and so won approval from the lower officials, they were also insisting that civil servants would have to be remunerated "on the basis of real accomplishments." This stab at the prorepublican SPD-patronized officials was obviously meant to mollify the nationalistic bureaucrats.[89] In a similar spirit, Jakob Sprenger, during a Reichstag debate in December 1930, castigated the rigid promotion system that trapped many a youthful civil servant in his first post with no chance of professional advancement for many years.[90]

Still, like the university professors, the other upper civil servants were somewhat slow in signing up for membership, at least until the summer of 1932.[91] Men who had dared to do so in the past were known to have been transferred; and so when Count Fritz-Dietlof von der Schulenburg joined the party in the fall of 1931, his action left his superior in a state of shock, for he fully anticipated Schulenburg's dismissal from state service. Another reason why Nazi-minded higher bureaucrats stayed out of Hitler's party was that they were often expressly asked to do so by local Nazi leaders, who believed that they could better serve the Nazi cause in a seemingly nonpartisan way. This, for example, was true of Dr. Benno Martin, then a young state counselor (*Regierungsrat*) in the Nuremberg police presidium, who later rose to prominence as Nuremberg's police chief and remained in this position until the end of the Third Reich.[92]

By 1933 Hitler had succeeded in maintaining and even in strengthening the ties between his party and important representatives of the still vastly influential social elite. This alliance bore all the marks of a marriage of convenience: Hitler needed patricians and mandarins to smooth his path to the top, and they in turn planned to use the Führer as a "drummer boy" for their own schemes, aimed largely at preserving the old order and neutralizing the threat of Communism.

The alliance was endangered several times in 1932, when elitist circles feared that the Nazi party was moving too close to the working class by championing the cause of hundreds of thousands of destitute unemployed. Members of the elite particularly feared the SA, which had begun to resemble a huge, disorganized band of desperadoes. And when Hitler's chief of staff, Gregor Strasser, tried in early December to come to some agreement with the new Chancellor, General von Schleicher, a reactionary who dallied with notions of populist "socialism," this did not warm the Führer's relationship with the influential few outside the Berlin cabinet. But Strasser's departure from the NSDAP after the talks with Schleicher proved abortive helped to bring about crucial meetings between key representatives of government, conservative vested interests, and the National Socialists.

As a result, Hitler was appointed Chancellor by Hindenburg on January 30, 1933. That evening thousands of National Socialists carried torches through the streets of the capital, past the chancellery in the Wilhelmstrasse where Hitler waved down to them from a balcony. He was greeting his supporters, Germans from all walks of life, many of whom had given him their unqualified backing throughout the Time of Struggle and who now celebrated with him their hard-earned triumph. And so the Nazi party, which had taken its name from the working class and had attained national prominence as a mass formation supported by the lower middle class, was finally elevated to the seat of power by the German elite.

4

THE PEACEFUL PERIOD
JANUARY 1933 TO SEPTEMBER 1939

After January 1933 the character of the National Socialist Workers' party changed. During the Weimar Republic it had served Hitler as an instrument to obtain political power by formal democratic means. He had been interested in attracting to it as many people as possible in order to gain strong electoral backing, people who came from every stratum in the German Reich, from both sexes, and from all age groups. But when the NSDAP became a state monopolist organization in a dictatorial system, it did not need popular support. Its political power was guaranteed by other agencies staffed by technocrats and by experts in terror and oppression — agencies such as the SS, the Gestapo, and to a certain extent the SA. And although the Nazi party lost importance vis-à-vis the SS and, after the onset of the war, the army, this did not mean that it became obsolete. Many administrative tasks remained within its sphere of competence, and new responsibilities were added as the regime progressed.

One of the party's functions was to serve as a link between the regime's political leadership and the German people. If a representive share of the people could be organized within the party's ranks, the leadership would be in a position to monitor, and thereby to quietly control, prevailing attitudes within the population — attitudes that indicated the degree of consensus between the people and their leadership. After 1932 the NSDAP became a measuring device as well as a steering mechanism in the relationship between Germans and their government. This raises three questions about the party's membership: the ultimate shape the party was to assume (elite or mass); the degree of choice embodied in a decision for or against membership; and the motives for taking up membership, including the play of social and economic factors in shaping these motives.

First, although by 1933 or 1934 the NSDAP had become an official monopolistic institution with a proclivity toward elitism, it still clung to its historic claim of being a mass movement, or at least the backbone of one. Second, German *Volksgenossen* (comrades-in-the-folk) were never forced to join the party, especially not collectively, although in the case of certain individuals and even certain subgroups strong suasion was applied in soliciting "voluntary" membership. This happened especially during three phases of the peaceful period of the Third Reich when the membership rolls were opened to all "Aryans" (non-Jewish German citizens): in the summer of 1933, in 1937, and in 1939. But in 1934–1936 and 1938 only young people (generally not older than twenty-one) and certain privileged members of NSDAP adjunct organizations, such as the Nazi Student Union (NSDStB), were permitted to sign up.[1]

Third, if NSDAP membership was by and large voluntary, what were the motives of the men and women who decided to join after the Time of Struggle? (Even in the best years their number never reached 10 percent of the population.) Before 1933 the party had represented a social and political protest movement, indeed, in 1932 a mass protest movement; but after 1932 this was not the case. If in that year the prevailing aim of Nazi newcomers had been to gain relief from desperate socioeconomic straits, the same motive would not have been valid in 1937 or 1939 after economic conditions had become bearable. Still, in 1933 when a great mass of Germans rushed to the party offices (see figure 1), the Great Depression had by no means passed. "Men joined the Party to get a job or to hold a job or to get a better job or to save themselves from getting a worse job, or to get a contract or to hold a contract, a customer, a client, a patient." This verdict voiced by Milton Mayer in 1955 suggests sociopolitical opportunism as a mainspring for action; yet it does not exclude the possibility of governmental pressure or ideological conviction as additional factors in the decisions of German men and women.[2]

The analysis of the social composition of the Nazi membership from 1933 to 1939 is empirically supported by data from the Reich, part of the larger Berlin Document Center sample described in the Introduction (table 7). This subsample of Nazi joiners was broken down by region to facilitate comparisons between large cities, towns, and the countryside (figures 2–5). To illustrate the case of medical doctors as a particularly Nazi-prone group, a separate figure (figure 6), incorporating data from the BDC subsample, was drawn up. These joiners should be viewed in the manner outlined at the beginning of chapter 3.

The new joiners' percentages have been supplemented with data on established Nazi members in Frankfurt/Main in 1940 and the Reich in 1942 (columns H and I, table 7). Finally, data on anti-Nazi (Communist) victims of the regime (columns J and K, table 7) have been added, in order to suggest comparisons between the social structure of the Nazis and that of the Communists.

THE WORKERS

Even though there is no evidence that members of the German working class were physically or psychologically compelled by functionaries of the regime to join the Nazi party between 1933 and 1939 (and later), the motivations underlying workers' voluntary NSDAP membership must be carefully evaluated. Is it correct, for instance, to say with Oxford historian Timothy W. Mason that the regime was both dependent on and afraid of the workers, and that it entered into a sort of operational relationship with them, mollifying them materially but at the same time threatening them with subjugation either then or in the future?[3] To answer this question it is necessary to examine the state of the workers and their attitudes toward the party before the war.

From 1933 to 1939 the working class was still underrepresented in the NSDAP, constituting between 30 and 40 percent of the entire new membership at the Reich level, as compared with about 54 percent of the German population as a whole (see figure 2 and tables 7 and 1). A sharp drop in representation had occurred between 1932 and 1933, but after 1933 what appeared to be a significant change took place and the new membership gradually increased up to the beginning of the war.[4] Between 1930 and 1933 the fall in new worker members appears to have been sharpest in the big cities and small towns (figures 3 and 4). In 1933 the German nonrural workers were shocked by the Nazis' destruction of organized labor: the KPD was proscribed in February and March, the trade unions were liquidated in early May, then the SPD was dissolved, and later on individual leftists and former socialist party and union members were persecuted.[5] Rural workers, by contrast, were not so severely affected by the restrictive measures taken against organized labor, which centered in the cities and towns, and so they were much less hostile toward the NSDAP in 1933 (figure 5).

After 1933 the city workers' sentiments toward the NSDAP improved markedly; in the country improvement was apparent after 1935.[6] This positive trend was the immediate result of the regime's relative success in battling unemployment, which was more prevalent in the industrialized urban areas than in the country.[7] Evidence suggests that in 1933 the workers were biding their time with regard to Nazism, waiting to see how the political leaders would deal with the problem of unemployment, and that they became more and more inclined to join the party as Hitler's job creation measures began to take effect.[8] From January 1933 to the declaration of the second Four-Year Plan in October 1936, the number of unemployed in the Reich was effectively reduced by four-fifths; from the end of August 1932 until the same month in 1937 the employment figure at the national level rose by almost 50 percent.[9] At the end of August 1938, there were only 179,000 jobless in the land, down from more than six million in January 1933.[10]

In spite of such imposing statistics, however, the government's handling of the unemployment question, after the initial period of spectacular success from 1933 to 1936, may have contributed as much to the alienation of some German workers from the party as it helped in attracting others. For one thing, as recent historical scholarship in eastern and western Europe has shown, the figures published by the Nazis were often deceptive because of inconsistent arithmetic or outright falsification.[11] Moreover, the benefits received by some workers' groups frequently meant losses for others, and there were also regional and local inequalities. Generally, the most qualified worker was the most easily employable; nobody bothered to train the unskilled laborer, to upgrade his expertise and improve his marketable skills. Those in seasonal employment remained precariously insecure, as did those who worked in industries handicapped by intermittent shortages of raw materials. Industries that did not play an essential part in the armament effort, particularly after the initiation of the second Four-Year Plan in 1936, could offer few opportunities to blue-collar workers in search of steady employment. Among such workers were the basket weavers of eastern Bavaria (1936), and the turnpike laborers, cement mixers, and tobacco handlers of Westphalia (1935–36).[12]

In this connection, two occupational groups, textile workers and miners, who had very little professional job training and ranked low on the early lists of key armaments industries, were in almost constant trouble. The textile industry, concentrated mainly in Rhineland-Westphalia, Saxony, and a few places in South Germany, was not cartelized, and because deliveries of raw materials were irregular it was forced periodically (even as late as November 1937) to dismiss workers and curtail production.[13] In mining, especially in the Ruhr, there were also sporadic layoffs. Both of these industries felt the economic strains of the Great Depression, which caused dislocations in heavy industry until 1936, when the rearmament effort gradually began to stimulate production. In addition, they were affected by the new rationalization of the German production systems, which reduced the customary demand for manpower. In 1925, for example, 460,000 miners had been called upon to produce 104 million tons of coal; in 1938, 127 million tons were produced by only 335,000 men. More coal was needed, but by the late 1930s many workers, long frustrated by stoppages, inclement working conditions, and low wages, had left the mines in search of easier and more lucrative jobs.[14]

One major reason why the total percentage of worker members in the NSDAP remained much below that of workers in the Reich as a whole was the comparatively bad economic conditions under which they labored, even when times were good. As circumspect historians have shown, this line of argumentation presupposes that the worker was primarily interested in his material well-being rather than in corporate class-consciousness or a distinctive sociopolitical system.[15] Masses of archival documents prove that, at least in the early years, the Nazis avoided any centralized direction of wages and prices lest the delicate alliance with private industry be put in jeopardy. By and large the regime adopted the wage and price policies inherited from the republican phase, although at first some insignificant changes were made to help curtail unemployment, mainly by keeping wages down. The government would have liked to see wages and prices remain low; but free-market competition reigned by 1935–36, and the leaders did little more than remind the people of the Führer's wish for moderation. This was the tenor of speeches by Göring in late 1936 and by Hess in early 1937.[16] As Mason correctly observes, one could not really speak of a "national wage policy" before June 1938.[17]

The development of inequalities in the employment and wage sector as a result of the operation of free-market mechanisms was allowed to run its course until the regime was forced to clamp down in the spring of 1938. As early as 1934 some Nazi officials had observed, as the first symptom of dwindling unemployment, a shortage of skilled labor in specific industries, notably metallurgy and the building trades, which were later to be deemed indispensable to the war effort. In these industries a wage pattern was established that was to be copied by other industries, especially those with high-volume state contracts: economically potent employers would hire the most qualified workers by offering higher and higher wages, outbidding one another and so leaving weak competitors behind. By 1937–38 some wages had slipped out of state control and were helping to drive up prices of consumer goods as well as to create a national wage spectrum that was marked by great extremes.[18] Beset by the requirements of mobilization after 1936, the regime attempted to cope with the problem of excessive labor fluctuation not by enforcing wage ceilings but by restricting the skilled workers' horizontal mobility. The culmination of a series of measures toward that goal was the decree given by Economic Plenipotentiary Göring on June 22, 1938, for the "security of the work force regarding projects of national political significance." For some occupations, such as mining, this decree resulted in a total mobility freeze by early 1939.[19]

As a consequence the entire working class suffered, though those whose professional skills remained underdeveloped were the worst off. If wages rose regionally and in certain trades, prices usually followed close behind, often pushed up by shortages of important foodstuffs and clothing, such as margarine and shoes. A multitude of documents testify to the plight of working families throughout the Reich that were trying to make ends meet on low weekly budgets. In some cases workers' wives had to go out to look for jobs — contrary to the Nazis' condemnation of working women. Among the hardest hit were, once again, the miners. A coal miner who was earning a daily gross wage of 5.40 marks five times a week in October 1933 had to pay 9.88 marks a week in taxes and dues and thus was left with a weekly wage of 17.12 marks. By early 1938, more than four years later, the miner's daily wage had risen only to 5.50 marks.[20] The judgment of disgruntled laborers near Hanover in the late summer of 1933 is symptomatic of the sentiments of workers in other regions of the Reich for the entire period of the first phase of the regime: "Sure enough, we may not be out of work any more, but with such low wages we are worse off than before, for in this kind of work our clothes and shoes wear out twice as fast. Where shall we find the extra pennies, what with most of us being married."[21] Scholars generally agree that if all factors are considered, the "real income" of the majority of workers fell between 1929 and 1938 with a resultant drop in the overall standard of living, though there may be disagreements as to the extent of the discrepancy.[22]

It has been claimed that in 1937–38 the average worker was left with more money — that is, more buying power after deductions — than in 1933; but such an "improvement" was achieved solely at the expense of leisure time, because laborers everywhere were working longer shifts.[23] In fact, the problems arising from low wages and high prices were compounded for the average working man by overtime hours that reduced the amount of time he could spend with his family.[24] Bad nutrition, not infrequently the result of a luncheon diet of black bread supplemented with cooked potatoes and cabbage but with little meat or fat, tended to increase the workers' chances of becoming ill.[25] To this was added an intolerably long and arduous trip to the workplace, especially for those who had been assigned to a job location that was not of their own choosing.[26] Some laborers who had been conscripted into armaments industries were removed physically from their families for long periods of time.[27] Under such circumstances, and even when the place of work was closer to the family, the worker's "home," for which he might have to pay a very high rent, was often a barracks in need of repair, sometimes well-nigh uninhabitable, and almost always crowded.[28]

Somewhat different circumstances prevailed in the countryside. The percentage of agricultural worker newcomers to the NSDAP was also down since 1930–1932, but it did not decline as drastically as that of big city and town workers and — as in the Weimar Republic — was still the highest of the three regionally defined lower-class groups. This was so because unemployment in the country never had been and never was to be a problem of the same magnitude as in the industrial cities. If the rural workers' joiner curve after 1932 dropped relative to those of the other two classes (lower middle class and elite) in the country, it was because of a significant deterioration of living and working conditions for farm laborers (figures 3–5). The temporary upswing in the farm laborers' new membership curve between 1935 and 1937 was doubtless a result of Göring's introduction of financial credits for farm workers with small houses. Generally, however, and especially for older married laborers, the housing problem, along with low wages and high prices, bore the major responsibility for the ever-increasing flight from the land. Ironically, only young, unmarried male laborers were mobile enough to head for urban areas in search of the higher wages offered by industry and particularly by armaments manufacture. The regime found itself unable to stem this tide, even though it went so far as to threaten runaway laborers with the concentration camp.[29]

If the living standards of both industrial and agricultural workers in the Third Reich gave them little incentive to join the NSDAP, neither did the educational and job training system, which, at least in certain sectors, purported to stand for equal social opportunity. This claim was initially based on Hitler's ideas in *Mein Kampf,* ideas he reiterated throughout the period of his rule.[30] Hence it was part of the programmatic goal of the Hitler Youth (HJ) to incorporate as many young workers as possible within its ranks and allow them to benefit from various social projects such as summer camps. But more often than not, the Hitler Youth leaders found that despite a heavy comple-

ment of young workers and workers' descendants among both the
rank and file and the leadership cadres, large groups of adolescents
were prevented from partaking fully in such activities: poverty often
made it impossible for them to purchase the required uniform, for instance.[31] The HJ itself, however, did not deny that workers' children
had the potential for a higher education, as was proved in a survey
conducted by the local HJ leadership in a Hagen public school around
Easter in 1938.[32] Significantly, although workers' sons were still
underrepresented in the HJ-directed "Adolf Hitler Schools," their
percentage was actually higher there than in the conventional upper
schools in 1939 and 1940.[33] In spite of newly created institutions like
the Langemarck Studium (1938), which was supposed to open the way
for workers' children to qualify for a university education, members
of the lower class remained as underrepresented at Germany's institutions of higher learning as they had been through the years of the
Weimar Republic.[34] Young workers may have been given a better
chance for economic and social advancement through the Reich Vocational Contest, held annually till the beginning of the war,[35] but with
very few exceptions opportunities for social mobility among workers
and their offspring remained as scarce as before; the Third Reich was
never able to provide what it claimed it would, a consistent "selection
of the fittest."[36]

Another grievance of the workers was directed against the German
Labor Front (Deutsche Arbeitsfront—DAF), created and ruled by Dr.
Robert Ley. Its functions were manifold; yet its two most important
aims were to act as a substitute organization for the shattered trade
unions (in this capacity controlling the workers' lives physically as well
as spiritually) and to serve as an intermediary between the workers and
their employers. At both levels the DAF was anything but successful.
From the outset it was caught in the middle. Workers regarded it with
suspicion as an artificial surrogate union into which they were increasingly being pressed: by 1935 DAF membership for workers (and
salaried employees) had virtually become obligatory. Entrepreneurs
considered it "leftist" because it was charged by the regime to act on
the workers' behalf in order to win proletarian loyalties; and entrepreneurial membership in the organization, though needed in order to
fulfill the cherished objective of a homogeneous Volksgemeinschaft,
could never be enforced.[37]

The ambivalent status of the DAF hardly contributed to its
popularity among the workers. The highly publicized commitment of
the ubiquitous Dr. Ley was viewed with skepticism in the early years,
when membership was still more or less voluntary, and ugly rumors

about corruption, favoritism in assigning jobs, and general inefficiency as well as ignorance on the part of the leaders made the rounds in the workers' quarters. As attempts at coercion from without and the degree of regimentation from within the DAF's ranks increased, so did the workers' hatred of an institution that was obviously not designed for their good. One characteristic indication of the workers' rejection was the contempt with which they treated DAF-organized shop-steward elections in the factories: usually they ignored them altogether.[38] A source of never-ending complaints was the comparatively high scale of dues to be paid for various purposes, in particular insurance. Miners, who were charged the highest premiums, received so little in times of need that they soon became the most embittered opponents of the DAF.[39]

Were these disadvantages outweighed by the benefits offered to the workers through the DAF's much advertised social policy programs sponsored by "Strength through Joy" (*Kraft durch Freude*—KdF)? It is true that KdF organized relatively inexpensive holidays for DAF members, taking some on steamship cruises to the Norwegian fjords or the Spanish islands, but the evidence points to a number of factors that must have detracted from the joys promised by the tour officials. Many workers complained that although the tours were indeed much cheaper than individually financed ones, only the cream—the highly paid, highly skilled laborers—could afford to participate. Even then, holidays often had to be taken during the annual vacation period; additional free days on the employer's time were not allowed. Invariably, the pressure from above did not subside during these journeys; "regimented joy" could amount to outright ideological indoctrination during a forced weekend visit to an SS training castle or to strenuous "recreation" events such as rifle-range exercises, sanctioned by the regime but hardly on the list or workers' relaxation priorities. In one documented case an East Prussian quarry worker was ordered by the DAF to participate in a journey to Silesia that he had not requested. After protesting, he was told by the authorities that the trip would be chalked up to his holiday allotment and that he would not be eligible for compensation for wages lost during his enforced absence from the worksite.[40] The deception practiced by the administrators of KdF was especially evident in the tragic Volkswagen scheme, in which, as is known today, hundreds of average Germans lost their savings. Even if the people's cars had ever been delivered to the hopeful shareholders, few of the low-paid workers would have been able to enjoy them. When in July 1939 the regime bragged that 59 percent of all KdF automobile investors were earning less than 300 marks a month, this was not good news for most workers: at that time, the average worker's monthly wage of 156.96 marks was far below that amount.[41]

What sort of protest was still possible under a regime that so tenaciously curtailed all forms of mobility and personal freedom? As the documents make clear, strikes and work stoppages still occurred, though they were spontaneous, of short duration, and not centrally and sometimes not even locally directed. Usually they were started by unskilled workers on autobahn construction sites, in textile mills, or in mining; but in 1935 one such strike was staged by the experienced Opel auto workers of Rüsselsheim. Invariably, strike instigators were ruthlessly prosecuted as "Marxists" by the authorities, and reports of the walkouts were hushed up lest the public should question the regime's success in keeping the social peace.[42]

This raises the issue of the workers' "resistance" to National Socialist rule. There is no doubt that such resistance existed, and that it was chiefly organized by the KPD, which had been driven underground and thus made illegal; as for the SPD, it was better concealed and less reckless, but also extensive. The most efficient method of "resisting," and for Communist saboteurs certainly the safest, was the composition and clandestine distribution of leaflets and flyers. Ingenious techniques were developed for passing these materials around. In one case a Berlin "washerwoman" carted masses of Marxist propaganda covered over with dirty laundry through the streets of Berlin. Often the message contained in the propaganda was seemingly innocent or shrouded in sardonic humor.[43] If the distributors were caught by the police, they were always dealt with unmercifully.[44] The efficacy of the Gestapo in stamping out Communist subversion can be measured by the number of those who were arrested for distributing leaflets from 1933 to 1936: in the first year a total of 663 persons were indicted in the courts; in 1934 the number rose to 2,045; but in 1935 it dropped to 540 and in 1936 to 267.[45]

The success of the Nazis against organized Marxism indicates something about the nature of the workers' opposition to the regime: they lacked either the physical courage or the moral conviction to make the effort required to regain their independent class status. A lack of physical courage would be understandable in view of the frightening Nazi terror machine. But it is questionable whether the workers were always fully convinced that such an effort ought to be made. Several factors support this view. First, the importance of the Communist resistance before 1939 in factories and shops has probably been overrated, both by the Nazi authorities and by post-1945 Marxist-inspired critics. (On the other hand, resistance by the Social

Democrats may well have been underrated, as the recently published reports of the SPD in exile suggest.) Second, the Nazis who laid an early claim to having achieved social peace within a harmonious Volksgemeinschaft in the nation tended, for ideological reasons, to label any malcontents among the working class as *political* trouble-makers in order to have the justification for putting them away. In this they had no choice, for any official admission of structural socioeco-nomic maladies would have amounted to shifting the blame away from the maladjusted elements in German society to the political lead-ership. Third, many of the alleged troublemakers may not have been "Marxists" and hence would not have been interested primarily in political conditions but rather in economic conditions that could be rectified at the worksite. But although as a rule the Nazis overreacted to "Communist" plots that were nothing more than tempests in tea-pots, they were at times realistic enough to acknowledge that the workers' protest was indeed economically motivated and devoid of political conspiracy.[46]

These considerations help in putting the rather obscure concept of "workers' resistance" into clearer perspective. In answer to East Ger-man interpretations and to Mason's recent assertion that workers in the Third Reich adopted a more or less permanent attitude of political resistance (even though this may have fed on socioeconomic dissatis-faction), it has been argued elsewhere that routine complaints and bickering in factories and plants were not necessarily linked to an underlying ideological class resentment of the regime but may have been the visible manifestations of overemployment and greed for ever-better wages, both of which were indicative of fairly good times.[47] In this context it is important to note that the strike phenomenon did not originate until 1935 when most of the formerly unemployed workers had returned to the active work force, and that some of the work stop-pages were started not by unskilled workers but by highly qualified, already well-paid skilled workers who craved even better pay.[48] Mason himself concedes that the Gestapo could have exaggerated some cases in which workers, perhaps in a state of drunkenness, de-scribed themselves as "Communists" in disagreements with the regime and thus, while they undeniably courted misfortune, contributed to the legend of a proletarian class-consciousness in constant readiness to fight the Nazi leadership on *political* terms.[49]

Such readiness is indeed doubtful. It must be remembered that many former KPD or SPD members were not sufficiently fortified ideologically to see through the tricks of the totalitarian dictatorship; they might have accepted some aspects of the Third Reich while at the same time retaining a partial allegiance to the KPD or SPD.[50] The German-Jewish physician Dr. Georg Löwenstein recalls that after the Nazis arrested him in Potsdam in April 1933 he was maltreated by former Social Democrats: "I just could not get over the fact that the very same workers to whom I had spoken at huge Social Democratic rallies had, all of a sudden, turned into National Socialists."[51] There is persuasive evidence to suggest that many more former Social Democrats and Communists would have jumped on the Nazi bandwagon had they not feared harassment by lower-class Nazis of long standing. The Third Reich lost countless potential sympathizers from among the working class who could not or would not present themselves as unequivocally in favor of the regime.[52]

There is no disputing the fact, however, that workers, though markedly underrepresented in the NSDAP, demonstrated a strong presence in it, as they had done during the Weimar Republic. Actually, their newcomers' curve for the Reich as a whole was on the rise between 1938 and 1939, during Germany's most intense preparation for the war effort, at a time when—as Mason has clearly shown—the workers were more hard-pressed than ever before (figure 2). In the textile town of Gronau in Westphalia, for example, the entire local NSDAP chapter was composed of blue-collar workers![53]

From 1933 to 1939 in various regions of the Reich, governmental and party authorities periodically reported, if not a state of euphoria among the workers, at least a sense of satisfaction with the regime, which was most immediately traceable to renewed employment and the material assistance rendered by such social welfare agencies as "Winter Aid" (Winterhilfswerk—WHW) and "People's Aid" (NS-Volkswohlfahrt—NSV). Commenting on the correlation between the fulfillment of physical needs and political allegiance, one NSDAP functionary wrote concerning East Prussian workers in the summer of 1933: "Because the worker has suffered economically for years, and because in times past he has been turned into a strictly materialistic being, he is inclined, without making any value judgment, merely to take the economic measures of the government into consideration." The writer then went on to state that for the time being the workers were happy because there were signs that unemployment was vanishing.[54] A good deal of the Nazis' relative success among the blue-collar workers was due, as before, to their prolabor propaganda, which, while bordering on social demagoguery, tended to improve the self-image of many workers who accepted adages like "the peerage of hard jobs" and were impressed by the officially decreed concept of communion between employers and employees—however vague and blatantly fraudulent that concept eventually became.[55] Nor was it all talk. In the Ruhr, many a plant manager complied with DAF objectives by serving free meals to his workers; and in Berlin as late as January 1938 workers displayed their good will toward the government by expressing a desire to read Rosenberg's *Myth of the Twentieth Century* — if, as one man wrote, they could understand it in spite of the many difficult words in it![56]

In this connection, the importance of KdF for the workers cannot altogether be belittled: although it is true that for many even KdF could do nothing, there were nevertheless hundreds of thousands of workers who thought they received some benefit from the organization over the years.[57] Moreover, KdF presented the regime's ultimate goal of social homogeneity to be realized through the creation of the Volksgemeinschaft better than did any other innovation offered by the Nazis to the workers. This is obvious from a letter written in September 1934 by a fifty-three-year-old Saxon laborer, a member of the SPD for eighteen years, who could not stop praising KdF and all it was supposed to epitomize.[58] The letter writer's contempt for the defunct SPD, which would never have provided him with the opportunity for an inexpensive holiday in the way the KdF did, highlights another important reason for the workers' partial attraction to, or at least acquiescence in, Nazism: a certain degree of disenchantment with former ADGB union bosses and leftist party functionaries. Some reasoned that if a Volksgemeinschaft was to be created, a corrupt and smugly entrenched SPD with an adjunct labor union wielding a high degree of power would be superfluous. Ironically, the suspicion with which some blue-collar workers regarded the DAF actually stemmed from painful experiences with the labor unions of the Weimar Republic, notably the ADGB, and when the ADGB was purged on May 2, 1933, many of the former rank and file expressed their satisfaction.[59]

Many German workers, like representatives of other social subgroups in the Reich who attempted to come to terms with the new conditions after January 1933, displayed a tendency to put their trust in the Führer of the NSDAP. They praised Hitler for all the positive developments in the land and blamed the party bureaucracy for everything that went wrong. Hitler's ability to play such an integrating role in society, a role so pervasive that it affected large segments of the proletariat, is only one aspect of a much broader subject that has been discussed elsewhere.[60] But there is no doubt that to a very large extent Hitler was personally responsible for the fact that workers bothered to join the NSDAP at all after 1933, and that they joined in increasing numbers after 1938. Especially for those workers, Hitler's very existence as Führer appears to have been quite sufficient to offset their socioeconomic adversities, the delays in their social progress, and the pressures of the war effort, which bore ever more heavily on the proletariat after September 1, 1939.[61]

To return to Mason's thesis that the German worker was a potential threat to the Nazi regime, it seems clear that this perception ought to be somewhat modified. In terms of sheer numbers the workers could have easily overthrown the regime. But for this to happen, they would have needed their organizations — their parties and their trade unions. Those were progressively destroyed by the Nazis after January 1933. The realization of this state of affairs surely dampened the workers' desire to oppose Hitler's regime. On the other hand, the absence of appropriate Marxist direction, the increase in economic stability, and the evident willingness, after 1935, on the part of many workers to make their social and political peace with Adolf Hitler, if not with his dictatorial system, added to the workers' reluctance to react violently. In the war years the personal bond between Hitler and the working class was to grow even stronger.

THE LOWER MIDDLE CLASS

During the peaceful regime phase of National Socialism the lower middle class increased its overall support for the NSDAP beyond the level prevailing between 1930 and 1932. Members of that class joined the party in even greater numbers than before (see tables 6 and 7), thus continuing to surpass their rate of representation in the Reich (42.65 percent, as in table 1). But this trend continued only until 1939, when the percentage of lower-middle-class party newcomers fell sharply.

An exception to this pattern was the behavior of the master craftsmen and other small independent shopkeepers (subgroups 4 and 8), whose Nazi joiners' pattern from 1933 to 1939 developed in marked contrast to that of the other occupational subgroups in the lower middle class. These subgroups showed less enthusiasm for the NSDAP from 1933 to about 1937, but thereafter its joiners' curve rose, peaking by 1939 (table 7). The reasons for this may be assumed to have been largely socioeconomic and institutional. Historians have described the small businessman's gradual decline as the result of a fatal clash between his interests and those of big business (in the case of the craftsman), or of high-volume trade (in the case of the merchant). While this theory holds largely true for the first few years of the regime, small business was certainly not wiped out by the growth of large corporations, at least not prior to the outbreak of World War II.[62]

It is well known that by 1934, after a short period of economic stimulation, the regime had made it increasingly obvious that a policy sanctioning the objectives of the small enterprising middle class, the policy advocated by the Nazis since before Hitler's takeover, was to be severely curtailed in the Third Reich. Henceforth, small traders and artisans were, in a sense, to become the ideological stepchildren of the nation — in sharp contrast to the positive propaganda image that the peasants continued to enjoy for many years.[63] In the independent crafts sector (subgroup 4) this reversal manifested itself until 1939 in the following ways, most of them institutional in nature: the inability of the Nazi artisans' organization to maintain an independent course of action within the party and to avoid control by the Labor Front (which became effective with the total absorption of the Nazi Tradesmen's and Craftsmen's Association, the NS-Hago, into the DAF in 1936); the forced reorganization of the guild system; a tightening of standards for master craftsmen's examinations; and the reduction of the number of independent artisans' shops.[64]

In the retail trade sector (subgroup 8) the main pressures came from unbridled competition by chain stores, which, contrary to pre-1933 election campaign promises, were not dissolved but merely "Aryanized" — a Nazi euphemism for expropriation from Jews. To a lesser degree, discontent also resulted from the decision by the regime to retain the cooperatives.[65] All small businesses, depending on the particular industry involved and on regional concentration, were victimized to some extent by exigencies that were noticeably absent from the operational fields of big business or large-volume trading. For example, a chronic shortage of ready cash or credit prevented many small businesses from expanding, from upgrading their production or marketing procedures, or in some cases from continuing to exist.[66] In addition, because of partial state controls that were designed to keep consumer-good prices low in order to depress the wage level, the profit margins of small businesses were often extremely narrow, and proprietors and masters found themselves paying more for food and having to raise salaries to keep their employees.[67] Additional difficulties were posed by shortages and delays in the delivery of raw materials. This particularly affected the craftsmen; large industries, especially those with armaments contracts, received preferential treatment from the state.[68] Small business people, too, were often obliged to pay an increasing number of dues to various official or semiofficial organizations, for many businessmen had been forced to subscribe to multiple memberships, benefits, pensions, and insurance plans. Compounding all this was the heavy tax burden.[69] It is not surprising that more and more small businesses were forced to close down because of extreme indebtedness or in the wake of rationalization. In the handicraft sector, for instance, many one-man shops had been squeezed out of existence by 1939.[70]

Ironically, the regime-sponsored consolidation process, whose goal it was to eliminate noneconomic businesses, actually contributed after 1938 to a rise in the NSDAP new members' curve for both the craftsmen and small merchants. As the uncompetitive small merchant left his store to become a salaried employee in a chain outlet, and as the hopelessly indebted baker closed his shop to work in a mechanized bakery for top wages, the surviving intermediate business proprietors with two employees or more came to enjoy a correspondingly higher level of production, a larger turnover with increased profits, and, concomitantly, a better standard of living. Similarly, for many if not all craftsmen, the restrictions imposed by the regime on the registration of new shops, as well as the reduction in the number of diploma master craftsmen resulting from a stricter selection process, proved to be virtual blessings. Businesses that managed to pull through until 1938–39 were able — along with large-scale industry — to share in the economic opportunities offered by the war effort, so that in real terms the quality of life for the surviving small businessmen improved as compared with 1933.[71] One can infer with a high degree of certainty that it was those men and women, the surviving "fittest," who joined the NSDAP in large numbers in 1939 when the membership rolls were reopened to the general public.

As in the case of the shopkeepers and craftsmen, there is no evidence that independently established peasants or farmers in the Reich (subgroup 9) were in any way compelled by the authorities to join the Nazi party. Relative to other occupational subgroups, the peasants' enthusiasm for the NSDAP dropped somewhat in 1933 as compared with the 1930–1932 level; it recovered between 1934 and 1936, only to sink to a new low thereafter. Just before World War II, however, a moderate increase in the number of party joiners occurred (tables 6 and 7).

Reports from various regions of the country help to illustrate and explain these developments. An official memorandum from Lower Saxony for August 1933 mentions much complaining among farmers, who still regarded governmental measures as "reactionary." But in 1934–35 peasants in Brunswick County were said to be satisfied with the recent course of events in the agrarian sector and to trust in the future policy of the government. By 1936–37, however, this favorable mood had changed again for the worse, not only around Brunswick but also in Southwest Germany, where Württemberg farmers displayed a distinct reluctance to support Nazi ancillary organizations such as the NSV. Similar attitudes were expressed in the rural areas of Thuringia. Indeed, during 1937 the authorities noted that farmers were visibly underrepresented in the SS, which always prided itself on its peasant roots. By late 1938 the mood of dejection among farmers in the Reich was on record as being "general throughout." And in the first few months of 1939 Bavarian peasants were said to be very embittered and quite unwilling to support the regime by joining the NSDAP or assisting its agencies.[72]

As in the case of merchants and craftsmen, the farmers' attitude toward the party was determined larely by considerations of material well-being, although, as with the other two groups of the old middle class, it is hard to ascertain whether their tendency to spurn the party in some years more than in others amounted to an actual underrepresentation in the NSDAP, as its leaders claimed in early 1935.[73]

In the first few months of 1933 the German farmers were somewhat reluctant to join the party for two reasons. First, they were suspicious of the direction of agricultural affairs by Reich Nutrition Minister Alfred Hugenberg, a member of the Papen cabinet whom Hitler kept until the end of June, when he was replaced by R. W. Darré. Second, they were still suffering from the aftermath of the rural depression, which lasted well beyond Hitler's assumption of power, forcing the new government to spend time devising corrective policies and making sure that they would have the desired effect.

Improvement did not come until the latter half of 1933, after the German farmers had had a good harvest and the early Four-Year Plan had reached the first stages of implementation. From 1933 to 1935–36 the governmental measures to reconstitute the agrarian economy included a fixed-price policy guaranteeing the farmers higher returns for agricultural products (especially fats, milk, and pork), debt and mortgage relief, tariff protection in accordance with the official goal of autarchy, and essential tax cuts. Indeed, up to 1936 production rose and was followed by a rise in income, and during the peak of this development, in 1934–35, agriculture was "doing better financially than other sectors of the economy."[74] In these years at least, the German farmers profited materially from the ideology of "blood and soil," which had become an official plank in the party program and was to remain so, if only theoretically, well into the war phase.[75] This propaganda had helped to spawn, by the end of 1933, the Reich Nutrition Estate (Reichsnährstand—RNS), organized along largely corporative lines. The RNS, led by Darré and other zealous officials, was responsible for the farmers' part in the "battle of production" within the first Four-Year Plan and it administered most of the policies affecting German agriculture until 1938, when Darré lost his powers to Göring, who took charge of the economy on behalf of the all-out war effort.[76]

The RNS was blamed by farmers everywhere when, after 1936–37, the coordination of the agrarian sector with other sectors of the national economy began to falter, much to the peasants' disadvantage.[77] Yet although the RNS was often inefficient, corrupt, and short-sighted, the root causes of the farmers' malaise lay once again in the collision between free-market mechanisms and the Nazi concept of rigid state control of the economy. The interventionist measures put forward by the regime were conceived in the interest, initially, of national convalescence after the Great Depression; next, of national autarchy; and, finally, of mobilization for war. Under the multiple systems of stepped-up regimentation, the German farmers lost their mobility, their prosperity, and eventually the sense of individuality and freedom that they had traditionally prized.

Regimentation began with the hereditary estate law (*Erbhofgesetz*), which was promulgated on September 29, 1933, as one of the first achievements of the new regime. It designated peasant estates between 7.5 and 10 hectares for permanent possession by their current owners, to be handed down only to first-born sons. Such hereditary farms could not be sold or exchanged, and no mortgages or loans could be drawn on them. The honorific title *Bauer* was bestowed on their owners, in contradistinction to the allegedly more humble label *Landwirt*, which pertained to "ordinary" peasants. If this differentiation— based more on muddled Nazi ideology than on pragmatic considerations—was arbitrary and, in practice, meaningless, the socioeconomic ramifications of being a "hereditary farmer" were grave, particularly over the long run and in the case of heirless estates. As David Schoenbaum has aptly written, "For the moment the farm was attached to the farmer; for the future, however, the farmer was attached to the land." One of the most serious complaints of the newly, if involuntary, privileged class of state kulaks was that they became ineligible for long-term credits for which their farms could have served as collateral. When they needed to borrow more money in order to buy machinery to offset the effects of the growing manpower shortage in the country, they could only get small sums in the form of personal loans. Lacking manpower or equipment, they harvested less and less, and their production volumes declined.[78]

The flight of hired help from the land—at first of young unmarried women (milkmaids), then of adventuresome young men, and finally of middle-aged *patresfamilias* to better-paying jobs in industrial areas — has already been mentioned in connection with the growing dearth of skilled labor in the cities, particularly after 1936.[79] In the countryside this was not a problem at the beginning because measures relegating many able-bodied men and women to agrarian worksites had been instituted in the early years of the regime to curb large-scale unemployment.[80] But eventually the economic lure of the city took its toll and concurrently the hereditary farm law went into effect. Thereafter a growing number of young men and women had no prospect of ever owning even a small plot of land, and many of them wandered off to the urban centers. The introduction of military conscription in March 1935 deprived the farms of still more young males. In 1936, as exorbitantly high industrial wages in the cities beckoned, more and more young and unattached people left the farms. In an effort to stem this exodus the farmers were forced — against all regulations imposed by the authorities — to raise agricultural wage rates. This, however, did little to solve the labor-force problem and drove up the overhead costs of the farmers, who were forbidden by law to pass on such increases to German consumers through a price hike on foodstuffs. Thus began the vicious inflationary spiral that could not be checked until after World War II began. Most farmers were affected, including especially the intermediate and smaller peasants who lacked the necessary capital to invest in farm machinery but were forced to pay their hired hands wages that in some cases, in late 1938, exceeded those of 1933 by about 100 percent. When the incoming contingents of Hitler Youth, Labor Service personnel, and, about 1938, foreign workers did little to remedy the situation — the HJ was lazy or inefficient, and Italians and Poles soon were asking as much remuneration as the Germans — the farm-labor shortage developed into the most crucial issue the farmers had faced since the Great Depression.[81]

The inflationary spiral that bedeviled the farming community, which was the unfortunate consequence of inconsistently applied state controls combined with acts of unchecked private initiative, suspended agricultural fortunes in a precarious balance. The mechanics of a free-market economy, which had led to a lack of farm labor, did not operate when the peasant wished to sell his beef, milk, or grain to wholesalers at acceptable prices, for the state had imposed low price ceilings. By contrast, the free-market laws did take effect when the same agricultural products were resold at much higher prices to consumers in the industrial cities. Understandably, the angry farmers wondered who was pocketing the difference. Again, the farmers were forced to buy electric power, fertilizer, fodder, or farm implements at prices seemingly dictated by a free-market economy, for if tractors or chemicals were in short supply they were very expensive. Yet if the farmer dared to adapt himself to a supply-and-demand pattern, he ran the risk of infringing the law and being fined. This might happen if he offered usurer's wages in order to attract labor — a practice that only the better-off establishments could indulge in without permanent economic damage. It might also happen if he attempted to market butter he had made himself. Instead of converting their milk to butter, farmers were compelled by the government to deliver it — for a song — to mechanized dairies, which would sell the butter or pasteurized milk through city outlets at what seemed to the farmer to be a huge profit. Many small estate owners, however, were already in possession of sophisticated butter-making equipment, especially in places where the journey to the dairy was long or hazardous and transportation was scarce or expensive. Thus when everything was reckoned up, the peasant was left with an unfair ratio between production costs and selling price, even though his own or his wife's labor was thrown in for nothing. The end results by the start of World War II were a distinct reduction in farmers' profits and a drop in the standard of living in German villages.[82]

By comparison, both social groups of the new middle class, the lower and intermediate civil servants (subgroup 7) and the white-collar workers (6), fared somewhat better under the NSDAP, though for different reasons. For the lower civil servants as a whole a sudden rise in the NSDAP newcomers' membership curve took place between 1930 and 1933, followed by a further rise up to 1937 and then a fall that reached its nadir in 1939. The curve then rose again, peaked in 1940–41, and thereafter fell to below the level of the thirties. In the second year of the war the lower civil servants were still overrepresented in the party, as compared with their national representation rate of about 5 percent (tables 7, 6, and 1). An exception to this pattern was the behavior of one section of this group, the teachers without university degrees. For them 1933 was the most popular year of joining; for lower civil servants as a whole, however, the most popular year was 1937. Before 1933 these public school and other lower and intermediate teachers joined the party in greater strength than all other civil servants; and in 1933 they virtually stormed the NSDAP. But after 1933 the percentage of all Nazi teachers who joined was only 22.6, whereas the corresponding percentage for other civil servants was 70.4.[83] By about 1939, 28.2 percent of the members of the Reich League of German Civil Servants (Reichsbund der Deutschen

Beamten—RDB), including those of the upper echelons, were members of the NSDAP; of all teachers, upper-school ones not excluded, 23.8 percent had joined by 1943.[84]

Although scores of officials (civil servants) at all levels may have welcomed the advent of the National Socialist regime in 1933, their position in the Third Reich was soon to become precarious. On paper, their constitutional functions and their significance were redefined by zealous Nazi ideologues—among them renowned university jurists such as Otto Koellreutter and Ernst Rudolf Huber—but in practice their fields of operation remained largely unchanged. The one important alteration (implemented as early as 1933) was that the civil service was to be thoroughly politicized in the spirit of Nazism, thus abolishing the traditionally neutral attitude of state officials toward political matters. Henceforth the raison d'être of the officials hinged on the tolerance of a monopolistic political party that already included in its ranks functionaries who would eventually rival the state officials. At a more theoretical level, it was argued by the apologists of the regime that the dynamics of the Hitler "movement" obviated the need for executors of the laws of state government, which were depicted as static. In day-to-day terms this meant that after a forced conversion to Nazism even the lowest official was left with a sense of being caught in the middle between party and state, which, if functionaries of Martin Bormann's ilk were to have their way, was to be definitely resolved in favor of the party.[85]

That state officials were not totally eliminated over the years was undoubtedly due to the fact that, particularly at the beginning, the new regime just could not function without them. The Nazi party lacked basic governmental expertise.[86] Thus, although Adolf Hitler, fully in accord with Rudolf Hess and later Bormann, derided the officials, Dr. Wilhelm Frick, the Reich's Interior Minister until 1943 and himself a veteran administrator, pushed for recognition of the civil service corps and toiled to preserve its socioeconomic status.[87]

Evidently, in deciding for or against party membership after January 1933, civil servants, unlike any other social group in Germany, were motivated less by immediate materialistic considerations than by a quasi-moral factor—the question of their future as indispensable cogs in the machinery of government. No doubt the lower civil servants, who joined the NSDAP in the early summer of 1933 at more than double their percentage in the population at large, did so because they felt the need to assure the new administration of their loyalty.[88] But the administration, suspecting opportunism, issued directives to the effect that newly committed civil-servant party members should be watched very closely for outward signs of insecurity and that future applicants should be carefully screened.[89] It could not have escaped the notice of the Nazi civil servants that the Old Fighters among them —people who had joined before January 1933—were now enjoying special privileges such as preferential appointments and faster promotions.[90] And it may have come as a relief to many civil servants that even before the opening of the membership rolls in 1937 the party once again encouraged them to join. Most of the ones who did so realized that in the Nazi state the future of a bureaucrat without party affiliation was likely to be very difficult.[91]

By virtue of their special status in the state, the lower civil servants' relationship with the party was always potentially dangerous. For instance, in 1937 when an application for membership was refused by the review board within the party hierarchy, the reasons for refusal went on record to count against the candidate in question, although it is not clear whether any further action was taken. And if for whatever reason a civil-servant party member elected to opt out of the party, he invariably lost his job. Worse still, if he was expelled from the party for a serious misdemeanor, confinement in a concentration camp was his most likely punishment. Even for minor disciplinary infractions all civil-service party comrades were subject to prosecution by the party courts in addition to their specific honor courts.[92]

Nor could officials be at ease after they had joined the party. As Nazi members they were expected to subscribe to the party paper, the *Völkischer Beobachter*, were supposed to enroll their children in the Hitler Youth (though before March 1939 membership in that organization was generally not compulsory), and were called upon to participate in other party or ancillary organizations' events, such as helping the NSV. Before a promotion the Main Office of Civil Servants in the party would be asked to report on the official's record; any objections that had been made on political grounds would count heavily against him.[93]

Turning again to the lower and intermediate school teachers, it is not easy to explain why they joined the Nazi party in smaller numbers after 1933 than did the regular civil servants. Perhaps in that year of political-power change, when they rushed to the party, they had expected that the ideological mandate that they claimed to hold in the area of education would shield them from the suspicion of being mere opportunists. As it turned out, this was not the case; after 1933, in fact, they were even more severely reprimanded by party leaders than were their administrative colleagues.[94] Perhaps such treatment was what prompted them to hold back in 1937, when the membership books were reopened. Moreover, there is little indication that before 1937 the teachers, who were organized in the National Socialist Teachers' League (Nationalsozialistischer Lehrerbund—NSLB) were pressured to join in the same way as the other civil servants.[95] It was quite obvious that the state still needed the administrators, who might as well be good Nazis or be made into such. The teachers, by contrast, became increasingly unpopular with the regime, and they were outperformed in the ideological arena by the functionaries of the Hitler Youth, who did everything in their power to neutralize the teaching profession altogether.[96]

Both the teachers and the government administrators demonstrated a marked tendency to move away from the party in 1939 (table 7), when new memberships were once again invited. For the teachers this development merely continued the previous trend. But for the regular civil servants it meant a direct reversal of that trend. There are several possible reasons for this. In 1939, unlike 1937, no special party pressure was placed on civil servants: those who were likely to take that step had already taken it, and the others saw no reason to commit themselves six years after Hitler's assumption of power. The reversal may also have been a symptom of the civil servants' disappointment with recent developments in the salary area. Despite Frick's efforts, the piecemeal salary reform of 1937–38 had in no way lived up to the expectations of the lower civil servants. Since the last years of the Republic they had continued to be underpaid. In fact, the partial reform of 1937–38 had merely brought their salary level somewhat more into line with that of other social groups.[97] A further reason for the reversal could have been that the lowest civil servants such as locomotive engineers were excluded from some of the state's innovative social policy measures, such as KdF benefits, although as a reward for good behavior they and their higher-placed colleagues continued to enjoy the security of their professions, job tenure and a guaranteed pension.[98] But probably the most plausible explanation of the declining interest by state servants in the Nazi party was the growing disinclination among Germany's youth to enter into a civil-service career. By 1938–39 poor salaries, the generally unfavorable conditions surrounding job tenure, and the low prestige of the bureaucracy in comparison with other professional positions made the civil service less attractive to younger Germans than the booming armaments industry, which offered much better advancement possibilities. Even as early as 1933 the civil servant trainee shortage—including that in the teaching realm—had been one of the most severe problems besetting the administration of the Reich as a whole.[99]

The other section of the new middle class, the white-collar workers or lower employees, were underrepresented in the NSDAP at first, but later they displayed a mounting interest in the party with the result that new white-collar members were overrepresented in the NSDAP from 1937 on (tables 7, 6, and 1). Unlike the lower civil servants, they were under no particular pressure from the state to join the party. More like the groups of the old middle class, their actions tended to be motivated by socioeconomic factors.

Several indicators support the assumption that lower employees were, in socioeconomic terms, among the most fortunate Germans in the Reich. To be sure, the fact that the official nomenclature had abolished the formal distinction between "worker" and "employee" by defining them all collectively as the "retinue" (*Gefolgschaft*) within the *völkisch* community, might have been interpreted by suspicious lower employees as an attempt by the regime to remove the cherished distinction between themselves and the proletariat, a distinction in which the self-esteem of white-collar workers was traditionally grounded.[100] But in the real world of labor relations the force of the new definition was only nominal; where it did seem to count, the clerks profited by being eligible for some of the benefits expressly reserved for the "workers." In addition, they benefited in some instances from some of the regulations affecting social groups above the blue-collar workers, such as the lower civil servants. It appears, then, that they came as close as possible to enjoying the best of two worlds between 1933 and 1939, assuming, of course, that these worlds were still as separate as they had been during the Weimar Republic. In being counted along with the blue-collar workers, lower employees shared some of the trials and tribulations of this occupational subgroup, notably in the early years of hardship preceding 1936–37. They, too, suffered at first from the high rate of unemployment, complained about their low salaries, which were totally out of line with the high prices, and eventually were affected by the same governmental measures restricting physical mobility as were the blue-collar workers.[101]

Yet the various stepped-up programs for economic reactivation and mobilization that brought an end to unemployment in the workers' sector also helped in solving the unemployment problem for the lower and intermediate employees. With an equally strong demand prevailing for both blue- and white-collar workers, the latter were destined to fare better because a smaller percentage of them had been unemployed in the first place, and of those who were without jobs there were fewer unskilled white-collar than blue-collar workers. In the early boom years of the Third Reich, when skill and experience were at a premium, out-of-work lower employees stood a better chance of finding well-paying jobs than did workers, a majority of whom were young and untrained. This was particularly true after the government introduced measures extending special job-finding assistance to employees over forty, who had faced singularly difficult problems in the last years of the Weimar Republic.[102]

By about 1937, as unemployment in the white-collar sector of the national economy was on the wane, and as the more experienced clerks became harder to find, the laws of supply and demand began to assert themselves; this was also the case in the blue-collar sector. There is evidence that by 1938 white-collar workers such as stenographers could command wages far beyond the officially prescribed scale, if their know-how warranted such wages and industry was willing to pay them.[103] More significantly, the wages of the lower employees rose faster during the Third Reich than those of the workers, and thus in the final analysis they enjoyed a higher standard of living.[104] Accordingly, in the fall of 1938 blue-collar workers near Munich complained, "Workers' pay will not be continued in case of a short-term conscription into the army whereas clerks, who are better off anyway, continue to receive part of their salary."[105]

The white-collar employee also received other benefits that the worker did not get. On the whole, he enjoyed better working conditions in cleaner surroundings, was entitled to better social insurance and pension schemes and longer work-breaks and holidays, and received superior job protection in that he could not be dismissed so easily. Moreover, an employee of the government could take advantage of the regulations on behalf of Old Fighters of 1934, if he qualified as a member of that group, to secure a promotion or a better position.[106] As a result, the old status distinctions between white- and blue-collar workers, which had been temporarily submerged, surfaced again in the last few years before the war. In February 1937, for example, blue-collar workers took exception to groups of lower employees who tended to keep to themselves, whereas the workers reportedly "did not wish to stand on a different social plane from the employee." Other laborers criticized the special fringe benefits for employees, such as the extraordinary free shipments of coal they received. These were envied both for materialistic and psychological reasons, since the coal not only warmed the employees but indicated their right to receive preferential treatment. In this connection it is also significant that in 1939 workers' sons were underrepresented in the regime's elite schools, while the children of clerks were heavily overrepresented in them.[107] The available evidence upholds the often repeated charge that it was not the workers but rather the members of the middle classes — that is, the lower and intermediate employees — who benefited most from the various programs offered by the DAF, including the KdF holidays.[108]

By 1937-38 the occupation of clerk had become one of the jobs most sought after by young men and women about to leave primary school. As the demand for office and sales clerks grew, candidates applied for job training who, in more normal circumstances, would have been eligible only for lower positions because they lacked the necessary intelligence or education. In 1938 stern warnings abounded that course-examination standards for shop assistants and accountants would have to be raised in order to improve the quality of the current generation of training-course leavers and to keep out the misfits. Still, the mobilization economy could absorb an ever-growing contingent of white-collar workers. Between 1929 and 1938, while the number of manual laborers only increased at an annual average growth rate of 1.1 percent, the number of small employees grew at the rate of 2.5 percent. Before the war the attraction of well-paid white-collar occupations was equaled only by that of the highly skilled technological jobs, many of which were held by craftsmen with long years of schooling behind them.[109]

THE ELITE

From 1933 to 1939 members of the upper middle class and former aristocratic elite tended to be heavily overrepresented in the Nazi party. Within this stratum there were significant variations, however. After the NSDAP came to power, business executives and entrepreneurs supported it with great enthusiasm, but university students, for instance, were much less attracted to it (table 7).

Information on students derives in the main from records dealing with institutions of postsecondary education and only rarely with upper schools. The rate of student newcomers to the NSDAP declined sharply from 1932 to 1933, and then, with the exception of 1934-1936, went down further until 1938 (tables 6 and 7).[110] But although a smaller percentage of new party members were students, a greater percentage of students became party members. This was the case because of university enrollment restrictions (such as those against women) and voluntary neglect of the universities by eligible young adults; these factors reduced the number of students by 5.5 percent between 1932 and 1933 and by almost 50 percent between 1933 and 1937.[111]

For a brief time there was elation among Germany's student population over Hitler's political success in January 1933. During the final years of the Weimar Republic many students had eagerly awaited the improvements that would follow a Nazi victory. And yet in 1933 the students' NSDAP recruitment rate dropped, probably because of the introduction of restrictions on their individual liberties, which the majority of them had not anticipated.[112] One of the harshest blows was dealt by the Stormtroopers (SA), whose plebeian character had made them less than popular with students even before 1933.[113] Soon after the Nazi takeover, when all responsibility for military sport (*Wehrsport*) was delegated to the SA leadership, that organization began to exert control not only over students who were SA members but also over those who were not members, by compelling the majority of male students to participate in drills and other extracurricular activities. Because these exercises interfered with serious study the students hated them and circumvented them whenever possible. Control by the SA continued until after the Röhm Purge of June 30, 1934. The institutionalized influence of the SA in Germany's centers of higher learning was removed in early 1935, thus freeing many would-be academics to leave the SA and to seek membership in the party or the Nazi Student Union (NSDStB), if not the SS. That chain of events is reflected by the rising percentage of NSDAP student joiners between 1933 and 1935 (table 7).[114]

After 1935 student membership again declined, plunging to a new low in 1937. One of the main reasons for this development was that after the introduction of military conscription in March 1935 the university's attraction as a career vehicle paled in relation to the army, which welcomed young officer recruits from the upper schools.[115] Another major reason was the systematic destruction of the fraternity system by the regime, a process that had begun as early as 1933 but was intensified, through various stages, in 1935. By the spring of 1936 the fraternities had all but vanished, having been either forcibly dissolved or driven to accept "voluntary coordination."[116]

The Nazi student unions or "comradeship units" (*Kamerad-schaften*) that were supposed to replace the fraternities were hardly suitable substitutes for the young generation of aspiring academics, who, in spite of their right-wing political rabble-rousing in Germany's republican past, had always prized their individual liberties. Among these, the most cherished and traditional privilege was the freedom to organize in whatever way they wished. On the student-government level, some of the Nazi student leaders of the two official representative bodies, the NSDStB and the German Student Body

(Deutsche Studentenschaft), were so corrupt and incompetent that the majority of ordinary students became embittered. A change came in April 1936 when Dr. Gustav Adolf Scheel, a young SS officer, united the rival factions under his newly created office of Reich Student Leader.[117] This change, however, turned out to be the stepping-stone to greater restrictions, which by 1939 included involuntary participation in governmental "vocational" contests, forced sports and military training competitions, agricultural and other labor service, and various activities relating to party life that took away valuable time from both the students' study periods and the semester breaks. And a sizable number of students sorely needed those breaks in order to earn money to help finance their studies. Even before the war, it became virtually impossible for a young person to enter a university without having previously performed work or paramilitary service or without being forced to do so after enrollment.[118] Further, in order to be eligible for financial assistance from the state or the NSDAP, the student's political record had to be spotless.[119]

There were few overt manifestations of student discontent before the outbreak of the war, but those that are recorded indicate the general mood in the lecture halls of the nation. In late 1934 students at Bonn University, mindful of their role in a state whose monopolistic party with its strong anti-intellectual tradition did not really cherish the presence of students in its ranks, staged a protest when the theologian Karl Barth was suspended from teaching.[120] Again in July 1935 students engaged in a demonstration at the Teachers' Academy in Lauenburg, and they enrolled in courses taught by the prominent anti-Nazi historian Gerhard Ritter in Freiburg in order to "shake off the fetters of party ideology." By 1936-37, according to reports from the authorities, protests were occurring less in the smaller university towns such as Marburg than in the larger cities, where there was greater immunity from close party screening.[121]

Toward 1938-39 perhaps the greatest cause of student disillusionment with the Nazi regime was the lowering of academic standards as a result of the overall politicization of the universities. Here everyone — students, administrators, the NSDAP and state authorities — was caught in a vicious spiral of escalating difficulties that had brought the entire higher educational system to a crisis point by the beginning of the war. As political obligations, which worked against both intellectual honesty and academic quality, increased within and beyond the institutions of higher learning, potential students began to look to the army and the booming armaments industry as more appropriate guarantors of economic security and social prestige.[122] Increasingly neglected, university personnel feared the loss of their monopoly on higher education and consequently of their social privilege. At the same time the party and government realized that a depletion of the regular stock of highly educated staff was not good for the regime in the long run, especially since war was threatening and there was a need for such skilled professionals as physicians, engineers, and lawyers. And so, in order to attract more students, university spokesmen called for a shortening of the prescribed term of studies and for lower examination standards in certain disciplines. As a result, conscientious upper-school graduates were even less inclined to enroll, especially in the humanities or such professional curricula as law and even medicine, which were becoming increasingly infected with ideological hogwash. The natural and applied sciences, by contrast, not only were less affected by the Nazi ideology but were also more suited to the needs of an entrenched war economy, so these pragmatic subjects became substantially more attractive to students than courses in the humanities. The cumulative annual average decrease in students in the humanities from 1933 to 1939 was 23.5 percent (calculated from enrollment figures), but it was only 18.1 percent in the natural and applied sciences.[123] This crisis in higher education (viewed so far only from the student side) was paralleled at a lower level by similar developments affecting secondary and primary schools. As a whole, the educational situation reflected a conflict of principle between representatives of the established order and of the monopoly state party, which was destined to win in the end. The university students were, to an increasing extent, the victims of these circumstances; and insofar as they perceived their position, they expressed dissatisfaction with the regime by abstaining from Nazi party membership whenever they were able to do so.[124]

Between 1933 and 1939, when the student presence in the NSDAP was relatively weak, two other elite subgroups, industrial managers and entrepreneurs (10 and 14), adopted a much more favorable attitude toward the Nazi party. A high peak in newcomer membership in 1933 and another somewhat lower peak in 1939 reflect two climaxes of satisfaction with the regime by these occupational strata, which were, on the whole, overrepresented in the NSDAP. In absolute numbers the two subgroups combined provided the largest component of elite support for Nazism.[125]

Paraphrasing Schoenbaum, one could say that large-volume business and commerce fared well in the National Socialist system of economics for the very same reasons that small business fared badly: big business's reasons for being attracted to the party were precisely those that kept small business away from it.[126] Yet, as in the case of the Weimar Republic, it is important to distinguish between two different groups of big businessmen — the large industrialists or leaders of diversified trusts, of whom there were few, and the private owners or managers of intermediate family businesses, such as large local wholesale merchants or factory owners, of whom there were many. For two reasons the supporting data for this study reveal primarily the political behavior of the medium private businessmen, not of the large industrialists. First, since the typical great German magnate could see no particular advantage in joining the party after January 1933 and even thought himself above it, only a small minority of this group actually filled out membership forms.[127] Second, those large industrialists who did become Nazi party comrades had little influence on the trends described in this chapter simply because their numbers were negligible. Still, in spite of the uneven data, it is possible to carefully weigh the evidence and thus to arrive at judgments that are valid for both groups of elite businessmen.

The peak in the new NSDAP membership curve for big businessmen in 1933 reflects nothing less than the tremendous expectations of success under the new regime on the part of all such business people.[128] They had good reason to be optimistic. Hitler himself, in meetings with important representatives of industry and commerce, had renewed the promises he had made before assuming power that he would not attack the principle of free, private enterprise but would in fact endorse the idea of capitalism with a minimum of interference by the state. To underline his intentions, in June 1933 the Führer appointed Dr. Kurt Schmitt as Reich Minister of Economics. Schmitt basically represented the interests of big business, but as an insurance executive he understood the goals of smaller entrepreneurs as well. There was, then, to be no break with the immediate capitalist past and the business practices associated with it; significantly, Schmitt spoke as late as March 1934 of the necessity of building on previous achievements. Consequently, during the first year of the Nazis' reign representatives of industry and commerce were happy to support Schmitt in his ministry and to convene caucuses to report on methods of economic revitalization that would benefit all but the small businesses. As paradoxical as it may sound, many business people joined the Nazi party in 1933 because they had high expectations for the regime and trusted that under the conditions guaranteed by Hitler the representatives of the party would stay out of entrepreneurial affairs.[129]

The effect of Schmitt's appointment as Economics Minister was

that by the end of 1933 corporative notions, which were favored by only a few representatives of heavy industry, notably Fritz Thyssen, had been discarded by the political leadership and that the chief protagonists of such ideas, Otto Wagener and Gottfried Feder, had been reduced to insignificance. As for the pseudo-corporate structure of Robert Ley's German Labor Front organization (DAF), whose apparently proworker policy was later to become suspect, it held little threat for entrepreneurs in 1933.[130] Besides, the DAF had had an important hand in dissolving the conventional trade unions, an event that was cheered by all business leaders right down to the smallest factory owner. As far as these men were concerned, the worker's job was to work and not to strike: the fact that Hitler's regime basically appeared to agree with this mainstay of capitalist philosophy made the newly established relationship between business and the party an even more amiable one.[131]

As entrepreneurs in general proceeded to benefit from the regime's job creation measures, particularly in highway construction and housing renovation, and as they experienced the economic relief deriving from price and wage stabilization enactments, they could not escape the conclusion that their early hopes had been justified. This was all the more true because even in 1933 Hitler had tied his economic recovery program to the beginnings of mobilization for war, the first visible manifestation of which was a gradual reduction in unemployment.[132] Moreover, there were side benefits of a new kind that had scarcely been envisaged before the coming of the Third Reich — for instance, the widespread profiteering that followed "Aryanization" procedures carried out against Jewish businessmen. Here the individual factory owner or wholesaler tended to reap greater rewards than the tycoon, at least in the beginning.[133] There is ample proof that in the early months of the regime intermediate as well as big business representatives made no secret of their satisfaction with Hitler's coming to power. They not only gave money to the party, which many of them joined at the same time, but they also expressed their appreciation for it. On May 9, 1933, for example, the president of the Kottbus chamber of commerce assured the authorities that his organization "joyfully espouses the goals and ideas of these new National Socialist times."[134]

After the first year of the regime the shape of the new membership curve indicates a somewhat greater reluctance on the part of businessmen to join the NSDAP, although these newcomers continued to be overrepresented in the party (tables 7 and 1).[135] The relative lack of interest shown by managers and entrepreneurs toward the Nazi party during the period between 1934-35 and 1939 resulted from a combination of two factors: the difficulties that businessmen had to grapple with at that time and the opportunities available to them. In this connection, the high point of 1939 was obviously related to the renewed impetus given to the national economy by the war effort. In the final analysis, however, businessmen emerged at the start of World War II as a winning, not a losing, social group.

On the positive side of the balance sheet, all big businessmen were able to point to remarkable profits, which accrued in direct proportion to the size of the business involved and to its share in the ever-increasing level of war production. The latter held true especially after 1936 when armaments industries became part of the long-range planning mechanisms of the second Four-Year Plan. In general, the larger a firm was and the more adaptable it was to the war economy, the greater was its profit potential. For example, a minor engine maker near Brunswick, who turned to the production of aircraft motors in 1935, had by 1936 become not only deeply involved in the rearmament program but also very wealthy. This particular factory owner, incidentally, had been a party member since 1934.[136]

On the negative side of the balance sheet, but hardly offsetting the positive side, were the recurrent demands made by the DAF upon all types of managers and entrepreneurs. While these demands were ostensibly in the social interest of the workers (who were not at all impressed), the employers saw them as an encroachment upon their preserves, as an attempt at state intervention in their business establishments.[137] These developments were particularly evident after 1933, when Ley's labor organization was bent on expansion on a huge scale, with the result that eventually it became the largest corporation of its type in the world. Businessmen were never quite sure whether the DAF would succeed in becoming a pseudo-trade union that might rescind the state's fixed wage policy to the detriment of the employer, or whether it would try to curtail their long-standing prerogative to hire and fire workers at will. DAF functionaries themselves issued many threats against recalcitrant business leaders: there were instances of DAF inspectors paying surprise visits to businesses, perhaps to check the overtime schedule, and of DAF appraisers assessing a firm's worthiness before the closing of a lucrative armaments deal. And just as profits were linked to size, so the degree to which a plant owner managed to evade DAF membership or shop surveillance was directly related to the size of his enterprise; as a rule, trusts and cartels were beyond the reach of the Labor Front.[138] The distress the DAF brought to some employers was only partially counterbalanced by the advantages offered them by the Law for the Organization of National Labor, which, after January 20, 1934, guaranteed the employer the honorific title of Führer ("leader of the business"), in contrast to his "retinue" (the employees). (In a budding labor dispute, for instance, the mechanisms set in motion by this law decidedly favored the employer's side in arbitration, and in essence the law perpetuated the pre-1933 status quo in labor relations, leaving the preeminent position of the employer unchanged.)[139]

Again on the negative side, spokesmen for business, commerce, and industry may have been somewhat divided because of the inequity between large and small businesses. Large businessmen, tied to armaments production and strategic key industries, were raking in greater profits, consolidating potentially monopolistic positions, and, in some instances, strengthening their influence with state authorities. The most celebrated example of this, evident as early as 1933, was the IG Farben chemical trust. Through a complicated chain of events dictated by the imminence of war, it prospered so well that in August 1938 its representative, Dr. Carl Krauch, became one of Göring's leading delegates in the area of national production control. Still, it would be wrong to look upon the IG Farben trust's unique role in the Nazi regime as typical of big business, defined, as East German historians are wont to see it, as "fascist monopoly capitalism."[140] No one can deny, however, that the slowly changing demand by the state for production rather than consumption goods eventually harmed smaller industries, including the textile mills and lumber companies.[141] In this respect the developments paralleled those in the realm of small and artisanal business described earlier. Because of their low-priority position by, say, 1937, the smaller industries were the first to be affected by the rationing of scarce raw materials, and they were less able than the larger industries to pay the exorbitant wages that skilled labor began to demand about the same time. In 1938 one sympathetic Nazi economist advised that the "smaller and medium entrepreneur should be made to feel more certain that now someone is looking after him and that he is being spoiled a little more than the large businessmen, who can easily help themselves."[142] To compound these economic problems, in the mid-thirties Germany was at a disadvantage vis-à-vis other exporting countries in the world market. As a result there was a shortage of foreign exchange, which made it even more difficult for commercial firms specializing in import consumption merchandise, such as the coffee wholesalers of Bremen, to prosper.[143]

The crunch for industry and business as a whole was felt by 1938, after Göring, at Hitler's behest, had transformed Germany into a virtually state-controlled economy. This transformation was the consequence of two events: the introduction of the second Four-Year Plan, which was supposed to speed up the nation's preparation for war, late in 1936; and Göring's activation of a secret memorandum from Hitler in mid-1937. The Four-Year Plan resulted in the resignation of Dr. Hjalmar Schacht, the last representative of unfettered private enterprise, as Reich Minister of Economics; but it hardly came as a surprise to those who had observed the state's gradual infringements on private enterprise after 1933 and become aware of the philosophy of the regime—namely, that business was free to go its own way provided it served the party's long-range aims. By this logic it should have been clear to most businessmen that the very introduction of the second Four-Year Plan would mean more frequent acts of state intervention in order to regulate production wherever self-regulation failed to bring the desired results. Göring's decision to act on Hitler's memorandum (dated August 1936), which revealed his resolve to implement a state-controlled economy, was taken in July 1937 when the shortage of foreign exchange had become serious (even though Germany was already headed toward the goal of economic self-sufficiency) and when the iron and steel trusts were falling behind in the output of needed raw materials. In that month Göring announced the creation of the "Mining Enterprises Hermann Göring," a move that heralded the establishment of similar state combines in other fields of vital war production. Following the pattern set by these two measures, actions taken after the start of World War II further reduced the independence of the industrialists, though at the same time they drew even intermediate businesses into the realm of rearmament. The net result for business was, as some historians have noted, a considerable loss of freedom, but concomitantly, as plants began to be used to maximum capacity, profits continued for all entrepreneurs.[144] The business euphoria resulting from the economic boom was reflected in higher Nazi membership statistics for 1939 (table 7).

To complete this picture of the big-business community, the situation of the large landowners must also be considered. Viewed as a historical stereotype, the East Elbian landowner or *Junker* with a large estate was socially a member of the former ruling class and politically an adherent of the DNVP. The situation varied in other parts of Germany. In Bavaria, for example, the place of the DNVP could be taken by the Bavarian People's Party (BVP). The documents show that although the large landowners may secretly have remained loyal to the restorationist, monarchic cause and bewailed the silent death of the old right-wing parties, they acquiesced in the advent of Hitler. Actually, they had much to gain. Because they were allowed to keep their large estates, they benefited from a partial exension of the Weimar Republic's Eastern Aid program, and at the same time their grain production was subsidized and competitive food imports were shut out by high tariff walls. Their willful, cavalier ways toward hired labor were left unchanged, so that their relationship with farm workers was affected only inasmuch as the hired hands were bound to want more money in good times, exactly as they did on smaller farms. Unlike the smaller farmer, who had difficulty in meeting such demands, the estate owner had plenty of capital to spend on wages or on necessary machinery to replace the thinning work force. Here the same market mechanism that turned the economic spiral in the wrong direction for the small farmer turned it in the right direction for the big one. If more credit was needed it could easily be obtained, for the Junkers had real estate collateral because they were under no pressure to maintain a nonmortgageable "hereditary farm." Materially, they may not have done so well as the industrial tycoons or very wealthy factory owners between 1933 and 1939, but in comparison with the ordinary farmers they were very well off indeed. If they kept quiet and avoided conflict with local or regional party hacks, they could even receive preferential treatment, as in the case of one Baron Durant and one Countess Bismarck, whose properties, thanks to effective influence in high places, were not touched by autobahn construction. Small wonder, too, that in the Prussian province of Pomerania the landed gentry, conservative to the core, allowed opportunism to get the better of them when their vested interests seemed threatened. Of one great landowner, who was by no means atypical, it is reported that he used to keep his Nazi party badge on his writing desk but would quickly transfer it to his lapel when the NSDAP's representative came to the door. Only the war and the aristocracy's role in the Resistance were to change all this.[145]

Another elite subgroup, the higher civil servants, following a slump in party interest in 1930-1932, approached the NSDAP in much greater numbers in 1933. They again lost interest in 1935 but bounded back in 1937. In 1938-39, however, these higher administrators stayed away from the party to such an extent that they were underrepresented among the joiners (tables 7, 6, and 1).

These civil servants' rekindled interest in 1933 can be attributed to their feeling of confidence in the new government. Hitler's political takeover ended recurrent phases of frustration for upper and lower administrators alike. Many judges and state counselors, disappointed and resentful over Germany's turbulent republican past and often supported by the DNVP, which had just allied itself to the Nazis, showed their elation over Hitler's victory by signing up at the nearest party headquarters. This euphoria was reflected in the intelligent musings of Count Fritz-Dietlof von der Schulenburg on the changes about to be experienced (which were, incidentally, inspired by official talk about an impending judicial reform), in the declarations of loyalty made by upper-school teachers, and in the support given to the local party by the Hamburg judges.[146] Naturally, there were many variations on this scheme. While some highly placed public servants, such as Baron Ernst von Weizsäcker of the Foreign Office, were still deliberating about party membership in the middle of June 1933, others, like Justice Senator Dr. Curt Rothenberger in Hamburg, rushed to oblige the new rulers by implementing Nazi-inspired legislation with a vengeance.[147] Moreover, the Law for the Reconstitution of the Civil Service of April 1933, which, especially in Prussia, forced many a would-be rival out of office on the basis of political conviction or race, found favor with numerous nationalistic and anti-Semitic mandarins.[148]

One major reason for the relative decline of administrative enthusiasm after 1933 was the regime's increasing arbitrariness. This development alienated the conservative, university-educated officials, most of whom had taken law degrees. In spite of their contempt for what they considered to be the aberrations of the parliamentary system of Weimar, they tended to react sensitively to issues of constitutionality and due process of law. In the long run, these sophisticated legal experts, who after 1933 came increasingly under suspicion for not being able to do without a "constitution," found it much more difficult to accept the manipulation of the judicial system by the totalitarian dictatorship than did the less educated lower and intermediate civil servants.[149] As the regime's extralegal activities, which had begun with the terror generated by the SA in 1933–34, multiplied, highly motivated top administrators had to endure ever-growing affronts to their sense of justice. The judges, who were stripped of their juridical independence by being required to make decisions in the spirit of National Socialism and to accept Adolf Hitler as the supreme judge in the land, probably suffered the greatest psychological shock. Although the government paid lip service to the importance of the law, it was obvious soon after January 1933 that "the law" was to be made subservient to party and state and that its administrators were to be reduced to the status of mere bureaucratic helots.[150]

The chain of events that offended the higher civil servants' professional ethos and eventually threatened their position in the nation was touched off by the installation of pseudo-legal auxiliary police drawn from the ranks of largely unemployed SA stalwarts, paralleled, at a higher lever, by special SA commissars in regional governments. The Röhm Purge of June 1934 removed these, but in doing so it presented the officials with a new problem revealing the ruthlessness with which Hitler was prepared to rule — even beyond the constraints of the law, if need be.[151] As time went on, political supervision and internal and external pressure increased for higher civil servants who were members of the NSDAP or of party ancillary organizations such as the Nazi Jurists' League. In some of these quasi-corporative organizations, joint membership with lower civil servants was encouraged by the regime to help break down class barriers. This goal, which was proudly proclaimed by Bavaria's new Justice Minister, Dr. Hans Frank, was loathed by the traditionally aloof, high-ranking officials. On January 26, 1937, after long delays, the new German Civil Service Law, which revised the system of promotions in the interest of high state officials, had finally been promulgated against the opposition of the party. But to offset this, in the last three years before the war the degree of lawlessness and of official contempt for traditional juridical procedures became staggering. Hence the prestige of the civil-service corps reached its prewar nadir, with the result that conscientious men like Schulenburg reinforced their resolve to oppose the dictatorship on all counts.[152]

In 1933 the mandarins had turned out voluntarily to pledge Nazi membership, but they became disenchanted with the regime earlier than the lower civil servants. Since, especially in 1937, they were not subjected to the same degree of official pressure to join as were their lower-placed colleagues, their interest in NSDAP membership subsided more quickly. By 1937 the party, represented chiefly by Bormann, loudly claimed that it, rather than the state, should have total control of the civil-service corps, a claim that Interior Minister Frick found difficult to deny. This stance, however, does not seem to have frightened the top officials into joining the party, for the figures for new members kept declining up to the outbreak of the war.[153] The decline is significant because Bormann had actually threatened the top officials with promotion delays unless they joined the party — a threat that was finally and authoritatively quashed by Hitler himself in 1939. There can be only one explanation for the higher officials' comparatively confident stance vis-à-vis the NSDAP: as the machinery of government became more complicated for the new rulers, expecially in relationship to the preparedness economy, the higher civil servants became even more indispensable to the state. Thus they were able to take greater political liberties, to maintain an attitude of quiet defiance, and to retain their social homogeneity, which was the basis of their unique esprit de corps.[154] After 1936 their relatively independent position was supported by declining enrollments in law and political science courses at the universities and by an apparent unwillingness by graduates to enter the state service on terms that were much less favorable than those offered by industry or private practice.[155]

Among the educated state officials or higher civil servants the university professors were in a slightly different situation from that of the upper-school teachers and administrators. First, they did not come under the same degree of direct political pressure, and second, they could not demonstrate, in the short or long run, that they were equally important to the survival of the dictatorship.[156] In the Weimar Republic, university professors had been either highly nationalistic adherents of the DNVP or else completely apolitical. The second attitude seemed to conform perfectly with the tradition of academic freedom that afforded scholars the privilege of impartiality. Indeed, some of the older professors who managed a smooth transition into the Third Reich used neutrality as an excuse for not joining the NSDAP, even though in their hearts they might have favored the movement.[157] Of the ones who did join the party, at least two groups are clearly distinguishable.

First, there was a small and very exposed handful of scholars, some of them leading authorities in their field, who had openly favored the Nazis before 1933 and who unabashedly embarked on a course of ideological fortification of the Nazi doctrine without express solicitation by the state. To this group belonged such well-known collaborators as Martin Heidegger, Ernst Krieck, Alfred Baeumler, and Adolf Rein, not to mention the university technocrats serving fulltime on Himmler's and Rosenberg's staffs, whose individual biographies are interesting but offer little insight into the behavior of the professional group as a whole.[158] Such higher academics evidently took seriously Hitler's motto of the twenties: "In science the folkish State has to see a means for the promotion of national pride."[159]

The second, and by far the larger, group of career scholars who joined the NSDAP after 1933 did so for opportunistic reasons—perhaps, for example, to secure an important chair that had formerly been held or coveted by a Jewish rival—while at the same time they remained essentially true to the academic standards demanded by their discipline.[160] Superficially, the evidence points to a correlation between youth and NSDAP membership: the younger the person and the more apparent his willingness to join the party, the better were his chances for academic promotion or professorial tenure. Ambitious university academics seem to have gone through the motions of accepting onerous and often humiliating party regimentation in the hope of rapid professional advancement.[161] Still, statistical details compiled by Reece C. Kelly leave little doubt about the reluctance of even the young lecturers to join the party after 1933, thus duplicating the trend that was characteristic of all the other high civil servants and indicating that the attraction of the NSDAP was well on the way to decline by 1937.[162]

As the regime kept pressing hopeful scholars either to join the party and its ancillary organizations or to partake in institutionalized paramilitary activities, and as scholars showed increasing hesitation or cynicism in complying, NSDAP officials could not refrain from expressing their suspicions concerning the nation's highest educators.[163] "At the university, Nazis are as rare as in the bureaucracy," exclaimed one party official before a congregation of schoolteachers in April 1936, and three years later a Hessian functionary complained that "to date university lecturers as a whole have shown few signs of being inspired by Nazism."[164] There may have been few cases of downright opposition to the regime, especially among Germany's younger university faculty members before 1939–40;[165] but it is much more significant that as academic freedom in the universities became further curtailed, more young scholars chose promising positions in industry and the army instead of embarking on a higher teaching career, so escaping the reach of the NSDAP. This act, too, was a form of protest behavior among Germany's young elite.[166]

The last subgroup of the elite, the academic professionals (12), included the most powerful representatives of that class in the NSDAP, second only to the entrepreneurs and managers combined. Among the newcomer academic professionals between 1933 and 1939, medical doctors (physicians, dentists, veterinarians) formed the largest single element, ranging from one-fifth of the total in 1935 to more than one-third in 1939 (figure 6).

Generally, all the highly qualified professionals looked upon NSDAP membership as a guarantee of individual professional liberties, with which the new regime on the whole interfered surprisingly little. In addition, the regime saw to it that unwanted competition from Jewish circles was effectively eliminated—a gradual process that was largely completed by 1939. Obvious benefits accrued from this, particularly to lawyers and physicians, if only because since the Weimar period their professions had been well staffed with Jewish colleagues. Fewer benefits accrued to engineers or architects and to independently established writers, journalists, or artists who had not experienced that kind of competition.

It is difficult to recreate the atmosphere in which writers and journalists lived and worked as a step toward finding out whether they joined the party out of conviction or sheer opportunism.[167] There is evidence that many free-lance writers for large daily papers, as well as competent editors, joined the NSDAP out of a sense of cynicism—an attitude that had guided them well in the last turbulent years of the republic. For example, a journalist who had attacked governmental measures under Brüning with vitriolic diatribes would tend to criticize the unsavory aspects of the new regime between the lines of his editorials or through literary devices such as metaphor and hyperbole. Other journalists, without recognizing the inherent contradiction in the situation, might find these "revolutionary" times exciting material, as long as their customary freedom of expression was not curtailed. And to get around the gagging press laws, party membership served many writers as an expeditious tool.[168] Politically less critical, not to say naive, artists could have been lured to the party by the proclaimed aims of a new German Culture, indeed by the very strong undercurrent of a neoromantic cultural mysticism that could be experienced, for example, through the invocation of Teutonic gods in Wagnerian opera. The paradox remains, however, that the intellectuals, though generally despised by the Nazis, often found "intellectual" reasons for justifying the "revolution" and subsequently joining the party.[169] This may explain the questionable loyalty expressed not only by someone like poet-laureate Gerhart Hauptmann but also by a lesser writer like Gottfried Benn. The example of Thomas Mann, who went into exile in Switzerland in 1933 and subsequently lost his Munich possessions, his honorary doctorate, and his German citizenship, remained anomalous because there are indications that he could have returned to the Reich under the patronage of Joseph Goebbels. Other writers such as Bertolt Brecht and Oskar Maria Graf did not have this choice. Actors and opera singers had to join the NSDAP if they wanted satisfying roles in the nation's better known theaters, then controlled by Goebbels and Göring. Here, too, one finds the characteristic mixture of inner conviction and shrewd calculation that motivated so many other social subgroups to enroll in the party.[170]

A regime that was technically oriented and sang the praises of technological progress had to find favor with technologists, and specifically with university-educated engineers and architects. If as a professional group they appear underrepresented in the NSDAP, as Karl-

Heinz Ludwig believes he can prove, this may have been due partly to the technicians' relative lack of interest in politics, which was traditional and is glaringly obvious in Albert Speer's memoirs. It is also true, however, that engineers and architects, unlike lawyers and doctors, would have had relatively little to gain from the regime's expressly anti-Semitic policy.[171]

If lawyers were overrepresented in the NSDAP—an assumption that cannot be conclusively proved on the basis of the present data—this must have been mainly because of a combination of two factors. After Hitler's assumption of power many lawyers, notably the young ones, experienced miserable economic conditions because there were still too many practicing attorneys in the Reich. These lawyers were therefore all the more eager to drive out Jewish competitors in the profession, an urge that harked back to Weimar days.[172] Prominent Nazis who claimed that even as late as January 1934 active Jewish lawyers in Prussia made up as much as 17.5 percent of the lawyer population could assume that their followers knew that the Jewish population was then less than 1 percent of the total Reich population.[173] Even if the Nazi political system always remained suspicious of the law, however, lawyers were needed as long as the customary legal and judicial procedures were left unchanged. Moreover, as cases of political prosecution in the courts continued to multiply, lawyers were called upon in greater numbers to defend clients. As it turned out in most cases, this was a mere formality, but it kept the legal profession flourishing. Joining the NSDAP could, besides helping to speed up the removal of unwanted Jewish colleagues, mean unlimited opportunities for professional advancement in the party's ancillary organizations such as the SS. Until 1939 lawyers were also needed for the shady deals surrounding "Aryanization" of Jewish businesses: party members stood a better chance of becoming involved in such ventures and could look forward to a handsome fee. In dealings of this kind, the original ideas of "law" and "justice" were twisted to suit the regime's needs, in conjunction with the reinterpretation of the ethical code by Nazi experts. These ideals were officially upheld by the Nazi Jurists' League, ruled by Hans Frank, who conveniently paid lip service to the ultimate goal of "law." In this spirit, prominent jurists such as Otto Koellreutter and Ernst Forsthoff did their utmost to "justify" the Führer state with legalistic sophistry.[174]

In the case of medical doctors, however, an overrepresentation in the NSDAP can be documented with a high degree of certainty. Approximately 45 percent of all physicians (excluding dentists and veterinarians) were members of the party during the Third Reich.[175] Moreover, from 1925 to 1944 there were proportionately almost three times as many doctors – that is, physicians, dentists, and veterinarians – in the party as in the population of the Reich.[176] Why the percentage of Nazi newcomer medical doctors of all types declined by 1935 is not yet entirely clear.[177] Possibly medical doctors were nervous about the forthcoming Physicians' Law (promulgated on December 13, 1935): they may have been concerned about the possible extent of the regulation of doctors' professional activities and about a change in the medical code of ethics.[178] As it turned out, such fears were unfounded. The doctors reemerged after the new legislation as one of the most privileged groups in German society, whose traditional sanctuaries would be no more violated than they had been in previous years, and whose monopoly in the "business" of life and death was, if anything, destined to be strengthened.

German doctors, craving higher earnings, were vehemently antagonistic toward their Jewish colleagues. A separate study is needed of the "Aryanization" of the German medical profession from 1933 to 1945,[179] but it is clear that German "Aryan" doctors went out of their way to rid themselves of Jewish colleagues who were, admittedly, still powerful and popular, especially in such cities as Frankfurt and Berlin.[180] Building on their prejudice and hatred toward Jewish fellow students in the medical faculties of the Weimar Republic, where the percentage of Jewish students had been the second highest of any faculty, "Aryan" doctors proceeded to implement the purge they might only have talked about as young interns before Hitler's assumption of power.[181] Jewish physicians were forced out of practice by harassment or other questionable means, often after the accusation that they provided free medical service to the needy and thus damaged the earning potential of their "Aryan" colleagues.[182] Even though many German doctors did not actually agree with what Dr. Franz Wertheim told interrogators after World War II (namely, that by upbringing and conviction "[I am] an anti-semite – mainly on 'aesthetic' grounds, for I am in favor of preserving racial purity and consider that as a race the Jews are inferior"), many other physicians deliberately compared Jewish doctors to crooks and felons.[183]

Before Jewish physicians began to be routinely rounded up for deportation to the East, and while the law still afforded them a measure of protection, their German colleagues, usually acting through their professional association, Kassenärztliche Vereinigung Deutschlands (KVD), used every legal pretext to get their rivals proscribed.[184] Where the law could be circumvented without risk, this was done. Jewish doctors lost their memberships or their functions in the professional associations, either as a result of decisions based on the legal precedent of the Law for the Reconstitution of the German

Civil Service (April 7, 1933) or related legislation, or as a consequence of "Aryan" physician membership petitions. In a case reported from Waldenburg (Lower Silesia) in 1934, a Jewish Dr. M., whom the current law would have allowed to remain in the physicians' association because he had served in the front lines during World War I, was forcibly denied the right to practice as a doctor for the state-sponsored health insurance plan on the ground that he had never seen war service. To justify its decision the Waldenburg KVD chapter wrote, "Under these circumstances [the physicians' association] cannot be blamed for wanting to exclude from its ranks a colleague who constantly harmed the honor and the prestige of the medical profession by his conduct."[185] What particularly irked the German doctors was that many a Gentile patient was reluctant to give up his or her trusted Jewish doctor, and that until the end of 1938 the law remained unclear as to whether German patients could visit Jewish doctors, or Jewish patients "Aryan" doctors.[186]

As Dr. Wertheim admitted candidly after the war, getting rid of Jewish colleagues was a paying proposition. Indeed, by 1943 when fewer doctors remained to tend to a larger number of patients, physicians were enjoying very high incomes.[187] Nor was a higher material standard of living through the elimination of the Jews the only benefit a German doctor derived from membership in the NSDAP. In the Upper Bavarian hamlet of Murnau in July 1933 a surgeon laid claim to the post of hospital physician not only on account of his long experience but also because of his "status in good standing as a party member."[188] And as the teaching of medicine changed to emphasize such subjects as hereditary hygienics and racial anthropology, and a host of openings in these new fields appeared with such paragovernmental and paramilitary agencies as the police and the SS, to say nothing of the Wehrmacht, a young intern could, at least until 1939, virtually pick and choose the sort of medical career he wished to follow.[189] It is therefore understandable that until well into the war years the medical profession remained the declared favorite of those young men and women who still bothered to attend a university. Throughout the Reich the percentage of medical students was always higher than that of any other students.[190]

By the fall of 1939 Hitler's party had lived through an eight-year period that, viewed in retrospect, was the most fortunate phase of its history. Even skeptics had to admit that the party had weathered many storms and achieved many important goals. In the main, it had consolidated its position within the Nazi system. It appeared to have resolved the vexing question of whether it was a party of the mass or of the elite by posing sometimes as one and sometimes as the other. In 1934 it had survived the crisis of the Röhm Purge that signified Hitler's determination to quash all manifestations of plebeian domination; and its pattern of absolute growth from 1934 to 1935 was one of the most impressive in its entire history (figure 1). Even as a monopolistic state party whose internal policies and regulations were often dictated by considerations beyond the control of its own hierarchy, it had been successful in attracting nearly representative groups from German society, though of course medical doctors were more in evidence than miners. Above all, the NSDAP had succeeded in maintaining, at least nominally, the preeminence in National Socialist Germany that it had possessed during the Time of Struggle — that is, the distinction of being the vanguard of the Nazi movement. The Führer himself never tired of assuring his people that this was so. Although rival organizations like the SS were much more conspicuous in 1939 than they had been in 1930, the NSDAP with its many official functions (including the monitoring and even policing of public opinion) was still at the top of the order.

As the specter of war appeared on the horizon, obvious dangers lay ahead for the NSDAP. The regular armed forces, which in their National Socialist form were a creation of the period after 1934, posed an institutional as well as a social threat. As an institution the new Wehrmacht could usurp much of the power of decision making that the party had enjoyed during its peaceful phase. As a social cosmos it could lure away from the NSDAP both established and potential young male members, thereby weakening the party's social fabric, which was predicated upon the twin principles of male superiority and youth. An even greater threat in this regard was posed by the SS, which had become unreservedly elitist in structure and character and, unlike the Wehrmacht, was ever ready to assume ideological tasks that the party regarded as its prerogative.

These were only a few of the specific problems that the NSDAP would face if Hitler's war turned out to be more than a transitory phenomenon. Although short-term adjustments would not be difficult, the very survival of the NSDAP as an ideologically determined formation of German men and women would be at stake if a long-lasting war were to strengthen the rival organizations. Yet in September 1939 no Nazi party member thought in these terms. Any of them would have found it difficult to imagine that Hitler's war could become a drawn-out affair or that he might possibly lose it.

5

THE WAR YEARS
SEPTEMBER 1939 TO 1945

In the autumn of 1939 the NSDAP entered its most critical period. It was apparent that the challenges of World War II could be met only by party members who were highly capable and unquestionably loyal to Hitler. Therefore, it came as a shock to the leadership that even after the membership rolls were opened to the general public in 1939, the number of party applicants remained well below their target figure of 10 percent of the Reich population. Moreover, there were signs that the party was losing its appeal as an instrument of social and political mobility for Germans with special qualifications or skills. In particular, it was becoming less popular with the younger generation, the men and women who were expected to safeguard the longevity of the Thousand-Year Reich.

To counteract these tendencies, the Nazi leaders decided in February 1942 to close the membership books once again to the general public in order to attract more young members. Only adolescents and mature Germans of special distinction were to be allowed to join up. This system of selective closure remained in effect until the end of the regime. In essence, it increased the pressure on Hitler Youth leavers to enter the party and deprived ordinary Germans of the opportunity to prove their loyalty to Hitler by becoming voluntary joiners. What still remains an open question is how many adult Germans would actually have become Nazi party comrades in the last years of the regime if they had been given a chance to do so.

In this chapter the analysis of the social composition of the party membership rests on the data displayed in table 7 for new joiners and established members and on figure 6, which illustrates the peculiar situation of medical doctors.

THE WORKERS

In 1939 the percentage of workers joining the Nazi party increased noticeably, starting a trend that did not end until 1944. But at no time during this period did the percentage of worker joiners come up to that class's percentage in the German population: the proletariat continued to be underrepresented in the party.[1]

One could argue that, as before, the workers' attitude toward the NSDAP was determined largely by socioeconomic considerations. Beginning with the outbreak of war the workers' socioeconomic conditions were obviously a function of two factors: the regime's need for increased armaments output and a growing shortage of skilled manpower to produce this output. The relative scarcity of trained German workers, compounded by necessary inductions into the armed forces for service at the fronts, was never sufficiently offset either by the influx of coopted or conscripted foreign laborers, such as the masses of prisoners of war from France, Poland, or Russia, or by the stepped-up utilization of native and alien concentration-camp inmates. The workers' awareness of their indispensability to the German war machine may have impelled a majority of them to capitalize on their favorable position by pressuring the regime to either maintain or improve wages and conditions of work. The regime in turn was well aware that the workers might try to exploit their monopolistic situation, and even before the autumn of 1939 the party condemned the materialism of the workers.[2]

It is true that by September 1939 the war economy had compelled German workers to submit to wage ceilings and the abrogation of overtime pay, as well as to other strictures. But two months later the restrictions were removed, and throughout 1940 additional work incentives were introduced. Although the eight-hour day remained the norm for wage calculations, overtime was richly rewarded. By 1943 a bonus wage system based on efficiency was established. All of this meant that at the height of the war a hard-working laborer, highly skilled and willing to work long hours, could earn plenty of money.[3]

But as the war progressed the worker could buy fewer and fewer things with his money; the rationing of goods, especially scarce foodstuffs, decisively curbed his purchasing power.[4] Moreover, the war brought hardships: forced separation from one's family, uncomfortable and tedious commuting procedures, and of course the dangers associated with armaments production, which was subject to enemy bombing raids. Since numerous complaints were made about the conditions — complaints that are as well documented as the conditions

themselves — it is highly unlikely that materialism was the only induce-
ment attracting a higher percentage of workers to the NSDAP after
1938.[5] Nor could the improved social services, such as the more
beneficial old-age pension scheme of 1940 and the DAF's heightened
activity on the workers' behalf, have caused the greater influx of proletarians into the Nazi party after 1938, for these measures were not
comprehensive enough.[6]

The very fact that during the war multitudes of workers were given
the opportunity to earn high wages, even though the cash they received did not translate into greater buying power, instilled in them a
feeling of being part of a "new" society in which social opportunities
had indeed increased for the man on the street. The systematic proscription of organized Marxism by the Nazis, an action that at least by
the advent of the war had weakened the KPD's and the SPD's influence among German workers, changed the proletariat's sense of class-
consciousness. In the absence of socialist counterpropaganda these
proletarians, far from rising against a government that had initially
made good its promise to remove unemployment, even though it had
not improved their material lot substantially and had subjected them
to the rigors of a costly war, tended slowly to fall prey to the Nazi
slogans calling for the removal of class barriers and for a united
Volksgemeinschaft.[7] The war, moreover, acted as a catalyst toward a
type of social consolidation that was based on nationalist and biological premises. This became obvious when workers from the Ruhr, for
instance, were promoted to supervisory positions in the newly conquered East.[8] In addition, not only did workers find it easy to identify
with the Führer's humble background, but Hitler and his cronies lost
few chances to demonstrate their appreciation of the men in blue over-
alls. As Hitler praised munitions laborers for being "soldiers on the
home front," the workers could gratefully compare their situation
with that of the soldiers in the trenches. Many a laborer who had initially been conscripted for front-line duty but had then been sent back
to coal pits in the Ruhr or to the Schweinfurt ball-bearing plant of
Fichtl and Sachs realized that, Allied air raids notwithstanding, his lot
at home was infinitely better than the hardships of the front. In this
comparison it was primarily the British bomber pilot who emerged as
a substitute for the hated figure of the exploiting entrepreneur conven-
tionally vilified by the Communists. Secondarily it was the German
war profiteer, stereotyped by the Nazi media as *Schieber* and *Kohlen-
klau*, whom the workers suspected of being still within the ranks of the
upper classes.[9] In fact, the most obvious representatives of that class
were the rich but harmless ladies who could afford to vacation at exclusive spas during the summer of 1943, or, perhaps, the corrupt

NSDAP functionaries, against whom the workers wished the Führer would initiate another purge. It may be that the solidarity between Führer and workers was corroded in the chaotic years after 1942, when the differences between the home front and the military front gradually became meaningless. But in light of the rising NSDAP joiner figures for workers (table 7), it hardly seems justifiable to speak, as some authors have done, of an inner proletarian "will to resist" the regime. The evidence points to the contrary, at least until 1942.[10] In this sense, then, the German workers proved to be just as patriotic during World War II as they had been during World War I.[11]

THE LOWER MIDDLE CLASS

Among the six occupational subgroups of the lower middle class the independent shopkeepers and retail merchants (subgroups 4 and 8) showed a greater willingness to join the NSDAP in 1939 than they had in the previous period, reflecting their expectation of commercial success as the war approached.[12] In fact, a boom in small business had begun that lasted into 1940, during which the surviving independent craftsmen had a share in war production and retail merchants did a brisk business with somewhat more affluent consumers who spent freely, spurred on by public fears that goods would become rarer as the war progressed. In the Upper Danube area, for instance, by December 1939 "all items that could be had in the stores were bought up, including those that formerly had never been touched. This is a consequence of higher earnings."[13]

Later in 1939, however, things began to become more difficult for both merchant and craftsman, with little prospect of improvement until after the end of the war. The squeeze earlier applied to smaller businesses by big business continued unabated, with party and state giving their blessings or passing legislation that put small businesses at a disadvantage. The result, naturally, was a drop in enthusiasm for the party among both shopkeepers and artisans.[14]

As war production became paramount and the need for skilled workers ever greater, the weeding-out procedures that had affected artisanal shops in the previous period were reactivated shortly after the beginning of the conflict. Often enough, the gains were meager. In December 1939 only 18 metal workers could be recruited from a total of 134 small independent shops in the district of Eberswalde (Brandenburg).[15] But on a national scale, craftsmen's shops lost about 1,400,000 trained employees between the summer of 1939 and the spring of 1942. The chronic shortage of certain skills formerly practiced in small craft shops, such as shoemaking and housepainting, became particularly irksome. There were attempts in 1941 to alleviate under-employment by freeing the children of artisans from obligatory Hitler Youth service, but the problem was not solved. In the face of these hardships, special ordinances, such as that of October 12, 1939, com-pelling bakers to resume daily delivery of fresh-made buns, created further confusion and dismay.[16]

In the course of time, still more shops were found to be super-fluous, either because they were engaged in nonessential activities or because they were already operating with a skeleton staff. From April 1939 to June 1941 the total number of active, independent shops was reduced from 1.5 million to 1.1 million. Toward the end of the war the surviving shops were relegated to the business of repairs, and their proprietors became justly worried about their future after the "Final Victory" despite promises that conditions would then return to nor-mal.[17] Because of the grim job prospects in certain crafts that were not considered important for the war effort, such as the building trade, young recruits were hard to find, but in some increasingly mechanized trades, such as baking, there was a surplus of young trainees even as early as 1940.[18]

At the retail-store level these consolidation proceedings were paral-leled by similar measures, though not so drastically. Stores that were deemed nonessential in wartime, such as confectionery outlets and perfumeries, were closed by special ordinances early in 1943. Such steps, however, were not taken solely in the interest of larger busi-nesses, because a large number of chain-store outlets, especially those clustered in city centers, were forced to close as well.[19] Still, in the case of the merchants as well as the craftsmen, one can argue, as a West German scholar has recently done, that until 1945 the remaining busi-nesses found competition easier and profits higher—provided, of course, they had goods or services to offer in spite of the restraints im-posed by bombing raids and supply quotas.[20]

The relative scarcity of consumer goods or foodstuffs that were salable over the counters and the shortage of raw materials curtailed more than ever before the potential for economic long-term planning of both retail merchants and master craftsmen. Although until 1943 plenty of consumer goods were still being manufactured in the Reich, the public could buy these only on ration cards, and often the stores had sold out their stock.[21] Among the craftsmen who were affected by chronic supply shortages were bakers (who needed coal), smiths (who needed iron and alloys), and shoemakers (who needed rubber, not to mention leather). With the intensification of air raids, the danger that stocks of such supplies would be destroyed grew daily. In Munich during March 1944 a clothing merchant was anxious to put on sale a large stock of rubber coats lest they should go up in flames during the next bombing attack, but he was prevented from doing so because there were not enough ration cards to go around.[22]

Because supplies and merchandise were limited, some enterprising small businessmen occasionally tried to sell popular items to favorite customers under black-market conditions, without demanding ration cards and at a higher price. In some cases barter replaced money transactions: for instance, greengrocers might part with their vegetables only if they received chicken, butter, or soap from their customers, who very likely were farmers or merchants specializing in the distribution of these commodities. Similarly, tradesmen might work only for payment in kind, particularly in the countryside. As these practices increased, the authorities clamped down heavily on the culprits, meting out prison sentences and fines. For example, shopkeeper G. of Neumarkt (Oberpfalz) was sentenced in early 1943 by a special court in Nuremberg to a year in prison and the loss of her commercial license for an additional three years "because of barter trade and for having exceeded maximum retail price levels."[23]

Independent farmers (subgroup 9) were attracted to the NSDAP at a steady rate from 1939 to 1944, about equaling the 1933 level, and they continued to be overrepresented in the party compared with their 7.70 percent representation in the Reich.[24] By and large they seem to have harbored neither an overly strong resentment toward the NSDAP nor an enormous fervor for it during wartime.

Economically, farmers fared somewhat better in this period than they had previously, but they still did not really prosper. There were no major droughts or bad harvest, but neither were there any particularly fine crops or herds of cattle. Marketing possibilities varied according to the region and the produce. Government delivery quotas of crops such as wheat, at fixed prices, continued to be in force, and this ensured nutritional standards for the Volksgemeinschaft, in particular for the armed forces, that were very high in comparison with those of other belligerent countries. During the course of the war some of the quotas were relaxed in the interest of higher profits for the farmers, and certain price ceilings were raised, as was the ceiling for milk in 1942, to guarantee better financial returns. Although complaints were made against forced requisitions of livestock (such as horses and steers) for purposes of war, these disadvantages were partly counterbalanced by special benefits accruing only in wartime, such as controlled price and consumption patterns. The scarcity of fodder and fertilizer continued to be felt, but the need for expensive mechanization was somewhat reduced because labor reserves could be increased by importing foreign farm workers. One decided advantage the farmer possessed over all the other social subgroups was that in emergencies he could rely on his own produce to ward off starvation. In a sense, he was the beneficiary of a microcosmic subsistence economy specific only to the countryside. Despite the official delivery quotas, the farmers not only ate better than the townspeople during the war, but they were also able, as barter trade became more common, to augment their purchasing power by exchanging hoarded produce for coveted manufactured goods, even though such a practice was not without risks. Farmers possessed a further advantage in that they were able to get alien laborers for unusually low wages. Most of the mony saved, however, went to the government by way of taxes and special surcharges; and besides, these foreign laborers, who were less efficient than the Germans they replaced, caused additional troubles.[25]

The problem of agricultural labor during the war probably gave the individual farmer more headaches than any other matter. This problem was multifaceted. During the first three years of the war, in an attempt to promote the national "Nutrition Battle," the conscription of farmers for military service was not uniformly enforced and some farmers, to their great relief, were able initially to retain civilian status. Later, however, they might be called up for active duty; their relief then changed to anger. This was especially true after the disaster of Stalingrad in February 1943, when the drafts in the agrarian sector were drastically increased, so that by mid-1943 a total of nearly two million men from agriculture had been inducted into the Wehrmacht.[26] Moreover, after the winter of 1939–40 had demonstrated huge gaps in the civilian agricultural labor force, farm labor was made available from POW camps or foreign sources. As a result, by the middle of 1941 about a million and a half foreign workers were being used in the Reich economy, of whom approximately half toiled on the soil; yet industry was receiving foreign workers at a faster rate on the whole than agriculture. And even though by 1944 one laborer in five in Germany was a stranger, agriculture's demands still could not be met by the end of the war.[27]

When farmers were conscripted the chores fell to the women who were left behind. Although they received some help from members of the various civilian and youth service programs, such as those for young girls, city women, university students, and the Hitler Youth, this aid was intermittent, unsystematic, and on the whole ineffective. Farmers' wives and daughters bore the brunt of responsibility for the farms, often working themselves into a state of total physical exhaustion.[28] Many of these women found themselves in a difficult situation: they had to gain the good will of the foreign help, whom they generally treated with kindness, but for this they were reprimanded — and in some cases even punished with lengthy terms in the penitentiary — by the authorities, who forbade fraternizing with the enemy. Moreover, they were apt to incur the wrath of their husbands or fiancés, who often suspected their women of having affairs with the Poles or Frenchmen. A large stock of documents shows the suspicions to have been quite well founded.[29]

The farmers, officially still the darlings of the nation as evidenced by many public addresses and special events held in their honor, found it increasingly difficult to comprehend a war that they had never wanted and that took them away from their farms for months at a time. Many became more and more apathetic as exaggerated demands were made upon their patriotism. When at home, for example, they displayed a marked aversion to work, especially on Sundays. Not surprisingly, neither their own children nor the young people from the cities showed much desire to learn farming. Although the regime kept painting the German farmer's future in a newly conquered European East in glowing colors and calling for a volunteer army of trainees, its spokesmen could not help noticing that the German peasant was seldom apt to look beyond his village steeple. "The peasant population knows precious little what this war is all about," wrote a Hessian *Oberbereichsleiter* in the summer of 1943. "It is quite likely — and this is even worse — that they do not *want* to know about this struggle. Despite the efforts of the party and its agencies, a large number of them just will not come out of their state of indifference as far as the great events of our day are concerned."[30]

Another section of the lower middle class, the lower and intermediate civil servants (subgroup 7), joined the NSDAP in greater numbers during the first months of the war and then turned their backs on the party after 1940-41. Nevertheless, they remained overrepresented in the NSDAP until 1942.[31] In all probability, their renewed faith in the party at the beginning of the war is traceable to the host of novel and interesting professional opportunities that awaited them in the administrative networks established in the wake of Germany's blitzkrieg victories, particularly in Poland and France.[32] A few scholars have held that some sort of "crisis" caused civil servants to ignore the party after 1941, but this view is open to question.[33] Yet it is clear that a combination of factors throughout the later years of the war did threaten German officialdom more than at any time since

1933. This is probably the most likely reason for the decline in new party membership after 1941.

In addition to the old problems that continued to plague civil servants under Nazi rule, there were new problems that increased in severity as the armed conflict developed. As civil servants were conscripted into the army to serve at the front, those who were left behind were faced with insuperable difficulties in a civilian administration that was made infinitely more complex by the demands of war. The skeleton staff left on the home front was more and more overworked as cases of political disobedience increased within the civilian sphere and had to be dealt with in the courts, including the Nazi "special courts." Figures from the Justice Ministry show, moreover, that the decreasing number of justice officials was less and less capable of coping with the rising multitude of infractions. In 1943 the combined losses of dead and wounded among justice officials through air raids alone were more than forty-five times higher than they had been in 1941. Up to July 31, 1944, the ministry suffered a total of 158,00 dead and 280,000 wounded as the result of air raids and front-line casualties.[34] If conditions in East Prussia were in any way typical, it is probable that as more and more administrators were drafted into the army for active service, more extracurricular responsibilities (dictated by the party and its adjunct organizations, such as the harvest service and NSV clothes collections) were added to the already heavy burdens of the steadily diminishing number of civilian officials.[35] Inevitably, therefore, these German officials began to suffer from fatigue, sickness, and the ill effects of premature aging.[36] And as young potential recruits continued to seek professional opportunities in private industry or the Wehrmacht rather than in the civil service, the problems of government staffing were further compounded.[37]

During the war years a major complaint of the officials was that although they were charged with the execution of more burdensome chores at the administrative centers of the Reich, their remuneration did not improve. Instead, it worsened in comparison with the prewar phase, despite a number of ordinances that nominally increased their salaries. Here, too, an irreversible trend set in, one that had started in peacetime and was at root caused by the Nazi regime's contempt for servants of the state. The party's attitude toward the question of pay for those under extreme duress is illuminated by a candid remark made by Joseph Goebbels in his diary. On January 25, 1942, he wrote: "Officials are now to work fifty-eight hours per week instead of forty-six. The Ministry of the Interior immediately proposed that twenty-five marks per month be paid them as so-called 'soup money.' I regard that as wrong. Officialdom should do its duty. If it is demanded of officials that they work a few hours more in wartime than under normal peace conditions, they ought to look upon that as a sort of service of honour."[38]

Goebbels's reference to the Reich Interior Ministry was a timely allusion to the tug-of-war between party and state over matters concerning the civil administration, which had commenced before 1939 and looked as though it was going to be won by the party. Bormann, whose power increased after Hess's flight to England in May 1941, knew that Hitler shared his own dislike of the bureaucracy, as much in wartime as during the years of peace. Yet although the NSDAP intensified its pressure on the officials in various ways and actually managed to draw them somewhat into the party's jurisdictional realm by burdening them with party functions on the home front, Bormann could never entirely control them. On the one hand, Interior Minister Frick could not stop Bormann's abuse of the officials, who as a service class suffered a further loss of prestige; but on the other hand, Frick was still able to shield his officials from the obligation of NSDAP membership as a precondition of employment or job tenure, one of Bormann's most sought-after goals. By 1943, however, a new membership ban was in effect that barred all those but the youngest civil-service recruits with a Hitler Youth background from entering the party. It is likely that if Germany had won the war Bormann would have succeeded in altogether eradicating the time-honored German civil service in its traditional form and in replacing it solely with party stalwarts. In such an event, the fundamental contest between party and state in the Third Reich would have been decisively resolved in favor of the party.

Two significant portents heralded such a development. First, Bormann's virtual elimination, in the spring of 1943, of the NSDAP-directed professional organizations for civil servants in general and schoolteachers in particular (the NS-Hauptamt für Beamte and NS-Hauptamt für Erzieher, including their ancillary agencies) can only be interpreted as a measure aimed at drastically reducing any opportunity for professional self-realization. In this way Bormann neutralized the potential of these institutions to become an interest lobby, a potential they had always possessed despite their NSDAP affiliations. Second, Bormann had in hand and could have used to his advantage the casualty statistics for drafted state bureaucrats, which compared unfavorably with those for party functionaries on active military duty. Figures from East Prussia suggest that between September 1939 and

December 1942 only 1.9 percent of all state officials in uniform had been lost at the fronts, while the corresponding percentage for the party functionaries in approximately the same time period was 5.5 percent.[39]

Turning to the white-collar workers or lower employees (subgroup 6), their newcomer rate in the Nazi party increased after the beginning of the war, and they continued to be overrepresented there (tables 1 and 7). Little is known about the socioeconomic position of shop clerks, sales personnel, and business employees during this period. The scarcity of documentation in comparison with other groups would suggest, however, that white-collar workers as an interest lobby had little either to fight for or to fight against; while they harbored few ambitions, they also had few complaints. Like the blue-collar workers they benefited from a situation in which marketable skills were in great demand and were, at least nominally, richly rewarded. By and large, it is fair to say that during the war the dividing line between blue- and white-collar workers continued to fade as both groups coordinated their value systems with a materialistic code of ethics that was dictated, to a certain extent, by the prerogatives of the regime. Though hard evidence is lacking, it can be said that the lower and intermediate employees, like the laborers, became more patriotic during the war and heartily supported Germany's war effort. This attitude was natural for employees, who had no tradition of opposition to the state: resistance fighters from this occupational subgroup were relatively scarce as compared with those from the working class.[40] Inasmuch as the Nazi regime guaranteed steady employment and decent, if not optimal, wage conditions, especially in wartime, lower and intermediate employees found an almost ideal employment situation. Assuming that a German shop clerk, for example, was able to rule out ideological and political qualms altogether — and the white-collar worker was more ready to do this than a representative of any other occupational subgroup — his life under National Socialism was better than it had ever been before. During the war the lower middle class was still the prototypical exponent of National Socialism, and the lower employee continued to represent the occupational stratum most likely to support the Nazi regime.[41]

THE ELITE

Of the three social layers, the elite was clearly the one element in German society that sharply turned its back on the National Socialist movement after the war started, even though in general it remained overrepresented in the party.[42] Some of the reasons for this change sprang from prewar developments; others were a function of the escalating conflict.

The university and upper-school students' declining interest in the NSDAP after 1939 was, in part, a consequence of the limited social and professional opportunities afforded them by the party in peacetime, coupled with the party functionaries' continued disrespect for all things intellectual.[43] As students were increasingly used, even abused, by party agencies in all sorts of auxiliary functions connected with the war effort, their contempt for the uncouth party hacks with whom they came into daily contact mounted, just as did the functionaries' suspicions of them as "intellectuals."[44] To a large extent, these feelings were socially motivated and derived from the ingrained prejudices of the old elites against their social inferiors, as well as from the long-established social and intellectual insecurity of the petits bourgeois vis-à-vis the conventional establishment. The judgment of the Munich-based "White Rose" student resistance group led by Hans and Sophie Scholl in the summer of 1942 that it was impossible to tackle the National Socialist movement on a spiritual plane because by its very nature it was "antispiritual" was as much a manifestation of the university students' intellectual disdain as it was a comment on the failure of the Nazi party to reach the hearts of Germany's young academic elite.[45]

One of the problems confronting students in those restless years was a disintegrating sense of identity: they were torn between the demands of the war, especially military or labor service at the fronts, and the demands made on them in seminars and lecture halls. Apart from medical students, who were needed more than others and were granted special allowances and leaves of absence, the adherents of all academic disciplines expressed more and more doubt over their socioeconomic roles in a future Reich.[46] As the conflict intensified and the Volksgemeinschaft assumed an increasingly martial character, civilian ideals gave way to military ones: the student began to envision himself more properly as a leader of men in the Wehrmacht than as an engineer, high-school teacher, or lawyer. Hence there was a continued shortage of upper-school graduates in most faculties, a shortage that could not be met by the increasing numbers of female students who came to take the place of their male cohorts serving at the fronts. As ideological regimentation escalated to meet the requirements of the totalitarian regime and as academic standards fell still further, the universities themselves approached another climax in what appeared to be a continuing crisis of higher education. Declining enrollments and smaller numbers of graduates testified to the basic insecurity of students and their discontent with the traditional temples of learning.[47]

Yet if students could more readily picture themselves as members of the military leadership echelons, a view in harmony with the treasured tradition of front-line soldiering during World War I, they found it difficult to see themselves as future functionaries of the monopolist state party, despite the appeal it made to them.[48] It is significant that the male members of the "White Rose" student resistance cell directed their protests not so much against the rapacious campaigns of the Nazi Wehrmacht, in which they were still serving, as against the odious behavior of leading party bosses who were attempting to extend their jurisdiction over local university affairs. And although the Scholls and their friends died on the scaffolds early in 1943, the vast majority of students refrained from active resistance, except for the tumultuous protest demonstrations held on campus, such as one in Göttingen late in 1939. Instead, they adopted a wait-and-see attitude. A contemporary of those times has recalled the general feeling of the student body: "We who studied in those days were far from considering an altruistic self-sacrifice, or from establishing a signal for all to see . . . We thought of survival without becoming implicated in the regime's crimes . . . We wanted to get through the dark tunnel without guilt because we knew that at the other end important tasks were waiting to be solved by us."[49]

Indeed, there is evidence to suggest that in the final years of the regime, students began to rally in an effort to revive the esprit de corps that had characterized them as a chosen if endangered species in the Weimar Republic. As many as 40 percent of all students may have been members of the Nazi party at the end of the Third Reich, the majority of them undoubtedly coerced to join from the Hitler Youth.[50] Without question a large percentage of those who clubbed together for a last-ditch stand against the invading Russians and Americans in the final months of the regime still fought as much for the preservation of the fatherland as for the future of their own group as academics. But in 1944–45 the idealism that, however misdirected, still inspired the students' perseverance in the People's Militia (Volkssturm), at the military fronts, or even in university lecture halls, was more reminiscent of 1813 or 1848 than of the Hitler Youth or Labor Service rollcalls in 1935. It was the same spirit that in the late forties was to motivate a whole generation of World War II front-line veterans, many of them close to middle age, to resume studying again in a society that, though not yet fully cleansed, was slowly beginning to readopt the institutions of democracy.[51]

After the beginning of the war two other subgroups of the elite class, entrepreneurs and managers, were among the staunchest supporters of the Nazi party, although their strength as joiners was on the wane during the last years of the conflict.[52] Fundamentally, the profitable alliance between the Nazi rulers and industry continued as before the war, to the benefit of both parties. When the Four-Year Plan of 1936 petered out in confusion in early 1940, Göring was removed from the economic power controls, and on March 20, 1940, the technocrat Dr. Fritz Todt, who was much more sympathetic to private enterprise, became Minister for Armaments and Munitions. His jurisdiction over economic planning then became paramount. Todt laid the groundwork for the system of "self-government for industry" (to quote Alan Milward) that came to typify the Speer era, for Speer assumed responsibility for the war effort and eventually, in February 1942, for the entire economy. Large and small businessmen were allowed complete freedom provided they produced the needed armaments at the fixed-price levels (operative in 1942) and according to the prescribed quotas. Since the change in emphasis from the production of consumer goods to armaments took place only gradually and consumer goods were always in demand (even though exports were restricted), the combined profits from both types of products remained very high.[53] It was not until 1944–45 that large industrialists and lesser businessmen alike realized that a Final Victory was not in store for them and that they would have to suffer, at least economically.[54]

One of the trends continuing from the prewar phase was rationalization of industry, which in conjunction with concentration of production meant that again the worst organized and smallest entrepreneurs fared comparatively badly. Medium-sized enterprises had to face constant inspections to determine their armaments production capability, and if they did not pass they were shut down. Thus in Swabia and Bavaria in 1942 pulp and paper processing plants that manufactured paper bags, as well as shoe factories, were marked for closure in order to free skilled workers for redeployment. In 1943–44, textile plants in Styria suffered the same fate. Other factories were put out of commission because they lacked coal or depended exclusively on the manufacture of consumer goods. As a rule, the larger a business the better were its chances for high-profit production of essential goods and hence for economic survival. In the war years, intermediate plants more often than not were relegated to maintenance and repair work with no prospect of expansion and with lower financial returns.[55]

Records show that after 1939 the profits of businesses that managed to withstand the weeding-out procedures increased many times over their prewar levels. In addition to stepping up both armaments production and the manufacture of consumer goods — many of which, like men's watches, could be declared to be commodities for service at the fronts — the Nazi Reich, already largely autarchic, was able to enlarge its internal market network through the subjugation of foreign territory and civilian populations. Newly won territories could figure in the imperialistic planning of the business leaders, just as alien peoples could be looked upon as a mass of potential consumers of German-made manufactures. The acquisition of "living space" hence was as much a paying proposition for both the large and the successful medium businessmen as it was a political power lever for the government and party leaders.[56]

One important factor in the increased profits of businesses that were well geared to the war effort was the improved cost efficiency that resulted from the influx of cheap foreign labor. Exploitation of human resources was even greater when concentration-camp inmates were used, for they were paid either nominal wages or no wages at all. The number of such conscripts in a plant depended upon its size and individual requirements, varying from a few hundred (BMW Abteroda) to between forty and fifty thousand. Altogether, at the high point of the German war effort, about half a million inmates were being used in this way. Even lesser manufacturers thought nothing of treating these unfortunate people like cattle. Early in 1945 an American psychologist, Saul K. Padover, then a member of the U.S. Army, was visiting the textile industrial sites in Rhenish Krefeld. When he raised the question of German mass murders in Poland with a young factory owner, the man expressed his disapproval: " 'Why did they do it? . . . Why kill them? We needed all kinds of workers. We were asking for more workers all the time. They should have sent them to us, instead of killing them uselessly like that. Such a waste of manpower!' "[57]

The escalation of the war created enormous opportunities for expansion, financial profits, and general material benefits, and as a result the pressure on businessmen lessened from the German Labor Front, as well as from other party or governmental sources.[58] Hence, business executives and independent entrepreneurs, well aware of their indispensability in wartime, hardly needed to bother to join the NSDAP. Yet they continued to do so, though at a lower rate after 1939–40 than before. For successful businessmen, a nominal party membership still provided the best protection against interference in their entrepreneurial activities,[59] and it spared them from further infringements on their liberties, such as the compulsory camp training that was instituted for state officials.[60]

For another subgroup of the elite, the higher civil servants, the NSDAP new-membership pattern from 1939 to 1945 was very similar to that of the lower civil servants, a fact that suggests parallels between these two groups in both political motives and behavior.[61] In the first place, the early successes of the war, coupled with the novel administrative tasks allocated to them in conquered enemy territory, seem to have lifted the morale of all the bureaucrats, at least temporarily. An increasing percentage of higher civil servants joined the party between 1938–39 and 1940–41 (table 7). For those who were qualified and willing, there were many opportunities. But political barriers to professional advancement still had to be circumvented: for example, if a party review of a higher official's ideological track record was negative, it could substantially delay his advancement.[62]

Second, as the war progressed and the regime became harsher, higher civil servants as well as lower became more and more frustrated in their attempts to salvage the last remnants of conventional jurisprudence and administrative integrity. When the machinations of the regime's functionaries pushed Germany closer and closer to a police state, the gap between representatives of the party and the old-style bureaucracy became unbridgeable. The term *Höherer Beamter* — higher civil servant — virtually became a dirty word within party circles, a development that Hitler did not oppose but rather encouraged. As early as the spring of 1941 Interior Minister Frick had all but given up his fight for the preservation of the civil-service corps, though he was not replaced by Police Chief Himmler until August 1943.[63] In this context, the subjugation of justice to the totalitarian goals of the regime was complete. As trained jurists were sent from the home courts to duty at the fronts, more and more cases of political justice had to be dealt with by fewer judges and by attorneys who were still civilians.[64] By April 1, 1944, roughly 5 percent of all formerly active judges in the Reich, 8 percent of all state attorneys, and 13 percent of junior juridical personnel with university degrees had died soldiers' deaths. Three years prior to this, as many as 132 of the 281 justices' posts in Berlin had been vacant. There is evidence, however, that in the last three years of the war the Nazi regime reduced its dependence on university-trained staff, in particular judicial experts, and increasingly sought to delegate their judicial responsibilities to police executives or members of the SS. Late in 1944 judges were actually removed from their posts and deployed to work at tasks completely unrelated to their training. For instance, in December of that year two Berlin justices were toiling away as lathe operators in an armaments factory, sorely missed by their former superiors in the Justice Ministry.[65]

There are indications that after the Final Victory Hitler would have completely done away with the judicial system inherited from the Weimar Republic. It could not be made to function in accordance with the regime's lawless requirements of summary prosecution and arbitrary persecution. The Führer's denigration of judges in private as well as in official circles during the war knew no limits, but he also talked about a new type of National Socialist jurist to be trained not in the universities of the past but in special party institutions. This was in keeping with the gradual perversion of the law, which by the war years had made lip service to the concept of "law" utterly farcical.[66] As the prestige of judges declined, the attraction of the judge's vocation and the readiness of academics to embark on a career in the judicial service also fell to a new low.[67]

At the same time, things also worsened for the higher civil servants — the professors — in the universities. Because Hitler's hatred of academic teachers was almost as great as his hatred of judges, learned exponents of the humanities and even of the natural sciences did not fare well in official circles. Yet although scholarly standards in general continued to fall, islands of prodigious scholarship did remain, quite beyond the reach of the party. Ironically, as in the case of many wartime entrepreneurs, conscientious scholars often found that an "ivory-tower" existence and immunity from party interference could only be ensured through full membership in the NSDAP. But there were plenty of lesser academics who joined the party out of conviction and for fast professional advancement. As a matter of fact, the professional stratum of the upper middle class, whose social prestige had suffered as much as that of the other academic subgroups, included some of the most ambitious and self-interested careerists. Toward the end of the war they compared especially unfavorably with the much more idealistically minded students. A Königsberg student leader, reporting on attempts to organize the defense of his university town against imminent Russian invasion, praised the students' sense of solidarity but complained about the reluctance of the academic teachers to help in that effort: whereas the students, some of them war cripples, did their utmost, "the professors to a large part had nothing better to do than flee the province, accompanied by their women and children."[68]

Finally, academic professionals and other intellectuals were one of the most disappointed subgroups of the elite class to be found in the Reich after the outbreak of World War II. Their initial fervor for the NSDAP, which had reached a high point in 1935, cooled considerably after 1938 and remained low until the end of the war.[69]

The reasons for this increasingly negative attitude toward the National Socialist regime were various, but in general they were the same as those that prompted the entire upper class to turn its back on the Hitler movement during World War II. In this sense the academic professionals appear to have been prototypical of the elite as a whole. Basically, the intellectuals, themselves held in disrepute by Hitler, Bormann, and even Dr. Goebbels, came to look down on and reject the regime's functionaries because of their lack of intelligence, esthetics, morality, religion, and social conscience. The academics' own intelligence and sense of morality enabled them to perceive that the gradual development of Hitler's autocratic rule — which they had first welcomed as a necessary remedy for social and economic ills — into a full-fledged regime of terror was undesirable and even wrong. An early indication of this downward path had been the Röhm Purge of 1934, which had startled many who were accustomed to forming independent opinions on social and political affairs. The coming of war was not generally welcomed by intellectuals since it entailed a state of belligerence with England, which many educated Germans, a few of them Rhodes Scholars, customarily admired. And even though Germany's swift victories over Poland and France did not greatly concern the academics (both countries ranked somewhat low on their lists), they did condemn the oppression and the frequent acts of brutality that followed. Hitler's attack on Russia appeared to many thoughtful intellectuals as an act of pure folly, and the tragedy of Stalingrad in February 1943 strengthened the view that Germany could never win the war. As the police state tightened its grip and as news about crimes of unheard-of proportions leaked out, the intellectuals became more and more despondent. The "mercy killing" of the disabled and the persecution of Jews, compounded by the sufferings inflicted upon churchmen of both faiths, caused such indignation that no one dared to write or speak about it.

For conscientious journalists who resented the restrictions placed by the state on freedom of speech and press, the situation could hardly be tolerated. On both esthetic and social grounds they despised the NSDAP functionaries and even Hitler himself as upstarts or parasites. With the press stifled, modern art smeared, twelve-tone music derided, Christianity assailed, and objective science and scholarship trodden underfoot, the value system of the former upper-bourgeois elite, in particular as it was subscribed to by the university-educated professionals, appeared to be in the greatest peril. After Stalingrad, the flirtation of most intellectuals with Nazism was over. Significantly, in August 1943, the same month in which Frick was replaced by Himmler as Interior Minister, Germany's most prestigious daily newspaper for the intelligentsia, the *Frankfurter Zeitung*, was dissolved. It was only after another year that some of the intellectuals got together in an attempt to topple the regime, an effort that came much too late and was destined to fail.[70]

Two parts of this professional elite, the lawyers and physicians, deserve closer examination. Lawyers in private practice were having an increasingly difficult time. Most of them, like the higher bureaucrats (including the judges), were caught in a dilemma: they were officially despised and yet officially needed. In fact, Hitler's, Goebbels's, Himmler's, and Bormann's hatred of lawyers during the war was only slightly less volatile than their hatred of public officials, and it stemmed from the same root: a fundamental disregard for normative constitutional and judicial thinking.[71] Although the beginning of the Third Reich had brought the lawyers professional and material benefits, Germany's entrance into the war meant, first, their conscription into the Wehrmacht and the loss of their normally high incomes without adequate compensation, and second, a greater general commitment to the war effort. Hence, by April 1, 1944, over 2 percent of all attorneys in the Reich had died at the war fronts (even though their casualty rate was only half that of the judges), and throughout the war, lawyers of civilian status were called upon to help with harvesting, snow removal, and canvassing for "donations."[72] These activities were usually supervised by the Nazi Jurists' League, the officious professional union that continued to be in charge of "ideological education" as well as "the awakening of an understanding of National Socialist legal thought."[73] During these years, when martial law and party jurisdiction were more important than the traditional civil and criminal codes, and when interest in the nation's law schools was receding, the future of the profession appeared bleak, especially in light of the regime's eventual resolve to run the ship of state without the aid of the old bureaucracy. Nevertheless, the lawyers were still formally required to be present in the courts of law; there, notably as counsels for already doomed political offenders, they played puppet and therefore futile roles that proved demoralizing to many of them.[74] On top of all this, the lawyers could no longer count on receiving their usual high incomes. Although some continued to charge and collect large fees, many complained that their earnings were declining — doubtless the result of disruptions caused by military service and the general difficulties of the times.[75]

And finally, there were the medical doctors. It can be demonstrated that their new-member representation in the NSDAP, which stood at 1 percent in 1937, fell sharply to about half that by 1939 and slightly decreased therafter (figure 6). This indicates that despite a continued overrepresentation in the party, the doctors' enthusiasm for the regime declined when the war broke out and continued to lessen as it progressed.

Although physicians were sorely needed at home—all the more so since the removal of their Jewish colleagues had unduly depleted their ranks—they were conscripted more heavily for active front-line duty than all the other professional groups. Generally, the younger a physician was, the higher was the likelihood of his being called to the colors, although provisions were made to ensure that medical students would have a chance to complete their medical course on furlough or special leaves of absence. In all, anywhere from 40 to 60 percent of the Reich's male doctors were at the fronts from 1939 to 1942, and after Stalingrad in early 1943 the percentage increased. After 1940, moreover, it became more and more difficult for a doctor in uniform to leave the front, even to give emergency assistance to the civilian population at home.[76]

The massive deployment of formerly civilian physicians for war purposes led to a change in the social role as well as in the self-image of doctors in Germany. One of the first visible manifestations of this metamorphosis was negative: a chronic understaffing of the civilian sector with competent doctors, an enormously increased medical workload for those at home, a predominance of older physicians (who worked less efficiently), and, stemming from all this, a decline in medical standards. Over the war years, German civilians increasingly complained that doctors worked sloppily and without care, that they followed a system of preference for patients of long standing, and that they overindulged in alcohol or hard drugs to help them through the day. Some physicians were said to be ailing and incapacitated as a result of either old age or front-line injuries and hence not to be fit to carry out their duties. Others were reported to have taken sexual advantage of their female patients. Preposterous situations were not uncommon: in 1940 there was only one ophthalmologist in an Upper Bavarian area inhabited by 150,000 people; in 1944 the kindergartens in Westphalia lacked medical care almost entirely, and among the miners in the Ruhr wrong diagnoses often were made by overtired doctors. Throughout the country the number of miscarriages was increasing, particularly among the hard-working peasant women.[77]

No doubt military staff physicians were shattered by the conditions they saw when they went home on furlough. More important, the medical profession's entrenched conception of itself as an oligarchic, male-dominated clique with monopolistic powers over life and death was destroyed when growing numbers of female doctors were allowed, even coaxed, to practice medicine and fill in for the missing male doctors. For although at the beginning of the regime Nazi ideology had censured female physicians (a practice in line with the misogynist sentiments of male medical students during the Weimar Republic), this policy was modified in the mid-thirties and was eventually totally reversed at the outbreak of war in 1939. At the height of the conflict, not only were there Hitler Youth, Red Cross, NSV, and other party-related female doctors in the service, but by September 1944 women doctors with children were also being called upon to resume their professional duties.[78]

Gradually, the priorities of war and the requirements of a regimented society imposed restrictions on the physician's freedom, limited his traditional prerogatives (a combination of large income and high prestige), exposed him to extreme physical and mental suffering while in combat, and eventually began to redefine the Hippocratic norms to conform to the regime's ultimate goals. When not enduring the hardships of the front, as he did most of the time, the average German doctor, already controlled by such state agencies as the Reichsärztekammer (Reich Physicians' Chamber), was drafted into additional service for the party or for one of its adjunct organizations such as the NSV. His professional mobility was hampered by an increasing shortage of drugs and materials like insulin, as well as by special curfews prohibiting practice, as, for instance, during air raids in major cities (in January 1945). In 1942 legislation by decree took away age-old privileges never before inveighed against by the state: in May of that year every doctor was forbidden to change his profession without prior consent from the authorities, and in December Hitler interfered in the private relationship between doctor and patient by rescinding the doctor's commitment to secrecy regarding his patient's health. The Nazi movement, it appeared, was in the process of destroying privileges that German doctors had enjoyed for centuries and that in quieter times the Nazi regime itself had purported to back. In November 1943 one observer of the medical profession, after a meeting with the famous surgeon Ferdinand Sauerbruch, remarked, not without justification: "Actually the big doctors and surgeons, like Sauerbruch, are the only people who enjoy a certain amount of freedom. No one can afford to mistreat them."[79]

Through two important processes the old image of the German physician had been changed and reshaped by the end of the war. First, although university students continued to turn to medicine as one of the more popular disciplines, they also tended right from the beginning of the war to extend their studies for as long a time as possible in order to avoid the exorbitant demands of a civilian job or, worse still, the rigors of the front. This attitude on the part of some, if not all, of the young medical students detracted from the quality of the profession as a calling.[80] Second, would-be trainees who were interested in a medical vocation were given a wider choice of opportunities than ever before, provided they committed themselves to becoming career physicians in paramilitary formations such as the SS, where the crassest personal ambitions could be more easily realized than anywhere else, or in the armed forces, which could offer special privileges and fast promotions. As a result, potential recruits took an interest in medicine for careerist reasons alone. In the absence of immediate material rewards that would guarantee a high civilian standard of living, egotistical considerations supplanted the desire to help people in distress. Medicine had become a technical instrument toward the attainment of personal influence and, in some cases, political power.[81]

The combination of these phenomena led to a perversion of the Hippocratic ideal of saving human lives—led to a state of *l'art pour l'art* where medical experimentation might be carried out for the sake of scientific inquiry without due regard for humanity. At the height of the war the doctors who subscribed to this view (still a comparatively small group) were to be found in the army, the Luftwaffe, and especially the SS. Beyond this perversion an extreme form of medical practice developed that totally inverted the doctor's original aim to save life. Motivated perhaps by sadism or the determination to destroy, or perhaps merely by career-mindedness and the clamor for personal power over life and death, German physicians acted as henchmen to the racist-eugenic ends of the dictatorship, killing and torturing in euthanasia centers, prisons, and concentration camps. In the words of a Polish psychologist who watched them at close range in Auschwitz, they "infringed the basic rules of medical and human ethics"; for them "the sick prisoner was a defective specimen of the labor force or experimental material." In this fashion, the once untarnished reputation of German medicine was debased and finally destroyed. A new and idealistic generation of physicians would be needed to rebuild a profession that by 1945 had sunk into total disrepute.[82]

The image of decline presented in early 1945 by the doctors, a group that had suffered from progressive stages of deprofessionalization, symbolizes the decline experienced by the whole National Socialist German Workers' Party. The disastrous outcome of the war, of course, determined the fate of Adolf Hitler and of the Third Reich, as well as of the party. Before committing suicide on April 30, 1945, the Führer declared Martin Bormann to be the de jure head of the NSDAP. This former aide to Rudolf Hess, who had never been allowed to succeed Hess officially, was at last given the satisfaction of witnessing the expulsion of his most hated rival, SS Chief Heinrich Himmler, from the Nazi movement and of seeing Himmler replaced by Karl Hanke, a Nazi Gauleiter and Bormann's nominal subordinate within the party hierarchy. But the triumph was short-lived. Bormann died during his attempt to escape from Berlin, and the Allied victors placed the party at the top of their list of six Nazi organizations that should be indicted and tried at Nuremberg for crimes against humanity.

6

SOCIAL PROFILE
OF THE RANK AND FILE
1919-1945

In chapters 1-5 the social profile of the Nazi Party has been analyzed primarily in terms of the two variables of class (as indicated by occupational subgroup) and region. But the sociography of the NSDAP between 1919 and 1945 would not be complete without a discussion of two additional variables: age and sex. Several questions arise in relation to these two variables. First, age: Was the NSDAP really a relatively youthful party during its Time of Struggle? What happened to its age structure during the Third Reich? Second, the role of women in the NSDAP: Although this subject has not been seriously explored, certain planks in the early Nazi Program suggested that the misogynist party would look down on women in its ranks; but did the attitude toward women in the general membership change when—especially after 1939—a majority of the men were drafted? And third, both age and sex: Did these two variables interact at certain times, and if so, how did this affect the party structure?

After these questions have been considered, the social features of the party's rank and file between 1919 and 1945 will be summarized by integrating the key information on all four variables—class, region, age, and sex.

THE AGE FACTOR

From its inception in 1919 the DAP/NSDAP purposely directed much of its propaganda toward the youth sector of German society. During the Time of Struggle (1919-1932) the NSDAP was a blatantly youthful party, as both contemporaries and post-1945 critics of the Nazi movement have observed.[1] It is now possible, through the use of fresh empirical data, to reconstruct the average age patterns of National Socialists fairly accurately.

The age of party members has been examined in a variety of ways. For regionally or nationally defined groups of established Nazi members or party newcomers in any given year or time period, average (mean) ages were computed if the year of birth for each of these members was known. In addition, age groups or cohorts could be identified for either members or joiners, in order to facilitate as direct comparisons as possible with similarly defined age cohorts in the Reich population. Although age values pertaining to joiners and those pertaining to established members are not statistically compatible, joiners' figures may, if viewed consistently over time, allow inferences as to the average age of all established Nazis in any given year.[2]

The men who founded the DAP in 1919 were in their early thirties: the average age of Nazi party comrades was about 33. In 1920 the average age of the total membership increased slightly to nearly 34, but afterward it began to fall. By August 1921 the gradual influx of very young joiners (men in their early twenties) had reduced the average age of all party members to about 32.[3] This trend continued until just before the Putsch of November 1923, when the mean age of party newcomers had fallen to just over 27. At that time, about 47 percent of all joiners were 23 or under.[4] After Hitler's reestablishment of the party in February 1925, he insisted that new comrades be at least 18 years old, and as a result the mean age of new party members for the Reich rose in that year, hovering around 29.[5] By contrast, for the highly industrialized areas of the Ruhr, where many skilled laborers were attracted by the party's intermittent "leftist" propaganda, the average age of new members was considerably lower: 23 in Mülheim/Ruhr and 22 in Langerfeld.[6] In Essen in early 1926 the average age for the party chapter, then 411 members strong, was 25.[7] Conversely, members tended to be older in those regions that were less industrialized but had a solid commercial core that traded with a productive rural hinterland. Thus in Brunswick the average age of joiners in 1925-26 was just under 33.[8]

Just as the membership of the Nazi party has been compared in previous chapters with the Reich population in terms of social class and occupation, so its age structure can be compared with that of the Reich population. In order to do this for the Time of Struggle, the age distribution of the German population, based on five age groups (18-29, 30-39, 40-49, 50-59, and 60 and over), has been considered the norm, and the percentage share of each of these age groups among newcomers to the party has been plotted in figure 7 for the years 1925 to 1932 as greater (+) or smaller (−) than that of the corresponding age group in the Reich population. Judging by new party joiners in any given year, the percentage share of the youngest group (18-29) is always much greater in the NSDAP than in the German population, while for the older groups the percentage share is generally less. Consequently, throughout the 1925-1932 period the party was much more youthful than the Reich population. The tendency toward youth increased appreciably between 1925 and 1927, but after 1927 the membership age began to move somewhat away from youth toward maturity, as seen by the generally declining percentage for the youngest group and the generally increasing percentages for most of the other age groups. In 1930, for the first time, the percentage of joiners in the second age group (30-39) exceeded the percentage of the same age group in the Reich population.

This national trend is duplicated by the data relating to the average age of party members (or joiners) in specific regions during the same time period (1925-1932). For example, between 1925 and 1928 the average age of joiners in Thuringia was 30, and in Greater Bochum (as well as in the entire Reich) it was 29.[9] Then between 1930 and 1932 a noticeable increase in average age occurred, probably because the party was appealing to the upper layers of society, whose members were generally older. The average age of party joiners jumped from somewhat over 30 in 1930 to almost 32 in 1932.[10] By May 1932 the mean age of the total NSDAP membership in the small North German town of Eutin was close to 35. On a national basis, over the entire 1925-1932 period the average age of joiners was just over 31.[11]

One explanation for the preponderance of youthful members in the NSDAP between 1925 and 1932 is demographic. There were more men and women between 18 and 29 in the German population during this period than in the period immediately before or immediately after. The oldest Nazi party recruits in the 18-29 age cohort would have been born in 1896, and the youngest in 1914. As Carl Mierendorff remarked in 1930, the NSDAP had its greatest attraction for members of the generation born between 1905 and 1912 — roughly the same age cohort.[12] According to demographic studies, the 1900-1914 generation in Germany was unusually large in the 1920s and early 1930s, partly because it had not been decimated by World War I and partly because its ranks were swelled by an influx of youthful German remigrants after the treaties of Versailles and St. Germain (1919). Hence, whereas in 1910 the 20–30 age cohort had accounted for 16.4

percent of the total population, by 1925 it accounted for 18.3 percent.[13]

The demographic factor, however, does not explain why the most youthful cohort (18-29) was consistently overrepresented in the party (figure 7). Contemporary and modern theories that have linked this phenomenon with the German youth movement of the 1920s are not convincing, since the Nazi party differed decisively from the predominantly bourgeois youth groups. For one thing, the youth groups were much younger: their upper age limit was in general only slightly above the Nazis' lower age limit of 18. And the two most important characteristics of the youth movement — introspection and the aim of sociocultural regeneration — were conspicuously absent from the Nazi movement. Instead, the Nazis valued politically motivated activism and a sense of realism and materialism, which were manifested in their special conceptions of education and training, occupational careers, and social progress.[14]

An old but still valid interpretation of the youth phenomenon in Nazism holds that the NSDAP, an overtly radical party, was able to absorb many of those youthful elements in German society that were thirsting for action and were disappointed by the complacency of the staid established parties. Among these the SPD was the most complacent. By the late 1920s it had reached a high level of physical and mental stagnation that — in combination with the high average ages of members and functionaries — was identified by many critics such as Robert Michels as the cause of its "embourgeoisement," a process that had begun before 1914.[15] As the SPD's age structure showed a marked bias toward middle and old age and a corresponding lack of youth, it compared especially unfavorably with that of the NSDAP.[16] A regional sample (membership statistics from the Saxon district of Oschatz-Grimma for the spring of 1931) indicates that the 18-30 age cohort was approximately three times as strong in the local Nazi chapter as in the local SPD chapter; for the age group 50 and over, however, the Nazi cohort was only one-third as strong as the corresponding group in the Social Democratic Party.[17]

In the late years of the Weimer Republic, after issues had become polarized, the radical KPD was the only political party that was in any way comparable in age structure to the NSDAP. Although members aged 50 and over seem to have been rare in both parties, the 30-49 age cohort was more heavily represented in the KPD than in the NSDAP, with the 18-29 cohort much less prominent. Doubtless this was because of the KPD's ideological tradition, harking back to the nineteenth century, to which the more mature Communist comrades could readily relate; the "revolutionary" Nazi leadership's advocacy of a complete rupture with Germany's bourgeois and monarchic past,[18] on the other hand, made its most lasting impact on a youth cohort bent on making radical changes through a chimerical "Third Reich."[19]

As for the overall pattern (all age groups) of the Nazi party membership during the period from 1919 to 1933, an outstanding question still remains to be answered: Why did the average age of Nazi recruits vary so much throughout the Time of Struggle? Why did it steadily decrease from 1925 until it reached a low point in 1927, and then increase sharply until 1929; and why, after that, did it increase less sharply till 1931, but then again more sharply till the end of 1932? The obvious answer to the last part of this multiple question is that the number of mature upper-middle-class newcomers increased toward the end of the Republic. What remains puzzling, however, is the relative prominence of the youngest Nazi party joiner cohort up to 1927 and its decline thereafter (figure 7).

One could assume, as Peter Loewenberg has done, that the 18-29 age cohort, too young to participate in World War I but by no means untouched by the traumatic side effects of the conflict, swelled the ranks of the Nazi party after its reestablishment early in 1925.[20] But then why did this development reach a climax toward the end of 1927? Obviously, these youthful party recruits were younger than the World War I veterans who are often said to have predominated in the membership at that time, most of whom would have been in their thirties.[21] University students, it is true, would generally have been in the right age cohort, but there were not enough of them to cause the expansion of this cohort that is indicated by figure 7. Besides, the university students did not start to join the party in significant numbers until 1928.[22] Nor is much light shed on the question by the various unsubstantiated and superficial economic explanations that have been put forward. For instance, a recent suggestion that youth flocked to the party because "younger Germans did not share proportionately in the economic prosperity of 1927 [and] it is probable that the high unemployment rates contained a disproportionately large percentage of young people" overlooks the fact that the 1925-1927 time span was not a period of high unemployment, and, further, that for the years when unemployment was severe — that is, after 1927 — the pattern plotted in figure 7 implies just the opposite effect — that youth did not join the party with such frequency.[23]

The likelihood of a close relationship between economic factors (the depression) and radical-right party membership during the last half of the Weimar Republic appears to be strengthened by the fact that among the Nazi joiners the youngest age cohort (18-29, figure 7) contained a significant number of unskilled laborers. (In the Berlin Document Center sample, these laborers were one of the youngest occupational subgroups that joined the party between 1925 and 1933).[24] But although it is generally true that during the depression the youngest were the hardest hit and that the young unskilled laborers were the hardest hit of all,[25] it is also true that the curve of the youngest cohort in figure 7 declined from 1927 to 1932. Evidently young industrial laborers showed comparatively little interest in the Nazi party at that time of great economic stress. Hence the depression as the exclusive explanatory factor in the rise of Nazism after 1928 is put in doubt.[26]

Still another fact, one having to do with the white-collar workers (clerks), seems to contradict the theory of the economic motivation of Nazi recruits. If the familiar statement is accepted that among the clerks who were threatened by economic displacement between 1925 and 1933, the older (those over 35) were worse off than the younger because they were more likely to be fired — a formula that is the reverse of the one applied to industrial laborers — a relatively high average age might be expected for those clerks who chose to join the NSDAP in that period.[27] But in actuality the mean age of the white-collar recruits in the sample was just under 29 — very low indeed, and only slightly higher than that of the industrialized unskilled laborers.[28] It appears, therefore, that the depression was not a strong enough force to prompt the older clerks to exchange their political loyalties to the DNVP (through their professional association, the DHV) for a pact with Nazism, at least in terms of membership. As Hans Speier has shown, it was the young rank-and-file adherents of the DHV who eventually became notorious for their criticism of the association's leaders and who by 1930 began to switch to the NSDAP. In that year, the Nazi leadership itself estimated that three-quarters of all young DHV members were Nazis, so that in 1931, in the words of Gordon A. Craig, "the DHV had become an adjunct of the NSDAP."[29]

This empirical examination of the age pattern of party joiners before 1933 has done little more than validate the known fact that the Nazi rank and file were younger than the members of all the other political parties except the KPD. A breakdown of the sample into different age cohorts displays variations in strength over time — variations that in themselves are interesting but without further analysis cannot be significantly linked to any known socioeconomic circumstances.

During the Third Reich (1933–1945) the NSDAP gradually

transformed itself from an evolutionary (if not a revolutionary) movement into a monopolistic state party. This process of quasi-institutionalization resembles the development of modern religious sects, or of modern bourgeois political parties, which, once established, begin to lose their original vigor and youthfulness and become conservative, complacent, and lethargic as the membership core grows older. In the case of National Socialism, despite several attempts by the Nazi leadership to regenerate the party through infusions of new blood, the average age of members increased from the low thirties in 1932–33 to the middle and late forties in 1942–43.[30] Statistically, this means that for the entire life of the Third Reich the party's average age remained almost static relative to the age of the regime. Judged by its age factor, the party stagnated: it was as if the old, tired cohorts were unwilling to make room for young and eager joiners.

Actually, of course, some exchange of old for young was taking place. What was lacking, however, was a consistent influx of young members, matched by a corresponding withdrawal of old members. Moreover, after 1939 the war absorbed not only a greater number of young people who were potential party comrade fledglings but also comparatively more of the young men who had already joined the NSDAP. The final consequence of these phenomena in 1944-45 was an acute leadership crisis, one that appeared impossible to solve.[31]

A careful interpretation of the figures contained in the official *Partei-Statistik* for 1934, early in the Third Reich, suggests that the party was still youthful.[32] Among the total party membership the 18-30 age group was overrepresented by 6.5 percent, the 31-40 group by 5.9 percent, and the 41-50 group by 2.5 percent; the 51-60 cohort, however, was underrepresented by 3.3 percent and the 61-and-over group by 11.6 percent.[33] But a regional sample of established party comrades from Tyrlaching and Tittmoning in Upper Bavaria, dated July 1, 1935, shows the relatively high average age of about 41.[34] During the same period the mean ages of two other closed political groups whose common denominator was Communism were considerably lower. One group, 283 concentration camp inmates near Eutin, had an average age of between 34 and 35 in 1933, and 331 resistance fighters (who were destined to suffer violent deaths during the Third Reich) had an average age of just under 35 in 1935 — clear indications that at the beginning of Hitler's regime the (illegal) KPD was continuing to attract youthful activists.[35]

By 1940 the NSDAP had matured noticeably. The average age of 1,118 established party members in and around Frankfurt was just over 47. It is interesting, however, that two years later the average age of 635 Nazis in the Reich who had served the party beyond the call of duty was still 47,[36] even though by that time the Reich average for the party was closer to 49. Probably the reason was that this group's party activities included such chores as cleaning up bombed areas after enemy raids, which required strenuous physical effort.

When the party membership rolls were opened to every adult in Germany, as was the case in 1933, 1937, 1939-1942, and to a more limited extent in 1935-36, the NSDAP acquired an overrepresentation of new members between the ages of 30 and 59 (figure 8), which would account for the trend toward middle age. In all those years the newcomer cohorts aged 30-39 and 40-49 were distinctly overrepresented. The first year of open candidature (1933) was exceptional in that the flow of the youngest group (18-29) into the NSDAP was well above the Reich average for that group, even though it was decisively below the 1932 level (figure 8). Not surprisingly, it was during the periods of general closure of membership rolls—in 1934, 1938, and after February 1942—that the youngest group of joiners was heavily overrepresented in the party. Then older applicants were barred from entrance and the younger candidates were encouraged, if not forced, to join.

The party's pressure on the youngest cohort mounted considerably after 1941.[37] In the Hitler Youth, membership for boys and girls up to and including the age of 18 had virtually become compulsory after March 1939. Henceforth, there was more pressure on HJ graduates— those who had reached the age of 18 or 19—to join the NSDAP, although outright force was now as sparingly applied as before March 1939.[38] But as early as 1934-35 party leaders had realized that younger NSDAP recruits would have to be sought out, and in 1937 Hess had expressly stated that during the new membership drive "younger comrades" would have to be actively wooed.[39]

By then it was clear that the state party should be a leadership cadre staffed exclusively by seasoned Hitler Youth veterans. The party was not to exceed 10 percent of the Reich population, a figure in line with the elite concept that had first been mentioned by party strategists in 1935.[40] The leaders of the regime became increasingly aware, however, that even this comparatively low percentage could not be reached on a voluntary basis and, further, that the very young (after 1938 mainly Hitler Youth leavers) were not joining the NSDAP with great enthusiasm. Resolute measures were adopted to correct these conditions. In the fall of 1941 when the general membership rolls were still open, party headquarters directed the Hitler Youth to increase its quota of HJ boys earmarked for party membership from 20 to 30 percent, in addition to the 5 percent quota for HJ girls. On February 2, 1942, when the rolls were closed finally for most Germans, the party began to depend principally on volunteers from the Hitler Youth, and in the spring of 1943 the HJ's quota of girls was stepped up to 7 percent. Moreover, the joining date for all HJ party recruits was changed from late September to April 20, the Führer's birthday. In 1944 the induction date was pushed up even further to February 27, and in addition Hitler ordered that members of the Hitler Youth who had reached the age of 17 should also be included on the new party rosters. Hitler planned that after the war only HJ members, soldiers of exceptional distinction, and selected members of NSDAP ancillary organizations up to the age of 36 should be permitted to join his "elitist" party. The NSDAP was not only to be youthful, it was also to be ideologically safe. Still, there is no hard and fast evidence, even for the final phase of party rule, that any HJ member was either compelled to join the party or conscripted automatically, although there can be no doubt that for promising Hitler Youth members the pressures were severe.[41]

The preferential treatment received by 18-year-old and sometimes 17-year-old recruits during certain years is evident in the overrepresentation of the youngest cohort in those years (1934, 1938, 1942-1944 — see figure 8). Yet despite such manipulation of the age structure of the party, it was not as a whole getting any younger, nor could it achieve its goal of a fixed, low average level. One crucial obstacle to this attainment was the disproportionate loss of younger lives in the war. A confidential Nazi report prepared in the spring of 1943 suggests that out of approximately six and a half million male party members sent to the military fronts, those under 38 years of age were the ones sent to the front lines. Not surprisingly, they also sustained the highest number of casualties.[42] These facts imply that, from 1939 to early 1943, the younger the party conscripts were, the greater were their chances of being killed or captured at the fronts; and, as a corollary, the greater the number of young party members the regime sent out to fight, the greater was the likelihood of the party's early senescence and consequently of the premature weakening of its social fabric.

This situation posed a special threat to the party's leadership capability. The 18-30 age cohort, which in 1934-35 was still overrepresented in the NSDAP at large, seemed only a few years later to be taking little interest in leadership challenges.[43] For example, in 1938 the youngest cohort was seriously underrepresented in classes at the party's five leadership centers (*Gauschulungsburgen*) at Dessau,

Schwerin, Seeburg, Düsseldorf, and Zenkau.[44] And during the war this group's interest in leadership fell even further as more and more of its members died at the front. By September 1943 Party Treasurer Schwarz admitted that it might become necessary to use the functionaries of the BDM (Bund Deutscher Mädel—League of German Girls) in positions of responsibility.[45] In this manner the traditional male—supremacist position of the NSDAP leadership cadre was seriously threatened by structural problems, problems that were as much a consequence of the war as of the party's unpopularity with the German people at the nadir of the Third Reich.

WOMEN IN THE NAZI PARTY

In the 1930s the young Social Democratic firebrand Carl Mierendorff remarked that women played "no significant role" in the Nazi party.[46] Usually the conspicuous absence of women from the NSDAP has been traced to a combination of misogyny on the part of the NSDAP leadership and a corresponding, seemingly natural, desire by women to abstain from participation in Nazi politics. The *männerbündische*, male-supremicist attitude among the Nazis, which always bordered on the homoerotic, originated to no small degree in Adolf Hitler himself, but it was also evidenced by Alfred Rosenberg, Hermann Esser, and other early party paladins.This sexist, militaristic sentiment was epitomized in Hitler's statements, made in *Mein Kampf*, that women were essentially breeding material for future warriors, and that their place was to be in the home, by the hearth and with the children, strictly subordinate to the male head of the household.[47] As early as January 1921 women were excluded from party leadership positions; and as late as August 1927, during a party rally in Nuremberg, although women and girls were allowed to join the SA parade in Nazi attire, they were prohibited from passing by the grandstand to salute their Führer.[48] In the subsequent history of the party, issues of political import remained a male preserve, at least according to the laws laid down by the party hierarchy. During the party rally of 1938 Deputy Führer Hess exhorted his followers: "In conversation with your wives, speak only of those matters which have been expressly marked for public distribution." Six months later, local Nazi leaders in East Prussia were reminded that "one does not chatter with women about politics; women must take care of their looks, politics is our business."[49]

Although after 1919 women constituted slightly more than half of the total German population, they were always vastly underrepresented in the Nazi party. Not until the very last years of the Third Reich did that situation begin to change. The empirical data do not permit a precise judgment with regard to the percentage of women in the NSDAP throughout the Reich in any given year, but it is possible to give approximate indications, based on local and regional figures. In the party's founding period from 1919 to 1923 the women party comrade share appears to have been close to 10 percent initially, but later it fell off to about half that value. Various national samples exhibit values of nearly 9 percent for women joiners in 1919, 12 percent in 1920, about 10 percent in 1921, and not quite 9 percent in 1922. On the regional level, a sample of established Munich members in January 1920 shows 10.5 percent women, and a more substantial membership list from Munich covering January 1920 to August 1921, analyzed by Donald M. Douglas, produces the exceptionally high value of nearly 14 percent. As for Cologne, by April 27, 1922, the established NSDAP chapter included fifty male and six female comrades, or almost 11 percent women.[50] The party records are often too sketchy to permit a reliable interpretation even on the local level; for Göttingen the party history reads: "In March 1922 Göttingen had become an outpost [*Stützpunkt*], in May of that year a chapter [*Ortsgruppe*] of the NSDAP . . . Among the first twelve members of the chapter there also was a woman, and when in November of that year the membership had grown to twenty-five, even more women belonged to the party."[51]

It appears that after 1921 women's interest in Nazi party matters declined sharply. A sample of 505 established members in Ingolstadt (Lower Bavaria) and its rural hinterland in 1922-23 yielded only 32 women, or just over 6 percent; and a sample of 4,726 Germans throughout the Reich (but mainly in South Germany) who joined the party between the end of September and the beginning of November 1923 showed only 4 to 5 percent women.[52] These figures, of course, are well below Douglas's 14 percent for 1920-21. One possible reason for this decline was the dawning awareness that the NSDAP was dominated by male values, a fact that became obvious after the creation of the paramilitary SA in the summer of 1921 and the party's increasing collaboration with the male-dominated combat leagues (*Wehrverbände*). The abortive Putsch of November 1923 was a partial consequence of these developments.[53]

When the party was being reestablished in early 1925 on a national scale, women again joined up; but the percentages varied from place to place, hardly anywhere exceeding the relatively high values of the founding phase. The reasons for the variations remain puzzling. One could speculate that the low value of 2.5 percent female membership for Essen (February 1926), or of 4.7 percent for Greater Bochum (1925-1928), may have been due to the largely proletarian nature of the population; yet this supposition is dubious because the value for Barmen, also in the Ruhr and only slightly less industrialized than Essen or Bochum, was very much higher, 13.3 percent in April 1925.[54] Speculations about variations between areas outside the Ruhr are equally doubtful: in North German Brunswick in 1925-26 women accounted for only about 3 percent of the founding members of the chapter, while at roughly the same time in nearby Hamburg they constituted close to 11 percent. For a more easterly region, Thuringia, from 1925 to 1928, the value appears to have been somewhere between these two figures, or about 5 percent.[55] A total membership count for Starnberg in Upper Bavaria undertaken by the regional Nazi leader Franz Buchner in July 1927 resulted in the unusually high value of over 18 percent women.[56] But other samples of joiners between 1925 and 1929 once more exhibit a distinct trend away from women's involvement in Nazi party politics, as shown by the following percentages of women: 8 percent in 1925, 5 percent in 1926, 4 percent in 1927, 4 percent in 1928, and 4 percent in 1929.[57] It seems likely that 1928-29 marked a low point in women's involvement in the party and that from then until Hitler's assumption of power they again turned to the party in greater strength. This is suggested not only by fairly high figures for women's memberships in random localities, such as Deutsch-Krone and Klausdorf (9 percent on May 28, 1931) and Eutin (almost 14 percent in May 1932), but also by figures of a more national character supplied by NSDAP statisticians. These experts calculated the women's share in the party membership to have been 5.9 percent from 1925 to September 13, 1930, and 7.8 percent on January 29, 1933.[58] There were at least three reasons for the increasing numbers of women in the party toward the end of the Republic. The NSDAP leadership's new and higher estimation of women as potential voters made them more interested in membership; the vigorous attempts made by women activists in the party to broaden the women's organizational base resulted in the growth of women's ancillary institutions; and finally, more and more upper-middle-class and aristocratic women joined the party, forming an educated and eloquent vanguard that attracted other women from all walks of life.

From the inception of the NSDAP, the age of women party members differed significantly from men's. The women were generally older. In Douglas's Munich sample for January 1920 male party comrades averaged just over 33 years of age and females nearly 36. By

August 1921 the discrepancy had widened somewhat: men averaged 32 as against the women's 36.[59] Among a group of 4,416 newcomers to the NSDAP in autumn 1923, the mean age of the men was 27.5 as opposed to 28.4 for the women. In that group, almost 48 percent of the males but only about 40 percent of the females were 23 or younger.[60]

This pattern persisted after the renaissance of the party early in 1925. In the Bochum sample the women were 3.2 years older than the men, in the Brunswick group 12.5 years, in the Hamburg chapter 5.2 years, and in Thuringia 5.7 years.[61] In Eutin in May 1932 the average age of the women was 5.0 years higher than the average of both men and women in the chapter (34.8 years).[62]

As one explanation for the age difference between Nazi men and women during the years before 1933, both contemporary and post-1945 critics have emphasized the dearth of marriageable young males during the 1920s which caused a surplus of marriageable women in the early 1920s.[63] According to the census of 1925, it was among the 30-34 age cohort that a surplus of marriageable women appeared; and women between 35 and 80 fared even worse: for every available male there were nearly two unmarried females.[64] The implication — supported by contemporary analysts — is that as unmarried women advanced in age, they were more likely to consider Nazi membership than (male) bachelors of comparable age.[65]

Between 1925 and 1932 women accounted for 7.8 percent of Nazi joiners; but in 1933, the first year of the Third Reich, their contribution dropped sharply to 5.1 percent (table 8). This decrease, matched of course by a comparable increase in the men's share, may be partly explained by the stronger tendency among men than among women to join the NSDAP for opportunistic reasons after January 1933. In addition, however, the party hierarchy decided in late 1934 that although in the past the overall share of women in the NSDAP had been 5.5 percent, in the future 5 percent would be a reasonable female recruitment quota.[66] From then on, the women newcomers' rate dropped, averaging only 4.4 percent for the two-year period ending in 1936 (table 8). In 1937, therefore, concerned party officials issued a special appeal to the lower ranks of functionaries who were about to begin the new membership drive: all "prejudices" were to be eliminated, and party membership was to be made attractive not only to certain occupational groups such as workers and farmers but also, and especially, "to the German woman."[67]

This ostensibly more tolerant attitude on the part of the Nazi regime was the result of the general labor shortage that was then threatening to disrupt the entire economy, and that led at first to greater job opportunities for women—a theme that has been sufficiently explored in the most recent critical literature.[68] Women who proved themselves capable of doing a job could also be of value to the NSDAP. By this logic many of the axiomatic Nazi tenets regarding the weaker sex were implicitly abrogated. Significantly, in 1937 the proportion of women newcomers to the party rose to 10 percent, almost double the 1933 value (table 8). In 1938 the proportion climbed even higher to 17.5 percent, with the majority of all joiners coming from the Hitler Youth. (The directives governing the recruitment of HJ veterans favored BDM members over civilian female applicants.)[69] The continuing high value of 16.5 percent for women joiners in 1939 can be explained as the result of a technicality in the membership rules. In that year many of the male applicants, having been hastily recruited for battle, were not allowed to become full members of the party because of their membership in the Wehrmacht; instead, they were to be admitted at a later date, perhaps after being reassigned to the home front. This technicality may also have been instrumental in further increasing the percentage of women during 1940-41, when, as in 1939, the membership rolls were opened to the general "Aryan" public.[70] The extremely high figure of 34.7 percent between 1942 and 1944 was due once again to the policy of coopted, if not forced, NSDAP membership for Hitler Youth: as of spring 1943, quotas for party candidature from the BDM were increased from 5 percent to 7 percent of all female HJ.[71] By the end of the war, the regime could not help noticing that the depletion of the male sector of German society was creating severe manpower and leadership problems and that basic functions of the regime could only be preserved by utilizing female talent in the economy, the professions, and even the party.[72]

The age gap between male and female NSDAP joiners began to narrow in 1933. From then on, whenever young cohorts were admitted to the party, the women tended to be even younger than the men. This condition obtained in 1934, 1938, and 1942 (figure 9).[73] Between 1937 and 1942, except for a slowdown in 1939, the representation of the youngest female newcomer group steadily increased over its male counterpart. Conversely, female representation declined vis-à-vis the males for all the medium and older age groups (figure 9).

It can be assumed, therefore, that from 1937 to 1942 and even to 1944 the average age of the female membership of the Nazi party was slowly falling. This conjecture, although difficult to document for the entire Reich, is supported by uneven data for 1939 and 1940 from the Frankfurt area. In 1939, in two out of three suburban Frankfurt party chapters, Berkersheim and Obermain, there were still more men than women under 30; only in the third, Riederwald, a decidedly pro-letarian district, was this ratio reversed.[74] But a year later in the greater Frankfurt region the men tended to be somewhat older than the women: among 1,118 party comrades the men's mean age was 47.5 and the women's 47.0.[75]

If women who were younger than men had continued to join the NSDAP beyond the expected Final Victory, the overall party structure would have changed in two significant ways. First, the progressive senescence so dreaded by the party leadership would have been ar-rested. Second, this would have been accomplished at the expense of male supremacy—a traditional hallmark of the NSDAP. Since any loss of male predominance in the Nazi movement would have been anathema to Hitler and his cronies, one cannot even imagine what the Nazi leadership would have done to escape from this new dilemma.

THE RANK AND FILE

What were the major features of the Nazi rank and file in each of the five periods into which its social history has been divided?

In the first period, 1919-1923, the social profile of the party was closely linked to its purpose as expressed in official speeches and the Nazi program: to achieve socioeconomic justice for Germans disadvantaged by the loss of World War I and to restore Germany to its former national grandeur. The party was successful initially in its appeal to the relatively young and, in fact, never lost its grip on the nation's youth. The earliest recruits were predominantly male—a characteristic that persisted throughout the Time of Struggle. In terms of occupational or class structure the party appealed originally to laborers in the birthplace of the DAP, the industrial core of the city of Munich. But party propaganda was not exclusively directed toward the working man; it was broad enough to attract representatives of the lower middle class and even of the elite. As the party grew and spread into the Munich hinterland, farmers and peasants, many of whom shared the value system of the lower middle class, were drawn to it. Yet the Nazis, especially after they began to break new ground in the northern and more industrialized regions of the country, continued to win over genuine members of the proletariat.

Although Hitler himself, by both upbringing and inclination, was primarily interested in the lower middle class (as well as what he chose to call the "workers"), he does not seem to have concentrated exclusively on the middle class in this earliest period in order to develop what Seymour Martin Lipset has described as an extremist political formation of the middle. Instead of that, he seems to have worked toward the creation of a "mass movement," with changing emphasis on different levels of society, as Albrecht Tyrell has more recently suggested.[76] As early as January 1922, for example, Hitler stated that he wanted "a *völkisch* movement built on a rigid social basis, encompassing the broadest masses."[77] Nevertheless, Hitler's own lower-middle-class background and leanings were evident in the phrasing of the party's program. From the beginning the NSDAP was in two senses a party of the lower middle class: this class was numerically larger than either of the other two layers, and it was consistently overrepresented in the party. This does not mean, of course, that the other two classes were unimportant. Members of the upper layers of society were also significantly overrepresented; and the workers, though underrepresented, made their presence strongly felt. Indeed, from 1919 to 1923 the Nazi party, far from being a perfect mirror image of the social profile of the nation, contained, albeit in varying proportions, elements of every important social segment in the country so that it potentially assumed an integrative function in German society. By the fall of 1923, it had even lost its exclusively urban quality: it was becoming better known in the countryside and was making progress outside Bavaria.

During the second period, 1924-1930, the NSDAP managed to retain its integrative potential in relation to all sections of society. But in this time of comparatively high economic stability—when only a few occupational groups, such as laid-off laborers and unemployed sales and technical clerks, were restive—the party did not attract those who felt especially alienated from society, with the possible exception of the university students and North German farmers. After the abortive coup of 1923, Hitler was obliged to broaden the mass appeal of his party in order to attain political power by legal means.[78] From then on, the Nazis more and more conceived of their party as a mass organization.[79]

Broadening the party's appeal meant not only paying greater attention in 1925-26 to the industrial proletariat in Germany's northwestern territories but also concentrating on such members of the lower middle class as the peasants. Although between 1927 and 1929 certain changes in emphasis were made in the propaganda, the lower classes were not overlooked by the Nazi leadership, nor were all members of the upper middle class and nobility courted.[80] The overriding principle seems to have been that the leadership would ingratiate itself with all segments of society simultaneously, making allowances for certain areas of concentration in special circumstances but not appealing to any one segment at the expense of another. Ideally, men (if not women) from all walks of life were to be accommodated.[81] Hence it is important not to overemphasize the degree of rational decision making within the party directorate, as some historians have done.[82] Nor is the theory of a rigid division in the party between "leftist" groups around Gregor Strasser and a "rightist" leadership core surrounding Hitler defensible. The lines of division were blurred.[83] Strasser, like his friend Karl Kaufmann, was not interested solely in the workers but, after 1925-26, forged important links between industrial circles and Hitler, and the Führer himself, before 1928, appealed directly to the workers.[84] Since Hitler's primary motivation was the urge for power, his strategy was as opportunistic as his tactics were improvisational: capitalizing on a local grievance here and a regional malcontent there, he worked to expand his party following in order to win elections at all governmental levels.

In the third period, 1930-1933, the Nazis not only continued to welcome representatives from all segments of society, thereby strengthening the party's integrative character, but were also quite successful in achieving their goal of organizing a mass movement. This mass base was evident in the absolute size of the membership, the extent of electoral support, and the increasing proportion of women joiners. By July 1932 the NSDAP, with over half a million members (figure 1), had become the largest party in the Reichstag.[85] There is general agreement on these facts, but two questions are still being asked about related issues. First, in what proportions were the classes represented within the party? Second, in what way, if at all, was this distribution a consequence of the economic hardships suffered by the German people during the last years of the Weimar Republic?

First, although the workers increased their share in the party, they were still underrepresented; the lower middle class, even though its share diminished somewhat, continued to be overrepresented, and the elite, which slightly increased its share, also continued to be overrepresented.

Second, it is difficult to judge the extent to which these class proportions were the result of economic disasters, particularly those of the Great Depression. Scholars have already produced evidence to show that certain Germans who felt socioeconomically threatened turned to the NSDAP rather than to one of the other political parties.[86] Indeed, on the surface the correlation seems obvious. In the Reichstag election of September 1930, when the depression was well under way, German voters increased the party's representation from

12 to 107 seats, and in July 1932, at the height of the economic crisis, they increased it further to 230 seats. But in the November elections of the same year, the national economy had improved slightly, and Nazi representation declined to 196 seats.[87] Furthermore, up to 1933, if the Nazi membership statistics published in 1935 are at all credible, the party joiners' curve vaguely patterned this voters' curve. Such conclusions, however, do not take into account the inaccuracy of the Nazi statistics resulting from the very erratic recording of member exits and reentries, a practice that concealed the party's growth in real numbers and made its membership bookkeeping for the whole Time of Struggle extremely unreliable.[88]

For proof of the interaction between socioeconomic hardship and rising membership in the party, it has been customary to cite the partisan behavior of farmers over the 1927-1932 period: as their (measurable) tribulations increased, so did their numbers in the NSDAP. The same can be observed for small-scale and intermediate businessmen and entrepreneurs, although they are not so easy to identify because of a potential confusion with salaried clerks.[89] Conversely, the magnates, who fared better during the depression, are known to have been more reticent about joining the NSDAP, a recognized protest movement.

Nevertheless, it is questionable whether economic factors bore the main responsibility for the growth of the NSDAP toward the end of the Republic. In one occupational group, the lower clerks, it was the younger clerks, those least affected by the depression, who were attracted to the NSDAP. And among the workers it was those living in country areas, where dislocations were least likely to occur, who joined the NSDAP in greatest strength (table 9). Moreover, in the period from 1930 to 1932 as opposed to that from 1925 to 1929 there was a general shift of NSDAP joiners away from the city and the small town to the country. This change, since all social classes contributed to it, militates against the economic motivation theory.[90] As for class representation in the party, the workers, who suffered most from the depression, continued to be underrepresented; the lower and upper middle classes, which suffered less, continued to be overrepresented.

These doubts regarding a close relationship between the economic effects of the depression and NSDAP growth are supported by an examination of the pattern of membership growth. Conventional wisdom has it that the party experienced its most rapid growth in the period between September 1930 and January 1933.[91] Yet, although the absolute figures tend to give that impression, the cumulative (compound) rate of growth in this last Weimar period was actually lower than it had been during the preceding period (1925-1930).[92]

In the light of these facts, the historian would do well to give special consideration to motives that were not directly related to depression-induced circumstances – for example, to the political disenchantment that prompted civil servants, especially those in the upper echelons, to listen to Hitler, and to the feeling of sociocultural alienation that after 1929 grew enormously among academically trained professionals. Some historians have already taken a new look at things. Some time ago Peter Loewenberg introduced his suggestive theory that post-World War I youth cohorts were predestined to become followers of Hitler for psychological reasons alone. More recently Peter H. Merkl has argued in favor of a thesis allowing for such motives as anti-Semitism, anti-Marxism, a high propensity for militarism and activism resulting from parental environment, and psychological phenomena like "traumas of war and defeat" and religious preferences. Significantly, all these variables may transcend the class barriers that are determined largely by economic criteria.[93] Although findings such as Merkl's do not yet constitute a substantial alternative to the theory of economic motivation, they do suggest that the social profile of the Nazi party before January 1933 cannot be explained entirely or even mainly in terms of socioeconomic frustrations.[94]

In the last two periods of Nazi social history, 1933-1939 and 1939-1945 (the regime phase, or Third Reich), the major features of the party were very closely related to both its growth and its class divisions. During the Third Reich Hitler and the leadership corps could never agree on the form that their monopolistic state party should take, that is, whether it should be an elite cadre with select membership or a mass organization built on a broad populist base. There are indications that in the early years of the regime Hitler entertained notions of building an elitist body; if so, that would account for the closing of the membership rolls between 1933 and 1937. Yet this closing order was never strictly enforced, and anyone who had influential friends could get into the party. Further, the motive for the reopening of membership in 1937 did not line up with elitist principles. By then, in all probability, the party needed money and hoped to raise it by attracting a greater number of Germans to its ranks, even while insisting on strict selection of the leadership corps. This contradictory policy in itself kept the NSDAP from becoming an exclusive party during the balance of the Nazi era.

Although the party was growing too large to be elitist, its pretensions in that direction raised doubts about its being a mass movement. In terms of absolute growth, its membership figures were impressive. Climbing from 849,009 in January 1933 to 2,493,890 in December 1934, the membership reached more than 5 million in 1939 and by early 1945 was past the 8 million mark (figure 1). Yet Hitler's goal of a party membership equal to 10 percent of the German population, which had been mentioned in 1935, had still not been reached by May 1943 (if one can believe Bormann), and may only have been approached by the end of the regime—though the figures for the final phase are very unreliable. This was the case in spite of the fact that membership was being increasingly opened to women.[95]

It can be argued that if the party had consistently followed a strategy of recruitment based on quality and had tightly restricted its numbers, the result would have been an oligarchic movement with elitist aspirations. In that case, the principle of voluntary membership by individual application, precluding external pressure, would have been the basis of recruitment. But the manner of induction that actually developed was based on both volition and coercion, combined in varying measures according to the time and circumstance. On the one hand, the political leadership always stressed the element of "choice"; on the other hand, it was implicit in the concept of a mass movement that every mature member of the public would join or be faced with social and political ostracism. True, it was technically impossible for a German citizen (man or woman) to be compelled to enter the party. Nevertheless, in any totalitarian system governed by a monopolistic state party, freedom of choice tends to approach obligation, obligation to approach pressure, and pressure to approach compulsion. And although the extremes of freedom of choice and compulsion can be easily defined, the intermediate positions are difficult to specify. In practice, the Janus-faced nature of the NSDAP as both an elitist party and a mass movement, based on a rationale of voluntary-obligatory candidature, complicated the everyday life of party members by presenting them with inherently paradoxical rulings. In November 1943, for example, a directive went out from a Kreisleiter in Frankfurt that ordered all local party comrades to participate in a planned party rally but emphasized the voluntary character of everyone's efforts.[96] Every party member knew, of course, that special party courts could enforce compliance with the NSDAP's demands, particularly in wartime, and that expulsion from the party—though rarely implemented—would mean political and social banishment.[97]

A Nazi party comrade who took his membership seriously and wished to avoid reprimand and retribution for slackness, apathy, or defiance had to conform to a pattern of behavior that required ever-greater service to the party as the war progressed. In return he could not expect to receive much, apart from an honorary party citation that did not even include a medal for his lapel. From November 1934 to November 1942, out of a probable membership of 7 million, only 508 comrades were fortunate enough to receive the Golden Party Badge, the highest and practically the only distinction bestowed by the party. In other words, only one of about 14,000 party members could hope to be singled out in this manner — a very poor prospect for ambitious Nazi followers.[98]

Party pressures may still have been comparatively light in the first two years of the war, but after 1941 they steadily increased. In the Speer era, when guns were becoming more important than butter, party members had to extend themselves beyond such customary activities as clothes collection and snow removal and to help rally the home front.[99] From 1942 on, a spate of directives, memoranda, and circulars multiplied the members' responsibilities, added task to task, and taxed the patience of ordinary party stalwarts to the breaking point. Required to be models of dedication and personal sacrifice, party comrades were called upon to put the good of the party and state before their private interests in constant day-and-night service. One of the last official duties assigned to them was the local organization and direction of the Volkssturm, the people's militia, whose purpose it was to hold out against invading enemy troops during the final hour at whatever cost.[100]

Yet it was not for this reason alone that the NSDAP became increasingly unpopular with its general membership. As the fortunes of war turned against Germany, the blame fell not on the Wehrmacht but on the Reich leadership core and the intermediate functionaries of the NSDAP, who were present everywhere on the home front. After the debacle of Stalingrad early in 1943, the popular appeal of the party sank to an unprecedented low, and every new adversity brought further disgrace. In 1943 party comrades began to hide their party badges, and by 1944 they were openly disclaiming membership. At that time the ban on general membership, which had been in effect since early 1942, saved the party leadership the embarrassment of having to witness the total dissolution of the voluntarist principle. Still, the fear of severe sanctions kept all but a handful of members from resigning from the party ranks.[101] Since influential and knowedgeable party leaders like Goebbels were fully aware of the leadership dilemma, particularly after 1943, there may be justification for characterizing the ensuing state of affairs as one in which the party, "as a political mass organization within the National Socialist regime, became almost devoid of political function."[102]

If this was the basic problem, it certainly cut across the lines of class division within the party, which continued to be dominated by the lower middle class.[103] The members of that class increased their share from 1932 to 1933 and thereafter maintained their high level, except for a slight decrease between 1941 and 1944 to a percentage close to that of 1930-1932.[104] Within the lower middle class the balance shifted among the five main occupational subgroups. The farmers, master craftsmen and merchants (shopkeepers), who were sometimes dissatisfied with National Socialist policy, were less conspicuous in the party ranks than the lower civil servants and lower employees (white-collar workers). The members of this last subgroup were exemplary followers of Hitler; in fact the white-collar worker of the lower middle class might be described as the typical Nazi. And during the Third Reich, as during the Weimar Republic, this class was consistently overrepresented in Hitler's party.[105]

The workers provide one of the few surprises of this study. Clearly underrepresented in the NSDAP from 1932 to 1933, they gained strength later, especially after the war began.[106] This suggests that the claims of antagonism between the National Socialist leadership and the proletariat have been vastly exaggerated. One crucial reason for the workers' growing acquiescence in Nazism was the personality of Adolf Hitler. As time went by, and especially during the war years, the workers found it increasingly easy to regard the Führer as one of them.

The relationship between the elite (upper middle class and former aristocracy) and the Nazi party is so puzzling and complex that it warrants special consideration. It is significant that the German social elite reacted with such enthusiasm to the establishment of the Third Reich that its newcomer strength in the party increased by about 50 percent from 1932 to 1933. After that, however, the percentage of new members decreased steadily, until by 1942 the upper layer's share of candidates approximately equaled its representation in the Reich.[107]

By tradition as well as temperament the NSDAP was anathema to the elite, just as the elite was suspect in the eyes of the party. Nevertheless, in the early years of the regime both sides consented to a temporary and rather precarious alliance. On the one hand, the elite, interested "in defending higher status and its perquisites against challenge from less privileged elements," supported the conservative and nationalistic aspects of the Nazi program in order to meet the threat both of Communism inside and beyond Germany's borders and of the rabble-rousing mob represented by the SA within the Nazi movement.[108] On the other hand, Hitler and his cohorts, while often venting their suspicions of the educated and propertied elite, were dependent upon that class to run the machinery of government, if not the party itself.[109]

The first of three major crises that were to shatter and finally destroy the uneasy understanding between the former ruling elite and the Nazi movement came in June 1934 — the so-called Röhm Purge.[110] Although many nationalistic hard-liners from the reactionary camp hailed the purge as a necessary act of vengeance against the despicably plebeian SA, the majority of the elite were repelled by the arbitrariness of the action and even more by the fact that members of their own class, such as General Kurt von Schleicher and General Kurt von Bredow, had been among its victims. The reaction of Count Lutz Schwerin von Krosigk, who was Finance Minister at the time, was typical. What appalled him was not that "Röhm and suspect figures like [SA leader] Heines in Silesia were removed as such . . . but *how* they were removed." Most members of the elite would have preferred a court trial by judge and jury even though such a court could have handed down the death sentence.[111]

From then on, the elite knew that rough times lay ahead. Local functionaries of the NSDAP proclaimed that the end would soon come for their long-standing rivals, the hated intellectuals. One recently appointed Nazi counselor of Berlin, Comrade Johannes Engel, stated in November 1934 that the "slimy bourgeoisie would have to watch out, the government officials of the future should be selected according to their Nazi ideological fortitude, not their professional expertise, and that for the old officials a "second June 30th" was in store, and then more heads would roll.[112]

Notwithstanding these threats, after the Röhm Purge the regime continued to rely on the former ruling class for the performance of functions in the military, governmental, industrial, and higher-education sectors of the Third Reich, as well as for the customary services offered by the classic academic professions. But as the elite's position in the nation became more difficult, their enthusiasm for the party waned.[113] A series of lesser events took place that served as portents of two greater tragedies to come. Shortly before his death early in 1935, the Bavarian Minister of Culture, Hans Schemm, a public school teacher and self-taught chemist, warned the mandarins, professionals, and academics who were allegedly trying to "infiltrate" National Socialism that their numbers were known and their names were on record.[114] On July 20, 1937, when the German resistance movement under the leadership of conservative members of the old privileged class was beginning to grow, Himmler decreed the final dissolution of the Masonic lodges, the mainstay of that class.[115] Then the campaign against the intellectuals was stepped up. On January 31, 1939, the *Berliner Tageblatt*, one of the bulwarks of educated circles all over the nation, was forced to suspend publication. A few months later the use of the term *Bildung*, which epitomized culture, etiquette, and higher education and applied exclusively to the upper classes, was seriously questioned in an officially sanctioned article that asked, "Has the term 'Bildung' any place in National Socialist thought, after all?" And in May 1939 the regime clamped down on the independent associations that had been founded by higher academics to organize advanced lectures for the educated. This last government measure nearly coincided with the decree ordering all 10- to 18-year-old sons and daughters of German citizens to enter the Hitler Youth, including those from privileged homes.[116]

The outbreak of war in the fall of 1939 brought on the second major calamity for the upper classes. Many of their members could applaud the early blitzkrieg victories, particularly those over Poland and France; but a conflict with England was viewed as folly, and to become involved in military action against Russia and the United States was considered by many to be a very grave political mistake. The military setbacks of 1943 proved those critics right. These setbacks, moreover, had been preceded by news about Nazi atrocities against the Poles, Russians, and Jews. And concurrently the resistance movement was continuing to grow. Although the motives of many members of the opposition to Hitler may be questioned on both moral and political grounds, the significant point is that his party was becoming more and more unpopular with the conservative elite.[117]

Probably no statistical device could measure the effects of the physical and psychological blows suffered by the elite after the abortive attempt on Hitler's life on July 20, 1944, nor could it gauge the resulting degree of alienation between the upper classes and the NSDAP. The failure of this attempt was the third and final catastrophe. It had already become obvious to many former patricians, or at least to their sons and daughters, that the party—despite its own chronic failures—was bent on replacing the administrative and military, and perhaps even the industrial, structure that bore the stamp of the traditional elites with new structures fashioned after the ideals of the Führer and his party. Had the loss of the war not prevented the implementation of such changes, planned for the period after the Final Victory, the shortage of suitable personnel to man the new structures of the regime might well have caused a crisis for the party. But inasmuch as Himmler had decided to found a new biologically selectable aristocracy, to be settled on the wide plains of Eastern Europe, strictly in accordance with Hitler's long-range goal to eliminate the German princely houses, plans to rid German society of its former ruling classes were on the books.[118]

The officer corps of the Wehrmacht most assuredly would have been neutralized after the Victory.[119] It was an integral part of the former ruling elite, and its representatives had played a significant and repugnant role in the assassination attempt of July 1944.[120] But there were still other considerations. The Wehrmacht had always been beyond the reach of the NSDAP despite certain attempts, made early in the regime by General Werner von Blomberg and General Walter von Reichenau, to Nazify it.[121] Not only had it been granted special status as one of the three pillars of the regime (the others being the NSDAP and the government), but it was able to suspend the party membership status of its enlisted men and officers for the duration of their service and to subject them to its own (rival) jurisdiction. The party functionaries' jealousy of the officer corps was as deeply ingrained as the officers' own contempt for those brown-uniformed party officials, who could never forget that Hitler's victory over Röhm in 1934 had also meant the triumph of the army over the SA.[122] Many officers may have been "fair-weather Nazis," as Hugh Trevor-Roper has called them; certainly many were totally apolitical. But it has also come to light that the army's complicity in specifically "Nazi" crimes, such as the ill treatment of Russian POWs, was much greater than had previously been believed.[123] Yet the army as an institution remained a potential haven for members of the former ruling class who wished to avoid any contact with the party after July 1944. To many it was an oasis of freedom in a landscape of unrelenting political pressure, a factor that helps to explain why many would-be academics preferred an active officer's career to one in the party or to a lengthy course of university studies.[124]

Another bulwark of the upper classes that would have been in great danger after a German victory was the established Christian Church, including both the Protestant and the Roman Catholic churches. In conformity with the party's more benevolent attitude toward the elite in the first phase of the regime, the government tried to demonstrate its good intentions toward both churches; the most impressive manifestation of this was the Concordat of July 1933 with the papacy. The regime's tactics did not necessarily mean that Hitler was serious in his endeavors, nor did it guarantee that the NSDAP would make peace with the Catholic and Protestant hierarchies. In fact, by about 1938, notwithstanding earlier promises and assurances on the part of the government, the "church struggle" between Nazism and the institutionalized Christian religion was well advanced, with Bormann acting as the chief henchman in the uneven battle. Whereas the organization of a Nazified Protestant church, the "German Christians," never came to fruition, the Confessional Church led by Pastor Martin Niemöller was subdued though not altogether suppressed. In the Catholic realm, Hitler used the arrangement with the Vatican to maintain a formal state of peace with the papacy while simultaneously transporting thousands of lower clergy to concentration camps. The involvement of individual church leaders in the events of July 1944, including Dr. Dietrich Bonhoeffer and Dr. Eugen Gerstenmaier on the Protestant side and Father Alfred Delp on the Catholic side, highlighted the degree of interrelationship between the upper classes and the Christian institutions, as well as their mutual rejection of National Socialism. Characteristically, after that tragic July the Kreisau Circle, which under the leadership of Count Helmuth James von Moltke played such an eminent role in the planning of the final coup against Hitler, became known as much for its social elitism as for its dedication to the Christian cause.[125]

With the upper classes' unpopularity with the party, as shown by their declining membership, and with a concomitant increase in the workers' share in the NSDAP, one might be tempted to conclude that the changes that had taken place in the social composition of the Nazi party after 1933 heralded a social revolution not only in the party but in German society as well. But by 1945 there had been no social revolution. Yet neither had the National Socialist regime attempted to rigidify the already existing class divisions for the sake of any one particular social layer at the expense of the others.[126] True, Hitler had proclaimed a racially and (implicitly) a socially homogeneous *Volk* early in his regime, but by 1944 any conscious attempts that might have been made in that direction by government and party had not succeeded. In the party itself, the representation of the workers may have increased as much as that of the elite had declined, but in society there had not been any significant change. Farmers continued, as before, to be suspicious of the strange ways of the higher-placed townspeople who were billeted in their homesteads at the height of the war, and the fur-coated lawyer's wife who was fortunate enough to be fed on the farmer's produce retained her customary aloofness. Judges who were working in a Berlin toolmaker's shop at the end of 1944 in aid of the war effort expressed their sympathy for the workers' harsh lot as they toiled side by side with them, but there was no doubt about their desire to return to their former professional positions. About this time an unsophisticated but observant young German, who had evidently been immersed in National Socialist ideology, summed up the situation succinctly. "The Labor Service," he noted in his diary, "once was organized for every German boy and every German girl . . . Was it not originally founded so that members of all occupations could unite to perform the same type of work, where the young would see no difference between high and low, poor and rich? To this day we see no indication whatsoever that this has happened." His words, spoken about German youth, were equally applicable to German society as a whole.[127]

II

SOCIAL PROFILE OF THE NAZI PARTY'S LEADERSHIP CADRES 1919-1945

7

THE EARLY YEARS TO POWER
1919 TO 1933

From the beginning of the Nazi party until Hitler's political takeover, party leadership was affected by three interrelated factors: the precariousness of the leaders' political position; leaders' frequently doubtful legitimacy within the party; and leaders' apparent dysfunctionality in the extremely unstable chain of command. These characteristics of NSDAP leadership varied inversely with a leader's degree of social standing, level in the party hierarchy, and size of the area of jurisdiction. For instance, functionaries who were the least educated, commanded the smallest units of the party, and were locally the most isolated were likely to enjoy the smallest measure of influence and consequently of security in the party echelons. Personnel turnover was greatest among the lowest ranks, especially the Ortsgruppenleiters (local chapter leaders). To the supreme leaders this insecurity was a necessary result of change, which was regarded as an intrinsic quality of the NSDAP as a dynamic "movement." The NSDAP, they believed, was a party that naturally resisted institutionalization, in marked contrast to the rigidly established bourgeois political parties. But this situation itself was to change after Hitler assumed the post of Reich Chancellor in January 1933 and the NSDAP became the monopolistic state party.

During its Time of Struggle (more properly called the "movement phase") the NSDAP experienced considerable difficulty in providing its functionaries, especially those on the local levels, with a sense of formal legitimacy traceable to the origin of power. At the bottom of the party leadership pyramid stood the Ortsgruppenleiters. They fitted in socially with the ordinary rank-and-file party comrades and were in rapport with them. At the top were the Gauleiters, the regional leaders. Even if they had worked their way up from local-leader status, they were more properly the creatures of Hitler and were regarded as his trustees. Their relationships with the local leaders varied. On the whole, there was no smooth transition of power from Hitler to the Gauleiters and from them to the local leaders. The fact that some links in this chain of command were missing gave rise to the existence of *Bezirksleiter*, subregional leaders, in some but not all of the regions. Between Ortsgruppenleiters and Gauleiters were the *Kreisleiter*, in charge of districts, and initially under the Bezirksleiters where those existed.[1] Often local party dignitaries were self-appointed, or they acquired their offices incidentally, perhaps because they were the only male party comrades available for active duty in a hamlet or city suburb. Decentralizing tendencies, which emanated from the helm of the Nazi party right from its birth up to 1931-32, led to a virtual absence of requirements for party office except that the candidate be a member in good standing.[2] For years, therefore, local party leaders and ordinary members were interchangeable. Reasons for an Ortsgruppenleiter's appointment to office were not needed between 1919 and 1932.

The following examples illustrate this point. Paul Strube in Melsungen (Hesse) had been a member of the Deutsch-Völkische Freiheitspartei, a Nazi substitute movement during the period of Hitler's imprisonment in Landsberg, and so he became an officer in the NSDAP in 1925. Party comrade Hesse became Ortsgruppenleiter in East Prussian Osterode in 1931 after a two-year stint as an SA man (and only one year's membership in the party). Another East Prussian local group leader seemed the natural choice for his job because his entire family, including parents-in-law, had helped in the daily chores of running the *Ortsgruppe* (local chapter), performing their clerical and menial tasks at home as in a family business. The earliest claim to fame of a later Gauleiter, Franz Schwede, was his instrumental role as cofounder of the Coburg Nazi branch late in 1922; he was then promoted to deputy Ortsgruppenleiter and, by Christmas 1923, to Ortsgruppenleiter. Kurt Schmalz, another future party leader, joined the NSDAP in Brunswick's hinterland a few months after its refounding in July 1925. No sooner had he dedicated his efforts to the growing Hitler Youth and made his way into the SA than he became Ortsgruppenleiter in Lower Lusatia. If the spirit moved them, some fanatical Nazi members founded Nazi chapters on their own. No one in the Munich leadership was likely to object to this, for individual initiative was one of the Social Darwinist principles subscribed to by the Nazi ideologues, in particular by Hitler, and capable leaders at any levels were scarce, as continued to be the case during the years of the Third

Reich.[3] Hence Hans Schemm, later to become Gauleiter and Bavarian Minister of Culture, established on his own authority an Ortsgruppe in his native Bayreuth soon after Hitler recalled his party faithfuls in February 1925.

In regional party administrations such as that of East Prussia, which, from 1925 on, was able to develop a firm hierarchy with command channels from the Gauleiter to the Bezirksleiters or Kreisleiters down to the local Ortsgruppenleiters, certain criteria of selection in the interest of stability were slowly introduced. Since one objective was the avoidance of too much change, candidates were actively sought who were reasonably well off and could afford to sustain an honorary party office without remuneration. Thus at one time in 1930 the criterion of "car owner" was emphasized because such a man would be able to cover the wide East Prussian plains and keep the flock together. Another standard observed by the higher leaders in East Prussia who assumed the right to appoint their own local deputies without interference from Munich was the service principle: on the lower levels of the hierarchy, old members were to enjoy seniority over new ones.

Yet while this suggests the shadow of a rationale for party appointments, entrance into the Nazi leadership corps at the lowest levels, even in East Prussia, still occurred more by chance than by any other method. As one contemporary described it at the beginning of the Third Reich: "In the fall [of 1928] the newly appointed regional leader of East Prussia held the first National Socialist meeting in Stallupönen. That day several fellow countrymen, as well as myself, became members of the party. The number was too small for a local group. My young compatriot and I, however, continued to work for the idea. *In the end he undertook the leadership of the new local.*"[4]

It is generally held that after the revival of the party early in 1925 Hitler followed a vague policy of division of regional authority. This tended to elevate his own status while allowing most Gauleiters unchecked sway in their domains as well as the freedom to act against one another. Their autocratic ways stopped short only where the Führer was concerned. Hitler was not wholly the initiator of this system, which was cryptofeudal in essence and provided the salient advantages of *divide et impera* — a principle that Hitler learned to put into practice early in his career. It was reinforced by the quasi-independent stance of the North German Arbeitsgemeinschaft (Cartel), to which after 1924 almost all of the powerful post-Putsch functionaries outside Bavaria belonged. Precisely because the chain of command between Hitler and the Gauleiters was weak in everyday party situations, the chain of command could be weak between a self-indulgent Gauleiter and equally self-indulgent local party chapter leaders. This improvised, unsystematic, and imperfect pattern of cohesion between the various levels of party administration, in which Hitler himself might at any time intervene, seems to have been sufficiently flexible to keep the party from disintegration and even to have provided for moderate growth in the years of relative quiet from 1925 to 1928. With their technical functions and their personal fates often hanging in the balance, if not in limbo, Ortsgruppenleiters and even Gauleiters were not likely to acquire the strong sense of self-esteem that they needed in order to become successful bureaucrats and politicans.[5]

Some scholars aver that Hitler decided as early as 1928 to cleanse his entire administration, starting logically (as he thought) with the Gaus or regions. The appointment of Gregor Strasser as party organization chief marked this new direction. The gradual tightening-up at Gauleiter level was appropriately paralleled by a similar weeding-out carried on by Gauleiters and their deputies at the district and local levels. The significant difference was that while Hitler's gradually escalated action was undoubtedly impelled by a desire for greater political efficiency, especially at election time, the Gauleiters' proscriptions were usually triggered by personal whims. Before Hitler took steps to relieve Gauleiter Paul Hinkler of his post in Halle-Merseburg, Hinkler had already succeeded in cementing a bulwark of local cronies, who bullied Ortsgruppenleiters and supported their leader when his designated successor appeared in February 1931. At the same time, the Gauleiter of South Hanover-Brunswick was putting pressure on his nominal surbordinates and singling out his favorites for special treatment. Gauleiter cliques were common after 1930, with many of the older, longer-serving comrades falling victim to the unbridled ambitions of younger, less inhibited men.[6]

When Theodor Heuss referred in 1932 to the "absolutist strength of the party leadership," implying the establishment of a monolithic structure and of the "leadership principle," he may well have been aware of the result of Gregor Strasser's long-awaited changes, which had begun with his reorganization of the Nazi Women's Movement in the fall of 1931 and had finally reached completion in the following summer. The application of the leadership principle meant in practice the introduction of a logical and cogent chain of command, from Hitler on down to the low Nazi chapter leader. This firm anchoring of military obedience patterns which included all but the unmanageable SA under Ernst Röhm and some loosely connected ancillary groups, was bound to assist the NSDAP in its last concerted efforts to win national political power, and it could not be shaken by the formality of relieving Strasser of his supervisory post on December 9, 1932. It seemed that by 1932, at last, every party stooge who cared for an assured and neatly defined place in "his" movement could feel that he had one, provided he had come through the shake-ups unscathed. But many of the party functionaries still suffered from an identity problem that affected them like a recurrent trauma: was their legitimacy firmly grounded in their historic roles as flag-bearers in the advance units of the "revolution"? In their haphazard way they were preparing themselves to adopt the stance of a much older and more firmly established ruling elite that had long since ceased to suffer from such qualms.[7]

Here the question of overall continuity presents itself. It stands to reason that continuity of the functionaries' corps could have been achieved through stability in office or promotion supported by merit, or a logical combination of both. Theoretically this should have been feasible even though men who were willing and able to serve were notoriously scarce, to the point where some individuals occupied more than one position, such as that of Ortsgruppenleiter and that of SA leader.[8] But because of the peculiar interaction of two conditions in the Nazi system — first, arbitrary decision making based on personal preference at all administrative party levels, and second, the normative bureaucratic mechanisms typical of well-ordered state administrations — no party servant, even a Gauleiter, could count on making a life career out of Nazi politics. Until at least 1933 this situation compounded the original instability of the Nazi leadership corps. Research has revealed that the Gauleiters were among the most stable groups of Nazi officials, even before 1933, and that the Ortsgruppenleiters showed the highest incidence of failure, causing a constant need for re-recruitment.[9] This fact, which clearly suggests a positive correlation between job importance and job tenure, raises the question whether such factors as academic or technical skills and social background also affected job tenure.

Conventional wisdom holds that Nazi functionaries of all ranks came from a predominantly lower-middle-class background.[10] Hence until the Putsch phase in November 1923, the "vulgarians in Hitler's retinue" (as Albert Speer called them) are said to have been exponents of a typical lower-middle-class way of life, value system, and economic disposition: they were craftsmen, lower civil servants, and white-collar workers. The sources indicate little change for the period after 1924. "The majority of the Nazi leadership of Hamburg in the years 1926-27," remarked former Gauleiter Albert Krebs, "derived from the middle and lower middle classes and still lived by values and goals that had been formed in the prewar era." In October 1929, the district leader in Saxon Freiberg was a master bookbinder; scarcely a year later, the local Nazi chapter leader in East Prussian Widminnen was a chimney sweep, and he was succeeded by a house painter.[11]

Although there is evidence that some workers held leadership positions, this seems to have been true only at the parochial levels and in areas with a heavy proletarian population, such as the Ruhr or the seaports. And, as a result of the modest publicity generated by Anton Drexler and his fellow Munich "workers," blue-collar laborers were most prominent as local leaders during the first three years of the party's existence, after which they were displaced by representatives of the lower middle class. In Bremen in November 1922, for example, two of the three local Nazi leaders were blue-collar workers, but subsequently their names disappeared from the records. After 1925 workers appear to have done somewhat better only at the local or regional *electoral* levels; possibly they were selected as candidates by the NSDAP leadership to polish the party's image as a "workers' party." Hence, among the twenty-one candidates who were hand-picked to run in the provincial elections in East Prussia in 1929, 33 percent were manual laborers. Following the Reichstag elections of 1930 and 1932 workers constituted 20 percent of the deputies: a low figure if compared with the percentage of workers in the Reich, but high in comparison with that of other political parties.[12]

In contrast to the obvious underrepresentation of workers among the Nazi leadership, the picture for the elite as portrayed by the conventional source material is not very clear. For instance, among intermediate party leaders below the highest rank of Gauleiter, men with academic backgrounds were reported in 1926-1928 for Hamburg and in 1930-31 for East Prussia and Thuringian Gera. For Eutin in the early thirties, Lawrence Stokes found that 12 percent of the Nazi leadership were members of the upper middle class, which would suggest an overrepresentation of the elite in this small-town area of Schleswig-Holstein.[13]

Because the conventional evidence, which has served as the basis for all previous historiography on this topic, is so spotty, a new set of figures drawn from more representative samples has been prepared for this study. Samples for the greater Bochum area, Thuringia, and the Reich between 1925 and 1928 indicate that the elite was much more heavily overrepresented among Nazi Gauleiters than in the general membership, while the converse was true of the workers (table 10, columns A, C, E; figure 10).[14] And although the lower middle class was slightly less prominent in the leadership than in the general membership, it was clearly overrepresented in both.[15] In 1929, for the Reich as a whole, the percentage of socially privileged (elite) men remained high among the Gauleiters alone, whereas the elite percentage was much lower among the regional and local Nazi functionaries taken as a whole—a mixed population including agitators and conveners as well as various ranks of NSDAP leaders and their deputies, ranging from Ortsgruppenleiter up to Gauleiter (table 10, columns G, I). In the same two groups both the lower middle class and elite were overrepresented, the latter heavily so, while the workers were underrepresented.[16] A positive correlation between class and operational function is also indicated by the 1930 percentages of the three classes in four different Nazi leadership groups—the Ortsgruppenleiters in Kassel and in Harburg, the agitators from Baden, and the Reich Gauleiters. The more important such party functions were, and the higher the party prestige resulting from them, the greater was the likelihood of elite membership. In these four corps of functionaries the elite was overrepresented and the workers were underrepresented (table 10, columns K, M, O, Q). Significantly, the workers were least in evidence in the most prestigious of the four groups, the Reich Gauleiters (where the elite predominated relative to the Reich population), and were best represented at the local chapter level. There the share of the elite was smaller than at the Gauleiter level, but that class was still overrepresented. For the lower middle class, too, representation diminished as rank advanced from the lowest cadres to the highest.[17]

In 1931 at Lüneburg the representation of elite functionaries fell below their percentage in the Reich, but this may have been because the elite was generally underrepresented in the region. By contrast, in the same year the elite was very heavily overrepresented among the Reich Gauleiters (table 10, columns S, U).[18]

Until the Reichstag elections of September 1930 the Gauleiters were beyond question the most important single body of party leaders upon whom Hitler could rely. But after these elections, as the NSDAP geared up for the influx of more and more upper-middle-class and aristocratic members and, concomitantly, for the kind of bourgeois respectability that was politically most useful through a strong presence in the local, regional, and nationally elected diets, the Gauleiters' exclusive functions were somewhat reduced. As a group they began to be outweighed by an ever-growing number of technocrats, many of whom were academically trained and had been recruited from the reservoir of employable, yet often unemployed, university graduates who made up the mass of pauperized students at the end of the Weimar era.[19] Viewed as a close group, these specialists, who for the purpose of this study will be called the "New Functionaries," soon superseded their ideologically stronger rivals from the Gauleiter camp in two important respects. First, instead of being assigned merely regionally, within the jurisdictional confines of a Gau, they were deployed both centrally and regionally across Gau divisional lines, thus potentially countermanding the Gauleiters' powers. Second, those who had a university education either tended to come from upper-middle-class and aristocratic homes more often than the Gauleiters did, or as a result of their education had reached a higher rung on the social ladder.[20] Among these New Functionaries the percentage of the lower middle class and especially of the workers lay well below their percentage of the Reich population.[21] Even in the Nazi party, apparently, efficiency could not be attained without sound education, and dogma was not a substitute for rationality.[22]

At every level of the Nazi hierarchy, functionality was closely linked either to some sort of specialist training or to status based on tangible socioeconomic assets, as further analysis of the data in table 10 reveals. It can be shown that in any one of the Nazi leadership corps the percentage of lower civil servants—a particularly articulate and upwardly mobile group, among whom the public school teachers played an eminent role because of their tradition of political participation—tended to rise in direct proportion to the operational significance of that particular corps.[23] For example, between 1925 and 1928 the lower civil servants' party membership rate was merely 7.3 percent in Bochum and 10.0 percent in Thuringia, but during the same period it was 27.8 percent in the Reich Gauleiters' cohort (table 10, columns A, C, E). In 1929 in the mixed functionaries' corps throughout the Reich, the rate was lower, namely 16.7 percent (column G). At both national and regional levels the type of bureaucratic experience that the state servants had was needed to run the party apparatus, while such experience was not necessarily required at the local levels of administration. In the organically closed unit of the village, for instance, the literary and vocal talents of the service class were less important than the respectability derived from long-standing residence and property ownership. The criteria of social standing in the locality, whatever they might be, were reflected in the Nazi leadership structure at the same local level. For example, master craftsmen, merchants, and farmers, in the socioeconomic substructure of the Kassel hinterland, constituted 59.3 percent of the group of Ortsgruppenleiters there (column K). In the Harburg area (column M) the most important groups were the workers, who probably commuted to the nearby port of Hamburg, and the established farmers of the surrounding villages in Schleswig-Holstein (61.9 percent), with the farmers at 38.1 percent being the stronger of the two. Within the group of Baden agitators (column O) the high percentage of merchants (23.7) is remarkable, probably reflecting the effects of economic depression on the Baden small-town infrastructure. The academic professionals, much more persuasive speakers than the merchants, showed the next highest percentage, 16.9.[24] Perhaps these academics were the vanguard, the first representatives, of those alienated intellectuals who began drifting into Hitler's party in greater numbers at the beginning of the thirties. And finally, in the case of the Lüneburg Ortsgruppenleiters (column S), it was once again the farmers who, in the rural hinterland of the seaport of Hamburg, were at the top of the social system and who emerged accordingly as the strongest occupational stratum in the local Nazi leadership.[25]

These findings support the contention that the social structure of the NSDAP functionary corps was closely related to the complex system of administrative tasks to be performed by the party hierarchy: the higher the degree of skill required, the more qualified and sophisticated were the administrative personnel. The NSDAP thus appears to have been ruled by the same laws of rationality that governed other institutions, corporations, and even other political parties in the Weimar Republic. In that sense the party displayed one of the key characteristics of modern industrial societies.[26]

This viewpoint is further corroborated by an examination of the age of Nazi functionaries. Generally, in keeping with the demands made upon them by various problems of leadership, functionaries were older than ordinary party comrades, even though they were much younger than their political opponents in popularly elected diets.[27] This was the case even in the pre-Putsch phase (before November 1923).[28] In Greater Bochum and Thuringia between 1925 and 1928 the average age of the common membership was 29 and 30 years respectively, while that of the Reich Gauleiters in the same period was 36 (table 10, columns B, D, F). In September 1930, according to Juan J. Linz, 36.8 percent of the rank-and-file Nazis, compared with only 26.2 percent of the leaders, were 30 or below.[29] And barely a year later, when the average Nazi functionary was nearing the end of his thirties, the ordinary comrades of the movement, if judged by the figure for Eutin, were less than 35.[30]

For the entire Time of Struggle the percentage of party members between 18 and 30 was 42.3, whereas the corresponding figure for the functionaries was only 16.6.[31]

Among the party functionaries age was usually correlated positively with position: the higher and more demanding the function, the older the person fulfilling it. At the lower levels of the hierarchy, the less important functionaries (Ortsgruppenleiters) tended to be younger than the more important ones (Kreisleiters).[32] In 1929, when the mixed group of Reich functionaries had a mean age of 33 years, the more prestigious Gauleiter corps had a mean age of 38 (table 10, columns H, J). In 1930 the average age of the eighty-three Ortsgruppenleiters in Kassel was 37,[33] whereas for the Reich Gauleiters it was 39 (column R). The Baden agitators (column P) were younger than both of these groups. Their mean age of 33 is explainable in terms of the relative immaturity of university students and recently graduated academic professionals, people who were well suited to dispense propaganda but were by no means typical of either the rank and file or the leaders at that time. In 1932 the Gauleiters' average age of 38 (see figure 11) differed little from that of all the National Socialist Reichstag deputies (39), a situation that was attributable to the exchangeability of Gauleiters and deputies during that phase of party history. Reichstag candidates were at least as important to a political party seeking public backing as were its top internal leaders; indeed, some Gauleiters such as Goebbels were made to serve in both positions simultaneously.[34] It is significant that in 1932 the New Functionaries (technocrats) in the Nazi hierarchy were not appreciably younger than the Gauleiters: their mean age of 37.3 years reflected not only their completion of academic training but also a considerable measure of professional experience.[35] Maturity and experience were essential preconditions for service in administrative positions within a party preparing for the takeover of the national government. An analysis of the age of Gauleiters by social class between 1925 and 1933 demonstrates that the more socially elevated and, presumably, the better educated a Nazi functionary was, the older and consequently more worldly-wise and urbane he tended to be (figure 12). Characteristically, the Gauleiters of proletarian background ranked low on this scale of interacting values, and the members of the elite ranked high.

It has often been said that during the Weimar Republic the Nazi functionaries, no matter what their social class association, came from broken backgrounds and were social outsiders or even outcasts. If this is true, it might be deduced that Nazism was fashioned as a "protest movement" by a handful of desperadoes who thought of themselves as a new "counter-elite" and who were reacting to socioeconomic ills that were, perhaps, the outgrowth of World War I and the upheavals that followed it. To this way of thinking, the depression that came after 1929 would only have accelerated a trend that had begun early in the decade.

This view might gain credibility if it could be proved that the socioeconomic situation of Nazi leaders of all ranks was bleak before they joined the party. Although a few examples of economic hardship can be found at the lower leadership levels, the documentary evidence is overwhelmingly in favor of the contrary view: Nazi leaders became impoverished as a result of their activities on behalf of the party.[36] Lower civil servants risked expulsion from the state bureaucracy and small merchants often lost their local clientele because of their active commitment to the Nazi cause. Working largely without regular pay and driven by a very personal sense of idealism and admiration for Hitler, local and regional party representatives often contributed money and produce to the party coffers. Such acts of private subsidy frequently bankrupted these functionaries, forcing them to resign their party position and concentrate on their own careers. Other leaders jeopardized their health by working for the party during the night and on weekends in addition to carrying on their regular occupational chores. In this sense the party functionaries resembled the more devoted rank-and-file comrades; but among the ordinary membership such sacrifices were less common whereas for the leadership core they were the rule. Such efforts, in fact, became an element of social distinction that defined the functionaries as a closely knit peer group. This pattern was consistent from the beginning of the Time of Struggle until Hitler's assumption of power. Since few accounts of such sacrificial service have been published, several examples will be cited here.

Of Hamburg's first Nazi leader, Josef Klant, it was said that in 1922 he did not "spare himself or his family and friends. His money is the party's money as well. The earnings from his little tobacco store are earnings for the party." Karl Lenz, born in 1899 in Heidelberg, a public school teacher and deputy Gauleiter in Baden (1927), suffered severe professional setbacks: "From 1923 till 1933 I was suspended from my job without pay for a total of seven years." Karl Holz, who was Streicher's deputy in Nuremberg, had joined the NSDAP in 1922; having been elected a Nuremberg councilman in 1924, he became so aggressive toward the lord mayor that he lost his permanent civilian position as town clerk. After World War II Karl Wahl, the former Swabian Gauleiter, recalled his situation in 1927: "I had no income, only expenses. My meager salary as a lawyer's assistant was hardly enough to provide a living, let alone to finance special expenses for party activities. My health had suffered much because of this demanding service. During the day I worked at my job, while at night I labored for the party, alone with a few of the faithfuls." "After six months as a municipal deputy," remembered Freiberg Kreisleiter Helmut Böhme toward the end of the 1920s, "I lost my employment as a master book binder on account of my NSDAP membership. Since then I have been jobless and on the dole." Onetime Gauleiter Rudolf Jordan recounted that two days before Christmas in 1929, when he was twenty-seven, his name was struck from the list of prospective schoolteachers by the government in Kassel "because of my propaganda efforts for the NSDAP." East Prussian Gau functionary Paul Gillgasch, a traveling salesman, complained in June 1930 that he could no longer pay for party telephone calls: "For the time being, I am supporting the business of the district office with the proceeds from the sale of razor blades, small portraits of Hitler, and leaflets." A fellow comrade in Tilsit protested in December of that year that he was incapable of any further extensions of credit out of his own savings to various nearby party chapters, especially because he always had to write "a dozen letters" to retrieve the money. And in January 1932 SA leader Viktor Lutze pleaded with the chief of the Hitler Youth on behalf of an old party stalwart who had served in various capacities and was then an Ortsgruppenleiter. "He is an old National Socialist who has sacrificed a lot for the movement," wrote Lutze. "But now he is at the end of his rope. Utterly penniless, he carries on a miserable existence with his family."[37]

Nor did the most onerous burdens fall entirely on the men least favored by family or professional fortune. Alwin Görlich, the owner of an internationally connected trucking company in Lower Rhenish Cleve and a veteran Ortsgruppenleiter and Bezirksleiter, stated in June 1932 that his business had suffered significant setbacks because he had shelled out "more than 10,000 marks as contributions for the struggle, all in the course of three years." A few months later a similar cry went out from Hans Wiemer, an Ortsgruppenleiter, after the two stores he owned in Lusatia had been sabotaged and nearly ruined. Clearly, as Martin Broszat has observed, neither opportunism nor materialistic greed played a role in motivating such men to enlist in the Nazi cause.[38]

Not infrequently, a Nazi leader's personal life was complicated by his real or alleged infractions of the law, committed in full knowledge of what he was doing, for which he might suffer restrictions on his freedom, court fines, and loss of job tenure. Civil and criminal suits were about equal in number.[39] For instance, in Nuremberg between 1926 and 1930 Harl Holz was sentenced seventeen different times, totaling four months in prison and 3,500 marks in fines, for anti-Semitic activities. His superior, Streicher, spent fourteen weeks in a prison cell for similar offenses in 1926.[40] In August 1927 Josef Grohé, the local Nazi leader of Cologne, wrote to his comrade, Bernhard Dicker, in care of Cologne's Klingelpütz jail, that he would soon join him for three weeks because he could not pay a penalty after having "allegedly" insulted a Jew. By the early thirties the number of law-offending party comrades had increased to such a point that regional Nazi auxiliary committees had to be set up to help their suffering families.[41] Police surveillance of local party activity was ever present, even in areas where the NSDAP was not legally proscribed by state governments. State servants who were also working for the party, such as tax clerk Hardtke in Darkehmen (East Prussia) in 1929, had to be especially wary of the authorities; they lived in constant fear of reprisals by the state.[42] Joseph Goebbels may well have expressed the Führer's own sentiments when in June 1932 he sent part of his royalties as a writer to eight Berlin co-fighters who were in prison. To one of them he wrote, "You have done more for the party than the party can ever do for you."[43]

For party workers there was no escape from these economic and legal dilemmas unless they either reached a fairly elevated level in the Nazi hierarchy or were successful in political elections. A key NSDAP position afforded some measure of economic protection, but public office or a deputyship was still better, providing not only token remuneration by the state but sometimes free railway passage and, within certain limits, immunity from public prosecution even for the most fanatical displays of partisanship. Since the NSDAP was notoriously short of funds after 1925, even a Gauleiter's position might be purely honorary or, at best, poorly paid. Only in extreme cases of need did the party come to a man's rescue. In 1932 a Saxon Kreisleiter, unemployed since 1930, was supporting his wife and two children on about 68 marks a month that he received from charity, until the party granted him an additional subsidy of 50 marks. At that time an unskilled laborer in the Reich with no job experience could expect to be earning about 100 marks a month. In 1927-28 Friedrich Hildebrandt, "honorary" Gauleiter of Mecklenburg, a farm helper, lived on 125 marks a month, supported by fellow workers and his patrons, the Counts Schulenburg.

In 1929-30 Gauleiters were put on the party's payroll. One such functionary, Rudolf Jordan, could count on receiving 300 marks a month in 1931. After 1930, when Reichstag and Landtag seats could be contested and won by Nazi representatives, who then, at the national level, might make up to 750 marks a month plus benefits, high-priority positions on the Nazis' candidate rosters were coveted by many an Old Fighter with hopes of just rewards. Under the Weimar election system the top-ranking candidates of a political party had the best chance of electoral success. Hence Hitler, counseled by the able Strasser, was expected to attempt judicious decision making, not to say arbitration, in rejecting and awarding candidacies. If party workers throughout the republican era generally displayed more altruism than avarice, the public elections at the end of the Weimar period brought a change of heart to many functionaries who believed that the harvest-time had come at last.[44]

In spite of all their problems, the Nazi functionaries of the Weimar era did not project the image of a group of losers living on the fringes of society. This was true, first of all, of the lower Nazi echelons, for not only their socioeconomic fortunes or misfortunes but also their nationalist proclivities were shared by millions of Germans of similar age, social background, and war-related experience. In this sense, then, the ranks from Ortsgruppenleiter to Kreisleiter tended to be rather typical of the masses of petty bourgeois and sometimes of workers whom they were seeking to represent politically.

The situation was somewhat more complicated at the highest levels of the party bureaucracy, where a comparatively large number of elite members were to be found.[45] In his classic study of 1951 the American sociologist Daniel Lerner established that the position of what he called Nazi "coercers" and "administrators," who would have included the Gauleiters and some of the New Functionaries, as a new social and functional elite was at best precarious. He claimed that they came from disrupted family and educational backgrounds and that, in particular, their broken World War I and Freikorps careers had turned them, not excluding the representatives of the old upper classes, into frustrated social misfits who had lost touch with the realities of the Weimar Republic, become disengaged from the conventional morality of the period, and espoused the Nazi movement as their last chance of survival. Altogether, Lerner drew the composite portrait of a group of "marginal men."[46] Recently this view has been challenged by Ronald Rogowski, who, in accordance with some of Peter Merkl's earlier findings, has deemphasized the significance of records of ruptured military service and other supposed indicators of social and psychological personality disturbance and instead, citing the case of the Gauleiters, has stressed the relative elasticity of the Nazi elite by pointing to their intergenerational upward mobility. "By the best estimates we can form," writes Rogowski, the Gauleiters "displayed before their entry into the NSDAP a degree of upward social mobility that considerably exceeded the German average of even the quite recent past."[47]

My position, based on an independent examination of the sources, falls somewhere between the two extremes presented by Lerner and Rogowski. The upward mobility of the Gauleiters between 1925 and 1933 was high, but not so high as that extrapolated by Rogowski.[48] Yet the present analysis agrees with his finding that among the vertically mobile Gauleiters those who were upwardly mobile far surpassed those who were downwardly mobile, and that in consequence these functionaries, as a close group, exceeded by a very significant margin the upward mobility standard set by the population at large.[49] Hence, in a formal sense at least, the Gauleiters could not have been socially so "marginal" as Lerner's collective biographies of the Nazi "administrators" would indicate.[50] At the same time, however, the social "stability" of the Gauleiters lacked some of the ingredients of permanence generally associated with elites of long standing. Not only because they had recently risen in the social scale but also because of the jump some of them had taken in the process of forging ahead many of the Gauleiters feared competition from the older, more secure cohorts. Although only 2 percent of all the members of the upper middle class (elite) in the Reich had moved up from the working class, this kind of movement was characteristic of the Gauleiters' thrust into the established social elite: 17.4 percent of all upper-class Gauleiters came from a workers' background (table 11). The fear these men had of being toppled from their elevated social position and being pushed back to their originally humble level must have been excruciating, and it must have contributed to an overall feeling of sociopsychological insecurity. Because of the possibility of friction between this smaller group of highly mobile Gauleiters (17.4 percent) and the established group of stable elite (39.1 percent), the cohesion of the Gauleiter corps must have been very tenuous.[51] As for the lower-middle-class segment of the Gauleiters, its degree of self-recruitment from its own class was not significantly different from that in the Reich populace.[52] What is startling, however, is the comparatively low influx of the working class into that segment of the corps (14.3 percent as opposed to 23 percent for the Reich population), and the correspondingly high percentage of socially demoted members of the upper class (14.3 percent as opposed to 5 percent). This shows a higher degree of downward mobility from elite status to the lower middle class in the Gauleiter corps than in the

Reich.[53] Furthermore, the Gauleiter corps had a greater proportion of working-class sons of elite fathers, indicating social demotion by two ranks (20 percent). For the Reich population, this extreme degree of downward mobility has not gone on record (0 percent – table 11). All these factors suggest that it was not so much the high degree of social mobility itself as the social polarities manifested by such patterns of movement that gave the Gauleiters a weak sense of social stability. Although such qualities as Bildung, commonly associated with elite status, were undoubtedly to be found within the Gauleiter corps, in practice its value system inclined toward that of the lower middle class because that class predominated in the corps numerically, absolutely as well as relatively.[54]

The same cannot be said of the technocratic specialists (New Functionaries) who flocked to the party in the last few years of the Republic. Relatively more of them than of the Gauleiters were university-trained and had upper-middle-class or aristocratic fathers.[55] They were socially more secure than the Gauleiters, and they were also more cynically opportunistic and more capable of doing difficult jobs quickly. Moreover, their wartime, Freikorps, or vigilante experience, however intermittent, had not caused a hiatus in personality development and hence "marginality," as Lerner's matrix of instability indicators would suggest, but rather the contrary: it had served as a character-building mechanism of the highest order.[56] After all, not just those male university students who openly sympathized with Hitler's cadres but all of those who sat in the lecture halls at the end of the 1920s had served in some military capacity or other, and on their own volition. The students with shattered psyches were, in fact, those who had not had a chance to serve. And had not even the *Zeitgeist* of the Weimar Republic extolled the ideal of the "heroic man" conjured up by intellectuals, bards, and poets who themselves never bothered to join the National Socialist camp – such men as Ernst Jünger, Friedrich Hielscher, Ernst von Salomon, and the Reverend Martin Niemöller?[57]

What was this "lower-middle-class mentality" that most of the Nazi functionaries shared with the petit bourgeois core of the rank and file and that constituted another normative criterion of their specific character as a cohort? It has already been suggested in the introduction that during the Weimar Republic a relationship existed between class and mentality. As Ralf Dahrendorf wrote in 1968, despite a lack of empirical evidence on which to base an exact examination of mentalities in terms of class criteria, a correlation between the two concepts did indeed exist: "There are certain economic, political, and social attitudes that adhere to social positions in society just as role expectations do."[58] Dahrendorf himself mentions industriousness or love of hard work; and for the German petit bourgeois of the 1920s and early 1930s other characteristics can be added — anti-intellectuality, ideological dogmatism, xenophobia, bureaucratic formalism, and authoritarian traditionalism.[59] These inclinations and their extensions constitute a catalogue of values that may be said, on the one hand, to have been germane to the German lower middle class and, on the other, to have possessed a special potential for breeding fascist proclivities.

The average Nazi functionary's attitude toward abstract thought was in keeping with the German petit bourgeois's customary rejection of all things intellectual. The absence of academic schooling led him to suspect formal knowledge as such, which could result in turn in the total replacement of rational categories by emotional and even magical values. The frequent emphasis by Nazi leaders on *Herzensbildung* or "education of the heart" as an antidote to intellect was as symptomatic of this distrust of rationality as was recourse to superstition, fable, or astrology. Hitler's secretary, Rudolf Hess, seriously believed in the supernatural power of the number three; Fritz Sauckel favored legends from the Germanic past over history; and Karl Wahl preferred "love" to analysis as a tool of persuasion.[60] Virtues of character were extolled rather than faculties of criticism; trustfulness was to supplant inquiry. As one East Prussian party organizer, by trade a door-to-door salesman, said in 1931, he preferred the "proved" fighters to latter-day converts, for the former possessed, "if not always the needed intelligence, a sense of fealty to a much higher degree." By the same token, a man who could demonstrate a good hand in writing documents and letters exhibited, by the accepted metaphysical laws of calligraphy, more the qualities of moral strength than of intellectual adroitness.[61]

Yet a basically ambivalent attitude on the part of the German petit bourgeois toward matters of the mind and their sociocultural derivatives, such as higher education and artistic creativity, has always been one of the quintessential characteristics of lower-middle-class mentality, thus compounding its complexity.[62] The capacity to begin a chain of thought without developing it to some definite conclusion distinguished the German *Kleinbürger* (petit bourgeois) both from the worker, who refused to think at all, and from the *Bildungsbürger* (man of culture), who thought sequentially. The *Halbbildung* — the half-education of many Nazi leaders — with its deep roots in the realm of the autodidactic, the axiomatic, and the apodictical, and with its characteristic absence of logic, was evident in the case of Hans Schemm, a Franconian public school teacher and later a Gauleiter. This amiable son of a master shoemaker, credited by his biographers with a "keen sense of imagination" as well as "spiritual agility," exceeded the formal requirements of a public school seminarist's training by becoming a devotee of chess as well as an admirer of Goethe, Nietzsche, and Richard Wagner. In the course of time he became a part-time chemist and, by way of a deep interest in bee cultures, something of a biologist. Mixing his acquired knowledge with the prejudices and convictions prevalent among his social peers, he not only became a fervent anti-Semite but was allegedly able to "prove" the validity of anti-Jewish thought by likening it to the biological processes revealed to him through his studies of insects. Magnetic and good-looking, Schemm gained a reputation for maturity and solid if unorthodox accomplishments in many areas of learning. At the height of his career he came closer to the *terribles simplificateurs* of Jacob Burckhardt's vision than any of the other Nazi leaders except Adolf Hitler, whom he resembled in charismatic appeal.[63] A kindred spirit of Schemm's, though certainly of lesser stature, was Karl Holz, the Nuremberg town clerk who prided himself on the daily "hour or two" of reading that he managed while in prison—preferably translations of novels by Charles Dickens—and who could pass as an artist. Another was salesclerk Josef Grohé of Cologne, of whom it was said that he excelled through a combination of "unerring instinct and rich knowledge, acquired by assiduously studying every available political publication, both books and journals."[64]

Nazi party leaders as a group lacked one of the essential qualifications of the true intellectual, namely, the capacity for "the independent and deliberate use of the word."[65] This characteristic was inversely related to the nature of Nazi ideology. Insofar as this ideology was the outgrowth of syncretistic thought (though, as Eberhard Jäckel has shown, it did not lack some inherently logical passages), it was a typical by-product of lower-middle-class thinking.[66] Moreover, the amorphous structure of the Nazi *Weltanschauung* as expressed in *Mein Kampf* could be digested piecemeal by the intermediate lower-middle-class functionary, who, never eager to comprehend the quintessence of an issue, was content to remember and regurgitate snippets of the doctrine to suit his immediate purpose.[67] It has been observed with some justification that one of the reasons for Alfred Rosenberg's failure to become a genuine Nazi "revolutionary" was the internal logic of his arguments, even though they were based on false premises. His main work, *Myth of the Twentieth Century*, was described by

Hermann Rauschning in 1937, not without a trace of sarcasm, as simply not irrational enough. In its relative cogency it smacked of the intellectual establishment, causing Rosenberg to be stigmatized as the "clandestine [upper-] middle class member of the Nazi elite" and to lead a precarious existence in the party.[68]

Rosenberg was not the only Nazi "intellectual" of upper-middle-class breeding who fared badly with the Führer even before 1933. Dr. Artur Dinter, a chemist, religious sectarian, and author of several racist novels, propagated an ideology of his own, which, though not essentially different from Hitler's, was more streamlined and far more convincing in its argumentation. In addition, by incorporating religious issues within its catechism, it could lay claim to a transcendental dimension, completely missing from Hitler's work, that would appeal to the formally educated elite.[69] Evidently afraid of competition, Hitler had Dinter fired as Gauleiter of Thuringia in October 1927.[70] Dinter happened to be an "intellectual" whose skills were not called for in the party's ranks. Other lesser leaders of some intellectual standing could flaunt their intellectuality at times without too much fear of internal repercussions. When Dr. Georg Usadel, an Insterburg upper-school teacher and local party boss, was attacked by his East Prussian district leader for being an "individualist" unsympathetic to the objectives of National Socialism, Usadel responded with a letter that was so sardonic as to be totally incomprehensible to the addressee. Usadel's use of irony as a tactical form of defense, which was utterly unlike the approach of the generally humorless rank and file, could only be matched by the pen of Dr. Joseph Goebbels, a fellow intellectual traveler who was equally untypical of the Nazi leadership.[71]

To the regular party worker, what mattered was not so much the content of the ideology as the method of disseminating it. The manner of presentation was the message, and emotional appeal was superior to dialectic. In this idiom Hitler had proved himself to be the ultimate master; his treatises on propaganda in *Mein Kampf* are admittedly among the most original pieces of composition in the entire book.[72] In addressing any given crowd, a showman's antics were of paramount importance. Hence Gera's Kreisleiter, the physician Dr. Engelstädter, was rated in the fall of 1931 not on his medical degree but on the "popular delivery of his speech."[73] Whenever political opponents refuted a Nazi's arguments in a systematic way, they were to be silenced not by logic but by high-volume rhetoric. This is implied when Nazi chroniclers report that in public rallies functionaries were able to rebut "in the sharpest and most successful manner," and that they "dispatched" their adversaries "in the most brilliant fashion."[74] It mattered little if the paragraphs of the party program or tenets of Hitler's *Kampf* were distorted beyond all meaning: as far as Nazism's economic theory was concerned, it was such a hodgepodge of ideas as to make sense only to its creators, and as late as 1927 *Mein Kampf* reportedly had not been read by a large majority of the highest-ranking Nazi leaders. Consequently, in 1925 a party convener was rumored to be speaking about the "Protocols of the White Goats" rather than the "Protocols of the Elders of Zion," and during the prosperity of 1927 another made the inane forecast of a "new inflation."[75] But these slips did not matter to the largely lower-middle-class crowd, whose value system was already attuned to the propaganda of proselytizing zealots who came from similar psychosociological backgrounds, and whose instructions at the highest Nazi indoctrination centers were low in dogmatic content but rich in mass psychology.[76]

The one ingredient of the Nazi Weltanschauung that matched the prefashioned world-view of both the functionaries and the party comrades was racism, in particular anti-Semitism, which sprang from a combination of xenophobia and simplistic Social Darwinist notions. Fear and hatred of strangers were commonplace among Germans of all walks of life after World War I, but they were most pronounced in lower-middle-class cohorts, who, unlike the elite, knew no foreign languages and had not traveled widely, and who, unlike the workers, felt a need to expand their geographic or linguistic horizons. Not only had a comparatively large number of Nazi leaders remigrated to Germany after having experienced the persecution syndrome of growing up German in a sea of unfriendly "natives"—a fate that the contemporary *völkisch* poet Hans Grimm dramatized in his best-selling novel, *Volk ohne Raum* (*People without Space*)—but many of them could not forget the Russians from the Eastern Front, the French they had fought after the invasion of the Ruhr, or the Poles they had confronted in the Silesian Freikorps units.[77]

A few of these leaders may have developed their contempt for Jews while struggling for economic survival in foreign lands.[78] But most of them thought they had found plenty of occasions at home to foster hatred of the Jews, a hatred so violent that in some cases it bordered on the pathological. Besides Streicher, whose demeanor toward Jews is easily traceable to sexual maladjustments, there was the Hamburg Gau leader, Klant, who in 1926 trained his cat to refuse fish that was announced as coming "from the Jews." Anti-Semitism was such a matter of conviction among Nazi functionaries that many of them knowingly staked their careers on it. Both Franz Schwede and Robert Ley jeopardized their civilian positions because of anti-

Jewish agitation, thus paving the way for their elevation to the uppermost strata of the Nazi leadership.[79]

Finally, these largely lower-middle-class functionaries possessed what has been called the "authoritarian personality." Patriarchal and prudish at home, which by no means precluded the possibility of a double standard in sexual relations for a *paterfamilias* beyond the confines of his private household, these men took full advantage of their elevated position in the family unit, one that had been established long before World War I. It was predicated upon a value system that was antiquated, antiemancipatory, antimodernist. The essence of their traditionalism was their illiberalism: the fundamental belief in natural inequalities. In small-town milieus, they frequently subscribed to a *Stammtisch-Kultur*, a beer-hall culture that came alive after 7:00 P.M. in neighborhood hangouts and that thrived only in the peer group to which every member belonged. It was in these exclusively male-dominated local gatherings in the backrooms of taverns, in glee clubs, and in various associations for the preservation of national-*völkisch* ideals, where the drinking was heavy and incidental vulgarities flourished, that irrational men generated antidemocratic demonstrations in which they participated with unbridled, self-indulgent sentimentality.[80] These local peer groups, where the individuality of a single member counted for nothing unless it could manifest itself in a collectively asserted force, served as germinal cells of a higher-purposed *Gemeinschaft*. The German Kleinbürger pubs of the Time of Struggle became, as it were, the seed beds of totalitarianism in the much wider landscape of National Socialist dictatorship. In such environs, pre-1933 Nazism celebrated its greatest triumphs and won over its most promising converts.

8

PEACETIME
JANUARY 1933 TO
SEPTEMBER 1939

With Hitler's assumption of the chancellorship on January 30, 1933, the NSDAP became the official state party, wielding clearly monopolistic powers. It underwent a multifaceted metamorphosis that affected the status of its common members and especially of its professional and semiprofessional functionaries. These changes came in the wake of expansion, which was needed in order to deal with the welter of new administrative problems that had to be solved in the Reich. By the end of 1934 the party apparatus increased its strength from a few hundred full-time workers to nearly three quarters of a million dedicated zealots (full-time and part-time). Less than five years later – shortly before the war – the party included 1.7 million officers, counting everybody from the regionally organized core leadership cadres to the various ancillary and adjunct organizations. This expansion resulted mainly from the creation and subsequent growth of two new types of Nazi "leaders" at the grass-roots level, below the Ortsgruppenleiters: *Blockleiter* (block leaders) and *Zellenleiter* (cell leaders).[1] These positions, established in 1933 to ensure closer contact with party members at large in everyday situations, were filled in 1934-35 by 204,359 block leaders and 54,976 cell leaders. By January 1939 there were 463,048 block and 89,378 cell leaders – increases of 126 and 62 percent respectively – while the ranks of Ortsgruppenleiter and *Stützpunktleiter* (outpost leader) together grew only from 20,724 to 28,376, representing a gain of only 37 percent.[2] The ranks above Ortsgruppenleiter increased even less spectacularly.[3]

A better understanding of the enlarged Nazi hierarchy after 1933 requires a more thorough explanation. After his assumption of power, Hitler, with the aid of Dr. Robert Ley (head of the party's organizational section), along with Rudolf Hess and Martin Bormann, covered Germany with a network of party administrative units. These units were organized according to much tighter hierarchical principles than those that had prevailed during the Time of Struggle.[4] The *Führerprinzip* (leadership principle), which required the delegation of authority from the supreme party leader down to the lowliest Blockleiter, was strictly followed. Hitler dealt directly with the *Reichsleiter* (Reich leaders) at the peak of the NSDAP's hierarchy, most of whom had been his personal friends and loyal cronies from the earliest days. Although the Reichsleiters worked from a central pivot (either Munich or Berlin), had specific tasks to perform, and were, by virtue of their rank as well as their ready access to the Führer, nominally superior to the regional party representatives, the Gauleiters, they exercised no jurisdiction over the Gauleiters in either a "constitutional" or a technical sense. In practice, the Gauleiters reported only to Hitler, with Hess or his chief aide, Bormann, acting not as superiors but merely as liaison officers. The Gauleiters, however, whose regions often coincided with the provinces and states, directly commanded the Kreisleiters (district leaders) within their regions. The Kreisleiters in turn gave orders to the Ortsgruppenleiters (chapter leaders), and the Ortsgruppenleiters gave orders to the Zellenleiters. By 1936 an Ortsgruppe encompassed about 1,500 households or family units. Depending on the density of the region, the Ortsgruppe might embrace only a city suburb or perhaps a few villages in the countryside. (If an Ortsgruppe was very small or was still in the process of formation, it was called a *Stützpunkt* — outpost — and its chief a *Stützpunktleiter*. Stützpunkts were found mainly in the countryside.)[5] Each Zellenleiter, in turn, oversaw between four and eight blocks, and a corresponding number of Blockleiters, on the lowest rung of the party ladder, reported to him. In 1936, after some organizational streamlining, one block comprised forty to sixty households. This rigid vertical structure, similar to a pyramid with Hitler at the peak and a veritable mass of party servants at the bottom, was augmented horizontally by a subsystem of deputies, wardens, and various kinds of specialists such as propaganda experts, so that theoretically not even a Blockleiter was without his consorts (the so-called *Blockwalter* — block guardians), who might represent the interests of ancillary organizations.[6]

The most significant change made after the takeover in 1933 had to do with the degree of authority enjoyed by the Nazi functionaries. The enlarged share of tangible power, much of it exercised by over 90 percent of the regionally deployed leadership corps, sprang from a dual conception of legitimacy: that based on the Nazi movement's

"revolution" and that arising from the linkage between the party and
the state offices that resulted from the Law for the Unification of Party
and State of December 1933.[7] Hence the infiltration of all levels of the
state bureaucracy by officials of the NSDAP was essential, and it was
supported post factum by such academic luminaries as Professor Carl
Schmitt. Gauleiters, for instance, might assume the responsibilities of
Länder premiers or commissars or could at least take on Länder
cabinet posts, and Kreisleiters could become county chiefs (*Landräte*).
Ortsgruppenleiters very often served as mayors, especially in the
smaller towns, and even Blockleiters assumed complementary posts in
municipal administrations.[8] Still, the party had to avoid emasculating
itself by overstaffing the governmental agencies with its functionaries.
Although the gradual usurpation of the traditional bureaucracy was
one of its declared goals, the double, triple, or even quadruple
workloads given to party workers often made them more than usually
inefficient. Consequently, in 1937 (February 19) in an attempt to prevent the NSDAP's already low prestige from falling even further, Hess
decreed that the posts of Kreisleiters and Landräte should no longer be
held by the same man. This measure, however, was hard to implement
because of the chronic personnel shortage.[9]

The public's low estimate of the NSDAP functionaries, as well as
of all kinds of party comrades, was largely a result of the way in which
party officials carried out their tasks. Although the higher officials, the
Gauleiters, were visible mainly through pomp and ceremony rather
than clearly recognizable administrative acts, the presence of the
Kreisleiters and Ortsgruppenleiters was directly felt, and the cell and
block leaders were active everywhere. Any Kreisleiter, for instance,
could make a ruling regarding the permanent employment of a
teacher, a ruling that was regarded as official. In the same educational
area an Ortsgruppenleiter was empowered to accept or reject parents
who wished to serve as school trustees. The Kreisleiters' realm also
included regional work-creation programs and the selection and
training of youthful party cadre recruits, and the Ortsgruppenleiters
routinely selected the cell and block leaders and supervised their work
in the Volksgemeinschaft.[10]

The institutionalization of block and cell leaders at the base of the
party pyramid was obviously meant to strengthen the party's hold on
the civilian populace by giving a huge number of small functionaries
power to virtually invade the family's private sphere. To the common
man the concept of totalitarianism was physically embodied between
1933 and 1945 by the insidious Blockleiter, who used the authority of
party and state to force an alliance between the masses and their rulers

by the application of outside pressure. The Blockleiter's official mandate required regular visits to the families of his precinct; he was to monitor the party activities of his charges and report them to his superiors. It was important to him whether or not the children were enrolled in the Hitler Youth (particularly before March 1939, when such service was not yet compulsory) and whether or not the head of the household donated money for party purposes. Ostensibly he ran small errands, selling badges, distributing leaflets, or disseminating details about ever-changing party regulations; in actuality he was always on the lookout for individuals who might be straying from the party line. His special rapport was with genuine Nazi party comrades to whom he gave advice and whose membership dues he collected, but he dealt with every adult German on a day-to-day basis. He was the party's town clerk, town crier, and mailman, and his overriding and securely anchored function was to be an unpaid stool pigeon. Altogether, his job was not an enviable one, and undoubtedly the reason many men became Blockleiters was to escape party harassment themselves. Morale was chronically low among these wretched party servants, and since masses of them were needed, the NSDAP even resorted at one time to hiring non-party members instead of the Old Fighters who were usually sought.[11]

A party functionary's membership number was an important indication of his status within the party hierarchy. According to the regime's criteria it was prestigious for a party servant to have joined the movement before January 30, 1933, and especially so before September 14, 1930, when the NSDAP won its first landslide victory in the Reichstag. As with any revolutionary elite that has assumed supreme power and subsequently embarked on a course of consolidation—a more recent example is Castro's elite in Cuba—the most attractive spoils had to go to the pioneers of the movement. Because of the relative corporate stability of the upper and intermediate leadership strata, Reichsleiters, Gauleiters, and most Kreisleiters and Ortsgruppenleiters were Nazi veterans of long standing, stamped by a tradition of unwavering dedication to Hitler's cause. But below the rank of Ortsgruppenleiter, the combination of high personnel turnover, constantly increasing recruitment needs, and comparatively low functional prestige caused a much greater influx (and outflow) of "new" party members and made these lower cadres much more heterogeneous. Thus a positive correlation existed between rank and corporate stability; the higher up the pyramid the party functionary group stood, the more uniform and entrenched it was.[12]

One might think that after 1933 the conceptions of social prestige usually associated with vertical mobility were not as important in the Nazi party as the "revolutionary" norms of in-group distinction represented by the label "Old Fighter." This calls for an analysis of the social composition of the newly augmented NSDAP hierarchy after Hitler's assumption of power, beginning with the Reichsleiters at the top. They constituted Hitler's camarilla, were formally sanctioned in the new system of party and state, either by being appointed to a cabinet post, as were Frick, Göring, and Goebbels, or by holding ministerial rank in a state government, as did Hans Frank (Bavaria's Minister of Justice), Franz Ritter von Epp (for a while State Commissar of Bavaria), Göring (Minister President of Prussia), and Karl Fiehler (Lord Mayor of Munich). (In addition, some Reichsleiters, such as Goebbels and Baldur von Schirach, doubled as Gauleiters, and Ley was a former Gauleiter.)[13]

The social composition of the Reichsleiter cadre demonstrates once again that the higher the rank, the greater was the proportion of the elite class (upper middle and former aristocracy) in it, and the smaller the proportion of the other two classes. Among these highest functionaries the elite was more than twenty-four times stronger than it was in the Reich population, whereas the lower middle class was heavily underrepresented (29 as opposed to 43 percent) and the workers were not represented at all.[14] There is little in the biographies of these Reichsleiters to suggest either professional or social uprootedness.[15]

Among the seventeen Reichsleiters who were members of the elite, all but three or four were so well established socially that they would certainly have succeeded in their chosen occupations; they did not need the Nazi party to embellish their careers. This applied in particular to five of the six retired senior officers above the rank of lieutenant (Walter Buch, Ritter von Epp, Göring, Konstantin Hierl, Adolf Hühnlein, and Ernst Röhm), one of whom was a general (Ritter von Epp) and another a colonel (Hierl). Of the eight university graduates, there was not one who either had not had a job before becoming active in the Nazi movement or was not intelligent enough to find one: Frank and Goebbels were young intellectuals with solid university records who, in spite of emotional imbalances, would have succeeded in any field or calling; Frick was a veteran senior administrator in the Bavarian government; Ley held a comfortable position with the IG Farben works in Leverkusen; Richard Walther Darré, Otto Dietrich, and Himmler, although not necessarily facing the brightest professional prospects, had the potential to establish themselves in respectable upper-middle-class positions. The only

merchant among the elite members of the cadre, Joachim von Ribbentrop, not actually of aristocratic birth (he had arranged to inherit his
"title" from an aristocratic namesake for professional and social
reasons), nevertheless, came from a very well established family and
had been able to make his way into the executive lounges of a major
company.

Within the elite group of Reichsleiters only Göring, Hess, Baldur
von Schirach, and Alfred Rosenberg might have become "marginal
men" (in Daniel Lerner's terminology) if they had not joined the party.
Despite Göring's talents as an aviator, which had brought him the
Pour le mérite, Germany's highest medal, during World War I, his
extravagant life-style might have led to economic trouble and social
decline had it not been for his marriage into the Swedish nobility early
in 1923. Hess, though a World War I lieutenant and something of a
flying ace, could have been counted as a member of the lower middle
class except for the fact that, while studying at the University of
Munich, he had been appointed assistant to a famous professor,
General Karl Haushofer; if he had not become a Nazi, he probably
would have completed his doctorate and become a professor under
Haushofer's patronage. As for Schirach, when he was studying
German literature in Munich he never came close to reaching the
university position Hess achieved and in fact devoted very little time to
his studies, but he did have some talent as a writer and would probably
have graduated along with the majority of his classmates. Besides, his
patent of nobility and his upbringing instantly identified him as a
member of the social elite. Rosenberg was a more problematical
figure. He had taken a Russian degree in architecture but had never
practiced his specialty. Living as a Baltic German émigré journalist in
Munich, he was hardly known for his writings before he met Hitler.
Still, when he did choose to organize his thoughts, he was a very competent writer and probably would have joined the editorial board of
some right-wing magazine, newspaper, or publishing house.

Within the other group of Reichsleiters, the seven that came from
the lower middle class, the career pattern seems to have been equally
undisturbed. Max Amann, a retired noncommissioned officer from
World War I days, was making his living in various businesses before
he joined the party; later, as head of the Nazi-owned Franz Eher
publishing house, he was to show an astonishing capacity for dynamic
management. Fiehler, Willy Grimm, and Franz Xaver Schwarz were
all well-placed lower and intermediate bureaucrats, the last honorably
retired. Philipp Bouhler, a former army lieutenant, was a white-collar
employee, and Viktor Lutze was a merchant. The only truly "mar-

ginal" individual was Martin Bormann, whose original trade was farming but who had become involved in the right-wing political *Feme* murders and had actually served time in jail before joining the Nazis.[16]

In considering the social mobility pattern of the Reichsleiters, one is impressed by the high degree of stability. Measured in terms of intergenerational mobility, 80 percent of all Reichsleiters were socially stable. Of those, 75 percent were cases of self-recruitment within the elite (upper middle class or aristocracy). The social mobility that did exist was exclusively positive – from lower to upper class. There were no workers in the Reichsleiters' families, either fathers or sons.[17] The intergenerational status continuity of this cohort appears to have been matched by its physical stability. During the whole of the period from 1933 to 1945 there were only three fundamental personnel changes: Röhm was murdered, Hess flew to England, and Lutze died.[18] Horizontal shifts in position also occurred, but they did not alter in any way the social homogeneity of the Reichsleiter caucus: for instance, Frank moved from Munich to Poland, Himmler and Rosenberg became cabinet ministers, and Schirach changed over from Berlin to Vienna.

Social homogeneity also existed, but to a lesser degree, in the Gauleiter corps. Next to the Reichsleiters, the Gauleiters remained the most physically stable group of functionaries in the party hierarchy after 1933, with the most important personnel changes resulting from corps enlargement after the Anschluss in 1938-39.[19] In terms of intergenerational social mobility, the pattern after 1933 was not very different from that of the Time of Struggle.[20]

It is interesting to compare the Gauleiters' social mobility with that of another Nazi elite cadre that was not composed of NSDAP functionaries: the SS officer corps (see table 11). While still more vertically mobile than the general German population, the SS leaders appear to have been more stable than the Gauleiters; moreover, in their social movement, whether upward or downward, they seldom crossed more than one class barrier.[21] This comparison not only underlines the social instability of the Gauleiters relative to the SS, but also indicates the somewhat more conservative character of the SS leadership corps as a status-enhancing vehicle: the SS, despite its quasi-revolutionary appeal, served more as an in-status recruitment mechanism, especially for the conventional elite, than as a vehicle of socioeconomic improvement for socially disadvantaged men – at least at the leadership level.[22]

This leads to the question of class representation and resultant functions in the party leadership corps below the rank of Reichsleiter. Generally, it can be said that one of the original laws governing leadership and management in the NSDAP was continued after January 1933: that the importance of a functionary's position correlated positively with his social status and acquired expertise. Early in 1935, for example, persons with administrative experience, such as civil servants (who belonged either to the lower middle class or the elite) were most common among the Gauleiters and least common among the rank and file.[23] As another example, in 1941 among the intermediate corps of Kreisleiters, the strength of the elite was a little more than half than what it was among the heavily upper-class Gauleiters, while in the next year, among the Gauleiters, the proportion of the elite was more than triple what it was among the Nazi members or rank and file (table 10). The elite also played a part in two other cadres, situated outside the vertically stratified order of Nazi core functionaries (whose responsibility and complementary range of qualifications decreased with the physical size of their jurisdictional area): the Reichstag deputies and the New Functionaries. After 1933 the Reichstag deputies played merely perfunctory roles on the political stage and therefore did not need much ability or training. Characteristically, their elite share in 1933 was somewhat smaller than that of the Gauleiters; and since, like the Reichsleiters and Gauleiters, they were a physically stable body, this ratio did not change significantly during the Nazi regime.[24] The New Functionaries or technical specialists were quite a different case. Because of the state's diversified requirements after Hitler's assumption of power, their ranks expanded through the absorption of highly qualified technocrats, who then superimposed themselves on the vertically stratified leadership corps. The newcomers to this group hailed almost exclusively from the higher circles of society, so that between 1932 and 1934 the corps of specialists as a whole increased its already high elitist proportion from 54.6 to 63.4 percent.[25] Because their administrative functions, if not necessarily their rankings, were higher than those of the Gauleiters, their elite representation also continued to be higher. By 1941 these experts, solidly established within the NSDAP leadership, were more or less identical with the service class of *Amtsleiter* or agency heads. In that year, by virtue of their high supervisory functions in both central and regional NSDAP offices, the Amtsleiters' elite percentage was appreciably higher than that of the Gauleiters (table 10).[26]

Two observations may be made about the percentage of workers within the various cadres of party leaders. First, workers continued to be visibly underrepresented in all cadres. Second, the evidence suggests some deviation from the earlier thesis that party rank correlated positively with class and expertise. For instance, in 1941, contrary to expectations, the proportion of workers in the Kreisleiter corps was actually lower than in the Gauleiter corps (table 10). Evidently, the work of the Kreisleiter appealed very much more to members of the lower middle class than to the working class. In other cases, however, the correlation formula still applied. At the humblest level of political representation in Nazi Germany, that of the local (municipal) diets, the appointed delegates, the majority of whom lived in the countryside and in small towns, had a much higher proportion of working-class members than did the Reichstag deputies, Gauleiters, New Functionaries, and Amtsleiters, who were all higher up the pyramid. Conversely, the local delegates' proportion of elite members was much lower (table 10). But in all of these groups except the New Functionaries the lower middle class was inordinately strong, in both absolute and relative terms; in fact, it was hardly ever under-represented at any level of the Nazi hierarchy.

The limitations of the data do not permit a comprehensive analysis of the social make-up of the administrative party ranks below that of Kreisleiter. This is unfortunate, since the Ortsgruppenleiters, Stützpunktleiters, Zellenleiters, and Blockleiters made up 99.7 percent of the regionally deployed, vertically stratified leadership at the lowest levels in 1934-35 and 99.8 percent of it in 1939.[27] Although it might be reasonable to assume that the lower the rank the more closely its sociological pattern coincided with that of the total membership and, beyond that, with the Reich population, there seem to have been exceptions that were determined by the peculiarities of the local or territorial socioeconomic infrastructure. Thus in the Reich at the end of 1934 the percentage of workers among Ortsgruppenleiters and Stützpunktleiters combined was about 10.8, well below the figure for ordinary Nazi party comrades (33.2 percent). Yet in Thuringia it was 14.3 percent, close to the 15 percent figure that was recorded some fifteen months later for the rural area around Memmingen (Bavaria). Since Memmingen was definitely rural and Thuringia was more rural (small-town and agrarian) than metropolitan, it is probable that the workers who collaborated with the Nazis by acting as low-level functionaries were not predominantly urban dwellers. Here, then, is a parallel to the situation of workers in the ordinary party membership after 1933. Conversely, however, in high-density city centers even the lower-level functionaries tended to come more often from the lower middle class and even from the elite, as exemplified by two party chapters in Munich in midsummer 1934: in the aggregate sample of thirty-three functionaries at or below the level of Ortsgruppenleiter, about one third were from the social elite.[28] A sociological congruence between regionally based functionaries' cadres and corresponding groups of ordinary members was most likely to occur when the lowest cadres in the leadership hierarchy, such as the block and cell leaders, were augmented horizontally by various auxiliary, volunteer, or other local party helpers such as wardens and deputies. Hence in Thuringia, where between 1934 and 1939 no more than 1,400 functionaries could have been Stützpunktleiters, Ortsgruppenleiters, and Kreisleiters, the total of all "Politische Leiters" (political leaders) has been documented as about nineteen times that number (table 12). Significantly, in early 1939 the social structure of these 26,000 or so "functionaries" of varying degrees of distinction appears to have been more like that of the total Thuringian NSDAP membership (87,258 in late 1934) than like the structure of the other leadership categories. Likewise, for the Bavarian rural district of Traunstein in 1937-38, in a regional sample of nearly five hundred offices maintained by the lower party functionaries from cell leader down to block guardian, about 39 percent of the offices were held by workers and the rest by members of the lower middle class, with the exception of some 5 percent held by the elite, including managers, higher civil servants, entrepreneurs, and academic professionals.[29]

It is fair to conclude that at least in the higher and intermediate echelons of Nazi leadership the prominent occupations were those that entailed either respectable local social standing or a sufficiently high degree of literacy. In this sense, the social tendencies of the Time of Struggle were actually strengthened and even quasi-institutionalized. This is hardly surprising, because after 1933 it was essential to introduce more rationality into the administrative processes of the party apparatus. Two examples of strongly represented occupations are farming and teaching. Farmers were relatively strong in the rural administrative areas of the party. Consequently, Stützpunkts, which were mostly rural, had a significantly large percentage of farmers as Stützpunktleiters.[30] As a rule, the percentage of civil servants in an NSDAP office was directly related to the prestige of that office, with teachers generally accounting for more than half of the civil servants in a cadre. The teachers' share — both within the Nazi civil-service group and within the functionary corps — appeared highest in those localities where teachers traditionally enjoyed relatively high prestige. It was probably among the Stützpunktleiters of the countryside that the teachers emerged in their greatest strength, though they were also well represented in the Kreisleiter corps. Generally speaking, in fact, civil servants were greatly overrepresented in all the functionary cadres compared with their position in the Reich, and the teachers as a separate occupational stratum were more heavily overrepresented in the total leadership corps than any other civilian profession in the Reich. This proves the existence, during the Nazi regime, of an interaction between the importance of administrative tasks to be performed at party levels and competency as manifested by literacy.[31]

In considering the age factor of the functionary corps from 1933 onward it might be asked whether the laws that governed the development of the age pattern before 1933 also applied during the Nazi regime. Three observations have already been made in regard to the earlier period: (1) the party leadership was generally older than the rank and file; (2) age correlated positively with rank and office; and (3) original social status (class) and age (maturity based on many years of training and expertise) were reciprocally related. Although there is less certainty that all these laws applied after 1933, it is clear that as far as age is concerned, all the leadership cadres stagnated between 1933 and 1945. Because of limited evidence, however, it is difficult to say whether the rate of ossification was faster among the functionaries than among the ordinary party comrades.[32]

What the data do suggest is that the most distinguished NSDAP cadres also tended to be the oldest, as had been the case before 1933. The prevailing Nazi recruitment processes perpetuated this condition, for the more prestigious a cadre formation was, the smaller was the likelihood that it would or could induct new members. Hence from 1933 to 1945 the Reichsleiters at the top of the hierarchy were not only the oldest peer group, relatively speaking, but also the most immobile from a recruitment point of view. Significantly, their rate of aging in this time span was higher than that of the Gauleiters, who came next in rank, average age, and turnover. In 1933 the mean age of Reichsleiters was 43 and that of Gauleiters 40; by 1944 these mean ages had shifted upward to 54 and 48 respectively.[33]

Various records pertaining to another leadership group, the Reichstag candidates, once again suggest a similarity between the Gauleiters and this national deputy cohort. For example, in 1933 a group of fifty-one Franconian Reichstag candidates (of whom only a small number were actually elected to office) had a mean age of 40, the same as the Reich Gauleiters'. Again, in 1938 the mean age of the Berlin Reichstag deputies was very close to the Gauleiters'—only two years younger.[34]

The average ages of Gauleiters and Kreisleiters (one rung apart on the ladder) may also be compared directly. In 1939 the Kreisleiters' mean age was 37.5 and the Gauleiters' 44. Two years later these values were 41 and 45 respectively.[35] The proportion of Kreisleiters in their twenties diminished from about 14 percent in 1934 to just under 8 percent in 1939, and finally to about 3 percent in 1941; for the 18- to 40-year-old group the proportion declined from 69.9 percent (end of 1934) to 64.5 percent (1939) and then to 52.6 percent (1941).[36]

For the ranks below Kreisleiter the figures are sparser, but the data indicate that in 1934-35 the strength of the prime age bracket (31-40) in the ranks from Kreisleiter on down gradually diminished from the top to the bottom level (table 13). Conversely, the lower ranks were stronger in the most promising age group (18-30), which would reach the desired level of operational maturity (31-40) ten years later.[37] Interestingly, counts that were made to establish the strength of the promising under-30 generation among mixed groups of political leaders up to the rank of Ortsgruppenleiter in three Frankfurt suburbs during the late summer of 1939 resulted in comparatively high percentages from that generation: 9.6 for Riederwald, 15.6 for Obermain, and 28.6 for Berkersheim.[38]

Undeniably, as the dictatorship moved from peace to war, the local ranks were growing relatively older, instead of remaining at a fixed level.[39] This phenomenon cannot be explained by pointing to the recruitment of youth and to the casualty figures for the forces. Such explanations would be tenable only if the party had contributed its leadership personnel to the military effort in the trenches at an unusually high rate. But such was not the case: the party not only sent a smaller share of its functionaries into battle than did the ordinary Nazi male membership, but also, of those who took up arms, fewer were lost.[40]

In actuality, the increasing age levels of the leadership cadres resulted from two factors that led potential young recruits to view a party career with increasing apathy. At the upper levels, from Reichsleiter down to Kreisleiter, the vertically stratified leadership core tended to be monopolized by Old Fighters who were generally reluctant to make room for young newcomers, while at the lower levels, from Ortsgruppenleiter down to block guardian, the incentives to young potential office holders were minimal. The levels of Reichsleiter or Gauleiter may in theory have held certain attractions for qualified young men with strong desires for influence and power, but those levels were closed so tightly that not a single applicant was considered who had not joined the NSDAP before January 1933. At the level of Kreisleiter, however, the rules for restaffing were not quite so strictly applied; and by 1941 Kreisleiter openings had begun to appear for post-1933 party joiners that back in 1934 had been exclusively staffed by Old Fighters.[41] Although from the point of view of age alone the need for constant personnel replenishment at all functionary levels was acknowledged in the highest party circles, and especially so as the war progressed, the younger men, gifted and highly trained, could not comprehend why they should have to stay in some lower party job, waiting for promotion, while higher-placed cronies refused to relinquish what appeared to be quite undeserved sinecures.[42] And positions at the Ortsgruppenleiter and lower levels, which would have welcomed even "New Fighters," simply did not appeal to young Germans, including the graduates of the Hitler Youth, as long as more rewarding, prestigious, and adventurous posts were offered first by the mobilization effort and then by the war economy.

The question remains whether class and age were positively correlated among the Nazi functionaries after January 1933. While such a correlation undoubtedly existed during the Time of Struggle, the data do not wholly support its continuation during the regime. Among the Gauleiters the elite stratum continued to be older than both the lower-middle-class and the working-class strata until 1937, when the average age of the lower-middle-class Gauleiters began to rise steadily above that of the two other social layers (figure 12). By 1937, too, the elite's representational curve had reached its nadir in a movement of gradual deterioration that had started well before 1933 (figure 10). Possibly, the group of socially superior Gauleiters who managed after 1937 to maintain their stance against their lower-middle-class colleagues were identical with the group of younger, allegedly more able Gauleiters who, as Bormann's fledglings, were instrumental in carrying out the new administrative tasks precipitated by mobilization and war.[43] That would, of course, reverse the third formula—that of a reciprocal relationship between social status and maturity—that had been in operation before 1933. But alternatively there may be no connection whatever between a decline in the proportion of elite-stratum Gauleiters and a decrease in the Gauleiters' average age. Indeed, some of the evidence indicates that after 1933, because of in-group closure at the upper end of the functionary body and chronic failure of self-recruitment at the lower end, the factors of social class distinction that might otherwise have had a bearing on age were entirely inoperative. In 1934 the additional group of New Functionaries that had joined the established cohort after January 1933 was collectively 43 years old—three years older than the

Gauleiter corps, a fact that would have coincided with the higher elite content of the New Functionary cadre, so that the expanded group of New Functionaries in 1934 was only six months older than the Gauleiters (40.5 years old as opposed to 40).[44] Yet comparisons for 1941 do not appear to sustain a continuation of this pattern. For in that year the Amtsleiters — virtually an extension of the earlier group of New Functionaries — had the same average age as the Gauleiters, namely 45, even though their elite segment was considerably stronger. A year later the situation was still more confusing, for then the Gauleiters were, on average, 46 years old, while the trusted party stalwarts and lower-grade functionaries, with their relatively small percentage of elitist members, were 47 (table 10). The data are no more enlightening at the Reichsleiter level. A juxtaposition of the average age figures of the (larger) elite stratum and the (smaller) lower-middle-class group shows that the elite Reichsleiters were on the whole a year older than those from the lower middle class, but this small difference over the entire regime period is too insignificant to support a positive correlation between age and social status.[45]

The value system predominating at the lower leadership levels of the Nazi party, the system that spread to the higher levels and worked even beyond the party to put its stamp on German society, was that of the lower middle class. For in spite of the relatively strong representation of the social elite (accompanied by a correspondingly weak representation of the working class), the lower middle class was consistently in the absolute majority in all but the very highest functionary bodies. This state of affairs, or rather mentality, was made possible by the political changes instituted after January 1933, which sanctioned the rule of the "plebeians," as Lerner termed the mass of Nazi leaders. As a consequence, despite the heavy numerical representation of the German elite at the top of the NSDAP leadership, the sociocultural value system to which that elite would normally have subscribed would have been completely overshadowed by the value system of the lower middle class, as had been the case before 1933.

Most functionaries, during their halcyon years of power preceding the war, retained many of the salient mental characteristics of their Time of Struggle predecessors. For all but the most intelligent and educated of them, a prefabricated ideology continued to be substituted for rational and independent thinking; prejudice, particularly the racial kind, supplanted objectivity. The concentric circles of paladins within Hitler's wide-ranging entourage, no less than the host of block and cell officials that comprised well over 90 percent of the entire Nazi leadership, were ill-read provincials who spurned books as well as art and music, despite occasional pretensions designed to demonstrate their *Kultur*. Speer recalls that even among Hitler's immediate associates anyone who had just returned from a vacation in Italy was regarded as an expert in foreign affairs by the rest of the camarilla. It was common knowledge among Hitler's intimates that the Führer held Joachim von Ribbentrop in high esteem as an Anglo-American specialist because of the latter's earlier activities as an odd-job man in Canada.[46] Often, when Nazi functionaries had to make important public statements, their specious, stilted speeches, reflecting their conventional education, caused great amusement in higher society. Yet what else could be expected when the erstwhile farmhand Hildebrandt, Gauleiter of Pomerania, was allowed to hold forth on "Nordic culture," and unsophisticated instructors of the upper Hitler Youth cadres, who at one time might have absorbed biographical tidbits about Schiller and Goethe, taught incorrectly that one had assassinated the other?[47] Figures of speech did not come easily to such pedants as Reich Party Treasurer Schwarz or Party Secretary Bormann, who excelled in the primary German virtue of industriousness. Heinrich Himmler left a plethora of supercilious memoranda and patronizing letters for posterity to read, but his allusions to established wisdom are forced and his historical parallels often miss the point. Himmler's style may have been unique; but he had tens of thousands of little epigones who reasoned in very similar fashion and, as was obvious to the more enlightened, with the same pathetic results.[48]

Hampered by such limitations, the functionaries were called upon first to train themselves, each rank teaching the next, right down to the most impenetrable Nazi party comrade, and then attempt to indoctrinate the whole adult population outside the party. As decreed by the regime, the ideological training of functionaries by functionaries—*Schulung*, as it was called—was an important ingredient within the broad spectrum of party activities. Its main precept was the idea of *Menschenführung*, leadership of men, by holding high the example of good character. It was believed that "good character" was the result of *Herzensbildung*—education of the heart, that archetypical ideal of the Time of Struggle.[49] Menschenführung stressed physical appearance and personal prowesss in leaders and their retinue, as evidenced by sports achievements and a healthy eugenic pedigree. In keeping with these vitalistic goals, a sense of discipline, propagandistic talent, ideological correctness, comradeship, and no more than a modicum of formal, institutionalized schooling were also desirable. To apply Menschenführung was the prerogative of Führers, of leaders, in a tight chain of command, and it had nothing whatever to do, as Hess once reminded his subordinates, with the rational act of "governing by fountain pen or typewriter." Because it was derived from character, Menschenführung as a moral category eluded all attempts at well-reasoned conceptualization; rather, it aspired to loftier, metaphysical planes. Bormann defined it concisely when he stated that Menschenführung was "not a question of science, but a question of the heart and political instinct." It came to serve as the guiding principle not only of leadership selection at most levels but also of functionary patronage and tenure in the case of loyal Old Fighters who really should have been dismissed for their governmental inadequacies.[50]

For want of qualified applicants at the lowest leadership levels, block and cell leaders often had to be appointed without the prerequisite party schooling. This defect might have been partly remedied during the Hitler Youth training, but since relatively few young men were coming from the HJ, older novices were appointed whose ideological slates bore only the most rudimentary Nazi notions. In those instances where Schulung did take place, it followed the stereotypical guidelines laid down by the Nazi leadership core. Records for 1936 that have survived from a Gau training center in East Prussia show that disciplines and routines conducive to Menschenführung in the historic Nazi context were taught above all else. Calisthenics, paramilitary skills, flag ceremonies, and marches and forays into "enemy" border areas abounded, all to be practiced as group activities under the command of a camp "leader." Beyond such physical and, in its broadest sense, sensual activity, appealing to instinct rather than reason, the only food for thought consisted of crass ideological subjects, including "race science, history, history of the Nazi movement, German, program content [*Programmatik* — ideological propaganda] and geopolitics."[51]

Within the Nazi party, the content of Schulung probably appealed to the lower-middle-class, parochial temperament of most trainees. But Schulung became more problematical when newly ordained functionaries acted as *praeceptores Germaniae* by preaching it to the various strata of German society in an effort to force the birth of the homogeneous Volksgemeinschaft. In the case of the general public the specifically Nazi value system clashed with conceptions held by those of other social classes and cultural traditions. These clumsy attempts at National Socialist proselytizing eventually became one of the chief reasons for the political leaders' growing unpopularity.[52] Simple-minded block leaders who went from house to house peddling their ideological wares were rebuffed by the more educated, or by those proud of their own social station, including even many workers.[53] The higher leadership must have realized that sociocultural harmonizing would be difficult, because they made attempts to have party representatives work with those of their own social background, and in particular to recruit block leaders from the upper layers of society in order to impress the elite. Not uncommonly, *faux pas* were committed by party hacks at the grass roots level in both the town and the country. Some overzealous Nazi officials who in 1937 denounced the Christian faith were no more appreciated by pious housewives in Hanover, Swabia, or eastern Bavaria than had been the East Prussian propaganda wardens who in 1933 lectured pompously on the "evils" of Judaism to dignified ladies already appalled by anti-Jewish demonstrations. It is true that occasionally these difficulties were sufficiently appreciated within the party hierarchy so that adjustments could be made. In the fall of 1933 in Bremen, NSDAP speakers of less than average intellect were very reluctant to hold forth on weighty issues of party and state, and a few years later the upper Nazi echelons directed their local representatives to avoid answering questions during field work, "unless one really knows what one is talking about."[54]

In the final analysis, however, the new functionaries could not realize their proclaimed aim of transforming German society because, even under the relatively stable conditions that preceded the war, when the country's prospects appeared bright to many Nazi sympathizers, they failed in trying to become the new, natural leaders of the people. They found it exceedingly difficult to don the robe of a "future upper class," to play the role of a "counter-elite" (Lerner), and to take over where the old elite had supposedly left off. While some of them were showing contempt for various forms of social intercourse customarily espoused by the upper class, such as the old-style dinner parties, others by contrast were lobbying for admission to the exclusive supper clubs and casinos of the old establishment, with no obvious intention of undermining them. Nothing expressed more succinctly the difficulties of transition from the old elite to the new than this contradiction in behavior. The attempt of some functionaries of the "revolution" to eliminate the traditional barriers to authority through insult and invective was really a symbol of their own impotence, not of their strength. In the hallowed temples of learning — bastions of the old ruling order — pathological Jew-baiters like Streicher publicly claimed that if the Führer's brain were placed in a set of scales, it would outweigh all the professorial brains in Berlin;

and the haughtily autocratic Bavarian Gauleiter Adolf Wagner threatened elite-conscious student fraternities with instant proscription unless they turned Nazi, and quickly.[55]

The petty, small-town mentality of the predominantly lower-middle-class leadership corps could not grasp the idea that efficacy was one of the key factors of rational administration—of just such an administration as that which had evolved logically from the principles practiced for decades in Germany. The Prussian and the Baden models were preeminent, and although before 1918 the one had leaned as much to the autocratic side as the other had inclined toward the liberal, they had both been the products of upper-class ingenuity. The Prussian model, extending from the reign of the Great Elector (1640-1688) to and beyond the post–World War I revolution, was famous for its neat delineation of bureaucratic and executive prerogatives, which in post-1918 constitutional terms translated into responsible functions for the representative parliament and in bureaucratic practice manifested itself in an optimal degree of precision and incorruptibility on the part of the state administration.[56]

The Prussian governmental system was the exact opposite of the haphazard governing scheme of the Nazi leaders at all levels of the hierarchy. Because some leaders claimed their authority from state positions held jointly with party office, they may have retained a vestige of the legality and efficiency accompanying the established bureaucratic norms that derived directly from pre-1933 governmental usage. But in the many more cases in which a leader's power rested solely on the putative legitimacy of the Nazi movement, administrative circumspection was supplanted by impulsive self-interest, and institutional jurisdiction tended to give way to arbitrary, and largely ineffectual, rule. The looser the ties were with traditional government and bureaucracy, the wider the areas of arbitrary power became and the greater the likelihood of this power being applied by brutal force and individual oppression.

This curiously dualistic character of Nazi authority, deriving from *both* party and state and blurring the margins of arbitrary power, constituted—so it has been convincingly argued—one of the cornerstones of the Hitlerian dictatorial system.[57] If it is accepted that Hitler allowed, indeed encouraged, a certain measure of administrative license to be built into the power base of every NSDAP functionary, it follows that the Führer not only tolerated but actively fostered the growth of the kind of Nazi leader who, while observing the strictest formal obedience to his superiors in the hierarchy, was at liberty to exercise what appeared to be personal, even whimsical, domination over his immediate subordinates. This was, in fact, the essential meaning of the leadership principle.[58] Only against this background can one comprehend the extent of indiscriminate political action at every leadership level, as well as the high degree of self-righteousness and the seeming absence of fear of censorship from above. Because party leaders of every kind, to a greater or lesser extent, followed the novel Nazi standards of public behavior, a specifically Nazi code of political ethics gradually developed that helped to shape their corporate identity as a socially homogeneous in-group.

It is, of course, a truism that the exercise of political power based on human egotism tends toward abuse of the governed rather than toward paternalistic benevolence. Significantly, the available empirical evidence indicates that Nazi leaders were rarely, if ever, motivated by benevolence. Yet two examples of kindly behavior by leaders at the lowest levels — behavior prompted by their negative reaction to irregularities from above — show that not all Nazi functionaries needed the officious but hollow exhortations issued by Hess and Ley to the effect that Nazi leaders should mix with the people and further their best interests.[59] In Westerland on the North Sea island of Sylt in the summer of 1936, Ortsgruppenleiter Jakobsen sided strongly with his charges, mainly blue-collar workers, after being subjected to the arrogant and insensitive conduct of visiting Cologne Gauleiter Grohé. And in the Upper Bavarian countryside, Stützpunktleiter Sturm, himself a laborer, was sympathetic to people trying to leave the farms in search of higher wages in the cities, in protest against "farmers who are living off the fat of the land and knowingly depriving their servants of the bare essentials."[60] More frequently, Nazi leaders, claiming to reconcile the natural opposites of populist appeal and stringent regimentation, boasted that they were fulfilling particular needs in their own precincts; in reality, though, they were simply feeding their own egos. Self-seeking Gauleiters even went so far as to set up foundations for the indigent, "in order to curry public favor."[61]

Hermann Rauschning's insight that the Nazi system worked well mainly because of its oppressive mechanisms, in which "everyone is the other man's devil, everyone supervises everybody," attains a new validity when one considers the many cases of frivolous abuse of power at all levels of leadership.[62] At the bottom of the hierarchy, the use of block and cell personnel as spies for the regime was a treacherous abuse of their position of trust vis-à-vis the people; the ubiquitousness of these nauseatingly inquisitive though bumbling tyrants cannot be overemphasized.[63] In February 1934, at a higher level, a rurally based Stützpunktleiter reported to his superiors the name of a traveling salesman who had just accused the Führer of overtaxation. At a still higher level the capricious acts of Ortsgruppenleiters ranged from reprimanding BBC listeners and informing on political attitudes to wanton shooting of Jews during the regime's anti-Semitic campaign of November 1938. Higher still, a Kreisleiter could do all this and more, including interfering out of sheer malice with the affairs of an ancillary organization, or dispatching men and women in droves to the concentration camps. Finally, a Gauleiter or Reichsleiter had almost unlimited power over the individual liberties of ordinary civilians; to the average German, such a leader's hostility could mean death instead of life. With these "little dictators," as Count Schulenburg called them in 1935, literally everywhere, unrestrained in the use of powers that could wreak havoc, it is not difficult to believe Hess's assertion, made in June 1935, that "the political evaluation of a fellow German very often is of the gravest consequences not only for his own future, but also for that of his family." Here was the origin of what was to become "prosecution of next of kin" during the final years of the Third Reich.[64]

The arbitrariness of the local and regional potentates manifested itself in other ways. Most of them ruled too much, but some of them ruled too little: absenteeism on the part of Gauleiters or even Kreisleiters was not unheard of.[65] And this fitted well into the picture of the Nazi regime as a system of competing rivalries, in which at a given leadership level everyone fought with everyone else, with Hitler presiding securely at the top of the pyramid. There was no end to petty party intrigues. Goebbels was known to despise all the other paladins because he deemed them more stupid than himself. Gauleiter Wahl of Swabia was almost cheated out of his office by Munich's Gauleiter Wagner, who conspired with Ley in this matter. Himmler and Rosenberg kept up a somewhat ludicrous battle over Nazi ideology. Gauleiters like Streicher, Bürckel, Mutschmann, and Koch became so successful at these games that, to all intents and purposes, they enjoyed absolute political power over their "subjects"; only Streicher, in the course of time, was tripped up by becoming involved in a monstrous case of corruption in his region. And it has aptly been said that one of the reasons why Hess flew to England in 1941 was that, not being adept at scheming, he was being overtaken by the unscrupulous Bormann.[66]

Corruption and graft, rampant in all ranks of the leadership, constituted merely another side of this phenomenon. They arose as a natural consequence of the Old Fighters' mentality, which was geared to the dictates of a spoils system: now was the time to reap the material rewards for the sacrifices of the Time of Struggle. This again correlated with the lower-middle-class mold of the leadership core; materialistically minded shopkeepers, white-collar workers, or even lower civil servants, who gradually entrenched themselves in positions of political power, found it harder to resist temptations to enrich themselves than had the members of the old elite, who were either too high-minded or too wealthy to succumb.[67] Possibly, as Rauschning suggested more than forty years ago, this was yet another function of Hitler's principle of *divide et impera*: to encourage the vanguards of the "revolution" to wrongfully enrich themselves, thereby creating a common consciousness of guilt that tied all the "culprits" to the supreme leader as the ultimate arbiter who could then grant them absolution.[68] Hitler was the charismatic leader who, as Max Weber has explained, "rejects as undignified all methodical rational acquisition, in fact, all rational economic conduct." By those terms, his underlings were the "charismatic warriors," for whom "booty is both means and end of the mission."[69]

It was not that Hitler's lieutenants were badly remunerated. Except for the bottom levels of block, cell, and local chapter leaders, where men tended to serve in an honorary capacity, the salaries and expenses paid to all NSDAP officials were more than enough to ensure them a comfortable existence.[70] As a rule, these were above the average paid for comparable positions in private industry or even in the conventional civil service. The higher the position, the better the emolument, and the greater the opportunity to accumulate riches and offices, including those of state. Reichsleiters and Gauleiters customarily could expect to be granted a Reichstag seat, which would bring them 500 to 600 marks monthly on top of their party salary. Thus the German Reichstag, having lost all of its former constitutional functions, was turned into an institution for rewarding proved Old Fighters. Other gratuities also accrued as a result of party office: a mansion, for instance, such as the one financed out of Cologne municipal funds for Gauleiter Grohé, or the one purchased with government money for the personal use of East Prussian Gauleiter Koch. In 1935 Hans Schemm, the Gauleiter and Bavarian Minister of Culture, was said to have earned 200,000 marks a year — 70,000 from his offices and the rest from his activities as a party journalist. If an official felt that his rewards were not high enough, he could always ask for more. In 1934 the former Gauleiter Paul Hinkler, who was not at that time a Reichstag delegate, complained that he could not subsist on the 500 marks (comparable to the stipend of a Kreisleiter) he was receiving as police chief of Altona-Wandsbek. Two years later, this former public school teacher was back in the ranks of the deputies, at a time when the unemployed in the national work-creation programs had to get along on less than 60 marks a month.[71]

Whatever graft and corruption occurred at the base of the hierarchy is understandable in light of the low financial compensation for those largely honorary jobs. But at the upper levels Hitler actually sanctioned financial abuse as a convenient method for deploying Nazi power. Of course, the origin of the post-1933 transgressions could be traced back to the irregularities practiced by a largely lower-middle-class leadership during the Time of Struggle, and therefore they were not unique.[72] But whereas those of the Time of Struggle had been haphazard, the later malefactions developed into a system. At the Kreisleiter level and below, such improprieties came to resemble common felonies, and hence the malefactors were more easily indicted by those who dared to indict them. At these levels concerned public prosecutors found it least difficult to stamp out petty crime. Thus it was possible for the Ortsgruppenleiter of Ebermannstadt in Bavaria to be successfully tried on charges of embezzlement and forgery in November 1935.[73] There is evidence to suggest that the higher party stooges, who committed the more serious acts of larceny, ended up beyond the reach of conventional justice and even without party disciplinary action because Hitler willed it so, despite the lip service that Hess paid to the ideal of personal incorruptibility after the Röhm affair.[74] Gauleiters like Erich Koch and Friedrich Karl Florian were particularly skillful in maintaining "special accounts" for large amounts of money that could not be traced and that even Party Treasurer Schwarz had difficulty in bringing under his control. Joseph Bürckel, who in 1938 was Gauleiter and State Commissar in Vienna, had at that time a million and a half marks at his disposal, stashed away in various bank safes and inaccessible for audit.[75]

The tastes of the party bosses became more expensive as they connived at laying their hands on ever-larger caches of funds. They developed an obvious predilection toward the way of life practiced by the old elite, and their attempts to imitate it marked them as true petty bourgeois parvenus. These bloated men attempted to live in opulent villas that before 1933 they could only have dreamed about but that became more readily attainable during the gradual expropriation of the German Jews. While it is true that only a few could afford the sort of grandiose dwelling that Bormann built for himself not far from Hitler's Berghof in Berchtesgaden, many tried to ape the pretentiousness of Göring's hideaway, Karinhall, albeit on a smaller scale, or to adopt the runic decor revived by Himmler's SS. Many aspired to set up a private hunt; most of them, in stark contrast to Hitler's frugality, enjoyed a heavily laden dinner table. At the Gauleiter level, ostentation reached absurd heights when someone like Wilhelm Kube ordered schoolchildren to stand at attention during his regular small-town visits and was attended by personal lackeys at mealtime.[76]

Finally, nothing characterized the self-seeking attitude of these petty despots better than their greed for illicit sexual adventure, for alcohol, and for oversized cars. These longings identified them as frustrated upstarts from the lower levels of German society who naively thought that if they adopted such tokens of upper-class superiority the ouster of the old ruling order would be as good as accomplished. Ironically but not untypically, they misjudged the social values attached to these symbols in the scale of prestige. Illicit sex was not so generally accepted by the German upper crust as it was, for instance, by the French *haute volée*. As for the use of alcoholic beverages, German etiquette demanded that quality should be considered above quantity and, above all, that personal composure should never be lost. And although large automobiles were undoubtedly a status symbol for the influential few, men of culture often spurned such vehicles in favor of more unobtrusive transportation. From 1933 to 1939, when material goods were still plentiful and the euphoria over the formal change in power had not yet died down, the caricature of the average Nazi party boss would have been that of a stocky Kreisleiter approaching middle age who after an evening of too much beer was making advances to a BDM leader in the back of his chauffeured limousine. Such were the by-products of intermediate political power prior to the outbreak of hostilities in the fall of 1939.[77]

9

WARTIME

SEPTEMBER 1939 TO 1945

World War II, not surprisingly, made an enormous impact on the social structure of the Nazi bureaucracy. The pressures imposed by the conflict naturally led both the general population and the regime to expect more from the party, and these increased demands necessitated changes in the pattern of leadership. Yet, although certain critical aspects of the bureaucrary changed during the course of the war, there was little change in the relationship between social status and administrative demands; class conditions throughout all leadership ranks remained remarkably stable not only from 1933 to 1939 but right on to the end of the Third Reich.

Much of the information in this chapter is anecdotal rather than empirical because archival sources are still comparatively barren with regard to the status of Nazi leaders during World War II. Yet whatever primary evidence does exist will be sufficient, in conjunction with (secondary) accounts from memoirs, diaries, and other nonprimary material, to document the history of the Nazi party functionaries through the war years — a history that is not at all inconsistent with that of the Nazi bureaucracy in peacetime.

The problem of leadership recruitment, which had been difficult even before the fall of 1939, was further complicated by the exigencies of war. One of the obvious reasons for this was that seasoned party officials of military age were being increasingly called to the colors, and that other potential replacements were young men who were leaving either school or the Hitler Youth or the special party training centers. After the introduction of general conscription in 1935, the NSDAP had been slow to commit its own staff for obligatory service in the newly formed Wehrmacht. This was partly due to the growing rivalry between the party and the armed forces, expressed especially in the leaders' jealousy of army prerogatives, a jealousy that the Wehrmacht officers met with expressions of contempt.[1] Until 1939 party leaders, who could claim exemption in a variety of ways, had been largely immune from the military draft. In addition, their paramilitary and premilitary schooling tended to be supervised not by the army but by the SA. This was changed, however, at the beginning of the conflict: on October 1, 1939, Hess rescinded the supervisory privileges of the SA. But even then, party leaders in training were put into a somewhat limited program that concentrated mainly on rifle skills. Eventually, however, these modest demands had to be stepped up considerably. Judged by data from southern Westphalia, whereas only about 15 percent of all political leaders had been conscripted by the beginning of 1940, by May 1943 the proportion had jumped to about 42 percent. Correspondingly, during the first ten months of 1942 the number of specifically draft-exempt key functionaries decreased by approximately one quarter.[2]

As a rule, military service at the front was not popular with Nazi party leaders, and they did everything in their power to postpone it or prevent it altogether, using as their chief excuse the allegedly more pressing problems of the home front. There is evidence to suggest that many leaders who were drafted served only in token capacities or for very short periods. While the ordinary conscript had no hope of ever returning from the trenches, a top functionary like Baldur von Schirach was able to resume civilian life after comparatively light military duties lasting for only six months between the victory over Poland and the capitulation of France. Similarly preferential treatment was accorded to lesser men, such as deputy Gauleiter Kurt Schmalz. But Kreisleiter Otto Dettmann, whose party position was somewhat less important, was obliged to take part not only in the conquest of Poland but also in the entire western campaign before being allowed to return home in 1941 and dedicate himself to the issues of his native Rostock.[3] A comparison of functionaries with common Nazi party comrades shows that throughout the war the functionaries had a better chance of escaping the draft, lost a smaller share of their men as casualties, and received a smaller number of military decorations.[4]

Archival records imply that when functionaries did report for war duty, they were quite successful in staying behind the lines, perhaps even in positions of relative comfort. In fact, Nazi leaders at the front came to be regarded by the regular soldiers as shirkers or cowards. At home, at the height of the conflict, it was rumored that if party bosses had to join the military, they usually managed to take over plush administrative posts in the newly acquired territories where fighting had ceased.[5] There were party men who served with distinction, who preferred to make the supreme sacrifice rather than return to the routine duties of the home front. Nevertheless, the typical leader claimed military exemption; this was done partly in order to maintain his seniority, which would have been suspended while he was in the Wehrmacht.[6]

For many leading functionaries the war turned out to be a blessing in disguise. Their already well-developed instincts for spoils led them into areas that offered lavish booty and extraordinary professional opportunities. The suspicions on the home front concerning the sybarite's diversions in the "new" territories were well founded. By reliable accounts, Poland was a favorite nesting ground for functionaries who, when drafted for war service, were able to land an armchair post, often as the consequence of a formal promotion in rank. For instance, a 35-year-old butcher who had attended the party training institute at Sonthofen was whisked into the position of Kreisleiter in a subdivision of newly acquired Polish Wartheland in 1940; and Kurt Schmalz's first wartime posting was that of a deputy Gauleiter in the same recently created Gau. Old Fighter Balnus, an Ortsgruppenleiter in Tiegenhof, also managed a promotion to deputy Kreisleiter in the formerly Polish district of Zempelburg, until he was forced to don a Wehrmacht uniform. After the invasion of Russia in the spring of 1941 these opportunities were further expanded. In September 1942 Kreisleiter Anton Gerriets of Kolberg (Pomerania) was inducted into military service not as a soldier in the armed forces but as "Deputy Director of the Work Area Nikolaiev" in the Ukraine, under the control not of an army general but of the party stooge and nominal East Prussian Gauleiter Erich Koch, Reich Commissar for the Nazi-occupied Ukraine. Indeed, the professional posts opened by the war to party zealots of proved loyalty and requisite experience in the leadership ranks seemed at first plentiful and lucrative: no sooner had the war begun than Martin Bormann's right-hand man, Helmuth Friedrichs, prepared a list of Old Fighters, all active in the NSDAP hierarchy at the level of Kreisleiter or higher, who were earmarked for extended missions with a view to enlarging their "personal horizons." This list of twenty-four names not only includes impeccable service credentials but reveals an average age for these men of slightly over 36, nearly two years below the norm for Kreisleiters at that time. Doubtless, the party assigned its top group to the most auspicious posts in what was expected to become a geopolitical expansion of gigantic proportions.[7] Even in the highest echelons, however, Hitler's cronies profited most.

Gauleiters Koch and Lohse moved from their East German provinces to the Baltic states and the Ukraine, where they virtually set up court. Hans Frank did the same in Cracow, although he came under certain restraints from the rival SS.[8]

With thousands of personnel being shifted from home ground to serve in the occupied territories and with increasing inductions of party staffers into the armed forces, the NSDAP leadership shortage in the Reich became more and more critical as the war dragged on. The dilemma was multidimensional. Because the inflow of new recruits was decreasing, the average age of officials was steadily increasing. The party leadership tried in every possible way to attract new, young recruits to its ranks. A freshly graduated throng of specially trained *Ordensjunker*—hopefuls just out of party finishing schools like the "Order Castle" at Sonthofen—was dispatched to Poland after September 1939, so that the more experienced administrators could stay at home. Beginning early in 1940 the NSDAP trained approximately one hundred functionaries in a series of ten-day courses at Sonthofen. At the same time, leading party strategists in Hess's office were emphasizing the immediate necessity of testing novice party leaders in action. When by the beginning of 1941 more territories had been added to the Reich, including some, such as Alsace, that contained German-speaking populations, hopes of new recruitment possibilities brightened. Still, the deficiencies persisted, and by 1942 they were noted especially at the block and cell leaders' levels. Around 1943, available and qualified men had become such a rarity that they were traded from one party agency to another, with arrangements being made over the incumbents' heads. In the spring of that year, according to Goebbels, Hitler had to acknowledge within the closely knit circle of his intimates "how extremely rare are men of real calibre." Luckily, in the summer of 1943, because of the elimination of several party affiliate offices, some five thousand functionaries were on hand for other party chores or, if need be, military service. But this did not help much. A year later, newly created "Political Squads," which were to be staffed exclusively by "fanatically dedicated National Socialists" and whose real purpose was paramilitary home defense, turned out to be nothing more than a chimera dreamed up by ambitious pencil-pushers working under Ley. In the fall of 1944, shortly before the end of the European war, Gestapo chief Ernst Kaltenbrunner conceded defeat in the area of leadership recruitment when he cabled Bormann from Vienna that it was not even possible to appoint a suitable Kreisleiter to replace a deputy Gauleiter, because there wasn't one around.[9]

The difficulties were compounded by the realization on the part of the NSDAP master-minds that if the war was to be won and the home front protected, the pseudo-bureaucratic principle of Menschen-führung on which so much of the regime's administration had been based in the initial years of the Third Reich had to be replaced by the governing principle of *Leistung,* or efficiency, as quickly and permanently as possible. Since this proposal went against the grain of the predominantly lower-middle-class mentality, it was accepted very reluctantly. In November 1939 the party chancellery still vehemently supported deputy Gauleiter Kurt Schmalz of Wartheland, formerly of South Hanover, on the basis of his character and his alleged ability to win the confidence of the man on the street, while at the same time admitting "the extent to which the party was now compelled to heed the principle of Leistung." In keeping with the old attitudes, the men surrounding Hess and Bormann still distrusted party leaders such as Dietrich Klagges, the Minister President of Brunswick, as a candidate for Gauleiter, "because his forte seems to lie more in the area of public administration than in Menschenführung."[10] In practical field work, however, such value systems proved less and less useful, as the case of Kreisleiter Hermann Bernhardt shows. In December 1940 Gauleiter Eggeling of Halle asked Reich Party Treasurer Schwarz whether he had a place for Bernhardt, who was unbearable in his current post. "Despite the best of human qualities," explained Eggeling, "he simply does not possess the aptitude necessary to deal with the issues arising in his office." Eggeling's concluding remarks were astute and to the point: "Today, many an old and decent party comrade carries on under the shadow of tragic failure. While I deplore that this is so, it does not alter the fact that such men are just not tolerable in the office of Kreisleiter." Schwarz's reply was sympathetic, but he was unable to help: it would be impossible to employ Bernhardt in the Munich party treasury "since his credentials in no way comply with the requirements governing my area of operations."[11] Yet by the end of 1942 Leistung had become more firmly anchored as a postulate of government and organization within the party. Even Hitler had ordered that in matters regarding personnel deployment "personality and performance would have to be the sole criteria of judgment." Henceforth, promotions through the ranks of the party were to be contingent on actual achievement instead of on seniority, as had been the custom. These tenets were reemphasized in July 1944, even though at that time their proper implementation seemed precarious and the results uncertain.[12]

In this final phase of the Third Reich the problem was too deep-seated to warrant a solution by decree. The belated infusion of rationality into the party apparatus was insufficient to entice prospective candidates to come and stay. In competition with lucrative and influential positions offered by industry and the armed forces, even a higher career in the party held few attractions for potential neophytes. Ever since 1933 the party's prestige within the population had been declining in direct proportion to the life of the regime. Where the incentives were puny, only the least qualified became interested in party chores, and "volunteers" at the lowest levels performed only under official pressure. "Suitable people there were plenty," recalls onetime Gauleiter Wahl in regard to the war period, "but they avoided an office. Hence our selection had to take place at the expense of talent." There were even cases, though they were rare, of well-placed party officials resigning in order to accept positions in industry. Increasingly, high-school graduates decided against a full-time occupation in the NSDAP. According to research conducted by the SS, the percentage of upper-school leavers contemplating a party career shrank from 1.1 in 1940 to 0.2 in 1942.[13]

The hopes of the top NSDAP leaders understandably rested upon the Hitler Youth as the foundation for mass recruitment. But after paramilitary training in the HJ these young men turned their attention instead to the Wehrmacht, which offered more instant and more conventional symbolic gratification, such as an officer's insignia. Not only did the HJ leadership itself become chronically understaffed, as most of its members were drawn to the front, but even the graduates of special HJ training institutes turned away from the NSDAP to fight the enemy in the trenches. By the spring of 1943 the top party echelons had become acutely aware of the likelihood that Hitler Youth veterans, while fulfilling their obligations in the army, would get so accustomed to a soldier's life as to be totally estranged from the ways of the party. Hence Ley made the futile recommendation that Kreisleiters in Germany should keep in touch with these youths by letter and personally look after them on furlough. "Through careful treatment of this *very important problem* a stage must be reached where these young men regard their principal tasks and their fortunes as lying chiefly with the party, so that they will remain unconditionally faithful."[14]

The central problem, of course, was still the closure of the entire leadership cadre at its upper end. The Gauleiters, those veritable models of Old Fighters, simply refused to make way for potential successors, and they were supported in this attitude by the Führer himself. Although the party chancellery's personnel officers came to recognize the need for implementing rational laws of selection and promotion, Hitler, despite the organizational chaos and wanton corruption all around him, remained convinced that the unflinching fealty of his oldest friends was more important to stable autocratic rule than the highest professional qualifications. Yet as long as the path to the peak of the pyramid remained blocked to younger, brighter, and more ambitious men, even the Führer could not completely close his eyes to the faults and shortcomings of his sycophants, who, as he exclaimed in 1942, represented the only dependable reservoir of administrative competence in the land. By 1943 it was obvious that some old Gauleiters were either too sick or too inadequate to carry on, while a few younger ones who were working along the lines of Leistung were putting in more creditable performances. In the last few years or the war — not that it would have mattered any more — Hitler, who had already been forced to part with Streicher, agreed to relieve Gauleiters Schirach and Weinrich, whose work in Vienna and in Hesse contrasted sadly with that of two of their highly dynamic colleagues, Lauterbacher of South Hanover and Hanke of Upper Silesia.[15] How much all of this affected the professional morale of the entire leadership corps had been revealed as early as 1939 by Bormann's caustic comment that Nazi functionaries had evidently learned to live with "the insecurity of a political leader."[16]

They had also learned to live with their own ineptitude. During a war requiring that leadership in both the military and the civilian and governmental sectors be firmly based on merit and performance, the mediocrity of many party functionaries became more and more glaringly obvious in spite of the gradual introduction of the criterion of Leistung. Their behavior fell far short of the standards of ingenuity and efficiency customarily espoused by the Wehrmacht, by industry, and by the conventional civil service. The representatives of the NSDAP floundered at every level of the hierarchy from the beginning to the end of World War II. Thus in the Eiffel Mountains west of the Rhine near Koblenz, Gauleiter Gustav Simon had acquired by 1940 the reputation of being Germany's sloppiest regional administrator. In the East at that time, Hans Frank and Arthur Seyss-Inquart, the governors of the Nazi-dominated Polish Generalgouvernement with headquarters in Cracow, cursed the day in October 1939 when they had brought in party "experts" to fill the new administrative posts opened by the Polish conquest, because since then nothing at all had been accomplished. On the home front the blocks and cells were often supervised by moronic party wardens who were too old and feeble to be sent to the trenches. Thus in May 1942, during a lecture on the reconstitution of Europe after the Final Victory, one block leader made himself the laughingstock of an educated audience in Berlin. "Before long he succumbed to a wild polemic against the Jews, who were held responsible for every conceivable ill," recorded one listener. "Jews who had been wounded in the Great War were said to be just as bad. It was almost as if he blamed those Jews especially for having got themselves wounded so they could use this as a cover for today. Anything is possible on the part of these brains. The man then paused, lost his thread, and simply left the stand." One Kreisleiter in a small Thuringian town who was obliged to make public speeches "tried hard and embroidered his rhetoric with lots of difficult words." In March 1943, Goebbels, Gauleiter of Berlin, ordered Kreisleiters and Berlin Gau personnel to report "for a good dressing-down." He immediately "dismissed two local leaders in western parts of the city who were altogether too lax." Seven months later the Kreisleiter in Frankfurt found occasion to reprimand his staff for not appearing in public and for generally neglecting their chores.

Meanwhile, in nearby Kassel Gauleiter Weinrich had failed completely at his task of civilian air-raid protection; and although assistance to the population during and after air raids was one of the most important responsibilities of NSDAP functionaries, Weinrich was not alone in losing his nerve. In Starnberg it was reported that every time the air-raid siren sounded, Kreisleiter Franz Buchner made a dash for the air shelter, "where he then would sit for a period staring into a corner. All of a sudden he would lie down on his back on a table-top and pump the air with his legs, before finally getting down and going home." Contemporary critics agreed that the inability of local party leaders to cope with the bombing problems was superseded only by their vainglorious attempts to cover up their ineptitude. "The bombing terror is the invention of Anglo-Saxons and Jews," a Stuttgart party boss assured his frightened flock in the summer of 1944. "And even if we shall be forced to live in shelters and in forests, we shall never surrender!" The unique combination of naiveté and fanaticism that characterized the wartime functionaries was neatly expressed by a joke that made the rounds of a heavily bombed Stuttgart during the last years of the war. Men, women, and children are huddled together in a bunker waiting for the enemy attack to end. In the midst of a long-winded speech rallying support and sympathy for the regime, the block leader asks: "And where would we be right now, if we didn't have our Führer?" Immediately a calm voice answers from the corner: "In bed." These simple-minded local and regional leaders still put their trust in Menschenführung. Significantly, the Berlin government's chief interpreter, Paul Schmidt, recalls a Kreisleiter who in April 1944 was responsible for a railway disaster because apparently "he knew more about the leadership of men than about leading a passenger train." At the height of the conflict even reasonably sophisticated insiders were under the erroneous impression that the party was being kept alive at home by the "sixth or seventh best" because the more qualified people were at the front.[17]

Yet while the overall capability of the NSDAP functionaries sank to a new low during the Second World War, the number and difficulty of their tasks actually surpassed the peacetime level. The complicated technical and organizational problems that had to be solved in order to protect the civilian population were too much for the average functionary, who in peacetime had had to deal with liturgy rather than logistics. After 1939, for instance, the ritualism of Schulung was replaced by a serious psychological effort to counteract the enemy's propaganda, an undertaking that tested not only the patience but the skills of any but the most cynical party representatives. Of even greater importance were the roles that Ortsgruppenleiters and Kreisleiters were expected to play in the procurement, safeguarding, and allocation of essential foodstuffs and fuels. And some party bosses had to oversee salvaging operations during natural emergencies, such as torrential floods, for the civilian members of the relief organization Technical Emergency Aid, which had mastered those crises in ordinary times, had long since been incorporated into the armed forces.[18]

By far the most crucial demands were made in the area of home defense. Until the front-line warriors assumed last-stand positions within the borders of the old Reich, this responsibility devolved entirely upon Hitler's lieutenants. Years before the war, farsighted planners had estimated that approximately eight million Germans of every walk of life would have to be involved in one way or another in air-raid protection activities; moreover, it was clearly incumbent upon local leaders below the rank of Ortsgruppenleiter to assume key functions.[19] But the demands that were made after 1940 on party cadres of all ranks far exceeded the forecasts of the greatest prewar pessimists. If there were any standards left by which party leaders could be judged in the discharge of their duties, it was their behavior before, during, and after an Allied air raid. While the Gauleiters, who were raised to the position of Reich defense commissars by 1942, were held responsible for the orderly evacuation of especially endangered urban centers, such as the old part of Magdeburg, it was the Kreisleiters who had to oversee the evacuation or rescue operations, with the Ortsgruppenleiters assisting them and cleaning up the rubble. In the last three years of the war, party recommendations for medals or promotions were based to a very large extent on an individual's performance as an air-raid warden. This was increasingly the case after Goebbels invoked Total War early in 1943. The fight-to-the-finish that was to symbolize the regime's unbending will to survive put unbearable burdens on the shoulders of the common functionary and singled him out, once again, as the vanguard of the movement.[20]

There is no question that the power held, whether legitimately or arbitrarily, by all political leaders increased substantially after the beginning of the war. Despite their failures in administering party and state, and despite their inferiority in internecine battles with such other bearers of authority as the Wehrmacht officer corps, Nazi functionaries were able to enlarge their sway over the civilian population, and this gave them an even more exaggerated sense of self-importance. Party bosses made up for whatever prestige they might have lost in internal party relationships by their petty autocracy over the people.[21]

It might seem that the large measure of personal power enjoyed by functionaries would have been enough to once again render the party cadres' position attractive, if only to those types of men who commonly thrive on the exertion of influence over their fellows. This power was particularly evident when professional careers, physical freedom, or life were at stake. Although overshadowed by the terror wielded by the Gestapo and SS since the beginning of the war, on which modern historiography has tended to concentrate, the part that the political leaders played in the subjugation of the common man — working hand in glove with the police and consigning many a political opponent of the regime to captivity, torture, or even death — has been generally overlooked.

After September 1939 the block and cell leaders intensified their control over every German man, woman, and child at all levels of everyday existence: in the street, on the apartment stairs, and, more and more, in the air-raid shelter. It was on the routine reports of these local leaders that the Ortsgruppenleiters' political assessments were based; and if those were unfavorable, a promising career, even one in the civil service, could be instantly cut short. Buoyed by their sense of authority, some local party leaders went so far as to exercise their prerogative by proxy, like a Zellenleiter near Würzburg who entrusted his 14-year-old daughter with the task of snooping on the neighbors.

At a slightly higher level the Ortsgruppenleiters, especially in rural areas, often ruled tyrannically. Of some it has recently been said that they "absolutely governed the village." Apart from their political evaluations, they could grant or withold moving permits, influence the type of accommodation available, and show bias in the distribution of fuels, foodstuffs, or clothing. An ordinary German who criticized an Ortsgruppenleiter openly during the war risked the concentration camp, or worse. The Ortsgruppenleiters' political significance vis-à-vis the public was further enhanced by their appointment as auxiliary justices at political trials during the last two years of the war. Hence in April 1944 when Erich Knauf, a democratically minded journalist, was sentenced to death by Roland Freisler's infamous People's Court, an Ortsgruppenleiter by the name of Winter was one of the officials responsible for the verdict.[22]

In keeping with their larger area of formal jurisdiction, the powers of the Kreisleiters were even broader. Kreisleiters had the right to use as instruments of prosecution, if not persecution, subdivisional party courts, the so-called *Kreisgerichte*; these courts had authority chiefly over party members, but certain of their recommendations, such as expulsion from the party, could trigger much more drastic actions by the Gestapo. Indeed, it was at the Kreisleiter level that the collaboration between the administrative party organs and the Gestapo appears to have taken place most frequently and most effectively. This was undoubtedly a function of the close interrelationship between the Kreisleiter's post and various fairly elevated state offices, such as the *Regierungsrat* (office of state counselor) at which the party official technically appeared as superior to the agent of the (state) police. An occurrence at Waldshut, a small Baden town on the Swiss border, is typical of many similar, well-documented cases. On January 17, 1942, the local bandage maker, F.S., who allegedly had refused to contribute wool cloths to the war effort, was dragged from his shop by a horde of party members at the behest of Kreisleiter Dr. E. After Kreis officials fastened a wooden gallows, three meters high, to a nearby fire hydrant, they subjected S. to death threats and demeaning treatment in a mock trial. While the Kreisleiter watched surreptitiously from a distance, the Ortsgruppenleiter of the town took actual charge of the proceedings, which also included an exhortation to surrounding schoolchildren to spit on the culprit. After the conclusion of this "celebration," as it was officially called, the craftsman was led away by an officer of the Gestapo, "whose presence there," according to a bystander's account, "obviously had not been entirely accidental." Kreisleiters are also reported to have directed the near-lynchings of German women who had been publicly accused of being "Polish whores," while in the eastern territories these functionaries might select Jews for execution and might violate and shoot non-Jewish prostitutes. Even more than Ortsgruppenleiters, Kreisleiters figured prominently as cojurors in political kangaroo courts; by 1944 they had helped to hand down innumerable death sentences.[23]

Naturally, the uses of power, implicitly justified by the demands of Total War, were even more far-reaching and potent at the highest administrative level of the Gauleiters. Commensurate with their multiple activities as territorial party administrators, defense commissars, and mobilization and armaments plenipotentiaries, they held instant authority over life or death. These powers have been grossly underestimated because they were surpassed by those of the more ferocious and lethal executors of the Nazi regime such as the SS. Yet at the height of World War II it could indeed be fatal to spread unpleasant truths about a Gauleiter who reigned over his region with the air of an autonomous potentate, strengthened by Hitler's constant support. Thus the hapless Hessians who in 1942 questioned the honor of the singularly corrupt Frankfurt Gauleiter, Jakob Sprenger, were instantly arrested and imprisoned. Generally, however, like the omnipotent princes of feudal times, Gauleiters took care to present themselves as popular rulers, for such was the latitude of their invested powers that they could afford to grant substantial favors to the people. For this reason the gratuitous favoritism dispensed at the Gauleiter level was as much a function of the willfulness of Nazi rule as were terror and oppression. These functionaries' urge to be universally recognized by their "subjects" not as tyrants but as benefactors inspired Gauleiter Robert Wagner to grant cash and letters of recognition to Germans who had been temporarily evacuated from the western borderland late in 1939; and whenever the general standard of living showed indications of a slump, the Gauleiters were the first to ostentatiously decry it.[24]

The party leaders' heightened consciousness of omnipotence during the war generated further and crasser acts of graft, corruption, and licentiousness, all in accordance with the laws that govern patterns of autocratic behavior. Although the party's remuneration to its full-time officers continued to be more than sufficient, with a Kreisleiter earning nearly double the salary of a schoolteacher and a Gauleiter receiving about six times as much, the war provided opportunities for self-aggrandizement far beyond those that had existed in peacetime.[25] These temptations were difficult to resist. Petty graft and embezzlement, involving local party funds, valuable raw materials collected for recycling, and stocks of groceries and alcohol, became general at the lower level of the hierarchy. The ration-card system was circumvented wherever possible; black-market dealings were a popular if somewhat risky supplement. By 1940 even Kreisleiters, shielded by their more experienced superiors, were helping themselves to monies out of illegitimate "special accounts" that Reich Party Treasurer Schwarz found hard to trace.[26]

To the general public, the plump cheeks and potbellies of ordinary party officials became as symbolic of Nazi prominence as did the automobiles requisitioned for "war purposes," sumptuous living quarters, and household servants that were otherwise in very short supply. Nowhere were these trappings more profligate than at the Gauleiter and Reichsleiter levels. In East Prussia, where he still officiated when he was not in the Ukraine, Gauleiter Koch resided in a villa, expropriated from the Polish Prince Czartorisky, that overawed the visitor with its huge marble hallway. In Vienna, Gauleiter von Schirach soon became the private owner of several mansions; at official dinners he showed off his Hapsburg imperial china and silverware while liveried servants attended his guests. Engaging in war-profiteering schemes on an immense scale, Hitler's paladins maintained private hunts, bought expensive paintings from the rapacious Göring's "personal" collection, hoarded the choicest of wines and liqueurs in huge quantities, and threw lavish parties lasting for nights on end, often, as in the case of deputy Youth Leader Artur Axmann, in the company of beautiful young actresses who were obliged to "entertain" the men. Sexual excesses, particularly among the higher functionaries, were more common now than before the war. The higher up the Nazi functionaries climbed, the more likely they were to be carrying on in the "life style of victors" long before the coming of the Final Victory. And the more clearly the average German citizen saw that the Nazi leaders' corruption was a direct denial of the much-celebrated Volksgemeinschaft, the greater became his contempt for the party. By May 1943 the security service of the SS in Kitzingen had reason to believe that the mounting feeling of disgust might soon lead to expressions of open revolt.[27]

As in peacetime, Hitler remained unopposed to this moral decline. In dealing with those cases of misconduct that came to his personal attention, he maintained the same ambivalent attitude that characterized his position on other weighty issues of party and state unless his charismatic authority was at stake. The evidence suggests that although Hitler acknowledged these irregularities to critics such as Goebbels or Schwarz and approved of their endeavors to eradicate the irregularities as well as to discipline the entire party cadres, he at the same time encouraged his cronies to stock up their larders. As long as the National Socialist state survived, Hitler regarded corruption and immorality as necessary functions of intraregime rivalries, which in the final analysis supported his own supremacy.

ı April 1940, when the war had barely begun, Hitler anxiously moralistic Hess to implement a "Führer Decree" curtailing the political leaders' right to wear uniforms in places of public entertainment such as dance halls or bars. At the same time Hitler delegated power to Schwarz to eradicate the secret accounts. But two years later, when the misappropriations of Erich Fischer, an official in the party's press section, were creating an internal scandal, Schwarz himself agreed with Goebbels that the affair should be hushed up. Nevertheless, Hitler was agitated enough to decide in July 1942 that in order to avoid conflicts of interest the high-ranking party administrators should no longer be permitted to serve on the controlling boards of private industry. Early in the following year, in a private conversation with Goebbels, Hitler went through the motions of condemning the high style of living so rampant in his entourage. The Führer was going to "forbid hunting for the duration of the war and the use of alcohol at any events sponsored by the party," wrote Goebbels in his diary, but then he concluded apprehensively: "The Führer is disgusted. I hope he will take proper measures." Indeed, a few days later, Hitler had State Secretary Lammers draw up an ordinance admonishing "prominent persons in the state and the Party to behave according to wartime requirements." But, noted Goebbels, "this decree is quite inadequate, and I demanded something more severe." Recognizing Hitler's utterances for what they were — mere lip service — Goebbels did not even bother to report to the Führer that high-ranking functionaries, among them Frick, Rust, Darré, and Hierl, had been put into a compromising position through their complicity in war profiteering. Finally, in the fall of 1943, the efficiency-minded Speer threatened to curb the territorial high-handedness of the Gauleiters and asked Hitler to admonish them concerning alcoholic excesses. But he got nowhere with the Führer. Reminiscing about this incident six years later in Spandau Prison, the former Reich Armaments Minister came to realize, as Rauschning had done much earlier, that Hitler "consciously tolerated or even deliberately promoted the corruption. It tied the corrupt men to him."[28]

But the denouement was near. In the National Socialist leadership corps the various crises of the past came to a head during 1944 and the first few months of 1945. In the aftermath of the abortive attempt on Hitler's life on July 20, 1944, which for a short while strengthened the emotional bonds between the Führer and his hierarchy, Hitler, ever more distrustful of the Wehrmacht, delegated still more authority to the Gauleiters, chiefly in the area of home defense, and they then commissioned their subordinate staff accordingly.[29] There can be no doubt that such formal amplification of power led to an even greater arbitrariness on the part of NSDAP leaders toward the hard-pressed civilian population. By the fall of 1944, while vindictive block and cell leaders continued to snoop into citizens' private affairs and filed endless reports on them, the agents of the Gauleiters in their capacity as regional defenders acquired the means to force all able-bodied civilians into the emergency paramilitary Volkssturm. Endowed with the powers of martial law, Kreisleiters and Gauleiters could put to death alleged war-shirkers or persons accused of "defeatism." Late in January 1945 this unfortunate fate befell the deputy mayor of Breslau, Dr. Spielhagen, who was executed by Gauleiter Karl Hanke for "attempting to flee." Gauleiter Lauterbacher of Hanover, too, threatened with death the war-weary Germans who had displayed white flags of surrender to the Allies in order to save their home towns.[30] Whether or not these measures were enacted in a mood of general despair is difficult to ascertain, but judging by the extent of corruption and immorality, the political leaders must have known that the *Götterdämmerung* was about to descend. The drinking bouts that were staged by Gauleiter Fritz Wächtler in Thuringia—until he himself was killed by the rival SS—and the plundering and hoarding of foodstuffs and valuables by intermediate cadres were evidently inspired by frustration and the fear of impending doom.[31]

In those final months of the regime the political leaders abandoned any attempts at rationality that might have been made early in the war and returned to their former superstition, emotionalism, and half-truths. These once again became the basis of their thoughts and actions. Menschenführung as an administrative principle triumphed in the end. Schulung was revived. Propaganda supplanted sensible politics. As a consequence the most absurd schemes took hold of those who had almost ceased to hope that they could stem the oncoming tide. Bavarian Kreisleiter Hans Dotzler, by trade a poultry farmer, conceived a plan early in 1945 whereby former Catholic priests serving with the SS were to be dropped behind Soviet enemy lines in order to incite Catholic Slavs against the Stalinist regime. Details of the stratagem were sent by Bormann to Himmler, who filed the letter without comment. Robert Ley, who was almost always drunk, worked on the project of a Freikorps to be made up of all those who could still pedal a bicycle, carrying a grenade and a rifle to fight tanks in close combat on the streets. After this was turned down, Ley waxed enthusiastic over the "invention" of a lethal radiation machine that Albert Speer was to adopt. When told about it, Speer went along in a show of mock support. This once ambitious Munitions Minister had long since given up hope, surrounded as he was by ignorance and stupidity, which, as he says, "flourished as the enemy approached."[32]

As it turned out, Schulung and Menschenführung were to fail the Ortsgruppenleiters, Kreisleiters, and Gauleiters in their last efforts to escape disaster. Acting through Bormann in September 1944, Gauleiter Koch persuaded Hitler not to delegate the final defense of towns and villages to the more rationally oriented SS and Wehrmacht but instead to authorize the Gauleiters themselves to organize and direct the Volkssturm, composed of invalids, boys, and old men. The Gauleiters and their helpers, however, long alienated from military practice, were incapable of getting the Volkssturm movement off the ground. They could hardly cope with the masses of refugees who were pouring into the heartland of the Reich from the surrounding territories, let alone resist the advancing tanks. Some tried, like Bürckel in the West, only to give up and resign; Bürckel died under mysterious circumstances before the year of the Allied invasion was out. When it finally dawned on the Gauleiters that the days of the Third Reich were numbered, most of them, like the hordes of lesser leaders, could think only of themselves and how to minimize their personal misfortunes. Gauleiter Jordan in Halle-Merseburg went through the motions of "defense" until, in early May, he simply laid down his arms, sent his men away, and went home to his family. Karl Hanke in Breslau put up a much stiffer resistance initially—so stiff, in fact, that Hitler and Goebbels raved about him as "the best of our Gauleiters"—but then in May he suddenly took off in a small aircraft and was never seen again. It was a most inglorious retreat for the petty Nazi potentates, who were so devoid of honor and any sense of personal responsibility that they could not face up to the consequences of their deeds. Only an old Kreisleiter near Halle accepted personal responsibility. He first delivered his town intact to the Americans, against his innermost convictions, and then he committed suicide. In early April 1945 Bormann, before Russian soldiers killed him in the streets of Berlin, issued what must have been his last directive to the NSDAP's political leaders: to fight on further, "either to victory or to death." On May 4, Gauleiters Koch and Lohse, lodging with the caretaker government of Admiral Dönitz in Flensburg, demanded the use of a submarine in order to escape to South America. The insanity of this idea was matched only by the greed and cowardice that had given it birth. Just three days later the Allies accepted the German Wehrmacht's capitulation. The Thousand-Year Reich had fallen, as had Hitler and the leaders of his movement.[33]

10

SOCIAL PROFILE
OF THE LEADERS
1919-1945

The social characteristics of the Nazi leadership cadres from 1919 to 1945 were determined fundamentally by the ordinary factors of social stratification. Like every other group of German society at the time, the Nazi functionary corps was composed of the usual three social layers: working class, lower middle class, and elite. These divisions belied the implications of Nazi propagandists that social differences or differentiations in rank inside the party cadres, as in the Volksgemeinschaft, were negligible, or that they would be neutralized by the common bond of the National Socialist idea.[1]

Although it would be incorrect to claim that the entire Nazi functionary corps was staffed by "typically frustrated, lower-middle-class individuals" or by "marginal petty bourgeois," there is no doubt that the representatives of that class were in the absolute majority.[2] Hence the leadership corps was stamped by the value system of the German lower middle class, and its political and administrative actions can be viewed as the product of lower-middle-class mentality. This judgment, however, requires three reservations, all of which emphasize the importance of the elite class in the leadership. First, the relative proportion of elite elements was higher among the leaders than in the party at large or in the Reich population. Second, the elite proportion tended to increase with rank. And third, the elite element was particularly influential when extraordinary leadership was called for, as in the period between 1932 and 1934. These three points show that even the monopolistic party of the Nazi regime, whose corporate behavior has been described as impulsive, disorderly, and confused, was affected by the elite's rules of rationality, performance, and efficiency.

In this correlation between general effectiveness and social stratification, the NSDAP was not different from other governing elites in Germany. But in order to form a judgment about the efficacy of the party's leadership corps, one must measure its efficiency against that of other groups or subgroups of German society — for instance, industrial trusts, cartels, or the army — or of other formations of the National Socialist regime such as the SS. For example, the precepts of rationality underlying the activities of certain Kreisleiters, as in the evacuation of civilians before Allied air raids, appear to have been sound by comparison with the antienemy propaganda gestures of confused block guardians; but they pale before the strategic decisions of Wehrmacht staff officers and the guidelines of the SS that activated the mass killings of Jews at Auschwitz.

Although the Nazi leadership corps comprised the same three classes as other German groups, the mechanics of social stratification could be superseded and either modified or entirely suspended by the various marks of in-group distinction. The most significant and powerful of these was the status of Old Fighter. As a rule, the lower an individual's NSDAP membership number was, the greater was his peer-group standing in the party and particularly in the leadership cadre. And since party rank correlated positively with Old Fighter status, the highest party cadres enjoyed not only the greatest authority but also the greatest measure of corporate stability and, in the last analysis, the most stable sense of collective identity. Old Fighter criteria of selection did not come into play at the bottom of the hierarchy, where personnel fluctuations were much greater, because party members of long standing had already risen to higher levels. These anomalies at both extremes of the hierarchy accentuated the recruitment problem that already was seriously complicated by other idiosyncrasies of the NSDAP structure.

The future of the party was especially threatened when the social cohesion of the leadership corps based on vertical, socioeconomic stratification interacted negatively with its corporate identity based on Nazi veteran status. Because Old Fighter status was associated with the lower-middle-class origins of the NSDAP, and because the Old Fighter (lower-middle-class) mentality eventually prevailed at the highest leadership levels, the Old Fighter element must have continually militated against the social homogeneity created at those levels by mutual upper-class consciousness. Perhaps one of the more important reasons for the eventual failure of the Nazi leadership body as a social unit was that its awareness of collegiality as Adolf Hitler's executive arm could at any time be punctured and even ruptured by conflicting allegiances — for instance, when the sentiments of conventional class distinction clashed with the peer-group pride of early joiners. Such inner contests, with their inevitable centrifugal ramifications — waged between groups, between groups and individuals, or between individuals (including top leaders of the party) — were marked by peculiarly ambivalent attitudes, half traditionalist and half revolutionary, half bourgeois and half bohemian, half pedant and half intuent. Never could the opposites be reconciled, as the example of Joseph Goebbels shows. How often this Propaganda Minister, well versed in the values of the upper middle class that had adopted him, and one of the early foot soldiers of the movement, went on record as opposing the small-mindedness of his fellow Old Fighters![3]

Yet beyond these conflicting determinants there were elements of social definition that came to have a more unifying effect on the conglomerate Nazi leadership. One was the shared experience of deprivation and suffering before Hitler's assumption of power. Years of personal sacrifice for the movement had united Hitler's followers and stamped them, even in the eyes of political adversaries, as martyrs for a cause. Even before 1933, tales of heroic sacrifice for the fascist ideal gave rise to the hushed stories that no charismatic movement can do without and that eventually merge with the legends of its origins.[4] The profligate post-1933 Nazi literature, portraying the years of struggle in highly subjective terms, bears witness to the impact of historical events on the hearts of men and women who were facing existential crises in their lives. Out of these stark realities there finally emerged the necessary myths on which the survival of the Nazi movement as a chiliastic phenomenon depended. That these myths, so cherished by their protagonists, defied intellectual analysis by more critical outsiders was again a function of the petit bourgeois mentality with its leaning toward half-truths grounded in folklore.

The stories of harassment and persecution prior to 1933 served as a hallmark of in-group distinction until 1945 and beyond, as every student of Neo-Nazism in West Germany knows. This unifying characteristic of Nazi cadre membership was reinforced, after 1933, by a new communality based on the accepted practice of graft and corruption. The fruits of these practices were viewed by the Nazi peer group as compensation for injuries sustained during the Time of Struggle, and for this reason Hitler's coming to power seemed to mark the beginning of a phase of requital.

Corruption became possible because the new leadership corps was invested with powers that allowed great latitude for abuse. The corps's unconscionable interpretation of such powers in its own interest denoted the watershed between the new-style and the old-style political bureaucracies. The exercise of political power that gave free rein to personal whims and the private satisfaction of sensual pleasures, that ran the gamut from relatively innocent illicit sex to sadistic acts inflicted upon unhappy victims, was utterly opposed to the standards of the ascetic administrators of the Prussian school, with their roots in the nobility and the *Bildungsbürgertum*, the cultured patriciate. Of course, the extent of such indiscriminate use of power can only be measured relatively. Hans Mommsen's recent verdict, "Party officials, unless they took on some additional state assignment, remained more or less impotent," emphasizes the importance of the NSDAP's relationship with other agencies of the regime, such as the Wehrmacht, the SS, or the members of the old bureaucracy of notables who were slowly being absorbed into the new state. After the SA had run its course by mid-1934, the party leadership's virtually unlimited power over the population was only exceeded by that of Himmler's police squads, but during the war the relative importance of the party receded. Future research may reveal whether or not it is justifiable to speak of a renaissance of party prerogative after the attempt on the Führer's life in July 1944. Certainly, by then the NSDAP had gained important ground in its struggle against the teachers, who, as civil servants, were representatives of the state; by then the NSDAP was preparing itself to assume authority in the realm of home defense; the Wehrmacht was suffering various degrees of undermining by party representatives; and in 1945 other state organs were effectively reduced to agents of the party.[5]

Can it then be deduced that the NSDAP leadership constituted a new elite in German society, as has been argued by a score of writers? No, that was not the case. The Nazi functionary corps was not a counterelite composed of "marginal men" on the fringe, from largely plebeian origins, as Daniel Lerner and others have stated.[6] Contrary to Nazi wisdom, the leadership was not even a collection of the most valuable party comrades.[7]

To classify as a counterelite, the leaders would have had to bring about the completion of the National Socialist revolution, but this they were not able to do.[8] And, coming after and aping in various respects their austere Prussian precursors, they retained far too many epigonal characteristics to be considered a new species. After the changeover from one elite to the other, the new leadership was unable to take up a truly contrary posture and thus to function as a counterelite. There were too many elements of accommodation, of fusion, of absorption. In social composition alone, the pattern of mutual interactions and interlockings between the two groups was nearer to collusion than to collision. This personnel crossover worked in one of two ways: either young party specialists with the requisite qualifications infiltrated the traditionalist bastions and slowly bent them toward the regime, or upper-class men joined the Nazi cadres and openly operated on the Third Reich's behalf. Often the lines were so blurred that no one could tell who the turncoats were. What about Count Fritz-Dietlof von der Schulenburg, for example? Did he embrace the Nazi movement as a scion of the old ruling clan, or did he attempt to win over his peers as a convinced Nazi follower? What about Albert Speer, the self-assertive "artist"? Was he a patrician first (as he consistently took pride in claiming) and a National Socialist second, or vice versa?[9]

Nor can it be maintained that the Nazi leadership corps was composed of marginal men of plebeian origin. The majority of the Nazi leaders were far removed from any Lumpenproletariat. These representatives of the German lower middle class were as typically self-complacent and secure as any of the other Kleinbürgers in city, town, or country. Lerner's allusion to "plebeian" connections between the Nazi leadership and the populace is grossly misleading in view of the very low proportion of blue-collar workers in any of the Nazi cadres.

This study has shown that the Nazi leaders became stuck midway in their journey toward the development of a truly innovative, even revolutionary, "elite," as did the "Nazi Revolution" they heralded. Although they acquired some authority in certain areas as well as a discernible measure of prestige, they did not succeed in becoming new role models for German society. The twelve-year Reich was unable to mobilize a quick, effective revolution. It lasted long enough to develop some evolutionary characteristics, but not long enough to sustain this evolutionary course. Nazi functionaries were, therefore, social hybrids — revolutionaries with the jargon and mannerisms of well-fed, premature pensioners. Instead of developing into a new functional species, they always retained the marks of recently initiated novices. This made them look awkward and unsure, even when they were very confident inwardly.[10] "Never forget it," exclaimed an East Prussian functionary at a party leaders' gathering in early 1939, "we are the exponents, the future upper class!"[11] As far as it went, this statement was indisputable. At that moment the speaker and his audience still had every reason to believe it.

CONCLUSION

This analysis of the social composition of the Nazi party's general membership and its leadership corps would not be complete without some last reflections. They refer to the differences between the two groupings, the unique role of the lower middle class in the party, and, more definitively, to the concept of a National Socialist "revolution." Although this phenomenon has already been mentioned in various contexts on these pages, a final consideration of the parts of all three social classes in it — either planned or real — would cast more light on the general theme of continuity and change in the history of German society since World War I.

There were no significant differences between the general membership and the functionaries with regard to their motivation for joining the party. Since the functionaries were usually recruited from the central membership core, the lines of division between membership and leadership became increasingly blurred after 1933. It was in the humble office of Blockleiter that ordinary members and leadership cadres most clearly merged, because that office was the easiest one for an ordinary party comrade to attain. Hence, although a block leader was technically an officer of the NSDAP, in more realistic terms he was an especially vulnerable party member. The functionary corps was thus a prominent extension of the general membership, and the membership was the popular fundament for the party officers. This view is strengthened by the Nazi leadership's own definition of party membership: every National Socialist, whether incorporated in the functionary echelons or not, was to be considered a part of the revolutionary vanguard. Indeed, the figures available for the months just before the war show that almost one-third of Nazi party comrades could be identified as members of the Political Leadership Corps.[1]

A superficial view of the party between 1919 and 1945 would lead one to conclude further that there were no discernible differences in social makeup between the rank and file and the functionaries. In both groups men predominated over women, the age structures were about the same, and the working class was underrepresented while the lower middle class and the elite were overrepresented. It would seem, then, that a judgment recently made concerning the SPD in the Weimar Republic could also be applied to the NSDAP: "There is very little evidence to suggest that the . . . leadership was unrepresentative of its membership."[2]

But the detailed examination of the party undertaken for this study has revealed that in several important respects there were significant differences between the party's rank and file and its leadership.

First, male supremacy was much more pronounced in the cadres than in the general membership. Although the cadres never included a single member of the female sex, women always made up a small proportion of the rank and file.

Second, there were differences between the age patterns of the two groups that were significant enough by 1939 to suggest that the survival of the Nazi party would be endangered by an extended period of military activity. Before 1933 the ages of both the functionaries and the ordinary members had tended to be comparatively low, although the functionaries were always a somewhat older group because of the requirement that office be commensurate with maturity. But after 1933 both groups found themselves in danger of senescence as the party gradually lost its appeal as a vehicle of social mobility for the young. And after 1939 the war, which drained off young men, compounded these problems, especially for the cadres. At this point the general membership turned, albeit reluctantly, to young women, the only available recruitment reservoir, and induced greater numbers of them to join the party. For the functionaries, such a move was impossible: Hitler could not part with the treasured notion of male supremacy in the highest party echelons. Consequently, although by 1944 the social structure of the common membership was changing noticeably —toward lower age levels and a larger share of women—no such changes were occurring in the leadership corps, which remained exclusively male and was growing increasingly older. A projection of these conditions in an undefeated German Reich well beyond May 1945 would portray the leadership as a near-gerontocracy and the ordinary membership as a massive retinue of youthful women. Though this projection is entirely hypothetical, it illustrates the divergent patterns of growth of the functionaries and general membership — patterns that conflict with the image of relative uniformity evident in the movement before 1933.

Third, there were differences in social stratification. While the elite was consistently overrepresented in the rank and file of the party, this situation was more evident in the cadres: the higher the cadre, the greater the degree of elite overrepresentation. The converse applied to the working class: always underrepresented in both formations, this class was far less in evidence in the cadres, and its representation there declined with increasing rank.

In previous chapters, these conditions have been linked, through the application of a formula equating upper-class status with rationality, to the persistence of a pattern of rational administration harking back to pre-Nazi days, without which the "revolutionary" NSDAP bureaucracy could not have functioned. The fact that this rationality, as symbolized by the principle of Leistung or efficiency, was overshadowed until the end of the Third Reich by the counterprinciple of Menschenführung ("leadership of men"), has been traced to the predominance of lower-middle-class elements in the NSDAP. These elements were about equally overrepresented in both the general membership and the leadership corps; in fact, their overriding presence in both formations suggests similarities rather than the differences between the NSDAP's mass base and its leaders. Moreover, the historically important role that representatives of the lower middle class played in the foundation of the party, their continued numerical strength in it, and the specific value system with which they imbued it mark this class as the single most important influence in the development of the NSDAP from 1919 to 1945.

Judged from the point of view of party membership (both rank and file and leadership corps), the National Socialist movement was indeed a preeminently lower-middle-class phenomenon, as several scholars, notably Seymour Martin Lipset, have already declared. Not only is there no "need to abandon the middle-class thesis of Nazism," as has most recently been urged, but it would be folly to do so. Insofar as National Socialism is concerned, Wolfgang Sauer's judgment is still valid "that the lower middle classes, both rural and urban, were at least one of the major social components of fascist movements."[3]

This reaffirmation of a well-established view must, however, be accompanied by some important qualifications. In principle, they revolve around the concept of revolution.[4] If the view is tenable that members of the lower middle class came to dominate National Socialism and the Third Reich to the point of neutralizing the power of the former ruling class, one might reasonably assume that they attained their positions of power through revolution. One argument against this view has been advanced by Arno Mayer, who holds that in modern Europe the lower middle class has been known for "a predisposition *against* revolutionary confrontation" rather than for revolution. At the most, Mayer thinks that the petite bourgeoisie has been capable of "negative unity in defense of the status quo against a revolutionary challenge."[5] A similar argument has been offered by Arthur Schweitzer, who claims that prototypical representatives of the lower middle class (the old middle class) have lacked revolutionary aims, inasmuch as National Socialism perpetuated such long established notions, as the "conservative ideology of status."[6]

But there is absolutely no doubt that Hitler and his followers perceived themselves as the revolutionary vanguard of a movement bent on effecting fundamental changes in the existing structure of society.[7] One of the objects of a Nazi "revolution" would have been the removal of the traditional elite and its replacement by the NSDAP functionaries. The key question, therefore, is whether the documentation of the *intent* of revolution is tantamount to saying that this revolution actually took place — and hence that the lower-middle-class functionaries of the NSDAP were genuine revolutionaries.

On this point, a few observations may be made. One of the more startling findings of this study has been the consistency of elite overrepresentation in the Nazi party from 1919 to 1945. There are three possible explanations for this phenomenon. (1) Whatever the (lower-middle-class) tenets of National Socialism may have been, many members of the elite felt a distinct affinity for them and were ready to forsake the elite value system that had governed the mentality and behavior of their predecessors. It is conceivable, for instance, that many of the New Functionaries who joined the Nazi corps toward the end of the Weimar Republic were of that ilk. For whatever reason, they were on the brink of losing, or had already lost, their faith in the old order while nominally belonging to it. Count Schulenburg and Albert Speer were probably among them.[8] (2) Since members of the elite were accustomed to ruling, they jumped on the National Socialist bandwagon in order either to avoid losing their old positions of influence or to gain new powers. Such an attitude of cynical opportunism was exemplified by Reinhard Heydrich, the former naval officer who became Himmler's deputy police chief, and by Dr. Werner Best, the administrative jurist who was appointed Nazi governor of Denmark. (3) Many members of the old elite teamed up with the Nazi party in order to protect themselves from physical extinction by "retarding the radicalization of the revolution," as Rauschning succinctly put it.[9]

The extinction of the old elite was indeed envisioned by the would-be revolutionaries. But it was impeded and temporarily halted by two factors that the Nazi rulers had not foreseen.[10] First, Hitler and his cronies had underestimated the extent to which members of the old ruling order would join the movement. To remove these members would have amounted to a partial purge of the party, and purges, while sometimes a necessary instrument of totalitarian rule, may be extremely dangerous for the leadership. Second, the Nazi rulers were always dependent on the old elite to maintain the essential functions of government, if not of the party, because the Nazi system itself failed to produce enough efficient leaders of the new type. This situation naturally increased Hitler's hatred of the old elite and strengthened his resolve to destroy it.[11] These two factors continued to restrain the Führer until after the Putsch of July 1944, when he finally undertook to eradicate the elite. In this area World War II, also, blocked the Nazi revolution rather than helping it along, as has sometimes been claimed.[12]

Finally, the Nazi "revolutionaries" intended to close the gap between the working class and the other classes — or rather, the only remaining class, the lower middle class — once the removal of the old elite had been accomplished. Ideally, the historic proletariat would have merged with the historic lower middle class to create the new Volksgemeinschaft. Judging by the party's membership, by about 1942 the Nazis had gone a long way toward attracting an ever-greater number of workers to their movement by offering them bread and circuses as well as managing to suppress Marxist dogma capable of deterring proletarian would-be converts from accepting Hitler's brand of socialism.[13] But in this respect, also, the Nazi revolutionaries were destined to fail. Till the end of the Third Reich the working class stayed underrepresented in the common membership, to say nothing of the leadership corps.

On balance, then, the Nazi revolution remained unfinished. Perhaps it was a partial revolution, and its flagbearers were partial revolutionaries. But it was not a permanent revolution, programmed to go on forever, as Rauschning had envisaged in 1937.[14] It is impossible to conceive, in fact, of the smugly entrenched Nazi bosses as a hard core of "permanent revolutionaries" and of the millions of common Nazi members as their loyal followers. Whatever else they may have been before January 1933, by 1944 the party officials obviously lacked the asceticism, the stamina, the determination, and, last but not least, the intelligence of the true revolutionary, even if they did not lack his ruthlessness. Yet even by the end of the Third Reich the Nazi party had not accomplished through brutality and force what it had failed to do through persuasion and direction: to remove the old class differences and forge a new *völkisch* community. Instead, the class conditions that had prevailed after 1918 and again after 1933 continued, to a large extent, to prevail after 1945.[15]

TABLES

Table 1. Frequencies and percentages of occupations and classes in gainfully employed German population, Reich, summer 1933.[a]

Class	Occupational subgroup	Frequency (N)	Percent of total
Lower	1. Unskilled workers	10,075,782	37.25
	2. Skilled (craft) workers	4,478,803	16.56
	3. Other skilled workers	203,737	0.75
Subtotal		14,758,322	54.56
Lower	4. Master craftsmen (independent)	2,585,551	9.56
middle	5. Nonacademic professionals	483,208	1.79
	6. Lower and intermediate (petty) employees	3,359,248	12.42
	7. Lower and intermediate (petty) civil servants	1,402,189	5.18
	8. Merchants (self-employed)	1,624,118	6.00
	9. Farmers (self-employed)	2,082,912	7.70
Subtotal		11,537,226	42.65
Elite	10. Managers	143,659	0.53
	11. Higher civil servants	128,794	0.48
	12. Academic professionals	259,310	0.96
	13. Students (university and upper school)	129,292	0.48
	14. Entrepreneurs	91,296	0.34
Subtotal		752,351	2.78
Total		27,047,899	100.00

Sources: (1) *Berufszählung: Die berufliche und soziale Gliederung des Deutschen Volkes: Textliche Darstellungen und Ergebnisse* (*Statistik des Deutschen Reichs: Volks-, Berufs- und Betriebszählung vom 16. Juni 1933*, vol. 458) (Berlin, 1937), pp. 48–51. (2) *Statistisches Jahrbuch für das Deutsche Reich 1934* (Berlin, 1934), pp. 534–540.

a. In the case of students, employable rather than employed.

Table 2. Percentages of members or joiners of DAP and NSDAP chapters by social class and occupational subgroup in various South German towns and the Reich, 1919–1923.[a]

Class	Occupational subgroup	(A) DAP Munich pre-Hit.[b]	(B) DAP Munich end 1919[c]	(C) DAP Munich Jan 1920[d]	(D) DAP Munich May 1920[e]	(E) DAP Munich 1920[f]	(F) NSDAP Munich 1920–21[g]
Lower	1. Unskilled workers	6.4	9.0	2.5	3.5	18.4	20.6
	2. Skilled (craft) workers	13.5	12.1	20.9	20.9	11.8	6.0
	3. Other skilled workers	4.3	5.6	q	q	5.1	1.9
Subtotal		24.2	26.7	23.4	24.4	35.3	28.6
Lower middle	4. Master craftsmen	7.8	7.0	12.1	12.1	6.8	3.4
	5. Nonacademic professionals	–	–	–	–	–	5.6
	6. Lower employees	–	–	–	–	–	11.8
	7. Lower civil servants	–	–	–	–	–	9.9
	8. Merchants	–	–	16.0	20.0	–	19.2
	9. Farmers	0	0	0	0	1.4	1.1
Subtotal		–	–	–	–	–	51.0
Elite	10. Managers	–	–	–	–	–	1.2
	11. Higher civil servants	–	–	–	–	–	1.7
	12. Academic professionals	8.5	7.3	14.5	10.4	5.7	6.5
	13. Students	8.5	6.7	7.0	8.8	8.7	10.4
	14. Entrepreneurs	–	–	–	–	–	0.5
Subtotal		–	–	–	–	–	20.4
Percent (total)		100	100	100	100	100	100
Frequency (N)		47	178	170	552	1,541	2,035

a. In cases marked by a dash (−), the subgroup percentages could not be ascertained. In those cases the percentages in the columns A–E and G–M do not add up to a total of 100. In column N, the percentage for subgroup 5 is hidden in percentages for other subgroups.

b. DAP in Munich and surroundings before the advent of Hitler in autumn 1919. Percentages calculated on the basis of data in James P. Madden, "The Social Composition of the Nazi Party, 1919–1930," Ph.D. dissertation, University of Oklahoma, 1976, pp. 69–70.

c. DAP in Munich and surroundings at end of 1919. For figures underlying percentage calculations see Madden, "Composition," pp. 73–74.

d. DAP in Munich and surroundings by January 1920. Percentages calculated on the basis of data in Georg Franz-Willing, *Die Hitlerbewegung: Der Ursprung, 1919–1922* (Hamburg and Berlin, 1962), p. 130.

e. DAP in Munich and surroundings by May 29, 1920. Percentages calculated on the basis of data in Werner Maser, *Die Frühgeschichte der NSDAP: Hitlers Weg bis 1924* (Frankfurt/Main and Bonn, 1965), p. 255.

f. DAP joiners in Munich and surroundings, for 1920. Percentages calculated on the basis of data in Madden, "Composition," pp. 80–81.

g. NSDAP joiners in Munich, January 1920 to August 1921. Percentages calculated on the basis of data in Donald M. Douglas, "The Parent Cell: Some Computer Notes on the Composition of the First Nazi Party Group in Munich, 1919–21," *Central European History*, 10 (1977), 62–65.

h. NSDAP joiners in Munich and surroundings, for 1921. Percentages calculated on the basis of data in Madden, "Composition," pp. 88–89.

(G) NSDAP Munich 1921[h]	(H) NSDAP Rosenheim 1922[i]	(I) NSDAP Passau 1922[j]	(J) NSDAP Landshut 1922[k]	(K) NSDAP Mannheim 1922[l]	(L) NSDAP Munich 1922[m]	(M) NSDAP Reich 1923[n]	(N) NSDAP Reich Fall 1923[o]	(O) NSDAP Ingolstadt 1922-23[p]
25.2	4.9	2.7	1.9	3.1	8.5	19.3	11.9	13.3
11.9	21.9	12.6	22.5	16.7	18.3	16.5	14.3	17.6
5.2	q	q	q	q	1.3	2.6	9.7	3.7
42.3	26.8	15.3	24.4	19.8	28.1	38.4	35.9	34.6
6.9	12.6	7.3	13.0	9.7	10.6	9.5	8.3	10.2
—	—	—	—	—	—	—	—	4.3
—	—	—	—	—	—	—	11.8	17.2
—	—	—	—	—	—	—	6.6	10.4
—	22.4	14.8	17.0	35.1	—	—	14.4	12.3
0.8	0.6	0	3.8	0.6	2.2	7.3	11.0	4.5
—	—	—	—	—	—	—	52.1	58.9
—	—	—	—	—	—	—	1.9	0.6
—	—	—	—	—	—	—	0.4	0.6
5.3	8.1	2.7	7.6	8.5	3.1	3.0	2.5	1.2
11.2	4.2	0	0	3.6	5.0	3.3	4.4	2.9
—	—	—	—	—	—	—	2.7	1.2
—	—	—	—	—	—	—	11.9	6.5
100	100	100	100	100	100	100	100	100
909	307	75	210	162	318	4,538	4,454	489

i. NSDAP in Rosenheim by August 2, 1922. Percentages calculated on the basis of data in Maser, *Frühgeschichte,* p. 255.

j. NSDAP in Passau by August 24, 1922. Percentages calculated on the basis of data in Maser, *Frühgeschichte*, p. 255.

k. NSDAP in Landshut by September 20, 1922. Percentages calculated on the basis of data in Maser, *Frügeschichte*, p. 255.

l. NSDAP in Mannheim by August 28, 1922. Percentages calculated on the basis of data in Maser, *Frügeschichte*, p. 255.

m. NSDAP joiners in Munich and surroundings, for 1922. Percentages calculated on the basis of data in Madden, "Composition," pp. 95–96.

n. NSDAP joiners in Reich, for 1923. Percentages calculated on the basis of data in Madden, "Composition," pp. 102–103.

o. NSDAP joiners in Reich, September 25 to November 9, 1923. Percentages calculated on the basis of data in Michael H. Kater, "Zur Soziographie der frühen NSDAP," *Vierteljahrshefte für Zeitgeschichte*, 19 (1971), 139.

p. NSDAP joiners in Ingolstadt and surroundings, January 1922 to October 1923 (presumed to be the total membership at that time). Percentages calculated on the basis of information in NSDAP Ingolstadt membership list, 1922-23, SAM, NSDAP/469.

q. Combined percentage figures are given for skilled (craft) workers (subgroup 2) and other skilled workers (subgroup 3) because specific data were lacking.

Table 3. Percentages of joiners of NSDAP chapters by social class and occupational subgroup in Reich, 1925-1930.

Class	Occupational subgroup	(A) Studen. 1925[a]	(B) Madden 1925[b]	(C) Studen. 1926[a]	(D) Madden 1926[b]
Lower	1. Unskilled workers	12.7	20.8	17.8	24.1
	2. Skilled (craft) workers	19.5	13.0	23.6	14.8
	3. Other skilled workers	—	3.5	—	4.6
Subtotal		32.2	37.3	41.4	43.5
Lower-	4. Master craftsmen	11.3	7.5	13.7	8.5
middle	5. Nonacademic professionals	—	—	—	—
	6. Lower employees	21.4	—	18.1	—
	7. Lower civil servants	11.4	—	5.2	—
	8. Merchants	11.3	—	8.5	—
	9. Farmers	3.6	3.9	6.1	6.7
Subtotal		59.0	—	51.6	—
Elite	10. Managers	—	—	—	—
	11. Higher civil servants	1.7	—	0.5	—
	12. Academic professionals	4.7	3.0	3.4	2.5
	13. Students	2.0	4.7	2.8	5.9
	14. Entrepreneurs	0.4	—	0.3	—
Subtotal		8.8	—	7.0	—
Percent (total)		100	100	100	100
Frequency (N)		22,795	4,744	19,528	4,052

a. Percentages are based on data pertaining to total populations, which were tabulated for Nazi internal purposes by Werner Studentkowski. The list, undated, is in BA, Schumacher/376. Also see Albrecht Tyrell, ed., *Führer befiehl . . . Selbstzeugnisse aus der "Kampfzeit" der NSDAP: Dokumentation und Analyse* (Düsseldorf, 1969), pp. 379–380, 388, and facsimile near p. 389. Percentage figures for other skilled workers (subgroup 3) and nonacademic professionals (subgroup 5) could not be ascertained. These

(E) Studen. 1927[a]	(F) Madden 1927[b]	(G) Studen. 1928[a]	(H) Madden 1928[b]	(I) Studen. 1929[a]	(J) Madden 1929[b]	(K) Studen. 1930[a]
19.1	26.6	18.7	21.9	18.7	20.5	14.4
23.5	15.3	19.7	12.9	20.0	13.3	20.7
–	4.0	–	3.4	–	2.8	–
42.6	45.9	38.4	38.2	38.7	36.6	35.1
13.5	8.9	11.4	7.5	11.6	7.7	12.0
–	–	–	–	–	–	–
19.1	–	17.2	–	14.6	–	14.5
5.0	–	4.9	–	5.5	–	4.2
8.3	–	8.1	–	11.1	–	13.8
5.2	6.1	13.3	16.0	12.0	18.4	12.2
51.1	–	54.9	–	54.8	–	56.7
–	–	–	–	–	–	–
0.4	–	0.7	–	0.7	–	0.7
3.1	1.6	2.9	1.9	2.1	1.3	2.6
2.4	3.2	2.7	4.5	2.5	3.8	2.5
0.4	–	0.4	–	1.2	–	2.5
6.3	–	6.7	–	6.5	–	8.3
100	100	100	100	100	100	100
15,900	3,728	27,349	5,813	61,785	11,277	187,602

figures are hidden in those for other subgroups. The figures for managers (subgroup 10) are included in those for lower and intermediate (petty) employees (subgroup 6).

b. Percentages are based on data from samples drawn by Madden, in "Composition," pp. 142–143, 154–155, 166–167, 200–201, 215–216, 237–239. Figures for subgroups 5–8, 10–11, and 14 could not be ascertained. For this reason the percentages do not add up to a total of 100.

Table 4. Percentages of members of NSDAP chapters by social class and occupational subgroup in various German towns, 1925–1929.

Class	Occupational subgroup	(A) Hamburg Mar 1925[a]	(B) Barmen [Apr 1925][b]	(C) Langerfeld Nov 1925[c]	(D) Mülheim Nov 1925[d]	(E) Brunswick 1925-26[e]	(F) Mettmann Feb 1926[f]	(G) Starnberg July 1927[g]	(H) Königsberg [1928][h]	(I) Königsberg Jun 1929[i]
Lower	1. Unskilled workers	17.9	10.7	27.0	15.6	13.3	28.6	14.8	5.6	2.5
	2. Skilled (craft) workers	13.8	28.7	27.0	28.9	13.9	14.3	21.1	22.7	21.4
	3. Other skilled workers	1.9	4.9	2.7	6.7	2.3	3.6	11.1	4.7	3.8
Subtotal		33.6	44.3	56.8	51.1	29.5	46.4	47.0	33.0	27.7
Lower middle	4. Master craftsmen	7.9	16.4	16.2	15.6	8.0	7.1	12.2	13.1	12.4
	5. Nonacademic professionals	0	0.8	2.7	2.2	2.3	0	0	3.9	1.7
	6. Lower employees	14.2	17.2	0	17.8	19.5	32.1	7.4	14.2	20.0
	7. Lower civil servants	8.5	2.5	5.4	2.2	11.7	7.1	11.1	5.6	6.7
	8. Merchants	30.2	17.2	13.5	11.1	15.6	0	0	14.2	18.3
	9. Farmers	0	0.8	0	0	7.8	3.6	0	4.3	0.8
Subtotal		60.8	54.9	37.8	48.9	64.9	50.0	30.7	55.3	59.9
Elite	10. Managers	0.9	0	0	0	1.6	0	0	0	0.4
	11. Higher civil servants	0.9	0	0	0	0	0	14.8	0.9	0.8
	12. Academic professionals	3.8	0	2.7	0	2.3	0	3.7	1.3	2.1
	13. Students	0	0.8	2.7	0	0.8	3.6	0	7.8	7.9
	14. Entrepreneurs	0	0	0	0	0.8	0	3.7	1.7	1.3
Subtotal		5.6	0.8	5.4	0	5.5	3.6	22.2	11.7	12.5
Percent (total)		100	100	100	100	100	100	100	100	100
Frequency (N)		106	122	37	45	128	28	27	232	240

a. NSDAP in Hamburg after refounding of party, February–March 1925. Percentages calculated on the basis of information in NSDAP Hamburg membership list, appended to letter, Klant to Amann, Hamburg, March 11, 1925, BA, Schumacher/201. Also see *The Infancy of Nazism: The Memoirs of Ex-Gauleiter Albert Krebs, 1923–1933*, ed. William S. Allen (New York, 1976), p. 65.

b. NSDAP in Barmen after refounding of party, April 1925. Percentages calculated on the basis of information in NSDAP Barmen membership list, [April 1925], HSAD, RW 23, NSDAP/Gauleitung Ruhr.

c. NSDAP in Langerfeld by November 1925. Percentages calculated on the basis of information in NSDAP Langerfeld membership list, November 18, 1925, HSAD, RW 23, NSDAP/Gauleitung Ruhr.

d. NSDAP in Mülheim-Ruhr by November 1925. Percentages calculated on the basis of information in NSDAP Mülheim membership list, November 23, 1925, HSAD, RW 23, NSDAP/Gauleitung Ruhr.

e. NSDAP in Brunswick, 1925–26. Percentages calculated on the basis of information in Kurt Schmalz, *Nationalsozialisten ringen um Braunschweig* (Brunswick, 1934), pp. 225–229. Personal details pertaining to 128 out of the 150 members listed in Schmalz's book were found in the NSDAP Master File of the Berlin Document Center and statistically processed.

f. NSDAP in Mettmann by February 1926. Percentages calculated on the basis of information in NSDAP Mettmann membership list, February 28, 1926, HSAD, RW 23, NSDAP/Gauleitung Ruhr.

g. NSDAP in Starnberg by July 1927. Percentages calculated on the basis of information in Franz Buchner, *Kamerad! Halt aus! Aus der Geschichte des Kreises Starnberg der NSDAP* (Munich, 1938), pp. 159–160.

h. NSDAP in the city of Königsberg by 1928. Percentages calculated on the basis of information in NSDAP Königsberg City membership list, [1928], SAG, SF 6818, GA/33.

i. NSDAP in Königsberg and surroundings by June 1929. Percentages calculated on the basis of information in NSDAP Greater Königsberg membership list, June 18, 1929, SAG, SF 6818, GA/33.

Table 5. Percentages of members of NSDAP chapters by social class and occupational subgroup in Greater Bochum and the State of Thuringia divided according to place of residence, 1925-1928.

Class	Occupational subgroup	Greater Bochum[a]				State of Thuringia[b]			
		(A) Region as a whole	(B) Cities	(C) Small towns	(D) Country	(E) Region as a whole	(F) Cities	(G) Small towns	(H) Country
Lower	1. Unskilled workers	17.4	11.5	17.1	24.0	10.9	18.9	8.7	11.4
	2. Skilled (craft) workers	17.7	15.3	18.7	18.4	18.8	10.8	11.9	23.6
	3. Other skilled workers	5.8	5.5	5.8	6.1	2.5	0	2.7	2.6
Subtotal		40.9	32.2	41.6	48.5	32.2	29.7	23.3	37.6
Lower middle	4. Master craftsmen	10.1	8.7	10.6	10.6	10.9	8.1	6.8	13.5
	5. Nonacademic professionals	4.3	5.5	5.2	1.7	2.5	0	4.1	1.8
	6. Lower employees	15.5	21.3	14.8	10.6	14.6	8.1	21.5	11.4
	7. Lower civil servants	7.3	5.5	8.4	7.3	10.0	29.7	16.0	4.7
	8. Merchants	15.2	18.6	14.5	12.8	14.3	8.1	17.4	13.2
	9. Farmers	1.3	0.5	0.6	3.4	7.3	2.7	0.5	11.7
Subtotal		53.7	60.1	54.2	46.4	59.7	56.8	66.2	56.2
Elite	10. Managers	0.7	0	1.3	0.6	1.4	0	2.3	1.0
	11. Higher civil servants	0.5	0.5	0.3	0.6	0.9	0	1.4	0.8
	12. Academic professionals	2.4	4.4	1.6	1.7	3.1	2.7	4.6	2.3
	13. Students	1.3	1.6	1.0	1.7	1.2	8.1	2.3	0
	14. Entrepreneurs	0.5	1.1	0	0.6	1.4	2.7	0	2.1
Subtotal		5.4	7.7	4.2	5.2	8.1	13.5	10.5	6.2
Percent (total)		100	100	100	100	100	100	100	100
Frequency (N)		672	183	310	179	642	37	219	386

a. Columns B, C, and D show the three types of residential area into which the whole region A was subdivided. (See Introduction at n. 49 for definition of these types.) Percentages were calculated on the basis of information in Friedrich Alfred Beck, *Kampf und Sieg: Geschichte der Nationalsozialistischen Deutschen Arbeiterpartei im Gau Westfalen-Süd von den Anfängen bis zur Machtübernahme* (Dortmund, 1938), pp. 17–28. Personal details pertaining to 672 out of the 820 members listed in Beck's book were found in the NSDAP Master File of the Berlin Document Center and statistically processed. The hypothesis of statistical independence of class and region was rejected ($\chi^2 = 11.807$; $df = 4$; $C = 0.131$; $P < 0.025$).

b. Columns F, G, and H show the three types of residential area into which the whole region E was subdivided. Percentages were calculated on the basis of information in Fritz Sauckel, ed., *Kampf und Sieg in Thüringen: Im Geiste des Führers und in treuer Kameradschaft gewidmet den thüringischen Vorkämpfern des nationalsozialistischen Dritten Reiches* (Weimar, 1934), pp. 27–37; also see pp. 41, 46. Personal details pertaining to 642 out of the 941 members listed in Sauckel's book were found in the NSDAP Master File of the Berlin Document Center and statistically processed. The hypothesis of statistical independence of class and region was rejected ($\chi^2 = 15.891$; $df = 4$; $C = 0.155$; $P < 0.005$).

Table 6. Percentages of NSDAP joiners in the Reich according to place of residence, and of NSDAP chapters in four communities, by social class and occupational subgroup, 1930-1932.

Class	Occupational subgroup	(A) Reich joiners 1930-32[a]	(B) City joiners 1930-32[a]	(C) Small-town joiners 1930-32[a]	(D) Country joiners 1930-32[a]	(E) NSDAP Dt.-Kr., Kl. May 1931[b]	(F) NSDAP Pahres May 1932[c]	(G) NSDAP Eutin May 1932[d]	(H) NSDAP Eltersdorf Jun. 1932[e]
Lower	1. Unskilled workers	15.4	12.6	9.9	18.2	22.8	23.5	12.4	13.3
	2. Skilled (craft) workers	18.1	15.0	18.4	19.5	25.5	22.4	22.0	21.2
	3. Other skilled workers	2.4	2.9	2.2	2.1	4.8	2.9	6.3	10.0
Subtotal		35.9	30.5	30.5	39.8	53.1	48.8	40.7	44.5
Lower middle	4. Master craftsmen	10.5	8.6	10.7	11.2	15.2	12.9	12.7	12.2
	5. Nonacademic professionals	4.2	7.0	5.1	2.7	2.1	0	0	0
	6. Lower employees	11.1	15.7	17.3	7.3	6.9	0	19.7	6.7
	7. Lower civil servants	4.6	5.4	6.1	3.7	4.1	0	3.3	0
	8. Merchants	11.9	16.3	16.3	8.7	4.1	2.9	12.0	13.3
	9. Farmers	12.6	1.0	4.2	20.4	11.0	32.4	1.4	20.0
Subtotal		54.9	54.0	59.6	54.0	43.4	48.2	49.1	52.2
Elite	10. Managers	0.9	2.3	1.0	0.3	0	0	0	0
	11. Higher civil servants	1.2	1.9	0.6	1.1	0	0	0	0
	12. Academic professionals	2.5	5.6	1.6	1.2	1.4	0	2.3	0
	13. Students	3.2	4.8	5.4	1.8	0.7	2.9	2.1	3.3
	14. Entrepreneurs	1.4	0.8	1.3	1.8	1.4	0	5.6	0
Subtotal		9.2	15.5	9.9	6.2	3.5	2.9	10.1	3.3
Percent (total)		100	100	100	100	100	100	100	100
Frequency (N)		1,954	516	313	1,125	145	34	426	30

a. NSDAP joiners in Reich, 1930–1932. Columns B–D indicate the regional breakdown of Reich joiners given in column A. Percentage figures were calculated on the basis of information obtained for a subsample, part of a larger sample (1925–1945), which I drew systematically from the NSDAP Master File in the Berlin Document Center. See Michael H. Kater, "Quantifizierung und NS-Geschichte: Methodologische Überlegungen über Grenzen und Möglichkeiten einer EDV-Analyse der NSDAP-Sozialstruktur von 1925 bis 1945," *Geschichte und Gesellschaft*, 3 (1977), 453–484; and the Introduction to this book at n. 47. The hypothesis of statistical independence and place of residence was rejected ($\chi^2 = 47.018$; $df = 4$; $C = 0.153$; $P < 0.001$).

b. NSDAP chapter in Deutsch-Krone and Klausdorf (East Prussia) by May 1931. Percentages calculated on the basis of information in (combined) NSDAP Deutsch-Krone and Klausdorf membership list, May 28, 1931, IfZ, MA-1217/207.

c. NSDAP chapter in Pahres (Franconia) by May 1932. Percentages calculated on the basis of information in NSDAP Pahres membership list, May 1, 1932, appended to letter, Ortsgruppe Pahres to Kreisleitung Neustadt-Aisch, July 20, 1942, SAN, 503/96.

d. NSDAP chapter in Eutin (Schleswig-Holstein) by May 1932. Percentages calculated on the basis of data in Lawrence D. Stokes, "The Social Composition of the Nazi Party in Eutin, 1925–32," *International Review of Social History*, 23 (1978), Part I, 6.

e. NSDAP chapter in Eltersdorf (Franconia) by June 1932. Percentages calculated on the basis of information in NSDAP Eltersdorf membership list, June 1, 1932, appended to memorandum Ortsgruppenleiter, Eltersdorf, June 19, 1942, SAN, 503/96.

Table 7. Percentages of NSDAP joiners, established Nazi members, and Communist opponents by social class and occupational subgroup in the Reich, Frankfurt, and Eutin concentration camp, 1933-1945.

Class	Occupational subgroup	(A) Joiners 1933[a]	(B) Joiners 1934-36[a]	(C) Joiners 1937[a]	(D) Joiners 1938[a]
Lower	1. Unskilled workers	12.6	16.6	15.7	13.7
	2. Skilled (craft) workers	15.4	15.3	15.1	15.7
	3. Other skilled workers	2.7	1.4	3.8	3.8
Subtotal		30.7	33.3	34.6	33.2
Lower	4. Master craftsmen	8.9	8.9	8.7	9.1
middle	5. Nonacademic professionals	4.2	2.8	3.4	3.4
	6. Lower employees	10.6	10.0	16.8	21.8
	7. Lower civil servants	11.7	14.0	16.3	10.3
	8. Merchants	12.8	9.0	5.5	5.1
	9. Farmers	8.9	12.3	6.7	8.1
Subtotal		57.1	57.0	57.4	57.8
Elite	10. Managers	2.3	1.2	1.6	1.7
	11. Higher civil servants	2.8	1.4	1.9	0
	12. Academic professionals	3.0	3.3	2.3	2.6
	13. Students	1.7	2.4	1.1	4.3
	14. Entrepreneurs	2.4	1.4	1.1	0.4
Subtotal		12.2	9.7	8.0	9.0
Percent (total)		100	100	100	100
Frequency (N)		3,316	422	3,977	234

a. NSDAP joiners in Reich in given years. Percentage figures were calculated on the basis of information obtained for a subsample, part of a larger sample (1925-1945), cited in table 6, note a.

b. Sample of NSDAP members in Frankfurt/Main, 1940, list in BA, Schumacher/202.

c. Sample of NSDAP members in the Reich, 1942, with a proved record of service to the party beyond the call of duty, drawn systematically from the so-called *Kleine Funktionärskartei* in the BDC.

d. Sample of (Communist) concentration camp inmates at Eutin camp, 1933-34, col-

(E) Joiners 1939[a]	(F) Joiners 1940-41[a]	(G) Joiners 1942-44[a]	(H) Members Frankfurt 1940[b]	(I) Members Reich 1942[c]	(J) Inmates Eutin camp 1933-34[d]	(K) Communist opponents 1933-45[e]
15.9	17.5	18.3	7.6	7.6	55.8	22.8
20.1	15.5	18.6	5.3	10.3	15.0	29.3
3.9	4.1	5.7	2.1	4.9	2.8	5.5
39.9	37.1	42.6	15.0	22.8	73.6	57.6
11.6	8.9	10.7	3.0	5.9	8.7	16.9
3.0	3.8	2.9	1.6	3.2	0.7	6.1
15.3	18.8	25.3	24.9	11.5	3.9	10.3
7.6	11.6	3.3	36.0	20.4	1.8	1.2
6.7	5.4	3.3	6.6	10.1	4.2	2.7
9.7	9.4	9.1	7.3	15.7	2.5	0.3
53.9	57.9	54.6	79.4	66.8	21.8	37.5
2.0	1.6	1.0	2.6	3.1	1.1	0
0.5	1.4	0.3	1.9	2.7	0.7	0.9
1.6	1.2	0.5	0.6	1.8	0.7	2.1
1.0	0.2	0.5	0	0.2	0.4	1.8
1.2	0.6	0.4	0.4	2.7	1.8	0
6.3	5.0	2.7	5.5	10.5	4.7	4.8
100	100	100	100	100	100	100
1,001	2,715	1,492	926	555	283	329

lected by Professor Lawrence D. Stokes (Dalhousie University, Halifax, Canada). Professor Stokes kindly supplied me with the socially relevant data of his sample, for which I am grateful. See his article, "Das Eutiner Schutzhaftlager 1933/34: Zur Geschichte eines 'Wilden' Konzentrationslagers," *Vierteljahrshefte für Zeitgeschichte*, 27 (1979), 570–625.

e. Group of Communist resistance fighters who lost their lives in their fight against the Nazi regime, 1933–45, and whose names and social data are contained in Heinz Schumann and Gerda Werner, eds., *Erkämpft das Menschenrecht: Lebensberichte und letzte Briefe antifaschistischer Widerstandskämpfer*, ([East] Berlin, 1958).

Table 8. Percentages of female and male Nazi joiners in Reich, 1925-1944.[a]

Sex	(A) 1925-32	(B) 1933	(C) 1934-36	(D) 1937	(E) 1938	(F) 1939	(G) 1940-41	(H) 1942-44
Women	7.8	5.1	4.4	10.0	17.5	16.5	19.6	34.7
Men	92.2	94.9	95.6	90.0	82.5	83.5	80.4	65.3
Percent (total)	100	100	100	100	100	100	100	100
Frequency (N)	2,339	3,502	450	4,330	314	1,231	3,271	2,818

a. Percentages were calculated on the basis of information obtained for the sample of NSDAP joiners (1925–1945) drawn systematically from the NSDAP Master File in the Berlin Document Center. See the Introduction to this book at n. 47; and table 3 in Kater, "Quantifizierung," p. 461.

Table 9. Percentages of NSDAP joiner classes in the Reich by place of residence, 1925–1929 and 1930–1932.[a]

Place of residence	All classes[b]		Lower class[c]		Lower middle class[d]		Elite[e]	
	(A) 1925-29	(B) 1930-32	(C) 1925-29	(D) 1930-32	(E) 1925-29	(F) 1930-32	(G) 1925-29	(H) 1930-32
City	28.9	26.4	28.8	22.5	28.5	25.9	31.8	44.4
Small town	21.6	16.0	20.5	13.6	21.2	17.4	27.3	17.2
Country	49.6	57.6	50.7	63.9	50.4	56.7	40.9	38.3
Percent (total)	100	100	100	100	100	100	100	100
Frequency (N)	232	1,954	73	701	137	1,073	22	180

a. Percentages were calculated on the basis of information for a subsample (2,186 N for 1925–1932), part of a larger sample (1925–1945) referred to in table 6, note a. Also see the Introduction at note 47.

b. The hypothesis of statistical independence of class and place of residence was rejected (χ^2 = 6.64; df = 2; C = 0.055; P < 0.05).

c. The hypothesis of statistical independence of class and place of residence was rejected (χ^2 = 5.23; df = 2; C = 0.081; P < 0.10).

d. The hypothesis of statistical independence of class and place of residence was accepted (χ^2 = 2.11; df = 2; C = 0.041; P < 0.50).

e. The hypothesis of statistical independence of class and place of residence was accepted (χ^2 = 1.84; df = 2; C = 0.095; P < 0.50).

Table 10. Percentages and ages of established Nazi members, functionaries, and deputies by social class and occupational subgroup in the Reich and selected regions and towns, between 1925 and 1942.

		Members Bochum 1925-28		Members Thur. 1925-28		Gaul. Reich 1925-28		Funct. Reich 1929		Gaul. Reich 1929		Ogrul. Kassel 1930		Ogrul. Harburg 1930		Agitat. Baden 1930		Gaul. Reich 1930		Ogrul. Lüneburg 1931	
Class	Occupational subgroup	(A) %[a]	(B) Age[b]	(C) %[c]	(D) Age[b]	(E) %[d]	(F) Age[b]	(G) %[e]	(H) Age[b]	(I) %[d]	(J) Age[b]	(K) %[f]	(L) Age[b]	(M) %[g]	(N) Age[b]	(O) %[h]	(P) Age[b]	(Q) %[d]	(R) Age[b]	(S) %[i]	(T) Age[b]
Lower	1. Unskilled workers	17.4	(27)	10.9	(29)	3.7	(28)	7.7	(30)	5.1	(30)	11.1	(—)	9.5	(—)	3.4	(37)	5.3	(31)	8.3	(—)
	2. Skilled (craft) workers	17.7	(25)	18.8	(27)	0	(0)	11.4	(28)	0	(0)	0	(—)	14.3	(—)	8.5	(31)	0	(0)	12.5	(—)
	3. Other skilled workers	5.8	(35)	2.5	(31)	1.9	(33)	3.7	(34)	2.6	(35)	0	(—)	0	(—)	3.4	(24)	2.6	(36)	2.8	(—)
	Subtotal	40.9	(—)	32.2	(—)	5.6	(—)	22.8	(—)	7.7	(—)	11.1	(—)	23.8	(—)	15.3	(—)	7.9	(—)	23.6	(—)
Lower middle	4. Master craftsmen	10.1	(38)	10.9	(38)	0	(0)	6.1	(34)	0		19.8	(—)	9.5	(—)	6.8	(34)	0	(0)	6.9	(—)
	5. Nonacademic professionals	4.3	(30)	2.5	(33)	3.7	(27)	2.0	(33)	0	(0)	0	(—)	4.8	(—)	5.1	(36)	0	(0)	1.4	(—)
	6. Lower employees	15.5	(26)	14.6	(26)	7.4	(32)	16.3	(31)	7.7	(33)	12.3	(—)	4.8	(—)	5.1	(28)	10.5	(33)	1.4	(—)
	7. Lower civil servants	7.3	(36)	10.0	(38)	27.8	(37)	16.7	(41)	38.5	(39)	3.7	(—)	4.8	(—)	8.5	(35)	36.8	(40)	1.4	(—)
	8. Merchants	15.2	(30)	14.3	(31)	9.3	(37)	14.6	(34)	5.1	(37)	12.3	(—)	4.8	(—)	23.7	(33)	5.3	(38)	15.3	(—)
	9. Farmers	1.3	(29)	7.3	(29)	0	(0)	6.9	(31)	0	(0)	27.2	(—)	38.1	(—)	8.5	(34)	0	(0)	48.6	(—)
	Subtotal	53.7	(—)	59.7	(—)	48.2	(—)	62.6	(—)	51.3	(—)	75.3	(—)	66.7	(—)	57.7	(—)	52.6	(—)	75.0	(—)
Elite	10. Managers	0.7	(41)	1.4	(36)	11.1	(33)	2.4	(32)	10.3	(39)	0	(—)	0	(—)	1.7	(55)	10.5	(40)	0	(—)
	11. Higher civil servants	0.4	(38)	0.9	(39)	13.0	(44)	2.0	(36)	15.4	(42)	0	(—)	0	(—)	3.4	(48)	15.8	(43)	0	(—)
	12. Academic professionals	2.4	(33)	3.1	(39)	14.8	(36)	4.9	(37)	10.3	(35)	8.6	(—)	9.5	(—)	16.9	(31)	7.9	(36)	0	(—)
	13. Students	1.3	(20)	1.2	(24)	3.7	(32)	2.8	(24)	0	(0)	1.2	(—)	0	(—)	1.7	(22)	0	(0)	0	(—)
	14. Entrepreneurs	0.4	(31)	1.4	(40)	3.7	(44)	2.4	(40)	5.1	(47)	3.7	(—)	0	(—)	3.4	(40)	5.3	(48)	1.4	(—)
	Subtotal	5.4	(—)	8.1	(—)	46.3	(—)	14.5	(—)	41.0	(—)	13.5	(—)	9.5	(—)	27.1	(—)	39.5	(—)	1.4	(—)
	Percent (total) and age	100	(29)	100	(30)	100	(36)	100	(33)	100	(38)	100	(—)	100	(—)	100	(33)	100	(39)	100	(—)
	Frequency (N)	672	(—)	642	(—)	54	(—)	246	(—)	39	(—)	81	(—)	21	(—)	59	(—)	38	(—)	72	(—)

Class	Occupational subgroup	Gaul. Reich 1931 (U) %d	(V) Age[b]	Local deputies Reich 1933 (W) %j	(X) Age[b]	Reichstag deputies Reich 1933 (Y) %k	(Z) Age[b]	Gaul. Reich 1933 (AA) %d	(BB) Age[b]	Kreisl. Reich 1941 (CC) %l	(DD) Age[b]	Agency heads Reich 1941 (EE) %m	(FF) Age[b]	Gaul. Reich 1941 (GG) %d	(HH) Age[b]	Members Reich 1942 (II) %n	(JJ) Age[b]	Gaul. Reich 1942 (KK) %d	(LL) Age[b]
Lower	1. Unskilled workers	9.3	(35)	8.7	(—)	6.0	(—)	11.4	(36)	2.0	(38)	0	(0)	7.0	(44)	7.6	(47)	6.7	(45)
	2. Skilled (craft) workers	0	(0)	13.0	(—)	5.6	(—)	0	(0)	7.3	(38)	3.1	(45)	7.0	(38)	10.3	(46)	6.7	(39)
	3. Other skilled workers	2.3	(37)	3.1	(—)	0.7	(—)	2.9	(39)	2.0	(37)	0.6	(42)	2.3	(47)	4.9	(44)	2.2	(48)
	Subtotal	11.6	(—)	24.8	(—)	12.3	(—)	14.3	(—)	11.3	(—)	3.7	(—)	16.3	(—)	22.8	(—)	15.6	(—)
Lower middle	4. Master craftsmen	0	(0)	7.5	(—)	3.5	(—)	0	(0)	4.0	(45)	1.2	(44)	0	(0)	5.9	(49)	0	(0)
	5. Nonacademic professionals	0	(0)	4.9	(—)	3.5	(—)	0	(0)	6.3	(43)	5.5	(43)	2.3	(32)	3.2	(50)	2.2	(33)
	6. Lower employees	11.6	(33)	10.1	(—)	10.6	(—)	14.3	(35)	16.3	(38)	17.8	(44)	14.0	(44)	11.5	(45)	13.3	(45)
	7. Lower civil servants	32.6	(39)	12.0	(—)	12.0	(—)	28.6	(41)	17.9	(42)	6.7	(46)	25.6	(48)	20.4	(48)	24.4	(49)
	8. Merchants	4.7	(39)	14.7	(—)	9.1	(—)	2.9	(44)	16.6	(42)	11.7	(43)	7.0	(45)	10.1	(47)	6.7	(46)
	9. Farmers	0	(0)	9.9	(—)	13.0	(—)	0	(0)	9.3	(40)	3.7	(47)	2.3	(57)	15.7	(48)	2.2	(58)
	Subtotal	48.8	(—)	59.1	(—)	51.7	(—)	45.7	(—)	70.4	(—)	46.6	(—)	51.2	(—)	66.8	(—)	48.8	(—)
Elite	10. Managers	9.3	(41)	3.4	(—)	1.8	(—)	11.4	(43)	2.7	(46)	6.7	(45)	4.7	(52)	3.1	(46)	4.4	(53)
	11. Higher civil servants	14.0	(40)	3.2	(—)	10.6	(—)	14.3	(44)	4.7	(40)	13.5	(49)	7.0	(41)	2.7	(49)	6.7	(42)
	12. Academic professionals	11.6	(34)	6.4	(—)	13.4	(—)	11.4	(33)	5.6	(41)	26.4	(42)	16.3	(43)	1.8	(42)	20.0	(42)
	13. Students	0	(0)	0	(—)	0.4	(—)	0	(0)	3.0	(34)	0	(0)	0	(0)	0.2	(41)	0	(0)
	14. Entrepreneurs	4.7	(49)	3.1	(—)	9.8	(—)	2.9	(54)	2.3	(48)	3.1	(54)	4.7	(48)	2.7	(50)	4.4	(49)
	Subtotal	39.6	(—)	16.1	(—)	36.0	(—)	40.0	(—)	18.3	(—)	49.7	(—)	32.6	(—)	10.5	(—)	35.6	(—)
	Percent (total) and age	100	(38)	100	(—)	100	(40)	100	(40)	100	(41)	100	(45)	100	(45)	100	(47)	100	(46)
	Frequency (N)	43	(—)	4,404	(—)	284	(—)	35	(—)	301	(—)	163	(—)	43	(—)	555	(—)	45	(—)

Table 10, *continued*

a. Percentages calculated on the basis of information in Beck, *Kampf,* pp. 17–28. Personal details pertaining to 672 out of the 820 members listed in Beck's book were found in the NSDAP Master File of the Berlin Document Center and statistically processed.

b. Mean age calculations are based on given frequencies (*N*).

c. Percentages calculated on the basis of information in Sauckel, ed., *Kampf,* pp. 27–37. Personal details pertaining to 642 out of the 941 members listed in Sauckel's book were found in the NSDAP Master File of the Berlin Document Center and statistically processed.

d. Percentages for all Nazi Gauleiters (1925–1945) calculated on the basis of data in Federal Archive Koblenz (BA), Berlin Document Center, and in the literature.

e. Percentages calculated on the basis of data in list, Gliederung, October 1, 1929, NHSA, Hann. 122a, XI, 79.

f. Percentages calculated on the basis of data in list, Ortsgruppenleiter, Regierungsbezirk Kassel, July 1930, in Eberhard Schön, *Die Entstehung des Nationalsozialismus in Hessen* (Meisenheim/Glan, 1972), p. 99.

g. Percentages calculated on the basis of data in list, Ortsgruppenleiter, Amtsbereich Harburg-Wilhelmsburg, in memorandum police president, Harburg-Wilhelmsburg, February 21, 1930, NHSA, Hann. 122a, XI, 79.

h. Percentages calculated on the basis of data in list of Nazi agitators and speakers in Baden, report of Baden police, Karlsruhe, August 19, 1930, SAF, 317/1257 d.

i. Percentages calculated on the basis of data in list, Ortsgruppenleiter, Raum Lüneburg, April 1, 1931, in Claus-Dieter Krohn and Dirk Stegmann, "Kleingewerbe und Nationalsozialismus in einer agrarisch-mittelständischen Region: Das Beispiel Lüneburg 1930–1939," *Archiv für Sozialgeschichte,* 17 (1977), 92–94.

j. Percentages of a sample of local (municipal) Nazi deputies, calculated on the basis of information in A. Görlitzer, ed., *Adressbuch der nationalsozialistischen Volksvertreter* (Berlin, 1933), pp. 161–670. Every tenth entry was drawn from the complete list of names and occupations.

k. Percentages calculated on the basis of data on all Nazi Reichstag deputies as of fall 1933, in Görlitzer, ed., *Adressbuch,* pp. 1–8, and in the Berlin Document Center.

l. Percentages of a sample of Kreisleiters, calculated on the basis of information in *Reichsband: Adressenwerk der Dienststellen der NSDAP. mit den angeschlossenen Verbänden des Staates: Reichsregierung – Behörden und der Berufsorganisationen . . . ,* 3d ed., 1941/42 (Berlin, 1942), at the Berlin Document Center. Personal data on every third name in this volume were culled from various personnel files in the Berlin Document Center.

m. Percentages calculated on the basis of data in list, "Aufstellung der vom Führer bestätigten Politischen Leiter bis einschliesslich Amtsleiter in den Dienststellen der Reichsleitung der NSDAP.," [1941], BA, Schumacher/372, and files in the Berlin Document Center.

n. See table 7, note c.

Table 11. Social mobility (inflow) of Gauleiters, SS officers, and Reich population by social class, between 1925 and 1944, in percent.

Mobility	Social Class	Gauleiters[a] (A) 1925-32	Gauleiters[a] (B) 1933-44	SS officers[b] (C) 1925-39	Reich population[c] (D) 1925-29
Upward	1. Members of elite with lower-middle-class fathers	43.5	42.1	60.9	44.0
	2. Members of lower middle class with working-class fathers	14.3	16.0	5.3	23.0
	3. Members of elite with working-class fathers	17.4	15.8	0.8	2.0
Downward	4. Members of lower middle class with elite fathers	14.3	16.0	6.6	5.0
	5. Members of working class with lower-middle-class fathers	20.0	14.3	60.7	21.0
	6. Members of working class with elite fathers	20.0	14.3	3.6	0

a. See chap. 7, note 48; chap. 8, note 20.

b. Mobility percentages calculated on the basis of figures contained in Gunnar Charles Boehnert, "A Sociography of the SS Officer Corps, 1925–1939," Ph.D. dissertation, University of London, 1977, p. 205, and in a letter from Dr. Boehnert to me, Guelph, February 15, 1980. I am grateful to Dr. Boehnert for his cooperation. Also see Boehnert, "An Analysis of the Age and Education of the SS Führerkorps 1925–1939," *Historical Social Research – Historische Sozialforschung*, no. 12 (October 1979), 4–17.

c. Figures adopted from Hartmut Kaelble, "Soziale Mobilität in Deutschland, 1900–1960," in Kaelble et al., *Probleme der Modernisierung in Deutschland: Sozialhistorische Studien zum 19. und 20. Jahrhundert* (Wiesbaden, 1978), p. 249.

Table 12. Percentages of Nazi members and functionaries in Thuringia by operationally (horizontally) classified occupation, 1925–1939.

Occupation[a]	(A) Members 1925–28[b]	(B) Members Dec. 1934[c]	(C) Stützpunkt-leiter Dec. 1934[d]	(D) Ortsgruppen-leiter Dec. 1934[d]	(E) Kreisleiter Dec. 1934[d]	(F) Politische Leiter April 1939[e]
1. Workers	32.6	36.5	16.5	11.9	8.0	27.2
2. Employees	16.2	19.6	8.9	20.2	28.0	22.3
3. Self-employed	32.6	19.9	14.6	25.5	20.0	16.1
4. Civil servants	11.0	14.3	27.5	25.4	36.0	23.7
(5. Of those, teachers)	(3.1)	(5.1)	(22.0)	(15.6)	(28.0)	(9.3)
(6. Teachers as percent of civil servants)	(28.6)	(35.5)	(80.0)	(61.5)	(77.8)	(39.2)
7. Farmers	7.4	9.7	32.4	17.1	8.0	10.6
Percent (total)	100	100	100	100	100	100
Frequency (N)	634	87,258	672	615	25	26,502

a. Exclusive of: pensioners, housewives, students, no indication.

b. Percentages calculated on the basis of figures in Sauckel, ed., *Kampf*, pp. 27–37, and in NSDAP Master File of Berlin Document Center. See table 5, note b.

c. Percentage calculations on the basis of data in *Partei-Statistik* I.

d. Percentage calculations on the basis of data in *Partei-Statistik* II.

e. Percentage calculations on the basis of data in Karl Astel and Erna Weber, *Die Kinderzahl der 29000 politischen Leiter des Gaues Thüringen der NSDAP und die Ursachen der ermittelten Fortpflanzungshäufigkeit* (Berlin, 1943), pp. 13–14. The N of 26,502 represents 91.1 percent of 29,098 Politische Leiters to whom questionnaires were sent.

Table 13. Percentages of Nazi members and functionaries by age group, December 31, 1934.

Age group	(A) Members[a]	(B) Stützpunkt- leiter[b]	(C) Ortsgruppen- leiter[b]	(D) Kreis- leiter[b]
1. 18-30	37.6	19.8	15.8	14.2
2. 31-40	27.9	44.6	47.0	55.7
3. 41-50	19.6	26.4	27.8	26.4
4. 51-60	11.2	8.1	8.4	3.4
5. 61 and over	3.7	1.1	1.0	0.3
Percent (total)	100	100	100	100
Frequency (N)	2,493,890	6,518	14,110	776

a. Figures adopted from *Partei-Statistik* I.
b. Figures adopted from *Partei-Statistik* II.

FIGURES

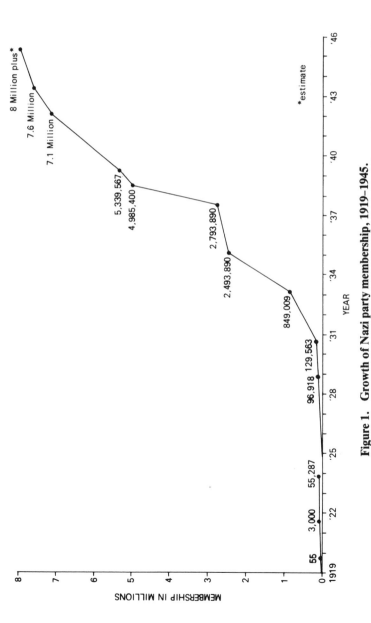

Figure 1. Growth of Nazi party membership, 1919–1945.

Sources: (1) Studentkowski list (see table 3) and other lists in BA, Schumacher/376. (2) *Partei-Statistik*, I (Munich, [1935]), 70. (3) Michael H. Kater, "Zur Soziographie der frühen NSDAP," *Vierteljahrshefte für Zeitgeschichte*, 19 (1971), 128. (4) Aryel L. Unger, *The Totalitarian Party: Party and People in Nazi Germany and Soviet Russia* (Cambridge, 1974), p. 84. (5) *Hitler: Sämtliche Aufzeichnungen 1905–1924*, ed. Eberhard Jäckel (Stuttgart, 1980), pp. 320, 448. (6) Doc. 7 (May 1930) in Ilse Maurer and Udo Wengst, eds., *Staat und NSDAP 1930–1932: Quellen zur Ära Brüning* (Düsseldorf, 1977), p. 67.

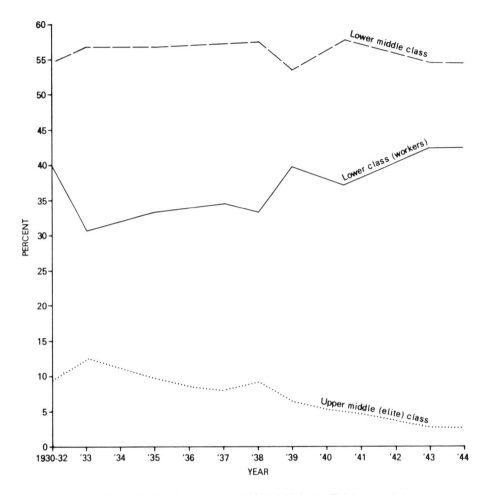

Figure 2.   Nazi newcomers, 1930–1944, in the Reich as a whole.

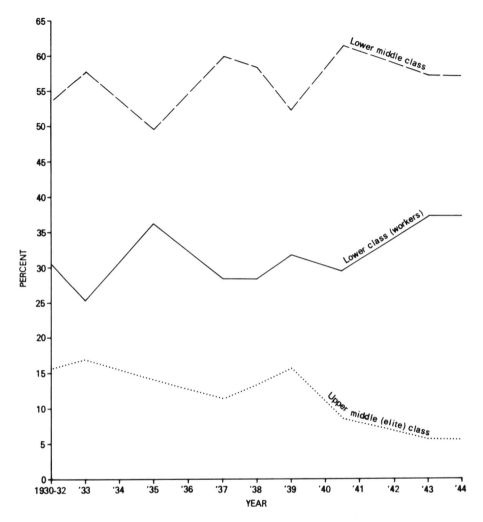

Figure 3.   Nazi newcomers, 1930–1944, in big cities.

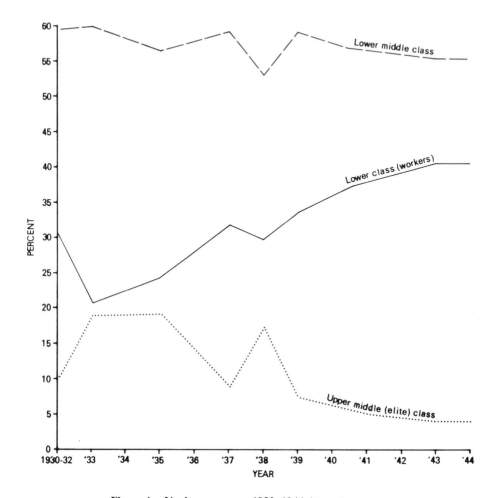

Figure 4. Nazi newcomers, 1930–1944, in small towns.

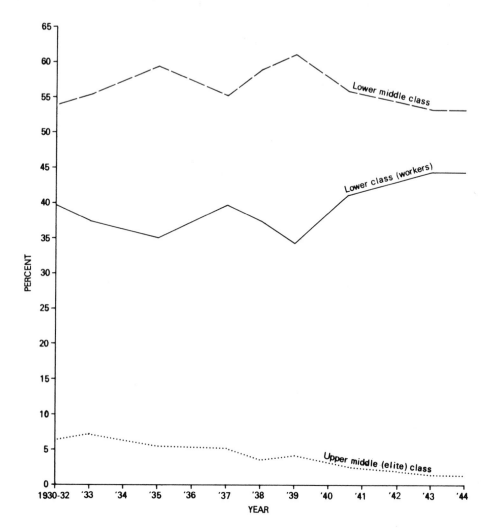

Figure 5. Nazi newcomers, 1930–1944, in the country.

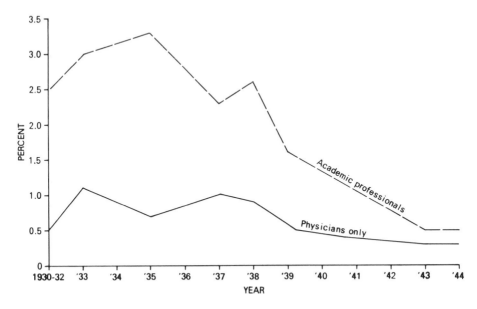

Figure 6. Nazi newcomers, 1930–1944: academic professionals and medical doctors.

Figure 7. Yearly percentage shares of five age groups of Nazi newcomers in relation to corresponding percentages in the Reich population, 1925–1932.
The 0 axis is based on German census figures for all age groups 18 to 60 and over, obtained for censuses of 1925 and 1933 from *Volkszählung: Die Bevölkerung des Deutschen Reichs nach den Ergebnissen der Volkszählung 1925*, Part II, *Textliche Darstellung der Ergbnisse* (*Statistik des Deutschen Reichs*, vol. 401, II) (Berlin, 1930), p. 557; *Statistisches Jahrbuch für das Deutsche Reich 1934* (Berlin, 1934), p. 12; *Statistisches Jahrbuch für das Deutsche Reich 1935* (Berlin, 1935), pp. 11–12. Census values were prorated for construction of the 0 axis. Nazi joiners' age groups were defined in the same terms as Reich age groups. For 1925–1929, because of a greater abundance of data, the Nazi joiners' age group fluctuations are based on figures extrapolated from values in Madden, "Composition," pp. 138, 150, 161, 197, 211. For 1930–1932, they are based on figures obtained for a subsample (2,095 *N*), part of a larger sample for 1925–1945, referred to in table 6, n. a. Also see Introduction of this book at n. 47.

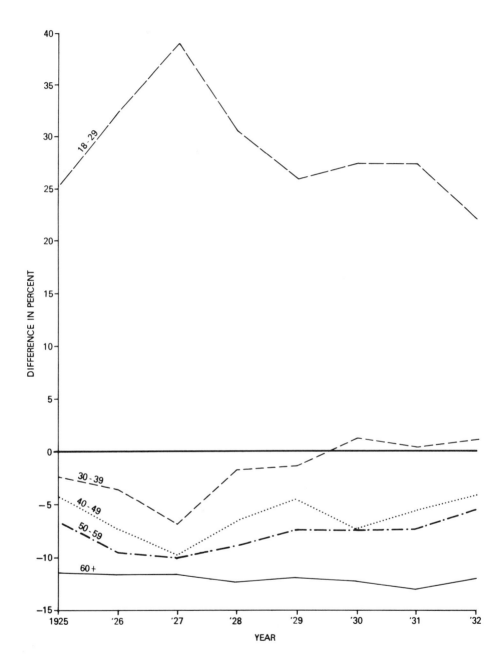

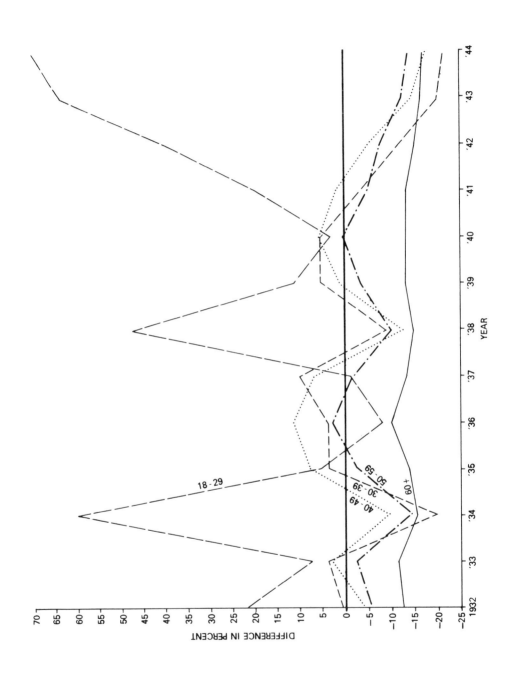

Figure 8. Yearly percentage shares of five age groups of Nazi newcomers in relation to corresponding percentages in the Reich population, 1932–1944.

The 0 axis is based on German census figures for all age groups 18 to 60 and over, obtained for censuses of 1933 and 1939 from *Volkszählung: Die Bevölkerung . . . 1925*, p. 557; *Statistisches Jahrbuch 1934*, p. 12; *Statistisches Jahrbuch 1935*, pp. 11–12; *Statistisches Jahrbuch für das Deutsche Reich 1941/42* (Berlin, 1942), pp. 24–25. Census values were prorated for construction of the 0 axis. Nazi joiners' age groups were defined in the same terms as Reich age groups. Nazi joiners' age group fluctuations are based on figures obtained for a subsample (16,821 *N*), part of a larger sample for 1925–1945, referred to in the Introduction at n. 47.

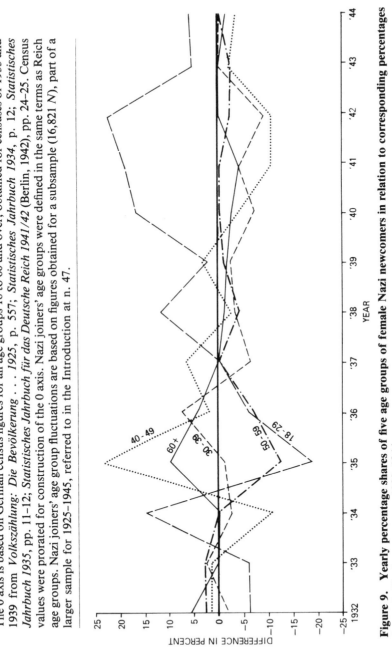

Figure 9. Yearly percentage shares of five age groups of female Nazi newcomers in relation to corresponding percentages for male Nazi newcomers, 1932–1944.

The 0 axis is based on figures for male Nazi newcomers from 1932 to 1944 (14,225 *N*). This subsample is part of a larger sample for 1925–1945, referred to in the Introduction at n. 47. Female joiners' age group fluctuations are based on figures obtained for a subsample (2,596 *N*), part of the larger sample for 1925–1945. Definition of male and female joiners' age groups is in the same terms as Reich age groups (see notes for figure 8).

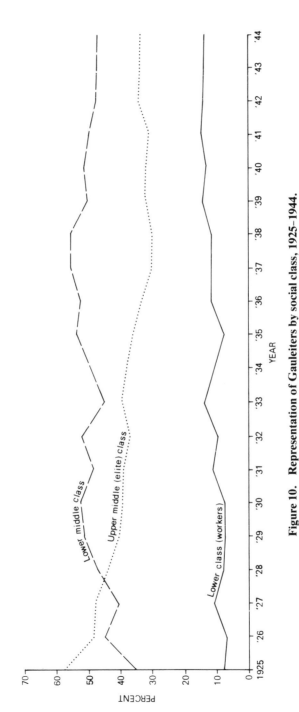

Figure 10. Representation of Gauleiters by social class, 1925–1944.
Based on data for Gauleiters (1925–1944) in Federal Archive Koblenz (BA),
Berlin Document Center, and the literature.

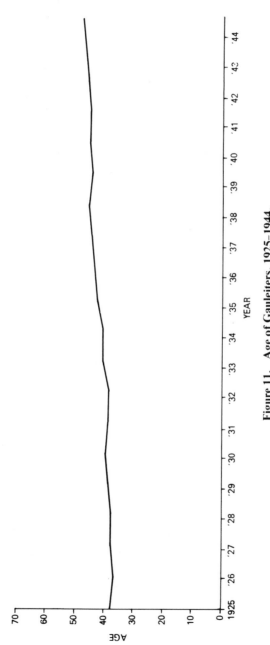

Figure 11. Age of Gauleiters, 1925–1944.

Based on data for Gauleiters (1925–1944) in Federal Archive Koblenz (BA), Berlin Document Center, and the literature.

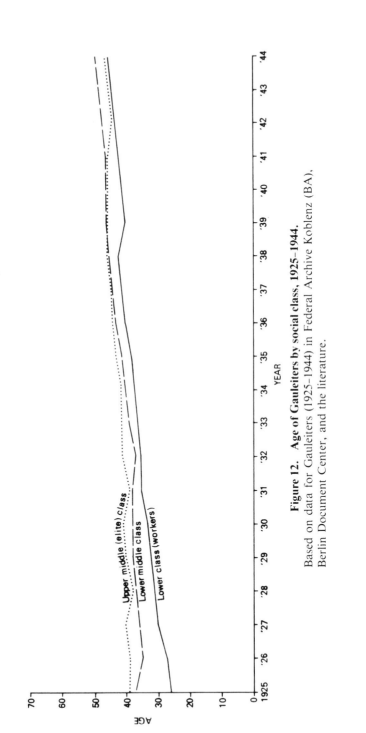

Figure 12. Age of Gauleiters by social class, 1925–1944.
Based on data for Gauleiters (1925–1944) in Federal Archive Koblenz (BA), Berlin Document Center, and the literature.

ARCHIVAL SOURCES

AJ	Archiv der Deutschen Jugendbewegung, Jugendburg Ludwigstein, Witzenhausen/Werra
	A 123/11 c
ARW	Archiv der Reichsstudentenführung und des Nationalsozialistischen Deutschen Studentenbundes, Universität Würzburg
	RSF II, A 17
BA	Bundesarchiv Koblenz
	NS 5 I/209; 212
	NS 8/197
	NS 19, Neu/1531
	NS 22/342; 860; 1046; 2007; 2008; 2011; 2017; 2022
	NS 26/148; 150; 151; 163; 170; 516; 517
	R 22/3356; 3364; 4003
	R 36/455
	R 43 II/556 b; 557; 940 b; 9566
	R 58/145; 146; 179; 182; 185; 190; 191; 193
	Schumacher/201; 202; 205; 213; 230; 368; 371; 372; 374–378; 392; 483
BAF	Bundesarchiv Freiburg – Militärarchiv
	RW6, V 67/2
BDC	Berlin Document Center
	Kleine Funktionärskartei
	Nationalsozialistischer Deutscher Lehrerbund (NSLB), Personalakten (PLA)
	NSDAP Master File
	Parteikanzlei (PK), Personalakten (PLA)
	Polizeiärzte (PAe), Personalakten (PLA)
	Reichsärztekammer (RÄK)
	SS-Akten (SSA)

BHSAM   Bayerisches Hauptstaatsarchiv München
       Sonderabgabe I/1758; 1868
       MInn, 73437/22

DAÖW   Dokumentationsarchiv des Österreichischen Widerstandes Wien
       1077; 1644; 1857; 1858; 1873; 1886; 1958; 1960; 1961; 1976;
       2007; 2128; 4447; 5025

FNSH   Forschungsstelle für die Geschichte des Nationalsozialismus in
       Hamburg
       964/NSLB

GLAK   Generallandesarchiv Karlsruhe
       309/1211
       465 d/114; 263

GSPKB   Geheimes Staatsarchiv Berlin, Stiftung Preussischer Kulturbe-
       sitz
       84a/3157
       84a/12002

GStAM   Geheimes Staatsarchiv München
       RE, 279/2

HHSAW   Hessisches Hauptstaatsarchiv Wiesbaden
       483/160; 191; 593; 874; 878; 996; 1659; 2654; 3159; 5536;
       5538; 5540–5542; 5544; 6453; 6454; 6458; 6482; 6533

HIS   Hoover Institution on War, Revolution and Peace, Stanford
       NSDAP Hauptarchiv, microfilms 12, 13, 18

HSAD   Hauptstaatsarchiv Düsseldorf
       RW 23, NSDAP/Gauleitung Ruhr

IfZ   Institut für Zeitgeschichte München
       microfilms MA-135; 227; 1217
       Fa 91/3

NA   National Archives Washington
       microfilms T-253/23; 30; 32

NAW   Niedersächsisches Staatsarchiv Wolfenbüttel
       12 A Neu, 13 h/1866; 18656; 19598; 19919; 48714

NHSA   Niedersächsisches Hauptstaatsarchiv Hannover
       Hann. 122a, XI, 79; 80
       Hann. 122a, XII, 32 m; 121; 122; 126
       Hann. 310 I, A 30; 32; 122 I
       Hann. 310 I, B 13

NSAO   Niedersächsisches Staatsarchiv Oldenburg
       320, 2, 2

OLA   Oberösterreichisches Landesarchiv Linz
       Pol. Akten/13–15; 80

SAB   Staatsarchiv Bremen
       3, E, 10, Nr. 36 /77/
       4, 65, II, A, 9, b
       N 7, Nr. 67 /60/

SAF   Staatsarchiv Freiburg/Breisgau
       317/1257 a/2
       317/1257 d; f

317/1267

350/657

SAG Staatliches Archivlager Göttingen, Gauarchiv Ostpreussen, Stiftung Preussischer Kulturbesitz (microfilms Niedersächsisches Staatsarchiv Bückeburg)

SF 6815, GA, A, 1a-1e

SF 6815, GA/6-9; 15

SF 6816, GA/11; 13

SF 6817, GA/17; 22; 25; 27

SF 6818, GA/29; 31-34

SF 6819, GA/34-37

SF 6826, GA/93; 98; 100; 101

SF 6827, GA/108; 110

SAL Staatsarchiv Ludwigsburg

PL/505

PL 509, 1/5; 1/6

PL 512/II, N, 98, 2; 5

SAM Staatsarchiv München

LRA/135116

NSDAP/11; 18; 31; 35; 54; 61; 79; 80; 84; 109; 113; 116-119; 122; 126; 348; 371; 431; 469

NSDAP/27 (SA); 28 (SA)

Pol. Dir. 6845

SAMs Staatsarchiv Münster i. W.

Gauleitung Westfalen-Nord, Gauamt für Volkswohlfahrt/7; 15

Gauleitung Westfalen-Nord, Gauinspekteure/102

Gauleitung Westfalen-Nord, Gauschulungsamt/15

Gauleitung Westfalen-Süd/1

NSF Westfalen-Nord/24; 122

Polit. Polizei, 3. Reich/109; 381; 428; 431; 433; 434; 440; 441

SAN Staatsarchiv Nürnberg

503/81; 96; 99; 112

SAPKG Staatliches Archivlager Göttingen, ehemaliges Staatsarchiv Königsberg, Stiftung Preussischer Kulturbesitz

240, D/116

SAS Staatsarchiv Sigmaringen

HO 235, I-VIII, F 7/1; 2

UK Unterlagen der Kassenärztlichen Vereinigung Deutschlands und der Reichsärztekammer (Berlin)

106

Personalakten (PLA) 130/123.02; 130/131.02; 207; 215; 217; 235; 243; 248

NOTES

INTRODUCTION

1. Notable sociohistorical exceptions are the pioneering works by William S. Allen, *The Nazi Seizure of Power: The Experience of a Single German Town 1930-1935* (Chicago, 1965); David Schoenbaum, *Hitler's Social Revolution: Class and Status in Nazi Germany 1933-1939* (Garden City, N.Y., 1966); Timothy W. Mason, *Arbeiterklasse und Volksgemeinschaft: Dokumente und Materialien zur deutschen Arbeiterpolitik 1936-1939* (Opladen, 1975). Richard Grunberger's book *The 12-Year Reich: A Social History of Nazi Germany 1933-1945* (New York, 1971), though useful for some facts, is not a scholarly work. Dietrich Orlow has written two well-researched books on the organizational history of the NSDAP: *The History of the Nazi Party: 1919-1933* (Pittsburgh, 1969), hereafter cited as Orlow I; and *The History of the Nazi Party: 1933-1945* (Pittsburgh, 1973), hereafter cited as Orlow II.

2. See the thought-provoking article by Heinrich August Winkler, "Extremismus der Mitte? Sozialgeschichtliche Aspekte der nationalsozialistischen Machtergreifung," *Vierteljahrshefte für Zeitgeschichte,* 20 (1972), 175-191; and the recent criticism by Pierre Ayçoberry, *The Nazi Question: An Essay on the Interpretations of National Socialism (1922-1975)* (New York, 1981), especially pp. 161-171.

3. For this study the boundaries of the German Reich are those of 1919-1945, including the Saar and the eastern provinces ceded to Poland. Austrians and Sudeten Germans have been added to the population after 1938. For the occupations the Reich census figures for 1933 had to be used because neither the census of 1925 nor that or 1939 offered explicit information on the occupations. For the purposes of this study it was assumed that if such data had been offered for 1925 and 1939, the percentage values for the individual occupations would not have significantly differed from those for 1933.

4. See Hans-Ulrich Wehler, "Vorüberlegungen zur historischen Analyse

sozialer Ungleichheit," in Wehler, ed., *Klassen in der europäischen Sozialgeschichte* (Göttingen, 1979), pp. 9-32; M. Rainer Lepsius, "Ungleichheit zwischen Menschen und soziale Schichtung," *Kölner Zeitschrift für Soziologie und Sozialpsychologie*, special issue, 5 (1961), 54-64.

5. Max Weber, *Economy and Society: An Outline of Interpretive Sociology*, ed. Guenther Roth and Claus Wittich (New York, 1968), I, especially 302-307, and II, especially 926-940. Horst Stuke speaks of the "gradation scheme," in his article "Bedeutung und Problematik des Klassenbegriffs: Begriffs- und sozialgeschichtliche Überlegungen im Umkreis einer historischen Klassentheorie," in Ulrich Engelhardt et al., eds., *Soziale Bewegung und politische Verfassung: Beiträge zur Geschichte der modernen Welt* (Stuttgart, 1976), p. 51.

6. Carl Dreyfuss, *Beruf und Ideologie der Angestellten* (Munich and Leipzig, 1933), p. 154.

7. Wehler, "Vorüberlegungen," p. 10; Ralf Dahrendorf, "Industrielle Fertigkeiten und Soziale Schichtung," *Kölner Zeitschrift für Soziologie und Sozialpsychologie*, 8 (1956), 540; Renate Mayntz, "Begriff und empirische Erfassung des sozialen Status in der heutigen Soziologie," *Kölner Zeitschrift für Soziologie und Sozialpsychologie*, 10 (1958), 62, 67; Hansjürgen Daheim, "Die Vorstellungen vom Mittelstand," *Kölner Zeitschrift für Soziologie und Sozialpsychologie*, 12 (1960), 244; Harriett Moore and Gerhard Kleinig, "Das soziale Selbstbild der Gesellschaftsschichten in Deutschland," *Kölner Zeitschrift für Soziologie und Sozialpsychologie*, 12 (1960), 88; Hans Peter Dreitzel, *Elitebegriff und Sozialstruktur: Eine soziologische Begriffsanalyse* (Stuttgart, 1962); Karl Martin Bolte, *Deutsche Gesellschaft im Wandel* (Opladen, 1966), p. 254; Seymour Martin Lipset, "History and Sociology: Some Methodological Considerations," in Lipset and Richard Hofstadter, eds., *Sociology and History: Methods* (New York and London, 1968), pp. 23-24; Heinrich August Winkler, *Mittelstand, Demokratie und Nationalsozialismus: Die politische Entwicklung von Handwerk und Kleinhandel in der Weimarer Republik* (Cologne, 1972), pp. 21-26; Werner Conze, "Beruf," in *Geschichtliche Grundbegriffe: Historisches Lexikon zur politisch-sozialen Sprache in Deutschland*, ed. Otto Brunner et al., I (Stuttgart, 1972), 490, hereafter cited as *Grundbegriffe*; Michael B. Katz, "Occupational Classification in History," *Journal of Interdisciplinary History*, 3 (Summer 1972), 63-88; Stephan Thernstrom, *The Other Bostonians: Poverty and Progress in the American Metropolis 1880-1970* (Cambridge, Mass., 1973), pp. 293-294; Jürgen Genuneit, "Methodische Probleme der quantitativen Analyse früher NSDAP-Mitgliederlisten," in Reinhard Mann, ed., *Die Nationalsozialisten: Analysen faschistischer Bewegungen* (Stuttgart, 1980), p. 50.

8. The class concept is critically discussed in Stuke, "Bedeutung," pp. 46-82. For the lower class or workers, see Werner Conze, "Arbeiter," in *Grundbegriffe*, I, 216-242.

9. The problem inherent in a proper translation of *Mittelstand* is alluded to by R.J. McKibbin, "The Myth of the Unemployed: Who Did Vote for the Nazis?" *Australian Journal of Politics and History*, 15 (1969), 26, n. 5.

10. See, for instance, the division employed by the compilers of *Deutsche Hochschulstatistik* (Summer 1931), p. *41.

11. Historical background material on *Mittelstand* and aristocracy is in Dreyfuss, *Beruf*, pp. 257–259; Dreitzel, *Elitebegriff*; Fritz K. Ringer, *The Decline of the German Mandarins: the German Academic Community, 1890–1933* (Cambridge, Mass., 1969), pp. 14–127; Ringer, "Bildung, Wirtschaft und Gesellschaft in Deutschland 1800–1960," *Geschichte und Gesellschaft*, 6 (1980), 5–35; Werner Conze, "Adel," in *Grundbegriffe*, I, 42–48; Conze, "Beruf," in *Grundbegriffe*, I, 504; Conze, "Mittelstand," in *Grundbegriffe*, IV (Stuttgart, 1978), 54–92; Rudolf Vierhaus, "Bildung," in *Grundbegriffe*, I, 519–555; Manfred Riedel, "Gesellschaft," in *Grundbegriffe*, II (Stuttgart, 1975), 796–798; Ralf Dahrendorf, *Society and Democracy in Germany* (Garden City, N.Y., 1967), pp. 217–226; A. J. Mayer, "The Lower Middle Class as Historical Problem," *Journal of Modern History*, 47 (1975), 424.

12. Theodor Geiger, *Die soziale Schichtung des deutschen Volkes: Soziographischer Versuch auf statistischer Grundlage* (Stuttgart, 1967; 1st printing, 1932), p. 27.

13. For the last observation, see Heinz Hamm, *Die wirtschaftlichen und sozialen Berufsmerkmale der kaufmännischen Angestellten (im Vergleich mit denjenigen der Arbeiter)* (Jena, 1931), pp. 17–18. In contradiction to Hamm, Geiger, from a socialist perspective, emphasized the similarities in life-style between workers on the one hand and lower employees on the other (*Schichtung*, p. 130). On the general problem of defining workers, see Ernst Lau, *Beiträge zur Psychologie der Jugendlichen*, 3d ed. (Langensalza, 1925), pp. 67–68; Hamm, *Berufsmerkmale*, p. 8; Theodor Geiger, "Zur Soziologie der Industriearbeit und des Betriebes," *Die Arbeit*, 6 (1929), 776; Franz Fendt, *Der ungelernte Industriearbeiter: Eine sozialökonomische Studie unter besonderer Berücksichtigung der gegenwärtigen deutschen Verhältnisse* (Munich and Leipzig, 1936); Dahrendorf, "Fertigkeiten"; Arthur Schweitzer, *Big Business in the Third Reich* (Bloomington, 1964), p. 63; Bolte, *Gesellschaft*, p. 278; Conze, "Arbeiter," p. 221; Ulrich Linse, *Die anarchistische und anarcho-syndikalistische Jugendbewegung 1919–1933: Zur Geschichte und Ideologie der anarchistischen, syndikalistischen und unionistischen Kinder- und Jugendorganisationen 1919–1933* (Frankfurt/ Main, 1976), p. 141; Gerhard Beier, "Das Problem der Arbeiteraristokratie im 19. und 20. Jahrhundert: Zur Sozialgeschichte einer umstrittenen Kategorie," in *Herkunft und Mandat: Beiträge zur Führungsproblematik in der Arbeiterbewegung* (Frankfurt/Main and Cologne, 1976), pp. 32, 51; Michael H. Kater, "Quantifizierung und NS-Geschichte: Methodologische Überlegungen über Grenzen und Möglichkeiten einer EDV-Analyse der NSDAP-Sozialstruktur von 1925 bis 1945," *Geschichte und Gesellschaft*, 3 (1977), 472–474; Genuneit, "Probleme," pp. 44–45.

14. In my two pilot studies, "Zur Soziographie der frühen NSDAP," *Vierteljahrshefte für Zeitgeschichte*, 19 (1971), 124–159, and "Sozialer Wandel in der NSDAP im Zuge der nationalsozialistischen Machtergreifung," in Wolfgang Schieder, ed., *Faschismus als soziale Bewegung: Deutschland und*

Italien im Vergleich (Hamburg, 1976), pp. 25-67, I had counted the labor aristocracy with the lower middle class. This was constructively criticized by Jürgen Kocka, "Zur Problematik der deutschen Angestellten 1914-1933," in Hans Mommsen et al., eds., *Industrielles System und politische Entwicklung in der Weimarer Republik: Verhandlungen des Internationalen Symposiums in Bochum vom 12.-17. Juni 1973* (Düsseldorf, 1974), p. 800, n. 13; and by Lutz Niethammer, "Faschistische Bewegungen der Zwischenkriegszeit in Europa," *Politische Bildung*, 1 (1972), 27. Hence I attempted a differentiation in "Quantifizierung," pp. 475-477. Evidently, Detlev Mühlberger was not aware of my changed approach when he wrote his otherwise perceptive article, "The Sociology of the NSDAP: The Question of Working-Class Membership," *Journal of Contemporary History*, 15 (1980), 493-511; see especially p. 495. On the phenomenon generally, see Georges Sorel, "The Decomposition of Marxism [1908]," in Irving L. Horowitz, *Radicalism and the Revolt against Reason: The Theories of Georges Sorel* (London, 1961), pp. 228-229; Robert Michels, *Zur Soziologie des Parteiwesens: Untersuchungen über die oligarchischen Tendenzen des Gruppenlebens*, 2d ed. (Leipzig, 1925), especially p. 368; Daheim, "Vorstellungen," p. 251; Moore and Kleinig, "Selbstbild," pp. 102-104; Gerhard Schulz, *Aufstieg des Nationalsozialismus: Krise und Revolution in Deutschland* (Frankfurt/Main, 1975), p. 198. Mayer still appears to follow Michels: "Lower Middle Class," p. 431.

15. See Geiger, "Soziologie," pp. 774-775; Svend Riemer, "Zur Soziologie des Nationalsozialismus," *Die Arbeit*, 9 (1932), 107-108; Karl Martin Bolte, "Die Berufsstruktur im industrialisierten Deutschland: Entwicklungen und Probleme," in Bolte et al., *Beruf und Gesellschaft in Deutschland: Berufsstruktur und Berufsprobleme* (Opladen, 1970), p. 107.

16. See, for instance, Riemer, "Soziologie," p. 104; Bolte, "Berufsstruktur," p. 107; Winkler, *Mittelstand*; and chaps. 1-5 of this book.

17. See Maria Regina Rumpf, "Die lebensalterliche Verteilung des Mitgliederzuganges zur NSDAP vor 1933, aufgezeigt an einer Grosstadt und einem Landkreis: Ein Beitrag zum Generationsproblem," Ph.D. dissertation, Heidelberg, 1951, p. 36; Genuneit, "Probleme," pp. 47-48; Kater, "Quantifizierung," pp. 473-474.

18. As they were counted in my first pilot study, "Soziographie," pp. 134, 139.

19. The formula is derived from census figures for 1925 published in A.R.L. Gurland et al., *The Fate of Small Business in Nazi Germany* (New York, 1975; 1st ed., 1943), p. 24. For a verification of those figures see Winkler, *Mittelstand*, p. 30; and Gerhard Starcke, *Die Deutsche Arbeitsfront: Eine Darstellung über Zweck, Leistungen und Ziele* (Berlin, 1940), p. 113. Geiger's estimate of ¾ to 1 million self-employed craftsmen (1932) appears too low: *Schichtung*, p. 85.

20. For the formula, see n. 38 below.

21. For the rationale see Kater, "Quantifizierung," pp. 474-475; Kater, "Soziographie," p. 135; J. F. Volrad Deneke, *Die freien Berufe* (Stuttgart, 1956), pp. 146, 159-166, 216; Karl Martin Bolte, *Sozialer Aufstieg und*

Abstieg: Eine Untersuchung über Berufsprestige und Berufsmobilität (Stuttgart, 1959), p. 28; Bolte, "Berufsstruktur," p. 109.

22. The last fact is rightly emphasized by Jane Caplan, "The Civil Servant in the Third Reich," Ph.D. dissertation, Oxford, 1973, pp. 57–58.

23. See Geiger, *Schichtung*, p. 57; Bolte, *Gesellschaft*, p. 278; Ulf Kadritzke, *Angestellte—Die geduldigen Arbeiter: Zur Soziologie und sozialen Bewegung der Angestellten* (Frankfurt/Main and Cologne, 1975), p. 368; Hans Speier, *Die Angestellten vor dem Nationalsozialismus: Ein Beitrag zum Verständnis der deutschen Sozialstruktur 1918–1933* (Göttingen, 1977), pp. 85–86; *Jahrbuch der Deutschen Sozialdemokratie für das Jahr 1930* [Berlin, 1931], p. 422.

24. See, in particular, Jürgen Kocka, "Angestellter," in *Grundbegriffe*, I, 112–128; and Kocka, *Die Angestellten in der deutschen Geschichte 1850–1980: Vom Privatbeamten zum angestellten Arbeitnehmer* (Göttingen, 1981), especially pp. 99, 130–140.

25. Many bank clerks called themselves *Bankbeamte* to simulate a generic kinship with the state officials.

26. See Hamm, *Berufsmerkmale*, pp. 3–6, 17–18; Geiger, "Soziologie," p. 780; Geiger, *Schichtung*, pp. 58, 130; Erich Engelhard, "Die Angestellten," *Kölner Vierteljahrshefte für Soziologie*, 10 (1932), 512–517; Dreyfuss, *Beruf*, pp. 153, 178, 256; Schweitzer, *Business*, p. 64; Bolte, "Berufsstruktur," pp. 46–47, 57; Speier, *Angestellten*, p. 21.

27. Most of the positions in question, up to the limit posed by the higher civil service, are conveniently listed in Arthur Rathke, *Wie werde ich Beamter? Ein Wegweiser durch die Vorbildungs-, Ausbildungs- und Laufbahnvorschriften der Beamtenberufe unter besonderer Berücksichtigung der technischen und der Beamtenlaufbahnen mit Hochschulbildung* (Berlin, 1940), pp. 19–24, from "Besoldungsgruppe 2 e" down to "Besoldungsgruppe 12" (with some overlapping with offices of the higher civil service at the upper end), and this work was used for the identification of lower-middle-class officials. See also ibid., p. 11; Heinrich Tisch, "Das Problem des sozialen Auf- und Abstieges im deutschen Volk, dargestellt an Hand einer Erhebung über die soziale Herkunft der Beamten in der Saarpfalz (Eine genealogisch-statistische Untersuchung als Beitrag zur Soziologie des deutschen Beamtentums)," Ph.D. dissertation, Heidelberg, 1937, pp. 18, 24, 32. The genesis of the modern German civil servant is succinctly explained in Bolte, "Berufsstruktur," pp. 74–75. Also see Riemer, "Soziologie," p. 106; Horst Krüger, *Das zerbrochene Haus: Eine Jugend in Deutschland*, 2d ed. (Munich, 1967), pp. 36–38; Genuneit, "Probleme," pp. 46–47.

28. See Kocka, "Problematik," p. 800, n. 13.

29. The formula is based on that percentage of self-employed persons (2.6%) who in 1937 earned at least 25,000.00 marks and paid the highest income tax rate in the Reich, between 22.2% and 32.9% per annum. See table 23 in *Statistisches Handbuch von Deutschland 1928–1944* (Munich, 1949), p. 564. Also see Geiger, *Schichtung*, pp. 35, 85; Riemer, "Soziologie," pp. 107–108; Genuneit, "Probleme," p. 49.

30. *Mithelfende Familienangehörige* were mentioned in the census records, with 5,312,116 *N* for 1933. See *Berufszählung: Die berufliche und soziale Gliederung des Deutschen Volkes: Textliche Darstellungen und Ergebnisse* (*Statistik des Deutschen Reichs: Volks-, Berufs- und Betriebszählung vom 16. Juni 1933*, vol. 458) (Berlin, 1937), p. 51. They were ignored in this study in the calculation of occupation or class because they could not easily be apportioned. For these problems, see Geiger, *Schichtung*, pp. 47–50.

31. The following works deal with the pertinent history of and problems involved in classifying farmers (peasants): Werner Conze, "Bauer," in *Grundbegriffe*, I, 407–439; Max Weber, *Wirtschaftsgeschichte*, ed. S. Hellmann and M. Palyi, 2d ed. (Munich and Leipzig, 1924), pp. 86–93; Gerhard Albrecht, "Das deutsche Bauerntum im Zeitalter des Kapitalismus," in *Grundriss der Sozialökonomik*, 9, no. 1 (Tübingen, 1926), 35–69; Riemer, "Soziologie," p. 108.

32. *Der Spiegel*, December 1, 1980, p. 19; Riemer, "Soziologie," p. 105; Geiger, *Schichtung*, p. 45; Bolte, "Berufsstruktur," p. 105; Genuneit, "Probleme," p. 45. Also see Kocka, *Angestellten*, especially pp. 110–114.

33. They are so treated in this book in the discussion of their relationship with National Socialism. See chaps. 1–5. The term "business leaders" is used by Hartmut Kaelble in his "Long-Term Changes in the Recruitment of the Business-Elite: Germany Compared to the U.S., Great Britain, and France since the Industrial Revolution," *Journal of Social History*, 13 (1980), 409. See also Fritz Croner, "Die Angestelltenbewegung nach der Währungsstabilisierung," *Archiv für Sozialwissenschaft und Sozialpolitik*, 60 (1928), 136–137; Geiger, "Soziologie," p. 774; Engelhard, "Angestellten," p. 480; Wilhelm Treue, "Der deutsche Unternehmer in der Weltwirtschaftskrise 1928–1933," in Werner Conze and Hans Raupach, eds., *Die Staats- und Wirtschaftskrise des Deutschen Reichs 1929/33* (Stuttgart, 1967), p. 92.

34. Rathke, *Beamter*, pp. 17–19; Dahrendorf, *Society*, p. 86; Karl Martin Bolte, "Berufsstruktur und Berufsmobilität," in Bolte et al., *Beruf und Gesellschaft*, p. 160.

35. See Geiger, *Schichtung*, p. 100; M. Rainer Lepsius, "Kritik als Beruf: Zur Soziologie der Intellektuellen," *Kölner Zeitschrift für Soziologie und Sozialpsychologie*, 16 (1964), 75–91; Michael H. Kater, *Studentenschaft und Rechtsradikalismus in Deutschland 1918–1933: Eine sozialgeschichtliche Studie zur Bildungskrise in der Weimarer Republik* (Hamburg, 1975), pp. 64, 68–73, 81–89.

36. *Hochschulstatistik*, p. *41; Bolte, *Aufstieg*, pp. 79–80, 98–99; Bolte, "Berufsmobilität," p. 160; Dreitzel, *Elitebegriff*; Deneke, *Freien Berufe*, especially p. 117.

37. See Engelhard, "Angestellten," p. 515.

38. Estimates according to figures in Karl-Heinz Ludwig, *Technik und Ingenieure im Dritten Reich* (Düsseldorf, 1974), p. 19, n. 6.

39. The rationale for this treatment is given in Kater, *Studentenschaft*; Kater, "The Work Student: A Socio-Economic Phenomenon of Early Weimar Germany," *Journal of Contemporary History*, 10 (1975), 71–94.

40. Figures were adopted from *Statistisches Jahrbuch für das Deutsche Reich 1934* (Berlin, 1934), pp. 534–540, for summer semester 1933.

41. Geiger counted just under 1% of the population of 1925 as "capitalists": *Schichtung*, pp. 72–73.

42. The figures were taken from *Berufszählung . . . 16. Juni 1933*, pp. 48–51, and, for students, from the source cited in n. 40. They were assumed to be constant for the periods 1919–1932 and 1933–1945 (see n. 3). Since the individual occupations in *Berufszählung* are numbered (101–509), it is possible to detail the counting procedure. Figures for the following occupational slots were consigned to subgroup 1: 104–108, 122, 133, 150, 166, 182, 184, 187, 193, 212, 216, 221, 232–234, 245–246, 251, 262–263, 268, 278, 281, 287, 304–306, 313, 318, 321, 323–325, 331–332 (females only), 333, half of 368 and 374, 387 (males only), 391, 394–395, 401–412, 417, 509. For subgroup 2: 63.4% each of 109, 131–132, 134–149, 151–164, 181, 183, 185–186, 188–192, 201–208, 211, 213–215, 217, 222–231, 235–244, 247–250, 261, 264–267, 269–270, 274–275, 277, 279–280, 282–286, 288, 392. For subgroup 3: 121, 165, 276, 289, 312, 314, 331–332 (males only), 377, 415–416. For subgroup 4: 36.6% each of the figures mentioned for subgroup 2. For subgroup 5: 167 (90,000 *N*), 272, 298, 319–320, 322, 353, 360, 361 (7,034 *N*), two-thirds of 362, 366, two-thirds of 369 and 370, 371–372, two-thirds of 373, half of 374 and 375, 382, 384, 386, 387 (females only), 388, 390 (3,693 *N*), 397. For subgroup 6: 103, 167 (52, 574 *N*), 172, 209, 273, 293–297, 316, 354–355, 367, half of 368, 376, 389, 390 (3,856 *N*), 393, 413–414, 506–508. For subgroup 7: 110, 311, 315, 317, 343–344, 346, 348–349, 358–359, 505. For subgroup 8: 292, 97.4% each of 299 through 301, 302, 303, 97.4% of 501. For subgroup 9: 97.4% of 101 and 102, 111. For subgroup 10: 291, 361(10,243 *N*), 503. For subgroup 11: 341–342, 345, 347, 350–351, 356–357, 504. For subgroup 12: 167 (60,000 *N*), 171, 271, 352, one-third of 362, 363–365, one-third of 369, 370, and 373, half of 375, 381, 383, 385, 396. For subgroup 13: 129,292 *N* (see n. 40; this figure replaces the original one for *Schulentlassene*, which was deleted). For subgroup 14: 2.6% each of 101–102, as well as 299 through 301, and 501. My method of creating a new vertical classification of occupations ignores the pattern of horizontal classification used in the official German statistics, which, taken from the 1925 census to the 1939 census, were anything but consistent: see Gerd Hardach, "Klassen und Schichten in Deutschland 1848–1970: Probleme einer historischen Sozialstrukturanalyse," *Geschichte und Gesellschaft*, 3 (1977), 516–517. For a discussion regarding the usefulness of that classification, also see: Bolte, "Berufssruktur," pp. 32, 103; Hans-Gerd Schumann, "Die Führungsspitzen der NSBO und der DAF," in *Herkunft und Mandat*, p. 159; Dietmar Petzina, *Die deutsche Wirtschaft in der Zwischenkriegszeit* (Wiesbaden, 1977), p. 33; Genuneit, "Probleme," pp. 35–36. This classification scheme was adopted by the Nazis for their own analysis of Nazi party membership in 1935 and constitutes one of the chief limitations of that work. See *Partei-Statistik*, I (Munich [1935]), 70, hereafter cited as *Partei-Statistik* I. One of the main reasons for the limited value of post.World War II analyses of Nazi party membership has been their uncritical adoption of the classifica-

tion scheme from *Partei-Statistik* I. See Wolfgang Schäfer, *NSDAP: Entwicklung und Struktur der Staatspartei des Dritten Reiches* (Hanover and Frankfurt/Main, 1957), p. 38; and Martin Broszat, *Der Staat Hitlers: Grundlegung und Entwicklung seiner inneren Verfassung* (Munich, 1969), p. 51. Also see n. 28 of chap. 8 below.

43. Bolte, "Berufsstruktur," p. 33.

44. Moore and Kleinig, "Selbstbild," p. 91; Ralf Dahrendorf, *Konflikt und Freiheit: Auf dem Weg zur Dienstklassengesellschaft* (Munich, 1972), p. 129; Morris Janowitz, "Soziale Schichtung und Mobilität in Westdeutschland," *Kölner Zeitschrift für Soziologie und Sozialpsychologie*, 10 (1958), 10; Dreyfuss, *Beruf*, p. 155; Geiger, *Schichtung*, p. 72. Also see n. 41 above.

45. For a similar treatment of Austrian Nazis before the *Anschluss*, see Gerhard Botz, "Die österreichischen NSDAP-Mitglieder: Probleme einer quantitativen Analyse aufgrund der NSDAP-Zentralkartei im Berlin Document Center," in Mann, ed., *Nationalsozialisten*, pp. 98–136; Botz, "The Changing Patterns of Social Support for Austrian National Socialism (1918–1945)," in Stein Ugelvik Larsen et al., eds., *Who Were the Fascists: Social Roots of European Fascism* (Bergen, 1980), pp. 202–225. Botz is preparing a full-scale study of the pre–1939 Austrian Nazis.

46. These 4,726 cases were out of a total membership of 55,287 in early November of 1923 (see figure 1). For social stratification analysis, only 4,454 cases could be used.

47. Details regarding the NSDAP Master File and my sampling and processing of case data are more fully explained in my article "Quantifizierung." Also see Botz, "NSDAP-Mitglieder." Facsimiles of membership cards are in Botz, "Probleme," on p. 116; and in James P. Madden, "The Social Composition of the Nazi Party, 1919–1930," Ph.D. dissertation, University of Oklahoma, 1976, pp. 298–299. The difficulties of sociologically assessing housewives and pensioners are briefly discussed in Dreitzel, *Elitebegriff*, p. 80.

48. The theoretical problems posed by social self-evaluation are discussed in: Hermann Schnaas, *Der Arbeitsmarkt der Angestellten und die Arbeitsmarktpolitik der Angestellten-Organisation, unter besonderer Berücksichtigung der Nachkriegszeit* (Münster, 1929), p. 3; Geiger, *Schichtung*, p. 13; Daheim, "Vorstellungen," p. 258; Moore and Kleinig, "Selbstbild"; Janowitz, "Schichtung," p. 13; Anna J. and Richard L. Merritt, eds., *Public Opinion in Occupied Germany: The OMGUS Surveys, 1945–1949* (Urbana, 1970), p. 125; Katz, "Classification," p. 71; Gunther Mai, "Die Sozialstruktur der württembergischen Soldatenräte 1918/1919," *Internationale wissenschaftliche Korrespondenz zur Geschichte der deutschen Arbeiterbewegung*, 14 (1978), 15–16; Genuneit, "Probleme," p. 41; Mathilde Jamin, "Methodische Konzeption einer quantitativen Analyse zur sozialen Zusammensetzung der SA," in Mann, ed., *Nationalsozialisten*, p. 94. Also see text of this Introduction near n. 28.

49. For regions, data from three censuses were used: (1) 1925 census, in *Statistisches Jahrbuck für das Deutsche Reich 1933*, pp. 11–13; (2) 1933 census, ibid., *1938*, pp. 16–18; (3) 1939 census, ibid., *1941/42*, pp. 17–20.

50. Peter H. Merkl, *The Making of a Stormtrooper* (Princeton, 1980), pp. 157–158, n. 57. Note, however, that my scheme of territorial subdivision seems to have agreed with Ayçoberry, *Nazi Question*, pp. 169–170, 226–227; and with Eike Hennig, "Regionale Unterschiede bei der Entstehung des deutschen Faschismus: Ein Plädoyer für 'mikroanalytische Studien' zur Erforschung der NSDAP," *Politische Vierteljahresschrift*, 21 (1980), 163.

51. This problem has lately been intelligently addressed by Schumann, "Führungsspitzen," p. 149; Annette Leppert-Fögen, *Die deklassierte Klasse: Studien zur Geschichte und Ideologie des Kleinbürgertums* (Frankfurt/Main, 1974), p. 323; Lawrence D. Stokes, "The Social Composition of the Nazi Party in Eutin, 1925–32," *International Review of Social History*, 23 (1978), Part I, 1; Ronald Rogowski, "The *Gauleiter* and the Social Origins of Fascism," *Comparative Studies in Society and History*, 19 (1977), 401.

52. As an example of this accepted view, see Jeremy Noakes and Geoffrey Pridham, eds., *Documents on Nazism, 1919–1945* (London, 1974), p. 114.

53. See text in chap. 7, between nn. 57 and 80. The legitimacy of sociocultural class typologies is discussed by Geiger, *Schichtung*, p. 5; and Bolte, *Gesellschaft*, p. 17. For interesting attempts at describing a specific lower-middle-class mentality, see Riemer, "Soziologie," p. 109; Schweitzer, *Business*, p. 76; Daheim, "Vorstellungen," p. 268; M. Rainer Lepsius, *Extremer Nationalismus: Strukturbedingungen vor der nationalsozialistischen Machtergreifung* (Stuttgart, 1966), pp. 13–14; Heinrich August Winkler, "From Social Protectionism to National Socialism: The German Small-Business Movement in Comparative Perspective," *Journal of Modern History*, 48 (1976), 15; Mayer, "Lower Middle Class," pp. 415, 425.

54. "National Socialism: Totalitarianism or Fascism?" *American Historical Review*, 73 (1967), 410–411.

1. THE BEGINNING: 1919 TO THE BEER HALL PUTSCH, NOVEMBER 1923

1. The values in columns A–D, H–K, and O in table 2 represent total populations (established local NSDAP chapter members) and should be treated in the same way as the values in table 4. The values in the remaining columns E–G and L–N of table 2 represent samples of newcomers or joiners within a specifically defined time period and should be treated in the manner of the Madden figures in table 3. See the beginning of chap. 2.

2. On the founding, see Heinz Spiess, "Der rechtliche und organisatorische Aufbau der Nationalsozialistischen Deutschen Arbeiterpartei," Ph.D. dissertation, Tübingen, 1936, p. 7; Ernst Rudolf Huber, "Die Rechtsgestalt der NSDAP," *Deutsche Rechtswissenschaft*, 4 (1939), 314.

3. On the deliberate attempt by the DAP/NSDAP to win workers, see Max H. Kele, *Nazis and Workers: National Socialist Appeals to German Labor, 1919–1933* (Chapel Hill, 1972), pp. 31–66; Geiger, *Schichtung*, p. 110; Orlow I, p. 19; Theodore Abel, *Why Hitler Came to Power* (New York, 1966; 1st printing, 1936), p. 170; Schulz, *Aufstieg*, p. 198; docs. 11, 14 in Albrecht

Tyrell, ed., *Führer befiehl . . . Selbstzeugnisse aus der "Kampfzeit" der NSDAP: Dokumentation und Analyse* (Düsseldorf, 1969), pp. 39, 51; Tyrell, *Vom "Trommler" zum "Führer": Der Wandel von Hitlers Selbstverständnis zwischen 1919 and 1924 und die Entwicklung der NSDAP* (Munich, 1975), pp. 21–22, 49–51; Reginald Phelps, "Hitler als Parteiredner im Jahre 1920," *Vierteljahrshefte für Zeitgeschichte*, 11 (1963), 274–330. Drexler's German job description was *Schlosser*; he called himself "a simple worker." See Anton Drexler, *Mein politisches Erwachen: Aus dem Tagebuch eines deutschen sozialistischen Arbeiters*, 4th ed. (Munich, 1937), pp. 3, 10; and Hans Frank, *Im Angesicht des Galgens: Deutung Hitlers und seiner Zeit auf Grund eigener Erlebnisse und Erkenntnisse* (Munich-Gräfelfing, 1953), p. 48.

4. See docs. 21, 25 in Ernst Deuerlein, "Hitlers Eintritt in die Politik und die Reichswehr," *Vierteljahrshefte für Zeitgeschichte*, 7 (1959), 213, 215; Deuerlein, ed., *Der Aufstieg der NSDAP in Augenzeugenberichten* (Düsseldorf, 1968), pp. 158–159; and the evidence in Harold J. Gordon, Jr., *Hitler and the Beer Hall Putsch* (Princeton, 1972), pp. 74–77.

5. *Bremer Zeitung*, November 5, 1922. The evidence in Wilfried Böhnke, *Die NSDAP im Ruhrgebiet 1920–1933* (Bonn and Bad Godesberg, 1974), pp. 41–54, supersedes that in Hans Graf, *Die Entwicklung der Wahlen und politischen Parteien in Gross-Dortmund* (Hanover and Frankfurt/Main, 1958), pp. 35–36, and the Nazi account in Friedrich Alfred Beck, *Kampf und Sieg: Geschichte der Nationalsozialistischen Deutschen Arbeiterpartei im Gau Westfalen-Süd von den Anfängen bis zur Machtübernahme* (Dortmund, 1938), pp. 210–234. Also see Alfred Rosenberg, *Letzte Aufzeichnungen: Ideale und Idole der nationalsozialistischen Revolution* (Göttingen, 1955), p. 98; John Farquharson, "The NSDAP in Hanover and Lower Saxony 1921–26," *Journal of Contemporary History*, 8, no. 4 (1973), 111, 113; "Die Frauenarbeit . . . 1922–35," HIS, 13/253.

6. See Tyrell, *Vom "Trommler,"* pp. 51–53, 68, 83; Riemer, "Soziologie," p. 111. Also docs. 100, 116 in *Hitler: Sämtliche Aufzeichnungen 1905–1924*, ed. Eberhard Jäckel (Stuttgart, 1980), pp. 133, 155–156, cited hereafter as *Hitler: Aufzeichnungen.*

7. Carl E. Schorske, *German Social Democracy 1905–1917: The Development of the Great Schism* (New York, 1965); Richard N. Hunt, *German Social Democracy 1918–1933* (Chicago, 1970); Ossip K. Flechtheim, *Die KPD in der Weimarer Republik* (Frankfurt/Main, 1969); Sigmund Neumann, *Die Parteien der Weimarer Republik* (Stuttgart, 1965; 1st printing, 1932), pp. 27–41, 87–95; Richard Breitman, *German Socialism and Weimar Democracy* (Chapel Hill, 1981).

8. This idea was by no means original. It had been enunciated by the Marxist-turned-racist Ludwig Woltmann in the early twentieth century, and others. See George L. Mosse, *Toward the Final Solution: A History of European Racism* (New York, 1978), p. 79.

9. See party program of February 24, 1920, especially paragraphs 4, 10, 11, in Gottfried Feder, *Hitler's Official Programme and Its Fundamental Ideas* (New York, 1978; 1st printing, 1934), pp. 30–40; *Hitler: Aufzeichnungen.* The

European tradition of anti-Semitic "finance capital" theory is explained in Mosse, *Solution*, pp. 152-154.

10. Feder, *Programme*, p. 40. Also Riemer, "Soziologie," p. 111; Leppert-Fögen, *Klasse*, p. 290. Kele, *Nazis*, pp. 37-38, grossly overestimates the significance of the party program for the workers.

11. Franz Neumann, *Behemoth: The Structure and Practice of National Socialism* (London, 1942), p. 107; Drexler, *Erwachen*, especially p. 60; docs. 19, 20 in Deuerlein, "Eintritt," pp. 211, 212; Riemer, "Soziologie," p. 111; Geiger, *Schichtung*, p. 119; Tyrell, *Vom "Trommler,"* pp. 21-22, 50-51; Erich Goldhagen, "Weltanschauung und Endlösung: Zum Antisemitismus der nationalsozialistischen Führungsschicht," *Vierteljahrshefte für Zeitgeschichte*, 24 (1976), 388. On the opposition of the SPD to anti-Semitism, see Donald L. Niewyck, *Socialist, Anti-Semite, and Jew: German Social Democracy Confronts the Problem of Anti-Semitism 1918-1933* (Baton Rouge, 1971), especially pp. 3-120. On Jewish intellectuals in the SPD, see Wilhelm Hoegner, *Flucht vor Hitler: Erinnerungen an die Kapitulation der ersten deutschen Republik 1933*, 2d ed. (Munich, 1978), p. 23.

12. Adolf Hitler, *Mein Kampf*, ed. John Chamberlain et al. (New York, 1939), pp. 873-875, 881-883; Tyrell, *Vom "Trommler,"* pp. 44-46; doc. 6 in Phelps, "Hitler," p. 303. On the problem of strikes and their resolution in the early Weimar Republic, see Michael H. Kater, "Die 'Technische Nothilfe' im Spannungsfeld von Arbeiterunruhen, Unternehmerinteressen und Parteipolitik," *Vierteljahrshefte für Zeitgeschichte*, 27 (1979), 30-78.

13. Geiger, *Schichtung*, p. 119.

14. See *Völkischer Beobachter*, August 21, 1921; Drexler, *Erwachen*; Tyrell, *Vom "Trommler,"* p. 49.

15. Drexler, *Erwachen*; Hitler, *Mein Kampf*. Also see docs. 79, 110 in *Hitler: Aufzeichnungen*, pp. 108, 149.

16. Quotation doc. 25 in Deuerlein, "Eintritt," p. 215. See Michels, *Soziologie*, pp. 344-365; Drexler, *Erwachen*, p. 10; Georg Franz-Willing, *Die Hitlerbewegung: Der Ursprung* (Hamburg and Berlin, 1962), p. 78; Schulz, *Aufstieg*, p. 198; Tyrell, *Vom "Trommler,"* p. 21; Kater, "Soziographie," p. 150.

17. *Political Man: The Social Bases of Politics* (Garden City, N.Y., 1960), pp. 134-136. Also see Friedrich Lütge, "An Explanation of the Economic Conditions Which Contributed to the Victory of National Socialism," in *The Third Reich* (London, 1955), p. 424; Lepsius, *Nationalismus*, p. 11; Schoenbaum, *Revolution*, p. 44; Leppert-Fögen, *Klasse*, p. 305; Francis L. Carsten, "Interpretations of Fascism," in Walter Laqueur, ed., *Fascism: A Reader's Guide: Analyses, Interpretations, Bibliography* (Berkeley and Los Angeles, 1976), p. 421; Geiger, *Schichtung*, pp. 110-122; Riemer, "Soziologie," pp. 110-112.

18. The accepted thesis was that the entire middle class was virtually wiped out through inflation. Winkler argues plausibly that this did not apply to those with real estate or debts that could be easily paid off with inflated currency, although in the case of the merchants and craftsmen he gives no indication how

large that fortunate segment of the small business community was. See *Mittelstand*, pp. 28, 109. Conventional views are in Gurland et al., *Fate*, p. 2; Lütge, "Explanation," p. 424; Schulz, *Aufstieg*, p. 252. For Hitler's appeal to *Mittelstand* and *Gewerbetreibende*, see docs. 136, 205, 405, 408, 544, 553, 566 in *Hitler: Aufzeichnungen*, pp. 193–194, 337, 691, 696–699, 945, 958–959, 1000–1001.

19. Winkler, *Mittelstand*, pp. 27–28, 31, 72–74, 77–78, 109; Kater, "Soziographie," pp. 138–139. For craftsmen among the newcomers of fall 1923 in the Bavarian countryside of Vilsbiburg, see Jürgen Genuneit, "Die Anfänge der NSDAP in Vilsbiburg," *Der Storchenturm: Geschichtsblätter für die Landkreise um Dingolfing, Landau und Vilsbiburg*, 12, no. 23 (1977), 56.

20. See Madden, "Composition," p. 82.

21. Werner T. Angress, "The Political Role of the Peasantry in the Weimar Republic," *Review of Politics*, 21 (1959), 533–539.

22. See Onno Poppinga, *Bauern und Politik* (Frankfurt/Main and Cologne, 1975), p. 42; Kater, "Soziographie," p. 142.

23. On the "Marxist" fears, Winkler, *Mittelstand*, p. 165. On the BVP, Falk Wiesemann, *Die Vorgeschichte der nationalsozialistischen Machtübernahme in Bayern 1932/33* (Berlin, 1975), pp. 15–67. See also Kater, "Soziographie," pp. 142–143; docs. 544, 561 in *Hitler: Aufzeichnungen*, pp. 945, 983, 988.

24. Arthur Dix, *Die deutschen Reichstagswahlen 1871–1930 und die Wandlungen der Volksgliederung* (Tübingen, 1930), p. 6; table in *Berufszählung . . . 16. Juni 1933*, p. 20; Eike Hennig, *Thesen zur deutschen Sozial- und Wirtschaftsgeschichte 1933 bis 1938* (Frankfurt/Main, 1973), p. 26.

25. Docs. 308, 408, 503, 505, 583 in *Hitler: Aufzeichnungen*, pp. 509, 696, 862, 865, 867–868, 1033; Broszat, *Staat*, p. 27; Kater, "Soziographie," pp. 144–145. Subjectively retrospective: Hans Fabricius, *Der Beamte einst und im Neuen Reich* (Berlin, 1933), pp. 46–53, 66–67.

26. E. Mursinsky and J. Brill, "Die Organisation der nationalsozialistischen Beamten," *Beamten-Jahrbuch*, 27 (1940), 149.

27. See the brilliant sketches in Siegfried Kracauer, *Die Angestellten: Eine Schrift vom Ende der Weimarer Republik*, 3d ed. (Allensbach and Bonn, 1959; 1st printing, 1930).

28. On the socioeconomic situation of the white-collar workers in general, see Dreyfuss, *Beruf*, pp. 210–211, 215; Bernhard Kockel, "Mittelstand und Nationalsozialismus," *Einheit*, 2 (1947), 180; Winkler, "Extremismus," p. 185; Speier, *Angestellten*, p. 93; Kater, "Soziographie," pp. 143–144; Kocka, *Angestellten*, pp. 142–176.

29. See Drexler, *Erwachen*; Phelps, "Hitler"; Otto Strasser, *Hitler und Ich* (Buenos Aires, 1940), pp. 17–18; Franz-Willing, *Hitlerbewegung*, pp. 79–80.

30. Mosse, *Solution*, pp. 166–167; Eugen Schmahl, *Entwicklung der völkischen Bewegung: Die antisemitische Bauernbewegung in Hessen von der Böckelzeit bis zum Nationalsozialismus* (Giessen, [1933]).

31. Iris Hamel, *Völkischer Verband und nationale Gewerkschaft: Der*

Deutschnationale Handlungsgehilfenverband 1893-1933 (Frankfurt/Main, 1967). For a connection between the anti-Semitism of the DHV and early Nazi propaganda, see doc. 1 in Phelps, "Hitler," p. 292.

32. See Kater, "Soziographie," pp. 145-148; Feder, *Programme,* pp. 38-43; Mosse, *Solution,* pp. 176-179; and the anti-Semitic witness accounts collected by Abel, *Hitler,* pp. 154-165. Friedrich Lütge's undocumented assertion of 1955 ("Explanation," p. 425) that it was "chiefly Jews from the East, who were frequently able to amass large fortunes without doing productive work, simply by deals on the Stock Exchange and by acting as middle-men in commercial activities, while the poverty of the masses became daily more acute" borders dangerously on the Nazi stock phrases contained, among others, in the Feder Program. In a similarly distorted vein, see Strasser, *Hitler,* p. 26.

33. Reinhold Schairer, *Die akademische Berufsnot: Tatsachen und Auswege* (Jena, [1932]), p. 14.

34. Donald M. Douglas, "The Parent Cell: Some Computer Notes on the Composition of the First Nazi Party Group in Munich, 1919-21," *Central European History,* 10 (1977), 60-61; Juan J. Linz, "Some Notes toward a Comparative Study of Fascism in Sociological Historical Perspective," in Laqueur, ed., *Fascism,* pp. 36-39; Günter Paulus, "Die soziale Struktur der Freikorps in den ersten Monaten nach der Novemberrevolution," *Zeitschrift für Geschichtswissenschaft,* 3 (1955), 696-699; Anselm Faust, *Der Nationalsozialistische Deutsche Studentenbund: Studenten und Nationalsozialismus in der Weimarer Republik,* I (Düsseldorf, 1973), 25-28; Jürgen Schwarz, *Studenten in der Weimarer Republik: Die deutsche Studentenschaft in der Zeit von 1918 bis 1923 und ihre Stellung zur Politik* (Berlin, 1971); Michael S. Steinberg, *Sabers and Brownshirts: The German Students' Path to National Socialism, 1918-1935* (Chicago and London, 1977), pp. 48-52; docs. 113, 119 in Ernst Deuerlein, ed., *Der Hitler-Putsch: Bayerische Dokumente zum 8./9. November 1923* (Stuttgart, 1962), pp. 357-358, 373-374.

35. On this, see Kater, *Studentenschaft,* pp. 59-66. For the pre-World War I period, see Konrad H. Jarausch, "Liberal Education as Illiberal Socialization: The Case of Students in Imperial Germany," *Journal of Modern History,* 50 (1978), 609-630; and Jarausch, *Students, Society, and Politics in Imperial Germany: The Rise of Academic Illiberalism* (Princeton, 1982).

36. See Linz, "Notes," p. 21; Winkler, *Mittelstand,* pp. 158-159; Schulz, *Aufstieg,* pp. 277-278; Franz-Willing, *Hitlerbewegung,* pp. 179, 185, 191-193; Hellmuth Auerbach, "Hitlers politische Lehrjahre und die Münchener Gesellschaft 1919-1923," *Vierteljahrshefte für Zeitgeschichte,* 25 (1977), 32-34. On the nature of the DNVP, see Lewis Hertzman, *DNVP: Right-Wing Opposition in the Weimar Republic, 1918-1924* (Lincoln, 1963).

37. See the percentages in table 2. Henry A. Turner, Jr., *Faschismus und Kapitalismus in Deutschland: Studien zum Verhältnis zwischen Nationalsozialismus und Wirtschaft* (Göttingen, 1972), pp. 10-13, 132; Heinrich August Winkler, "Unternehmerverbände zwischen Ständeideologie und Nationalsozialismus," *Vierteljahrshefte für Zeitgeschichte,* 17 (1969), 369;

Wolfgang Horn, *Führerideologie und Parteiorganisation in der NSDAP (1919–1933)* (Düsseldorf, 1972), pp. 94, 151. Dirk Stegmann, "Zum Verhältnis von Grossindustrie und Nationalsozialismus 1930–1933," *Archiv für Sozialgeschichte,* 13 (1973), 403–404, distorts the picture by overemphasizing Hitler's role as a mere puppet of German high finance.

38. "Die Wirtschaftsauffassung der NSDAP," *Politik und Zeitgeschichte,* B 9 (1975), 5–6.

39. See, for instance, docs. 11, 14 in Tyrell, ed., *Führer,* pp. 39, 51.

40. Douglas, "Notes," p. 64. Compare the relatively high percentages of academic professionals for Munich, 1920–21, with the relatively low ones for Ingolstadt, 1922–23, in table 2.

41. Alastair Hamilton, *The Appeal of Fascism: A Study of Intellectuals and Fascism 1919–1945* (New York, 1971), pp. 103, 109–110, 125. Also see Ernst Hanfstaengl, *Unheard Witness* (Philadelphia and New York, 1957); Auerbach, "Lehrjahre," p. 33; Linz, "Notes," p. 40.

42. The Nazis themselves used this argument to explain the poor performance of the party among (higher) civil servants. See Beck, *Kampf,* p. 179. Critically: Broszat, *Staat,* p. 27. Also see Hans Mommsen, "Beamtentum und Staat in der Spätphase der Weimarer Republik," *Deutsche Verwaltungspraxis,* no. 8–9 (1981), pp. 195, 196.

43. On the economic plight of the higher civil servants, see Alfred Weber, *Die Not der geistigen Arbeiter* (Munich and Leipzig, 1923), especially pp. 41–51; Thomas Childers, "National Socialism and the New Middle Class," in Mann, ed., *Nationalsozialisten,* p. 22; and Mommsen, "Beamtentum," p. 197. On the predicament of university professors see Reece Conn Kelly, "National Socialism and German University Teachers: the NSDAP's Efforts to Create a National Socialist Professoriate and Scholarship," Ph.D. dissertation, University of Washington, 1973, pp. 43–45; Ringer, *Decline,* pp. 63–64. See also Alan D. Beyerchen, *Scientists under Hitler: Politics and the Physics Community in the Third Reich* (New Haven and London, 1977), p. 122; Fabricius, *Beamte,* pp. 52, 60, 74, 76; Georg Franz-Willing, *Krisenjahr der Hitlerbewegung 1923* (Preussisch-Oldendorf, 1975), pp. 150–151. The specific brand of anti-Semitism within the educated elite is touched upon in Neumann, *Behemoth,* pp. 108–109; Stegmann, "Verhältnis," pp. 403–405. On the anti-Semitism among the *völkisch* intellectuals as represented by the Deutschvölkischer Schutz- und Trutzbund, see Uwe Lohalm, *Völkischer Radikalismus: Die Geschichte des Deutschvölkischen Schutz- und Trutzbundes 1919–1923* (Hamburg, 1970).

2. THE MIDDLE YEARS:
1924 TO THE FALL ELECTIONS OF 1930

1. See Reinhard Kühnl, *Die nationalsozialistische Linke 1925–1930* (Meisenheim/Glan, 1966); Spiess, "Aufbau," pp. 8–9; Kele, *Nazis,* pp. 76–77; doc. 38 in Tyrell, ed., *Führer,* pp. 93–94, and also p. 96; Böhnke, *NSDAP,* p. 198. Orlow I, p. 92, and chap. 4, "Urban Plan," overestimates the "planning" incentive of the party leaders, especially Hitler's own, after 1925.

2. For Hitler's speech, see Walter M. Espe, *Das Buch der N.S.D.A.P.: Werden, Kampf und Ziel der N.S.D.A.P.* (Berlin, 1934), p. 237. For the "leftist" appeal by the party to the workers throughout Germany from 1926 to 1929, see docs. in HSAD, RW 23 NSDAP/Gauleitung Ruhr; police report, Bremen, June 14, 1926, SAB, 4, 65, II, A, 9, b; report Baden interior ministry, [Karlsruhe], May 1, 1927, SAF, 317/1257 d; Gillgasch to Heidrich, Insterburg, June 3, 1929, SAG, SF 6818, GA/34; H. Spethmann, ed., *Die Stadt Essen: Das Werden und Wirken einer Grosstadt an der Ruhr* (Berlin, 1938), p. 35; Kele, *Nazis,* pp. 104-105, 108-126; Martin Broszat, "Die Anfänge der Berliner NSDAP 1296/27," *Vierteljahrshefte für Zeitgeschichte*, 8 (1960), 85-119; Rainer Hambrecht, *Der Aufstieg der NSDAP in Mittel- und Oberfranken (1925-1933)* (Nuremberg, 1976), pp. 234-235; Herbert Kühr, *Parteien und Wahlen im Stadt- und Landkreis Essen in der Zeit der Weimarer Republik: Unter besonderer Berücksichtigung des Verhältnisses von Sozialstruktur und politischen Wahlen* (Düsseldorf, 1973), p. 141; Farquharson, "NSDAP," p. 119; *The Infancy of Nazism: The Memoirs of Ex-Gauleiter Albert Krebs 1923-1933*, ed. William S. Allen (New York, 1976), p. 79, hereafter cited as Krebs, *Infancy*; Böhnke, *NSDAP*, pp. 83, 177; Eberhard Schön, *Die Entstehung des Nationalsozialismus in Hessen* (Meisenheim/Glan, 1972), p. 165; Peter D. Stachura, "Der kritische Wendepunkt? Die NSDAP und die Reichstagswahlen vom 20. Mai 1928," *Vierteljahrshefte für Zeitgeschichte*, 26 (1978), 72.

3. See "Die internationale Lüge des 1. Mai. Schaffende Deutschlands, wacht auf!" [1926], SAB, 4, 65, II, A, 9, b; also Krebs, *Infancy*, pp. 76-77; Böhnke, *NSDAP*, pp. 214-219; Deuerlein, ed., *Aufstieg*, p. 287. On March 2, 1925, Hitler declared before a throng of 1,500 Nuremberg followers that everyone wishing to pledge loyalty to the Nazi movement would have to regard himself as a worker, whether of brain or of fist (police report Nuremberg-Fürth, Abt. II, Nuremberg, March 3, 1925, SAN, 503/99). Hitler's overall attitude toward workers at this time is best analyzed in Timothy W. Mason, *Sozialpolitik im Dritten Reich: Arbeiterklasse und Volksgemeinschaft,* 2d ed. (Opladen, 1978), pp. 48-50. On the efforts by the Strasser brothers, see Gerhard Schildt, "Die Arbeitsgemeinschaft Nord-West: Untersuchungen zur Geschichte der NSDAP 1925/26," Ph.D. dissertation, Freiburg i.Br., 1964, pp. 72-75; Kühnl, *Linke;* Kühnl, "Zur Programmatik der nationalsozialistischen Linken," *Vierteljahrshefte für Zeitgeschichte*, 14 (1966), 317-333. Kühnl tends to overstate the importance of the "leftist" appeal by the Strasser group. The position of the workers is explained in Lepsius, *Nationalismus*, pp. 26-31.

4. See tables 1, 3-5. See also Broszat, *Staat*, pp. 51-52; Orlow I, pp. 136-139; Kele, *Nazis*, p. 121; Winkler, "Protectionism," p. 9; Jeremy Noakes, *The Nazi Party in Lower Saxony 1921-1933* (Oxford, 1971), pp. 104-105, 148, 246; John E. Farquharson, *The Plough and the Swastika: The NSDAP and Agriculture in Germany 1928-45* (London and Beverly Hills, 1976), p. 3; Thomas Childers, "The Social Bases of the National Socialist Vote," *Journal of Contemporary History*, 11, no. 4 (1976), 26; Stokes, "Composition," p. 23. Also see n. 16 below.

5. The case of Thuringia is atypical (see table 5).

6. Günter Plum, *Gesellschaftsstruktur und politisches Bewusstsein in einer katholischen Region 1928–1933: Untersuchung am Beispiel des Regierungsbezirks Aachen* (Stuttgart, 1972), pp. 21, 23, 67. Mason attempts a short typology of the agrarian-based worker in *Sozialpolitik*, pp. 59–60. Also see Geiger, *Schichtung*, pp. 92–93; Heinrich Striefler, *Deutsche Wahlen in Bildern und Zahlen: Eine soziographische Studie über die Reichstagswahlen der Weimarer Republik* (Düsseldorf, 1946), pp. 40–46; Graf, *Entwicklung*, p. 39; Broszat, *Staat*, p. 52; Schoenbaum, *Revolution*, pp. 26–27; Kühr, *Parteien*, pp. 282–298; Schulz, *Aufstieg*, p. 553; Böhnke, *NSDAP*, pp. 179–180; Werner Stephan, "Zur Soziologie der Nationalsozialistischen Deutschen Arbeiterpartei," *Zeitschrift für Politik*, 20 (1931), 797–798; Ellsworth Faris, "Takeoff Point for the National Socialist Party: The Landtag Election in Baden, 1929," *Central European History*, 8 (1975), 163; Stachura, "Wendepunkt," pp. 86–88. From a contemporary Nazi point of view, see the candid admission by Beck, *Kampf*, p. 367. The partially agrarian character of the Ruhr region is dealt with by Gregor Böttcher, "Die Umschichtungen der Agrarproduktion im mittleren Ruhrrevier durch den Einfluss der Industrie," in Paul Busch et al., *Bochum und das Mittlere Ruhrgebiet: Festschrift zum 35. Deutschen Geographentag vom 8. bis 11. Juni 1965 in Bochum* (Paderborn, 1965), p. 50.

7. Hans Jäger, *Das wahre Gesicht Hitlers und der NSDAP.* (Prague, [1933]), pp. 48, 55, 65–66; Broszat, *Staat*, p. 52; Kater, "Wandel," p. 31.

8. Some of the documents collected on this point pertain strictly to industrialized urban settlements: see Schubert to NSDAP office in Elberfeld, Langerfeld, December 8, 1925; Essig to Lutze, Herne, June 21, 1926, HSAD, RW 23, NSDAP/Gauleitung Ruhr; Hermann Okrass, *Das Ende einer Parole: "Hamburg bleibt rot,"* 2d ed. (Hamburg, 1935), p. 186 (corroborated by Krebs, *Infancy*, pp. 82-83); KPD report Baden, May 25, 1926, SAF, 317/1257 d. Other documents leave the question of the social target group in doubt: file NHSA, Hann. 310 I, A 30; newspaper excerpt "Hitlerleute in Heilsberg," June 1930, SAG, SF 6826, GA/96; newssheet no. 1 of the district of Greater Königsberg, February 23, 1929, SAG, SF 6818, GA/33; Fischer to Gauleitung Königsberg, Marienburg, January 12, 1930; report Weitzel, Insterburg, September 1, 1930, SAG, SF 6818, GA/34; minutes of speech by Grohé in Cologne municipal council, December 30, 1929, in Peter Schmidt, *Zwanzig Jahre Soldat Adolf Hitlers: Zehn Jahre Gauleiter: Ein Buch von Kampf und Treue* (Cologne, 1941), p. 138.

9. Details in Plum, *Gesellschaftsstruktur*, p. 56; Heinz Günter Steinberg, *Die Entwicklung des Ruhrgebietes: Eine wirtschafts- und sozialgeographische Studie* (Düsseldorf, 1967), pp. 57–60; Otto Winzer, *Zwölf Jahre Kampf gegen Faschismus und Krieg: Ein Beitrag zur Geschichte der Kommunistischen Partei Deutschlands 1933 bis 1945*, 4th ed. ([East] Berlin, 1957), p. 13; Böhnke, *NSDAP*, pp. 89–90; Erwin Rawicz, *Die deutsche Sozialpolitik im Spiegel der Statistik* (München-Gladbach, 1929), pp. 121–122; Ludwig Preller, *Sozialpolitik in der Weimarer Republik* (Stuttgart, 1949), p. 165.

10. See the documents relating to Baden, especially Mannheim-Ludwigshafen, in SAF, 317/1257 f; Kühr, *Parteien*, pp. 138, 142.

11. W. Kaasch, "Die soziale Struktur der Kommunistischen Partei Deutschlands," *Kommunistische Internationale*, May 9, 1928, pp. 1052, 1054; Eva Cornelia Schöck, *Arbeitslosigkeit und Rationalisierung: Die Lage der Arbeiter und die kommunistische Gewerkschaftspolitik 1920-28* (Frankfurt/Main, 1977), p. 227. As with the tables for this chapter, Kaasch's and Schöck's percentage entries for "miscellaneous" and "housewives" were discarded and the remaining percentage figures readjusted.

12. Noakes, *Nazi Party*, p. 68; Kele, *Nazis*, pp. 87–89.

13. Regierungspräsident Stade to Oberpräsident Hanover, Stade, April 14, 1930, NHSA, Hann. 122a, XI, 79. A similar situation was reported for the following plants in Hanover: Continental, Hanomag, Hannoversche Strassenbahn, Elektrizitätswerk, and plastics factory Benecke. NSBO cells that reportedly had been formed were deemed so insignificant that chances for the next shop steward election were regarded as very low (Polizei-Präsident to Regierungspräsident, Hanover, March 19, 1930, ibid.). See also Schulz, *Aufstieg*, p. 549; Hans-Gerd Schumann, *Nationalsozialismus und Gewerkschaftsbewegung: Die Vernichtung der deutschen Gewerkschaften und der Aufbau der "Deutschen Arbeitsfront"* (Hanover and Frankfurt/Main, 1958), pp. 34–36; Gerhard Starcke, *NSBO. und Deutsche Arbeitsfront*, 2d ed. (Berlin, 1934), pp. 9–20; Böhnke, *NSDAP*, pp. 170, 172; Schön, *Entstehung*, pp. 168–169; Orlow I, p. 169; Kühr, *Parteien*, p. 156; Kocka, "Problematik," p. 798.

14. Kater, "Die 'Technische Nothilfe,' " pp. 30–31. The Nazis' condemnation of Technische Nothilfe appears in: excerpt, police report no. 24, April 1, 1925, SAB, 4, 65, II, A, 9, b; G. Strasser to NSDStB, Munich February 6, 1928, ARW, RSF II, A 17.

15. Kele, *Nazis*, pp. 122–123; Böhnke, *NSDAP*, pp. 217–218; Schoenbaum, *Revolution*, p. 31.

16. Doc. 70b in Tyrell, ed., *Führer*, p. 188; NSDAP chapter Neukirchen-Vluyn to Kaufmann, June 19, 1928; NSDAP chapter Brunswick to Kaufmann, September 7, 1928, HSAD, RW 23, NSDAP/Gauleitung Ruhr; minutes of speeches by Grohé in Cologne municipal council, December 30, 1929, and April 14, 1930, in Schmidt, *Jahre*, pp. 139, 141–142; *Regensburger Anzeiger*, June 6, 1929; Arendt to Heidrich, Tannenhof, February 17, 1930, SAG, SF 6818, GA/34; "Der deutsche Mittelstand zum Tode verurteilt!" [September 1930], SAG, SF 6826, GA/100; Hambrecht, *Aufstieg*, pp. 238–239; Schön, *Entstehung*, pp. 162–163; Kater, "Wandel," pp. 27–28. Further documentation for the above is in nn. 17 and 18 below.

17. Winkler, *Mittelstand*, pp. 30, 79, 104–106; Winkler, "Vom Protest zur Panik: Der gewerbliche Mittelstand in der Weimarer Republik," in Mommsen et al., eds., *System*, p. 786. Between 1925 and 1928 the collective national income in the Reich rose by 25%. Dieter Petzina, "Germany and the Great Depression," *Journal of Contemporary History*, 4, no. 4 (1969), 59. Friedrich-Wilhelm Henning, *Das industrialisierte Deutschland 1914 bis 1927* (Pader-

born, 1974), p. 83, has correctly observed that even owners of real estate — as long as they were not large-scale entrepreneurs or calculating profiteers — at best could only salvage what they had previously possessed. Also see Henning, pp. 88-90.

18. Noakes, *Nazi Party*, pp. 110-111. Winkler, too, concedes the importance of the subjective sentiment as a motive for radical rightist behavior within this group, even though he has, correctly, emphasized the objective factors: *Mittelstand*, pp. 79-82, 119, 139; and "Protest," p. 786. Also see the qualifying remarks by Childers, "Bases," p. 21.

19. Gurland et al., *Fate*, p. 3; Noakes, *Nazi Party*, p. 127; Dörte Winkler, *Frauenarbeit im "Dritten Reich"* (Hamburg, 1977), p. 35; Carl Mierendorff, "Gesicht und Charakter der nationalsozialistischen Bewegung," *Die Gesellschaft*, 7 (1930), Part I, 494. For chain stores, see Heinrich Uhlig, *Die Warenhäuser im Dritten Reich* (Cologne and Opladen, 1956), pp. 24-70.

20. A typical manifestation of an artisan's anti-Semitism is the linoleum carving by painter apprentice Fr. B., attached to letter dated Krefeld, January 14, 1928, to Gauleitung Ruhr, HSAD, RW 23, NSDAP/Gauleitung Ruhr, depicting a swastika-brandishing horseman riding over a dragon. To B., this represented "the triumph of Nazism over the Jew." Examples of shopowners who suffered temporarily because of sacrifices for Nazism are in L. Lorösch, "Die Geschichte der N.S. Frauenschaft . . . ," enclosed with letter, Lorösch to party archive, Hanau, September 21, 1935, HIS, 13/254; Albert Hellweg, *Vom Kampf und Sieg des Nationalsozialismus im Kreise Lübbecke* (Lübbecke, [1934]), p. 46; Okrass, *Ende*, p. 154; Abel, *Hitler*, p. 89. This is not to say that Nazi membership might not have led to a (new) Nazi clientele: see newssheet 1 of the district of Greater Königsberg, February 23, 1929, SAG, SF 6818, GA/33. According to table 3, (columns G, I, K), the newcomer Nazi merchant percentage jumped from 8.1% in 1928 to 11.1% in 1929 and 13.8% in 1930. The corresponding figures for master craftsmen are 11.4%, 11.6%, and 12.0%.

21. In this case, the otherwise not reliable figures in *Partei-Statistik* I, 70, document the development. This runs counter to Broszat's assertion, *Staat*, p. 37, that the party did not put itself on the map in the countryside until 1929-30.

22. Winkler, *Frauenarbeit*, p. 35; McKibbin, "Myth," p. 33; Johann Dorner, *Bauernstand und Nationalsozialismus*, 2d ed. (Munich, 1930), pp. 12-13, 22, 40-41; Angress, "Role," pp. 538-540; Plum, *Gesellschaftsstruktur*, pp. 96-99; Poppinga, *Bauern*, pp. 44-45; Hans-Jürgen Puhle, *Politische Agrarbewegungen in kapitalistischen Industriegesellschaften: Deutschland, USA und Frankreich im 20. Jahrhundert* (Göttingen, 1975), p. 90; Noakes, *Nazi Party*, pp. 108-110, 126-127, 151; Farquharson, *Plough*, p. 26; Larry E. Jones, "Inflation, Revaluation, and the Crisis of Middle-Class Politics: A Study in the Dissolution of the German Party System, 1923-28," *Central European History*, 12 (1979), 146-147; Rudolf Heberle, *Landbevölkerung und Nationalsozialismus: Eine soziologische Untersuchung der politischen Willensbildung in Schleswig-Holstein 1918-1932* (Stuttgart, 1963). See also *Wehlauer Tageblatt*, January 3, 1930.

23. This is documented in Gerhard Stoltenberg, *Politische Strömungen im schleswig-holsteinischen Landvolk 1918-1933: Ein Beitrag zur politischen Meinungsbildung in der Weimarer Republik* (Düsseldorf, 1962); Puhle, *Agrarbewegungen*, p. 90; Plum, *Gesellschaftsstruktur*, pp. 97-99; Angress, "Role," pp. 540-542; Noakes and Pridham, eds., *Documents*, pp. 91-92; Lepsius, *Nationalismus*, pp. 22-23.

24. Excerpt, police presidium report, Hanover, December 8, 1925, SAB, 4, 65, II, A, 9, b.

25. Schön, *Entstehung*, p. 87; Adalbert Gimbel, ed., *So Kämpften Wir! Schilderungen aus der Kampfzeit der NSDAP. im Gau Hessen-Nassau* (Frankfurt/Main, 1941), p. 21.

26. Heberle, *Landbevölkerung*, pp. 160-161; Stachura, "Wendepunkt," p. 79.

27. Memorandum of Nazi chapter Bielefeld, [summer 1928], HSAD, RW 23, NSDAP/Gauleitung Ruhr. Also see doc. 72b in Tyrell, ed., *Führer*, p. 193; Baden police report, Karlsruhe, January 9, 1928, SAF, 317/1257 d; Stachura, "Wendepunkt," p. 79; Noakes and Pridham, eds., *Documents*, pp. 91-92; Orlow I, pp. 158-159; Schäfer, *NSDAP*, p. 13; Schön, *Entstehung*, pp. 96-97.

28. "An die deutsche Bauernschaft"; and "Deutscher Bauer!" [summer 1928], SAG, SF 6826, GA/101. See also Werner Willikens, "Nationalsozialismus und Landvolk," *Nationalsozialistisches Jahrbuch*, 3 (1929), 192-199.

29. Program is reprinted verbatim in *Völkischer Beobachter*, March 7, 1930. Critical evaluations are in Heberle, *Landbevölkerung*, p. 163; Schulz, *Aufstieg*, pp. 560-562; Horst Gies, "Der Reichsnährstand — Organ berufsständischer Selbstverwaltung oder Instrument staatlicher Wirtschaftslenkung?" *Zeitschrift für Agrargeschichte und Agrarsoziologie*, 21 (1973), 217-228.

30. Horst Gies, "NSDAP und landwirtschaftliche Organisationen in der Endphase der Weimarer Republik," *Vierteljahrshefte für Zeitgeschichte*, 15 (1967), 341-376.

31. See the documents for spring and summer 1930 in Franz Josef Heyen, ed., *Quellen zur Geschichte des Nationalsozialismus vornehmlich im Raum Mainz-Koblenz-Trier* (Boppard, 1967); report of Weitzel, Insterburg, September 1, 1930, SAG, SF 6818, GA/34. The difficulties in Bavaria are depicted in Dorner, *Bauernstand*, p. 52; Geoffrey Pridham, *Hitler's Rise to Power: The Nazi Movement in Bavaria, 1923-1933* (London, 1973), especially pp. 57-58, 83, 114-126, 224-226; Farquharson, *Plough*, p. 4. Typical is the recollection by S. Schr. in his letter to Decker, Thansau, April 19, 1937, SAM, NSDAP/28 (SA). For difficulties in the northern, Franconian part of Bavaria, see Hambrecht, *Aufstieg*, pp. 240-243, 305.

32. See the contemporary analysis in Stephan, "Soziologie," pp. 794-796; Hans Neisser, "Sozialhistorische Analyse des Wahlergebnisses," *Die Arbeit*, 7 (1930), 659. Examples of election propaganda: flyers "Deutsche Bauern!" [September 1930]; "Bauer erwache!" [September 1930], SAG, SF 6826, GA/100. Critically: Hennig, *Thesen*, p. 42.

33. Memorandum Heitelmeier, Dinkelsbühl, March 16, 1942, SAN, 503/96; Franz Buchner, *Kamerad! Halt aus! Aus der Geschichte des Kreises Starnberg der NSDAP* (Munich 1938), pp. 159–160.

34. See Michael H. Kater, "Hitlerjugend und Schule im Dritten Reich," *Historische Zeitschrift*, 228 (1979), 607–608.

35. See chap. 1 at n. 25; Hans Mommsen, *Beamtentum im Dritten Reich: Mit ausgewählten Quellen zur nationalsozialistischen Beamtenpolitik* (Stuttgart, 1966), p. 21.

36. *Mein Kampf*, pp. 12, 387, 443.

37. Fabricius, *Beamte*, p. 55.

38. Heinrich Müller, *Beamtentum und Nationalsozialismus*, 6th ed. (Munich [1933]; 1st ed., 1931), pp. 22–23; Pridham, *Rise*, p. 193; Childers, "Bases," p. 23; Noakes and Pridham, eds., *Documents*, p. 90; Hans Mommsen, "Die Stellung der Beamtenschaft in Reich, Ländern und Gemeinden in der Ära Brüning," *Vierteljahrshefte für Zeitgeschichte*, 21 (1973), 154–155; Mommsen, "Beamtentum," pp. 197–199; Hambrecht, *Aufstieg*, p. 239.

39. Background and details in Stokes, "Composition," p. 12; Kurt Haentzschel, "Darf der Beamte einer revolutionären Partei angehören?" *Reichsverwaltungsblatt und Preussisches Verwaltungsblatt*, 51 (1930), 509–513; Rudolf Morsey, "Staatsfeinde im öffentlichen Dienst (1929–1932): Die Beamtenpolitik gegenüber NSDAP-Mitgliedern," in Klaus König et al., eds., *Öffentlicher Dienst: Festschrift für Carl Hermann Ule zum 70. Geburtstag am 26. Februar 1977* (Cologne, 1977), especially pp. 115–116; Karl Dietrich Bracher, *The German Dictatorship: The Origins, Structure, and Effects of National Socialism* (New York and Washington, 1972), p. 185; Fabricius, *Beamte*, pp. 57, 78; file in GSPKB, 84a/3157; Prussian state order, July 3, 1930, BHSAM, Sonderabgabe I/1758; Beck, *Kampf*, p. 180. Regarding Baden, see *Vossische Zeitung*, July 5, 1930; Baden police report, Karlsruhe, August 19, 1930, SAF, 317/1257 d.

40. Cuno Horkenbach, ed., *Das Deutsche Reich von 1918 bis Heute* (Berlin, 1930), p. 299; Georg Witzmann, *Thüringen von 1918–1933: Erinnerungen eines Politikers* (Meisenheim/Glan, 1958), pp. 153–174.

41. Case of Hanoverian police detective, June 1930, in *Vorwärts*, June 28, 1930; case of Stade inspector Hasse, August 1930, in Hans Henningsen, *Niedersachsenland, du wurdest unser! Zehn Jahre Nationalsozialismus im Gau Ost-Hannover: Streiflichter aus der Kampfzeit* (Harburg, [1935]), p. 93; case of Hattingen public school teacher Schepmann, in Beck, *Kampf*, p. 230. More general: Müller, *Beamtentum*, p. 24.

42. Noakes, *Nazi Party*, pp. 131–136; Karl Fiehler, "Unsere Stellung zum Berufsbeamtentum," *Nationalsozialistisches Jahrbuch*, 4 (1930), 168–173.

43. See table 5, especially the figures for Greater Bochum. Confidence interval tests (at a confidence level of 95%) for the value of 14.6% for Thuringia show fluctuations between 11.8% and 17.4% (table 5). The hypothesis that there was an overrepresentation of Thuringian white-collar workers in the Nazi party is not supported (Reich level: 12.42% – table 1).

44. Croner, "Angestelltenbewegung," pp. 112–114; Hamm, *Berufsmerkmale*, pp. 22–23.

45. Schnaas, *Arbeitsmarkt*, pp. 10-11, 23; Josef Nothaas, "Die Stellenlosigkeit der Angestellten," *Allgemeines Statistisches Archiv*, 16 (1927), 294, 306; Croner, "Angestelltenbewegung," pp. 104, 108, 141; Kadritzke, *Angestellte*, p. 353.

46. Croner, "Angestelltenbewegung," pp. 130, 142; Schnaas, *Arbeitsmarkt*, pp. 44-45; Nothaas, "Stellenlosigkeit," pp. 309, 320; Hamm, *Berufsmerkmale*, pp. 13-15; Speier, *Angestellten*, pp. 71-73; Kadritzke, *Angestellte*, pp. 369-370, 377.

47. See doc. 6 (April 28, and 29, 1930) in Ilse Maurer and Udo Wengst, eds., *Staat und NSDAP 1930-1932: Quellen zur Ära Brüning* (Düsseldorf, 1977), p. 36; Kocka, "Problematik," p. 798; Franz Stöhr, "Geistige Strömungen in der Angestelltenbewegung," *Nationalsozialistisches Jahrbuch*, 2 (1928), 135-136; Hamel, *Verband*, pp. 190-192, 226-258; Krebs, *Infancy*, pp. 9-25. Childers somewhat discounts the importance of the DHV and stresses instead the significance of the Allgemeiner freier Angestelltenbund (AfA), which organized white-collar workers with leftist leanings. "National Socialism," pp. 20-21, 23.

48. For typical examples of jobless clerks who were attracted to the NSDAP because of their economic misery during this period, see the short case histories of K. Bernhardt ("Mein Lebenslauf," Kölleda, April 25, 1934, BDC, PK, PLA K. Bernhardt) and O. Dettmann (Wernick to NSDAP-Reichsschatzmeister, Schwerin/Meckl., July 8, 1937, BDC, PK, PLA O. Dettmann). But see the discussion in chap. 6 at nn. 27-29.

49. See table 3 in Kater, *Studentenschaft*, p. 209.

50. For background see ibid., and Kater, "Der NS-Studentenbund von 1926 bis 1928: Randgruppe zwischen Hitler und Strasser," *Vierteljahrshefte für Zeitgeschichte*, 22 (1974), 148-190. See also Faust, *Studentenbund*; Steinberg, *Sabers*, pp. 48-86; Hans Peter Bleuel and Ernst Klinnert, *Deutsche Studenten auf dem Weg ins Dritte Reich: Ideologien — Programme — Aktionen 1918-1935* (Gütersloh, 1967). For Freiburg, see the case study by Wolfgang Kreutzberger, *Studenten und Politik 1918-1933: Der Fall Freiburg im Breisgau* (Göttingen, 1972).

51. Quotation from Mierendorff, "Gesicht," p. 496.

52. Kater, *Studentenschaft*, p. 117, and table 13 on p. 221 of that book.

53. This has been the tenor of the works by Eberhard Czichon, *Wer verhalf Hitler zur Macht? Zum Anteil der deutschen Industrie an der Zerstörung der Weimarer Republik* (Cologne, 1967); Dietrich Eichholtz, *Geschichte der deutschen Kriegswirtschaft 1939-1945*, I, *1939-1941* ([East] Berlin, 1969); and Eichholtz and Wolfgang Schumann, eds., *Anatomie des Krieges: Neue Dokumente über die Rolle des deutschen Monopolkapitals bei der Vorbereitung und Durchführung des zweiten Weltkrieges* ([East] Berlin, 1969). Although Stegmann has on the whole been critical of the East German approach, he himself tends to overstate the heavy-industrial character of the magnates supporting Hitler after 1926. See his article "Verhältnis," and Henry A. Turner's criticism of Stegmann in "Grossunternehmertum und Nationalsozialismus: Kritisches und Ergänzendes zu zwei neuen Forschungs-

beiträgen," *Historische Zeitschrift*, 221 (1975), 18–68. On the East German interpretations, see the critiques by Hennig, *Thesen*, pp. 46–48; Dieter Gessner, *Das Ende der Weimarer Republik: Fragen, Methoden und Ergebnisse interdisziplinärer Forschung* (Darmstadt, 1978), p. 55. See also Heinrich August Winkler, *Revolution, Staat, Faschismus: Zur Revision des Historischen Materialismus* (Göttingen, 1978), pp. 65–117, 137–159. Among the cities in the Ruhr less favored by entrepreneur newcomers to the NSDAP, Bochum appears to have been the exception (table 5). In this connection, see n. 58 below.

54. Avraham Barkai, "Sozialdarwinismus und Antiliberalismus in Hitlers Wirtschaftskonzept: Zu Henry A. Turner Jr. 'Hitlers Einstellung zu Wirtschaft und Gesellschaft vor 1933,' " *Geschichte und Gesellschaft*, 3 (1977), 410; Dieter Petzina, *Autarkiepolitik im Dritten Reich: Der nationalsozialistische Vierjahresplan* (Stuttgart, 1968), p. 21; Schweitzer, *Business*, p. 99; Schulz, *Aufstieg*, p. 497.

55. Schubert to Goebbels, Langerfeld, September 12, 1925, HSAD, RW 23, NSDAP/Gauleitung Ruhr.

56. Doc. 65 in Tyrell, ed., *Führer*, pp. 168–173; doc. 3 in Schumann, *Nationalsozialismus*, pp. 166–167; Turner, *Faschismus*, pp. 35, 66; Schulz, *Aufstieg*, p. 498; Stegmann, "Verhältnis," p. 411; Schoenbaum, *Revolution*, pp. 25–26. The Hamburg address is in *Im Kampf um die Macht: Hitlers Rede vor dem Hamburger Nationalklub von 1919*, ed. Werner Jochmann (Frankfurt/ Main, 1960), pp. 69–121. In light of this, Turner's remark that in February 1926 Hitler "practically had no contact with entrepreneurial circles" approaches understatement: "Hitlers Einstellung zu Wirtschaft und Gesellschaft vor 1933," *Geschichte und Gesellschaft*, 2 (1976), 105.

57. Stegmann, "Verhältnis," pp. 412–413.

58. The April speech took place on the 27th in Essen at the instigation of the Bochum factory owner G. Neuhaus (Geschäftsführer Gau Ruhr to Constabel [Essen], April 22, 1927, HSAD, RW 23, NSDAP/Gauleitung Ruhr; Böhnke, *NSDAP*, p. 113). According to one interpretation, Hitler later met Kirdorf at Frau Bruckmann's Munich villa on her initiative, and it was here that Kirdorf asked Hitler to author the lengthy memorandum on the state of the economy that was later presented, in printed form, to the industrialists in Essen. See Turner, *Faschismus*, pp. 66–67, 70. Kirdorf's importance is exaggerated in Stegmann, "Verhältnis," pp. 412–414, but is put into proper perspective in Turner, *Faschismus*, pp. 85–86. Hitler's memorandum, "Der Weg zum Wiederaufstieg," is reprinted in *Faschismus*, pp. 45–59. It is possible that Hitler had his first important talk with Kirdorf not through the good offices of Elsa Bruckmann in Munich but through mutual acquaintances in the Ruhr. In a letter from Karl Kaufmann to Hitler dated September 3, 1927 (HSAD, RW 23, NSDAP/Gauleitung Ruhr), the writer recalled that he (as the son of a textile manufacturer from Elberfeld) had approached a factory director named Arnold in Hattingen, where the NSDAP was well entrenched, asking him to prevail upon Kirdorf to receive Hitler. As a result, Kirdorf is said to have met Hitler in the company of Josef Terboven, the future Gauleiter of Essen, and an unnamed person. The subject of the conversation is said to have

been money. According to Kaufmann's letter, Kirdorf expressed displeasure to Arnold later on because he had not been able to meet with Hitler in private.

59. Nazi chapter Rheinhausen to Gau Ruhr Elberfeld, Rheinhausen, November 11, 1927, HSAD, RW 23, NSDAP/Gauleitung Ruhr; *Völkischer Beobachter*, December 10, 1927. The meeting in Nuremberg is documented in file BA, NS 26/517; minutes of speech by Hitler, December 8, 1928, SAN, 503/99; Hambrecht, *Aufstieg*, p. 237.

60. Stegmann, "Verhältnis," p. 415; Barkai, "Wirtschaftsauffassung," p. 7; Feder, *Programme*, pp. 40–41; and this chapter at n. 27.

61. My own view agrees with Turner's balanced thesis in *Faschismus*. Also see Schulz, *Aufstieg*, p. 500; Stachura, "Wendepunkt," pp. 76–77.

62. See the case of an unknown letter writer of Gau Westfalen Süd/Düsseldorf (to Florian, October 12, 1927, BDC, PK, PLA F. K. Florian), in which Florian was asked to approach the Opel auto works for a car, in return for Nazi assurances regarding "future protection of the German automobile industry" and the party's intention "to wean the German worker away from Marxism."

63. On Pietzsch, see Neumann, *Behemoth*, p. 316; *Wer ist's?* 10th ed., ed. Herrmann A. L. Degener (Berlin, 1935), pp. 1212–13; and (for the post-1932 period) *Deutschland-Berichte der Sozialdemokratischen Partei Deutschlands (Sopade)*, 5th ed. (Salzhausen and Frankfurt/Main, 1980), II (1935), 890–891. The list of financial contributors to the NSDAP from the Rheinland published by Horst Mazerath and Henry A. Turner, Jr., "Die Selbstfinanzierung der NSDAP 1930–1932," *Geschichte und Gesellschaft*, 3 (1977), 65, contains mostly names of medium businesses. See also Jäger, *Gesicht*, p. 49, and the file in NHSA, Hann. 310 I, A 30, for the names of German firms anticipating business with the NSDAP, such as providing it with goods and services (1929).

64. On the whole, large farmers had been able to survive economic difficulties much more comfortably than small-scale farmers, especially because of more generous credit support. See Poppinga, *Bauern*, p. 44; Schulz, *Aufstieg*, pp. 619–622; Puhle, *Agrarbewegungen*, pp. 90–91; Schäfer, *NSDAP*, p. 13; Farquharson, *Plough*, p. 26. On Nazi propaganda attempts in East Prussia in early 1930, see Gillgasch to Heidrich, Insterburg, March 30, 1930, SAG, SF 6818, GA/34; Bergel to Gau Ostpreussen, Klein Klitten, June 23, 1930, SAG, SF 6819, GA/35.

65. See, for instance, Hitler, *Mein Kampf*, pp. 612, 640–643; and Turner's comment, "Einstellung," p. 96. Also see minutes of Hitler's Nuremberg speech, March 23, 1927, SAN, 503/99; diary Ziegler, "Aus dem Kampf der Heidelberger SA Pfingsten 1925 bis März 1933," regarding Hitler's speech in Heidelberg, August 6, 1927, GLAK, 465d/114 (pp. 41–43). Regarding Hitler's speech in Munich, March 9, 1927, see Deuerlein, ed., *Aufstieg*, p. 274.

66. Ruge to Luetgebrune, Munich, September 2, 1927, NA, T-253/30.

67. An example is Hitler's statement against all counselors, September 1928: *Völkischer Beobachter*, September 2–3, 1928. Also see Schulz, *Aufstieg*, pp. 420–421; and Hamilton, *Appeal*, p. 110, for an evaluation of Rosenberg,

Feder, etc., vis-à-vis the educated. Of paradigmatic significance is the view expressed by Major F. Bucher in letter to Hitler, Hamburg, July 20, 1929, doc. 94, in Werner Jochmann, ed., *Nationalsozialismus und Revolution: Ursprung und Geschichte der NSDAP in Hamburg 1922–1933: Dokumente* (Frankfurt/ Main, 1963), pp. 283–286. A reflection of the Nazis' erstwhile attitude toward "intellectuals" is to be found in the contemporary Third Reich writings of such Nazis as Hans Schemm and Helmut Stellrecht: Schemm, "Gedankensammlung," February 22, 1935, BDC, PK, PLA H. Schemm (p. 24); Helmut Stellrecht, *Neue Erziehung* (Berlin, 1942), p. 197.

68. See the example from Krefeld in memorandum NSDAP-Bezirksleitung Nieder¡hein, Goch, July 25, 1927, HSAD, RW 23, NSDAP/Gauleitung Ruhr.

69. See Walter Struve, *Elites against Democracy: Leadership Ideals in Bourgeois Political Thought in Germany, 1890–1933* (Princeton, 1973); Klaus Bergmann, *Agrarromantik und Grosstadtfeindschaft* (Meisenheim/Glan, 1970); George L. Mosse, *The Crisis of German Ideology: Intellectual Origins of the Third Reich* (New York, 1964); Rolf Geissler, *Dekadenz und Heroismus: Zeitroman und völkisch-nationalsozialistische Literaturkritik* (Stuttgart, 1964), pp. 121–129; Wanda von Baeyer-Katte, *Das Zerstörende in der Politik: Eine Psychologie der politischen Grundeinstellung* (Heidelberg, 1958), pp. 40–44; Karl Otto Conrady, "Deutsche Literaturwissenschaft und Drittes Reich," in Eberhard Lämmert et al., *Germanistik — eine deutsche Wissenschaft* (Frankfurt/Main, 1967), p. 87; Eva Pfeifer, "Das Hitlerbild im Spiegel einiger konservativer Zeitungen in den Jahren 1929–1933," Ph.D. dissertation, Heidelberg, 1966, p. 10; Hamilton, *Appeal*, pp. 123, 136; and the essays in Karl Corino, ed., *Intellektuelle im Bann des Nationalsozialismus* (Hamburg, 1980). Rolf Boelcke, "Die Spaltung der Nationalsozialisten," *Die Tat*, 22 (1930), 365, speaks of the "despairing intellectuals." Paradigmatic is the case of the young physician Franz Wertheim, as described in Louis Hagen, *Follow My Leader* (London, 1951), pp. 45–46. See also Deuerlein, ed., *Aufstieg*, p. 271. The manifestations of the "cultural depravity" of the "Jazz Age" in postwar Germany, particularly Berlin, against which these men militated, are described in Walter Laqueur, *Weimar: A Cultural History 1918–1933* (London, 1974); Peter Gay, *Weimar Culture: The Outsider as Insider* (New York and Evanston, 1968); Otto Friedrich, *Before the Deluge: A Portrait of Berlin in the 1920's* (New York, 1972); PEM [Paul Erich Marcus], *Heimweh nach dem Kurfürstendamm: Aus Berlins glanzvollsten Tagen und Nächten* (Berlin, 1962). Also see Strasser, *Hitler*, pp. 31–32; and *Der Spiegel*, August 16, 1982, pp. 154–163.

70. The League of National Socialist German Jurists (BNSDJ) was formed in 1928 at the behest of a young Nazi lawyer, Dr. Hans Michael Frank, Hitler's personal lawyer and the future governor of Nazi-occupied Poland. Background is in *Völkischer Beobachter*, September 2–3, 1928; Gerhard Schulz, "Die Anfänge des totalitären Massnahmestaates," in Karl Dietrich Bracher et al., *Die nationalsozialistische Machtergreifung: Studien zur Errichtung des totalitären Herrschaftssystems in Deutschland 1933/34*, 2d ed. (Co-

logne and Opladen, 1962), p. 518; Christoph Klessmann, "Der General-gouverneur Hans Frank," *Vierteljahrshefte für Zeitgeschichte*, 19 (1971), 249; Beck, *Kampf*, p. 184. The League of National Socialist German Physicians was founded in August 1929 by Dr. Ludwig Liebl of Ingolstadt. See Hans Volz, *Daten der Geschichte der NSDAP*, 9th ed. (Berlin and Leipzig, 1939), pp. 26–27; file in BA, Schumacher/213; Kater, "Wandel," pp. 34–35.

71. See Volz, *Daten*, pp. 24, 27; Rosenberg to "Werter Parteigenosse," Munich, October 14, 1927, HSAD, RW 23, NSDAP/Gauleitung Ruhr; Reinhard Bollmus, *Das Amt Rosenberg und seine Gegner: Studien zum Machtkampf im nationalsozialistischen Herrschaftssystem* (Stuttgart, 1970), p. 27; Kater, "Wandel," p. 29; Daniel Horn, "The National Socialist *Schüler-bund* and the Hitler Youth, 1929–1933," *Central European History*, 11 (1978), 355–375.

72. Horkenbach, ed., *Reich* (Berlin 1930), p. 316; Attila Chanady, "The Dissolution of the German Democratic Party in 1930," *American Historical Review*, 73 (1968), 1433–53.

73. On intellectual and socioeconomic discontent as well as the political allegiance of professors and higher bureaucrats to the conservative bourgeois parties until the end of the twenties, see Mommsen,"Beamtentum," p. 197; Hans Peter Bleuel, *Deutschlands Bekenner: Professoren zwischen Kaiserreich und Diktatur* (Berne, 1968); Ringer, *Decline*, pp. 76–80, 201–227, 242–252. Also Kelly, "National Socialism," p. 45; Fabricius, *Beamte*, p. 75; Okrass, *Ende*, pp. 188–189; minutes of speech by Grohé in Cologne municipal council, April 14, 1930, in Schmidt, *Jahre*, pp. 141–142; Schön, *Entstehung*, p. 162. A telling document from the Nazi point of view is Meyer, "Zur Parteigeschichte Winkelhaid," [before 1932], SAN, 503/96.

74. Example of this for February 1930 is in Horn, "*Schülerbund*," p. 361. Also see Kühr, *Parteien*, p. 144; Hambrecht, *Aufstieg*, p. 239; Jäger, *Gesicht*, p. 61; Müller, *Beamtentum*, p. 25; Beyerchen, *Scientists*, pp. 97–98; Fabricius, *Beamte*, pp. 51, 53, 62.

75. The most up-to-date and succinct characterization of Brüning as a politician is in Gordon A. Craig, *Germany 1866–1945* (New York and Oxford, 1978), pp. 535–543, 553–568.

3. THE RISE TO POWER: SEPTEMBER 1930 TO 1933

1. This increase is not readily apparent from a comparison of the figures in tables 3 (columns A–K), 4 (columns A–I), and 5 (columns A, E) with those in table 6 (column A). The reason is that the primary BDC sample of 1,954 N for 1930–1932 is not immediately compatible with the secondary samples used in analyzing the previous phases of NSDAP development. Confidence interval tests (at the 95% confidence level) indicate that the figure of 35.9% for the lower class may have been either as low as 33.7% or as high as 38.1%. But if this figure is compared with a compatible one taken from the larger BDC sample (see Introduction at n. 47) for the period from 1925 to 1929, the increase becomes visible: according to this sample of 232 N, the percentage of the lower

class for 1925–1929 was 31.4. Because of its extremely low N, however, this sample was not used in the construction of any of the tables. Further statistical support for the increase of workers in the NSDAP after September 1930 is in *Partei-Statistik* I, 70, although the figures indicated there have to be used with caution: if categories 7 and 8 (pensioners and housewives — p. 70) are discounted, the Nazi category of workers (no. 1) increases from 27.7% of total membership from before September 14, 1930, to 34.4% between that date and Hitler's assumption of power. Also see Alexander Weber, "Soziale Merkmale der NSDAP-Wähler: Eine Zusammenfassung bisheriger impirischer [sic] Untersuchungen und eine Analyse in den Gemeinden der Länder Baden und Hessen," Ph.D. dissertation, Freiburg i.Br., 1969, p. 72; Kele, *Nazis*, p. 210; Böhnke, *NSDAP*, p. 199; Schulz, *Aufstieg*, p. 721; Noakes, *Nazi Party*, p. 159; Pridham, *Rise*, p. 186; Kurt Hiller, "Über die Ursachen des nationalsozialistischen Erfolges," *Die Weltbühne*, 28 (1932), 271.

2. See Hennig, *Thesen*, pp. 52, 55, 60–61, 64–66, 72–75. According to Hennig's tables 6 and 7(a), the average annual (compound) decrease in the national income from 1928 to 1932 was 12.0% and the increase in unemployment from February 1926 to February 1932 was 17.7%. Calculation according to Roderick Floud, *An Introduction to Quantitative Methods for Historians* (Princeton, 1973), pp. 91–92. Also see Dieter Petzina, "Hauptprobleme der deutschen Wirtschaftspolitik 1932/33," *Vierteljahrshefte für Zeitgeschichte*, 15 (1967), 18; Petzina, "Germany," pp. 59–74; Rudolf Vierhaus, "Auswirkungen der Krise um 1930 in Deutschland: Beiträge zu einer historisch-psychologischen Analyse," in Conze and Raupach, eds., *Staats-und Wirtschaftskrise*, pp. 155–175. Further, see Kele, *Nazis*, p. 189; Henning, *Deutschland*, pp. 96–97, 127–130; Preller, *Sozialpolitik*. As an example of regional development (Lower Silesia), see Landrat Jerschke to Regierungspräsident in Liegnitz, Glogau, November 17, 1931, BA, NS 26/516.

3. See Mason, *Sozialpolitik*, pp. 89–91; Spethmann, ed., *Essen*, pp. 66, 317; Graf, *Entwicklung*, p. 37; Kurt Klotzbach, *Gegen den Nationalsozialismus: Widerstand und Verfolgung in Dortmund 1930–1945: Eine historisch-politische Studie* (Hanover, 1969), p. 40; Steinberg, *Entwicklung*, p. 58–62; Böhnke, *NSDAP*, pp. 139–141; Weber, "Merkmale," pp. 93–94; Pridham, *Rise*, p. 188.

4. See Böhnke, *NSDAP*, pp. 141–142; Graf, *Entwicklung*, pp. 40–42; Steinberg, *Entwicklung*, p. 62; Kele, *Nazis*, p. 208; Peter D. Stachura, " 'Der Fall Strasser': Gregor Strasser, Hitler and National Socialism 1930–32," in Stachura, ed., *The Shaping of the Nazi State* (London and New York, 1978), p. 103.

5. Kele, *Nazis*, pp. 204–208; Schulz, *Aufstieg*, p. 558. Also see n. 13 below. According to Childers's analysis, "Bases," p. 28, the SPD lost no *voters* to the NSDAP, but this indicates nothing regarding *membership*. Moreover, Childers's study does not encompass agrarian regions. The counterargument for the (Lower Saxon) countryside is made by Günther Franz, *Die politischen Wahlen in Niedersachsen 1867–1949*, 2d ed. (Bremen-Horn, 1953), pp. 63–64.

6. See figures for the Reich, 1930-1932, in table 6. While there is no difference between the workers' percentages in city and small town (30.5), the percentage for the country is considerably larger (39.8). The higher figures for workers in table 6 pertaining to agrarian-based party chapters (columns E-H) are also significant. Also see Jerschke to Regierungspräsident in Liegnitz, Glogau, November 17, 1931, BA, NS 26/516; Beck, *Kampf*, p. 230; Heberle, *Landbevölkerung*, pp. 113-114; Schulz, Aufstieg, pp. 721-722; Weber, "Merkmale," p. 98; Childers, "Bases," p. 29.

7. McKibbon, "Myth," pp. 28, 30; Hennig's remarks in Frank Deppe et al., eds., *Marburger Gespräche aus Anlass des 70. Geburtstags von Wolfgang Abendroth* (Marburg/L., 1977), p. 407; Winkler, *Mittelstand*, p. 177; Winkler, "German Society, Hitler and the Illusion of Restoration 1930-33," *Journal of Contemporary History*, 11, no. 4 (1976), 2; Franz, *Wahlen*, p. 64; Mason, *Sozialpolitik*, p. 54.

8. Geiger, *Schichtung*, p. 111. Also see Baden police report for Baden Interior Minister, Karlsruhe, December 21, 1932, SAF, 317/1257a/2; Franz, *Wahlen*, p. 61; Henning, *Deutschland*, p. 135.

9. See Hellweg, *Kampf*, especially pp. 64-65, 72, 74, 79-80; Bracher, *Dictatorship*, p. 188; Merkl, *Making*.

10. Kele, *Nazis*, pp. 186-187; Bracher, *Dictatorship*, p. 198; Cuno Horkenbach, ed., *Das Deutsche Reich von 1918 bis Heute: 1932* (Berlin, 1933), p. 357; Flechtheim, *KPD*, pp. 273, 285; Joseph Goebbels, *Vom Kaiserhof zur Reichskanzlei: Eine historische Darstellung in Tagebuchblättern (Vom 1. Januar 1932 bis zum 1. Mai 1933)* (Munich, 1934), pp. 191-195, 198; Schumann, *Nationalsozialismus*, p. 40; Craig, *Germany*, p. 564.

11. *Jahrbuch Sozialdemokratie 1930*, pp. 3-54; Horkenbach, ed., *Reich* (Berlin, 1930), p. 305; Hunt, *Social Democracy*, pp. 185-187; Breitman, *Socialism*, pp. 152-160.

12. See the figures in Striefler, *Wahlen*, table 1; and Beier, "Problem," p. 59, table VIII. Also see Hunt, *Social Democracy*, p. 168; Hennig, *Thesen*, p. 65; Heinrich Brüning, *Memoiren 1918-1934* (Stuttgart, 1970), p. 480; Henning, *Deutschland*, p. 133; Allen, *Seizure*, pp. 48-49, 110-111; Schulz, *Aufstieg*, pp. 553-557; Hiller, "Ursachen," p. 270; Eiji Ohno, "The Social Basis of Nazism," *Kyoto University Economic Review*, 42 (1972), 21. As examples of the Nazis' effective propaganda thrust against the SPD, particularly in 1932, see the flyers and handbills in SAG, SF 6826, GA/98, 100, 101. In 1930, about 59% of the SPD membership consisted of workers: *Jahrbuch Sozialdemokratie 1930*, p. 194; it was thus much more pronouncedly a "workers' party" than the NSDAP and would remain so, despite present and impending losses to other parties. See also Weber, "Merkmale," p. 73; Schulz, *Aufstieg*, p. 557.

13. See table 6 (columns D-H); Ohno, "Basis," pp. 23-24; Weber, "Merkmale," pp. 99-100; Schulz, *Aufstieg*, p. 722; Bezirksleiter, activities report, Tilsit, February 10, 1931; Fuchs to Gau East Prussia, Insterburg, April 1, 1931, SAG, SF 6818, GA/33. In a medium-sized thermometer factory in Ilmenau (Thuringia), approximately 100 workers had switched over to the Nazis

by March 1932, while the remaining 500 had stayed with the KPD and SPD. See Hoesrich to Gauleitung Weimar, Roda (Thuringia), March 1, 1932, IfZ, MA-135/136685-87. In rural Winkelhaid near Nuremberg, all the resident workers were still "red" at the time of the founding of the local Nazi chapter in April 1931. Meyer, "Zur Parteigeschichte Winkelhaid," [before 1932], SAN, 503/96. Yet that could change quickly: see the high figures for workers in the NSDAP chapters in Franconian Pahres and Eltersdorf (1932) in table 6. On the special problems of agricultural workers, who were more dependent on wages-in-kind and subsistence privileges resulting from their semifeudalistic dependence on their employers, especially in the German East, see Heinrich Bennecke, *Wirtschaftliche Depression und politischer Radikalismus 1918-1938* (Munich and Vienna, 1970), pp. 239-240.

14. The Landtag election in Prussia, two Reichstag elections, and two presidential elections, all in 1932.

15. For examples of the customary anti-Semitic hate propaganda, see von Pappenheim to Prussian Regierungspräsident, Erfurt, June 8, 1931, SAS, HO 235, I-VIII, F 7/1; "Aufruf! An alle sozialdemokratischen u. kommunistischen Arbeiter Deutschlands!" [1932], SAG, SF 6826, GA/101.

16. *Preussische Zeitung*, March 30, 1932. Also see the multitude of leaflets and propaganda materials in SAG, SF 6815, GA/7 and in SF 6826, GA/98, 100, 101.

17. On the approach to the miners, see Kele, *Nazis*, p. 195. For an example of a "mistake" the Nazis made in Kehrberg and came to regret, see minutes of Schmalfeldt, Lindenberg, [end of 1931], BA, NS 22/1046.

18. Starcke, *NSBO.*, p. 27; Udo Kissenkoetter, *Gregor Strasser und die NSDAP* (Stuttgart, 1978), pp. 78-80; Böhnke, *NSDAP*, pp. 170-175. Also see Schulz, *Aufstieg*, p. 610; Schumann, *Nationalsozialismus*, pp. 36-41; Okrass, *Ende*, p. 243; Broszat, *Staat*, pp. 64-65; Kele, *Nazis*, pp. 170, 198, 200; Hambrecht, *Aufstieg*, p. 235. The Nazis' condoning of strike action can be gleaned from: Muhs to Gaupropagandaleitung Süd-Hannover-Braunschweig, Hanover, October 21, 1932, NHSA, Hann. 310 I, A 122 I. The party's attitude toward conventional unions is made clear in a flyer, "Schaffen und Raffen. NSDAP. und Gewerkschaften," [1932], SAG, SF 6826, GA/100.

19. *Ostdeutscher Beobachter*, December 13, 1930; Kiefert to Nazi chapters of Tilsit district, Tilsit, January 8, 1931, SAG, SF 6818, GA/33; Gillgasch to Fuchs, [Königsberg], December 19, 1931, SAG, SF 6819, GA/37; Allen, *Seizure*, p. 70.

20. See Böhnke, *NSDAP*, pp. 175-176; Wirth to state governments, Berlin, August 29, 1931; Baden police report for Baden Interior Minister, Karlsruhe, December 21, 1932, SAF, 317/1257a/2.

21. See explanation in n. 1 above. According to *Partei-Statistik* I, the percentages for the following occupations (largely lower middle class) were down: employees; independent craftsmen; merchants; civil servants; farmers. The percentage for the lower middle class between 1925 and 1929 according to the sample described in n. 1 above was 59.2, as opposed to 54.9 between 1930 and 1932 (table 6, column A). Also see Pridham, *Rise*, p. 186.

22. See Stokes, "Composition," p. 25.

23. See Winkler, *Mittelstand*, pp. 31, 35, 172; Winkler, "Protest," p. 789.

24. Allen, *Seizure*, pp. 69, 132–133. Also Winkler, *Mittelstand*, p. 34; Böhnke, *NSDAP*, p. 142; Hambrecht, *Aufstieg*, p. 188.

25. Winkler, *Mittelstand*, p. 34; Gerhard Friters, "Who are the German Fascists?" *Current History*, 35 (1932), 533; Alfred Braunthal, "Die ökonomischen Wurzeln des nationalsozialistischen Wirtschaftsprogramms," *Die Gesellschaft*, 7 (1930), Part II, 487; Böhnke, *NSDAP*, p. 142.

26. Brettschneider to Heidrich, Elbing, January 23, 1931, SAG, SF 6819, GA/35.

27. See Hambrecht, *Aufstieg*, pp. 188–189; Heberle, *Landbevölkerung*, p. 135.

28. The value of 8.7% for Nazi merchant newcomers in the country can be shown, by a confidence interval test (95% confidence level), to be significantly smaller than the value of 16.3% for those in the city and small town (table 6, columns B–D). The test demonstrates no significant difference between the values of 8.6%, 10.7%, and 11.2% pertaining to craftsmen (table 6, columns B–D).

29. Flyer announcing Koch's speech for December 12 [1930]; flyer, "Handwerksmeister und Gesellen! Kleingewerbetreibende!" [March 1932]; flyer, "Wir Nationalsozialisten geben Euch," [March 1932], SAG, SF 6826, GA/100; *Wirtschaftliches Sofortprogramm der N.S.D.A.P.: Ausgearbeitet von der Hauptabteilung IV (Wirtschaft) der Reichsorganisationsleitung der N.S.D.A.P.* (Munich, 1932), pp. 29–30; *Bremer Nationalsozialistische Zeitung*, September 20, 1932; minutes of speech by Grohé in Cologne municipal council, April 22, 1931, in Schmidt, *Jahre*, p. 193; doc. 12 in Noakes and Pridham, eds., *Documents*, p. 106; Braunthal, "Wurzeln," p. 488; Winkler, *Mittelstand*, pp. 153, 167–168, 170, 173, 177; Hambrecht, *Aufstieg*, p. 238; Claus-Dieter Krohn and Dirk Stegmann, "Kleingewerbe und Nationalsozialismus in einer agrarisch-mittelständischen Region: Das Beispiel Lüneburg 1930–1939," *Archiv für Sozialgeschichte*, 17 (1977), 60.

30. Details in Winkler, *Mittelstand*, pp. 167–175, 180; Winkler, "Protest," pp. 789–790; Winkler, "Der entbehrliche Stand: Zur Mittelstandspolitik im 'Dritten Reich,' " *Archiv für Sozialgeschichte*, 17 (1977), 3; Krohn and Stegmann, "Kleingewerbe," pp. 60–62; doc. 13 in Noakes and Pridham, eds., *Documents*, pp. 106–108; Noakes, *Nazi Party*, pp. 170–173; circular, Hierl to the delegates, Munich, October 24, 1931, SAMs, Gauleitung Westfalen-Nord, Gauamt für Volkswohlfahrt/15.

31. See *Partei-Statistik* I, 70.

32. Because of low *N*, the percentages based on this count are, in the final analysis, not reliable. See table 3 in Kater, "Wandel," p. 30.

33. Jerschke to Regierungspräsident in Liegnitz, Glogau, November 17, 1931, BA, NS 26/516; Noakes, *Nazi Party*, pp. 167–168; Poppinga, *Bauern,* pp. 45–48; Heberle, *Landbevölkerung*, pp. 124–129, 165–166; Pridham, *Rise,* p. 232; Bennecke, *Depression*, pp. 237–238; Hambrecht, *Aufstieg*, p. 189; Braunthal, "Wurzeln," p. 491; Petzina, *Wirtschaft*, pp. 99–100; Friters,

"Fascists," p. 533.

34. Jerschke to Regierungspräsident in Liegnitz, Glogau, November 17, 1931, BA, NS 26/516; Heberle, *Landbevölkerung*, pp. 169-171; Gies, "Reichsnährstand," pp. 220-228; Gies, "NSDAP," pp. 360-368; Schön, *Entstehung*, pp. 154, 194. For South Germany: Meyer, "Zur Parteigeschichte Winkelhaid," [before 1932], SAN, 503/96; Hambrecht, *Aufstieg*, p. 242; Pridham, *Rise*, pp. 224-236, 282-283; Wiesemann, *Vorgeschichte*, pp. 97-106.

35. Puhle, *Agrarbewegungen*, p. 91; Gies, "NSDAP," p. 368.

36. See report regarding state of agriculture in Brunswick, October-November 1932, NAW, 12 A Neu, 13h/48714; Petzina, "Hauptprobleme," pp. 31-34; Petzina, *Wirtschaft*, p. 114; Gies, "Reichsnährstand," p. 224.

37. See n. 32 above.

38. Pridham's suggestion that the Bavarian farmers stayed away from NSDAP membership for lack of money is not very plausible in the light of evidence concerning the even poorer Nazi party comrades in the cities. On the whole, however, his observations are correct: *Rise*, pp. 236, 282. Also see Schön, *Entstehung*, p. 201; Ortwin Domröse, *Der NS-Staat in Bayern von der Machtübernahme bis zum Röhm-Putsch* (Munich, 1974), pp. 296-297; Elke Fröhlich and Martin Broszat, "Politsche und soziale Macht auf dem Lande: Die Durchsetzung der NSDAP im Kreis Memmingen," *Vierteljahrshefte für Zeitgeschichte*, 25 (1977), 552; flyer, "Ostpreussens Landwirtschaft stirbt!!!" [fall 1932], SAG, SF 6826, GA/98.

39. *Beamten-Jahrbuch*, 26 (1939), 169. An increase for 1932 is indicated in table 3 in Kater, "Wandel," p. 30. Also see Mommsen, "Beamtentum," p. 199.

40. Report, Hasse to Regierungspräsident in Liegnitz, Glogau, November 19, 1931, BA, NS 26/516; Müller, *Beamtentum*, pp. 6-7; C.W. Guillebaud, *The Economic Recovery of Germany: From 1933 to the Incorporation of Austria in March 1938* (London, 1939), p. 24; Broszat, *Staat*, p. 28; Bennecke, *Depression*, pp. 118-119; Pridham, *Rise*, p. 193; Rainer Bölling, *Volksschullehrer und Politik: Der Deutsche Lehrerverein 1918-1933* (Göttingen, 1978), pp. 196-203.

41. Background history is in *Jahrbuch Sozialdemokratie 1930*, pp. 168-174.

42. Report of Bevik, Insterburg, October 18, 1930, attached to letter, Heidrich to Bezirksleitung Nordost, Insterburg, October 20, 1930, SAG, SF 6818, GA/34.

43. See chap 2 at n. 36.

44. On Esser, see Unknown to Hess, March 21, 1932, BA, NS 22/859. Also see Police President Hanover to Regierungspräsident, Hanover, December 17, 1931, NHSA, Hann, 122a, XI, 80; Hambrecht, *Aufstieg*, p. 349. See the anti-Nazi arguments published by enemies of Nazism, particularly the strong civil servants' lobby Reichsbund Deutscher Beamter, in Helmut Klotz, *Nationalsozialismus und Beamtentum* (Berlin, 1931), pp. 4-5, 7; "Achtung, Beamte! Ein paar Minuten Gehör!" [March 1932], SAG, SF 6827, GA/108; "Die politische Haltung der Nationalsozialisten: Theorie und Praxis—Worte und Taten," [last half of 1932], SAG, SF 6817, GA/27.

45. Müller, *Beamtentum*, pp. 33, 61–62; "Pressenotiz: Nationalsozialismus und Berufsbeamtentum," Gelsenkirchen, November 12, 1931, SAMs, Gauleitung Westfalen-Nord, Gaumt für Volkswohlfahrt/15; Mommsen, "Stellung," pp. 151–165.

46. Freiherr von Oeynhausen to Ortsgruppenleiter, Grevenburg, February 10, 1932, and to Bezirksfachberater, April 8, 1932, SAMs, Gauleitung Westfalen-Nord, Gauamt für Volkswohlfahrt/15; "Der Nationalsozialismus – eine Gefahr für das Berufsbeamtentum?" [April 1932]; "Die Auflösung des Berufsbeamtentums," [April 1932], SAG, SF 6826, GA/100; "Kollegen!" [April 1932], SAG, SF 6826, GA/101; "Beamte erwacht!" [June/July 1932], SAG, SF 6826, GA/98. Also see n. 39 above.

47. Computed on the basis of figures in Schemm, circular 8, Bayreuth, March 1, 1932, HIS, 12/243; *Berufszählung . . . 16. Juni 1933*, p. 49 (figures for teachers according to national census of 1933). Also see Bölling, *Volksschullehrer*, pp. 203–219. Among the restrictive measures by governments, among which the Reich's again stood out as the most lenient, see Morsey, "Staatsfeinde," pp. 121–133; *Frankfurter Zeitung*, October 6, 1932 (for Hesse); doc. 34 in Henning Timpke, ed., *Dokumente zur Gleichschaltung des Landes Hamburg 1933* (Frankfurt/Main, 1964), pp. 181–190 (for Hamburg). On the development of the Nationalsozialistische Beamtenabteilung, which was formed by the consolidation of various local groups at the regional and national levels, see Fabricius, *Beamte*, p. 79; Beck, *Kampf*, pp. 181–183; Gau-Organisationsleiter I to Bezirks- und Kreisleiter of Gau Süd-Hannover-Braunschweig (circular 6), Hanover-Döhren, December 11, 1931, NHSA, Hann. 122a, XI, 80; Freiherr von Oeynhausen to Bezirksfachberater, Grevenburg, April 8, 1932, SAMs, Gauleitung Westfalen-Nord, Gauamt für Volkswohlfahrt/15. Regarding examples of local concentration of Nazi lower civil servants, see Ernst-August Roloff, *Bürgertum und Nationalsozialismus 1930–1933: Braunschweigs Weg ins Dritte Reich* (Hanover, 1961), p. 81 (Holzminden police academy); Hambrecht, *Aufstieg*, p. 312 (Ebrach foresters); Pridham, *Rise*, p. 193 (Starnberg administrators); "Achtung! Ostpreussische Beamte!" [November 1932], SAG, SF 6826, GA/101 (declared Nazi lower civil servants in East Prussia). On the problems of disciplinary action against lower civil servants in this period: Reinhard Neubert, "Beamtentum und Nationalsozialismus," *Deutsches Recht*, 1, no. 4–5 (1931), 77; Gauverband Westfalen-Nord, NSDStB to all Gruppenführer, Gelsenkirchen, February 1932, SAMs, Gauleitung Westfalen-Nord, Gauamt für Volkswohlfahrt/15; Scheerschmidt to NSDAP Munich, Neuvorwerk, September 12, 1931, BDC, NSLB, PLA K. Scheerschmidt; Pietsch to Kreisleitung Mühldorf, n.d., BDC, PK, PLA W. Pietsch. For developments in Bavaria, see Pridham, *Rise*, p. 193.

48. Compare the figures in *Partei-Statistik* I, 70, and table 3 in Kater, "Wandel," p. 30.

49. Documentation for the above is in Vierhaus, "Auswirkungen," pp. 170–171; Kele, *Nazis*, pp. 201–203; Dreyfuss, *Beruf*, p. 166; Weber, "Merkmale," pp. 95–96; Winkler, *Mittelstand*, p. 35; Speier, *Angestellten*, pp.

71-73; Kocka, "Problematik," p. 796. Examples of Nazi propaganda for white-collar workers in 1931-32: "3 Millionen Arbeitslose! — Zusammenbruch der Wirtschaft!" [1931], SAG, SF 6826, GA/101; "Waren- und Kaufhaus-Angestellte!" [March 1932], SAG, SF 6826, GA/100; *Preussische Zeitung*, November 17, 1932.

50. See the innovative study by Richard F. Hamilton, *Who Voted for Hitler?* (Princeton, 1982).

51. According to data in table 3 in Kater, "Wandel," p. 30, the (statistically not reliable) percentage fluctuations for the "upper middle class" from 1925 to 1933 were as follows: 1925-1929, 7.4%; 1930, 8.0%; 1931, 8.1%; 1932, 7.9%; 1933, 10.4%. Data from the sample mentioned in n. 1 above (2,186 *N*) indicate an only slightly higher value for 1925-1929 (9.5%) than for 1930-1932 (9.2% — see column A in table 6).

52. On the depression and heavy industry, see Mason, *Sozialpolitik*, pp. 93-96; Bernd Weisbrod, *Schwerindustrie in der Weimarer Republik: Interessenpolitik zwischen Stabilisierung und Krise* (Wuppertal, 1978), pp. 479-501. See also text in chap. 2 between nn. 52 and 64.

53. Controversy concerning these issues has not yet been resolved, owing chiefly to the disappearance of the party treasury records. While Turner has cautioned against overestimating the role of the industrialists, Stegmann's interpretation strongly accuses big business of complicity in the rise of Nazism. In view of the evidence presented, Turner's more temperate judgment constitutes a sounder argument than Stegmann's. For the above, see Turner, *Faschismus*, pp. 139-140; Stegmann, "Verhältnis," pp. 416-426. Also see Volker Hentschel, *Weimars letzte Monate: Hitler und der Untergang der Republik*, 2d ed. (Düsseldorf, 1979), pp. 103-104, n. 3; Broszat, *Staat*, pp. 78, 222; Schulz, *Aufstieg*, pp. 623-624; Hans-Erich Volkmann, "Das aussenwirtschaftliche Programm der NSDAP 1930-1933," *Archiv für Sozialgeschichte*, 17 (1977), 274; Schweitzer, *Business*, p. 101; and the good summary in Thomas Trumpp, "Zur Finanzierung der NSDAP durch die deutsche Grossindustrie: Versuch einer Bilanz," *Geschichte in Wissenschaft und Unterricht*, 32 (1981), 227-230. On the contacts between big business and Gregor Strasser see Stachura, "Strasser," pp. 94-95; Kissenkoetter, *Strasser*, pp. 125-126; Hentschel, *Monate*, pp. 110-111.

54. Regarding Hitler's interests, see his address to the industrialists in the influential Düsseldorf Industry Club, on January 26, 1932, in which he paid lip service to the ideals of private property and initiative: *Vortrag Adolf Hitlers vor westdeutschen Wirtschaftlern im Industrie-Klub zu Düsseldorf am 27.* [*recte: 26.*] *Januar 1932* (Munich, [1932]), especially pp. 8, 10, 18-19, 26-27. Also see Schweitzer, *Business*, p. 100; Hentschel, *Monate*, pp. 119-120; Trumpp, "Finanzierung," p. 232.

55. Divergent views on these developments are in Turner, *Faschismus*; Stegmann, "Verhältnis." Leaning toward Turner and on the whole more persuasive are Winkler, "Unternehmerverbände"; Alan S. Milward, "Fascism and the Economy," in Laqueur, ed., *Fascism*, p. 389; Lipset, *Man*, pp. 148-149; Hentschel, *Monate*, pp. 112-117, 128-138; Trumpp, "Finanzierung," pp.

230–235. Leaning toward Stegmann: Hennig's remarks in Deppe et al., eds., *Gespräche*, pp. 406–407; Schweitzer, *Business*, pp. 102–105. Also see Eichholtz and Schumann, *Anatomie*, pp. 92–98; Broszat, *Staat*, p. 30; Volkmann, "Programm," pp. 270–272; Treue, "Unternehmer," pp. 122–125; Hans Mommsen, "Die Sozialdemokratie in der Defensive: Der Immobilismus der SPD und der Aufstieg des Nationalsozialismus," in Mommsen, ed., *Sozialdemokratie zwischen Klassenbewegung und Volkspartei: Verhandlungen der Sektion "Geschichte der Arbeiterbewegung" des Deutschen Historikertages in Regensburg, Oktober 1972* (Frankfurt/Main, 1974), pp. 107–108. Recently, the debate has centered on the importance of the so-called Keppler Circle as representatives of big business instrumental in Hitler's rise to power. See Turner, "Grossunternehmertum," pp. 23–35; Stegmann, "Verhältnis," pp. 426–430, 434, 438–439. On the genesis and history of this circle, see Michael H. Kater, "Heinrich Himmler's Circle of Friends 1931–1945," *MARAB: A Review* [published by the Univeristy of Maryland Abroad], 2, no. 1 (1965–66), 76–77; Reinhard Vogelsang, *Der Freundeskreis Himmler* (Göttingen, 1972).

56. Linz, "Notes," p. 78, quotes Turner's findings that among 92 big business executives associated with the Nazi party until 1945, only 12% had in fact joined the NSDAP before 1933. An even lower percentage (7.4%) is given for Ruhr industrial leaders by Hans Mommsen, "Zur Verschränkung traditioneller und faschistischer Führungsgruppen in Deutschland beim Übergang von der Bewegungs- zur Systemphase," in Schieder, ed., *Faschismus*, p. 179, n. 39.

57. See Treue, "Unternehmer," pp. 122–123; Schulz, *Aufstieg*, pp. 623–627; Winkler, "Unternehmerverbände," p. 363. Also see circular, Hierl to delegates of Wirtschaftliche Abteilung et al., Munich, October 24, 1931, SAMs, Gauleitung Westfalen-Nord, Gauamt für Volkswohlfahrt/15.

58. Preller, *Sozialpolitik*, pp. 360, 400.

59. Ernst Lange, "Die politische Ideologie der deutschen industriellen Unternehmerschaft," Ph.D. dissertation, Greifswald, 1933, p. 36; Jäger, *Gesicht*, p. 54; Stegmann, "Verhältnis," pp. 428–429, 435–437; Turner, *Faschismus*, p. 30; Stokes, "Composition," p. 25; Hambrecht, *Aufstieg*, pp. 153, 312. See the interesting case of thermometer manufacturer Carl Hoesrich: Hoesrich to Gauleitung Weimar, Roda (Thuringia), March 1, 1932, IfZ, MA-135/136685–87.

60. Typical is the letter by Arendt to Heidrich, Tannenhof, September 27, 1930, SAG, SF 6818, GA/34: "[Brewery owner D.] does not wish his contribution [of 500 marks to the NSDAP] to show up anywhere in Königsberg, as he will not enter it in his books . . . In the presence of others he will deny any connection with the NSDAP." A similar verdict regarding the construction firm of O. is in Arendt to Gauleitung Königsberg, Tannenhof, November 11, 1930, SAG, SF 6818, GA/34. The case of a jobless builder is in Behr, "Geschichte der Ortsgruppe Widminnen," p. 28, SAPKG, 240, D/116.

61. On the support schemes, see Dieter Petzina, "Elemente der Wirtschaftspolitik in der Spätphase der Weimarer Republik," *Vierteljahrshefte für Zeitgeschichte*, 21 (1973), 130–131.

62. Guillebaud, *Recovery*, p. 19; Schulz, *Aufstieg*, pp. 621–622; Broszat, *Staat*, p. 29; Hans Beyer, "Die Agrarkrise und das Ende der Weimarer Republik," *Zeitschrift für Agrargeschichte und Agrarsoziologie*, 13 (1965), 88–89; Bennecke, *Depression*, p. 241; Behr, "Widminnen," p. 22 (see n. 60 above); Winkler, "Society," p. 7; Brüning, *Memoiren*, pp. 640, 642–643; Petzina, "Hauptprobleme," pp. 36–37; Petzina, *Wirtschaft*, p. 100. The relationship between large farmers and National Socialism is analyzed from a DNVP point of view, by estate owner [Ewald] von Kleist-Schmenzin, in "Rednerinformation der G.P.L.," no. 2, Stettin, May 27, 1932, SAG, SF 6815, GA/7.

63. See the timely observation by Theodor Heuss, *Hitlers Weg: Eine Schrift aus dem Jahre 1932*, ed. Eberhard Jäckel (Tübingen, 1968; 1st printing, 1932), p. 122.

64. Indicative of this is a statement made by the municipal caucus of Protestant organizations in Hanover, in letter to NSDAP chapter Hanover, October 15, 1929, NHSA, Hann. 310 I, A 30: "We are in any case very interested in further cooperation with political candidates of a decidedly Protestant conviction, including those in your party, and we would appreciate it if you could point out such people to us so that we may get in touch with them." See also Schulz, *Aufstieg*, pp. 695, 700; Plum, *Gesellschaftsstruktur*, p. 36. The entire Protestant church issue is ably discussed in Klaus Scholder, *Die Kirchen und das Dritte Reich*, I (Frankfurt/Main, 1977).

65. Feder, *Programme*, p. 43; *Westdeutscher Beobachter*, September 4, 1931; *Evangelisches Kirchenblatt für Württemberg*, 92 (1931), 33; doc. 3 in Noakes and Pridham, eds., *Documents*, p. 69; Hans Buchheim, *Glaubenskrise im Dritten Reich: Drei Kapitel nationalsozialistischer Religionspolitik* (Stuttgart, 1953), p. 66; Leonore Siegele-Wenschkewitz, *Nationalsozialismus und Kirchen: Religionspolitik von Partei und Staat bis 1935* (Düsseldorf, 1974), p. 13; Schulz, *Aufstieg*, pp. 696, 700.

66. See flyer, "Sage mir mit wem Du umgehst, Und ich sage Dir wer du bist!" [April 1932], SAG, SF 6826, GA/100; Konrad Heiden, *A History of National Socialism* (London, 1971; 1st printing, 1934), p. 153; Buchheim, *Glaubenskrise*, pp. 64–65; Schön, *Entstehung*, p. 192; Siegele-Wenschkewitz, *Nationalsozialismus*, pp. 24–26; Schulz, *Aufstieg*, pp. 697–698; Broszat, *Staat*, p. 46; Noakes, *Nazi Party*, p. 206–207; Hambrecht, *Aufstieg*, pp. 245–246; Broszat et al., eds., *Bayern in der NS-Zeit: Soziale Lage und politisches Verhalten der Bevölkerung im Spiegel vertraulicher Berichte* (Munich and Vienna, 1977), p. 371.

67. Buchheim, *Glaubenskrise*, pp. 67, 69–78; Noakes, *Nazi Party*, p. 208; Siegele-Wenschkewitz, *Nationalsozialismus*, pp. 23, 66–67; Schulz, *Aufstieg*, pp. 694–695.

68. For North Germany, see Noakes, *Nazi Party*, pp. 207–208; *Bremer Nationalsozialistische Zeitung*, June 3, 1931; activities report, Gau Süd-Hannover-Braunschweig, Hanover, May 9, 1931, NSHA, Hann. 310 I, B 13. For Franconia: Hambrecht, *Aufstieg*, pp. 287–292. For Baden: Maier to district offices et al., Karlsruhe, December 5, 1931, SAF 317/1257 b. For Hesse: Schön, *Entstehung*, pp. 191–193; *Westdeutscher Beobachter*,

September 4, 1931. For West Germany: Möller to Reichsjugendführer, Soest, December 6, 1933, HIS, 18/339. For Thuringia: Siegele-Wenschkewitz, *Nationalsozialismus*, p. 23. For Pomerania: Siegele-Wenschkewitz, *Nationalsozialismus*, p. 22; doc. 118 (VII) in Robert Thévoz et al., eds., *Pommern 1934/35 im Spiegel von Gestapo-Lageberichten und Sachakten (Quellen)* (Cologne and Berlin, 1974), p. 384. For East Prussia: correspondence Pfarrer Michalik–Gauleiter Koch (1931–32), SAG, SF 6818, GA/27. Also see Buchheim, *Glaubenskrise*, pp. 42, 63, 66–69.

69. Siegele-Wenschkewitz, *Nationalsozialismus*, p. 25.

70. See "Christentum und Nationalsozialismus," [1931–32], and flyer, "Evangelische! Was ist mit Hitler?" [1932], SAG, SF 6817, GA/27; Siegele-Wenschkewitz, *Nationalsozialismus*, p. 27.

71. Alfred Rosenberg, *Der Mythus des 20. Jahrhunderts: Eine Wertung der seelisch-geistigen Gestaltenkämpfe unserer Zeit*, 41st and 42d eds. (Munich, 1934; 1st ed., 1930). Also see *Westdeutscher Beobachter*, September 4, 1931; Heiden, *History*, pp. 152–153; Schulz, *Aufstieg*, pp. 698–702; Ernst-Wolfgang Böckenförde, "Der deutsche Katholizismus im Jahre 1933: Eine kritische Betrachtung," *Hochland*, 53 (1961), 217, n. 5; Hambrecht, *Aufstieg*, pp. 247, 248–287; Linz, "Notes," pp. 85, 88. Also see Samuel Alexander Pratt, "The Social Basis of Nazism and Communism in Urban Germany: A Correlational Study of the July 31, 1932, Reichstag Elections in Germany," M.A. thesis, Michigan State College of Agriculture and Applied Science, 1948, p. 85, for the comparatively more negative effect of the Nazis in Catholic (electoral) districts.

72. Rosenberg, *Mythus*, pp. 129, 183–185, 622, 626, 685.

73. Buchheim, *Glaubenskrise*, pp. 63–64; Schulz, *Aufstieg*, p. 697. This is not to say that there were no serious Protestant Christians who repudiated Nazism and Rosenberg's ideas on sincere religious grounds: see "Christentum und Nationalsozialismus," [1931–32], SAG, SF 6817, GA/27; "Rednerinformation der G.P.L.," no. 2, Stettin, May 27, 1932, SAG, SF 6815, GA/7. Also see *Evangelisches Kirchenblatt für Württemberg*, 92 (1931), 65.

74. See figures in table 3, Kater, "Wandel," p. 30.

75. Quotation is from Unknown to Mittelstrass, Berlin-Grunewald, October 8, 1931, AJ, A 123/11 c. Also see: Steinberg, *Sabers*, p. 111–112; Kater, *Studentenschaft*, p. 173.

76. The Nazi doubts are reflected in Rüger to Bormann, Erfurt, December 18, 1930, SAM, Pol. Dir. 6845; Wagner to Parteigenosse, April 21, 1931, GLAK, 465d/263. In retrospect, Beck, *Kampf*, p. 178.

77. On this as well as the plight of intellectuals and their relationship to Nazism, see Jäger, *Gesicht*, p. 57; Laqueur, *Weimar*, pp. 527–564; Hambrecht, *Aufstieg*, pp. 260–261; preelection flyer, addressed to "Sehr geehrter Herr," [October–November 1932], SAG, SF 6815, GA/7; directive, Hess, Munich, July 1932, SAG, SF 6818, GA/31.

78. On the development of the Jurists' League, see Beck, *Kampf*, pp. 187–189; membership list BNSDJ, January 1, 1931, BA, NS 26/517 (209 members); the same for October 1, 1931, BHSAM, Sonderabgabe I/1868 (253

members); Hitler, "Gewährung von Rechtsschutz durch die National-
sozialistische Deutsche Arbeiterpartei," Munich, November 30, 1930, NHSA,
Hann. 310 I, A 32; Füchte to Alle Fachberater für Rechtsschutz, Gelsenkir-
chen, November 16, 1931, SAMs, Gauleitung Westfalen-Nord, Gauamt für
Volkswohlfahrt/15. On the architects' and engineers' association, see Feder
and Hierl, Anordnung Nr. 1, Munich, November 2, 1931; memorandum,
"Kampfbund der deutschen Architekten und Ingenieure," Munich, [1932],
SAMs, Gauleitung Westfalen-Nord, Gauamt für Volkswohlfahrt/15; Ludwig,
Technik, pp. 65–66, 90–94.

79. See Otto Büsch and Gerald Feldman, eds., *Historische Prozesse der
deutschen Inflation 1914–1924: Ein Tagungsbericht* (Berlin, 1978), p. 251;
Gerald Schröder, "Die 'Wiedergeburt' der Pharmazie – 1933 bis 1934," in
Herbert Mehrtens and Steffen Richter, eds., *Naturwissenschaft, Technik und
NS-Ideologie: Beiträge zur Wissenschaftsgeschichte des Dritten Reichs*
(Frankfurt/Main, 1980), pp. 168–169, 183 (n. 17). On the Nazi Physicians'
League in this period, see *Der Freiheitskampf*, September 9, 1931. I owe the
insight regarding a fear of socialized medicine to a conversation with Professor
Fridolf Kudlien in May 1982, a historian of medicine at the University of Kiel,
who has done extensive research in this area. On this, see also Eckhard Hansen
et al., *Seit über einem Jahrhundert . . . : Verschüttete Alternativen in der Sozialpolitik: Sozialer Fortschritt, organisierte Dienstleistermacht und nationalsozialistische Machtergreifung: Der Fall der Ambulatorien in den
Unterweserstädten und Berlin* (Cologne, 1981).

80. Peter Hüttenberger, "Interessenvertretung und Lobbyismus im Drit-
ten Reich," in Gerhard Hirschfeld and Lothar Kettenacker, eds., *Der
"Führerstaat": Mythos und Realität: Studien zur Struktur und Politik des
Dritten Reiches* (Stuttgart, 1981), p. 431; Füchte to Alle Fachberater für
Rechtsschutz, Gelsenkirchen, November 16, 1931, SAMs, Gauleitung
Westfalen-Nord, Gauamt für Volkswohlfahrt/15.

81. On this, see the illuminating example in Hambrecht, *Aufstieg*, p. 310.

82. This is documented, above all, in the editorials of four right-of-center
bourgeois papers, which show a gradual inclination toward the Nazis till 1933.
See the excellent analysis by Pfeifer, "Hitlerbild"; also Professor Wilhelm
Burmeister, "Der Kandidat der deutschen Künstler: Adolf Hitler," February
13, 1932, doc. 108, in Jochmann, *Nationalsozialismus*, pp. 366–370; Müller,
Beamtentum, p. 38, Hamilton, *Appeal*, pp. 124, 142–143; von Baeyer-Katte,
Politik, pp. 36–37, 41; Riemer, "Soziologie," p. 117; Mommsen,
"Verschränkung," p. 165; Daniel Lerner, *The Nazi Elite* (Stanford, 1951), pp.
30–32; Klaus Fritzsche, *Politische Romantik und Gegenrevolution:
Fluchtwege in der Krise der bürgerlichen Gesellschaft: Das Beispiel des
"Tat"-Kreises* (Frankfurt/Main, 1976), pp. 237–259; Modris Eksteins, "All
Quiet on the Western Front and the Fate of a War," *Journal of Contemporary
History*, 15 (1980), 355. The mood of despondency is captured well in the
otherwise critical memoirs of Harry [Graf] Kessler, *In the Twenties: The
Diaries of Harry Kessler* (New York, 1971), pp. 239–438. On Jünger, see the
poignant analysis by Struve, *Elites*, pp. 377–414. A figure similar in type to

Jünger but much less prolific was Dr. Kleo Pleyer, like Jünger a dedicated youth leader, who in the Third Reich would take over Professor Hans Rothfels's chair in history at the University of Königsberg and who was fated to die a hero's death at the eastern front in 1942. See Michael H. Kater, "Bürgerliche Jugendbewegung und Hitlerjugend in Deutschland von 1926 bis 1939," *Archiv für Sozialgeschichte*, 17 (1977), 142–143, 160–161, 167 (n. 272). Regarding Spengler, it is interesting that Hitler professed *not* to be an adherent of the ideas of the "prophet of doom." See *Hitler aus nächster Nähe: Aufzeichnungen eines Vertrauten [Otto Wagener] 1929–1932*, ed. Henry A. Turner, Jr. (Frankfurt/Main, 1978), p. 290, hereafter cited as Wagener, *Hitler*.

83. See the retrospective comments by Professor Carl Schmitt, one of the most brilliant advocates of dictatorship among the educated elite at the end of the Weimar Republic: *Staat, Bewegung, Volk* (Hamburg, 1935), p. 31. Also Pfeifer, "Hitlerbild," pp. 130, 180, 183–185; Hambrecht, *Aufstieg*, p. 309; Noakes and Pridham, eds., *Documents*, p. 139; "Die Flucht aus der NSDAP.," [November 1932], SAG, SF 6827, GA/105; NSDAP Gau Ostpreussen, Information 5/32, Königsberg, October 1, 1932; report Gau East Prussia, Königsberg, November 10, 1932, SAG, SF 6815, GA/7.

84. Kater, "Hitlerjugend," p. 25; Weigand von Miltenberg [Herbert Blank], *Adolf Hitler Wilhelm III.* (Berlin, 1932; 1st printing, 1930), p. 91. Example of Nazi propaganda directed at academically trained teachers: "Erzieher!" [1932], SAG, SF 6826, GA/101. On the relationship between lower-school teachers and prorepublican parties (DDP, SPD), see Bölling, *Volksschullehrer*.

85. Rector Technische Hochschule Braunschweig to Flechsig, Brunswick, September 28, 1938, NAW, 12 A Neu, 13 h/18656. Also see Johannes Stark, "Die Verjudung der deutschen Hochschulen," *Nationalsozialistische Monatshefte*, 1 (1930), 360–370; Karl Otmar Freiherr von Aretin, "Die deutsche Universität im Dritten Reich," *Frankfurter Hefte*, 23 (1968), 694; Uwe Dietrich Adam, *Hochschule und Nationalsozialismus: Die Universität Tübingen im Dritten Reich* (Tübingen, 1977), pp. 24, 31, 175; Beyerchen, *Scientists*, pp. 20–21; Hajo Holborn, "Origins and Political Character of Nazi Ideology," *Political Science Quarterly*, 79 (1964), 544 (n.5); Krebs, *Infancy*, p. 126; Kelly, "National Socialism," pp. 46–49; Wolfgang Kunkel, "Der Professor im Dritten Reich," in Helmut Kuhn et al., *Die deutsche Universität im Dritten Reich: Acht Beiträge* (Munich, 1966), pp. 106–113; Kurt Sontheimer, "Die Haltung der deutschen Universitäten zur Weimarer Republik," in *Universitätstage 1966: Nationalsozialismus und die deutsche Universität: Eine Veröffentlichung der Freien Universität Berlin* (Berlin, 1966), pp. 24–42.

86. See table 3 in Kater, "Wandel," p. 30, which contains figures for all higher civil servants, including teachers, professors, and clergy.

87. Neubert, "Beamtentum," p. 78; Klotz, *Nationalsozialismus*, p. 5; Albert Krebs, *Fritz-Dietlof Graf von der Schulenburg: Zwischen Staatsraison und Hochverrat* (Hamburg, 1964), pp. 75–76, 79, 82, 84–86; Domröse, *NS-Staat*, p. 321; Broszat, *Staat*, p. 28; Mommsen, "Stellung," p. 151. Note the cynicism in Ernst Rudolf Huber, "Bedeutungswandel der Grundrechte," *Archiv*

des öffentlichen Rechts, n.s. 23 (1923), 54-55.

88. Mommsen, "Stellung"; Mommsen, "Beamtentum," p. 198. For Papen's decrees, see Petzina, "Hauptprobleme," p. 20; Huber, "Bedeutungswandel," pp. 55-56.

89. "Die Auflösung des Berufsbeamtentums," [April 1932], SAG, SF 6826, GA/100. Also see: "Der Nationalsozialismus—eine Gefahr für das Berufsbeamtentum?" [April 1932], ibid.; "Korruptionsergüsse aus dem Kreise Stuhm," [1932], SAG, SF 6826, GA/98; Müller, *Beamtentum*, p. 35.

90. Müller, *Beamtentum*, p. 32.

91. See the observation by Geiger, *Schichtung*, p. 121.

92. In one case, Justice Dr. Wollmann tried to express his pro-Nazi sentiments in a letter to SA-Gruppenführer Heines, whose men he was forced to try in a republican court of law: Wollmann to Heines, Schweidnitz, November 22, 1932, NA, T-253, 23/1473946. Also see the case of Potsdam judge Fuhrmann, who was punitively transferred in early 1932, in Hagen, *Leader*, p. 290. The case of Lindau mayor Ludwig Siebert, who became a Nazi party comrade in 1931, is in Mommsen, "Verschränkung," p. 166. On Schulenburg, see Krebs, *Schulenburg*, pp. 75, 84-86. On Martin, see Hambrecht, *Aufstieg*, p. 313; and Edward N. Peterson, *The Limits of Hitler's Power* (Princeton, 1969). Further: Caplan, "Civil Servant," p. 81.

4. THE PEACEFUL PERIOD: JANUARY 1933 TO SEPTEMBER 1939

1. While the NSDAP purported to represent the masses, its actual membership was always small enough to justify elitism. A detailed discussion of this isssue is in chap. 6, at nn. 95-97.

2. Milton Mayer, *They Thought They Were Free: The Germans 1933-45* (Chicago and London, 1955), p. 85.

3. Mason, *Arbeiterklasse*, pp. 1-173.

4. Table 7 (columns A-E), figure 2.

5. See Bracher, *Dictatorship*, pp. 197-198, 218-221; Schumann, *Nationalsozialismus*, pp. 49-75; Timpke, ed., *Dokumente*, pp. 75-79, 82-90, 92-119. A local example of occupation of ADGB headquarters (Hanover, May 1933) is in Gerda Zorn, *Stadt im Widerstand* (Frankfurt/Main, [1965]), p. 30. Also see Graf, *Entwicklung*, p. 48; and the documents cited in nn. 43 and 45 below. For the SPD, see Hoegner, *Flucht*.

6. See figures 3-5.

7. In January 1933 rural areas held only about 5% of the total unemployed. Farquharson, *Plough*, p. 183.

8. Winzer, *Jahre*, p. 105. On the job creation measures, see Fritz Reinhardt, *Die Arbeitsschlacht der Reichsregierung* (Berlin, 1933); Reinhardt, *Generalplan gegen die Arbeitslosigkeit: Vortrag gehalten im Klub zu Bremen* (Oldenburg, 1933); Jürgen Stelzner, "Arbeitsbeschaffung und Wiederaufrüstung 1933-1936: Nationalsozialistische Beschäftigungspolitik und Aufbau der Wehr- und Rüstungswirtschaft," Ph.D. dissertation, Tübingen, 1976,

pp. 53–268; Petzina, "Hauptprobleme," p. 48; Petzina, *Wirtschaft*, pp. 112–114.

9. According to Hans Kühne, "Der Arbeitseinsatz im Vierjahresplan," *Jahrbücher für Nationalökonomie und Statistik*, 146 (1937), 690; and doc. 68 in Mason, *Arbeiterklasse*, p. 505. Typical local figures, in this case for Wiesbaden (1932–33), are in Kater, "Wandel," p. 45. For the area of Harz Mountains (1933) see Gau Süd-Hannover-Braunschweig, situation report for August 1933, NHSA, Hann. 310 I, B 13; for Bavaria (1934, 1936) see the documents in Broszat et al., eds., *Bayern*, pp. 89, 219.

10. Doc. 146 in Mason, *Arbeiterklasse*, p. 845; Kühne, "Arbeitseinsatz," p. 690. There were 338,000 "registered unemployed" by April 1938. Guillebaud, *Recovery*, p. 111. Also see Neumann, *Behemoth*, pp. 354–356.

11. See Mason, *Arbeiterklasse*, pp. 47–48. Karl Lärmer of East Germany can show that the Nazis vastly exaggerated the significance of the autobahn construction program in unemployment reduction. *Autobahnbau in Deutschland 1933 bis 1945: Zu den Hintergründen* ([East] Berlin, 1975), pp. 54–55. As a source, Lärmer's book is useful but has faults typical of East German historiography. See the review by Karl-Heinz Ludwig in *Archiv für Sozialgeschichte*, 18 (1978), 738–739.

12. Docs. 8, 10 in Thévoz et al., eds., *Quellen*, pp. 114, 147; Scholtz-Klink, monthly report NSF (hereafter cited as Scholtz-Klink/NSF) for September–October 1936, BA, NS 22/860; activities report NSF Westfalen-Nord, July–August 1935, SAMs, NSF Westfalen-Nord/122; Fischer to Gestapa, Münster, February 5, 1936, SAMs, Polit. Polizei, 3. Reich/441. Also see Mason, *Arbeiterklasse*, p. 72; doc. 40, p. 355; doc. (October 1933) in Broszat et al., eds., *Bayern*, p. 217; situation report for November 1936, Gau Westfalen-Nord, SAMs, Gauschulungsamt/15; Scholtz-Klink/NSF for May 1937, BA, NS 22/860.

13. Westphalia (1935): Stosch to Gestapa, Recklinghausen, May 6, 1935, SAMs, Polit. Polizei, 3. Reich/433; Pomerania (1935): doc. 9 in Thévoz et al., eds., *Quellen*, p. 131; Franconia (1936): doc. (September 19, 1936) in Broszat et al., eds., *Bayern*, p. 259; Saxony (1936): Scholtz-Klink/NSF for September–October 1936, BA, NS 22/860; Bavaria (1937): doc. 27 in Mason, *Arbeiterklasse*, p. 290; Westphalia (1937): Scholtz-Klink/NSF for November 1937, BA, NS 22/860.

14. Steinberg, *Entwicklung*, pp. 61, 64–65; Stosch to Gestapa, Recklinghausen, March 6 and May 6, 1935, SAMs, Polit. Polizei, 3. Reich/431 and 433; Scholtz-Klink/NSF for March–April 1937, BA, NS 22/860; doc. 47 in Mason, *Arbeiterklasse*, 401, also p. 69. For miners in Central Germany, see Eichholtz, *Geschichte*, I, 28.

15. Schoenbaum, *Revolution*, pp. xii–xiii; Arthur Schweitzer, *Die Nazifizierung des Mittelstandes* (Stuttgart, 1970), p. 149.

16. Doc. 5 in Mason, *Arbeiterklasse*, p. 219; minutes of speech by Rudolf Hess at Nuremberg Party Rally, printed by Bormann, April 15, 1937, BA, NS 22/2011 (pp. 7–8). Also see doc. 60 in Mason, *Arbeiterklasse*, p. 463.

17. Mason, *Arbeiterklasse*, p. 745; also see p. 66; Hilde Oppenheimer-Bluhm, *The Standard of Living of German Labour under Nazi Rule* (New York, 1965; 1st printing, 1943), pp. 8–9.

18. See docs. (1936–1938) in Mason, *Arbeiterklasse*, pp. 198–201, 239, 307, 312, 350, 401–402, 411, 527; and docs. (1935–36) in Broszat et al., eds., *Bayern*, p. 242, 260. Also Kühne, "Arbeitseinsatz," pp. 693, 696; [Werner] Mansfeld, "Sicherung des Gefolgschaftsbestandes," *Der Vierjahresplan*, 1 (1937), 154; Schumann, *Nationalsozialismus*, pp. 143–144; Timothy W. Mason, "Labour in the Third Reich, 1933–1939," *Past and Present*, 33 (1966), 126–129; Dietmar Petzina, "Die Mobilisierung deutscher Arbeitskräfte vor und während des Zweiten Weltkrieges," *Vierteljahrshefte für Zeitgeschichte*, 18 (1970), 446.

19. Kühne, "Arbeitseinsatz," pp. 696–697; Mansfeld, "Sicherung"; Schumann, *Nationalsozialismus*, p. 144; Göring's decree reprinted as doc. 110 in Mason, *Arbeiterklasse*, pp. 669–670; Mason, "Labour," p. 130; Schoenbaum, *Revolution*, p. 97; Petzina, *Wirtschaft*, pp. 145–146; Lärmer, *Autobahnbau*, p. 60; Gustav Hermann Seebold, *Ein Stahlkonzern im Dritten Reich: Der Bochumer Verein 1927–1945* (Wuppertal, 1981), pp. 154–156.

20. Figures according to: activities report Gau Süd-Hannover-Braunschweig for October 1933, NHSA, Hann. 310 I, B 13; doc. 150 in Mason, *Arbeiterklasse*, p. 871. More on the miners' wages in: situation report for November 1936, Gau Westfalen-Nord, SAMs, Gauleitung Westfalen-Nord, Gauschulungsamt/15; doc. (July 5, 1937) in Broszat et al., eds., *Bayern*, p. 266; Scholtz-Klink/NSF for September–October 1936 and May 1938, BA, NS 22/860; docs. 33, 47, 85 in Mason, *Arbeiterklasse*, pp. 327, 402, 571; Wolfgang Jonas, *Das Leben der Mansfeld-Arbeiter 1924 bis 1945* ([East] Berlin, 1957), pp. 333–348. In early 1938 regulatory measures by the government improved the lot of the miners slightly: Karl Teppe, "Zur Sozialpolitik des Dritten Reiches am Beispiel der Sozialversicherung," *Archiv für Sozialgeschichte*, 17 (1977), 234. Marlies G. Steinert's undocumented assertion that miners' wages ranged at the very top in the Reich's economy is completely erroneous. *Hitlers Krieg und die Deutschen: Stimmung und Haltung der deutschen Bevölkerung im Zweiten Weltkrieg* (Düsseldorf and Vienna, 1970), p. 61.

21. Cited in activities report, Gau Süd-Hannover-Braunschweig, for August 1933, NHSA, Hann. 310 I, B 13. Similar complaints for: East Prussia (1933): Scholz to Kreisleitung NSBO, Königsberg, July 14, 1933, SAG, SF 6817, GA/17; Thuringia (1934): doc. (March 13, 1934) in Broszat, *Staat*, p. 197; Pomerania (1934): doc. 3 in Thévoz et al., eds., *Quellen*, p. 51; Silesia (1934): Lärmer, *Autobahnbau*, p. 62; Saar (1935): p. 61; Westphalia (1935): activities report NSF Westfalen-Nord, July–August 1935, SAMs, NSF Westfalen-Nord/122; Franconia (1936): doc. (September 19, 1936), in Broszat et al., eds., *Bayern*, p. 259; Weser-Ems (1937): Scholtz-Klink/NSF for May 1937, BA, NS 22/860; East Prussia (1937): doc. 52 in Mason, *Arbeiterklasse*, p. 435; Oberdonau (1938–39): police station Kirchdorf to Landrat, Kirchdorf, February 23, 1939, OLA, Pol. Akten/13; Upper Bavaria (1939): Gau

München-Oberbayern, situation report Altötting for January–March 1939, SAM, NSDAP/126.

22. Oppenheimer-Bluhm, *Standard*, p. 41, puts the difference in "real income" at 2%. Mason, working with more up-to-date data, puts the real-wages index at 118 in 1929, and at 107–108 in 1936. *Arbeiterklasse*, pp. 62–64. Also see Petzina, *Wirtschaft*, pp. 121–122, 146–147; Mason, "Women," p. 104; Schumann, *Nationalsozialismus*, p. 144; Thomas E.J. de Witt, "The Economics and Politics of Welfare in the Third Reich," *Central European History*, 11 (1978), 271.

23. See Neumann, *Behemoth*, p. 356; Schoenbaum, *Revolution*, pp. 102–103, 105–106; Winzer, *Jahre*, p. 132; and Mason, *Arbeiterklasse*, p. 64.

24. Scholtz-Klink/NSF for March–April 1939, BA, NS 22/860; Martin Gumpert, *Heil Hunger! Health under Hitler* (New York and Toronto, 1940), p. 60; Oppenheimer-Bluhm, *Standard*, p. 28; Lärmer, *Autobahnbau*, pp. 63–64.

25. Mason, *Arbeiterklasse*, p. 72, docs. 85, 150, also pp. 568–569, 870–871; Scholtz-Klink/NSF for September–October 1936, BA, NS 22/860; Gumpert, *Hunger*, pp. 62–64; Lärmer, *Autobahnbau*, pp. 65–67. Also see Jonas, *Leben*, pp. 409–439; *Deutschland-Berichte*, II (1935), 786, 788.

26. On the effects of the loss of mobility, see docs. 27, 145 in Mason, *Arbeiterklasse*, pp. 289, 842. On commuting hardships and costs, see situation report, Gauleitung Westfalen-Nord, for November 1936, SAMs, Gauleitung Westfalen-Nord, Gauschulungsamt/15; Rottmann to Franke, July 9, 1938, SAMs, Gauleitung Westfalen-Nord, Gauinspekteure/102; *National-Zeitung*, February 10, 1938; doc. (January 1939) in Broszat et al., eds., *Bayern*, p. 280; Lärmer, *Autobahnbau*, pp. 64, 67.

27. Scholtz-Klink/NSF for September–October 1936 and January–February 1937, BA, NS 22/860; Kühne, "Arbeitseinsatz," p. 692; Gumpert, *Hunger*, pp. 61–62.

28. Situation report of Betriebsblock Strassenbahn, Königsberg, July 17, 1933, SAG, SF 6817, GA/17; Scholtz-Klink/NSF for March–April 1937, BA, NS 22/860; minutes of speech by Hess at Nuremberg Party Rally, printed by Bormann, April 15, 1937, BA, NS 22/2011 (p. 9); doc. (January 1939) in Broszat et al., eds., *Bayern*, p. 280; doc. 123 in Mason, *Arbeiterklasse*, p. 723; also pp. 76–77; Steinert, *Krieg*, p. 63; *Deutschland-Berichte*, II (1935), 554.

29. See docs. 4, 7, 9, 10, 15 in Thévoz et al., eds., *Quellen*, pp. 64, 92, 130, 143, 145, 171; Frieda Wunderlich, *Farm Labor in Germany, 1810–1945* (Princeton, 1961), pp. 281–283, 292–303; Poppinga, *Bauern*, p. 55; Schoenbaum, *Revolution*, pp. 174–179; Petzina, *Autarkiepolitik*, p. 93; activities report Gau Süd-Hannover-Braunschweig for December 1933, NHSA, 310 I, B 13; Mason, *Arbeiterklasse*, pp. 75, 111–112; Falk Wiesemann, "Arbeitskonflikte in der Landwirtschaft während der NS-Zeit in Bayern 1933–1938," *Vierteljahrshefte für Zeitgeschichte*, 25 (1977), 577, 583–589.

30. Hitler, *Mein Kampf*, pp. 637–638. Also Hitler in conversations with O. Wagener, Wagener, *Hitler*, pp. 423–434. Further see Struve, *Elites*, pp. 428–429.

31. Melita Maschmann, *Account Rendered: A Dossier on my Former Self* (London, 1965), pp. 35–36; Führer des Bannes B 1 to Kammerer, Laufen, August 5 and 6, 1935, SAM, NSDAP/348; Standortführer HJ-Bann 75 to Heider, Bremen, December 9, 1935, SAB, N 7, Nr. 67 /60/; Verordnungsblatt Gau Süd-Hannover-Braunschweig, Amt NSBO, March 15, 1939, BA, Schumacher/202 (p. 7).

32. *Das Junge Deutschland* (1939), pp. 282–285.

33. Harald Scholtz, *Nationalsozialistische Ausleseschulen: Internatsschulen als Herrschaftsmittel des Führerstaates* (Göttingen, 1973), pp. 133, 245. See the illuminating example in activities report NSDAP Kreis Wilhelmshaven, November 1939, NSAO, 320, 2/2.

34. Ulrich Gmelin, "Das Langemarck-Studium," *Der Deutsche Hochschulführer: Lebens- und Studienverhältnisse an den Deutschen Hochschulen*, 21 (1939), 18–20; Hanns Streit, "Das Reichsstudentenwerk," ibid., 25; *Das Junge Deutschland* (1937), p. 512; Gustav Adolf Scheel, "Der NSD.-Studentenbund," in Rudolf Benze and Gustav Gräfer, eds., *Erziehungsmächte und Erziehungshoheit im Grossdeutschen Reich als gestaltende Kräfte im Leben des Deutschen* (Leipzig, 1940), pp. 204–205; Adam, *Hochschule*, p. 118; Kater, *Studentenschaft*, pp. 40–42. Schoenbaum, *Revolution*, pp. 274–275, notes a decline in the percentage of workers' children in the universities since the Weimar era. Similarly, and more up to date, Aharon F. Kleinberger, "Gab es eine nationalsozialistische Hochschulpolitik?" in Manfred Heinemann, ed., *Erziehung und Schulung im Dritten Reich*, II (Stuttgart, 1980), 21.

35. On its origins see Michael H. Kater, "The Reich Vocational Contest and Students of Higher Learning in Nazi Germany," *Central European History*, 7 (1974), 225–226; also "Rednermaterial zum Reichsberufswettkampf 1936," HIS, 18/342; Baldur von Schirach, *Revolution der Erziehung: Reden aus den Jahren des Aufbaus*, 2d ed. (Munich, 1939), p. 66; Georg Ebersbach, "Woher kommen die Besten? Die soziale Herkunft der Gausieger – Zentrale Förderung zwingend geboten," *Das Junge Deutschland* (1939), 276–278.

36. The official term was "Auslese der Tüchtigsten." On this failure, see Hartmut Kaelble, "Chancenungleichheit und akademische Ausbildung in Deutschland, 1910–1960," *Geschichte und Gesellschaft*, 1 (1975), 141–144; Michael H. Kater, "Die deutsche Elternschaft im nationalsozialistischen Erziehungssystem: Ein Beitrag zur Sozialgeschichte der Familie," *Vierteljahrschrift für Sozial- und Wirtschaftsgeschichte*, 67 (1980), 509–512.

37. Huber, "Rechtsgestalt," p. 340; Wiesemann, "Arbeitskonflikte," pp. 588–589; Schweitzer, *Business*, p. 380; Schweitzer, *Nazifizierung*, pp. 149, 152; Mason, *Arbeiterklasse*, pp. 82–83.

38. Stosch to Gestapa, Recklinghausen, May 6, 1935, SAMs, Polit. Polizei, 3. Reich/433; docs. 9, 17 in Thévoz et al., eds., *Quellen*, pp. 130, 181; activities report Kreis Wasserburg for June–July 1935, SAM, NSDAP/118; memorandum Reiser, Thalheim, January 6, 1936, SAM, NSDAP/443; Fischer to Gestapa, Münster, February 5, 1936, SAMs, Polit. Polizei, 3. Reich/441; Scholtz-Klink/NSF for September–October 1936, BA, NS 22/860;

doc. 44 in Mason, *Arbeiterklasse*, p. 380, also p. 37.

39. The typical case of an Essen miner who had paid almost a day's wage per month for accident insurance and after a mishap in early 1939 had to be hospitalized for several weeks, while his family received only 80 pfennigs per day, is related in Scholtz-Klink/NSF for January–February 1939, BA, NS 22/860. Also see Stosch to Gestapa, Recklinghausen, March 6, 1935, SAMs, Polit. Polizei, 3. Reich/431; doc. 27 in Mason, *Arbeiterklasse*, p. 287; Gumpert, *Hunger*, p. 62; Teppe, "Sozialpolitik," p. 234.

40. Case of worker Blum is in correspondence regarding B., February–March 1934, BA, R 36/455. Also see Fischer to Gestapa, Münster, February 5, 1936, SAMs, Polit. Polizei, 3. Reich/441; Scholtz-Klink/NSF for January 1938, BA, NS 22/860; "Jahresfahrtenprogramm [KdF] 1938 Kreis Düren," BA, NS 5 I/212; Oppenheimer-Bluhm, *Standard*, p. 65; Schoenbaum, *Revolution*, pp. 111–112; Michael A. Merritt, "Strength through Joy: Regimented Leisure in Nazi Germany," in Otis C. Mitchell, ed., *Nazism and the Common Man: Essays in German History (1929–1939)* (Minneapolis, 1972), p. 67; *Deutschland-Berichte*, II (1935), 175–177, 845–851, 1457–61.

41. Details on the KdF car may be found in Walter Henry Nelson, *Small Wonder: The Amazing Story of the Volkswagen* (Boston and Toronto, 1965), pp. 18–96. Also see Deutsches Nachrichtenbüro, July 21, 1939 , Nr. 1076, BA, R 43 II/556 b. Calculation of 1939 average wage is according to figures in *Statistisches Handbuch*, p. 469.

42. See docs. (1936–1939) in Broszat et al., eds., *Bayern*, pp. 256, 262–263, 272, 274, 284; docs. 27, 41 in Mason, *Arbeiterklasse*, pp. 290, 292, 363; Scholtz-Klink/NSF for June 1937, BA, NS 22/860; Grunberger, *Reich*, p. 199; Winzer, *Jahre*, pp. 77, 96–99.

43. Examples of the "wooden suit" in Lower Danubian Austria, correspondence of June 1939 in DAÖW/1644. Also see docs. 3, 29 in Jörg Schadt, ed., *Verfolgung und Widerstand unter dem Nationalsozialismus in Baden: Die Lageberichte der Gestapo und des Generalstaatsanwalts Karlsruhe 1933–1940* (Stuttgart, 1976), pp. 63, 176; doc. (January 11, 1937) in Broszat et al., eds., *Bayern*, p. 261; docs. 103, 123 in Mason, *Arbeiterklasse*, pp. 634, 724. Also see p. 123; and Winzer, *Jahre*, pp. 76, 136; Heinz Gittig, *Illegale antifaschistische Tarnschriften 1933 bis 1945* (Leipzig, 1972), pp. 15, 29–30, 79, 127–128; *Deutschland-Berichte,* II (1935), 663–664; Hans Mommsen, "Politische Perspektiven des aktiven Widerstandes gegen Hitler," in Hans Jürgen Schultz, ed., *Der Zwanzigste Juli: Alternative zu Hitler?* (Stuttgart and Berlin, 1974), p. 27; *Der alltägliche Faschismus: Frauen im Dritten Reich* (Berlin and Bonn, 1981), pp. 165–175; and the important new study by Detlev Peukert, *Die KPD im Widerstand: Verfolgung und Untergrundarbeit an Rhein und Ruhr 1933–1945* (Wuppertal, 1980), especially pp. 13–324, 420–429.

44. See the documents cited in n. 43 above.

45. According to the table in Gittig, *Tarnschriften*, p. 38.

46. Hence one has to read critically reports containing allegations against "Communists" and talking of "political" protest or strike. See activities report

Gau Süd-Hannover-Braunschweig for July to September 1933, NHSA, Hann. 310 I, B 13; doc. (July 31, 1936) in Broszat et al., eds., *Bayern*, p. 94; Winzer, *Jahre*, pp. 99, 101. Also docs. 67, 68 in Timpke, ed., *Dokumente*, pp. 285–305. Examples of realistic situation assessments by the Nazis are in Winzer, *Jahre*, p. 137; doc. 2 in Thévoz et al., eds., *Quellen*, p. 39; doc. 44 in Mason, *Arbeiterklasse*, p. 380. On the SPD resistance, see *Deutschland-Berichte*, I–VII (1934–1940).

47. See Eichholtz, *Geschichte*, I, 28, who speaks of "class struggle" and "united action" by the workers. Similarly, although more temperately, Mason, *Arbeiterklasse*, pp. 1–173. See the critiques by Ludolf Herbst, "Die Krise des nationalsozialistischen Regimes am Vorabend des Zweiten Weltkrieges und die forcierte Aufrüstung: Eine Kritik," *Vierteljahrshefte für Zeitgeschichte*, 26 (1978), 372; and Peter Hüttenberger in *Vierteljahrschrift für Sozial- und Wirtschaftsgeschichte*, 64 (1977), 125; Hüttenberger, "Nationalsozialistische Polykratie," *Geschichte und Gesellschaft*, 2 (1976), 440.

48. Docs. 2, 3 in Mason, *Arbeiterklasse*, pp. 195, 200.

49. Mason, "Labour," p. 132. A documented example of such inadvertent "resistance" is in the report of SS-Oberscharführer Stein, Freilassing, May 16, 1935, SAM, NSDAP/119.

50. This point is well argued by Andrew G. Whiteside, "The Nature and Origins of National Socialism," *Journal of Central European Affairs*, 17 (1957), 73, who in turn relies on observations by Karl Bednarik. In a more general context but applicable to the workers' situation, see the argument in Sebastian Haffner, *Anmerkungen zu Hitler*, 17th ed. (Munich, 1978), pp. 45–46. Also see the memoirs of Friedrich Christian Prinz zu Schaumburg-Lippe, *Zwischen Krone und Kerker* (Wiesbaden, 1952), pp. 165–166; and Domröse, *NS-Staat*, p. 331.

51. Georg Loewenstein, *Kommunale Gesundheitsfürsorge und sozialistische Ärztepolitik zwischen Kaiserreich und Nationalsozialismus — autobiographische, biographische und gesundheitspolitische Anmerkungen (Forschungsschwerpunkt Reproduktionsrisiken, soziale Bewegungen und Sozialpolitik an der Universität Bremen: Arbeitsbericht zu verschütteten Alternativen in der Gesundheitspolitik*, III, ed. Stephan Leibfried and Florian Tennstedt) (Bremen, [1980]), 24. Also see the examples in Hoegner, *Flucht*, p. 205; *Der alltägliche Faschismus*, p. 27; *Deutschland-Berichte*, II (1935), 298, 420, 426, 1079–80.

52. See doc. 2 in Thévoz et al., eds., *Quellen*, p. 39; Hoegner, *Flucht*, p. 127; Steinert, *Krieg*, p. 62; case of imprisoned former KPD member A.L. who promised allegiance to the new regime and eventually was released: correspondence Emmendingen, March–April 1933, SAF, 350/657.

53. Fischer to Gestapa, Münster, February 5, 1936, SAMs, Polit. Polizei, 3. Reich/441. In 1936, with a population of approximately 18,000, Gronau was the 321st-largest town in the German Reich. The figures are from various editions of *Statistisches Jahrbuch für das Deutsche Reich*; and "Alphabetisches Verzeichnis der Gemeinden," *Statistisches Jahrbuch Deutscher Gemeinden: Amtliche Veröffentlichung des Deutschen Ge-*

meindetages, 32 (1937), Part I.

54. Report about the current attitude within the Königsberg population, in particular the Königsberg workers, Königsberg, July 18, 1933, SAG, SF 6817, GA/17. Also see doc. (April 20, 1933) in Broszat et al., eds., *Bayern*, p. 210; activities report Gau Süd-Hannover-Braunschweig for December 1933, NHSA, Hann. 310 I, B 13; police station St. Pankraz to regional police, St. Pankraz, July 23, 1938, OLA, Pol. Akten/13; situation reports for Freilassing, Landsberg/Lech, and Altötting (1938–39), SAM, NSDAP/126; Steinert, *Krieg*, p. 61. Without qualification, I would not go as far as Hamilton, *Appeal*, p. 163, who writes that "the industrial workers . . . were, on the whole, satisfied with the new régime," a second-hand judgment based not on archival materials but on an opinion voiced by A. J. Nicholls.

55. The "Law for the Organization of National Labor," promulgated on January 20, 1934, was entirely in that propagandistic vein; it is reprinted in Rolf Fritzsche, *Aufbau der Wirtschaft im Dritten Reich* (Berlin-Charlottenburg, 1934), rp. 92–125. Choice examples of Nazi propaganda toward the workers after 1933 in: flyer, "Adolf Hitler und der Arbeiter," [1933], SAG, SF 6826, GA/98; speech by Ley, May 16, 1934, in Robert Ley, *Durchbruch der sozialen Ehre: Reden und Gedanken für das schaffende Deutschland*, ed. Hans Dauer and Walter Kiehl (Berlin, 1935), p. 139; report regarding Kreistagung for Ammersee on October 9, 1936, SAM, NSDAP/117. Critical reflections in: Broszat, *Staat*, p. 182; Schoenbaum, *Revolution*, pp. 80–81; Schweitzer, *Nazifizierung*, p. 140; Petzina, "Mobilisierung," p. 444; Mason, *Arbeiterklasse*, p. 5–6.

56. Fischer to Gestapa, Recklinghausen, June 6, 1935, SAMs, Polit. Polizei, 3. Reich/434; Scholtz-Klink/NSF for January 1938, BA, NS 22/860.

57. The more positive side of Kdf for the workers becomes apparent in a letter by Minister of Finance to presidents of Landesfinanzämter, Berlin, February 5, 1934, BA, R 43 II/557; "Was der K.D.F.-Fahrer wissen muss," [1937], BA, NS 5 I/212; Willy Müller, *Das soziale Leben im neuen Deutschland unter besonderer Berücksichtigung der Deutschen Arbeitsfront* (Berlin, 1938), p. 182; Hans Krapfenbauer, "Die sozialpolitische Bedeutung der NS.-Gemeinschaft 'Kraft durch Freude,'" Ph.D. dissertation, Nuremberg, 1937, p. 23; Merritt, "Strength," p. 66; Broszat, *Staat*, p. 204.

58. Anonymous letter to Boege, Leipzig, September 12, 1934, printed in Ley, *Durchbruch*, pp. 215–216.

59. On the "conversion" of former leftist party adherents and attitudes toward old-style unions, see Blank to Prussian ministry of the interior, Stolzenhagen, March 27, 1933, BDC, PK, PLA F. Heermann, report NSDAP-Ortsgruppe Judithen, Königsberg, July 14, 1933; situation report of Betriebsblock Strassenbahn, Königsberg, July 17, 1933, SAG, SF 6817, GA/17; acitvities report Gau Süd-Hannover-Braunschweig for May 1933; situation report Gau Süd-Hannover-Braunschweig for August 1933, NHSA, Hann. 310 I, B 13; Fritsch to Streicher, Erlangen, May 8, 1934, SAN, 503/81.

60. In my article "Hitler in a Social Context," *Central European History* 14 (1981), 243–272.

61. Positive sentiment toward Hitler on the part of the workers is expressed in the following sources, among others: report about the current attitude within the Königsberg population, in particular the Königsberg workers, Königsberg, July 18, 1933, SAG, SF 6817, GA/17; doc. (May 18, 1934) in Broszat, et al., eds., *Bayern*, p. 220; docs 2 and 3 in Thévoz et al., eds., *Quellen*, pp. 38 and 51.

62. See Winkler, "Stand." Also see Schweitzer, *Business*, pp. 146, 163; Schoenbaum, *Revolution*, p. 136; Broszat, *Staat*, pp. 217-218; Grunberger, *Reich*, pp. 169-170. From the East German point of view Lärmer argues a thesis of total subjection of small business by "monopoly capitalism," *Autobahnbau*, p. 40.

63. For an example of occasional, haphazard attempts by Nazi ideologues to change this, see Joseph Otto Plassmann, "Geleitwort," in Eugen Weiss, *Heute ist Richtfest* (Berlin-Lichterfelde, 1937), p. 7. For the peasants, see n. 76 below.

64. See Neumann, *Behemoth*, pp. 231-233; Gurland et al., *Fate*, p. 57; Winzer, *Jahre*, p. 133; Schweitzer, *Business*, pp. 142-144, 160-162, 176-177, 231; Schweitzer, *Nazifizierung*, pp. 154-170; Winkler, "Stand." Details on the coordination and National Socialist reconstruction of artisans' organizations after January 1933 are in Hans Meusch, "Das Handwerk im neuen Reich," *Jahrbücher für Nationalökonomie und Statistik*, 141 (1935), 301-331; Felix Schüler, *Das Handwerk im Dritten Reich: Die Gleichschaltung und was danach folgte* (Bad Wörishofen, 1951); Valentin Chesi, *Struktur und Funktionen der Handwerksorganisation in Deutschland seit 1933: Ein Beitrag zur Verbandstheorie* (Berlin, 1966).

65. Activities report Gau Süd-Hannover-Braunschweig for August 1933, NHSA, Hann. 310 I, B 13; Oberpräsident Ostpreussen to Dargel, Königsberg, July 16, 1934, SAG, SF 6816, GA/11; *Deutschland-Berichte*, II (1935), 1345. Official anti-chain store and co-op diatribes are in information reports of NSF, 11, Munich, April 8, 1933, HIS, 13/254; Konrad Mass, *Das erste Jahr der Regierung Hitler* (Munich, 1934), p. 10. Nazi apologies in defense of the institutions are in: directives, Berlin, July 23, 1934, BA, Schumacher/205; "SA. der NSDAP. Gruppe Südwest, Führungsabteilung," Stuttgart, March 29, 1936, SAL, PL/505 (pp. 8-11). Critical evaluations of the issue are in Gurland et al., *Fate*, pp. 51-53; Uhlig, *Warenhäuser*, pp. 71-182; Schweitzer, *Business*, p. 120; Broszat, *Staat*, pp. 212-213; Winkler, "Stand," pp. 5, 10; Schoenbaum, *Revolution*, pp. 141-147.

66. Activities report Gau Süd-Hannover-Braunschweig for November 1933, NHSA, Hann. 310 I, B 13; doc. 10 in Thévoz et al., eds., *Quellen*, p. 142; doc. 145 in Mason, *Arbeiterklasse*, p. 843; Gurland et al., *Fate*, pp. 61, 63-64; Domröse, *NS-Staat*, p. 319.

67. On price and wage levels, see Petzina, *Autarkiepolitik*, pp. 163-168. Also see doc. (June 1934) in Broszat et al., eds., *Bayern*, p. 224; doc. 8 in Thévoz et al., eds., *Quellen*, p. 114; Schelle to Gestapa, Münster, January 7, 1936, SAMs, Polit. Polizei, 3. Reich/440; "SA. der NSDAP. Gruppe Südwest, Führungsabteilung," Stuttgart, March 29, 1936, SAL, PL/505 (p. 7); doc. 30

in Schadt, ed., *Verfolgung*, p. 182; doc. 151 in Mason, *Arbeiterklasse*, p. 903; Gurland et al., *Fate*, pp. 62, 66–67; Schweitzer, Business, pp. 163, 184–187, 194–195; Schoenbaum, *Revolution*, pp. 139–140; Broszat, *Staat*, p. 212; Krohn and Stegmann, "Kleingewerbe," pp. 77–78.

68. Activities report Gau Süd-Hannover-Braunschweig for October 1933, NHSA, Hann. 310 I, B 13; doc. (January 12, 1934) in Broszat et al., eds., *Bayern*, p. 65; doc. 19 in Thévoz et al., eds., *Quellen*, p. 194; doc. 52 in Mason, *Arbeiterklasse*, p. 433; Scholtz-Klink/NSF for July–September 1937 and January–February 1939, BA, NS 22/860; situation report Landsberg/Lech for January–March 1939, SAM, NSDAP/126; *Deutschland-Berichte*, II (1935), 1345–48; Winkler, "Stand," p. 32.

69. Activities report Gau Süd-Hannover-Braunschweig for June 1933, NHSA, Hann. 310 I, B 13; activities report Kreis Wasserburg/Inn, October 1934, SAM, NSDAP/118; Stosch to Gestapa, Recklinghausen, June 6, 1935, SAMs, Polit. Polizei, 3. Reich/433; doc. 5 in Thévoz et al., eds., *Quellen*, p. 79; doc. (June 3, 1935) in Broszat et al., eds., *Bayern*, p. 83; Scholtz-Klink/NSF for July–September 1935, BA, NS 22/860; Gurland et al., *Fate*, pp. 58–59; Schweitzer, *Business*, p. 145.

70. Activities report Gau Süd-Hannover-Braunschweig for August 1933, NHSA, Hann. 310 I, B 13; Scholtz-Klink/NSF for March–April 1937, BA, NS 22/860; docs. 45, 104, 144, 151 in Mason, *Arbeiterklasse*, pp. 390, 642, 836, 899; Gurland et al., *Fate*, pp. 30–32, 59; Neumann, *Behemoth*, pp. 217–218, 231–232.

71. Hence the gloomy picture painted by Winkler, "Stand," appears considerably brighter in light of the following evidence: docs. 4, 5 in Thévoz et al., eds., *Quellen*, pp. 66, 78; Gau Westfalen-Nord, situation report for November 1936, SAMs, Gauleitung Westfalen-Nord, Gauschulungsamt/15; *Bremer Nachrichten*, January 22, 1936; situation report Freising for July–September 1938, SAM, NSDAP/126; Leitner to Stegerling, August 23, 1939, OLA, Pol. Akten/13; Theodor Noé, "Die Organisation der Reichsbetriebsgemeinschaft Handwerk," in *Festbuch zum Reichshandwerkertag 12. bis 23. Juni 1935 Frankfurt a. M.* [Berlin, 1935], pp. 57–58; Felix Schüler, "Die wirtschaftliche Entwicklung des Handwerks seit dem 30. Januar 1933," in *Festbuch zum Reichshandwerkertag*, p. 82. Also see the enlightening commentaries by Gurland et al., *Fate*, p. 100; Schweitzer, *Nazifizierung*, pp. 165, 171, 177; Mason, *Arbeiterklasse*, pp. 115–118; Krohn and Stegmann, "Kleingewerbe," p. 86.

72. Activities report Gau Süd-Hannover-Braunschweig for August 1933, NHSA, Hann. 310 I, B 13; reports about agriculture in Brunswick, 1934–1937, NAW 12 A Neu, 13 h/48714, cited hereafter as RAB; report Schwaermeyer, Hechingen, March 1, 1937, SAS, HO 235, I–VIII, F 7/2; Scholtz-Klink/NSF for March–April 1937 and January–February 1939, BA, NS 22/860; Schoenbaum, *Revolution*, pp. 163–164; doc. 150 in Mason, *Arbeiterklasse*, p. 865; doc. (June 27, 1939) in Broszat et al., eds., *Bayern*, p. 130. See also Domröse, *NS-Staat*, pp. 316, 318. On the SS emphasis on "peasant roots," see *Statistisches Jahrbuch der Schutzstaffel der NSDAP 1938* [Berlin, 1939], p. 103 (copy in IfZ); Heinrich Himmler, "Wesen und Aufgabe der SS und der

Polizei," [January 1937], in *Sammelheft ausgewählter Vorträge und Reden für die Schulung in nationalsozialistischer Weltanschauung und nationalsozialistischer Zielsetzung* (Berlin, 1939), pp. 151–152, 162–163; Michael H. Kater, "Die Artamanen — Völkische Jugend in der Weimarer Republik," *Historische Zeitschrift*, 213 (1971), 577–638.

73. See *Partei-Statistik* I, 137. Farquharson's assertion of a "general acceptance of the party on the land," *Plough*, p. 251, is somewhat dubious. According to tables 1 and 7 (columns A–E), farmer newcomers to the party were overrepresented from 1933 to 1936 and again in 1939, but underrepresented in 1937. For 1938 no significant deviations are discernible (according to a confidence interval test at the 95% level).

74. Farquharson, *Plough*, p. 67, also pp. vi, 53, 66. See the original reports: docs. 2, 3, 12, 13, 17 in Thévoz et al., eds., *Quellen*, pp. 39, 51, 159, 163, 181; docs. (October 1935) in Broszat et al., eds., *Bayern*, p. 87; Schelle to Gestapa, Münster, January 7, 1936, SAMs, Polit. Polizei, 3. Reich/440; RAB (October 1933 to November 1936). Also: Mass, *Jahr*, p. 48; Guillebaud, *Recovery*, pp. 154–165; Schoenbaum, *Revolution*, pp. 170–171; Poppinga, *Bauern*, p. 50; Petzina, "Hauptprobleme," pp. 39, 51–53; Petzina, *Wirtschaft*, p. 114–116; Jürgen von Kruedener, "Zielkonflikt in der nationalsozialistischen Agrarpolitik: Ein Beitrag zur Diskussion des Leistungsproblems in zentral gelenkten Wirtschaftssystemen," *Zeitschrift für Wirtschafts- und Sozialwissenschaften* (1974), 348.

75. Hence the overrepresentation of farmer newcomers to the party, 1933–1936: as in n. 73 above.

76. On the profarmer propaganda, see Fritzsche, *Aufbau*, pp. 36–37; entry for May 29, 1934, in *Das politische Tagebuch Alfred Rosenbergs 1934/35 und 1939/40*, ed. Hans-Günther Seraphim (Göttingen, 1956), p. 24. Also see *Nationalsozialistische Erziehung* (Osthannover), June 18, 1939, p. 287; Karlheinz Schmeer, *Die Regie des öffentlichen Lebens im Dritten Reich* (Munich, 1956), pp. 87–91; Schoenbaum, *Revolution*, pp. 48, 160–161. On the RNS and the regime's agrarian concepts, see Gies, "Reichsnährstand," pp. 229–233; Gies, "Aufgaben und Probleme der nationalsozialistischen Ernährungswirtschaft 1933–1939," *Vierteljahrschrift für Sozial- und Wirtschaftsgeschichte*, 66 (1979), 466–499; Puhle, *Agrarbewegungen*, p. 100; Poppinga, *Bauern*, p. 63.

77. See docs. (February 10 and December 6, 1937) in Broszat et al., eds., *Bayern*, pp. 361, 364; Oberpräsident Ostpreussen to Dargel, Königsberg, July 16, 1934, SAG, SF 6816, GA/11; Broszat, *Staat*, pp. 237–238; Domröse, *NS-Staat*, p. 317. Also the reflection in the general downward trend of new-membership figures in table 7, columns A–E.

78. Quotation from Schoenbaum, *Revolution*, p. 165. Also see pp. 164, 166–169; Friedrich Grundmann, *Agrarpolitik im "Dritten Reich": Anspruch und Wirklichkeit des Reichserbhofgesetzes* (Hamburg, 1979); RAB, such as for August–September 1937; Ortsgruppenleiter Wartenberg to Kreisleiter Erding, Wartenberg, November 30, 1933, SAM, NSDAP/443; docs. (1933–34) in Broszat et al., eds., *Bayern*, pp. 343, 346, 348; Karl Hopp, "Erbhofrecht in

Zahlen," *Deutsche Justiz*, p. 98 (1936), 1563–68; Broszat, *Staat*, pp. 236–237; Kruedener, "Zielkonflikt," pp. 341–345; Poppinga, *Bauern*, pp. 50–51; Domröse, *NS-Staat*, p. 316; Farquharson, *Plough*, pp. 138–140, 201.

79. See text at n. 29.

80. See especially the periodic reports RAB, January 1933 to about summer 1935.

81. RAB, summer 1935 to August 1938. Also see doc. (March 3, 1938) in Broszat et al., eds., *Bayern*, p. 367; Huber to Kreisleitung Traunstein, Heretshain, May 15, 1934, SAM, NSDAP/27 (SA); docs. 3, 10, 14 in Thévoz et al., eds., *Quellen*, pp. 51, 146, 166; Scholtz-Klink/NSF for March–April 1937, November–December 1938, January–February 1939, BA, NS 22/860; voluminous materials pertaining to Upper Austria in OLA, Politische Akten/13; situation report Altötting for January–March 1939, SAM, NSDAP/126; docs. 27, 36, 47, 96, 102, 150 in Mason, *Arbeiterklasse*, pp. 284, 336, 405, 614, 631–632, 867; Kühne, "Arbeitseinsatz," pp. 704–705; Gertrud Zypries, "Der Arbeitsdienst für die weibliche Jugend," in Paul Meier-Benneckenstein, ed., *Das Dritte Reich im Aufbau: Übersichten und Leistungsberichte*, II (Berlin, 1939), 420–426; Elisabeth Steiner, "Agrarwirtschaft und Agrarpolitik: Innere Zusammenhänge in der Agrarwirtschaft und ihre Tragweite für die Agrarpolitik," Ph.D. dissertation, Jena, 1939, pp. 25–28; *Das Junge Deutschland* (1939), p. 137; Poppinga, *Bauern*, p. 54; Farquharson, *Plough*, pp. 184–190, 197–198, 200; Wiesemann, "Arbeitskonflikte," pp. 573–590.

82. See RAB, 1935 to August 1938. Also: doc. (September 26, 1936) in Broszat et al., eds., *Bayern*, p. 96; Kreisleitung Wilhelmshaven, activities report April 1938, NSAO, 320, 2/2; Schelle to Gestapa, Münster, January 7, 1936, SAMs, Polit. Polizei, 3. Reich/440; Scholtz-Klink/NSF for March–April, July–September, November 1937, and April, May 1938, BA, NS 22/860; docs. 96, 104, 150 in Mason, *Arbeiterklasse*, pp. 620, 647, 866, also pp. 111–112; Steiner, "Agrarwirtschaft," p. 30; Schoenbaum, *Revolution*, pp. 171–173; Poppinga, *Bauern*, pp. 57, 59–61; Gies, "Aufgaben," pp. 470–495; Farquharson, *Plough*, pp. 79, 173, 192–197, 226. My findings contradict the earlier verdict by Petzina, *Autarkiepolitik*, p. 95, that profits in agriculture on the whole rose by 25% from 1935–36 to 1939.

83. Results of an analysis of BDC sample described in the Introduction near n. 47 and in Kater, "Quantifizierung" (for 1925–1944), and in table 4 in Kater, "Hitlerjugend," p. 614.

84. Figures for 1939 from *Beamten-Jahrbuch*, 26 (1939), 171, which refers to the 350,164 members of the RDB who belonged to the NSDAP, out of a total of 1.5 million RDB members. Since the RDB was a voluntary organization, the percentage of NSDAP members among civil servants in the Reich may be assumed to have been lower. On the genesis of the RDB, see Mursinsky and Brill, "Organisation." The percentages of 63% and 11% (members of civil service in the NSDAP, after and before January 1933, respectively), quoted by Schoenbaum, *Revolution*, p. 205, refer *only* to higher civil servants (on those, see text after n. 145). Schoenbaum has adopted these

figures uncritically from Gerhard Schulz, "Die Anfänge des totalitären Massnahmenstaates," in Karl Dietrich Bracher et al., *Die nationalsozialistische Machtergreifung: Studien zur Errichtung des totalitären Herrschaftssystems in Deutschland 1933/34*, 2d ed. (Cologne and Opladen, 1962), pp. 507–508, who in turn assumed them uncritically from [Erwin] Schütze, "Beamtenpolitik im Dritten Reich," in Hans Pfundtner, ed., *Dr. Wilhelm Frick und sein Ministerium: Aus Anlass des 60. Geburtstages des Reichs- und Preussischen Ministers des Innern Dr. Wilhelm Frick am 12. März 1937* (Munich, 1937), p. 56. Also see Kater, "Hitlerjugend," pp. 607–608.

85. See doc. (August 31, 1935) in Broszat et al., eds., *Bayern*, p. 85; Amt für Beamte to Gauleitung Süd-Hannover-Braunschweig, Hanover, December 7, 1933, NHSA, Hann. 310 I, B 13; minutes of speech by Rudolf Hess at Nuremberg Party Rally 1938, SAG, SF 6815, GA/6 (p. 7); Hermann Neef, *Das Beamtenorganisationswesen im nationalsozialistischen Staat: Vortrag . . . gehalten an der Verwaltungs-Akademie Berlin am 29.1.1935 im Rahmen einer Vortragsreihe "Das Dritte Reich"* (Berlin, 1935), pp. 8–9; Neef, *Die politisch-weltanschauliche Reorganisation der deutschen Beamten im Sinn und Geist des Nationalsozialismus: Rede gehalten auf dem Reichsparteitag 1935* (Berlin, 1935), p. 14; Otto Koellreutter, *Deutsches Verfassungsrecht: Ein Grundriss*, 2d ed. (Berlin, 1936), p. 163; Reinhard Höhn, "Der Beamte," *Deutsches Recht*, 7 (1937), 101–102; Schütze, "Beamtenpolitik," p. 51; Arnold Köttgen, "Die Stellung des Beamtentums im völkischen Führerstaat," *Jahrbuch des öffentlichen Rechtes der Gegenwart*, 25 (1938), 19, 22, 27–28, 52; Mursinsky and Brill, "Organisation," p. 155; Ernst Rudolf Huber, *Die verfassungsrechtliche Stellung des Beamtentums* (Leipzig, 1941), pp. 20–21, 24–30, 33, 45; Broszat, *Staat*, pp. 316–319. A caricature of the unchanged "apolitical" official is in Krüger, *Haus*, p. 30.

86. See the admissions by Fabricius, *Beamte*, p. 93; Huber, *Stellung*, p. 20; Rudolf Jordan, *Erlebt und erlitten: Weg eines Gauleiters von München bis Moskau* (Leoni, 1971), pp. 125–126.

87. On Hitler: Broszat, *Staat*, p. 160; Albert Speer, *Inside the Third Reich: Memoirs* (New York, 1970), pp. 53, 63. Aping Hitler was the Saxon Gauleiter Martin Mutschmann. See Bauer to Hess, Dresden, March 18, 1935, BDC, PK, PLA M. Mutschmann. On Frick: Mommsen, *Beamtentum*, p. 31; Broszat, *Staat*, p. 306, 313; Jane Caplan, "Bureaucracy, Politics and the National Socialist State," in Stachura, ed., *Shaping*, pp. 234–256; Caplan, "Civil Servant."

88. All the more so, since before the national elections of March 1933 the Nazis distributed a flyer in civil-service circles, attempting to counter the "lie" which was allegedly going around to the effect that the Nazi regime would dismiss all officials "who do not belong to the NSDAP." Flyer, "Deutsche Beamte erwacht!" [early March 1933], SAG, SF 6826, GA/98. Also see tables 6 and 7 (columns A–E); activities report Kreis Wasserburg/Inn, October 1934, SAM, NSDAP/118; Saul K. Padover, *Experiment in Germany: The Story of an American Intelligence Officer* (New York, 1946), pp. 151–152; Peter Diehl-Thiele, *Partei und Staat im Dritten Reich: Untersuchungen zum Verhältnis*

von NSDAP und allgemeiner innerer Staatsverwaltung 1933–1945, 2d ed. (Munich, 1971), p. 59. Diehl-Thiele's assumption (p. 59, n. 80) that officials might have been forced to join the party collectively is erroneous. See text of this chap. at n. 1 and chap. 6 at nn. 41 and 96. The pressures toward new political loyalties are well characterized in Krüger, *Haus,* p. 29. The mixed feelings with which many of the lower administrators served the Nazi regime, after an initial phase of elation, are sketched in Erwein von Aretin, *Krone und Ketten: Erinnerungen eines bayerischen Edelmannes,* ed. Karl Buchheim and Karl Otmar Freiherr von Aretin (Munich, 1955), pp. 230, 244–245.

89. *Partei-Statistik* I, 75; Mommsen, *Beamtentum,* p. 83.

90. Fabricius, *Beamte,* p. 97; Reich Interior Minister to Oberste Reichsbehörden et al., Berlin, March 20, 1934, GSPKB, 84a/12002; *Deutsche Justiz: Justizministerialblatt,* no. 13 (1934), p. 403; *Bayerische Staatszeitung,* June 9, 1934; OKH to special representative of Gauleiter . . . East Prussia, Berlin, April 21, 1938, SAG, SF 6817, GA/25; Walter Sommer, "Die NSDAP. und das Deutsche Beamtengesetz," *Deutsche Verwaltungsblätter,* 85 (1937), 83; Köttgen, "Stellung," p. 48; Rathke, *Beamter,* pp. 10, 31–32; docs. 1, 7, 9, 10, 11 in Mommsen, *Beamtentum,* pp. 166, 173, 175–178, also p. 31.

91. The German Civil Service Act of January 26, 1937, had made it very clear that civil servants were expected to be good National Socialists, if not Nazi party members. See Huber, *Stellung,* pp. 23–24; Sommer, "NSDAP.," pp. 81–82; Köttgen, "Stellung," p. 3; Schütze, "Beamtenpolitik," p. 60. In light of this, the situation reports by director of penal institutions Freiburg, Freiburg i.Br., January 24 and May 23, 1936 (GLAK, 309/1211) are highly significant.

92. *Die Deutsche Höhere Schule,* 3 (1936), 312–313; Pfundtner to Landesregierungen, Berlin, May 4, 1939, NAW, 12 A Neu, 13 h/19919; Verordnungsblatt Gau Süd-Hannover-Braunschweig, Parteigericht, August 1, 1939, BA, Schumacher/202; Bormann to all Reichsleiter and Gauleiter, Munich, July 4, 1935, BA, Schumacher/377; Huber, *Stellung,* p. 41; case of a Reichbahnassistent (March 1938), documented in Heyen, ed., *Quellen,* pp. 237–238; Diehl-Thiele, *Partei,* pp. 55–56.

93. Docs. (September 4, 1934 and March 1939) in Broszat et al., eds., *Bayern,* pp. 74, 520; activities report Gau Süd-Hannover-Braunschweig for November 1933, Hanover, December 19, 1933, NHSA, Hann. 310 I, B 13; doc. 10 in Thévoz et al., eds., *Quellen,* p. 140; Sperling to Fachschaftsleiter et al., Laufen/Obb., February 26, 1935, SAM, NSDAP/371; circular, Link to "Herr Berufskamerad!" Laufen/Obb., August 26, 1936, SAM, NSDAP/118; Gauamtsleiter, Amt für Beamte, to Gauleitung, Personalamt, Geisenfeld, November 6, 1936, SAM, NSDAP/28 (SA); Bavarian ministry of interior to subordinate agencies, Munich, January 5, 1936, BHSAM, MInn, 73437/22; Neef, *Reorganisation,* p. 22; Schütze, "Beamtenpolitik," p. 60; Gerhart Wehner, "Die rechtliche Stellung der Hitler-Jugend," Ph.D. dissertation, Leipzig, 1939, p. 112; Mommsen, *Beamtentum,* p. 75; Caplan, "Civil Servant," pp. 197, 330–332. Also see Jochen Klenner, *Verhältnis von Partei und Staat 1933–1945: Dargestellt am Beispiel Bayerns* (Munich, 1974), p. 191.

94. *Partei-Statistik* I, 75.

95. A rare example of pressure: Mansfeld, "An die Vertrauensleute in den Schulen!" Hamburg, June 10, 1937, FNSH, 964/NSLB.

96. Kater, "Hitlerjugend."

97. Doc. 132 in Mason, *Arbeiterklasse*, p. 771; Gauleitung Westfalen-Nord, situation report for November 1936, SAMs, Gauleitung Westfalen-Nord, Gauschulungsamt/15; Oppenheimer-Bluhm, *Standard*, pp. 19, 69; Steinert, *Krieg*, p. 65; Caplan, "Civil Servant," pp. 176–212; Caplan, "Bureaucracy," p. 249.

98. See Kerrl to Reich Minister of Finance, Berlin, May 8, 1939, BA, R 43 II/556 b; Sommer, "NSDAP.," p. 82; Huber, *Stellung*, p. 28.

99. See Hanns Anderlahn, "Der Volksschullehrer," *Das Junge Deutschland* (1938), 574; *Beamten-Jahrbuch*, 26 (1939), 170; Mommsen, *Beamtentum*, p. 192; Caplan, "Civil Servant," pp. 190–191, 205. Regarding the loss of prestige of the civil service corps, see Walter Tiessler, "Klassenkampf," *Der Hoheitsträger* (June 1939), 10; Huber, *Stellung*, p. 50; Broszat, *Staat*, p. 323. In order to attract more civil-service recruits, training periods were shortened and standards lowered by 1938–39. See *Nationalsozialistisches Bildungswesen*, 3 (1938), 503; *Der Deutsche Erzieher* (1939), 183–184. In view of these developments, Rathke's assessment of the recruitment situation in 1940 was totally unrealistic, *Beamter*, pp. 10, 31–32, 55.

100. Law for the Organization of National Labor, January 20, 1934, § 1, printed in Fritzsche, *Aufbau*, p. 92. A Nazi interpretation of this is in Mass, *Jahr*, pp. 39–40. Also see speech by Ley, May 16, 1934, in Ley, *Durchbruch*, pp. 142–143, 146; Bernhard Köhler, "Das Recht auf Arbeit als Wirtschaftsprinzip," in Meier-Benneckenstein, ed., *Das Dritte Reich im Aufbau*, I, 210–211; Otto Jamrowski, ed., *Handbuch des Betriebsführers: Betriebsführer-Lexikon* (Berlin, 1940), p. 44: Schoenbaum, *Revolution*, p. 65. Also see Kocka, *Angestellten*, pp. 178–180.

101. See Ortsgruppenbetriebswart, situation report for July 1933, Königsberg, July 14, 1933, SAG, SF 6817, GA/17; doc. 47 in Mason, *Arbeiterklasse*, p. 408; Mansfeld, "Sicherung," p. 154.

102. See: doc. 4 in Thévoz et al., eds., *Quellen*, p. 66; docs. 2 [*recte*: 3], 14, 40, 68 in Mason, *Arbeiterklasse*, pp. 194, 209, 235, 356, 505; Kühne, "Arbeitseinsatz," pp. 708–710; Jamrowski, ed., *Handbuch*, pp. 33–34; Kocka, *Angestellten*, pp. 183–184. Schoenbaum, *Revolution*, p. 98, writes that some of these older employees were used in blue-collar jobs. Also see text in chap. 6 at n. 27.

103. Docs. 96, 104, 150, 156 in Mason, *Arbeiterklasse*, pp. 619, 643–645, 873, 946.

104. This is based on an analysis of figures in Richard Bargel, *Neue deutsche Sozialpolitik: Ein Bericht über Grundgedanken, Aufbau und Leistungen* (Berlin, 1944), p. 53: the compound average annual rate of growth in percent for the highest-paid category of employees between 1933 and 1938 was 17.5%, the corresponding one for workers only 14.1%. Whereas there was no decrease in the category of lowest-paid workers, there was a compound

average annual decrease of 2.5% in that of the employees (calculations according to the formula in Floud, *Introduction,* p. 91). Also see the figures presented by Oppenheimer-Bluhm, *Standard,* pp. 41–43; and Grunberger, *Reich,* pp. 195–196.

105. Situation report for Freising, July–September 1938, SAM, NSDAP/126.

106. Hanns Hastler, *Grundriss des deutschen Arbeitsrechts* (Berlin-Charlottenburg, 1934), pp. 50, 84; Hastler, *Grundriss des deutschen Arbeitsrechts: Nachtrag* (Berlin-Charlottenburg, [1935]), pp. 15–16; *Materialien für den Erlass von Betriebsordnungen* (Berlin-Charlottenburg, 1934), pp. 26–27, 32, 59–61; Arthur Schöller, *Führer durch die Krankenversicherung* (Berlin, 1935), pp. 57–58; doc. 54 in Mason, *Arbeiterklasse,* p. 445; *Deutsche Justiz: Justizministerialblatt,* no. 13 (1934), p. 403; Schoenbaum, *Revolution,* pp. 115–116; Grunberger, *Reich,* pp. 195–196; Kocka, *Angestellten,* pp. 180, 185.

107. The figures were 19.5% for workers' sons and 28% for employees' sons in the Adolf-Hitler-Schulen. Similar percentages obtain for the elite schools Nationalpolitische Erziehungsanstalten (NPEA). See Scholtz, *Ausleseschulen,* p. 133; and text near n. 33. Also see Scholtz-Klink/NSF for January–February 1939, BA, NS 22/860. The quotation is from doc. 27 in Mason, *Arbeiterklasse,* p. 288.

108. During a trip from Saxony to the Black Forest in May 1935, blue-collar and white-collar workers were represented in the ratio of about 2:1. A similar ratio is reported for holiday hikes in Saxony throughout 1938. See Krapfenbauer, "Bedeutung," pp. 25–26; annual report 1938 of KdF Saxony, BA, NS 5 I/209 (p. 6). In October 1933, blue-collar and white-collar workers were represented in the DAF in the ratio of 3.7:1. Calculated according to figures in Schumann, *Nationalsozialismus,* p. 168. Also see Kocka, *Angestellten,* p. 186; Kater, "Wandel," pp. 49–50, 65, n. 156, and text near n. 40.

109. Rates of growth were calculated according to figures in Oppenheimer-Bluhm, *Standard,* p. 42 (procedure as indicated in n. 104 above). On the declining standards, see *Das Junge Deutschland* (1938), 567. Also see Schoenbaum, *Revolution,* pp. 114–115. The overall increase of clerks occurred notwithstanding the reduction of certain branches of white-collar employment, such as shop assistanceships, which decreased by 9% from 1933 to 1939. Broszat, *Staat,* p. 217.

110. The peak in 1938 represents a statistical distortion caused by the virtual absence of Nazi party newcomers from other occupational subgroups within the elite due to membership roll closure. In that year, primarily young people and Austrians (the latter of whom are not included in these figures) after the Anschluss of March 1938 were allowed to join. See tables 1, 6, and 7 (columns A–E). Also see n. 135.

111. Counts are from winter semester 1932–33 to summer semester 1933, and again to summer semester 1937. Calculated according to figures in *Statistisches Jahrbuch für das Deutsche Reich 1933,* pp. 523, 525; ibid., *1934,* pp. 534, 536; as well as Jacques R. Pauwels, "Women and University Studies

in the Third Reich, 1933-1945," Ph.D. dissertation, York University, 1976, p. 430. Details on the decline of university graduates are in Charlotte Lorenz, *Zehnjahres-Statistik des Hochschulbesuchs und der Abschlussprüfungen,* II (Berlin, 1943), 11-23, 38-43, 63-64. Only traditional and technical universities were considered. Until summer semester 1939, the decrease from 1933 was 50.1%. Also see Schoenbaum, *Revolution,* p. 273; Steinberg, *Sabers,* p. 153; *Das Junge Deutschland* (1938), 479, 482; Werner Lottmann, "Die Ausbildungsdauer auf den Hochschulen: Ein Problem der Bevölkerungspolitik und Begabtenförderung," *Das Junge Deutschland* (1938), 413; Christian Gizewski, "Zur Geschichte der Studentenschaft der Technischen Universität Berlin seit 1879," in Reinhard Rürup, ed., *Wissenschaft und Gesellschaft: Beiträge zur Geschichte der Technischen Universität Berlin 1879-1979,* I (Berlin, 1979), 133-140. The NSDAP membership figures mentioned in my article, "Contest," p. 247, are wrong, as they are based on a misinterpretation of data in Schoenbaum, *Revolution,* p. 72.

112. To a large degree the elation was based on the early decision of the regime to restrict the percentage of Jewish students who had been fiercely battled by the "Aryan" student population in the republican era. See Kater, *Studentenschaft,* pp. 145-162; Bleuel and Klinnert, *Studenten,* p. 246. Its most significant manifestation was the burning of "un-German" books on most campuses in May 1933. On this and the anti-Jewish measures see: docs. in Joseph Wulf, ed., *Literatur und Dichtung im Dritten Reich: Eine Dokumentation* (Gütersloh, 1963), pp. 41-56; Hans-Wolfgang Strätz, "Die studentische 'Aktion wider den undeutschen Geist' im Frühjahr 1933," *Vierteljahrshefte für Zeitgeschichte,* 16 (1968), 347-372; Manfred Franze, *Die Erlanger Studentenschaft 1918-1945* (Würzburg, 1972), pp. 185-188, 190-191; Faust, *Studentenbund,* II, 121-122; Steinberg, *Sabers,* p. 140; "Preussische Studentenrechtverordnung," April 12, 1933, in Joachim Haupt, *Neuordnung im Schulwesen und Hochschulwesen* (Berlin, 1933), p. 17; Albrecht Götz von Olenhusen, "Die 'nichtarischen' Studenten an den deutschen Hochschulen: Zur nationalsozialistischen Rassenpolitik 1933-1945," *Vierteljahrshefte für Zeitgeschichte,* 14 (1966), 175-206.

113. Kater, *Studentenschaft,* pp. 186-196.

114. Judging from figures for Erlangen in Franze, *Studentenschaft,* p. 214, anywhere from a quarter to a third of all male students were SA members in the summer of 1933. If the majority of these left the SA to enter the NSDAP, this would have increased the student newcomer contingent to a peak that year. See columns A and B of table 7. On SA pressures and organizational history at the universities, see Franze, *Studentenschaft,* pp. 215, 219-220; Bleuel and Klinnert, *Studenten,* p. 256; Faust, *Studentenbund,* II, 127; Steinberg, *Sabers,* pp. 147-148.

115. Grunberger, *Reich,* pp. 317-318; Anderlahn, "Volksschullehrer," p. 574.

116. Details are in: Bleuel and Klinnert, *Studenten,* pp. 249-255, 258-259; Otto B. Roegele, "Student im Dritten Reich," in Kuhn et al., *Universität,* pp. 158-160; Franze, *Studentenschaft,* pp. 254-288; Steinberg, *Sabers,* pp. 148,

151, 154-172; Faust, *Studentenbund,* II, 131-132. A telling example from Greifswald is in doc. 1 in Thévoz et al., eds., *Quellen,* p. 33.

117. Details on student government are in Franze, *Studentenschaft,* pp. 289-317; Faust, *Studentenbund,* II, 132; Steinberg, *Sabers,* pp. 142-144, 152. On the influential function of Scheel's office in recruiting new Nazi comrades, see Biller, circular 93, Munich, June 8, 1937, SAM, NSDAP/84.

118. See Haupt, *Neuordnung,* pp. 18, 22; Gauleitung Weser-Ems, activities report, April 1938, NSAO, 320, 2/2; Franz Alfred Six, "Nachwuchs und Auslese auf den deutschen Hochschulen," *Der deutsche Student,* 3 (1935), 192-193; Franze, *Studentenschaft,* pp. 224, 320-324, 330, 341-342; Bleuel and Klinnert, *Studenten,* pp. 253-257; Roegele, "Student," pp. 152-158; Kater, "Contest"; Schoenbaum, *Revolution,* pp. 84, 272-273; Steinberg, *Sabers,* pp. 141, 145, 151-152. The general atmosphere of regimentation is ably reflected in the documents in Guido Schneeberger, ed., *Nachlese zu Heidegger: Dokumente zu seinem Leben und Denken* (Berne, 1962).

119. Otto Reise, "Reform der Studienförderung," *Das Junge Deutschland* (1938), 427; Lottmann, "Ausbildungsdauer," pp. 425-426; *Der Deutsche Hochschulführer: Lebens- und Studienverhältnisse an den Deutschen Hochschulen,* 21 (1939), 27; Steinberg, *Sabers,* p. 145; Adam, *Hochschule,* pp. 108-109. On the Nazi institution of the (free) pre-university preparatory *Langemarck-Studium* (1938) and its ineffectiveness, see *Das Junge Deutschland* (1938), 482; Roegele, "Student," pp. 164-165; Schoenbaum, *Revolution,* pp. 274-275. A breakdown of an average student's semester expenses is in *Der Deutsche Hochschulführer,* p. 23.

120. See Biller, circular 93, Munich, June 8, 1937, SAM, NSDAP/84; Roegele, "Student," pp. 154-155; Geoffrey J. Giles, "The Rise of the National Socialist Students' Association and the Failure of Political Education in the Third Reich," in Stachura, ed., *Shaping,* p. 181.

121. Examples are in Gerhard Ritter, "Der deutsche Professor im 'Dritten Reich,'" *Die Gegenwart,* December 24, 1945, p. 24 (quotation); Steinberg, *Sabers,* pp. 137-138; doc. 16 in Thévoz et al., eds., *Quellen,* p. 178; anonymous report regarding conditions at the University of Marburg, [1936-37], IfZ, MA-227/5005329-31. Also see *Deutschland-Berichte,* II (1935), 702-706; entries for July 20 and August 22, 1935, in *In the Twenties: The Diaries of Harry Kessler,* pp. 471, 474; and for July 4, 1939, in Ulrich von Hassell, *Vom Andern Deutschland: Aus den nachgelassenen Tagebüchern 1938-1944,* 3d ed. (Zurich, 1947), p. 63. In light of this more up-to-date information, my earlier judgment regarding a comparatively firm loyalty by students toward the regime until 1943 has to be modified, "Contest," p. 247.

122. Typical is the case of "Jürgen" mentioned in Ursula von Kardorff, *Berliner Aufzeichnungen: Aus den Jahren 1942 bis 1945,* 3d ed. (Munich, 1962), p. 8: "Actually, he wanted to study history. In order to escape from the party, he joined the army full-time. After having served for two years and having been promoted to lieutenant, the war broke out." Also see Joachim Werner, "Zur Lage der Geisteswissenschaften in Hitler-Deutschland," *Schweizerische Hochschulzeitung,* 19 (1945-46), 79; Roegele, "Student,"

p. 165. On the function of the army as a refuge beyond the reach of the NSDAP, see Klaus-Jürgen Müller, *Das Heer und Hitler: Armee und national-sozialistisches Regime 1933–1940* (Stuttgart, 1969); Müller, *Armee, Politik und Gesellschaft in Deutschland 1933–1945: Studien zum Verhältnis von Armee und NS-System* (Paderborn, 1979), especially pp. 39–40, 43.

123. In this context, the following statement by a Nazi jurist is illuminating: "Only in those areas in which reason employs nothing but arithmetic computation, such as in mathematics, chemistry, physics, and astronomy, is the question of the *Volk* without significance." Robert Keimer, "Das Recht und der Nationalsozialismus," in Josef Wagner, ed., *Hochschule für Politik der Nationalsozialistischen Deutschen Arbeiterpartei: Ein Leit-faden,* 3d ed. (Munich, 1934), p. 82.

124. Calculations on the basis of figures in *Statistisches Handbuch,* p. 622. The school parallel is described in Kater, "Hitlerjugend." Also see: NS-Altherrenbund, circular II/38, Munich, September 23, 1938, SAM, NSDAP/119; *Das Junge Deutschland* (1938), 479–481; Rathke, *Beamter,* p. 89; Schoenbaum, *Revolution,* p. 274, n. 99; Bleuel and Klinnert, *Studenten,* p. 256; Kater, "Contest," pp. 241–242, 248, 258; Kleinberger, "Hoch-schulpolitik," pp. 18–19; and the case of Otto von H. (1934) in Erich Eber-mayer, *Denn heute gehört uns Deutschland . . . Persönliches und politisches Tagebuch: Von der Machtergreifung bis zum 31. Dezember 1935* (Hamburg and Vienna, 1959), pp. 440–441.

125. Tables 7 (columns A–E) and 1.

126. Schoenbaum, *Revolution,* p. 156.

127. See Linz, "Notes," p. 78, reporting the findings of Henry A. Turner, Jr. Typical of this attitude is the answer reported to have been given by Dr. Max Winkler, who later collaborated with the Nazis in occupied Poland, to Walther Funk, who asked for his cooperation in early 1933: "I am not a Nazi and will not join the party under any circumstances." Quoted in Margret Boveri, *Wir lügen alle: Eine Hauptstadtzeitung unter Hitler* (Olten and Freiburg i.Br., 1965), p. 230. The case of Dr. Ernst Leitz, Sr., owner of the Leica camera works in Wetzlar, is similar: Gaupersonalamt to Gauwirt-schaftsberater, Frankfurt/Main, November 26, 1942, HHSAW, 483/874. As an example of an industrial leader who made a point of joining the party in 1933 one could name Fritz Thyssen. See Turner, *Faschismus,* p. 106.

128. See the figures for managers and entrepreneurs in table 6 (column B) and table 7 (columns A–E).

129. Typical is the case of Dr. I. J., a medium entrepreneur in the Southwest German iron industry, as described in Gaupersonalamt to Gauwirt-schaftsberater, Frankfurt/Main, November 18, 1942, HHSAW, 483/874. Also see speech by Schmitt in Fritzsche, *Aufbau,* pp. 69–71, and see p. 21; doc. 21 in Eichholtz and Schumann, *Anatomie,* p. 106; doc. XIX in Stegmann, "Verhältnis," pp. 481–482; Max Frauendorfer, "Ständischer Auf-bau," *Grundlagen, Aufbau und Wirtschaftsordnung des nationalsozia-listischen Staates,* 3, no. 47 (1936), 17; Schweitzer, *Business,* pp. 124–125; Broszat, *Staat,* pp. 218–222; Turner, *Faschismus,* pp. 25–30;

Petzina, "Hauptprobleme," pp. 41, 46; Petzina, *Autarkiepolitik,* p. 22; Mason, *Arbeiterklasse,* p. 38.

130. Raimund Rämisch, "Der berufsständische Gedanke als Episode in der nationalsozialistischen Politik," *Zeitschrift für Politik,* n.s. 5 (1957), 269–272; Schweitzer, *Business,* pp. 249, 252; Broszat, *Staat,* pp. 193, 222. Formally, Feder did not lose his position as State Secretary in the Economics Ministry until after the Röhm affair, 1934. See Albrecht Tyrell, "Gottfried Feder and the NSDAP," in Stachura, ed., *Shaping,* pp. 78–79.

131. Schweitzer, *Business,* pp. 359, 367; Mason, *Arbeiterklasse,* p. 38; Udo Wengst, "Der Reichsverband der Deutschen Industrie in den ersten Monaten des Dritten Reiches: Ein Beitrag zum Verhältnis von Grossindustrie und Nationalsozialismus," *Vierteljahrshefte für Zeitgeschichte,* 28 (1980), 101. On the attitude of business, including intermediate business, toward strikes in the Weimar Republic, see Kater, "Die 'Technische Nothilfe,' " pp. 35–48, 73–75.

132. On that interrelationship, see Petzina, "Hauptprobleme," pp. 42–43. A more extreme (East German) interpretation is in Eichholtz, *Geschichte,* I, 37; and Eichholtz and Schumann, *Anatomie,* p. 14.

133. Neumann describes the atypical: *Behemoth,* p. 226. Typical of local businessmen who profited is the case of real estate broker Hans Koenig, related in Padover, *Experiment,* pp. 56–57. Also see Bernt Engelmann, *Deutschland ohne Juden: Eine Bilanz* (Munich, 1974), pp. 348–352. On the relationship between gradual economic recovery, business interests, and Nazi party membership in general, see Petzina, "Hauptprobleme," pp. 47–48; Padover, *Experiment,* p. 236.

134. Quotation is from Lange, "Ideologie," p. 81; also see p. 82. Also typical is the example of a bedding firm in Wiesbaden, related in Werner to Kreisleiter Wiesbaden, Wiesbaden, October 21, 1933, HHSAW, 483/2654. Further see Schweitzer, *Business,* p. 249; Schulz, "Anfänge," p. 649; Noakes and Pridham, eds., *Documents,* pp. 378–379.

135. The low point in the development for managers and entrepreneurs in 1938 is, mathematically, the result of a disproportionately greater influx of younger persons, mostly Hitler Youth students, and youngish intellectuals (see table 7 and n. 110). On the 1938 entrance regulations, see Anton Lingg, *Die Verwaltung der Nationalsozialistischen Deutschen Arbeiterpartei,* 2d ed. (Munich, 1940), p. 164; regulation Hess, August 11, 1937, in *Verfügungen/Anordnungen Bekanntgaben,* I (Munich, n.d.), 551–552. For regulations governing Austria, see only "Mitteilungsblatt des Gaues Niederdonau der NSDAP, Sondernummer," September 1, 1941, BA, Schumacher/206 (pp. 4–5). On the occasional contravention of these regulations, see the example for Berlin in Scholtz-Klink/NSF for May 1938, BA, NS 22/860.

136. Case is reported in Hagen, *Leader,* pp. 122–123. Also see Schweitzer, *Business,* pp. 398–399; Schoenbaum, *Revolution,* p. 156; Broszat, *Staat,* p. 229; doc. 131 in Mason, *Arbeiterklasse,* p. 768, and item 7 in table on p. 61 of that book.

137. See text near n. 37.

138. Speeches by Ley, April 14, 1934 (Düsseldorf); May 16, 1934 (Berlin), in Ley, *Durchbruch,* pp. 127-130, 140; doc. 3 in Thévoz et al., eds., *Quellen,* p. 51; Gau Westfalen-Nord, situation report for November 1936, SAMs, Gauleitung Westfalen-Nord, Gauschulungsamt/15; doc. 65 in Mason, *Arbeiterklasse,* pp. 485-486, also see pp. 32, 37, 41. On the good track record with DAF of Dr. E. L. (Wetzlar), see Gaupersonalamt to Gauwirtschaftsberater, Frankfurt/Main, November 26, 1942, HHSAW, 483/874. Further see *Deutschland-Berichte,* II (1935), 424; Schweitzer, *Nazifizierung,* pp. 144, 146-150; Grunberger, *Reich,* p. 194; Domröse, *NS-Staat,* p. 314; Wengst, "Reichsverband," p. 96; Hüttenberger, "Polykratie," p. 426.

139. Mass, *Jahr,* pp. 39-41; Schoenbaum, *Revolution,* pp. 92-93; Schweitzer, *Nazifizierung,* pp. 140-141.

140. See Winzer, *Jahre,* p. 131; Eichholtz and Schumann, *Anatomie,* p. 211; Eichholtz, *Geschichte,* I, 42-48. More temperately the West German historian Petzina, *Autarkiepolitik,* pp. 27, 118-124. The East German interpretation is briefly, if convincingly repudiated by Schoenbaum, *Revolution,* pp. 157-158; Andreas Dorpalen, "Weimar Republic and Nazi Era in East German Perspective," *Central European History,* 11 (1978), 223-224.

141. The changeover in actual production is demonstrated by the figures in Petzina, *Autarkiepolitik,* pp. 185-187; Mason, *Arbeiterklasse,* p. 61.

142. Quotation is from Rudolf Brinkmann, *Staat und Wirtschaft: Vortrag gehalten am 21. Oktober 1938 in Düsseldorf anlässlich der Reichstagung des Fachamtes Banken und Versicherungen in der Deutschen Arbeitsfront* (Stuttgart and Berlin, [1938]), p. 20. Examples of consumer production plants that were at a disadvantage are in docs. 33, 41, 45, 108 in Mason, *Arbeiterklasse,* pp. 324, 336, 360, 365, 395, 658; docs. 5, 11, 18, 19 in Thévoz et al., eds., *Quellen,* pp. 77, 155, 190, 194.

143. See Stosch to Gestapa, Recklinghausen, September 1, 1934, SAMs, Polit. Polizei, 3. Reich/428; Petzina, *Autarkiepolitik,* p. 33-34, 110-111. Also see Petzina, *Wirtschaft,* pp. 70-71; Berenice A. Carroll, *Design for Total War: Arms and Economics in the Third Reich* (The Hague and Paris, 1968), pp. 87-92.

144. Broszat, *Staat,* p. 230; Schoenbaum, *Revolution,* pp. 157-158. Also see Carroll, *Design,* pp. 126-158; Dieter Petzina, "Hitler und die deutsche Industrie: Ein kommentierter Literatur- und Forschungsbericht," *Geschichte in Wissenschaft und Unterricht,* 17 (1966), 489; Alan S. Milward, *The German Economy at War* (London, 1965), p. 3; Fritzsche, *Aufbau,* pp. 24-25, for signs of state decisionism in 1933-34. Further see: Broszat, *Staat,* pp. 223-225; Petzina, *Autarkiepolitik,* pp. 45-51, 102-105, 116. Hitler's memorandum of August 26, 1936, is printed as doc. 48 in Eichholtz and Schumann, *Anatomie,* pp. 146-150.

145. Robert Thévoz et al., eds. *Pommern 1934/35 im Spiegel von Gestapo-Lageberichten und Sachakten (Darstellung)* (Cologne and Berlin, 1974), p. 78; activities report Gau Süd-Hannover-Braunschweig for November 1933, NHSA, Hann. 310 I, B 13; docs. 5, 9 in Thévoz et al., eds., *Quellen,*

pp. 74, 130; doc. (September 3, 1937) in Broszat et al., eds., *Bayern,* p. 105; *Deutschland-Berichte,* II (1935), 271, 1500-03; Petzina, "Hauptprobleme," pp. 51-52; Schoenbaum, *Revolution,* pp. 180-182; Poppinga, *Bauern,* 59, 61, 64; Lärmer, *Autobahnbau,* p. 45; Puhle, *Agrarbewegungen,* pp. 95-96, 98-102. Also see the sketch in Ilse McKee, *Tomorrow the World* (London, 1960), pp. 24-25.

146. See Krebs, *Schulenburg,* pp. 101-103; Orlow II, p. 24; Dr. Pfeiffer to Landrat, Emmendingen, March 29, 1933, SAF, 350/657. On the planned reform, destined never to be carried out, see Frank, *Angesicht,* p. 179; Wilhelm Frick, *Der Neubau des Dritten Reiches: Vortrag, gehalten vor Offizieren der Reichswehr am 15. November 1934* (Berlin, 1934), p. 15; *Heeresadjutant bei Hitler 1938-1943: Aufzeichnungen des Majors Engel,* ed. Hildegard von Kotze (Stuttgart, 1974), p. 120.

147. *Die Weizsäcker-Papiere 1933-1950,* ed. Leonidas E. Hill (Frankfurt/ Main, 1974), p. 73; doc. 63 in Timpke, ed., *Dokumente,* pp. 272-273.

148. This law affected higher civil servants much more decisively than lower and intermediate ones. See Huber, *Stellung,* pp. 21-22; Köttgen, "Stellung," p. 22; doc. 7 in Mommsen, *Beamtentum,* p. 147; Schütze, "Beamtenpolitik," pp. 51, 55-56; Broszat, *Staat,* p. 306; Caplan, "Civil Servant," pp. 129-130; Wolfgang Runge, *Politik und Beamtentum im Parteienstaat: Die Demokratisierung der politischen Beamten in Preussen zwischen 1918 und 1933* (Stuttgart, 1965), pp. 239-244. Many of the dismissed jurists were forced to devote themselves to private law practice, and even that was made difficult for them. Karl Siegfried Bader, *Die deutschen Juristen* (Tübingen, 1947), p. 34; Hoegner, *Flucht,* pp. 217-218.

149. One contemporary party opinion was, "A part of the bureaucracy just cannot get over the fact that our Reich is without a 'constitution' " — confidential report from Ley's office, [August 1939], BA, Schumacher/375. In a similar vein: Schmitt, *Staat,* p. 6. To be sure, for anyone who could grasp this strange logic, Nazi jurists argued that the NSDAP had assumed the functions of the constitution: "[Die NSDAP] ist die verfassungstragende Bewegung des völkischen Reiches," Huber, "Rechtsgestalt," p. 324. Also see text near n. 85.

150. See Huber, *Stellung,* pp. 23, 25, 30, 38, 41; Otto Koellreutter, *Deutsches Verwaltungsrecht: Ein Grundriss* (Berlin, 1936), p. 37; Koellreutter, *Verfassungsrecht,* p. 177; Curt Rothenberger, *Der Deutsche Richter* (Hamburg, 1943), pp. 16-17, 43, 49-51; William Sweet, "The Volksgerichtshof: 1934-45," *Journal of Modern History,* 46 (1974), 315-317; Hans Peter Bleuel, *Strength through Joy: Sex and Society in Nazi Germany* (London, 1973), p. 147. Top Nazi jurist Hans Frank's protestations after the war, expressed in his memoirs, *Angesicht,* pp. 169-180, 342, that he had constantly tried to stand up for "The Law" only to bring upon himself the Führer's wrath, are belied by his contemporary statements, as in Frank, *Recht und Verwaltung: Rede, gehalten anlässlich der Schulungstagung für Rechtswahrer der Verwaltung der deutschen Ostmark und des Sudetengaues in Berchtesgaden am 5. Dezember 1938* (n.pl., [1939]), p. 7; and in Rudolf Schraut, ed., *Deutscher Juristentag 1933: 4. Reichstagung des Bundes Nationalsozialistischer Deutscher Juristen*

e. V.: Ansprachen und Fachvorträge (Berlin, 1933). The various commentaries in this volume convey an excellent impression of the perversion of the legal system under Nazi rule. Also see *Beamten-Jahrbuch,* 26 (1939), 201–202.

151. Michael H. Kater, "Ansätze zu einer Soziologie der SA bis zur Röhmkrise," in Engelhardt et al., eds., *Bewegung,* p. 825; Broszat, *Staat,* p. 310. On the impact of the Röhm affair on the German intelligentsia, see text in chap. 6 at n. 110.

152. See Krebs, *Schulenburg,* pp. 127–139, 154–177; Frank, *Recht,* p. 14; Mursinsky and Brill, "Organisation," pp. 159–160; Neumann, *Behemoth,* pp. 309–310; Broszat, *Staat,* p. 323; and the examples Dr. Zaeschmar (1939) in Ebermayer, *Deutschland,* p. 430; and Assessor M., in folder Hugo Mailinger (1938–39), SAM, NSDAP/28 (SA); Mommsen, *Beamtentum,* pp. 91–123.

153. See text near nn. 85–93; table 7.

154. On this, see Tisch, "Problem," p. 57; Broszat, *Staat,* pp. 306–307, also pp. 294–297, 311, 313; docs. 3 f, 3 k in Mommsen, *Beamtentum,* pp. 188, 192–193, also p. 82; Jochen von Lang, *The Secretary: Martin Bormann: The Man Who Manipulated Hitler* (New York, 1979), p. 109; case histories in: correspondence, head, Freiburg correctional institutions (1936–37), GLAK, 309/1211; Peterson, *Limits,* pp. 308–309, 360–361, 393; Orlow II, p. 226.

155. See text near nn. 122–124. Also the following documents relating specifically to the higher civil-service trainee sector: Otto von H. to Ebermayer, Berlin, November 26, 1934, in Ebermayer, *Deutschland,* pp. 440–441; "Denkschrift an Reichsführer-SS. Erziehungsnachwuchs 1942. Abgeschlossen 15.3.42," BA, NS 19, Neu/1531; Martin Jonas, "Die Justizausbildungsordnung vom 22. Juli 1934," *Deutsche Justiz: Rechtspflege und Rechtspolitik,* 96 (1934), 996; Schütze, "Beamtenpolitik," pp. 57–58; *Nationalsozialistisches Bildungswesen,* 1 (1936), 737, and 3 (1938), 478; *Berliner Tageblatt,* July 23, 1937; docs. 3 k, 7 in Mommsen, *Beamtentum,* pp. 147, 192; Rothenberger, *Richter,* p. 55; Caplan, "Civil Servant," pp. 190, 265–266, 306.

156. Unfortunately, empirical data on professors were not available in sufficient plenitude to warrant a separate examination of their NSDAP membership pattern. But since their situation was in many ways similar to that of the academically schooled professionals, one may imagine their new party membership pattern to have been somewhere between that of the high state officials (of whom they formed a part) and that of the academic professionals. See table 7 (columns A–E).

157. See the incisive comment in Andreas Feickert, *Studenten greifen an: Nationalsozialistische Hochschulrevolution* (Hamburg, 1934), p. 32; and the intelligent reflections in Aretin, "Universität," p. 694; and Anselm Faust, "Professoren für die NSDAP: Zum politischen Verhalten der Hochschullehrer 1932/33," in Heinemann, ed., *Erziehung,* II, 31–49.

158. Details in Otto Koellreutter, "Grundfragen unserer Volks- und Staatsgestaltung," in Meier-Benneckenstein, ed., *Das Dritte Reich,* I, 88–89 (on Koellreutter); Martin Heidegger, *Die Selbstbehauptung der deutschen Universität: Rede, gehalten bei der feierlichen Übernahme des Rektorats der Universität Freiburg i. Br. am 27.5.1933* (Breslau, 1934); Schneeberger, ed.,

Nachlese; Hamilton, *Appeal,* pp. 146–149 (on Heidegger); Geoffrey J. Giles, "University Government in Nazi Germany: Hamburg," *Minerva,* 16 (1978), 196–221 (on Adolf Rein); Ernst Nolte, "Zur Typologie des Verhaltens der Hochschullehrer im Dritten Reich," *Aus Politik und Zeitgeschichte: Beilage zur Wochenzeitung Das Parlament,* November 17, 1965, pp. 3–14 (on Baeumler, Krieck, and the general issue); Adam, *Hochschule,* pp. 34, 40, 173 (on various prominent scholars at Tübingen University); Franze, *Studentenschaft,* pp. 345–351 (on various prominent scholars at Erlangen University); Kater, "Contest," pp. 235–236, 253–254; Grunberger, *Reich,* pp. 307–309; Gerd Rühle, *Das Dritte Reich: Dokumentarische Darstellung des Aufbaues der Nation* (Berlin, 1933), p. 157. Also see Michael H. Kater, *Das "Ahnenerbe" der SS 1935 bis 1945: Ein Beitrag zur Kulturpolitik des Dritten Reiches* (Stuttgart, 1974); and Volker Losemann, *Nationalsozialismus und Antike: Studien zur Entwicklung des Faches Alte Geschichte 1933–1945* (Hamburg, 1977).

159. Hitler, *Mein Kampf,* p. 635.

160. The Law for the Reconstitution of the Civil Service of April 7, 1933, inasmuch as it removed Jewish academics from university positions, catered especially to the traditional anti-Semitic sentiments of many of Germany's higher academics. See text near n. 85 in chap. 3. Also see Koellreutter, "Grundfragen," pp. 93–94; Ernst von Hippel, *Die Universität im neuen Staat* (Königsberg, 1933), pp. 19–20; Wolfgang Trillhaas, *Aufgehobene Vergangenheit: Aus Meinem Leben* (Göttingen, 1976), p. 169; Adam, *Hochschule,* p. 79; Steinberg, *Sabers,* p. 136; Franze, *Studentenschaft,* p. 343; Grunberger, *Reich,* pp. 308–309. Paragraphs 1–7 of the law of April 7, 1933, are reprinted in Rühle, *Das Dritte Reich,* pp. 112–113.

161. Joseph Pascher, "Das Dritte Reich, erlebt an drei deutschen Universitäten," in Kuhn et al., *Universität,* pp. 53–55; Paul E. Kahle, *Bonn University in Pre-Nazi and Nazi Times (1923–1939): Experiences of a German Professor* (London, 1945), pp. 16–17; Friedrich Neumann, "Die Deutsche Hochschule," in Benze and Gräfer, eds., *Erziehungsmächte,* pp. 178–179; Trillhaas, *Vergangenheit,* pp. 164–167; Adam, *Hochschule,* pp. 122, 136–137, 207; Kelly, "National Socialism," pp. 66–68, 96–98, 100, 108, 338–339. Some qualifications are in Kater, "Machtergreifung," pp. 69–70. The unfortunate case of nonjoiner Dozent Dr. Lysinski (Mannheim) is treated in Reinhard Bollmus, *Handelshochschule und Nationalsozialismus: Das Ende der Handelshochschule Mannheim und die Vorgeschichte der Errichtung einer Staats-und Wirtschaftswissenschaftlichen Fakultät an der Universität Heidelberg 1933/34* (Meisenheim/Glan, 1973), pp. 115–116, n. 308.

162. Kelly, "National Socialism," pp. 374–375.

163. See ibid., p. 318; also Trillhaas, *Vergangenheit,* pp. 162–165; Reich Education Minister to subordinate agencies, Berlin, June 24, 1938; director, prehistoric section of Brunswick museum, to Brunswick Minister of Education, Brunswick, October 24, 1938, NAW, 12 A Neu, 13 h/1866; Volker Losemann, "Zur Konzeption der NS-Dozentenlager," in Heinemann, ed., *Erziehung,* II, 87–109.

164. "Aussprache der Kreisamtsleiter mit den Referenten der Behörden am 6. April 1936 auf der Insel Reichenau," SAL, PL 512/II, N, 98, 2; memorandum by NSDAP-Kreisleitung Wetterau for May–June 1939, HHSAW, 483/5536. Also see Rühle, *Das Dritte Reich,* p. 156; Haupt, *Neuordnung,* p. 22; M. Boveri's observations in *Berliner Tageblatt,* 1933 and 1936, reprinted in Boveri, *Wir Lügen,* pp. 98, 505; Schumann, report NSLB Meissen for May 1934, HIS, 13/248; Kater, "Contest," pp. 250–252; Kelly, "National Socialism," pp. 106, 376–377.

165. Details regarding exceptions, notably that of psychology professor Wolfgang Köhler, pertain to older faculty: Köhler himself was close to retirement. See Mary Henle, "One Man against the Nazis—Wolfgang Köhler," *American Psychologist* (October 1978), 940–943; *Deutsche Allgemeine Zeitung,* April 28, 1933; Adam, *Hochschule,* pp. 202, 204; Giles, "University Government," p. 202; Kelly, "National Socialism," pp. 54, 103. Also Pascher, "Das Dritte Reich," pp. 64–66; Kahle, *Bonn University,* p. 34–35; Karl Saller, *Die Rassenlehre des Nationalsozialismus in Wissenschaft und Propaganda* (Darmstadt, 1961), pp. 43–46.

166. See Lottmann, "Ausbildungsdauer," p. 421; Feickert, *Studenten,* p. 35; Neumann, "Hochschule," p. 178–179.

167. For the general problems of intellectuals in the first few years of the Third Reich, see Michael H. Kater, "Anti-Fascist Intellectuals in the Third Reich," *Canadian Journal of History,* 16 (1981), 263–277; Wolfgang Schieder, "Schriftsteller im Dritten Reich," in Werner Link, ed., *Schriftsteller und Politik in Deutschland* (Düsseldorf, 1979), 83–99; and the essays in Corino, ed., *Intellektuelle.* Also see *Deutschland-Berichte,* II (1935), 226–229.

168. On the situation of journalistic writers, see Karl-Dietrich Abel, *Presselenkung im NS-Staat: Eine Studie zur Geschichte der Publizistik in der nationalsozialistischen Zeit* (Berlin, 1968), pp. 29–37, 60–68, 71–72; Boveri, *Wir Lügen,* especially pp. 177, 185, 256, 271; Bella Fromm, *Blood and Banquets: A Berlin Social Diary,* 2d ed. (New York and London, 1942), p. 103; Ebermayer, *Deutschland,* p. 537; Norbert Frei, *Nationalsozialistische Eroberung der Provinzpresse: Gleichschaltung, Selbstanpassung und Resistenz in Bayern* (Stuttgart, 1980), pp. 15, 182–183, 307–313; Jochen Klepper, *Unter dem Schatten deiner Flügel: Aus den Tagebüchern 1932–1942* (Stuttgart, 1965), pp. 33–796; and the characteristic remarks by the editorial staff of *Kölnische Zeitung,* May 20, 1933, in *Sechs Bekenntnisse zum neuen Deutschland: Rudolf G. Binding, E. G. Kolbenheyer, Die "Kölnische Zeitung," Wilhelm von Scholtz, Otto Wirz, Robert Fabre-Luce antworten Romain Rolland* (Hamburg, 1933), pp. 9–13.

169. See the acid commentary by Hermann Rauschning, *Die Revolution des Nihilismus: Kulisse und Wirklichkeit im Dritten Reich,* 4th ed. (Zurich and New York, 1938; 1st ed., 1937), pp. 144–145.

170. Doc. 151 in Mason, *Arbeiterklasse,* p. 898; Hamilton, *Appeal,* pp. 150–154, 164–166; Ebermayer, *Deutschland,* p. 249; Fritz Kortner, *Aller Tage Abend,* 2d ed. (Munich, 1959), pp. 425–426; Laqueur, *Weimar,* pp. 267–268; Mosse, *Final Solution,* p. 196. On Benn, see Jürgen Schröder, "Benn in den

dreissiger Jahren: Klaus Ziegler zum Gedenken," in Corino, ed., *Intellektuelle,* pp. 55–59. On Mann, see Paul Hübinger, "Thomas Mann und Reinhard Heydrich in den Akten des Reichsstatthalters v. Epp," *Vierteljahrshefte für Zeitgeschichte,* 28 (1980), 111–143; Thomas Mann, *Tagebücher 1933–1934,* ed. Peter de Mendelssohn (Frankfurt/Main, 1977); and Kater, "Intellectuals," pp. 270–271. Also see the scathingly critical novel by Thomas Mann's son Klaus Mann, *Mephisto: Roman einer Karriere* (Amsterdam, 1936), allegorizing stage actor Gustav Gründgens's career in the Third Reich. On Brecht and Graf, see Günter Albrecht et al., *Lexikon deutschsprachiger Schriftsteller: Von den Anfängen bis zur Gegenwart,* I, 2d ed. (Leipzig, 1972), 102, 283. Examples of an "intellectual's" rationalization of Nazi doctrine are in Hermann Schwarz, *Christentum, Nationalsozialismus und Deutsche Glaubensbewegung,* 2d ed. (Berlin, 1938); Schwarz, "Zur philosophischen Grundlegung des Nationalsozialismus," in Meier-Benneckenstein, ed., *Das Dritte Reich,* I, 13, 15, 28. This attitude is all but ridiculed by a Nazi critic, Andreas Pfenning, "Gemeinschaft und Staatswissenschaft: Versuch einer systematischen Bestimmung des Gemeinschaftsbegriffes," *Zeitschrift für die gesamte Staatswissenschaft,* 96 (1936), 301–302. See the incisive comment by Neumann, *Behemoth,* p. 379.

171. See Ludwig, *Technik,* pp. 105–106, 130, 136–137; the essays in Mehrtens and Richter, eds., *Naturwissenschaft;* and the prewar chapters in Speer, *Reich.* Hermann Rauschning's observation, "it is curious to note how many engineers Hitler drew into his select circle"—*Men of Chaos* (Freeport, N.Y., 1971; first published, 1942), p. 230—deserves consideration in this context.

172. The evidence on membership is scant, but locally revealing: of 148 jurists in Munich and Upper Bavaria that were sampled for 1938–39, 52.7% had either taken out Nazi party membership or had applied for it. File sheets in SAM, NSDAP/54. Also see Hüttenberger, "Interessenvertretung," pp. 431–432.

173. Speech by Wagner at Reich Party Rally 1934, in Leonardo Conti, ed., *Reden und Aufrufe: Gerhard Wagner 1888–1939* (Berlin and Vienna, 1943), p. 85.

174. On the unpopularity of lawyers with the regime, see Tiessler, "Klassenkampf," p. 10. Undoubtedly, even some Nazi lawyers tried to help their clients in and out of court and some even risked concentration camp internment. See Thévoz et al., eds., *Darstellung,* p. 188; Baden Minister of the Interior to district offices et al., Karlsruhe, February 7, 1934, SAF, 317/1267; Gertraud and Erwin Herrmann, "Nationalsozialistische Agitation und Herrschaftspraxis in der Provinz: Das Beispiel Bayreuth," *Zeitschrift für Bayerische Landesgeschichte,* 59 (1976), 239; Hoegner, *Flucht,* pp. 211–212; case of Dr. Valentin Heins in Hübinger, "Thomas Mann"; and the highly moving accounts in Dietrich Güstrow, *Tödlicher Alltag: Strafverteidiger im Dritten Reich* (Berlin, 1981). On Koellreutter, Forsthoff, et al., see A. Voigt, "Die Staatsrechtslehrer und das Dritte Reich: Eine Auswahl," *Zeitschrift für Religions- und Geistesgeschichte,* 31 (1979), 195–202; Erich Döhring, *Geschichte der juristischen Fakultät 1665–1956* (Neumünster, 1965),

pp. 209–219. The "Jewish problem" in the legal profession surfaces in Beck, *Kampf,* p. 184; docs. (1933–1935) in Broszat et al., eds., *Bayern,* pp. 433–435, 442; Klipp to Grote, Weimar, November 16, 1934, UK, PLA/215. The debarring process for Jewish attorneys-at-law took place from November 1938 to February 1939. See "Fünfte Verordnung zum Reichsbürgergesetz," September 27, 1938, in Johannes Buettner, ed., *Der Weg zum nationalsozialistischen Reich: Dokumente zur Verwirklichung des Programms der NSDAP.* (Berlin, 1943), I, 151. A successful Nazi lawyer's career is described in Henry V. Dicks, *Licenced Mass Murder: A Socio-Psychological Study of Some SS Killers* (Sussex, 1972), p. 205. Also see Aretin, *Krone,* pp. 237, 250–251, 258–259. On the BNSDJ after 1933 and on Frank's role there, see Schulz, "Anfänge," p. 518; Frank, *Angesicht,* pp. 164–165, 169. The perversion of the law is manifest in Keimer, "Recht," pp. 81–82.

175. The figure is based on personal details recorded on membership cards of 4,177 members of the Reich Physicians' Chamber (Reichsärztekammer — RÄK), to which all practicing physicians in the Third Reich had to belong. See Bauer, Cropp, and Walther, *Der Arzt* (Berlin, 1938), p. 55. The sample of 4,177 represents a total of about 79 million membership cards housed in the BDC. My findings on the Reich scale are supported by the following local figures: a list of physicians from Laufen and Berchtesgaden (Upper Bavaria) indicates that in February 1935, of a total of 32 doctors, 16 belonged to the NSDAP. The list is in SAM, NSDAP/371.

176. The calculation (0.72% doctors in the NSDAP; 0.26% doctors in the Reich population) is based on a count of physicians, dentists, and veterinarians in the BDC sample (1925–1944) described in the Introduction at nn. 46–47, as well as on figures for those groups in *Berufszählung . . . 16. Juni 1933,* pp. 48–51, 108 (figures for 1933 census). In the overall counts, only gainfully employed persons and students were considered.

177. See figure 6.

178. "Reichsärzteordnung," December 13, 1935, *Reichsgesetzblatt* (1935), Part I, 1433–44.

179. There is convincing documentation regarding the questionable activities of the Association of German Health Insurance Physicians (Kassenärztliche Vereinigung Deutschlands — KVD) in the private archives of the Bundeskassenärztliche Vereinigung Deutschlands in West Berlin. Also see the articles in Gerhard Baader and Ulrich Schultz, eds., *Medizin und Nationalsozialismus: Tabuisierte Vergangenheit — Ungebrochene Tradition?* (Berlin, 1980).

180. In 1933, about 14% of all physicians in the Reich were Jewish. Siegfried Ostrowski, "Vom Schicksal jüdischer Ärzte im Dritten Reich: Ein Augenzeugenbericht aus den Jahren 1933–1939," *Bulletin des Leo Baeck Instituts,* 6 (1963), 314. On January 1, 1934, as many as 46.8% of all practicing physicians in Berlin were said to be Jewish. Speech by G. Wagner at Reich Party Rally 1934, in Conti, ed., *Reden,* p. 85. A partisan Nazi doctors' functionary mentioned a figure for Berlin of 65–70% for March 1934. See Vorsitzender to Schmeller, Berlin, March 21, 1934, UK, PLA/207. From the Berlin

Charité hospital, 96 Jews were dismissed on March 31, 1933, leaving 181 Gentiles behind. Gert H. Brieger, "The Medical Profession," in Henry Friedlander and Sybil Milton, eds., *The Holocaust: Ideology, Bureaucracy, and Genocide* (New York, 1980), p. 145. Until 1945, 5,500 Jewish doctors had been eliminated from the German medical scene. Grunberger, *Reich,* p. 220. Also see Engelmann, *Deutschland,* pp. 71–98. The figure of 10,000 Jewish doctors (as opposed to 38,000 "Aryan" ones), presented by Gumpert, *Hunger,* p. 115, is probably exaggerated.

181. Jews constituted 7.8% of all medical students in the winter semester of 1932–33. The faculty with the highest percentage of Jewish students (10.4%) was the philosophical one. See table 11 in Kater, *Studentenschaft,* pp. 218–219.

182. The social-mindedness of Jewish doctors in Berlin is vouched for by Ostrowski, "Schicksal," p. 314.

183. Statement by Wertheim as quoted in Hagen, *Leader,* p. 47.

184. Jewish physicians were not legally prohibited from practicing medicine until September 30, 1938. "Vierte Verordnung zum Reichsbürgergergesetz," July 25, 1938, in Buettner, *Weg,* I, 150. The entire process of legalistic and arbitrary proscription is well detailed in Ostrowski, "Schicksal," pp. 319–351.

185. KVD chapter Waldenburg to KVD Lower Silesia, Waldenburg, September 5, 1935; declaration of 14 "Aryan" doctors, Waldenburg, September 22, 1934, and other documents relating to case of Dr. M., in UK, PLA/235. Also see case of Dr. G. B. (1937–38), UK, PLA/130/131.02; case of Dr. O. (1933–1935), UK, PLA/217; case of Dr. W. (1937), UK, PLA/248; case of Dr. St. (1933–1938), UK, PLA/130/123.02; case of Dr. T., whose file contains an interesting letter by Behrendt to Schulz, Berlin, February 10, 1938, PLA/243, according to which it was the principle of the KVD to make compensation payments due to Jewish physicians "only if the association has actually been forced to do so by court order." Also see Oskar Karstedt, "Die Durchführung der Arier- und Kommunistengesetzgebung bei den Kassen-Ärzten, -Zahnärzten usw.," *Reichsarbeitsblatt,* 2 (*Nichtamtlicher Teil*) (1934), 179–183.

186. See Dr. Althen to members of Wiesbaden chapter of Nazi Physicians' League, Wiesbaden, August 11 and 30, 1934, as well as other materials from this file, HHSAW, 483/3159; directive Dr. Staeckert, KVD Erfurt, October 20, 1934, UK, PLA/215; Kreisamtsleiter to Dr. Dürring, August 30, 1935, BDC, PAe, PLA Dürring; doc. (January 7, 1939) in Broszat et al., eds., *Bayern,* p. 477; testimony of Hildegard Trutz in Hagen, *Leader,* pp. 254–255; Krüger, *Haus,* p. 18; Ostrowski, "Schicksal," p. 339. The traditional relationship between Jewish doctors and non-Jewish patients reached back long before 1933. See Ostrowski, "Schicksal," p. 315. Further documentation on the activities of German against Jewish physicians is in docs. (1935–36) in Broszat et al., eds., *Bayern,* pp. 454, 459; Swoboda to Bayerische Politische Polizei, Munich, October 13, 1933, SAM, LRA/30656; Hermann Stresau, *Von Jahr zu Jahr* (Berlin, 1948), pp. 95–96, 140–141; and the enlightening article by Florian Tennstedt and Stephan Leibfried, "Sozialpolitik und Berufs-

verbote im Jahre 1933: Die Auswirkungen der nationalsozialistischen Machtergreifung auf die Krankenkassenverwaltung und die Kassenärzte," *Zeitschrift für Sozialreform,* 25 (1979), 129–130, 138, 212–238.

187. Wertheim's testimony is in Hagen, *Leader,* p. 50. In 1935, the average German physician's annual gross income was 11,608.00 marks; in 1938 it was 14,940.00 marks. Doc. 201 in Walter Wuttke-Groneberg, ed., *Medizin im Nationalsozialismus: Ein Arbeitsbuch* (Tübingen, 1980), p. 347. These figures compare very favorably with those for higher civil servants, for instance. In 1940, the range for the highest-paid bureaucrats was from 8,400.00 to 12,600.00 marks a year. This would have included consuls-general, police presidents, and the director of the Reich Archive. Rathke, *Beamter,* p. 17.

188. Dr. E. to Mayor Wust, Murnau, July 10, 1933, SAM, NSDAP/84. From a Jewish doctor's point of view, see the example in Alexander Hohenstein, *Wartheländisches Tagebuch aus den Jahren 1941/42* (Stuttgart, 1961), p. 160.

189. On the new direction in medicine, see Bauer, Cropp, and Walther, *Arzt;* H. W. Kranz, " 'Einkehr' und 'Umkehr,' " *Ziel und Weg,* 4, no. 2 (1934), 38–40; Karl Kötschau, *Zum nationalsozialistischen Umbruch in der Medizin* (Stuttgart and Leipzig, 1936), especially pp. 38–49, 66–67, 86–89. Model careerists with the police and the SS respectively are described in the files of Stabsarzt der Polizei Dr. Josef Fischer (1938–39), BDC, PAe, PLA J. Fischer; and Dicks, *Mass Murder,* pp. 143–144. Also see Grunberger, *Reich,* pp. 220–221.

190. See *Das Junge Deutschland* (1938), 480–481; "Denkschrift an Reichsführer-SS. Erziehungsnachwuchs 1942. Abgeschlossen 15.3.42," BA, NS 19 Neu/1531; Grunberger, *Reich,* p. 220.

5. THE WAR YEARS: SEPTEMBER 1939 TO 1945

1. Table 1; table 7 (columns A–I); figure 2.

2. See SD report 25 of December 6, 1939, BA, R 58/145. Similarly: doc. (April 22, 1941) in Heinz Boberach, ed., *Meldungen aus dem Reich: Auswahl aus den geheimen Lageberichten des Sicherheitsdienstes der SS 1939–1944* (Neuwied and Berlin, 1965), p. 137. On the growing worker shortage and its consequences for the war economy, as well as details on foreign workers, see Walter Stets, "Die Lenkung des Berufsnachwuchses 1941: Richtlinien für Jungen," *Das Junge Deutschland* (1940), 256; Informationsdienst Nr. 12, Munich, March 30, 1942, SAM, NSDAP/79; Speer, *Reich,* pp. 219–220; Milward, *Economy;* Petzina, *Autarkiepolitik,* p. 160; docs. 108, 111 in Eichholtz and Schumann, eds., *Anatomie,* pp. 230, 237; Mason, *Arbeiterklasse,* p. 731; Edward L. Homze, *Foreign Labor in Nazi Germany* (Princeton, 1967).

3. Docs. 188, 201, 205, 208, 224, 229, 239, 242 in Mason, *Arbeiterklasse,* pp. 1095, 1132–33, 1144, 1150, 1183–85, 1196, 1218, 1227, also pp. 1233–34; doc. (May 24, 1943) in Boberach, ed., *Meldungen,* pp. 398–401; Neumann, *Behemoth,* pp. 282–286; Max Seydewitz, *Civil Life in Wartime*

Germany: The Story of the Home Front (New York, 1945), pp. 163-184; Eichholtz, *Geschichte,* I, 74-78; Grunberger, *Reich,* p. 201; Petzina, "Mobilisierung," p. 452; Petzina, *Autarkiepolitik,* p. 191; Milward, *Economy,* pp. 111-112, 142, 148; Jonas, *Leben,* pp. 387-388; Wunderlich, *Labor,* pp. 240-245.

4. On this phenomenon, see *Frankfurter Zeitung,* March 19, 1942.

5. Docs. (1940-1943) in Broszat et al., eds., *Bayern,* pp. 294, 300, 303, 642; doc. 52 in Schadt, ed., *Verfolgung,* p. 219; docs. 84, 127, 218, 232 in Mason, *Arbeiterklasse,* pp. 559, 736, 1174, 1204-5; docs. (1940-1942) in Boberach, ed., *Meldungen,* pp. 35, 91, 93, 112, 137, 147, 162, 177, 242, 272, 295; directive Kreisleiter, Wetzlar, November 23, 1939, HHSAW, 483/5550; activities report NSDAP Kreis Wilhelmshaven, November 1939, NSAO, 320, 2/2; SD report 25, December 6, 1939, BA, R 58/145; police station Windischgarsten (Oberdonau) to Landrat, October 7, 1940, OLA, Pol. Akten/14; Gestapo Vienna, Tagesrapport Nr. 2, November 2-4, 1940, DAÖW/1873; Scholtz-Klink/NSF for January-March 1942, BA, NS 22/860; homework essays by Bochum primary-school pupils, enclosed with memorandum SD Dortmund, May 11, 1942, SAMs, Polit. Polizei, 3. Reich/381; also see memorandum SD Dortmund, May 18, 1942, in the same file; Gauleitung Hessen-Nassau, circular 83/43, Frankfurt/Main, June 2, 1943, HHSAW, 483/5542; Hanssen to Reich Justice Minister, Berlin, May 31 and September 25, 1943, BA, R 22/3356; Steinert, *Krieg,* pp. 120, 164-165, 198, 213-214; Jonas, *Leben,* pp. 409-439; Seydewitz, *Life,* p. 181; Wunderlich, *Labor,* pp. 270-271; Stefan Karner, "Bemühungen zur Ausweitung der Luftrüstung im Dritten Reich 1940/41: Die Flugmotorenwerke Ostmark und ihr Marburger Zweigwerk 1941-45," *Zeitgeschichte,* 6 (1979), 323-324; Oppenheimer-Bluhm, *Standard,* pp. 52-54, 56.

6. See "Kinderlandverschickung der Partei auch im Krieg," Artikeldienst of NSV IV, 2/22407, July 20, 1940, HIS, 13/258; entry for July 30, 1944, in Kardorff, *Aufzeichnungen,* p. 176; minutes of speech by Friedrichs at Führer headquarters, March 23, 1944, BA, Schumacher/368; Schumann, *Nationalsozialismus,* p. 145; Schweitzer, *Nazifizierung,* p. 172; Wunderlich, *Labor,* pp. 276-280; Jay W. Baird, *The Mythical World of Nazi War Propaganda 1939-1945* (Minneapolis, 1974), p. 26.

7. Although there were occasional work stoppages, strikes, and increasing evidence of local absenteeism, these attitudes and activities appear to have been more economically than politically motivated and very often were the result of plain fatigue from overexertion. This is not to say that there was no Communist-inspired subversion among workers in the plants. Even the terror generated by Gestapo and SS could not eradicate this. It is significant, however, that the majority of workers tended to regard hapless Marxist agitators arrested by the police and eventually tried by the courts more as traitors to a fatherland at war than as benefactors to the cause of working-class solidarity. See "Stimmungsmässige Auswirkung der Verhängung von Todesstrafen gegen Kommunisten" (Austria), [1942-43], DAÖW/4447. Also documents pertaining to Communist resistance fighters arrested or before the

courts: DAÖW/2007, 1960, 1958, 1886, 1858, 1857, 1961. See also docs. 215, 224, 243, 244 in Mason, *Arbeiterklasse,* pp. 1169, 1184, 1230–31, also pp. 172–173; Winzer, *Jahre,* pp. 198, 229; Baird, *World,* p. 209; Schweitzer, *Nazifizierung,* p. 153; Seydewitz, *Life,* pp. 175–176, 182; entry for September 21, 1943, in *The Goebbels Diaries,* ed. Louis P. Lochner (London, 1948), p. 372; Steinert, *Krieg,* pp. 121, 554; Stefan Karner, "Arbeitsvertragsbrüche als Verletzung der Arbeitsdienstpflicht im 'Dritten Reich': Darstellung und EDV-Analyse am Beispiel des untersteirischen VDM-Luftfahrtwerkes Marburg/Maribor 1944," *Archiv für Sozialgeschichte,* 21 (1981), 297–308, 313–323.

8. In this context, the statement by Wunderlich, *Labor,* p. 353, assumes special significance: "Compared with the exploited foreign worker . . . the German farm worker was still a privileged group." Regarding the workers' potential for nationalism, see Geiger, *Schichtung,* p. 129.

9. The German terms mean "profiteer" and "coal snatcher."

10. This is the underlying assumption of the commentary by Mason, *Arbeiterklasse,* pp. 170–173, although his study only touches upon the first few months of the war. The accounts in Seydewitz, *Life,* pp. 177, 190, 192, from an exiled Social Democrat's perspective, are grossly exaggerated. The quotation is from Seydewitz, *Life,* p. 171. Karner ("Arbeitsvertragsbrüche," pp. 322–323) is critical of this view. An indication that the workers' mood had started to change by 1943–44 is given in Victor Klemperer, *LTI* ([East] Berlin, 1949), p. 102. Also see docs. (1943) in Broszat et al., eds., *Bayern,* pp. 645, 650, 656; and docs. (February 15 and July 26, 1943) in Boberach, ed., *Meldungen,* pp. 358, 421. The documents in Broszat et al., eds., *Bayern;* Kardorff, *Aufzeichnungen;* Steinert, *Krieg,* pp. 555–556, on the other hand, suggest continued support among the workers for the NSDAP beyond 1942.

11. Scholtz-Klink/NSF for period ending December 31, 1939, BA, NS 22/860; docs. 174, 242 in Mason, *Arbeiterklasse,* pp. 1044, 1228; police station Windischgarsten to Landrat, April 22, 1940, OLA, Pol. Akten/14; Eigruber, "An das Landvolk von Oberdonau!" Linz, May 16, 1940, OLA, Pol. Akten/15; Informationsdienst Nr. 9, Munich, February 20, 1942, SAM, NSDAP/79; homework essays by Bochum primary-school pupils, enclosed with memorandum SD Dortmund, May 11, 1942, SAMs, Polit. Polizei, 3. Reich/381; docs. (1939–1943) in Boberach, ed., *Meldungen,* pp. 18, 36, 243, 260, 303, 307–308, 352; docs. (November 13, 1943; August 26, 1944) in Broszat et al., eds., *Bayern,* pp. 590, 659; *Nationalsozialistisches Jahrbuch,* 18 (1944), 167, 169; entry for May 19, 1944, in Kardorff, *Aufzeichnungen,* p. 151; Hitler's remarks of May 19, 1942, in Henry Picker, *Hitlers Tischgespräche im Führerhauptquartier 1941–42: Im Auftrage des Deutschen Instituts für Geschichte der nationalsozialistischen Zeit geordnet, eingeleitet und veröffentlicht,* ed. Gerhard Ritter (Bonn, 1951), p. 285, hereafter cited as *Hitlers Tischgespräche;* Neumann, *Behemoth,* p. 285; Seydewitz, *Life,* p. 170; Petzina, "Mobilisierung," p. 448; Steinert, *Krieg,* pp. 555–556; Grunberger, *Reich,* pp. 39, 201. Among the blue-collar workers, the miners seem to have been the hardest to reach for the NSDAP. See the trustworthy report by

NPEA inmate H. Martens, Plön, 1942, BA, R 43 II/9566.

12. Table 7 (columns A-G); and text at nn. 62–71 in chap. 4.

13. Ecklbaur to Landrat, Steyrling, December 4, 1939, OLA, Pol. Akten/13.

14. This is reflected by the declining new-membership figures in table 7 (columns E-G).

15. SD report 25, December 6, 1939, BA, R 58/145.

16. Figures are from Milward, *Economy*, pp. 46–47. Also see SD reports 27, December 11, 1939, BA, R 58/146; and 7–10, December 13, 1943, BA, R 58/191; doc. 118 in Boberach, ed., *Meldungen*, p. 98; "Richtlinien für eine Befreiung vom Dienst in der Hitlerjugend," December 10, 1941, NSAW, 12 A Neu, 13 h/19598; Der Berichterstatter, 68, January 7, 1943, issue A, BA, NS 26/163; Gauleitung Ostpreussen, "Vertraulicher Informationsdienst," Königsberg, October 11, 1943, SAG, SF 6815, GA/8; Venter, report regarding journey, December 1943, Berlin-Köpenick, December 29, 1943, HIS, 13/260; monthly report of Regierungspräsident, Regensburg, February 10, 1944, BA, Schumacher/483.

17. See Winkler, "Stand," pp. 34, 38; Gurland et al., *Fate*, pp. 115–116; doc. 357 in Boberach, ed., *Meldungen*, p. 356; Georg Ebersbach, "Wettkampf in Treue zur Front," *Das Junge Deutschland* (1943), 264; "Die Rationalisierungs-Massnahmen in den Wehrkreisen VII und XIII," [1942], SAM, NSDAP/79; Milward, *Economy*, p. 92. For an example of a shop (copper smithy) that not only survived but expanded as a result of war-related production, see Eberle to Kanzlei des Gauleiters, Munich, March 24, 1944, SAM, NSDAP/18.

18. Stets, "Lenkung," pp. 256–257.

19. SD reports 90–92, April 12, 1943, BA, R 58/182; and 7–10, December 13, 1943, BA, R 58/191; entry for April 12, 1943, in Hans-Georg von Studnitz, *Als Berlin brannte: Diarium der Jahre 1943–1945* (Stuttgart, 1963), pp. 61–62; Uhlig, *Warenhäuser*, pp. 185–187.

20. See Winkler, "Stand," p. 36.

21. See Milward, *Economy*, pp. 106–108.

22. This example is in Natzinger to Flemisch, Dachau, March 31, 1944, SAM, NSDAP/31. Also see SD reports 30, December 18, 1939, BA, R 58/146; and 353, January 25, 1943, BA, R 58/179; docs. (1939–40) in Boberach, ed., *Meldungen*, pp. 23, 26–27, 98, 143; plenipotentiary for the leather trade to Oberpräsidenten et al., Berlin-Charlottenburg, February 9, 1940, SAM, NSDAP/61, Kreisleitung Limburg-Unterlahn, political situation report, Limburg, January 24, 1940, HHSAW, 483/5544; monthly report of Regierungspräsident, Regensburg, February 10, 1944, BA, Schumacher/483; Seydewitz, *Life*, p. 119.

23. Monthly report of Regierungspräsident, Regensburg, March 10, 1943, BA, Schumacher/483. Also see NSDAP Kreis Wilhelmshaven, activities reports of October and November 1939, NSAO, 320, 2/2; monthly report of Regierungspräsident Ansbach for August 1939; monthly report Regierungspräsident, Regensburg, September 8, 1939, GStAM, RE, 279/2;

docs. 67, 110 in Boberach, ed., *Meldungen*, pp. 56, 91; docs. (January 16, 1941; November 2, 1942) in Broszat et al., eds., *Bayern*, pp. 162, 609.

24. Tables 1 and 7 (columns A-I).

25. Monthly report of Regierungspräsident Ansbach for August 1939, GStAM, RE, 279/2; various situation reports regarding Oberdonau (1939-40) in OLA, Pol. Akten/13, 14; RNS, "Stimmungsbericht aus dem Gebiet der Landesbauernschaft Hessen-Nassau vom 1. Dezember 1939," HHSAW, 483/5550; the same for January 1, 1940, HHSAW, 483/5550; doc. 47 in Boberach, ed., *Meldungen*, pp. 41-42; Tagesrapport Nr. 2, November 2-4, 1940, DAÖW/1873; Tagesrapport Nr. 7, October 15-16, 1940, DAÖW/1858; Informationsdienst Nr. 9, Munich, February 20, 1942; Nr. 11, Munich, March 20, 1942; Nr. 13, Munich, April 25, 1942, SAM, NSDAP/79; monthly report Regierungspräsident, Regensburg, March 10, 1943, BA, Schumacher/483; situation report for the period ending June 1, 1943, Linz, June 9, 1943, OLA, Pol. Akten/80; docs. (1941-1942) in Broszat et al., eds., *Bayern*, pp. 195-197, 247-253; Farquharson, *Plough*, pp. 225, 227, 230-231, 239.

26. The last figure is according to Farquharson, *Plough*, p. 234. Also: Heller to Landrat, Kremsmünster, September 11, 1939; situation report Raml for Landrat, Grünberg, September 25, 1939, OLA, Pol. Atken/13; Neubauer to Landrat, Klaus, February 24, 1940, OLA, Pol. Akten/15; docs. (May 26, 1940; January 26, 1941; November 29, 1942) in Broszat et al., eds., *Bayern*, pp. 139, 144-145, 163, Homze; *Labor*, pp. 209-210.

27. Political situation report, Kreisleitung Limburg-Unterlahn, January 24, 1940, HHSAW, 483/5544; various docs. in OLA, Pol. Akten/15; "Vertraulicher Informationsdienst," Gauleitung Ostpreussen, Könisberg, June 11, 1943, SAG, SF 6815, GA/8; Homze, *Labor*, pp. 32, 34, 46, 49, 231, 234-236; Wunderlich, *Labor*, pp. 338, 343-350; Steinert, *Krieg*, p. 121; Farquharson, *Plough*, pp. 235, 239.

28. "Der soziale Einsatz des weiblichen Arbeitsdienstes," Artikeldienst of NSV X/22407, June 25, 1940, HIS, 13/258; docs. (August 31 and September 2, 1940) in Broszat et al., eds., *Bayern*, p. 143; "Richtlinien für eine Befreiung vom Dienst in der Hitler-Jugend," December 10, 1941, NAW, 12 A Neu, 13 h/19598; Tritschler, "Bericht über den Kriegseinsatz der Hitlerjugend des Standortes Soldau (Kartoffelernte) 1943," Soldau, October, 5, 1943, SAG, SF 6827, GA/110; Hauptstellenleiter to Hämer, September 29, 1944; Der Beauftragte des Kreisleiters für die bäuerliche Nachwuchssicherung to Rauber, January 20, 1945, HHSAW, 483/6458; Winkler, *Frauenarbeit*, pp. 108, 116, 130.

29. Docs. 183 and of April 20, 1944, in Boberach, ed., *Meldungen*, pp. 142, 505; "Vertrauliche Information," Gauleitung Ostpreussen, November 15, 1941, SAG, SF 6815, GA/8; Scholtz-Klink/NSF for October-December 1941 and January-March 1942, BA, NS 22/860; docs. (January 31 and September 29, 1942) in Broszat et al., eds., *Bayern*, pp. 154-155, 160; report Landrat Müldorf for Regierungspräsident, February and for March 1943, SAM, LRA/135116; Elise Bock to Feldpost-Nr. 08000, Altenburg, November 14, 1944, HHSAW, 483/6453. Homze's assertion, *Labor*, pp. 168-176, 297,

that conscripted foreign laborers were generally maltreated in the Reich must be qualified with a view to conditions in the countryside.

30. Weekly report Bürtz, Lauterbach, June 9, 1943, HHSAW, 483/5538. In a similar vein: doc. (April 26, 1942) in Broszat et al., eds., *Bayern*, p. 156; doc. (April 20, 1944), in Boberach, ed., *Meldungen*, p. 503. Also see Weixelbaumer to Gestapo, Kirchdorf/Krems, February 28, 1940; Eigruber, "An das Landvolk von Oberdonau!" Linz, May 16, 1940, OLA, Pol. Akten/15; entry for October 14, 1940, in Willi A. Boelcke, ed., *Kriegspropaganda 1939–1941: Geheime Ministerkonferenzen im Reichspropagandaministerium* (Stuttgart, 1966), p. 549; Gauleiter, circular 141/42, Frankfurt/Main, September 10, 1942, HHSAW, 483/5540; Landesbauernschaft Hessen-Nassau to Orlikowski, Frankfurt/Main, July 29, 1943, HHSAW, 483/6453; Eichenauer to Kreisleitung Alsfeld-Lauterbach, Rixfeld, October 15, 1944, HHSAW, 483/6454; Buchberger to Eberstein, Munich, October 20, 1943, SAM, NSDAP/11; doc. (November 14, 1944) in *Verfügungen/Anordnungen*, VII, 199; Stets, "Lenkung," p. 256; Wunderlich, *Labor*, pp. 196–197, 309–310.

31. Tables 1 and 7 (columns A–I).

32. The experiences related in the first half of Hohenstein, *Tagebuch*, are prototypical. Also see Hitler's remark of August 1, 1941, in *Hitlers Tischgespräche*, p. 195; Generalstaatsanwalt, Kammergericht to Reich Justice Minister, Berlin, February 1, 1940, BA, R 22/3356. Seydewitz's assertion, *Life*, p. 324, that "not more than 50 per cent" of all officials were Nazis by 1943, while indicating a high rate, is unsubstantiated.

33. See Seydewitz, *Life*, p. 324.

34. Calculated on the basis of figures in information service of Reich justice ministry, no. 47, [summer 1944], BA, R 22/4003.

35. Till the end of December 1939, 5,308 East Prussian officials (including higher ones) had been drafted; till the beginning of December 1942, this number had risen to a cumulative total of 20,350. At the same time, officials employed in extracurricular party activities in 1939–40 totaled 9,653, a number that rose cumulatively to 19,091 till December 1942. Dragg to Gauarchiv, Königsberg, December 21, 1942, BA NS 26/151.

36. August Kubizek, *The Young Hitler I Knew* (Westport, Conn., 1976), p. 295; *Das Junge Deutschland* (1942), 180; entry for January 25, 1942, in *Goebbels Diaries*, p. 15; Dragg to Gauarchiv, Königsberg, December 18, 1942, BA, NS 26/151; docs. (January 31 and June 1, 1942), in Broszat et al., eds., *Bayern*, pp. 155, 158; Generalstaatsanwalt, Kammergericht to Reich Justice Minister, Berlin, February 1, 1940; Hanssen to Reich Justice Minister, Berlin, May 31, 1944, BA, R 22/3356.

37. *Das Junge Deutschland* (1941), 304–305; ibid. (1942), 180–182; Gauleitung Westfalen-Nord, circular 100/42 Münster, July 24, 1942, SAMs, Gauleitung Westfalen-Nord, Gauamt für Volkswohlfahrt/7; Peterson, Limits, p. 99.

38. *Goebbels Diaries*, p. 15. On the question of the relatively low standard of living enjoyed by officials during the war also see: Hölscher to Gürt-

ner, Berlin, January 4, 1941, BA, R 22/3356; Warsemann to Reich Justice Minister, Frankfurt/Main, March 28, 1942, BA, R 22/3364; Gauleitung Westfalen-Nord, circular 100/42, Münster, July 24, 1942, SAMs, Gauleitung Westfalen-Nord, Gauamt für Volkswohlfahrt/7; Steinert, *Krieg*, p. 165; Grunberger, *Reich*, pp. 127–128.

39. For the last group, the count included all cases up to May 1, 1943. Computations according to figures in Dragg to Gauarchiv, Königsberg, December 21, 1942, BA, NS 26/151; confidential report, "Einsatz und Bewährung der Parteigenossen im Wehr- oder anderweitigem Kriegsdienst seit dem 1. September 1939 nach dem Stande vom 1. Mai 1943," BA, Schumacher/374. Also see NSDAP Kreis Wilhelmshaven, activities report, October 1940, NSAO, 320, 2/2; Hitler's remark of August 1, 1941, in *Hitlers Tischgespräche*, p. 195; entry for June 3, 1942, in Hohenstein, *Tagebuch*, p. 283; Dragg to Gauarchiv, Könisgberg, December 18, 1942, BA, NS 26/151; circular NSLB 151/42, Bayreuth, November 28, 1942, HIS, 12/242; Ley, directive 4/43, Munich, April 24, 1943, BA, NS 22/2008; Wegerle to Zellen- und Blockwalter, Frankfurt/Main, November 6, 1943, HHSAW, 483/1659; Striewe, "Nachwuchs der Partei aus der Hitler-Jugend," Munich, June 12, 1944, HIS, 18/339; *Nationalsozialistisches Jahrbuch*, 17 (1943), 206; Arnold Köttgen, *Deutsche Verwaltung*, 3d ed. (Berlin, 1944), pp. 109, 112; Broszat, *Staat*, pp. 323–325; Lang, *Secretary*, p. 110; Kater, "Hitlerjugend," especially pp. 599–623.

40. Table 7 (columns J and K, lines 6 and lower-class subtotal).

41. Although there is room for a large-scale monographic treatment of this problem, the following documents throw some light on the situation of white-collar workers from 1939 to 1944: police station Windischgarsten to Landrat, Windischgarsten, October 7, 1940, OLA, Pol. Akten/14; docs. 224, 385 in Boberach, ed., *Meldungen*, pp. 179, 401; docs. (May–September 1940; June 1, 1942; November 1, 1943) in Broszat et al., eds., *Bayern*, pp. 158, 295, 656; Hölscher to Gürtner, Berlin, January 4, 1941, BA, R 22/3356; "Denkschrift an Reichsführer-SS. Erziehungsnachwuchs 1942. Abgeschlossen 15.3.42," BA, NS 19 Neu/1531; Landrat Mühldorf to Regierungspräsident, monthly report July 1943, SAM LRA/135116; Stets, "Lenkung," p. 257; Steinert, *Krieg*, p. 165; Mason, *Arbeiterklasse,* p. 106; Kocka, *Angestellten*, pp. 181–183, 186–188.

42. Tables 1 and 7 (columns A-G).

43. Table 7 (columns A-G).

44. Doc. 202 in Ursula von Gersdorff, *Frauen im Kriegsdienst 1914–1945* (Stuttgart, 1969), pp. 415–417; "Aufstellung . . . Gau Mecklenburg," NSDStB, n.d., BA, NS 26/150; "Übersicht zum Kriegsdiensteinsatz des NSD.-Studentenbundes im Gau Mainfranken für die Zeit vom 1.11.39–31.12.42"; "Einsatz der Studentenschaft. Nationalsozialistischer Gaudienst, Gau Mainfranken," January 30, 1943, BA, NS 26/148; Wille, "Semesterbericht der Gaustudentenführung Ostpreussen für die Monate Juni, Juli, August und September 1944," Königsberg, September 27, 1944, BA, NS 26/151; docs. (August 31 and September 2, 1940) in Broszat

et al., eds., *Bayern*, p. 143; docs. (April 22 and May 24, 1943) in *Verfügungen/Anordnungen*, IV, 261–262; Franze, *Studentenschaft*, pp. 366–371.

45. Quotation is from flyer signed by Hans Scholl and Alexander Schmorell, Munich, summer 1942, printed in Christian Petry, *Studenten aufs Schafott: Die Weisse Rose und ihr Scheitern* (Munich, 1968), p. 156. Also see Wille, "Semesterbericht der Gaustudentenführung Ostpreussen für die Monate Juni, Juli, August und September 1944," Könisgberg, September 27, 1944, BA, NS 26/151; entry for September 20, 1944, in Klaus Granzow, *Tagebuch eines Hitlerjungen 1943–1945* (Bremen, 1965), p. 109.

46. Regarding medical students, see the qualifying remarks in the text at n. 80.

47. Memoranda by Berlin professors W. Guertler and O. Ritter von Niedermayer, November 1939 and April 20, 1940, BA, R 43 II/940 b; Pauwels, "Women," pp. 315–423; entry for September 16, 1943, in *Goebbels Diaries*, p. 365; docs. (April 22 and May 24, 1943) in *Verfügungen/Anordnungen*, IV, 261–264; "Denkschrift an Reichsführer-SS. Erziehungsnachwuchs 1942. Abgeschlossen 15.3.42," BA, NS 19 Neu/1531; doc. 202 in Gersdorff, *Frauen*, pp. 415–417; Schäfer to Kreisjugendberufswarte und -innen, Frankfurt/Main, March 5, 1945, HHSAW, 485/6453; Franze, *Studentenschaft*, pp. 369–370; Hellmut Seier, "Der Rektor als Führer: Zur Hochschulpolitik des Reichserziehungsministeriums 1934–1945," *Vierteljahrshefte für Zeitgeschichte*, 12 (1964), 144–145; Hans Ebert and Hermann-Josef Rupieper, "Technische Wissenschaft und nationalsozialistische Rüstungspolitik: Die Wehrtechnische Fakultät der TH Berlin 1933–1945," in Rürup, ed., *Wissenschaft*, I, 474, 485–487; Pascher, "Das Dritte Reich," p. 66; Roegele, "Student," p. 170.

48. See Schwarz, *Studenten*, pp. 21–57; entry for March 17, 1943, in *Goebbels Diaries*, p. 234; doc. (June 11, 1943) in *Verfügungen/Anordnungen*, IV, 259; memorandum Mauer for Friedrichs, Munich, July 20, 1944, BA, Schumacher/368.

49. The quotation is from Roegele, "Student," pp. 171–172. On the "White Rose" and other examples of active student resistance, see Petry, *Studenten*; Klaus Vielhaber, ed., *Gewalt und Gewissen: Willi Graf und die "Weisse Rose"* (Freiburg i.Br., 1964); Fritz Leist, "Möglichkeiten und Grenzen des Widerstandes an der Universität," in Kuhn et al., *Universität*, pp. 177–213; Ursel Hochmuth, *Candidates of Humanity: Dokumentation zur Hamburger Weissen Rose anlässlich des 50. Geburtstages von Hans Leipelt* (Hamburg, 1971); doc. regarding the indictment of students Leberstorfer, Hoffmann, Popper, Vienna, September 25, 1940, DAÖW/1976; "Bericht über die Tätigkeit der Gruppe Mayer-Thanner im Rahmen der Widerstandsgruppe Johann Müller," n.d., DAÖW/2128. On less overt forms of student defiance, see entry for December 11 and 12, 1939, in Boelcke, ed., *Kriegspropaganda*, pp. 239, 241; entry for May 15, 1943, in Kardorff, *Aufzeichnungen*, p. 49; Pascher, "Das Dritte Reich," p. 66; Sarah Mabel Collins, *The Alien Years: The Autobiography of an Englishwoman in Germany and Austria: 1938–1946* (London, 1949), p. 117; Pauwels, "Women," p. 403.

50. According to figures computed on the basis of Reichsstudentenwerk (student aid) data in Bundesarchiv Koblenz by Gerhard Arminger (Gesamthochschule Wuppertal). See his "Quantitative Approaches to and Inferences from Student Data: Involvement of German Students in Nazi Organizations Based on the Archive of the Reichsstudentenwerk" (paper presented at the Social Science History Association Annual Meeting, Nashville, Tenn., October 24, 1981).

51. This mood is well depicted in the reminiscences of Heidelberg historian Werner Conze, in *Rhein-Neckar-Zeitung*, May 12 and 13, 1979. Also see: Wille, "Semesterbericht der Gaustudentenführung Ostpreussen für die Monate Juni, Juli, August und September 1944," Königsberg, September 27, 1944, BA, NS 26/151; Götz von Olenhusen, "Studenten," p. 203; entry for February 28, 1944, in Else R. Behrend-Rosenfeld, *Ich stand nicht allein: Erlebnisse einer Jüdin in Deutschland 1933–1944*, 2d ed. (Frankfurt/Main, 1963), pp. 245–246.

52. Table 7 (columns A–I).

53. Details in Petzina, *Autarkiepolitik*, pp. 148–149, 156; Milward, *Economy* (quotation on p. 62); Seydewitz, *Life*, pp. 131–134; docs. 111, 197 in Eichholtz and Schumann, eds., *Anatomie*, pp. 238, 282–283; *Nationalsozialistisches Jahrbuch*, 18 (1944), 151; entry for October 20, 1947, in Albert Speer, *Spandau: The Secret Diaries* (New York, 1976), pp. 76–77; Speer, *Reich*, p. 339. Todt's rise to power is described by Carroll, *Design*, pp. 213–231. The "confusion" of early 1940 is reflected in entry for March 11, 1940, in Hassell, *Deutschland*, p. 134.

54. Milward, *Economy*, pp. 125, 162–163, 165–166; Milward, "Fascism," p. 398; Grunberger, *Reich*, p. 183; Lang, *Secretary*, p. 297.

55. Doc. 54 in Boberach, ed., *Meldungen*, p. 49; "Die Rationalisierungs-Massnahmen in den Wehrkreisen VII und XIII," [1942]; Informationsdienst Nr. 12, Munich, March 30, 1942, SAM, NSDAP/79; Gurland et al., *Fate*, pp. 94–95; Seydewitz, *Life*, pp. 130–133; Karner, "Bemühungen," pp. 329–330; Milward, *Economy*, pp. 92, 94–95, 106–110.

56. See Kreisleiter Wetzlar, memorandum Punkt 21, Wetzlar, November 23, 1939, HHSAW, 483/5550; Gaupersonalamt to Gauwirtschaftsberater, Frankfurt/Main, March 26, 1943, HHSAW, 483/878; doc. (February 1, 1944) in Broszat et al., eds, *Bayern*, p. 178; Petzina, *Autarkiepolitik*, pp. 143–144; Milward, *Economy*, pp. 29–31, 72; Grunberger, *Reich*, pp. 177–180; Seydewitz, *Life*, p. 162; and the example in Baeyer-Katte, *Politik*, pp. 158–159. Also see the interesting documents in Eichholtz and Schumann, eds., *Anatomie*, although their own commentary, from the East German point of view, is somewhat exaggerated: pp. 19–20, 24, 32–33, 292–293. Similar overstatements are in Eichholtz, *Geschichte*, I, such as on p. 63.

57. Padover, *Experiment*, p. 330. The figures are according to doc. 268 in Eichholtz and Schumann, eds., *Anatomie*, pp. 471–476, see also p. 26. Further see entry for November 1, 1941, in Hassell, *Deutschland*, p. 235; Grunberger, *Reich*, p. 182; Milward, *Economy*, pp. 112–113; Seydewitz, *Life*, pp. 134–135; memorandum Himmler, Führer headquarters, December 5,

1941, DAÖW/1077; Enno Georg, *Die wirtschaftlichen Unternehmungen der SS* (Stuttgart, 1963). The ramifications of the use of female labor in the war are discussed in Winkler, *Frauenarbeit*, pp. 97–98, 139–140, 148. Also see Seebold, *Stahlkonzern*, pp. 159–173.

58. An example of DAF interference is in DAF-Kreisobmann to Kausemann, Gelnhausen, December 22, 1939, HHSAW, 483/5550.

59. This is suggested by an analysis of several business leaders' curricula vitae (executives and factory owners from Hesse), some without NSDAP membership, in HHSAW, 483/874 and 878. Also see assessment of twenty-nine party comrades in Gauwirtschaftsberater Hessen-Nassau to Gauper-sonalamt, Frankfurt/Main, April 30, 1940, HHSAW, 483/593.

60. The self-confidence even of smaller industrialists is reflected in: situation report for the period ending June 1, 1943, Linz, June 9, 1943, OLA, Pol. Akten/80. Also see Schwarz to Höllerich, Munich, November 16, 1939, SAN, 503/81; and entry for September 22, 1940, in Hassell, *Deutschland*, pp. 162–163.

61. Table 7 (columns E-G).

62. Docs. (May 21 and August 29, 1941) in *Verfügungen/Anordnungen*, II, 288–292, 305–306; cases of F.K., Dr. F.G., Dr.W.-T. in Gauwirtschafts-berater to Gaupersonalamt, Frankfurt/Main, April 30, 1940, HHSAW, 483/593; doc. [early 1941] in Broszat et al., eds., *Bayern*, pp. 612–613.

63. Excerpt of Frick's letter to Hitler, spring 1941, is in Broszat, *Staat*, p. 234. Also see Potjan to Reich Justice Minister, Berlin, April 1, 1940, BA, R 22/3356; point 24 in Gauwirtschaftsberater to Gaupersonalamt, Frankfurt/Main, April 30, 1940, HHSAW, 483/593; *Das Junge Deutschland* (1942), 181–182; entry for February 21, 1943, in *Die Weizsäcker-Papiere*, p. 325; Boberach, ed., *Meldungen*, p. 381, n. 6; docs. (October 5 and 23, 1943) in Broszat et al., eds., *Bayern*, pp. 583, 653; Venter, report regarding journey, December 1943, Berlin-Köpenick, December 29, 1943, HIS, 13/260; Schulen-burg's letter dated April 4, 1943, excerpted in Krebs, *Schulenburg*, p. 247; Bohle to Himmler, Berlin, September 25, 1944, BDC, SSA E.W. Bohle; Caplan, "Civil Servant," p. 224.

64. Sweet, "Volksgerichtshof," pp. 327–328. From 1943 to the middle of November 1944 alone, cases of "high treason" increased from 211 to 505, and those of "defeatism" from 241 to 893. Block to Thierack, Berlin, December 2, 1944, BA, R 22/3356.

65. Percentage and other figures are from: "Informationsdienst des Reichsministers der Justiz, Beitrag 5," [1944], BA, R 22/4003; Hölscher to Schlegelberger, Berlin, July 2, 1941, BA, R 22/3356. Also see Generalstaatsan-walt to Reich Justice Minister, Berlin, February 1, 1940, BA, R 22/3356.

66. See Hitler's tirades expressed on March 29, and May 22 and 31, 1942, in *Hitlers Tischgespräche*, pp. 211–212, 245–246; also entries for January 3 and 4, February 22, August 20, and September 2, 1942, in *Adolf Hitler: Monologe im Führerhauptquartier 1941–1944: Die Aufzeichnungen Heinrich Heims*, ed. Werner Jochmann (Hamburg, 1980), pp. 172, 293, 350–354, 381, cited hereafter as Hitler, *Monologe*; and entry for April 21, 1942, in *Heeresad-*

jutant bei Hitler, p. 120. Also see *Nationalsozialistisches Jahrbuch*, 17 (1943), 207; and *Nationalsozialistisches Jahrbuch*, 18 (1944), 210; doc. [early 1941] in Broszat et al., eds., *Bayern*, pp. 612–613; Steinert, *Krieg*, pp. 290–292; Hans Bernhard Brausse, *Die Führungsordnung des deutschen Volkes: Grundlegung einer Führungslehre* (Hamburg, 1940), pp. 128–129; Klessmann, "Frank," p. 258; Hüttenberger, "Polykratie," p. 430; Sweet, "Volksgerichtshof," p. 321; Grunberger, *Reich*, pp. 125–126.

67. *Das Junge Deutschland* (1942), 181–182; Warsemann to Reich Justice Minister, Frankfurt/Main, March 28, 1942, BA, R 22/3364; Caplan, "Civil Servant," especially pp. 242–243, 291–293, 306.

68. Semester report Wille, Königsberg, September 27, 1944, BA, NS 26/151. Typical example: entry for April 26, 1945, in Margret Boveri, *Tage des Überlebens: Berlin 1945* (Munich, 1968), p. 72; and memoranda by Berlin professors W. Guertler and O. Ritter von Niedermayer, November 1939 and April 20, 1940, BA, R 43 II/940 b. Hitler's derogatory remarks are in *Hitlers Tischgespräche* (entry for February 17, 1942), pp. 205–206. Generally, see Kater, *Das "Ahnenerbe,"* pp. 145–301; *Nationalsozialistisches Jahrbuch*, 17 (1943), 202; and *Nationalsozialistisches Jahrbuch*, 18 (1944), 204; entries for May 12 and 22, 1943, in *Goebbels Diaries*, pp. 295, 308; Giles, "University Government," p. 220; Steinert, *Krieg*, pp. 440–441; Grunberger, *Reich*, pp. 311–312; Helmut Heiber, *Walter Frank und sein Reichsinstitut für Geschichte des neuen Deutschlands* (Stuttgart, 1966); Kelly, "National Socialism," pp. 378–379, 459–464. Characteristically, a Bormann aide in early 1944 spoke of the "universally despised academics at the universities," Leitgen(?), memorandum for Bormann, Munich, January 12, 1944, BA, Schumacher/371.

69. The figures in table 7 (columns A-G) show that in 1942–1944 joiners from the academic professions were underrepresented in the NSDAP — for the first time in the history of Nazism. Also see table 1 and figure 6.

70. Adam von Trott zu Solz, the resistance fighter (1944), was a German Rhodes scholar. See docs. (May 14 and June 11, 1943) in Broszat et al., eds., *Bayern*, pp. 578, 640; docs. (April 19, May 6, November 22, 1943; and February 7, 1944) and docs. 377, 381 in Boberach, ed., *Meldungen*, pp. 383, 387, 456, 483; entry for May 9, 1942, in Stresau, *Jahr*, p. 291; entry for May 10, 1944 in Kardorff, *Aufzeichnungen*, p. 147; Boveri, *Wir lügen*, especialy pp. 226, 546, 600; Baeyer-Katte, *Politik*, pp. 142–143; Abel, *Presselenkung*, pp. 84–96. Also see the pathetic address of Berlin Geheimrat (secret counselor) Dr. O., recently evacuated to the countryside, to a group of Nazi women, sometime between 1942 and 1944. It is obvious that the words "Führer" and "Nationalsozialismus" toward the end of the speech were uttered with great reluctance. Osterheit, "Meine sehr verehrten Damen der Frauenschaft!" [Gerdauen], n.d., SAG, SF 6818, GA/31. Lawrence D. Stokes, "The German People and the Destruction of the European Jews," *Central European History*, 6 (1973), 167–191, has attempted to answer the question of how much about anti-Jewish Nazi crimes the German people really knew.

71. Hitler's diatribes of March 29 and July 22, 1942, are in *Hitlers Tischgespräche*, pp. 211–213, 259–260. Also see Hitler, *Monologe*; entry for

April 21, 1942, in *Heeresadjutant bei Hitler*, p. 120; entry for September 23, 1943, in *Goebbels Diaries*, p. 384; Steinert, *Krieg*, p. 292; doc. [1941] in Broszat et al., eds., *Bayern,* pp. 612–613; Gaupersonalamt to Gauwirtschaftsberater, Frankfurt/Main, January 25, 1943, HHSAW, 483/878; Felix Kersten, *Totenkopf und Treue: Heinrich Himmler ohne Uniform* (Hamburg, n.d.), p. 132; Lang, *Secretary*, p. 167.

72. See text near n. 65; "Informationsdienst des Reichsministers der Justiz, Beitrag 5," [1944], BA, R 22/4003; "Aufstellung [der Kriegsleistungen] . . . Gau Mecklenburg, Mitglieder NS-Rechtswahrerbund," n.d., BA, NS 26/150; Wicklmayr, "Übersicht zum Kriegseinsatz des NS-Rechtswahrerbundes im Gau Mainfranken für die Zeit vom 1.9.1939–31.12.1942," Würzburg, March 13, 1943, BA, NS 26/148.

73. Quotations are from *Nationalsozialistisches Jahrbuch*, 17 (1943), 207; and ibid., 18 (1944), 210.

74. The practice of appointing *Pflichtverteidiger* (obligatory counselors) for culprits whose fate had been sealed beforehand was continued to the end of the war. For an example of such an appointment, see legal file Leberstorfer, Hoffmann, Popper, and Czernohorsky, especially memorandum Engel, Vienna, November 1, 1940, DAÖW/1976. Frau Dr. W., then a young woman lawyer in Berlin, told the author in Heidelberg (1966) about the agony she went through when she failed to save the life of Erich Maria Remarque's sister in People's Court. Eventually, Ms. Remark was decapitated for allegedly having plotted against the regime.

75. Conflicting reports are in Hölscher to Gürtner, Berlin, March 5, 1940; Hanssen to Reich Justice Minister, Berlin, May 31, 1943, BA, R 22/3356.

76. Entry for September 1, 1939, in Klepper, *Schatten*, p. 796; entry for December 12, 1939, in Boelcke, ed., *Kriegspropaganda*, p. 241; SD report 29, December 15, 1939, BA, R 58/146; doc. 133 in Gersdorff, *Frauen*, p. 318; Dr. Wolf to Landrat, Traunstein, December 13, 1940, BDC, PAe, PLA Jäger; memorandum, minutes of remarks made by Oberstabsarzt Dr. Ehrle, November 24, 1942; Sievers to Dr. Bruns, Hanover, December 4, 1942, NHSA, Hann. 122a, XII/32 m; Dr. Bäuml, Informationsdienst Nr. 41, Munich, September 21, 1944, SAM, NSDAP/31.

77. SD report 28, December 13, 1939, BA, R 58/146; doc. 1 in Boberach, ed., *Meldungen*, p. 6; Dr. Wolf to Landrat, Traunstein, December 13, 1940, BDC, PAe, PLA Jäger; Ohlendorf to Klopfer, Berlin, [October–November 1942], BA, R 22/4203; Sievers to Dr. Bruns, Hanover, December 4, 1942, NHSA, Hann. 122a XII/32 m; Beer to Reichsärztekammer, Munich, August 27, 1943, BDC, PAe, PLA Heiler; SD report 86–88, March 2, 1944, BA, R 58/193; Wanjek to NSV Münster, Ibbenbüren, March 29, 1944; NSV Höxter-Warburg to NSV, Gau Westfalen-Nord, Bad Driburg, April 11, 1944, SAMs, Polit. Polizei, 3. Reich/109; Dr. Bäuml, Informationsdienst Nr. 41, Munich, September 21, 1944, SAM, NSDAP/31; doc. 1 in Volker R. Berghahn, "Meinungsforschung im 'Dritten Reich': Die Mundpropaganda-Aktion im letzen Kriegshalbjahr," *Militärgeschichtliche Mitteilungen*, 1 (1967), 97; case of Dr. Guttmann (1944), BDC, PAe, PLA Guttmann.

78. Michael H. Kater, "Krisis des Frauenstudiums in der Weimarer Republik," *Vierteljahrschrift für Sozial- und Wieschaftsgeschichte*, 59 (1972), especially 217–218, 223; Pauwels, "Women," pp. 39–41, 58, 80–84, 284, 331; doc. 133 in Gersdorff, *Frauen*, p. 318; entry for September 1, 1939, in Klepper, *Schatten*, p. 796; case of Dr. Annemarie Sossinka in Schneider to Munich manpower office, September 17, 1942 (date of postage stamp), BDC, PAe, PLA Sossinka; Dr. Bäuml, Informationsdienst Nr. 41, Munich, September 21, 1944, SAM, NSDAP/31; Günter Kaufmann, *Das kommende Deutschland: Die Erziehung der Jugend im Reich Adolf Hitlers*, 3d ed. (Berlin, 1943), p. 90; Kurt Hass, ed., *Jugend unterm Schicksal: Lebensberichte junger Deutscher 1946–1949* (Hamburg, 1950), p. 17.

79. Quotation comes from entry for November 6, 1943, in Kardorff, *Aufzeichnungen*, pp. 84–85. For corroboration, see Ferdinand Sauerbruch, *A Surgeon's Life* (London, 1953), pp. 215–216, 230–233, 242–246. Also see "Verordnung zur Sicherstellung der ärztlichen Versorgung der Zivilbevölkerung vom 27. Mai 1942," *Deutsches Ärzteblatt*, 72 (1942), 241–242; Hitler's decree, Führer headquarters, December 23, 1942, in Reich Interior Minister to Oberpräsidenten et al., Berlin, January 14, 1943, NHSA, Hann. 122a, XII/122; "Das Hohelied des Arztes," Artikeldienst, Hauptamt für Volkswohlfahrt — Hauptstelle Presse, [1940–41], HIS, 13/258; "Pflege der Volksgesundheit," Nationalsozialistischer Gaudienst, Gau Mainfranken, January 30, 1943, BA, NS 26/148; "Mitteilungen an die Ärzte Süd-Hannover-Braunschweigs," Hanover, September 1, 1944 (p.1) and January 1, 1945 (p.1), NHSA, Hann. 122a, XII/126; *Nationalsozialistisches Jahrbuch*, 18 (1944), 189–190, 208–209; Gumpert, *Hunger*, p. 115; case of Dr. Wertheim in Hagen, *Leader*, pp. 54–61; front-line letters by Dr. Gruner (1942–43) in Walter and Hans W. Bähr, eds., *Kriegsbriefe gefallener Studenten 1939–1945* (Tübingen and Stuttgart, 1952), pp. 278–281; Ernst-Günther Schenck, *Ich sah Berlin sterben: Als Arzt in der Reichskanzlei* (Herford, 1970), pp. 46–47. During the war the average income of civilian physicians in the Reich appears to have declined in comparison with the prewar period. In 1938 the gross annual income of doctors in the Reich was 14,940.00 marks (see n. 187 in chap. 4). But in 1943 the average annual gross salary for all of Augsburg's 103 state-insurance-plan physicians was 14,854.37 marks, and for all of Goslar's 9 physicians it was 12,957.75 marks. These last figures are from "Saldenauszug aus dem Ärztekontokorrent zum 31.12.43, KVD Braunschweig [und Augsburg], Bilanz und Erfolgsrechnung . . . 3. Vierteljahr," UK, 106.

80. Doc. 55 in Helmut Heiber, ed., *Reichsführer! . . . Briefe an und von Himmler* (Stuttgart, 1968), p. 69; "Denkschrift an Reichsführer-SS. Erziehungsnachwuchs 1942. Abgeschlossen 15.3.42," BA, NS 19 Neu/1531; entry for September 16, 1943, in *Goebbels Diaries*, p. 365; Reich Interior Minister to Prussian Oberpräsidenten et al., Berlin, July 2, 1943, NHSA, Hann. 122a, XII/121; Werner, "Lage," p. 79.

81. Examples of quick careers in army or party service are contained in: Schwebel to Gaupersonalamt, November 24, 1942, HHSAW, 483/191; curricula vitae and personal files for Drs. Boye, Schöndorf and Strack, in BDC,

PAe; Hagen, *Leader*, pp. 51-53. Also see "Wer will Sanitätsoffizier der Luftwaffe werden?" *Deutsches Ärzteblatt*, 71 (1941), 175.

82. The quotation is from Anna Pawełczyńska, *Values and Violence in Auschwitz: A Sociological Analysis* (Berkeley and Los Angeles, 1979), p. 73. Also see Kater, *Das "Ahnenerbe,"* pp. 227-264; Alexander Mitscherlich and Fred Mielke, eds., *Medizin ohne Menschlichkeit: Dokumente des Nürnberger Ärzteprozesses* (Frankfurt/Main and Hamburg, 1962); Klaus Dörner, "Nationalsozialismus und Lebensvernichtung," *Vierteljahrshefte für Zeitgeschichte*, 15 (1967), 121-152; Lothar Gruchmann, "Euthanasie und Justiz im Dritten Reich," *Vierteljahrshefte für Zeitgeschichte*, 20 (1972), 235-279; Walter von Baeyer, "Die Bestätigung der NS-Ideologie in der Medizin unter besonderer Berücksichtigung der Euthanasie," in *Universitätstage 1966*, pp. 69-74; Dicks, *Mass Murder*, pp. 143-157. F. Sauerbruch, *Life*, p. 249, writes: "This is not the place to discuss the trial of the doctors at Nuremberg, but I should like to point out that many doctors who were certainly not less 'guilty' than those who suffered their sentence, are now peacefully practising their profession."

6. SOCIAL PROFILE OF THE RANK AND FILE, 1919-1945

1. Josepha Fischer, "Die nationalsozialistische Bewegung in der Jugend," *Das Junge Deutschland* (1930), 343-352; Neisser, "Analyse," p. 658; Jäger, *Gesicht*, pp. 68-70; Hans Gerth, "The Nazi Party: Its Leadership and Composition," *American Journal of Sociology*, 45 (1940), 529. For observations by post-1945 historians, see Krebs, *Infancy*, p. 242; Petzina, "Germany," p. 73; Hambrecht, *Aufstieg*, p. 304; Noakes, *Nazi Party*, p. 60; Allen, *Seizure*, p. 72; Peter Loewenberg, "The Psychohistorical Origins of the Nazi Youth Cohort," *American Historical Review*, 76 (1971), 1469-71. See also Bracher, *Dictatorship*, p. 96.

2. In this respect, the treatment of joiners regarding age resembles that of joiners regarding class and occupational subgroup, as explained at the beginning of chap. 2.

3. Compared with the accurate computations by Douglas, "Notes," pp. 70-71, on which this text is based, the figures provided earlier by Franz-Willing, *Hitlerbewegung*, p. 129, and Werner Maser, *Die Frühgeschichte der NSDAP: Hitlers Weg bis 1924* (Frankfurt/Main and Bonn, 1965), p. 175, are out of date.

4. Kater, "Soziographie," pp. 155, 157. The age of 27.5 is given for Vilsbiburg (Bavaria) in Genuneit, "Anfänge," p. 55.

5. Doc. 56 in Tyrell, ed., *Führer*, p. 137; Krebs, *Infancy*, p. 51. See Joseph Nyomarkay, *Charisma and Factionalism in the Nazi Party* (Minneapolis, 1967), p. 74, n. 8. According to the Hamburg sample (table 4, n. a), the average age of Hamburg party members in 1925 was about 28. Also see Joachim C. Fest, *Hitler* (New York, 1974), p. 275.

6. Membership lists for Mülheim/Ruhr, November 1925, and Langerfeld, November 1925, as cited in table 4, nn. c and d.

7. Calculated on the basis of figures for party membership in the Essen chapter, November 1925 to February 1926, HSAD, RW 23, NSDAP/Gauleitung Ruhr.

8. According to figures in the Brunswick sample (table 4, n. e).

9. Thuringia and Bochum samples (table 5, columns A and E). For the Reich see table 2 in Kater, "Wandel," p. 27. Compare Eutin's average member's age of 31.0 (1925–1928), as calculated by Stokes, "Composition," p. 26.

10. Table 2 in Kater, "Wandel," p. 27.

11. Stokes, "Composition," p. 18; table 6 in Kater, "Quantifizierung," p. 467. In light of these findings, my earlier assumption of a gradual rejuvenation of the NSDAP from 1925 to 1933 ("Soziographie," p. 157), recently reiterated by Douglas, "Notes," p. 71, has to be dismissed. Also, Noakes's assertion, *Nazi Party*, p. 159, that "during the period 1930–3 . . . the average age of [the NSDAP's] recruits went down still further" is not defensible. Figure 7 shows that the age breakdown published in *Partei-Statistik* I, 162, is unreliable for this period, and there are inconsistencies and faults in the construction of its table; for one thing, the perimeters of the age brackets do not conform with those generally adopted by Reich statisticians. Theodore Abel's age breakdown published by Peter H. Merkl, "Die alten Kämpfer der NSDAP: Auswertung von 35 Jahre alten Daten," *Sozialwissenschaftliches Jahrbuch für Politik*, 2 (1970), 497, must be considered a biased one. In it, the age groups 31–50 are overrepresented, compared with my own statistics. This is understandable because middle-aged people over 31 were likely to respond more readily to Abel's questions than the less literate and expressive young people under 31.

12. "Gesicht," p. 497.

13. Herbert Moller, "Youth as a Factor in the Modern World," *Comparative Studies in Society and History*, 10 (1968), 243–244. My percentage calculation is based on figures in Rawicz, *Sozialpolitik*, pp. 23–24.

14. Among contemporary observers who lumped the young Nazis together with other youth groups was Dix, *Reichstagswahlen*, p. 43. More recently, this interpretation has been upheld by Franz-Willing, *Hitlerbewegung*, p. 137, for the period before 1924; and Merkl, "Kämpfer," p. 506, for the period from 1925 to 1933. Also see Merkl, *Political Violence under the Swastika: 581 Early Nazis* (Princeton, 1975). The difference between Hitler Youth and bourgeois youth is explained in Kater, "Jugendbewegung," pp. 131–155.

15. On this, see Schorske, *Social Democracy*; Hunt, *Social Democracy*; Geiger, *Schichtung*, p. 132; Hoegner, *Flucht*, pp. 26–33; Craig, *Germany*, pp. 499–502.

16. See the age breakdown for the SPD (1930) in *Jahrbuch Sozialdemokratie 1930*, p. 195. Also Hunt, *Social Democracy*, pp. 106–107; table 2 in Gerth, "Nazi Party," p. 530; Kaasch, "Struktur," p. 1052; and table II-1 in Merkl, *Making*, p. 60. The SPD age figures are not directly comparable to the NSDAP figures because they represent not newcomers but total

membership for the years indicated. On the ossification of the SPD, Center Party, DVP, and DNVP see Jäger, *Gesicht*, pp. 69, 73; Plum, *Gesellschafts-struktur*, p. 30; Dirk Blasius, "Psychohistorie und Sozialgeschichte," *Archiv für Sozialgeschichte*, 17 (1977), 399–400; Mommsen, "Sozialdemokratie," pp. 124–127; Mommsen, "National Socialism: Continuity and Change," in Laqueur, ed., *Fascism*, pp. 186–187.

17. *Partei-Statistik* I, 157.

18. See Hitler's diatribes against Germany's nineteenth-century political traditions, as well as against the more recent republican past, in *Mein Kampf*.

19. See Kaasch, "Struktur," pp. 1051–52; Hermann Weber, *Die Wandlung des deutschen Kommunismus: Die Stalinisierung der KPD in der Weimarer Republik*, I (Frankfurt/Main, 1969), 281–282; Blasius, "Psychohistorie," p. 400; Siegfried Bahne, *Die KPD und das Ende von Weimar: Das Scheitern einer Politik 1932–1935* (Frankfurt/Main and New York, 1976), p. 15; Mommsen, "National Socialism," p. 187.

20. In "Cohort," p. 1458, Loewenberg writes: "The new adults who became politically effective after 1929 . . . were the children socialized in the First World War." In light of the data presented here, one would have to predate Loewenberg's statement without changing its essential meaning: it now appears that these "new adults" became "politically effective" as early as 1925–26.

21. See, for example, Jäger, *Gesicht*, pp. 71–72.

22. Table 13 in Kater, *Studentenschaft*, p. 221.

23. The quotation is from Madden, "Composition," p. 161. See Dietmar Keese, "Die volkswirtschaftlichen Gesamtgrössen für das Deutsche Reich in den Jahren 1925–1936," in Conze and Raupach, eds., *Staats- und Wirtschaftskrise*, pp. 38–39.

24. Table 6 in Kater, "Quantifizierung," p. 466.

25. Hermann Maass, "Hilfe für die erwerbslose Jugend," *Das Junge Deutschland* (1931), 14–15; Hennig, *Thesen*, pp. 44–45; Loewenberg, "Cohort," p. 1468; Petzina, "Germany," p. 73; Irmtraud Götz von Olenhusen, "Die Krise der jungen Generation und der Aufstieg des Nationalsozialismus: Eine Analyse der Jugendorganisationen der Weimarer Zeit," *Jahrbuch des Archivs der deutschen Jugendbewegung*, 12 (1980), 61–65.

26. Such doubts were articulated in 1967 by Werner Conze, "Die politischen Entscheidungen in Deutschland 1929–1933," in Conze and Raupach, eds., *Staats- und Wirtschaftskrise*, p. 177.

27. See Schnaas, *Arbeitsmarkt*, pp. 42–44; Dreyfuss, *Beruf*, pp. 174–177, 219; Mierendorff, "Gesicht," p. 495; *Preussische Zeitung*, November 17, 1932. The Reich Relief Ordinance (*Kündigungsschutzgesetz*) of July 9, 1926, which was supposed to extend special protection to employees over 30, seems to have had little, if any, effect. See Croner, "Angestelltenbewegung," pp. 145–146; and especially Preller, *Sozialpolitik*, p. 368.

28. Table 6 in Kater, "Quantifizierung," p. 466.

29. Speier, *Angestellten*, p. 118. Also see Craig, *Germany*, p. 551. There is a possibility that the young clerks who joined the NSDAP during the

depression were those who could not yet benefit from the system of social insurance, notably unemployment insurance after 1927, to the same degree as
could their seniors because they had not paid their premiums for the required
twelve months and lacked the seniority protected by the *Betriebsrätegesetz*
(Works Counselors' Ordinance). I owe this insight to a letter from Herr
Rudolf Bree, Königswinter, December 21, 1979, who experienced these conditions as a young white-collar worker during the depression. See also Croner,
"Angestelltenbewegung," pp. 145–146. If the link between the circumstances
described by Bree and Nazi party membership as it is reflected in the statistical
data could be further documented, the weight of the argument would again
shift in the direction of an economic explanation.

30. For 1932–33, see text near n. 10. For 1942–43, the average ages were
computed for established Frankfurt/Main party members for 1940
(age = 47.4, N = 1,118; see table 7, n.b) and established Reich party members
for 1942 (age = 47.3, N = 635; see table 7, n. c, and table 10, column JJ).

31. See the warning contained in Himmler's letter to Berger, August 26,
1942, doc. 139 in Heiber, ed., *Reichsführer*, p. 142.

32. Since the data from samples of new and established party members in
table 7 cannot be consistently interpreted on a cumulative basis from year to
year, it is impossible to derive from them the average age of the NSDAP for
any given point in time between 1933 and 1945.

33. *Partei-Statistik* I, 158.

34. The membership list contains eighty-six names. SAM, NSDAP/109.

35. The figure for Eutin was computed from data kindly supplied to me
by Professor Lawrence D. Stokes, Dalhousie University, Halifax. The average
for the Communists of 1935 was computed from the data as indicated in table
7, n. e.

36. See n. 30 above.

37. Kater, "Quantifizierung," pp. 453–484.

38. See Kater, "Jugendbewegung," pp. 169–171; Spakowsky, circular
14/33, Hamburg, September 11, 1933, BA, Schumacher/377.

39. *Partei-Statistik* I, 166; Hess, directive 24/37, Munich, February 9,
1937; Reichinger to Gauamtsleiter et al., Munich, February 13, 1937, SAM,
NSDAP/84.

40. See *Partei-Statistik* I, 44; text in chap. 4 at n. 1; and the beginning of
chap. 5.

41. This renders doubtful the assertion by one young man that after its
members' senior matriculation (*Abitur*) on March 23, 1942, the school class
was collectively "consigned" to the NSDAP. See Hass, ed., *Jugend*, p. 52.
Also see the beginning of chap. 4 at n. 1. For 1941, a much more plausible account of pressure being applied while one was still in the HJ is in McKee,
World, pp. 45–46. Also see Kater, "Quantifizierung," pp. 479–481, and n. 96.

42. "Vertraulich. Einsatz und Bewährung der Parteigenossen im Wehr-
oder anderweitigem Kriegsdienst seit dem 1. September 1939 nach dem Stande
vom 1. Mai 1943," BA, Schumacher/374.

43. See n. 33 above. In the Reich population, the 18- to 30-year-old

cohort's proportion was somewhat higher in the late 1930s than before World War I, according to the 1910 general census and the diagram in Lottmann, "Ausbildungsdauer," p. 415.

44. Computation on the basis of data (194 *N*) in Rudolf Proksch, "Der Erziehungsauftrag der NSDAP.," in Benze and Gräfer, eds., *Erziehungsmächte*, pp. 230–231.

45. Schwarz to Ecksturm, Munich, September 17, 1943, BA, Schumacher/377. On the BDM, see Jutta Rüdiger, "Der Bund Deutscher Mädel in der Hitler-Jugend," in Meier-Benneckenstein, ed., *Das Dritte Reich*, II, 395–413; Maschmann, *Account*.

46. "Gesicht," p. 501.

47. Kubizek, *Hitler*, pp. 152, 186; Hitler, *Mein Kampf*, pp. 616, 621; Hitler, *Monologe*, p. 235; Rosenberg, *Mythus*, pp. 482–522. Also Rosenberg, *Aufzeichnungen*, pp. 182, 185; Krebs, *Infancy*, p. 256; Hans Beyer, *Die Frau in der politischen Entscheidung* (Stuttgart, 1933), pp. 72–75; Heuss, *Weg*, pp. 133–135; Aretin, *Krone*, pp. 188–189; Padover, *Experiment*, p. 143; Kater, "Krisis," pp. 247–248; Richard J. Evans, "German Women and the Triumph of Hitler," *Journal of Modern History*, accepted for demand publication, abstract printed in vol. 48, no. 1 (March 1976); Timothy W. Mason, "Women in Germany, 1925–1940: Family, Welfare and Work," Part I, *History Workshop*, 1 (1976), 87–88; Winkler, *Frauenarbeit*, pp. 28–29.

48. Franz-Willing, *Hitlerbewegung*, p. 82. There seem to have been a few local exceptions to the leadership rule: in May 1922 the leadership of the Dortmund chapter included, besides six men, one woman, if only until the end of August: Böhnke, *NSDAP*, p. 47. On Nuremberg, see the document in Deuerlein, ed., *Aufstieg*, p. 279.

49. Minutes of speech by Hess, Reich Party Rally 1938; "Stichworte für Rede Ortsgruppenleiter-Tagung 14.&15.1.1939," SAG, SF, 6815, GA/6.

50. Table 5 in Kater, "Soziographie," p. 152; Madden, "Composition," pp. 75, 78, 86, 93; Franz-Willing, *Hitlerbewegung*, p. 129; Douglas, "Notes," pp. 65, 67; Runge to Staatskommissar für öffentliche Ordnung, [Cologne], April 27, 1922, printed in Schmidt, *Jahre*, pp. 44–45.

51. "Die Frauenarbeit . . . 1922–35," HIS, 13/253.

52. List of Ingolstadt Nazi members (505 *N* were utilized out of a total of 535 entries), see table 2, n. p. Also see Kater, "Soziographie," p. 127, and table on p. 151. In light of this and the above evidence, Claudia Koonz's figure of 20% for women in the early 1920s stands corrected: "Mothers in the Fatherland: Women in Nazi Germany," in Renate Bridenthal and Koonz, eds., *Becoming Visible: Women in European History* (Boston, 1977), p. 448.

53. See Gordon, *Hitler*, especially pp. 88–119; Orlow I, pp. 40–45; Fest, *Hitler*, pp. 142–146, 168–189. Subjectively: Ernst Röhm, *Die Geschichte eines Hochverräters*, 4th ed. (Munich, 1933), pp. 164–300.

54. For Bochum sample, see table 5, column A. Essen sample (377 *N*—total membership from November 1925 through February 1926), HSAD, RW 23, NSDAP/Gauleitung Ruhr. The Essen value must be judged in terms of the preponderance of women in the area, as described in Spethmann, ed.,

Essen, p. 312. For Barmen sample (in this case $N = 135$) see table 4, n. b.

55. See Brunswick, Hamburg, and Thuringia samples, as described in table 4, nn. a and e, and table 5, column E. As in the case of Essen (n. 54), in Brunswick's civilian population the percentage of women was slightly higher than in the Reich's: 52.9% as opposed to 51.6%. *Die Stadt Braunschweig in der Zeit vom 1. April 1921 bis 31. März 1926: Verwaltungsbericht im Auftrage des Rates der Stadt bearbeitet vom Städtischen Statistischen Amt* (Brunswick, 1929), pp. 16–17; table 6 in Kater, "Soziographie," p. 152.

56. Total membership of the Starnberg chapter on July 1, 1927, was thirty-three. See Buchner, *Kamerad*, pp. 159–160.

57. Madden, "Composition," pp. 138, 150, 160, 196, 211.

58. *Partei-Statistik* I, 16. The 1933 value is corroborated in Kater, "Quantifizierung," p. 482, especially n. 86. Also see Deutsch-Krone and Klausdorf sample ($N = 155$), table 6, n. b; table 4 in Stokes, "Composition," p. 18 ($N = 469$). Schoenbaum's figure of 3.0% for 1932 is obviously wrong: *Revolution*, p. 37.

59. Douglas, "Notes," p. 70.

60. Kater, "Soziographie," pp. 156–157.

61. See nn. 54 and 55 above.

62. Stokes, "Composition," p. 18. This difference is corroborated by the values displayed for the entire period, 1925–1933, in table 8 in Kater, "Quantifizierung," pp. 470–471, where the discrepancy between men and women is 4.1; between the total average age and the women's average age it was 3.7. Also see table 6, "Quantifizierung," pp. 466–467. As well, see data from the NSDAP chapters of (1) Frankfurt-Berkersheim, (2) Frankfurt-Obermain, (3) Frankfurt-Riederwald, August–September 1939: (1) 23.3% of all male members were under 30, compared to none of the female ones; (2) 22.1% of all male members were under 30, compared to 20.4% of the female ones; (3) 18.2% of male members were under 30, compared to 54.1% of female ones. Total N of all three chapters = 1,286. Lists are in HHSAW, 483/160.

63. Hertha Siemering, *Deutschlands Jugend in Bevölkerung und Wirtschaft: Eine statistische Untersuchung* (Berlin, 1937), p. 217. Also see table 4 in Karl Astel and Erna Weber, *Die Kinderzahl der 29000 politischen Leiter des Gaues Thüringen der NSDAP und die Ursachen der ermittelten Fortpflanzungshäufigkeit* (Berlin, 1943), p. 20.

64. See the table in Rawicz, *Sozialpolitik*, p. 27, and also p. 26. Clifford Kirkpatrick, *Nazi Germany: Its Women and Family Life* (Indianapolis and New York, 1938), pp. 126–127.

65. Hermann Rauschning, *Gespräche mit Hitler* (Zurich, 1940), p. 240. The credibility of this book as an historical source is vouched for by Theodor Schieder, *Hermann Rauschnings "Gespräche mit Hitler" als Geschichtsquelle* (Opladen, 1972). Also see Kirkpatrick, *Nazi Germany*, p. 48; and Otto Dietrich, *The Hitler I Knew* (London, 1957), p. 219.

66. A membership list of 120 members for Amerang (Bavaria) for March 8, 1934, SAM, NSDAP/80, displaying a percentage for women of merely 2.5%, was not typical of conditions in the Reich at that time. See *Partei-*

Statistik I, 16, 44.

67. Directives by Schwarz and Buch, Munich, April 20, 1937, BA, Schumacher/377.

68. Pauwels, "Women," pp. 51–55; Winkler, *Frauenarbeit*, pp. 55–60.

69. See Kater, "Quantifizierung," pp. 482–484, for full documentation.

70. A directive of April 1940 once again favored BDM members over civilian young women for party entrance. RF, circular F 42/40, Berlin, April 19, 1940, BA, Schumacher/230.

71. Kater, "Quantifizierung," p. 481.

72. See "Informationsdienst des Reichministers der Justiz," [1944], BA, R 22/4003. It is still very difficult to establish cumulative percentages for female party members for any given point in time after 1934. Records thus far available are not representative enough and too unevenly distributed over time. For three different Frankfurt/Main suburban party chapters three different values were computed for memberships just before World War II: (1) 3.9% women, (2) 7.2% women, and (3) 8.1% women among members of good standing. See Ortsgruppen-Organisationsbericht O I for (1) Frankfurt-Berkersheim, September 4, 1939, (2) Frankfurt-Obermain, August 29, 1939, and (3) Frankfurt-Riederwald, September 10, 1939, HHSAW, 483/160. In 1940, the percentage of women in a sample of 1,118 established party members in the greater Frankfurt area (see table 7, n. b.) was 8.9.

73. Also see table 8 in Kater, "Quantifizierung," p. 470.

74. According to figures in Ortsgruppen-Organisationsbericht O I as in n. 72 above.

75. List of party members in greater Frankfurt area (see table 7, n. b).

76. Tyrell, *Vom "Trommler,"* pp. 52, 133; Auerbach, "Lehrjahre," p. 28; Horn, *Führerideologie*, p. 91.

77. Doc. 340 in *Hitler: Aufzeichnungen*, p. 542.

78. See Winkler, "Extremismus," p. 188; Tyrell, *Vom "Trommler,"* p. 174; Orlow I, p. 90; Stachura, "Wendepunkt," pp. 70–71; Stachura, "The Political Strategy of the Nazi Party, 1919–1933," *German Studies Review*, 3 (1980), 268.

79. NSDAP chapter Rheinhausen to Gauleitung Ruhr, Rheinhausen, May 18, 1927, HSAD, RW 23, NSDAP/Gauleitung Ruhr; report Baden interior ministry, [Karlsruhe], January 15, 1929, SAF, 317/1257 d; Schwarz's remarks regarding "mass attraction" in *Völkischer Beobachter*, April 29, 1930; [police] report, Munich, May 23, 1930, BHSAM, Sonderabgabe I/1758.

80. See chap. 2. Also Kater, "NS-Studentenbund," pp. 188–189; Stachura, "Wendepunkt"; regional order, northeastern region of NSDAP, Insterburg, July 9, 1930, SAG, SF 6818, GA/34; "An den deutschen Arbeiter," [September 1930], SAG, SF 6826, GA/100.

81. See doc. 56 in Tyrell, ed., *Führer*, pp. 136–141; *Völkischer Beobachter*, December 10, 1927; excerpt from bimonthly report 613, [Munich], April 22, 1930, BHSAM, Sonderabgabe I/1758; flyer, "An die Volksgenossen aus Neu-Kirchen-Vluyn!" [June 1928], HSAD, RW 23, NSDAP/Gauleitung Ruhr; "Betrogene! Sparer! Mittelständler! Bauern und

Arbeiter!" [September 1930], SAG, SF 6826, GA/100; Jäger, *Gesicht*, pp. 50–51; Krebs, *Infancy*, p. 63; Hambrecht, *Aufstieg*, p. 248; Böhnke, *NSDAP*, p. 230; Childers, "Bases," p. 25.

82. See Orlow I, pp. 116–120, 136–139, 174. On p. 174, for instance, Orlow makes the indefensible assertion that the NSDAP (in 1929) was "shedding the last vestiges of its socialist past." Similarly, Winkler,"Protectionism," p. 9; Noakes, *Nazi Party*, p. 148. Most recently, Stachura, "Strategy."

83. These divisions are stressed by Kühnl, *Linke*. For recent revisions of this theory, see Broszat, *Staat*, p. 38; Kater, "NS-Studentenbund," pp. 178–179; Tyrell, "Feder," pp. 72–73; Barbara Miller Lane, "Nazi Ideology: Some Unfinished Business," *Central European History*, 7 (1974), 20–21; Mason, *Sozialpolitik*, pp. 64–65; and especially Stachura, "Strasser." There is no question, however, that Strasser's more radical brother Otto deviated sufficiently from the party line to have a falling-out with Hitler in May–July 1930. How much of this disagreement is attributable to sheer aspects of party discipline rather than ideology has yet to be determined. See O. Strasser's own account in *Hitler*, pp. 100–117; Kater, "NS-Studentenbund," p. 179.

84. See n. 2 in chap. 2; Orlow I, pp. 87–120; Bouhler to all Gaus and NSDAP chapters, Munich, May 7, 1928, BA, Schumacher/374; Noakes, *Nazi Party*, p. 73.

85. See Heuss, *Weg*, p. 164; activities report Gau Süd-Hannover-Braunschweig, December 12, 1931, NHSA, Hann. 310 I, B 13; flyer, "Wir treten an!" [early January 1933], SAG, SF 6826, GA/93; Stephan, "Soziologie," p. 793; Riemer, "Soziologie," p. 111; Jäger, *Gesicht*, pp. 40, 44–45; Bracher, *Dictatorship*, pp. 152–191; Schoenbaum, *Revolution*, p. 45; Reinhard Figge, "Die Opposition der NSDAP im Reichstag," Ph.D. dissertation, Cologne, 1963, pp. 157–159; Böhnke, *NSDAP*, p. 191; Winkler, "Society," p. 1; Hambrecht, *Aufstieg*, pp. 236, 409.

86. For example, Petzina, "Germany," pp. 67–68.

87. Linz, "Notes," p. 89; Childers, "Bases," pp. 29–30. For the actual voting patterns, see Striefler, *Wahlen* (table 1); Ohno, "Basis," (especially table 1 on p. 2). Also Bracher, *Dictatorship*, p. 178. Details on the development of the national economy are in Petzina, "Hauptprobleme," pp. 20–36; Petzina, "Germany," p. 69.

88. According to Studentkowski's list, n. d., BA, Schumacher/376, the membership inflow from 1925 to 1930 was as follows: 26,796 for 1925; 22,044 for 1926; 17,888 for 1927; 30,190 for 1928; 67,378 for 1929; 196,042 for 1930. Up to and including 1930, altogether 230,775 persons had joined the NSDAP, but, according to *Partei-Statistik* I, 70, by September 1930 the party was left with only 129,563 members, which means that 101,212 had dropped out by then. Madden is the first to have examined this problem in detail, "Composition," pp. 258–268. Also see Pratt, "Social Basis"; and the beginning of chap. 2.

89. See Introduction at n. 28.

90. See columns A and B in table 9. Nothing decisive can be said about the lower middle class and the elite because data for them in table 9 lack

statistical significance according to chi-square tests. Possibly the lower middle class did, but the numerically insignificant elite did not contribute to this shift.

91. See Mason, *Sozialpolitik*, p. 62. Also see Bracher, *Dictatorship*, p. 133.

92. Since February 1925, the party increased to 129,563 in September 1930, and to 849,009, on January 30, 1933. Partially misleading figures are in Linz, "Notes," p. 60. From 1925 to 1933 the combined cumulative average monthly growth rate of the NSDAP was 15.5% In the first period, the party rose by 19.4%, while in the second this rate dropped to 6.8%. Calculations on basis of figures in *Partei-Statistik* I, 27, 69–70; and the compound growth formula in Floud, *Introduction*, p. 91. Compare this with a rate of only 0.3% for the SPD from April 1, 1925, to January 1, 1931 (calculations based on figures in Schöck, *Arbeitslosigkeit*, p. 229), and, for the KPD, about 0.14% from the end of 1924 to the beginning of 1931 (based on figures in Flechtheim, *KPD*, p. 347).

93. See, in particular, Merkl's conclusion in *Violence*, pp. 668–716 (quotation on p. 670). More recently, Merkl, *Making*, pp. 158, 191–194. Merkl's argument is weakened by the fact that his total sample of 581 early Nazis (and even fewer Stormtroopers) is skewed toward the pre-1930 period (*Violence*, p. 668). Also see Loewenberg, "Cohort."

94. See my review of Merkl, *Violence*, in *Social History* (Hull), 2 (1977), 700–702; also Ayçoberry, *Nazi Question*, pp. 180–182; and my review of Merkl, *Making*, in *American Historical Review*, 86 (1981), 161.

95. See Kater, "Wandel," pp. 43–44; Kater, "Quantifizierung," p. 454, n. 4, and p. 480, n. 71. Also "Vertraulich. Einsatz und Bewährung der Parteigenossen im Wehr- oder anderweitigem Kriegsdienst seit dem 1. September 1939 nach dem Stande vom 1. Mai 1943," BA, Schumacher/374; Bormann to Sauckel, May 27, 1943, BA, Schumacher/378.

96. Kreisleiter, circular 8/91/43, Frankfurt/Main, November 11, 1943, HHSAW, 483/5541. On the dual nature of the NSDAP, also see directives by Schwarz and Buch, Munich, April 20, 1937, BA, NS 22/2011; Lingg, *Verwaltung*, pp. 332–334; doc. (August 19, 1944) in *Verfügungen/Anordnungen*, VII, 172–173. Noncredible claims by party members after 1945 that they had been forced into the party without their knowledge or possibility of appeal are in Pascher, "Das Dritte Reich," p. 53; Hass, ed., *Jugend*, p.52. On the voluntary character of Nazi party membership see Rudolf Nissen, *Helle Blätter—dunkle Blätter: Erinnerungen eines Chirurgen* (Stuttgart, 1969), p. 120. Also see n. 41 above.

97. On the former, see Donald M. McKale, *The Nazi Party Courts: Hitler's Management of Conflict in His Movement, 1921–1945* (Lawrence, Kansas, 1974), pp. 172–173. On the latter, see Trinker to Schneider, Tilsit, February 17, 1933, SAG, SF 6817, GA/22; directive Hess, Munich, April 18, 1934, SAM, NSDAP/122; memorandum Kreisleiter Wetzlar, November 23, 1939, HHSAW, 483/5550.

98. The figure is from a list, [December 1942], BA, Schumacher/392. Regarding party citations, see *Kleine Funktionärskartei*, BDC. For the period

up to early 1935, see *Partei-Statistik* I, 220 (regarding a lower decoration).

99. Example for snow removal is in [Illegible] to Wagner, [Meerholz], December 13, 1941, HHSAW, 483/6482.

100. For a representative selection of ordinances, see *Verfügungen/Anordnungen*, IV, 4–7, 79–84; ibid., VII, 29; Ortsgruppenleiter, service order, party chapter Nordwest, Frankfurt/Main, October 12, 1943, HHSAW, 483/1659; enclosure 4 in Hans Kissel, *Der Deutsche Volkssturm 1944/45: Eine territoriale Miliz im Rahmen der Landesverteidigung* (Frankfurt/Main, 1962), pp. 100–103.

101. See, typically, political situation report, Kreisleitung Limburg, January 24, 1940, HHSAW, 483/5544; SD reports: 26, December 8, 1939, BA, R 58/146; and 9–12, June 17, 1943, BA, R 58/185; docs. (1941, 1943) in Boberach, ed., *Meldungen*, pp. 145, 418, 430; docs. (1943–44) in Broszat et al., eds., *Bayern*, pp. 179, 580, 659; docs. 1, 4 in Berghahn, "Meinungsforschung," pp. 96, 112. Also see Steinert, *Krieg*, p. 406; Peter Hüttenberger, *Die Gauleiter: Studie zum Wandel des Machtgefüges in der NSDAP* (Stuttgart, 1969), p. 160. Regarding party badges, see Verordnungsblatt Gau Süd-Hannover-Braunschweig, Geschäftsführung, January 1, 1939, BA, Schumacher/202; ordinance Ley 9/44, Munich, March 2. 1944, BA, NS 22/2008; Steinert, *Krieg*, p. 582; Baird, *World*, p. 210.

102. The quotation is from Mommsen, "National Socialism," p. 182. Also see pp. 195, 200 of that illuminating article. For Goebbels's insight, see entries for March 2 and 3, 1943, in *Goebbels Diaries*, pp. 202–203. See minutes of speech by Friedrichs (Bormann's assistant) at Führer headquarters, March 23, 1944, BA, Schumacher/368.

103. In considering the class criteria of the NSDAP from 1933 to 1945, one must remember that statistically representative samples of joiners were obtainable only for the years with open membership (1933, 1937, 1939–1941). Frequencies for the other years refer mainly to youth or are biased in favor of specific groups, such as members of the veterans' organization, *Stahlhelm* (1934–35). The social composition of those groups, particularly of youth, was not necessarily congruent with that of the NSDAP joiners at large. In spite of these caveats, however, it is still possible to arrive at a fairly accurate portrait of the party based on social-class criteria.

104. Table 7 (columns A–G); figure 2.

105. Table 7 (columns A–I); table 1.

106. Table 7 (columns A–G); table 1; figure 2.

107. Ibid.

108. The quotation is from Talcott Parsons, "Some Sociological Aspects of the Fascist Movements," *Social Forces*, 21 (December 1942), 145–146.

109. On the attitude of the elite, see entries for February 13 and March 5, 1933, in Ebermayer, *Deutschland*; Pfeifer, "Hitlerbild," pp. 52–55, 186–188; Frank, *Angesicht*, p. 143; Mason, *Sozialpolitik*, p. 81, Georg H. Kleine, "Adelsgenossenschaft und Nationalsozialismus," *Vierteljahrshefte für Zeitgeschichte*, 26 (1978), 117–121, 133–135; Klaus Hildebrand, "Die ostpolitischen Vorstellungen im deutschen Widerstand," *Geschichte in*

Wissenschaft und Unterricht, 29 (1978), 216–221. On the attitude of the Nazi leaders, see Schoenbaum, *Revolution*, p. 288, n. 2; Struve, *Elites*, pp. 428, 441; Mommsen, "National Socialism," pp. 183, 200–201. Also see Dr. Schmitt to Kreisleitung Rosenheim, [Munich], March 17, 1938; NS-Altherrenbund der Deutschen Studenten, circular II/38, Munich, September 23, 1938, SAM, NSDAP/119. Examples of members of the elite, as they were snobbishly laughing off the Nazis as a passing phenomenon at the beginning of the regime, are in Boveri, *Wir lügen*, pp. 45–46. Schweitzer's well-known thesis regarding a regular "coalition" between the "upper class" and the Nazis during the first phase of the Third Reich constitutes too much of an overstatement, *Business*, p. 43.

110. This is reflected by the decline in the figures for the elite in table 7 (columns A-C), and in the elite's curve in figure 2.

111. Quotation is from Lutz Graf Schwerin von Krosigk, *Es geschah in Deutschland: Menschenbilder unseres Jahrhunderts* (Tübingen and Stuttgart, 1951), pp. 206–207, also see pp. 208–209. Also: *Deutschland-Berichte*, II (1935), 1277; Krebs, *Schulenburg*, p. 114; Herbert von Borch, *Obrigkeit und Widerstand: Zur politischen Soziologie des Beamtentums* (Tübingen, 1954), pp. 217–218; Boveri, *Wir lügen*, p. 186; Dicks, *Mass Murder*, p. 151; Padover, *Experiment*, p. 227; Petzina, "Hitler," p. 487; Petzina, *Autarkiepolitik*, p. 22; Mason, *Arbeiterklasse*, p. 34; Hanfstaengl, *Witness*, pp. 262, 269–270; Annedore Leber, ed., *Das Gewissen steht auf: 64 Lebensbilder aus dem deutschen Widerstand 1933–1945*, 9th ed. (Berlin and Frankfurt/Main, 1960), p. 108; Hamilton, *Appeal*, p. 158; Rudolf-Christoph Freiherr von Gersdorff, *Soldat im Untergang* (Frankfurt/Main, 1977), p. 55; Mommsen, "National Socialism," p. 192. Also see doc. 9 in Thévoz et al., eds., *Quellen*, p. 135; and text at n. 151 in chap. 4.

112. According to letter by chief of Heeres-Personalamt to Wehrmachts-Amt, Berlin, November 9, 1934, BAF, RW6, V 67/2, these threats were part of a speech delivered by Engel at a DAF convention on November 6.

113. Table 7 (columns A–G); figure 6.

114. Schemm, "Gedankensammlung," February 22, 1935, BDC, PK, PLA H. Schemm.

115. Heydrich to Staatspolizeistellen et al., Berlin, July 20, 1937, SAS, HO 235, I–VIII, F 19; Mommsen, "Perspektiven," p. 28.

116. Boveri, *Wir lügen*, p. 608; Walter Reichert, "Bildung," *Nationalsozialistisches Bildungswesen*, 4 (1939), 332; correspondence regarding Deutscher Vortragsverband e. V. (founded 1876), May–June 1939, BA, NS 8/197; Kater, "Jugendbewegung," pp. 169–171. Also see the text in Introduction at n. 10.

117. As in n. 113 above.

118. In this sense, Goldhagen's interpretation in "Weltanschauung," pp. 394–395, must be fully agreed with. See Hassell, *Deutschland*, pp. 17, 21, 23, 91, 222, 300. Theodor Eschenburg, "Die Rede Himmlers vor den Gauleitern am 3. August 1944: Dokumentation," *Vierteljahrshefte für Zeitgeschichte*, 1 (1953), 366; entry for August 6, 1942, in Hitler, *Monologe*, p. 332; Dahren-

dorf, *Society*, p. 413; Wolfgang Zapf, *Wandlungen der deutschen Elite 1919-1961: Ein Zirkulationsmodell deutscher Führungsgruppen 1919-1961* (Munich, 1965), p. 181; Rauschning, *Revolution*, p. 91; John S. Conway, "Frühe Augenzeugenberichte aus Auschwitz: Glaubwürdigkeit und Wirkungsgeschichte," *Vierteljahrshefte für Zeitgeschichte*, 27 (1979), 260; Kersten, *Totenkopf*, pp. 97-104, 156-171; Schaumburg-Lippe, *Krone*, pp. 295-296, 299, 306; Mommsen, "Perspektiven"; Aretin, *Krone*, especially p. 151; Steinert, *Krieg*, pp. 468, 554; entry for July 13, 1942, in Stresau, *Jahr*, p. 303; Fritz Wiedemann, *Der Mann der Feldherr werden wollte: Erlebnisse und Erfahrungen des Vorgesetzten Hitlers und seines späteren persönlichen Adjutanten* (Velbert and Kettwig, 1964), pp. 96-97; Speer, *Reich*, pp. 256-257.

119. This assumption is substantiated by comments by Goebbels and Himmler late in the war. See Joseph Goebbels, *Tagebücher 1945: Die letzten Aufzeichnungen* (Hamburg, 1977), p. 273; Eschenburg, "Rede Himmlers," pp. 360, 388. In late September 1944, Bormann began to force more party functionaries into officer positions. Lang, *Secretary*, p. 299.

120. The best treatment of this problem is still in Peter Hoffmann, *The History of the German Resistance 1933-1945* (London, 1977), pp. 315-534.

121. Among the 518 former officers who were reinstated in the army, then still officially known as the Reichswehr, in 1934, 341 (65.8%) had joined the NSDAP before 1933. Hess to all Reichsleiters and Gauleiters, Munich, July 5, 1935, SAG, SF 6815, GA, A, 1a-1e. Also see Müller, *Heer*, pp. 61-87; William Carr, "National Socialism: Foreign Policy and Wehrmacht," in Laqueur, ed., *Fascism*, p. 171.

122. In Nazi literature, the three-pillar theory sometimes appears modified to allow for only two pillars, those of the Wehrmacht and the NSDAP. The confusion typifies the constitutional inconsistencies that were, however, of serious concern only to conservative jurists. See directive Schwarz, September 21, 1933, contained in "Politik in der Wehrmacht," Kornelimünster, April 8, 1954, BA, Schumacher/378; Koellreutter, *Verwaltungsrecht*, p. 40; Huber, "Rechtsgestalt," pp. 325, 327-328; Schoenbaum, *Revolution,* p. 218; Carr, "National Socialism," p. 171. On the army in the Röhm affair, see Müller, *Heer*, pp. 88-141.

123. See the excellent book by Christian Streit, *Keine Kameraden: Die Wehrmacht und die sowjetischen Kriegsgefangenen 1941-1945* (Stuttgart, 1978); also Helmut Krausnick and Hans-Heinrich Wilhelm, *Die Truppe des Weltanschauungskrieges: Die Einsatzgruppen der Sicherheitspolizei und des SD 1938-1942* (Stuttgart, 1981), especially pp. 13-278.

124. Regarding the Wehrmacht as an escapist mechanism, see the examples in Boveri, *Wir lügen*, p. 86; Kater, "Intellectuals," pp. 273, 276; Hamilton, *Appeal*, p. 159; and the almost incredible account in Friedrich Hielscher, *Fünfzig Jahre unter Deutschen* (Hamburg, n.d.), pp. 426-433. Baron von Gersdorff's memoirs attest as much to the political naiveté of the German officer corps as to the character of the army as a closed and anti-Nazi-oriented caste: *Soldat*, especially pp. 51-52, 56-57, 62-63. Also Steinert, *Krieg*, p. 278. On the preference for an officer career, see "Denkschrift an

Reichsführer-SS. Erziehungsnachwuchs 1942. Abgeschlossen 15.3.42," BA, NS 19 Neu/1531.

125. Minutes of speech by Hess at Nuremberg Party Rally 1938, SAG, SF 6815, GA/6; docs. (1934–35) in Thévoz et al., eds., *Quellen*, pp. 43, 173, 189; doc. 4 in Schadt, ed., *Verfolgung*, p. 70; Mass, *Jahr*, pp. 29, 52–53; entry for Jaunary 3, 1934, in Klepper, *Schatten*, p. 141; Broszat, *Staat*, p. 289; Buchheim, *Glaubenskrise*; Siegele-Wenschkewitz, *Nationalsozialismus*; John S. Conway, *The Nazi Persecution of the Churches 1933–45* (Toronto, 1968).

126. As early as 1942 Franz Neumann argued that Nazism attempted to act on behalf of an entrenchment of the "ruling class": *Behemoth*, p. 298.

127. Quotation is from entry for September 20, 1944, in Granzow, *Tagebuch*, p. 109. The other examples are from Hanssen to Reich Justice Minister, Berlin, January 27, 1944; Block to Thierack, Berlin, December 2, 1944, BA, R 22/3356; SD report 6–9, September 9, BA R 58/190; Oberlandesgerichtspräsident to Reich Justice Minister, Linz, December 11, 1944, OLA, Pol. Akten/80. Also see minutes of Hitler's address to German youth in *Der Kongress zu Nürnberg vom 5. bis 10. September 1934: Offizieller Bericht über den Verlauf des Reichsparteitages mit sämtlichen Reden* (Munich, 1934), p. 166; Schoenbaum, *Revolution*, pp. 59–60; Winkler, *Frauenarbeit*, p. 142; Heinrich August Winkler, "Vom Mythos der Volksgemeinschaft," *Archiv für Sozialgeschichte*, 17 (1977), 489; *Der alltägliche Faschismus*, p. 139.

7. THE EARLY YEARS TO POWER: 1919 TO 1933

1. Technically speaking, a Gauleitung was to encompass several German states (Länder) or parts thereof, a Bezirksleitung several Kreise (administrative units within a state), and an Unterbezirksleitung usually one Kreis. By about October 1931, this seems to have been only a theoretical division. After January 1933, there were no Bezirksleiters left. See Spiess, "Aufbau," p. 21.

2. Details on decentralization are in: Tyrell, *Vom "Trommler"*; Orlow I; Horn, *Führerideologie*.

3. Hitler's theory of natural selection (1929) is expounded in Wagener, *Hitler*, p. 44.

4. Quotation is from Abel, *Hitler*, p. 79 (italics mine). Also see police reports of January 25, 1923 and April 1, 1925, SAB, 4, 65, II, A, 9, b; Wiemer to Baron Michel-Kissling, Berlin-Lichtenberg, August 10, 1939, BDC, PK, PLA H. Wiemer; curriculum vitae Kurt Schmalz, Munich, June 28, 1943, BDC, PK, PLA K. Schmalz; Baehr, "Geschichte der Ortsgruppe Widminnen," p. 16, SAPKG, 240, D/116; curriculum vitae Hesse, Königsberg, n.d., SAG, SF 6817, GA/22; Gillgasch to Heidrich, Insterburg, March 30, 1930, SAG, SF 6818, GA/34; Dr. Naunin to Gauleitung Königsberg, Marienwerder, [June 1930], SAG, SF 6819, GA/34; Gillgasch to Wehner, [Königsberg], December 16, 1931, SAG, SF 6819, GA/36; Gillgasch to Seiler, [Königsberg], November 17, 1931, SAG, SF 6819, GA/37; Hermann Krüger, ed., *Wir waren dabei . . . Berichte über die nationalsozialistische Bewegung und Entwicklung*

im ehemaligen Kreise Isenhagen (Wittingen, [1934]), pp. 10–11; Gimbel, ed., *Wir*, p. 49; Spiess, "Aufbau," p. 21; Karl Heinz Albrecht, *Zehn Jahre Kampf um Gera: Eine Geschichte der NSDAP im Thüringer Osten* [Gera, 1933], pp. 63–64; Herbert Gaede, *Schwede – Coburg: Ein Lebensbild des Gauleiters und Oberpräsidenten von Pommern* (Berlin, 1939), p. 10; Hambrecht, *Aufstieg*, p. 139; Noakes, *Nazi Party*, p. 90. The scarcity of leadership potential is documented in: Koch to Kiewitt, [Königsberg], November 27, 1930, SAG, SF 6818, GA/33; Rosenberg to Luetgebrune, Munich, January 16, 1928, NA, T-253, 32/1482628; Hitler to Wagener, late 1931, in Wagener, *Hitler*, p. 413; Darré to Schwarz, Munich, October 10, 1932, BA, Schumacher/375; Tyrell, *Vom "Trommler,"* p. 167; Horn, *Führerideologie*, p. 287. The high degree of personnel turnover, especially at the lowest party levels, is evident from Baehr, "Widminnen," p. 6; Bezirksleiter Nordost, Gau Ostpreussen, to Gau Ostpreussen, Königsberg, November 15, 1930, SAG, SF 6818, GA/33; Gillgasch to Seiler, [Königsberg], July 10, 1931, SAG, SF 6819, GA/37; Liebel to Koch, Königsberg-Sackheim, September 9, 1932, SAG, SF 6815, GA/9; Hambrecht, *Aufstieg*, pp. 148–150.

5. Nyomarkay, *Charisma*, especially p. 30; Schildt, "Arbeitsgemeinschaft Nord-West," especially p. 41; Hüttenberger, *Gauleiter*, especially p. 31; doc. 83 a in Tyrell, ed., *Führer*, pp. 230–232. The cases of Klant, who exercised arbitrary and irrationally motivated power in Hamburg (1926), of Hessian Gauleiter Friedrich Ringshausen, who battled not the Führer but part of his Munich camarilla (1927), and of Halle-Merseburg Bezirksleiter Hans Wiemer, who continued on as party agitator after having been fired by his Gau (1929), are illustrations of trespasses of blurred lines of authority. See Krebs, *Infancy*, p. 39; doc. 90 in Tyrell, ed., *Führer*, p. 242; Gau Halle Merseburg to NSDAP-Reichsleitung, Halle, September 12, 1929, BDC, PK, PLA H. Wiemer. Rogowski's view, "The *Gauleiter*," p. 405, reportedly supported by Tyrell, that the bonds of authority tightened as early as summer 1926 is not, as he writes, "generally held," and, in light of my evidence, incorrect.

6. Horn, *Führerideologie*, p. 286; Stachura, "Strategy," pp. 279–280; Kissenkoetter, *Strasser*, pp. 35–40, 71–72; correspondence regarding P. Hinkler (1930-31), BDC, PK, PLA P. Hinkler; case of Ortsgruppenleiter F.K. in Schmidtke to Gauleitung Ostpreussen, Organisationsabteilung I, Tilsit, September 15, 1931, SAG, SF 6819, GA/36; Noakes, *Nazi Party*, p. 158; Hüttenberger, *Gauleiter*, p. 56.

7. Quotation is from Heuss, *Weg*, p. 120. Also see Horn, *Führerideologie*, pp. 286, 381–385; Hüttenberger, *Gauleiter*, p. 58; Tyrell, ed., *Führer*, p. 369; Hentschel, *Monate*, p. 80; Kissenkoetter, *Strasser*, pp. 65–82. Dr. Albert Krebs, Gauleiter of Hamburg, was dismissed by Hitler from party offices and from the party itself in the spring of 1932, as an alleged exponent of an older order. Krebs's reaction is in *Die junge Mannschaft* (June, 1932), 126–128; also see Krebs, *Infancy*, pp. 133–137, 188–189.

8. Examples of "regular" promotion in Görlich to G. Strasser, Cleve, June 18, 1932, BDC, PK, PLA A. Görlich; Hambrecht, *Aufstieg*, p. 142; Krebs, *Infancy*, p. ix; curriculum vitae Karl Lenz, BDC, SSA K. Lenz; cur-

riculum vitae Hesse, Königsberg, n.d., SAG, SF 6817, GA/22; curriculum vitae Kurt Schmalz, Munich, June 28, 1943, BDC, PK, PLA K. Schmalz. For men with double functions, see Kasche to G. Strasser, Sorau, December 19, 1928, BD C, PK, PLAS. Kasche; Lutze to Renteln, Hanover, January 9, 1932, HIS, 18/340; "Parteigeschichte der N.S.D.A.P. Ortsgr. Altenthann," n.d., SAN, 503/96.

9. See Horn, *Führerideologie*, p. 286

10. See, for instance, Ernest M. Doblin and Claire Pohly, "The Social Composition of the Nazi Leadership," *American Journal of Sociology*, 51 (1945), 49; and Zapf, *Wandlungen*, pp. 51, 179.

11. Quotations are from entry for April 24, 1966, in Speer, *Spandau*, p. 442; and Krebs, *Infancy*, p. 47. For the Munich/Bavarian scenario till fall 1923, see Franz-Willing, *Hitlerbewegung*, pp. 130–131; for Cologne March 1921, see Schmidt, *Jahre*, p. 44; for Nuremberg February 1922, see Robin Lenmenn, "Julius Streicher and the Origins of the NSDAP in Nuremberg, 1918–1923," in Anthony Nicholls and Erich Matthias, eds., *German Democracy and the Triumph of Hitler: Essays in Recent German History* (London, 1971), p. 139. Further, see Böhme to G. Strasser, Frieberg, August 5, 1932, BDC, PK, PLA H. Böhme; curriculum vitae Hesse, Königsberg, n.d., SAG, SF 6817, GA/22; Baehr, "Geschichte der Ortsgruppe Widminnen," pp. 6, 14 (see n. 4 above); Gimbel, ed., *Wir*, pp. 89–90.

12. My analysis for 1930 and 1932 is according to figures in Max Schwarz, *MdR: Biographisches Handbuch der Reichstage* (Hanover, 1965); and *Reichstags-Handbuch* (Berlin, 1928 through 1936). Although Weber's count of workers, "Merkamale," p. 74, is even more conservative than mine, he compares the NSDAP favorably with all other parties except for the KPD. Calculations for East Prussia according to figures in Penier to Gauleitung Königsberg, October 14, 1929, SAG, SF 6815, GA/7. Also see *Bremer Zeitung*, November 5, 1922; Böhnke, *NSDAP*, pp. 48, 52, 131, 198, 201.

13. See Dr. Naunin to Gauleitung Königsberg, Marienwerder, [June 1930], SAG SF 6819, GA/34; Schmidtke to Organisationsabteilung I, Gauleitung Ostpreussen, Tilsit, September 15, 1931, SAG, SF 6819, GA/36; Albrecht, *Kampf*, pp. 63–64; Krebs, *Infancy*, p. 50; Stokes, "Composition," p. 16.

14. Compare table 1. A list of ninety-two Thuringian Ortsgruppenleiters for the summer of 1924, a period of illegitimacy for the Nazis, shows an elite proportion of 22.8%. IfZ, MA-135/136514-15.

15. See table 10 (columns A, C, E); figure 10; table 1.

16. Compare table 1.

17. Differences between the two Ortsgruppen areas, Kassel and Harburg, may be explained in terms of regional conditions. For instance, the rate of Harburg's proletarian Ortsgruppenleiters was higher than Kassel's because of Harburg's greater percentage of "workers" in the gainfully employed population. The presence merely of "unskilled" workers in the Kassel group suggests a high proportion of farm hands. But a more diversified industrial grid such as Harburg's required craft workers, whose strong presence in the region is in

fact reflected in Harburg's Ortsgruppenleiter group. As calculated on the basis of figures for the census of 1933 in *Berufszählung: Die berufliche und soziale Gliederung der Bevölkerung in den Ländern und Landesteilen: Provinz Hannover* (*Statistik des Deutschen Reichs: Volks-, Berufs- und Betriebszählung vom 16. Juni 1933,* vol. 455/14) (Berlin, 1936), pp. 48–49, 51.4% of Harburg and precisely the environment from which the Ortsgruppenleiters came (Kreis Harburg; Stadtkreis Harburg-Wilhelmsburg) were "workers" according to the official definition. By the same definition, and calculated on the basis of figures for the same census in *Berufszählung . . . Landesteilen: Provinz Hessen-Nassau* (*Statistik des Deutschen Reichs . . . ,* vol. 456/25) (Berlin, 1936), pp. 42–43, the percentage of "workers" in Regierungs-Bezirk Kassel (origin of Kassel Ortsgruppenleiters) was 44.6%. In both cases, only full-time, gainfully employed men and women were counted.

18. Like Harburg, Lüneburg was partially dependent on Hamburg's marine-related industry, with a fair share of skilled and craft workers commuting to the metropolis, while unskilled rural laborers undoubtedly toiled in the fields. The percentage of "workers" in Lüneburg (Stadt- und Landkreis Lüneburg) was 48.0%, lower than Harburg's, but higher than Kassel's. See *Berufszählung . . . Hannover* (as in n. 17 above), pp. 48–49 (counting procedure as indicated in n. 17).

19. See Zapf, *Wandlungen*, p. 144.

20. Data for the "New Functionaries" were taken from *Deutsches Führerlexikon 1934/35* (Berlin, 1934). All men with an NSDAP affiliation were counted, but not state- and church-affiliated men. The total universe arrived at up to and including 1934 was 639 N. The social composition of this group up to and including 1932 (443 N) was as follows: elite, 54.6%; lower middle class, 38.8%; workers, 6.5%. As is apparent from figure 10, the percentages for the Gauleiters in 1932 were 37.5%, 52.5%, and 10.0%, respectively.

21. Table 1 and n. 20 above.

22. Kater, "Wandel," pp. 36–39.

23. The traditionally high-profile role of public school teachers in political parties before 1933 is discussed in Bölling, *Volksschullehrer*.

24. In Baden according to the census of 1933, all *Selbständige* (self-employed) within the gainfully employed population made up 24.5%. See *Berufszählung: Die berufliche und soziale Gliederung der Bevölkerung in den Ländern und Landesteilen: Land Baden* (*Statistik des Deutschen Reichs: Volks-, Berufs- und Betriebszählung vom 16. Juni 1933*, vol. 456/32) (Berlin, 1935), p. 3. These would have included merchants and self-employed academic professionals.

25. For the numerical strength of persons active in farming in that region, see column 16 for Stadt- und Landkreis Lüneburg in *Berufszählung . . . Hannover* (as in n. 17 above), p. 49. Although the presence of public school teachers in the Nazi party must not be overrated, there is no question that they played a key role in the development of the Nazi leadership apparatus at all levels. See my remarks in *American Historical Review*, 85 (1980), 152–153, as

well as my article "Hitlerjugend," pp. 607-608, 613-614. Also see exemplary case histories contained in Scheerschmidt to NSDAP-Reichsgeschäftsstelle, Neuvorwerk, September 12, 1931, BDC, NSLB, PLA K. Scheerschmidt; curriculum vitae Bernhardt, Kölleda, April 25, 1934, BDC, PK, PLA K. Bernhardt. Further: Pridham, *Rise*, pp. 191-192; Böhnke, *NSDAP*, p. 47; Hambrecht, *Aufstieg*, p. 36; Linz, "Notes," pp. 48, 56. In light of my findings with respect to the lower echelons of the NSDAP in Harburg and Lüneburg, Linz's statement that "none of the [fascist] parties recruited its leaders among rural society" ("Notes," p. 55) has to be modified. More accurate in this regard is Lepsius, *Nationalismus*, p. 23, n. 27.

26. See Dreitzel, *Elitebegriff.*

27. Only the Communist deputies were generally younger still. For 1924 to 1930, see Doblin and Pohly, "Composition," p. 43. For 1930, see Heinrich Geiger, "Der Reichstag der alten Herren," *Die Tat*, 22 (1930), 285-289; Geiger, "Streifzug im verjüngten Reichstag," *Die Tat*, 22 (1931), 811-816. According to figures in Schwarz, *Handbuch*, and *Reichstags-Handbuch* (1928-1932), I have calculated the average ages of Reichstag deputies for all of 1932 as follows: Nazis, 39.2 years; DNVP, 52.0; DVP, 53.5; Center, 51.4; Economic Party, 51.3; DDP/Deutsche Staatspartei, 50.1; SPD, 50.3; KPD, 36.9; *all* deputies, 45.4.

28. Compare Kater, "Soziographie," p. 156; and Gordon, *Hitler*, p. 71. Unfortunately, Gordon fails to provide average age values for the forty-five Ortsgruppenleiters he mentions.

29. Linz, "Notes," p. 81.

30. See Stokes, "Composition," p. 18; Zapf, *Wandlungen*, p. 169; Doblin and Pohly, "Composition," p. 49.

31. Calculated according to figures in *Partei-Statistik* I, 162; and *Partei-Statistik* II, 336, 376. In the latter case, only Kreisleiters and Ortsgruppenleiters were considered. In Franconia between 1925 and 1931, 63.8% of the general Nazi membership was between 21 and 30 years of age, whereas the leaders in that district varied in age from 34 to 44 years. Hambrecht, *Aufstieg*, p. 304.

32. Between 1925 and the first month of 1933, 14.2% of all Kreisleiters as compared to 16.8% of all Ortsgruppenleiters were between the ages of 18 and 30. See *Partei-Statistik* II, 336, 376. The figures refer only to party personnel still in office by the end of 1934.

33. Age of Kassel Ortsgruppenleiters according to Schön, *Entstehung*, p. 98.

34. The average age of Nazi deputies in the Reichstag for all of 1932 was 39.2 (see n. 27 above). Also see Doblin and Pohly, "Composition," p. 49.

35. Calculations for New Functionaries on basis of figures in *Deutsches Führerlexikon 1934/35* (see n. 20 above).

36. For the exceptions, see Herbert Schwarzwälder, *Die Machtergreifung der NSDAP in Bremen 1933* (Bremen, 1966), p. 122; Hans Wolfram von Hentig, "Beiträge zu einer Sozialgeschichte des Dritten Reiches," *Vierteljahrshefte für Zeitgeschichte*, 16 (1968), 49-50.

37. The above examples are documented in their order of occurrence in

Okrass, *Ende*, p. 68; curriculum vitae Karl Lenz, n.d., BDC, SSA K. Lenz; Hambrecht, *Aufstieg*, p. 123; Karl Wahl, ". . . *es ist das deutsche Herz*": *Erlebnisse und Erkenntnisse eines ehemaligen Gauleiters* (Augsburg, 1954), p. 53; Böhme to G. Strasser, Freiberg, August 5, 1932, BDC, PK, PLA H. Böhme; Jordan, *Erlebt*, p. 22; Gillgasch to Gauleitung Königsberg, Insterburg, June 20, 1930, SAG, SF 6818, GA/34; Kiefert to Paltinat, Tilsit, December 29, 1930, SAG, SF 6818, GA/33; Lutze to Renteln, Hanover, January 9, 1932, HIS, 18/340.

38. Broszat, *Staat*, pp. 52–53. Also see Görlich to G. Strasser, Cleve, June 18, 1932, BDC, PK, PLA A. Görlich (quotation); Wiemer to Baron Michel-Kissling, Berlin-Lichtenberg, August 10, 1939, BDC, PK, PLA H. Wiemer; Gimbel, ed., *Wir*, pp. 32–33, 89–90; Böhnke, *NSDAP*, p. 202.

39. On constitutional grounds Nazi speakers were often condemned for violating the Law for the Protection of the Republic. See the case of Haselmeyer (1926) in Schön, *Entstehung*, p. 89. Background on indictment on constitutional grounds is in Gotthard Jasper, *Der Schutz der Republik: Studien zur staatlichen Sicherung der Demokratie in der Weimarer Rebublik 1922-1930* (Tübingen, 1963), pp. 106–210.

40. Hambrecht, *Aufstieg*, p. 123; and Holz to Frau Lämmermeyer, [Nuremberg jail], cell 258, December 22, 1930, HIS, 13/255. Also Streicher's own testimony in Jay W. Baird, "Das politische Testament Julius Streichers: Ein Dokument aus den Papieren des Hauptmanns Dolibois," *Vierteljahrshefte für Zeitgeschichte*, 26 (1978), 688.

41. Grohé to Dicker, Cologne, August 18, 1927, in Schmidt, *Jahre*, pp. 93-94; Koch to Bezirk Nordost, [Königsberg], December 18, 1930, SAG, SF 6818, GA/32.

42. See memorandum Kriminal-Oberkommissär, Passau, March 15, 1932, BDC, PK, PLA M. Moosbauer; Gillgasch to Pg. [*Parteigenosse*], Insterburg, May 6, 1929, SAG, SF 6818, GA/34.

43. Goebbels to Born, Berlin, June 9, 1932, facsimile in A. Piontek, "Das Recht der alten Kämpfer! Volksgemeinschaft bedeutet nicht Ellbogenfreiheit für jeden Neuling!" *Arbeitertum*, February 1, 1934, p. 7.

44. Average wage figures for late 1932 were calculated according to *Statistisches Jahrbuch für das Deutsche Reich 1933*, p. 273. Also see doc. 83 a in Tyrell, ed., *Führer*, p. 231; Memmel to Gradl, Würzburg, October 11, 1932; Ennerst to Gradl, Kitzingen, October 11, 1932, SAN, 503/112; Hildebrandt to G. Strasser, Parchim, April 27, 1928, BDC, PK, PLA F. Hildebrandt; A. H. Schultz, "Friedrich Hildebrandt," in Klaus Ekkehard, ed., *Die Reichsstatthalter: Ein Volksbuch* (Gotha, n.d.), p. 47; Krebs, *Schulenburg*, p. 303; Böhme to G. Strasser, Freiberg, August 5, 1932, BDC, PK, PLA K. Lenz; [Schultz] to Jordan, Munich, February 11, 1931, BDC, PK, PLA R. Jordan; Jordan, *Erlebt*, p. 14; Wahl, *Herz*, pp. 53, 61; Heuss, *Weg*, p. 120; Figge, "Opposition," pp. 133-135; Herrmann, "Agitation," p. 225; Kissenkoetter, *Strasser*, pp. 62-64.

45. See table 10; figure 10; and n. 20 above.

46. Lerner, *Elite*, especially pp. 84-91. On the basis of less persuasive

evidence, a similar view was earlier expressed by Gerth, "Nazi Party." See, for example, p. 524. Lerner's interpretation influenced, to a greater or smaller degree, the historiography on the "Nazi Elite" for over two decades to follow. See Zapf, *Wandlungen*, pp. 51–54, 176–177; Broszat, *Staat*, pp. 53–54; Hüttenberger, *Gauleiter*, pp. 119; Winkler, *Mittelstand*, p. 164; Linz, "Notes," pp. 46–47. Schumann's analysis of Nazi labor (NSBO) functionaries, "Führungsspitzen," pp. 159–162, was governed by similar criteria of social stability.

47. Rogowski, "The *Gauleiter*," especially p. 415. Also see Merkl, *Violence*, p. 623.

48. Whereas Lerner considered every tenth name mentioned in *Deutsches Führerlexikon 1934/35* (a total N of about 160), rendering a main sample that was then supplemented by subsamples, I analyzed the social, if not the military and educational, backgrounds of *all* NSDAP or NSDAP-related office holders (639 N — see n. 20). Out of the total of 75 Gauleiters from 1925 to 1932, 56 could be considered for my mobility study, whose paternal occupations were discovered through research. Rogowski, on the other hand, included only 42 Gauleiters in his working sample. See Lerner, *Elite*, pp. 1–2; and Rogowski, "The *Gauleiter*," p. 413. I am greatly indebted to Professor Rogowski as well as to several West German communal registries for their help in my attempt to enlarge my Gauleiter sample. According to my analysis, the total mobility of the Gauleiters in the Time of Struggle was just under 43%, not as high as 61%, the figure extrapolated by Rogowski.

49. Rogowski computed an upward in-mobility rate (measuring inflow) of 40% for the Gauleiters, and he quotes a Reich population upward in-mobility rate of anywhere from 13 to 20–25%, on the basis of information from Nothaas and Zapf. See "The *Gauleiter*," p. 414. While I could not establish the upward in-mobility rate for the Reich population with the aid of figures published recently by Hartmut Kaelble, "Soziale Mobilität in Deutschland, 1900–1960," in Kaelble et al., *Probleme der Modernisierung in Deutschland: Sozialhistorische Studien zum 19. und 20. Jahrhundert* (Wiesbaden, 1978), pp. 235–327, I can demonstrate, with the use of some of Kaelble's data, a higher overall in-mobility rate (*both* upward and downward) than in the Reich population: in 1925–1932 the Gauleiters' in-mobility rate was 42.8%, that of the Reich population in 1925–1929 was 24.0%. (This last figure is from Kaelble, p. 255.)

50. Lerner, *Elite*, p. 80. It remains questionable what Lerner's criteria for social classification were, that is, what he meant by "plebeian origins." On p. 81, for instance, he describes Heinrich Himmler as a man of such origins which he believes "to conform to those of Nazi administrators generally." The truth is that Himmler's father was a widely respected Bavarian upper-school teacher and that Himmler himself benefited from a *completed* university education. See Kater, *Das "Ahnenerbe,"* p. 17.

51. According to my computations, 39.1% of all elite Gauleiters 1925–1932 were socially stable: elite sons of elite fathers.

52. According to my calculations, 71.4% of all lower-middle-class

Gauleiters 1925–1932 were self-recruited from that class. According to calculations by Kaelble, "Mobilität," p. 254, the corresponding percentage for the Reich population 1925–1929 was 72%.

53. For the Reich figures, see Kaelble, "Mobilität," p. 254.

54. Tables 1, 10 (columns E, I, Q, U); figure 10. Also see Kater, "Wandel," pp. 36–38.

55. See text near n. 20, and n. 20.

56. Lerner, *Elite*, pp. 98–99.

57. For the military or paramilitary background of all manner of Nazi functionaries see the examples selected at random from a huge biographical source material: curriculum vitae Hesse, Königsberg, n.d., SAG, SF 6817, GA/22; Liebel to Koch, Königsberg, September 9, 1932, SAG, SF 6815, GA/9; Ullmer to Schwarz, Buchen, February 8, 1939, BDC, PK, PLA A. Ullmer; judgment of Gaugericht Hessen-Nassau, Frankfurt/Main, October 14, 1943 (case of Karl Walther), BDC, PK, PLA K. Walther; Krebs, *Infancy*, p. 136. On the "heroic ideal" see the revealing remarks regarding "voluntary service" in Hielscher, *Jahre*, p. 21; Franz von Salomon, *Fragebogen* [*The Questionnaire*] (New York, 1955), pp. 86–87. Also see Robert G. L. Waite, *Vanguard of Nazism: The Free Corps Movement in Postwar Germany 1918–1923* (Cambridge, Mass., 1952), pp. 41–42. On Jünger, see Struve, *Elites*, pp. 377–414; on Niemöller, Bracher, *Dictatorship*, p. 380. See also Rauschning, *Revolution*, pp. 264–296.

58. Dahrendorf, *Society*, p. 93. Also see Geiger, *Schichtung*, pp. 5, 77–138.

59. Dahrendorf, *Society*, p. 367. The judgment on the petit bourgeois agrees with Mayer, "Lower Middle Class," p. 432.

60. Minutes of speech by Nazi party comrade Max Kolb (Bayreuth) on the island of Reichenau, April 5, 1936, SAL, PL 512/II, N, 98, 2; entry for November 18, 1964, in Speer, *Spandau*, p. 417; Wahl, *Herz*, pp. 61, 150; Hüttenberger, *Gauleiter*, p. 46. For Dahrendorf's criticism of *Herzensbildung* as a sham *Bildung*, see *Society*, p. 363. In terms of the history of ideas, *Herzensbildung* is traceable, by way of the concepts of Paul de Lagarde and other nationalistic, postromantic thinkers, to the German *Vormärz* (pre-1848–49 revolutionary era) as a reaction to the formalistic (rational) *Bildung* that was a product of the *Aufklärung* (German Enlightenment). See Vierhaus, "Bildung," in *Grundbegriffe*, I, 537–538, 548, 550; and text in the Introduction near n. 10.

61. Gillgasch to Wehner, [Königsberg], December 16, 1931, SAG, SF 6819, GA/36; Baehr, "Geschichte der Ortsgruppe Widminnen," p. 16 (see n. 4 above).

62. With reference to Nazi leaders, see *Prisma*, no. 11 (September 1947), p. 37.

63. Schemm's intellectual profile can be gleaned from Hans Schemm, "Deutsche Erziehung! Warum nationalsozialistisches Wollen?" *Nationalsozialistische Monatshefte*, 1 (1930), 370–374; Schemm, "Gedankensammlung" (1934–35), BDC, PK, PLA H. Schemm; Bernd Lembeck,

Hans Schemm: Ein Leben für Deutschland (Munich, 1936), pp. 5–27; Benedikt Lochmüller, *Hans Schemm*, I and II (Munich, 1940); Gertrud Kahl-Furthmann, ed., *Hans Schemm spricht: Seine Reden und sein Werk*, 11th ed. (Bayreuth, 1942). Also see Aretin, *Krone*, pp. 186–187. Hambrecht, *Aufstieg*, pp. 139–140, probably overestimates Schemm's "mobility of mind."

64. Holz to Frau [*Professor!*] Lämmermeyer, [Nuremberg jail], cell 258, October 20, 1930, HIS, 13/255; artistic sketch of Holz's prison cell signed "Karl Holz," July 12, 1927, BDC, PK, PLA K. Holz; Schmidt, *Jahre*, p. 56.

65. Dahrendorf, *Society*, p. 281.

66. Eberhard Jäckel, *Hitler's "Weltanschauung": A Blueprint for Power* (Middletown, Conn., 1972). Also see Ernst Nolte, *Three Faces of Fascism: Action Française, Italian Fascism, National Socialism* (New York, 1966), pp. 402–425.

67. See M. Rainer Lepsius, "From Fragmented Party Democracy to Government by Emergency Decree and National Socialist Takeover: Germany," in Juan J. Linz and Alfred Stepan, eds., *The Breakdown of Democratic Regimes* (Baltimore and London, 1978), p. 63.

68. Rauschning, *Revolution*, p. 450. A similar evaluation of Rosenberg's work was offered as early as 1934 by Heiden, *History*, p. 41. In light of these astute contemporary perceptions, Schulz's superficial analysis of Rosenberg's work in *Aufstieg*, p. 420, is wide off the mark. The relatively low esteem that Rosenberg's book enjoyed among Old Fighters after its first appearance was the subject of one of Hitler's evening monologues during the war: entry for April 11, 1942, in *Hitlers Tischgespräche*, p. 275. Also see Wiedemann, *Mann*, pp. 193–194.

69. See Dinter's own claim in his letter to Streicher, Dörrberg, June 28, 1928, BDC, PK, PLA A. Dinter. At the core of Dinter's "theosophy" lay the alleged polarity between (Aryan) Christianity and (non-Aryan) Judaism and their perennial battle for superiority. By virtue of restricting himself to this main theme alone, Dinter's argumentative thrust was potentially much more powerful than Hitler's, provided the reader appreciated his peculiar logic. Dinter's main line of thought may be gleaned from his widely read book, *Die Sünde wider das Blut: Ein Zeitroman*, 3d ed. (Leipzig, 1919).

70. Tyrell, ed., *Führer*, p. 149.

71. Gillgasch to Usadel, Insterburg, March 24, 1931; Usadel to Gillgasch, Insterburg, April 2, 1931, SAG, SF 6818, GA/33.

72. Hitler, *Mein Kampf*, pp. 695–716, 846–867; Werner Maser, *Hitlers Mein Kampf: Entstehung, Aufbau, Stil, Änderungen, Quellen, Quellenwert, kommentierte Auszüge*, 2d ed. (Munich and Esslingen, 1966), pp. 210–225.

73. Albrecht, *Kampf*, pp. 63–64.

74. Case of Grohé in Schmidt, *Jahre*, p. 56; case of Weissel in report of Weissel, Insterburg, September 1, 1930, SAG, SF 6818, GA/34.

75. In 1925 the confusion resulted from a misreading of the German "Protokolle der Weisen von Zion" as "Protokolle der Weissen Ziegen." Examples are from Krüger, ed., *Wir*, p. 11; Bremen police report, October 8, 1927, SAB, 4, 65, II, A, 9, b. Also see Volkmann, "Programm," p. 252;

Strasser, *Hitler*, p. 60; Wiedemann, *Mann*, pp. 55–56; Karl Lange, *Hitlers unbeachtete Maximen: "Mein Kampf" und die Öffentlichkeit* (Stuttgart, 1968), pp. 30–31.

76. See Hierl to Gauleiters, Munich, December 23, 1930, SAMs, Gauleitung Westfalen-Nord, Gauamt für Volkswohlfahrt/15; Gutterer, "Richtlinien für die Propaganda durch Kleinarbeit," Hanover, November 26, 1932, NHSA, Hann. 310 I, A 122 I.

77. See curriculum vitae Hesse, Königsberg, n.d., SAG, SF 6815, GA/9. The hero of Grimm's novel is Cornelius Friebott who as a young man seeks his fortune in South Africa where he is constantly maligned for a multiplicity of reasons, among them his display of German "virtues," such as industriousness (see n. 59): Hans Grimm, *Volk ohne Raum* (Gütersloh, 1926). Also see Geissler, *Dekadenz*, pp. 142–150.

78. See the example of Edgar Brinkmann (Hamburg, 1926) in Krebs, *Infancy*, p. 45.

79. On Streicher, see Himmler to Ortsgruppe Nürnberg, [Munich], December 28, 1926, BDC, PK, PLA J. Streicher; Wagener, *Hitler*, p. 180; Strasser, *Hitler*, p. 41; Hoegner, *Flucht*, p. 67; Baird, "Testament." Streicher was particularly fond of uncovering "ritual murders" of Christian boys, allegedly committed by orthodox Jews: see correspondence "Der Stürmer/Gau-Propagandaleiter Ostpreussen" (December, 1932), SAG, SF 6818, GA/29. The quotation regarding Klant is from Krebs, *Infancy*, p. 40. On Schwede and Ley, see Gaede, *Schwede-Coburg*, p. 9; Schmidt, *Jahre*, p. 27; Albrecht Tyrell, "Führergedanke und Gauleiterwechsel: Die Teilung des Gaues Rheinland der NSDAP 1931," *Vierteljahrshefte für Zeitgeschichte*, 23 (1975), 360. Also see Holz to Frau Lämmermeyer, [Nuremberg jail], cell 258, December 22, 1930, HIS, 13/255; Henningsen, *Niedersachsenland*, p. 71; Schön, *Entstehung*, p. 89; Hambrecht, *Aufstieg*, p. 141.

80. On the authoritarian father image, see Robert G. L. Waite, *The Psychopathic God: Adolf Hitler* (New York, 1977), pp. 295–300. Kurt Sontheimer, *Antidemokratisches Denken in der Weimarer Republik: Die politischen Ideen des deutschen Nationalismus zwischen 1918 und 1933*, 4th ed. (Munich, 1964), pp. 43–53, 72–78, has pointed to the connection between an irrational attitude and antidemocratic thought in the Weimar Republic. Problems with alcohol among functionaries are indicated in Gaugeschäftsführer to Arendt, [Königsberg], January 5, 1931, SAG, SF 6818, GA/34; Gillgasch to Usadel, Insterburg, March 24, 1931, SAG, SF 6818, GA/33; Schmidtke to Gauleitung Ostpreussen, Tilsit, September 15, 1931, SAG, SF 6819, GA/36.

8. PEACETIME: JANUARY 1933 TO SEPTEMBER 1939

1. A prototype of the post-1933 Blockleiter had existed since 1932. See doc. 127 in Tyrell, ed., *Führer*, p. 305–306.

2. Computations are based on figures in: *Partei-Statistik* II, 7; *Beamten-Jahrbuch*, 26 (1939), 170; Diehl-Thiele, *Partei*, pp. 164–165. Intermediate figures for April 1937 are in Gerth, "Nazi Party," p. 522.

3. From January 1, 1935, to January 1, 1939, Gauleiters increased from 30 to 39 (23%), Kreisleiters from 827 to 903 (8%), Ortsgruppenleiters and Stützpunktleiters combined (on the latter, see n. 5) from 20,724 to 28,376 (37%). Figures are from *Partei-Statistik* II, 7; Diehl-Thiele, *Partei*, pp. 164-165; "Die Reichsstellen der NSDAP," [1939], BA, Schumacher/374; *Reichsband: Adressenwerk der Dienststellen der NSDAP. mit den Angeschlossenen Verbänden des Staates der Reichsregierung — Behörden und der Berufsorganisationen* . . . [Berlin, 1939] (copy in BDC).

4. Ley had succeeded G. Strasser in that post after the latter's resignation in December 1932. Technically, Hitler put himself in Strasser's position and appointed Ley as his chief of staff (*Stabsleiter*). See Gerd Rühle, *Das Dritte Reich: Dokumentarische Darstellung des Aufbaues der Nation: Die Kampfjahre 1918-1933* (Berlin, [1936]), p. 290.

5. *Partei-Statistik* II, 405. Nazi Stützpunkte were known before 1933 (comprising from 4 to 14 members), but they seem to have been very insignificant, because they invariably rose to the level of Ortsgruppen (from 15 members upward) or simply adopted that label. Spiess, "Aufbau," p. 21.

6. See: directive Hess, Munich, April 14, 1934, SAG, SF 6815, GA, A, 1a-1e; Ley, directive 12, Munich, May 1, 1936; Gauleitung Mainfranken, "Vertraulich. Block-und Zellenneuordnung der N.S.D.A.P.," Würzburg, November 26, 1936, BA, Schumacher/375; "Das Gesicht der Partei," n.d., BA, Schumacher/374 (pp. 7-10); "Anweisung an die Ortsgruppenorganisationsleiter," [before World War II], BA, Schumacher/372; Helmut Mehringer, *Die NSDAP als politische Ausleseorganisation* (Munich, 1938), p. 104; *Nationalsozialistisches Jahrbuch*, 18 (1944), 178; Gerth, "Nazi Party," pp. 521-522; Neumann, *Behemoth*, pp. 304-305; Krosigk, *Deutschland*, pp. 242-244; entry for December 14, 1947, in Speer, *Spandau*, p. 84; Speer, *Reich*, pp. 86-88; Orlow II, p. 134; Tyrell, "Führergedanke," p. 341.

7. The percentage figure is based on data in *Partei-Statistik* II, 7.

8. Schmitt, *Staat*, p. 16. Also see Gaede, *Schwede-Coburg*, p. 21; Broszat, *Staat*, pp. 142, 146-148; Fröhlich and Broszat, "Macht," p. 560; doc. (November 4, 1935) in Broszat et al., eds., *Bayern*, p. 88. This complex is comprehensively treated in Diehl-Thiele, *Partei*; and Mommsen, *Beamtentum*.

9. Minutes of speech by Hess at Nuremberg Party Rally 1938, SAG, SF 6815, GA/15 (p. 3); Klenner, *Verhältnis*, pp. 258-261; Hüttenberger, *Gauleiter*, p. 118.

10. Activities report Gau Süd-Hannover-Braunschweig for August 1933, Hanover, September 12, 1933, NHSA, Hann. 310 I, B 13; Ley, directive 12, Munich, May 1, 1936, BA, Schumacher/375; Arbeitsanweisung 13/1938, Munich, October 19, 1938, BA, NS 22/2022; Seier, "Rektor," pp. 120-121; Aretin, "Universität," p. 694; Rolf Eilers, *Die nationalsozialistische Schulpolitik: Eine Studie zur Funktion der Erziehung im totalitären Staat* (Cologne and Opladen, 1963), p. 73. Also see Orlow II.

11. Blockleiters' functions are explained in Ley, directive 12, Munich, May 1, 1936, BA, Schumacher/375; Hess, directive 134/39, June 23, 1939, in Verordnungsblatt Gau Süd-Hannover-Braunschweig, July 15, 1939,

Schumacher/202; "Das Gesicht der Partei," n.d., BA, Schumacher/374 (pp. 8–9); "Anweisung an die Ortsgruppenorganisationsleiter," n.d. [before World War II], BA, Schumacher/372; Kahl-Furthmann, ed., *Schemm*, p. 337; Wahl, *Herz*, p. 186; Collins, *Years*, p. 45; Eilers, *Schulpolitik*, p. 86; Krüger, *Haus*, p. 46; Christabel Bielenberg, *The Past is Myself* (London, 1968), p. 51. On the decreasing popularity of Blockleiters and problems of recruitment, see: covering letter, Ley, directive 12 (as above); decree Lutze, Munich, June 1, 1936; Gauleitung Mainfranken, "Vertraulich. Block- und Zellenneuordnung der N.S.D.A.P.," Würzburg, November 26, 1936, BA, Schumacher/375; situation report Gau Westfalen-Nord for November 1936, SAMs, Gauleitung Westfalen-Nord, Gauschulungsamt/15; Forstner to Kreisleitung Wasserburg, Aham, March 2, 1937, SAM, NSDAP/109; activities and situation report Kreis Wilhelmshaven, [April 1938], NSAO, 320, 2/2; political situation report Ortsgruppe Rothenburg/Tauber for February 1939, BA, Schumacher/372. For an example of an incompetent though well-meaning block leader instructed to report on Freiburg historian Gerhard Ritter, see Ritter, "Professor," p. 23.

12. The corporate stability manifested itself through peer association of long standing. While 71.4% of all Kreisleiters by early 1935 had joined the NSDAP between 1925 and the September elections of 1930, the corresponding percentages for Ortsgruppenleiters were 29.5%, for Stützpunktleiters 11.7%, and for ordinary party members 5.2%. Of the Kreisleiters, 28.6% had joined between September 1930 and January 30, 1933. For the remaining three groups the corresponding percentages were: 54.9%, 44.7% and 28.1%. See *Partei-Statistik* I and II. Also see Proksch, "Erziehungsauftrag," p. 214. The useful analysis in Schäfer, *NSDAP*, pp. 45–46, is based on figures in *Partei-Statistik* II. See also text below at n. 41, and n. 41.

13. The original number of names in list, "Reichsleiter der NSDAP," n.d., BA, Schumacher/368, was twenty. Because they performed Reichsleiters' functions within Hitler's entourage, I added the names of Hess (Hitler's secretary from 1925 on and deputy Führer after 1933), Röhm (SA Chief of Staff from 1931 until his death in 1934), von Ribbentrop (special adviser on foreign affairs from 1933 till his appointment as Foreign Minister in 1938), and Göring (Hitler's personal representative in Berlin after 1927). See also a somewhat similar list in Neumann, *Behemoth*, pp. 306–307.

14. After 1933, the following seventeen Reichsleiters, making up 70.8% of the total, belonged to the elite (occupations of fathers are indicated in parentheses): Walter Buch, b. 1883, retired major (President of Senate); Richard Walther Darré, b. 1895, univ.-grad. agronomist (import-export wholesaler); Otto Dietrich, b. 1897, PhD, univ.-grad. political scientist (not known); Franz Ritter von Epp, b. 1868, aristocrat, retired general (artist); Hans Frank, b. 1900, LLD, univ.-grad. lawyer (lawyer); Wilhelm Frick, b. 1877, LLD, univ.-grad. higher civil servant (primary-school teacher); Paul Joseph Goebbels, b. 1897, PhD, univ.-grad. German literature critic (lower civil servant); Hermann Göring, b. 1893, retired captain (higher civil servant);

Rudolf Hess, b. 1894, retired lieutenant, university assistant (import-export wholesaler); Konstantin Hierl, b. 1875, retired colonel (judge); Heinrich Himmler, b. 1900, univ.-grad. agronomist (upper-school teacher); Adolf Hühnlein, b. 1881, retired major (not known); Robert Ley, b. 1890, PhD, univ.-grad. chemist (farmer); Joachim von Ribbentrop, b. 1893, entrepreneur (lieutenant colonel); Ernst Röhm, b. 1887, retired captain (lower civil servant); Alfred Rosenberg, b. 1893, univ.-grad. architect (business executive); Baldur von Schirach, b. 1907, aristocrat, university student (theater director). The remaining seven Reichsleiters, 29.2% of the total, belonged to the lower middle class (occupations of fathers in parentheses): Max Amann, b. 1891, merchant (not known); Martin Bormann, b. 1900, farmer (lower civil servant); Philipp Bouhler, b. 1899, retired lieutenant (colonel); Karl Fiehler, b. 1895, lower civil servant (preacher); Willy Grimm, b. 1889, lower civil servant (not known); Viktor Lutze, b. 1890, merchant (master shoemaker and farmer); Franz Xaver Schwarz, b. 1875, retired lower civil servant (master baker). The mean birth year of the group of twenty-four was 1890. Sources for the information: BDC; IfZ; list, "Reichsleiter der NSDAP," n.d., BA, Schumacher/368; *Deutsches Führerlexikon 1934/35*; Erich Stockhorst, *Fünftausend Köpfe: Wer war was im Dritten Reich* (Velbert and Kettwig, 1967); *Wer ist's* (1935).

15. Contrary to the long-accepted interpretation by Konrad Heiden, *Der Fuehrer: Hitler's Rise to Power* (Boston, 1944), pp. 258–259, and his many epigones.

16. Details on these individuals' World War I and postwar careers are in Bradley F. Smith, *Heinrich Himmler: A Nazi in the Making, 1900–1926* (Stanford, Cal., 1971); Kater, *Das "Ahnenerbe,"* pp. 24–25; George W.F. Hallgarten, *Als die Schatten fielen: Erinnerungen vom Jahrhundertbeginn zur Jahrtausendwende* (Frankfurt/Main, 1969), pp. 34–39 (Darré and Himmler); Helmut Heiber, *Joseph Goebbels* (Berlin, 1962), chap. 1 and 2 (Goebbels); Walter Laqueur, *Russia and Germany: A Century of Conflict* (Boston and Toronto, 1965), pp. 69–75; Bollmus, *Rosenberg*, pp. 17–18 (Rosenberg); Martin H. Sommerfeldt, *Hermann Göring: Ein Lebensbild*, 7th ed. (Berlin, n.d.), pp. 13–43; Fanny Gräfin von Wilamowitz-Moellendorff, *Carin Göring* (Berlin, 1934), pp. 50–62 (Göring); Lang, *Secretary*, pp. 24–40 (Bormann); Joachim C. Fest, *The Face of the Third Reich: Portraits of the Nazi Leadership* (New York, 1970), pp. 227–228; Kater, *Studentenschaft*, pp. 132–133 (Schirach); Wolf Rüdiger Hess in Ilse Hess, *Antwort aus Zelle Sieben: Briefwechsel mit dem Spandauer Gefangenen* (Leoni, 1967) pp. 16, 26 (Hess); Klessmann, "Frank," pp. 246–249; Werner Präg and Wolfgang Jacobmeyer, eds., *Das Diensttagebuch des deutschen Generalgouverneurs in Polen 1939–1945* (Stuttgart, 1975), pp. 23–24; Domröse, *NS-Staat*, p. 302 (Frank); *Max Amann: Ein Leben für Führer und Volk* (Munich, n.d.), pp. 23–50; Oron J. Hale, *The Captive Press in the Third Reich* (Princeton, 1964), pp. 1–75 (Amann); Paul Schwarz, *This Man Ribbentrop: His Life and Times* (New York, 1943), pp. 26–70 (Ribbentrop).

17. The analysis is based on the data in n. 14.

18. See Zapf, *Wandlungen*, p. 125; Dahrendorf, *Society*, p. 226.

19. Horn, *Führerideologie*, p. 286; Tyrell, "Führergedanke," p. 341; Hüttenberger, *Gauleiter*, p. 57.

20. According to my calculations: While in 1925–1932, 42.8% of the Gauleiters (a total of 56 N) had been socially mobile (see nn. 48, 49 of chap. 7), 41.2% (of a total of 51 N) were socially mobile in 1933–1944 (in-mobility). In the first period, 32.1% had been upwardly and 10.7% downwardly mobile; in the second period, 29.4% were upwardly and 11.8% downwardly mobile. Hence in the first period 57.1% and in the second 58.8% of the Gauleiters were stable. Independently of my analysis, William Jannen, Jr., "National Socialists and Social Mobility," *Journal of Social History*, 9 (1976), 341–342, has noted an equally upward mobility trend for the Gauleiters after 1933 as Rogowski has for those before 1933. I am aware that socially classifying individual Gauleiters — or other functionaries, for that matter — in rigid fashion for the period after 1933 is as precarious as for the period before 1933. A complex (if typically difficult) example is that of Karl Hanke, born August 24, 1903, Gauleiter in Lower Silesia from 1941 to 1945. Although he was counted among the lower-middle-class Gauleiters in this study, his complicated case would warrant some qualifications. As the son of a locomotive engineer on the upper fringe of the proletariat (although, technically, Hanke senior was a lower civil servant), Karl worked his way up from miller's apprentice, via seven years of upper school, to the position of senior trade instructor, thus showing a remarkable degree of intragenerational upward mobility. After Freikorps and "Black Reichswehr" experience, he joined the NSDAP in 1928 (party no. 102606) and soon became a favorite of Goebbels in Berlin. He joined the SA in 1929, and, like so many others who wished to rid themselves of the stigma of Ernst Röhm, he joined the SS in 1934. If the rules of hypergamy had applied to men in his situation then, Hanke might well have risen into the social elite by virtue of his marriage to the daughter of a Berlin University lecturer in Oriental languages. Later in his career, Hanke — for a short while — managed to become the lover of the high-class Magda Goebbels, Joseph's wife. According to Speer, whose personal friend he became, Hanke displayed unusually refined tastes for a dyed-in-the-wool Nazi, such as a predilection for Bauhaus wallpaper. Also see the favorable appraisal by the Jewish physician Siegfried Ostrowski, "Schicksal," p. 323, which represents the opposite of Boveri's judgment in *Wir*, p. 604; and Hassell's entry for May 29, 1941, in *Deutschland*, p. 210. Speer's observations are in *Reich*, pp. 21–22, 146, 149–150. Also see *Wer ist's* (1935), p. 592; Stockhorst, *Wer*, p. 176.

21. In 1933–1944, 58.8% of the Gauleiters were stable (see n. 20 above). Among the SS officers (1925–1939) examined by Gunnar C. Boehnert (see table 11, n. b), 67.8% were stable. The stability percentage of the Reich population (1925–1929) according to Kaelble, "Mobilität," p. 255, was 76. Only 0.8% of all elite-class SS officers came from working-class fathers, as compared with 2% of the Reich population and 15.8% of the Gauleiters (assuming the figures for the SS to be compatible with my own for the Gauleiters and Kaelble's for the Reich). Only 3.6% of "worker" SS officers had elite-class

fathers, but 14.3% of all working-class Gauleiters did (table 11).

22. See also Michael H. Kater, "Zum gegenseitigen Verhältnis von SA und SS in der Sozialgeschichte des Nationalsozialismus von 1925 bis 1939," *Vierteljahrschrift für Sozial- und Wirtschaftsgeschichte*, 62 (1975), 372–375.

23. 36.1% of all Gauleiters were civil servants, compared with 22.3% of all Kreisleiters, 18.4% of all Ortsgruppenleiters, 18.0% of all Stützpunktleiters, and 13.5% of the rank-and-file membership, according to figures in *Partei-Statistik* I and II ("Others," "No Indication," "Pensioners," "Housewives" and "Students" were not counted). Also see the generally higher percentage figures for the elite in the case of the Gauleiters, and the generally lower ones for both the lower middle class and workers in the case of all other groups of functionaries referred to in table 10, for 1933–1942.

24. Table 10 (columns Y, AA). The relative stability of the deputies over time may be ascertained by analyzing the data in *Reichstagshandbuch* (1933–1943); and Schwarz, *Handbuch*.

25. The analysis is on the basis of 443 *N* for 1932 and 196 *N* for the period from January 30, 1933 to the end of 1934 (see n. 20 of chap. 7).

26. According to table 10 (columns EE, GG); 49.7% versus 32.6%.

27. Computations on the basis of figures in sources mentioned in n. 3 above.

28. In this case, the calculation of the workers' percentage figures does not follow the procedures outlined in the Introduction but rather the (horizontal) classification system regularly used by Reich and NSDAP statisticians. See Genuneit, "Probleme," pp. 35–40; and the latter part of n. 42 of the Introduction, above. This is so not by choice but by necessity because here the classification scheme was dictated by *Partei-Statistik*. The evidence presented in the text is therefore suggestive rather than indicative. Still, since my definition of workers does not deviate significantly from that of the Reich and NSDAP statisticians, the figures for workers mentioned here are thought to be compatible with those contained in the tables and figures. Also see nn. 17, 18, 24 of chap. 7. Percentages for workers among Reich Nazi party comrades, Stützpunktleiters, and Ortsgruppenleiters were computed on the basis of data in *Partei-Statistik* I and II. For the counting procedure, see the middle of n. 23 above. The percentage for Thuringia was calculated according to figures in Astel and Weber, *Kinderzahl*, p. 13 (also see table 12). The percentage for Kreis Memmingen-Land (October 1, 1935) is according to figures in Fröhlich and Broszat, "Macht," p. 560. Percentage for Munich Ortsgruppen Königsplatz and Laim-West (June [1934]) is according to figures in files, SAM, NSDAP/431.

29. Calculations according to figures in lists for Ortsgruppe Traunstein, [1937–38], SAM, NSDAP/113.

30. See *Partei-Statistik* II, 406; the figure for farmers in column C of table 12; and those in Fröhlich and Broszat, "Macht," p. 560. What has been said about the definition of workers in n. 28 applies to that of farmers in this case.

31. The distribution of civil servants and teachers in the NSDAP, by

December 1934, according to *Partei-Statistik* I and II and Gauleiter group for 1934 (36 *N* — see table 10, n. d), was as follows:

	Rank and file	Stütz-punkt-leiter	Orts-gruppen-leiter	Kreis-leiter	Gau-leiter
Civil servants	13.5	18.0	18.4	22.3	36.1
Of those, teachers only	3.7	12.6	7.8	10.9	14.8
Teachers as % of all civil servants	27.4	69.8	42.5	48.8	40.9

Also see table 10 (columns W, Y, AA, CC, EE, GG, II, KK); lists Ortsgruppe Traunstein, [1937–38], SAM, NSDAP/113; table 12. On the high profile of civil servants, especially teachers, in the Nazi leadership corps, see further: Kater, "Hitlerjugend," pp. 606–614; *Beamten-Jahrbuch*, 26 (1939), 171–172; Proksch, "Erziehungsauftrag," p. 214; doc. (1935) in Broszat et al., eds., *Bayern*, p. 534; monthly report Gessner, Döbeln, March 3, 1934, HIS, 13/245; Eilers, *Schulpolitik*, p. 74; report of Count Schwerin in Thévoz et al., eds., *Darstellung*, pp. 74–75. In the past, the role of elementary-school teachers, high as it admittedly was, has frequently been exaggerated by critics of the regime. A typical example is in Neumann, *Behemoth*, p. 304, whose surmise is based on a good deal of factual error.

32. On the age stagnation as such, see Lerner, *Elite*, p. 86; Rauschning, *Revolution*, p. 83.

33. This implies that the average annual rate of growth for the Reichsleiters' collective age was 2.09%, while that of the Gauleiters was only 1.67%. Calculations according to the formula in Floud, *Introduction*, pp. 91–92. See figure 11. Calculation of Reichsleiters' mean ages on the basis of values in n. 14 above. Speer, *Reich*, p. 312, thinks he can distinguish between an older, pre-1933 group of Gauleiters and a younger, post-1932 one principally reared and tended by Bormann. Figure 11 would suggest that in 1933–34 and then again in 1938–1941 the Gauleiter corps as a whole was reinforced by younger men, occasioned in the first instance, despite the generally nominal functions of the Gauleiters, by the beginning of the "regime phase," and in the second by the accumulation of new territory in need of administration (Austria, Sudetenland), and eventually by the necessities arising from early successes in World War II.

34. Calculation for 1933 acording to "Listen Wahlvorschlag für Wahlkreis 26, Franken, für Reichstagswahl [March 1933]," SAN, 503/112. Also see Doblin and Pohly, "Composition," p. 42; figure 11, table 10.

35. According to information kindly supplied to me by Professor Nobuo Noda, Kyoto University (Japan), in his letter of December 17, 1977. Also see his article, "District Leaders of the Nazi Party," *The Shirin or the Journal of History*, 61 (May, 1978), 113–131. Noda's sample of 90 Kreisleiters in 1939 was drawn systematically at the BDC from a total population of 802 Kreisleiters, whose names are contained in *Reichsband: Adressenwerk* (1939). Noda excluded cadres for Austria and the Sudentenland. The other data are taken from figure 11 and table 10 (columns DD, HH).

36. Calculations according to figures in *Partei-Statistik* II, 331–332; Noda, "District Leaders," p. 129 (Noda's age categories are slightly, but not significantly different from the ones used for this study); the author's BDC Kreisleiters' sample (301 *N*) described in table 10, n. 1.

37. Officially, the age bracket from 31 to 40 was regarded as the most ideal one, at least for Kreisleiters. See *Partei-Statistik* II, 332.

38. The total frequencies for each leadership corps were, in order: 94; 96; 21. See lists in HHSAW, 483/160. In April 1939, 9% of all married and 42% of all unmarried cadres in Thuringia were between 20 and 30 years old. Astel and Weber, *Kinderzahl*, pp. 15, 17.

39. See Schäfer, *NSDAP*, p. 48.

40. See text in chap. 9 at nn. 2–6.

41. Of 776 Kreisleiters counted at the end of 1934, 100% had joined before January 30, 1933 (according to *Partei-Statistik* II, 330). Of 89 counted in 1939, 98.9% joined before that date (according to Noda, "District Leaders," p. 129). The corresponding percentage for 295 Kreisleiters counted in 1941 whose party entrance years could be gleaned from the BDC files (see table 10, n. 1) was 93.6.

42. See entry for March 27, 1945, in Goebbels, *Tagebücher*, p. 393; Orlow II, p. 168; and, with regard to SS functionaries' age, doc. 139 in Heiber, ed., *Reichsführer*, p. 142; as well as text in chap. 9 at nn. 9–16.

43. See n. 33 above.

44. For the Gauleiters, see figure 11. My calculations of the New Functionaries' ages are based on the frequencies mentioned in n. 25 of this chap., and n. 20 of chap. 7.

45. Calculation of Reichleiters' ages on the basis of information in n. 14 above.

46. See Rauschning, *Revolution*, pp. 146, 258; Speer, *Reich*, pp. 60, 121–122. Also see Gaupropagandaleiter Ostpreussen to Behrend, Königsberg, April 20, 1933, SAG, SF 6818, GA/29; Goldhagen, "Weltanschauung," p. 393. Pretensions of *Bildung* are reproduced in the memoirs of two Gauleiters: regarding Kleist see Wahl, *Herz*, p. 106; Jordan, *Erlebt*, p. 169.

47. Rauschning, *Gespräche*, p. 131; Maschmann, *Account*, pp. 21–22. Also see entry for mid-May 1939 in *Tagebuch Alfred Rosenbergs*, p. 66; Hanfstaengl, *Witness*, p. 219. An example of bad diction is in an outpouring by HJ functionary Trude Bürkner (1937), doc. 49 in Hans-Jochen Gamm, *Führung und Verführung: Pädagogik des Nationalsozialismus* (Munich, 1964), p. 282.

48. For a typical example at this lower level, see "Stichpunkte für Rede Ortsgruppenleiter-Tagung 14.-15.1.1939," SAG, SF 6815, GA/6. On the pedantry of Schwarz, Bormann, Himmler, and lesser functionaries, see Ulf Lükemann, "Der Reichsschatzmeister der NSDAP: Ein Beitrag zur inneren Parteistruktur," Ph.D. dissertation, Berlin, 1963, p. 15; Lang, *Secretary*, pp. vi, 88; Kersten, *Totenkopf*, pp. 152-153; director of Volksschule Balingen to Huber and Plenske, Balingen, December 6, 1938, BDC, NSLB, PLA Scheerer. Also see Himmler's correspondence in Heiber, ed., *Reichsführer*.

49. See text in chap. 7 at n. 60.

50. Quotations are from minutes of speech by Hess at 1938 Party Rally, SAG, SF 6815, GA/6 (p. 4); Bormann to Rosenberg, Munich, November 23, 1938, NA, T-454, 65/650-51. The connection between *Herzensbildung* and *Menschenführung* is ably drawn by former Gauleiter Wahl in *Herz*, pp. 150-151. A most complete if somewhat long-winded definition of *Menschenführung* is in "Dienstanweisung betr. Gesellschaftserziehung," enclosed with letter Kaehne to Leiter der Kreishauptstellen et al., Würzburg, June 1, 1938, BA, Schumacher/372. Also see "Anweisung an die Ortsgruppenorganisationsleiter," [before World War II], BA, Schumacher/372. Criteria of personnel selection are in: "Richtlinien für die Auswahl, Ausmusterung und Einberufung der Anwärter für die Ordensburgen," Munich, October 19, 1938, BA, NS 22/2022; "Beurteilungsbogen, Gauschulungsamt Bayreuth" [in this case for Kreisamtsleiter Alfons Hinderberger], Weismain, November 6, 1938, BDC, PK, PLA A. Hinderberger. Regarding sport see Reichinger to Kreisleiter, Munich, December 19, 1935, SAM, NSDAP/122. The following two documents exemplify the priority of "character" over critical faculties in a functionary's curriculum vitae: directive Hess, Munich, April 14, 1934, SAG, SF 6815, GA, A, 1a-1e; Gau-Organisationsleiter to Aldag, Königsberg, December 1, 1938, SAG, SF 6816, GA/13. Typical, too, is the case of Starnberg Kreisleiter (and mayor) Franz Buchner who was known by his superiors to be incompetent but nevertheless was kept in office, presumably because of his low NSDAP membership number: Reichsleiter [Fiehler] to Nippold, Munich, [1935], BDC, PK, PLA F. Buchner.

51. "Lehrplangestaltung der Gauführerschule Lärchenwalde," appended to Gauführerschule Lärchenwalde to Gauleiter Ostpreussen, Lärchenwalde, April 29, 1936, SAG, SF 6816, GA/11. See also Bezirksbauernführer Laufen, Laufen, March 5, 1936, SAM, NSDAP/118; Reichinger to Kreisleiter, Munich, September 11, 1936, SAM, NSDAP/122; Kreispersonalamtsleiter to Michlbauer, [Upper Bavaria], February 11, 1938, SAM, NSDAP/109; Baeyer-Katte, *Politik*, p. 256.

52. See Ley, directive 12, Munich, May 1, 1936, BA, Schumacher/375.

53. Bielenberg, *Past*, pp. 51-57, writes about the benign contempt with which she, a *Frau Doktor*, treated "her" Blockleiter.

54. Quotation is from "Anweisung an die Ortsgruppenorganisationsleiter," [before World War II], BA, Schumacher/372. Also see: Hoffmann, "O.-Rundschreiben Nr. 62. An alle Redner der N.S.D.A.P., Kreis

Bremen," Bremen, September, 11, 1933, SAB, 3, E, 10, Nr. 36 /77/, 11; Scholtz-Klink/NSF for January–February 1937; March–April 1937; October–December 1941, BA, NS 22/860; correspondence K. Behrend-Gauleitung Ostpreussen (March–April 1933), SAG, SF 6818, GA/29.

55. The last two examples are from Steinberg, *Sabers*, p. 165, and memorandum Oskar Ritter von Niedermayer, Berlin, November 1939, BA, R 4311/940 b. Also see Peterson, *Limits*, p. 304. Quotation "future upper class" is from "Stichpunkte für Rede Ortsgruppenleiter-Tagung 14.–15.1.1939," SAG, SF 6815 GA/6. Also see directive Hess, Munich, May 30, 1934, SAG, SF 6815, GA, A, 1a–1e; "Anweisung an die Ortsgruppenorganisationsleiter für die fachliche Organisationsschulung," [before World War II], BA, Schumacher/372.

56. Characteristics of the ideal typical bureaucrat were spelled out as late as 1936 in Ernst von Harnack, *Die Praxis der Öffentlichen Verwaltung*, 2d ed. (Schwenningen, 1951; 1st ed., 1936), especially pp. 7–95. Also see Runge, *Politik*, pp. 209–218; Reinhart Koselleck, *Preussen zwischen Reform und Revolution: Allgemeines Landrecht, Verwaltung und soziale Bewegung von 1791 bis 1848* (Stuttgart, 1967); Walter L. Dorn, "The Prussian Bureaucracy in the Eighteenth Century," in Herman Ausubel, ed., *The Making of Modern Europe*, I (New York, 1956), 358–381; Bolte, "Berufsstruktur," pp. 74–75. The historian Otto Hintze and his contemporary, the sociologist Max Weber, have analyzed the phenomenon of efficiency in the Prussian-German bureaucracy most thoroughly. The reader may prefer to consult the excellent, and much briefer, analysis by Jürgen Kocka, "Otto Hintze, Max Weber und das Problem der Bürokratie," *Historische Zeitschrift*, 233 (1981), 65–105.

57. See text at nn. 7 and 8 above.

58. See Rudolf Vierhaus, "Faschistisches Führertum: Ein Beitrag zur Phänomenologie des europäischen Faschismus," *Historische Zeitschrift*, 198 (1964), 621; Robert L. Koehl, "Feudal Aspects of National Socialism," *American Political Science Review*, 54 (1960), 921–933.

59. Ley, directive 12, Munich, May 1, 1936, BA, Schumacher/375; minutes of speech by Hess at 1938 Party Rally, SAG, SF 6815, GA/6 (pp. 3–4).

60. Jakobsen to Kreisleitung Niebüll, Westerland, July 9, 1936, BDC, PK, PLA J. Grohé; quotation is from Fröhlich and Broszat, "Macht," p. 557.

61. Quotation is from de Witt, "Economics," p. 262. Also see Führungs- und Betätigungszeugnis for Dr. Paul Müller, Kronach-Teuschnitz, April 17, 1934, BDC, PK, PLA P. Müller; minutes of speech by Gauleiter [Röver] in Cloppenburg on November 25, 1936, SAG, SF 6817, GA/27; Gaede, *Schwede-Coburg*, p. 24.

62. *Revolution*, p. 73.

63. Evidence bearing precisely on that aspect of the block and cell leaders' multiple functions is in the first four documents mentioned in n. 11 above. Also see Reichsorganisationsleiter to NSDAP-Kreisleitung Munich, Munich, July 30, 1937, BA, Schumacher/375. Individual examples of block and cell leaders' powers are in Aeckter to Bürgermeister, Heiligkreuz, May 30, 1934,

SAM, NSDAP/119; Blockleiter to Breitenstein, August 9, 1935, SAM, NSDAP/84; Oberleitner to Nazi party comrades of Munich chapter, April 11, 1937, SAM, NSDAP/431; Erika Mann, *School for Barbarians* (New York, 1938), pp. 22, 35; Bielenberg, *Past*, p. 51.

64. The Third Reich term was *Sippenhaft*. Hess's statement is from his directive 119/35, Munich, June 14, 1935, SAG, SF 6815, GA, A, 1a-1e. Quotation Schulenburg is from letter Schulenburg to Koch, December 31, 1935, partially reprinted in Krebs, *Schulenburg*, p. 134. Also see Ortsgruppenleiter Olbersdorf to Heinz Kater, Olbersdorf, September 27, 1938 (threat against addressee for having listened to the BBC), in private possession of the author; activities report Gau Süd-Hannover-Braunschweig for July 1933, Hanover, August 10, 1933, NHSA, Hann. 310 I, B 13; Schäfer to Polster, Selm, September 17, 1933, SAMs, NSF Westfalen-Nord/24; Stützpunktleiter Schönram to Kammerer, Schönram, February 16, 1934, SAM, NSDAP/119; minutes of speech by Hess at Nuremberg Party Rally, printed by Bormann, April 15, 1937, BA, NS 22/2011 (p. 10); Ortsgruppenleiter to Personalamt Wiener Neustadt, n.pl., February 15, 1939, DAÖW/5025; Rauschning, *Gespräche*, p. 87; Ostrowski, "Schicksal," p. 348; Thévoz et al., eds., *Darstellung*, pp. 74-75; Joseph Peter Stern, *Hitler: The Führer and the People* (Glasgow, 1975), p. 162. Bonn University professor Paul E. Kahle was forced out of office and into exile in 1938-39: "The Ministry in Berlin was completely powerless against the local Nazi authorities." Kahle, *Bonn University*, p. 35.

65. Examples are in: Oberste Leitung Partei-Organisation, circular 26, Munich, July 6, 1933, BA, NS 22/342; Bauer to Hess, Dresden, March 18, 1935, BDC, PK, PLA M. Mutschmann; doc. (September 26, 1936) in Broszat et al., eds., *Bayern*, p. 96

66. This opinion is in Lang, *Secretary*, p. 67. Leading contemporary figures certainly would have concurred in this view. See, for instance, entry for November 11, 1939, in *Tagebuch Alfred Rosenbergs*, p. 89; Wiedemann, *Mann*, p. 197. See also Bollmus, *Rosenberg*, pp. 236-250; Hüttenberger, *Gauleiter*, p. 198; Wahl, *Herz*, pp. 90-92; entries for October 15, 1938, December 29, 1939, January 22-28, 1939, in Hassell, *Deutschland*, pp. 27, 42, 46; Bauer to Hess, Dresden, March 18, 1935, BDC, PK, PLA M. Mutschmann; Kater, *Das "Ahnenerbe*,*"* pp. 21-24, 139-144; Schweitzer, *Business*, p. 514; Speer, *Reich*, p. 45. For Hitler's attitude toward Gauleiter rule after 1933 see Hitler's statement of June 24, 1942, in *Hitlers Tischgespräche*, p. 252.

67. On this, see the astute observation by Fritz Stern, *The Failure of Illiberalism: Essays on the Political Culture of Modern Germany* (New York, 1972), pp. 31-32. Typically, Speer's reaction: entry for January 3, 1949, in *Spandau*, p. 116.

68. Rauschning, *Gespräche*, pp. 89-93; and the examples in Wiedemann, *Mann*, pp. 75, 95, 194-196. A somewhat different, modern reinterpretation of this position is in Hüttenberger, "Polykratie," p. 431.

69. *Economy*, III, 1113. See also p. 1119. Also see Nyomarkay, *Charisma*, p. 29.

70. This is not to say that Kreisleiters could not serve in an honorary capacity—a tradition that stemmed from the Time of Struggle. Frequently, their positions were converted to full-time ones with the advent of the war. See Gerstner to NSDAP-Reichsleitung, [Munich], October 17, 1940, BDC, PK, PLA M. Gerstner; as well as "Feststellung über die Anzahl der zur Wehrmacht einberufenen Politischen Leiter," for Gau Westfalen-Süd, up to February 1, 1940, SAMs, Gauleitung Westfalen-Süd/1.

71. On this and Hinkler, see doc. 17 in Thévoz et al., eds., *Quellen*, p. 181; Hinkler to Daluege, Altona, February 8, 1934, BDC, PK, PLA P. Hinkler; Stockhorst, *Wer*, p. 199. Also see activities report Gau Süd-Hannover-Braunschweig for June 1933, NHSA, Hann. 310 I, B 13; directive Hess, Munich, April 14, 1934, SAG, SF 6815, GA, A, 1a–1e; report Kreis Untertaunus for May/June 1939, HHSAW, 483/5536; Krebs, *Schulenburg*, p. 133; Grunberger, *Reich*, p. 94; Orlow II, p. 218 and table on p. 219. On Schemm, see *Deutschland-Berichte*, II (1935), 498. On the Reichstag as a ready-made berth for Old Fighter sinecurists, see Orlow II, p. 175; Koellreutter, *Verfassungsrecht*, p. 146; Kater, "Wandel," p. 62, n. 92; and Hitler's own revealing remarks about the function of the British Upper House as an institution for the distribution of "spoils," entry for February 8, 1942, in Hitler, *Monologe*, p. 273.

72. See Baehr, "Geschichte der Ortsgruppe Widminnen," p. 10 (see n. 4 of chap. 7); Lükemann, "Reichsschatzmeister," p. 53; Hüttenberger, *Gauleiter*, p. 48; Konrad Heiden, *Geschichte des Nationalsozialismus: Die Karriere einer Idee* (Berlin, 1932), p. 244; doc. 96 in Jochmann, ed., *Nationalsozialismus*, pp. 292–293; Krebs, *Infancy*, pp. 70, 85.

73. Doc. (November 4, 1935) in Broszat et al., eds., *Bayern*, p. 88. See also correspondence regarding Alfred Gross (summer 1934), BDC, PK, PLA A. Gross; doc. 10 in Schadt, ed., *Verfolgung*, p. 115; trial records regarding Dotzer et al., December 1934, BDC, PK, PLA Dotzer; entry for September 15, 1933, in Ebermayer, *Deutschland*, p. 594; docs. 4, 5 in Thévoz et al., eds., *Quellen*, pp. 62, 76; Thévoz et al., eds., *Darstellung*, pp. 48, 63–64; docs. (February 3 and March 3, 1936) in Broszat et al., eds., *Bayern*, pp. 89–90; Beauftragter des Reichsschatzmeisters to Gauleitung Magdeburg-Anhalt, October 29, 1938, BDC, PK, PLA Walter Sommer; Padover, *Experiment*, p. 57; Schäfer, *NSDAP*, p. 42; Orlow II, p. 153.

74. See directives Hess of July 19 and November 23, 1934, SAM, NSDAP/122 and SAG, SF 6815, GA, A, 1a–1e. Also see Gaede, *Schwede-Coburg*, p. 44; *Nationalsozialistisches Jahrbuch*, 18 (1944), 178; Orlow II, p. 8.

75. Hüttenberger, *Gauleiter*, p. 130; Lükemann, "Reichsschatzmeister," pp. 54–64; Krebs, *Schulenburg*, pp. 129–130; Grunberger, *Reich*, p. 91; Orlow II, p. 124; Lang, *Secretary*, p. 134.

76. Excerpted memorandum of July 1935, BDC, SSA W. Kube; Wahl, *Herz*, pp. 124–127; Baeyer-Katte, *Politik*, p. 161; Krebs, *Schulenburg*, p. 112; Speer, *Reich*, p. 58; Lang, *Secretary*, pp. 96–97. Also see Aretin, *Krone*, p. 234.

77. Evidence for all three areas of overindulgence is in: situation report of Ortsgruppe Maraunenhof, [summer 1933], SAG, SF 6817, GA/17; minutes of case Oberstes Parteigericht versus Herbert Albrecht, Munich, April 27, 1934, BDC, PK, PLA H. Albrecht; directive Hess, Munich, May 30, 1934, SAG, SF 6815, GA, A, 1a–1e; docs. 11, 19 in Thévoz et al., eds., *Quellen*, pp. 153, 197; unknown to Oberstes Parteigericht, n.pl., January 10, 1935, BDC, PK, PLA F. K. Florian; case of Werner Schmuck (1935), BDC, PK, PLA W. Schmuck; Schwarz(?) to Hellmuth, [Munich], January 19, 1937, BDC, PK, PLA O. Hellmuth; Kreisleiter Marienwerder to Moser, Marienwerder, June 24, 1937, SAG, SF 6816, GA/13; *Deutschland-Berichte*, II (1935), 486, 499, 503, 552, 600; Heinrich Hoffmann, *Hitler was my Friend* (London, 1955), p. 97; Schaumburg-Lippe, *Krone*, p. 163; Albert Zoller, *Hitler privat: Erlebnisbericht einer Geheimsekretärin* (Düsseldorf, 1949), p. 105; Krebs, *Schulenburg*, pp. 113, 132–133; Grunberger, *Reich*, pp. 62, 65, 96. Concerning Hitler's cynical approval, see entry for November 1, 1946, in Speer, *Spandau*, pp. 15–16.

9. WARTIME: SEPTEMBER 1939 TO 1945

1. See entry for September 17, 1938, in Hassell, *Deutschland*, p. 19; and text in chap. 6 at nn. 121–124.

2. For the figures, see Gau Westfalen-Süd, "Feststellung über die Anzahl der zur Wehrmacht einberufenen Politischen Leiter," as of February 1, 1940, SAMs, Gauleitung Westfalen-Süd/1; "Einsatz und Bewährung der Parteigenossen im Wehr- oder anderweitigem Kriegsdienst seit dem 1. Sept. 1939 nach dem Stande vom 1. Mai 1943," BA, Schumacher/374; Orlow II, p. 341. Also see Gauleitung Westfalen-Nord, situation and activities report for November 1936, SAMs, Gauleitung Westfalen-Nord, Gauschulungs-amt/15; Jamrowski, ed., *Handbuch*, p. 599; Reichsorganisationsleiter to Gauleiters, Munich, March 26, 1940, BA, NS 22/2017; Grunberger, *Reich*, p. 69.

3. In his memoirs, Schirach makes a lot out of having spent a few weeks in front-line duty during the western campaign. Baldur von Schirach, *Ich glaubte an Hitler* (Hamburg, 1967), pp. 251–263; curriculum vitae Schmalz, Munich, June 28, 1943, BDC, PK, PLA K. Schmalz; NSDAP recommendations for party comrade Otto Dettmann, December 23, 1941, and June 23, 1942, BDC, PK, PLA O. Dettmann. Also see the valid observation about Gustav Adolf Scheel in Bollmus, *Handelshochschule*, p. 97.

4. All this is apparent after an analysis of figures in: "Einsatz und Bewährung der Parteigenossen im Wehr- oder anderweitigem Kriegsdienst seit dem 1. Sept. 1939 nach dem Stande vom 1. Mai 1943," BA, Schumacher/374. For instance, according to the figures mentioned in this document, which are complete ones for the time from September 1, 1939, to May 1, 1943, of a total of 6,542,261 ordinary Nazi party comrades, 49.9% had to serve in active combat, whereas of 1,551,709 political leaders, only 42.0% had to serve. Among active soldiers, 6.9% of those from the party rank and file were lost in battle,

compared with 5.8% for the functionaries. The values for functionaries are included in those for *all* Nazi members. The party may have been correct in claiming that Nazi party members altogether put in heavier front service and suffered greater casualties than non-party members. See *Völkischer Beobachter*, Berlin, December 24, 1943.

5. Entries for December 5 and 13, 1939, in Boelcke, ed., *Kriegspropaganda*, pp. 238, 243; doc. (October 31, 1940) in Broszat et al., eds., *Bayern*, p. 604; doc. (July 8, 1943) in Boberach, ed., *Meldungen*, pp. 418–419; Hagen, *Leader*, p. 231–232; *Der alltägliche Faschismus*, pp. 50–51, 60.

6. See Charles W. Sydnor, Jr., *Soldiers of Destruction: The SS Death's Head Division, 1933–1945* (Princeton, 1977), p. 73; Ley, directive 18/42, Munich, December 10, 1942, BA, NS 22/2007. In the following, cases are documented of functionaries who (a) wished to serve at the fronts to escape intraparty intrigues at home; (b) were redeployed to their "civilian" position of Kreisleiter evidently against their will; (c) fought in the front lines in a spirit of dedication to Hitler, expecting imminent death in battle; (d) died peacefully (and more typically) as the result of a medical operation, in the course of party duty in their home Gau: Hildebrandt to Bormann, Schwerin, April 13, 1943, BA, Schumacher/205 (a); correspondence O.R. with others (1943), SAL, PL 509, 1/3 (b); "Vermächtnis des Kreisschulungsleiters Pg. K.G., Bayerische Ostmark, an seine Frau und Kinder," in Gauschulungsamt . . . Württemberg-Hohenzollern, Schulungsunterlagen des Gauschulungsamtes, Folge 7/43, SAL, PL 509, 1/5 (c); obituaries for Ernst Penner in *Preussische Zeitung*, November 27, 1940 (d).

7. List signed Friedrichs, Berlin, September 17, 1939, BA, Schumacher/371; also see n. 37 of chap. 8. See entry for December 18, 1940, in Hohenstein, *Tagebuch*, p. 21; Volkmann et al., Strafsache Balnus, Munich, October 28, 1942, BDC, PK, PLA Balnus; Kommandierung Gerriets, signed Friedrichs, Munich, September 3, 1942, BDC, PK, PLA A. Gerriets; curriculum vitae Schmalz, Munich, June 28, 1943, BDC, PK, PLA K. Schmalz. For an example of promotion as a result of administrative needs in newly conquered territory, see case of former Osnabrück Kreisleiter Münzer, who in July of 1940 became an aide to the Reich Commissar in Holland, Arthur Seyss-Inquart. Karl Kühling, *Osnabrück 1933–1945: Stadt im Dritten Reich* (Osnabrück, 1969), p. 152. Also see entry for January 19, 1941, in Hassell, *Deutschland*, p. 179; Alexander Dallin, *German Rule in Russia 1941–1945: A Study of Occupation Policies* (London and New York, 1957), pp. 101–103; Martin Broszat, *Nationalsozialistische Polenpolitik 1939–1945* (Stuttgart, 1961), pp. 49–57; Steinert, *Krieg*, pp. 280–281; Orlow II, p. 264.

8. Dallin, *Rule*, p. 103; Broszat, *Polenpolitik*, pp. 80–84; Präg and Jacobmeyer, eds., *Diensttagebuch*.

9. See entry for May 9, 1943, in *Goebbels Diaries*, p. 285 (first quotation). This is corroborated in Bormann(?), memorandum for Friedrichs, Führer headquarters, May 11, 1943, IfZ, Fa 91/3. Circular O 45/44, Organisationsamt, Gauleitung Franken, Nuremberg, June 9, 1944, BA,

Schumacher/372 (second quotation). Bormann(?), memorandum for Friedrichs, Berlin, November 10, 1941, BA, Schumacher/372; Bewes to Plenske, Crailsheim, January 23, 1942, SAL, PL 512, II, N, 98/5; deputy Gauleiter Westfalen-Nord, circular 69/42, Münster, June 22, 1942, SAMs, Gauleitung Westfalen-Nord, Gauamt für Volkswohlfahrt/7; Reichsorganisationsleiter [Ley], circular 10/42 to all Gauleiters, Munich, July 8, 1942, BA, NS 22/2007; Wegener to Backe, Oldenburg, February 22, 1943, BDC, PK, PLA H. Voss; cable Kaltenbrunner to Bormann, [Vienna], September 14, 1944, BA, Schumacher/371; Orlow II, pp. 273, 341, 424.

10. Bormann(?), memorandum for Friedrichs, Berlin, November 10, 1939; memorandum Friedrichs, Munich, December 2, 1939, IfZ, Fa 91/3. Also see Mommsen, *Beamtentum*, p. 115.

11. Eggeling to Schwarz, Halle/Saale, December 18, 1940; Schwarz to Eggeling, [Munich], January 6, 1941, BDC, PK, PLA H. Bernhardt.

12. Ley, directive 18/42, Munich, December 10, 1942, BA, NS 22/2007; directive 6/44 (March 10, 1944), in *Verfügungen/Anordnungen*, VI, 39; circular 146/44 (July 9, 1944), in *Verfügungen/Anordnungen*, VII, 53. As late as 1941, Professor Ernst Rudolf Huber, the leading academic jurist in the Third Reich, upheld the pseudo-constitutional but clearly anachronistic distinction between *Menschenführung* and *Sachgestaltung*: *Stellung*, pp. 46–47.

13. Quotation is from Wahl, *Herz*, p. 63. Also see: Reichsorganisationsleiter [Ley], circular 10/42 to all *Gauleiters*, Munich, July 8, 1943, BA, NS 22/2007; Saller to Zentralpersonalamt, Reichsschatzmeister, Reichenberg, January 21, 1942, BDC, PK, PLA K. Höss; "Denkschrift an RFSS. Erziehungsnachwuchs 1942. Abgeschlossen 15.3.42," BA, NS 19 Neu/1531. On the unpopularity of the roles lower functionaries played in the course of performing their daily routines among the people, see doc. (November 25, 1940), in Broszat et al., eds., *Bayern*, p. 608.

14. Quotation is from circular Ley 5/43, Munich, April 8, 1943, BA, NS 22/2008 (italics as in the original). Also see Mauer and Schenke, "Stichwortartige Gesichtspunkte für Rede Friedrichs," Munich, October 5, 1943; memorandum Mauer for Friedrichs, Munich, July 20, 1944, BA, Schumacher/368; Orlow II, p. 425; Brausse, *Führungsordnung*, p. 178; Kater, "Hitlerjugend," pp. 617–622.

15. Schirach fell out of grace, never to be replaced as Gauleiter of Vienna. Bormann(?), memorandum for Friedrichs, Berlin, November 10, 1939; memoranda by Bormann(?), Berlin, December 4 and 5, 1939; memorandum Bormann(?) for Friedrichs, Führer headquarters, May 11, 1943, IfZ, Fa 91/3; entries for May 5 and 9, and June 24, 1942, in *Hitlers Tischgespräche*, pp. 238–240, 251–252, 254; entry for May 17, 1942, in *Goebbels Diaries*, p. 162; Hüttenberger, *Gauleiter*, p. 195; Speer, *Reich*, pp. 261, 276, 313; Orlow II, pp. 357–358, 424–428. An example of a Gauleiter who refused to relinquish his position, yet finally was (reluctantly) forced by Hitler to do so (Josef Wagner, who made room for Karl Hanke in Silesia), is in Wagner to Hess, Berlin, November 11, 1939, IfZ, Fa 91/3; and BDC, PK, PLA J. Wagner.

16. Bormann(?), memorandum for Friedrichs, Berlin, November 10,

1939, IfZ, Fa 91/3.

17. Quotations from the top: entry for May 9, 1942, in Stresau, *Jahr*, pp. 291–292; McKee, *World*, p. 38; entry for March 3, 1943, in *Goebbels Diaries*, p. 204; Himmler to Giessler, November 7, 1943, BDC, PK, PLA F. Buchner; O.R., "Luftkriegserfahrungen in Stuttgart. Gedankengliederung," Stuttgart, June 25, 1944, SAL, PL 509, 1/6; Hans-Jochen Gamm, *Der Flüsterwitz im Dritten Reich* (Munich, 1963), p. 157; Paul Schmidt, *Statist auf diplomatischer Bühne 1923–45: Erlebnisse des Chefdolmetschers im Auswärtigen Amt mit den Staatsmännern Europas* (Bonn, 1949), p. 579; Maschmann, *Account*, p. 22. Also see: Orlow II, p. 320; Broszat, *Polenpolitik*, pp. 70–74; Kreisleiter Gross-Frankfurt, circular 1/25/43, Frankfurt/Main, October 5, 1943, HHSAW, 483/5541; entries for November 2 and 6, 1943, in *Goebbels Diaries*, pp. 400, 403; Lang, *Secretary*, p. 251.

18. Recommendation for Kreisleiter August Schultheiss, November 2, 1940, BDC, PK, PLA A. Schultheiss; Bormann, circular 105/41, Führer headquarters, August 27, 1941, HIS, 12/242; Sprenger, circular 107/42, Frankfurt/Main, July 21, 1942, HHSAW, 483/5540; Gauhauptamtsleiter, Gau Westfalen-Nord, circular 69/42, Münster, June 22, 1942, SAMs, Gauleitung Westfalen-Nord, Gauamt für Volkswohlfahrt/7; "Die Mitglieder-Versammlung der NSDAP. Eine Dienstanweisung für die Ortsgruppen, bearbeitet von Oberbereichsleiter Otto Schmidtke [Gauleitung Ostpreussen]," Königsberg, [1943], BA, Schumacher/375 (p. 19); minutes of speech Friedrichs at Führer headquarters, March 23, 1944, BA, Schumacher/368; Stokes, "People," p. 189; Kater, "Die 'Technische Nothilfe,'" p. 77.

19. Otto A. Teetzmann, *Der Luftschutz-Leitfaden für alle* (Berlin, n.d.), pp. 93, 135–136.

20. On Goebbels, Total War, and ramifications for the party cadres, see the docs. (January–March 1943) in Willi A. Boelcke, ed., *"Wollt Ihr den totalen Krieg?" Die geheimen Goebbels-Konferenzen 1939–1943* (Stuttgart, 1967), pp. 316–348; entry for March 13, 1943, in *Goebbels Diaries*, p. 227; circular (March 1, 1943) in *Verfügungen/Anordnungen*, IV, 4–5. Counter-air-raid functions of NSDAP personnel are documented in: Schrimpf, "Bericht über den Kriegseinsatz der Bewegung im Kreise Emden," Emden, February 18, 1943, BA, NS 26/163; minutes of speech held by O.R. before the NSDAP functionary corps of Kreis Balingen on February 3, 1944, February 8, 1944, SAL, PL, 509, 1/6; Kreisleitung Mannheim, "Bericht über Anordnungen, Massnahmen und Erfahrungen bei Luftangriffen," Mannheim, March 5, 1944, HIS, 13/260; Jordan, *Erlebt*, pp. 228–233. Characteristic examples of "recommendation" are those of Gerhard Buscher, May 20, 1942, BDC, PK, PLA G. Buscher; and Erich Börger, June 13, 1942, BDC, PK, PLA E. Börger. More examples of this kind may be found in the BDC's *Kleine Funktionärskartei*.

21. This thesis is on the whole concurred in by Orlow II, p. 264. Also see entry for January 16, 1941, in Hohenstein, *Tagebuch*, p. 57.

22. Quotation is from Collins, *Years*, p. 170. Also see p. 116; doc. (October 17, 1940) in Broszat et al., eds., *Bayern*, p. 602; Ortsgruppenleiter Unterschleichach to Kreisleitung Schweinfurt, Unterschleichach, May 27,

1942, BDC, NSLB, PLA E. Bachmann; entry for May 9, 1942, in Stresau, *Jahr*, pp. 292–293; docs. (February–April 1944) in Leber, ed., *Gewissen*, pp. 52–59. Rich documentation concerning the political evaluation of Germans of all walks of life by NSDAP personnel may be found in SAM; see, for instance, NSDAP/113; NSDAP/109; NSDAP/28 (SA). Also see *Der alltägliche Faschismus*, pp. 135–136.

23. Case of F.S. is documented in report by Reg.-Assessor Dr. B., Waldshut, January 21, 1942, SAF, 317/1267. Also see entry for December 5, 1939, in Hassell, *Deutschland*, p. 107; entries for January 7, 1941, March 18 and May 5, 1942, in Hohenstein, *Tagebuch*, pp. 28, 240, 251; Ley, circular 8/42, Munich, May 15, 1942, BA, NS 22/2007; entry for November 16, 1942, in Klepper, *Schatten*, pp. 1120–1121; doc. (July 1, 1943) in Broszat et al., eds., *Bayern*, p. 173; doc. (April 1, 1944) in Leber, ed., *Gewissen*, p. 53; Hagen, *Leader*, pp. 231–232; McKale, *Party Courts*, pp. 182–183; Bleuel, *Strength*, p. 232. For the example of a benevolent Kreisleiter who used his powers for the good of the civilian population and who as a result was "popular," see McKee, *World*, pp. 36–38.

24. For the last-mentioned examples, see SD report 32, December 22, 1939, BA, R 58/146; Milward, *Economy*, p. 10. In this context, also see Eberle to Kanzlei des Gauleiters [Adolf Wagner], Munich, March 24, 1944, SAM, NSDAP/18; entry for July 25, 1944, in Kardorff, *Aufzeichnungen*, p. 173. Regarding the nature of their power vis-à-vis the Volksgemeinschaft, see Speer, *Reich*, pp. 315, 412; Orlow II, p. 409; Koehl, "Feudal Aspects," p. 928; Seydewitz, *Life*, pp. 147–149; Hüttenberger, *Gauleiter*, especially pp. 147, 161, 168, 172, 199–200. Paradigmatic for conditions in the Gaus is a letter from Saxon Gauleiter Mutschmann to Schwarz pleading for a further extension of the regional NSDAP (Gau) executive, Dresden, February 7, 1944, BDC, PK, PLA Elsner.

25. The salary of a primary-school teacher was about 450 marks a month, that of a Kreisleiter was 800 or more. Gauleiter Florian, for example, received 2,820 marks gross salary in October 1942. See Gerstner to Zentral-Personalamt, Reichsschatzmeister, [Munich], October 17, 1940, BDC, PK, PLA M. Gerstner; Gauschatzmeister Mark Brandenburg to Heermann, March 4, 1942, BDC, PK, PLA F. Heermann; Schwarz to Florian, [Munich], October 22, 1942, BDC, PK, PLA F. K. Florian.

26. Martens, "Bericht über den Bergwerkseinsatz der NPEA Plön 1942," BA, R 43 II/9566; Hildebrandt to Bormann, Schwerin, April 13, 1943, BA, Schumacher/205; memorandum regarding Kreisleiter Alfons Schaller, Munich, May 4, 1943, BDC, PK, PLA A. Schaller; situation report for Thierack for the period up to June 1, 1943, Linz, June 9, 1943, OLA, Pol. Akten/80; Seydewitz, *Life*, pp. 124, 151–153; Theo Findahl, *Letzter Akt—Berlin 1939–1945* (Hamburg, 1946), p. 17; Lükemann, "Reichsschatzmeister," pp. 65–66; Boberach, ed., *Meldungen*, p. 430.

27. This is according to doc. (May 14, 1943) in Broszat et al., eds., *Bayern*, p. 640. Quotation is from Speer, *Reich*, p. 185, see also pp. 178, 216–217, 221; entry for September 22, 1940, in Hassell, *Deutschland*, pp.

163-164; anonymous letter regarding Schirach, [April/May 1944], BA, Schumacher/371; Bormann to Terboven, Führer headquarters, April 12, 1941, BDC, PK, PLA J. Terboven; Bernsdorff to Brandt, Berlin, September 29, 1942, BDC, PK, PLA M. Mutschmann; Lükemann, "Reichsschatzmeister," pp. 67, 80-86; Krebs, *Schulenburg*, pp. 205-206; Maschmann, *Account*, pp. 87-88, 148-149; Steinert, *Krieg*, p. 281. While party leaders such as Ley, Bormann, and Goebbels enjoyed more extended sexual escapades, functionaries' wives partook of the material fruits of corruption, but otherwise stayed meekly in the background, so much so that the Nazi women's organization complained. See *The Bormann Letters: The Private Correspondence between Martin Bormann and His Wife from January 1943 to April 1945*, ed. Hugh R. Trevor-Roper (London, 1954); Scholtz-Klink/NSF for September–December 1941, BA, NS 22/860; doc. 213 in Gersdorff, *Frauen*, pp. 434-435; Sprenger, circular 83/84, Frankfurt/Main, June 2, 1943, HHSAW, 483/5542; Collins, *Years*, p. 130; Baeyer-Katte, *Politik*, p. 164. The case of a typically promiscuous intermediate wartime functionary is in Strafsache Balnus, Munich, October 28, 1942, BDC, PK, PLA Balnus. Also see the accusations leveled against promiscuous Gauleiters by illegal "White-Rose" resistance flyer composed by Professor Kurt Huber [Munich, February 1943], in Petry, *Studenten*, p. 166. At least three Gauleiters were said, by the highest NSDAP leadership, to be unduly influenced by their wives: Josef Wagner, Martin Mutschmann, and Emil Stürtz. See BDC, PK, PLA J. Wagner; entry for December 12, 1942, in *Goebbels Diaries*, p. 179; memorandum Friedrichs for Walkenhorst, Munich, April 20, 1944, BA, Schumacher/205.

28. Quotations from the top: entry for March 9, 1943, in *Goebbels Diaries*, p. 217; entry for March 17, 1943, ibid., p. 234; entry for January 3, 1949, in Speer, *Spandau*, p. 116. Also see Hess to Politische Leiter, May 6, 1940, BA, Schumacher/372; entry for February 25, 1942, in *Goebbels Diaries*, p. 62; entry for July 26, 1942, in *Hitlers Tischgespräche*, p. 262; "Die Mitgliederversammlung der NSDAP," p. 31 (see n. 18); Lükemann, "Reichsschatzmeister," p. 67; Speer, *Reich*, p. 313.

29. For the immediate effect of the anti-Hitler plot on the party hierarchy, see entry for July 30, 1944, in Kardorff, *Aufzeichnungen*, p. 175; Eschenburg, "Rede Himmlers," for instance p. 385; Bormann, confidential circular 41/44, Munich, August 7, 1944, SAM, NSDAP/31.

30. Examples of very detailed questionnaires to be used by block and cell leaders in reporting on their charges exist for August 31 and September 1, 1944, regarding L.M. and A.B., in HHSAW, 483/996. Also see Bormann, circular 49/45, Führer headquarters, February 1, 1945, SAM, NSDAP/35; "Lieber Tot als Sklav. Der Gauleiter [Lauterbacher] ruft alle Volksgenossen zum fanatischen Einsatz auf," Hanover, April 5, 1945, doc. 79 in Gamm, *Führung*, pp. 375-377; similarly, Gauleiter Hellmuth's declaration, Würzburg, March 28, 1945, in Max Domarus, *Der Untergang des alten Würzburg: Im Luftkrieg gegen die deutschen Grosstädte*, 4th ed. (Würzburg, 1978), p. 153; Hüttenberger, *Gauleiter*, pp. 191, 193; Hans von Ahlfen and Hermann Niehoff, *So kämpfte Breslau: Verteidigung und Untergang von Schlesiens*

Hauptstadt (Munich, 1959), p. 50; Baird, *World*, p. 251.

31. See memorandum Weicker regarding Kreisleiter Fritz Schulte, Munich, December 12, 1944, BDC, PK, PLA F. Schulte; dok. 380 a in Heiber, ed., *Reichsführer*, pp. 304-305; doc. 4 in Berghahn, "Meinungsforschung," p. 108; Hüttenberger, *Gauleiter*, p. 209; Lang, *Secretary*, pp. 311-312.

32. Quotation is from Speer, *Reich*, p. 465. Also see memorandum Mauer for Friedrichs, Munich, July 20, 1944, BA, Schumacher/368; Ley to Bormann, Berlin, November 19, 1944, BDC, PLA K. Holz; Bormann, circular 49/45, Führer headquarters, February 1, 1945, SAM, NSDAP/35; Schlenker, Kreuter, Frey to Mitglieder unseres Sozialgewerks, Gelnhausen, March 11, 1945, HHSAW, 483/6533; Dotzler, "Vorschläge zum Aufbau einer Widerstandsbewgung in den von den Bolschewisten besetzten deutschen Ostgebieten," Berlin, January 23, 1945, enclosed with letter Bormann to Himmler, Führer headquarters, January 27, 1945, BDC, PK, PLA H. Dotzler; entry for March 29, 1945, in Goebbels, *Tagebücher*, p. 447.

33. Top quotation is from entry for March 30. 1945, in Goebbels, *Tagebücher*, p. 460; also see pp. 101, 325, 416, 503. Bottom quotation is from "Siegen oder fallen," April 3, 1945, in Heinz Blank, ed., *Augenzeugenberichte vom Kriegsende 1945 im Markt Gangkofen: Eine Dokumentation: Ein Beitrag zur Zeitgeschichte des Marktes Gangkofen* (Gangkofen, November 1975), p. 4 (copy in IfZ). See also: cable Kaltenbrunner to Bormann, [Vienna], September 14, 1944, BA, Schumacher/371; directives Bormann of October 1944 regarding formation of Volkssturm, SAM, NSDAP/31; Bormann to all Gauleiters, Führer headquarters, February 16, 1945, SAM, NSDAP/35; doc. 79 in Gamm, *Führung*, pp. 375-377; Salomon, *Fragebogen*, pp. 314-315; Domarus, *Untergang*, p. 154; Ahlfen and Niehoff, *Breslau*, pp. 49-50, 57; McKee, *World*, pp. 141-142; Jordan, *Erlebt*, pp. 266-267, 270-272; Hüttenberger, *Gauleiter*, pp. 188-194, 211; Speer, *Reich*, pp. 441-442, 446-450, 475, 496; Baird, *World*, pp. 249, 251-252; Gersdorff, *Soldat*, pp. 170, 180.

10. SOCIAL PROFILE OF THE LEADERS, 1919-1945

1. Kahl-Furthmann, ed., *Schemm*, p. 337; Gauleitung Mainfranken, "Block- und Zellenordnung der NSDAP," Würzburg, November 26, 1936, BA, Schumacher/375.

2. The first quotation is from Orlow II, p. 38. In this case, Orlow applies the label to the Kreisleiters. More simplistically: Steinert, *Krieg*, p. 602. The second quotation is from Dahrendorf, *Society*, p. 226.

3. *Das Tagebuch von Joseph Goebbels 1925/26*, ed. Helmut Heiber, 2d ed. (Stuttgart, 1961); Goebbels, *Kaiserhof*; Goebbels Diaries; Goebbels, *Tagebücher*.

4. See Vierhaus, "Führertum," p. 630.

5. Quotation is from Mommsen, "National Socialism," p. 194. Also see Kater, "Hitlerjugend," p. 617-623; Hüttenberger, *Gauleiter*, pp. 192, 195; Zapf, *Wandlungen*, p. 56; Manfred Messerschmidt, *Die Wehrmacht im NS-Staat: Zeit der Indoktrination* (Hamburg, 1969), pp. 463-480; Jeremy Noakes,

"Oberbürgermeister and Gauleiter: City Government between Party and State," in Hirschfeld and Kettenacker, eds., *Der "Führerstaat,"* pp. 224–225. Jannen, "Mobility," p. 344, contradicts Mommsen's thesis of global NSDAP impotence.

6. See Linz, "Notes," p. 43; Vierhaus, "Führertum," pp. 619, 625, 627.

7. For this Nazi view, see Mehringer, *NSDAP*, pp. 40, 44.

8. For more on this aspect, see the Conclusion of this book.

9. See entry for May 3, 1949, in Speer, *Spandau*, p. 128.

10. This becomes very obvious after studying documents regarding the relationship between NSDAP functionaries and the Wehrmacht in East Prussia (1937–1939), SAG, SF 6817, GA/25.

11. "Stichworte für Rede Ortsgruppenleiter-Tagung 14./15.1.1939," SAG, SF 6815, GA/6.

CONCLUSION

1. At that time, the party had 1.7 million political leaders. See text in chap. 8 at n. 1. According to figure 1, the total membership then was just over five million.

2. Breitman, *Socialism*, p. 7.

3. The first quotation is from Mühlberger, "Sociology," p. 504. The second quotation is from Sauer, "National Socialism," p. 410.

4. David Schoenbaum is still the foremost scholar to have put forth the view of a "social revolution" through Nazism, in his book *Revolution*. For various criticisms of this view, see Winkler, "Mythos," p. 490; Schweitzer, *Nazifizierung*, pp. 137–138; Karl Dietrich Bracher, "The Role of Hitler: Perspectives of Interpretation," in Laqueur, ed., *Fascism*, p. 220; and Grundmann, *Agrarpolitik*, p. 157. Rauschning, much earlier, talked about a revolution-in-the-making in his major work *Revolution*. Parallel to Schoenbaum, Dahrendorf, *Society*, pp. 402–428, advanced his controversial view of Nazism as a (social) revolutionary vanguard of "modernity." Several arguments could be made against this view. The principal one based on the thesis of this study would be that since modernity is predicated on rationality, modernization in Germany could not have been precipitated by the irrational, lower-middle-class men who constituted the core of Hitler's leadership cadres. See Dreitzel, *Elitebegriff*; and Wolfgang Schluchter, "Der Elitebegriff als soziologische Kategorie," *Kölner Zeitschrift für Soziologie und Sozialpsychologie*, 15 (1963), 241–243. Dahrendorf's view has been criticized in Schweitzer, *Nazifizierung*, pp. 136–137; Struve, *Elites*, p. 443; Grundmann, *Agrarpolitik*, pp. 156–157; Bracher, "Role," p. 220; and especially Turner, *Faschismus*, pp. 162–175. Before Dahrendorf published his thesis, Gerhard Ritter held that the destruction wrought by the collapse of the Third Reich created the basis for a more modern, democratic society after 1945. See his *Das deutsche Problem: Grundfragen des deutschen Staatslebens gestern und heute*, 2d ed. (Munich, 1966; 1st ed., 1962), pp. 209–210; and also Peter Stern, *Hitler*, p. 173.

5. "Lower Middle Class," p. 435. Italics as in the original.

6. *Nazifizierung*, pp. 177-178.

7. See Pfenning, "Gemeinschaft," pp. 310-311; Schoenbaum, *Revolution*, p. xxii; Bracher, "Role," p. 220; Mommsen, "National Socialism," p. 190; Merkl, *Making*, p. 148.

8. See text in chap. 10 at n. 9.

9. *Revolution*, p. 93.

10. This is somewhat different from saying, as Fritz Stern, *Failure*, p. 194, does: "Traditional beliefs and institutions were subverted and the old ruling classes gradually replaced by a new Nazi elite." Rauschning, *Revolution*, p. 86, argued wrongly that the old elite was as good as "obliterated," as early as 1937. Closer to my point of view are the qualifying remarks by Schieder, *Geschichtsquelle*, p. 52; and Müller, *Armee*, pp. 46-47.

11. In this connection, see his remarks (early 1934) as reported in Zoller, *Hitler privat*, p. 163.

12. See the correct interpretation by Schieder, *Geschichtsquelle*, p. 52.

13. A typical Nazi document praising the main achievements so far accomplished along such lines is "Sonderabgabe des NS-Gaudienstes über die Kriegsarbeit der Partei im vergangenen Jahr [for Gau München-Oberbayern 1942]," December 1942, BA, NS 26/170. Also see Martin Broszat, "Soziale Motivation und Führer-Bindung des Nationalsozialismus," *Vierteljahrshefte für Zeitgeschichte*, 18 (1970), 397.

14. *Revolution*, pp. 302, 323.

15. For the period after 1918, see Runge, *Politik*; Breitman, *Socialism*, pp. 136-139; Zapf, *Wandlungen*, p. 140. For the period after 1945, see Lewis J. Edinger, "Post-totalitarian Leadership: Elites in the German Federal Republic," *American Political Science Review*, 54 (1960), 71, 75.

INDEX OF AUTHORS CITED

GENERAL INDEX